- Offset
- Lehren
- Colletr

D.

The Trustee Guide to Investment

The Trustee Guide to Investment

Andrew Clare

and

Chris Wagstaff

First published 2011 by
PALGRAVE MACMILLAN

Palgrave Macmillan in the UK is an imprint of Macmillan Publishers Limited,
registered in England, company number 785998, of Houndmills, Basingstoke,
Hampshire RG21 6XS.

Palgrave Macmillan in the US is a division of St Martin's Press LLC,
175 Fifth Avenue, New York, NY 10010.

Palgrave Macmillan is the global academic imprint of the above companies
and has companies and representatives throughout the world.

Palgrave® and Macmillan® are registered trademarks in the United States,
the United Kingdom, Europe and other countries.

ISBN 978–0–230–24424–5

This book is printed on paper suitable for recycling and made from fully
managed and sustained forest sources. Logging, pulping and manufacturing
processes are expected to conform to the environmental regulations of the
country of origin.

A catalogue record for this book is available from the British Library.

A catalog record for this book is available from the Library of Congress.

10   9   8   7   6   5   4   3   2   1
20   19   18   17   16   15   14   13   12   11

Printed and bound in Great Britain by
CPI Antony Rowe, Chippenham and Eastbourne

Contents

Acknowledgements   xiii

Introduction   xiv

1   **The Pension Promise: How Do Pension Liabilities Arise?**   1
    Learning outcomes   1
    Who believes in the pension fairy?   1
    Defined benefit pension arrangements   2
    Defined benefit summary   10
    Defined contribution pension arrangements   11
    Defined contribution default funds and lifestyling   15
    Defined contribution starting to dominate the pensions landscape   19
    The shape and size of the pension industry   21
    Key points   22

2   **Trustee Knowledge and Understanding and Investment
    Governance: What Do Trustees Need to Know?**   25
    Learning outcomes   25
    Trustee knowledge and understanding   25
    Investment governance   29
    Investment governance for defined contribution schemes   32
    Summary   34
    Key points   34

3   **The Main Parties Trustees Deal with on Funding and
    Investment Issues: Who are the Main Pension Players?**   37
    Learning outcomes   37
    Introduction   37
    The Pensions Regulator (tPR)   38
    The sponsor   39
    The covenant consultant   40
    The Pension Protection Fund (PPF)   42
    The pensions manager   43
    The scheme secretary   43
    The scheme actuary   43
    The investment consultant   45
    The fund managers   46

The de-risking consultant 47
The scheme lawyer 47
The custodian 48
The investment banks 48
The scheme auditor 48
The professional independent trustee 49
Key points 49

4 The Macroeconomic Background to Pensions: Why Economics Matters **51**
Learning outcomes 51
What is economics? 51
Growth 52
Inflation 61
Macroeconomic policy 69
The 'state of the art': Inflation targeting 72
The price of inflation targeting 74
Fiscal policy 75
Summary 77
Key points 77

5 Cash: The Most Liquid of All the Asset Classes **79**
Learning outcomes 79
Introducing traditional asset classes 79
Introducing cash 80
Cash deposits 81
The money markets 82
Money market funds 84
Key points 85

6 Bonds: The Asset Class Trustees Fear the Most **87**
Learning outcomes 87
Introduction 87
Bond characteristics 88
The cash flow from plain vanilla bonds 89
The global bond market 90
Bond types 93
Corporate bonds and credit risk 97
The price of a bond 101
Bond prices and returns 103
Duration – the key bond risk parameter 105

Yield curves and the yield curve family 111
Zero coupon, spot or cash rates 112
Forward interest rates and the forward yield curve 116
The relationship between forward and zero coupon curves 119
What factors determine the shape of the yield curve? 120
Summary 124
Key points 124

7 Equities: The Traditional 'Growth' Asset Class 125
Learning outcomes 125
Introduction 125
What are equities? 126
The structure and size of the world's equity markets 128
Analyzing ordinary shares 132
Equity investment styles 139
The Dividend Discount Model (DDM) 143
Equity returns – the importance of dividends 150
Longer term equity valuation metrics 152
Key points 153

8 Real Estate: Putting Your Faith in Bricks and Mortar 155
Learning outcomes 155
Introduction 155
Distinguishing features 156
The case for real estate 158
Investing in real estate 160
Investment styles 167
Real estate market sectors 167
Investing globally in real estate 172
Concluding comments 174
Key points 174

9 Risk and Risk Management: Trustees as Risk Managers 175
Learning outcomes 175
Risk is one word but not one number 175
Not so 'modern portfolio theory' 177
Measuring risk 177
Interpreting standard deviation 179
Covariance and correlation 181
Diversification 183
Efficient portfolios 186

Reward and risk   189
The Capital Asset Pricing Model (CAPM) and risk-adjusted
    returns   191
Value at Risk (VaR)   197
Quantitative risk measures summary   201
Other, less quantifiable risks   201
Soft risks   205
Summary: A word of warning   207
Key points   209

10   Asset Allocation: The Big Decision   **211**
Learning outcomes   211
Introduction   211
Asset allocation in practice   212
Strategic asset allocation   214
Long-term expected returns   216
The expected, riskless real return   216
Expected inflation   218
The expected return on cash   220
Risk premia   221
Index-linked government bonds   222
Conventional government bonds – the inflation risk premium   222
Summary so far   225
Corporate bonds – the credit risk premium   225
Equities – the equity risk premium   228
Putting it all together   230
Volatility and correlations   231
Putting it all together to produce a strategic investment
    portfolio   234
Strategic versus tactical asset allocation   235
Strategic asset allocation summary   237
A tactical asset allocation process   237
Asset allocation summary   247
Key points   248

11   Derivatives: Instruments of Mass Destruction?   **249**
Learning outcomes   249
Introduction   249
Forwards and futures   250
Hedging with futures   253
Closing out   254

Futures margins   255
Equity index futures contracts   256
Long bond futures contracts   259
Options   263
Credit default swaps   272
CDSs as insurance   273
CDS payments   275
CDS maturities   275
Trading CDSs   276
Issues with respect to CDSs   277
Summary   278
Key points   278

12 Interest Rate and Inflation Swaps: Swapping Payments You Don't Want for Those That You Do   **279**
Learning outcomes   279
Introduction   279
Swap basics   281
What is *the* swap rate?   286
Inflation swaps   289
Using swaps to transform cash flow profiles   292
The investment context of interest rate and inflation swaps   301
Summary   302
Key points   302

13 Alternative Asset Classes: An Alternative to What?   **305**
Learning outcomes   305
Why invest in alternative asset classes?   305
The Yale Endowment Fund   308
Risk and return   310
Hedge funds   311
Private equity   323
Commodities   331
Foreign exchange   336
Integrating alternatives with traditional asset classes   341
Summary   344
Key points   345

14 Portfolio Management: Analyzing and Generating Returns   **347**
Learning outcomes   347
Introduction   347

Performance evaluation 348
Measuring absolute returns 349
Money-weighted rate of return (MWRR) 350
Time-weighted rate of return (TWRR) 351
TWRR versus MWRR 352
Measuring relative returns 352
Index weightings and return averaging 355
Performance attribution 358
Risk-adjusting returns 362
Active fund management 363
Active fund manager performance 366
Performance persistence 368
The search for alpha 370
Are the academic tests fair? 372
The performance of pension fund managers 374
Active fund management summary 376
Passive fund management 377
Combining active and passive management 383
Summary 388
Key points 389

15 Liability Driven Investment (LDI): An Exercise in Risk Management 391
Learning outcomes 391
Introduction 391
Liability driven investment 392
Interest rate risk 393
Inflation risk 395
Longevity risk 397
What are trustees to do? 398
The science of LDI 399
Value at Risk (VaR) 400
Stress/scenario testing 404
'PV01' and focusing more specifically on the risks embodied in the liabilities 406
Interest rate and inflation hedging instruments 408
Inflation swaps 409
Interest rate swaps 410
The impact of executing interest and inflation swaps on scheme VaR 411

Hedging longevity risk   412
Summary: the science of LDI   415
The practicalities of implementing a de-risking programme   415
What about the growth assets?   426
Summary   427
Key points   427

16 **Integrating Environmental, Social and Corporate
    Governance (ESG) Factors into the Investment Decision
    Making Process: An Altruistic Exercise?**   **429**
    Learning outcomes   429
    Introduction   429
    Incorporating ESG factors into investment decision
       making and disclosing the scheme's ESG policy   431
    What ESG comprises and why it matters   434
    Corporate governance   434
    Sustainable and responsible investing (SRI)   442
    Summary   449
    Key points   449

17 **Behavioural Finance: How Investors Really
    Make Investment Decisions**   **451**
    Learning outcomes   451
    Introduction   452
    The efficient market hypothesis   452
    What is behavioural finance?   458
    The social aspect of human behaviour   459
    Is behavioural finance a new phenomenon?   460
    The main behavioural biases   460
    Heuristics   461
    Framing   466
    So what can behavioural finance help explain?   468
    Being influenced by others   468
    The wisdom of crowds   469
    Why do financial markets fail to exhibit the wisdom of
       the crowd?   471
    The expert problem   474
    Decision making within Trustee Boards and Investment
       Committees   477
    Why hasn't behavioural finance become more mainstream?   481
    What is the future for behavioural finance?   482

Will we ever get a new theory?   483
Key points   484

**18 Manager Selection: How Do You Choose
a Good Fund Manager?**   **485**
Learning outcomes   485
Introduction   485
Selecting a passive fund manager   486
Selecting an active fund manager   487
Relying on past performance: The role of luck and skill   488
Investment philosophy and process (IP&P)   490
Index huggers or active fund managers?   492
Investment style   493
There's no 'I' in team   495
Behavioural biases   497
Capacity constraints   498
Risk management   499
Fees   500
And finally: sex   502
So what makes a good fund manager?   505
Some final thoughts   506
Key points   506

19 Conclusion   **509**

Glossary   513

Index   561

Acknowledgements

In writing this book, we are deeply grateful to all of those who graciously shared their time, knowledge and valuable insights with us, as well providing their thoughts and often detailed feedback on the draft manuscript. Many went far beyond the call of duty. Particular thanks should go to Rob Gardner, Mark Herne, Dawid Konotey-Ahulu, Georgina Marshall, Janet Measom, Nick Motson, Iain Richards, Meadhbh Sherman, David Skinner, Anita Skipper, Matthew Tatnell, Crawford Taylor, Peter Weiner, Bill Whitehead and Steve Waygood. We would also like to thank all of the data and information providers for the valuable facts and statistics that we have been able to draw upon in making this a more complete text.

We would like to thank Farida Ahmed for her invaluable help in the preparation of our manuscript. We'd also like to thank our publishers and copy-editors Keith Povey and Carol Thomas for their guidance throughout and, of course, our families, for their patience, encouragement and unwavering support.

Finally, we should add that nothing we say in the book should be construed as investment advice or as a recommendation to adopt a particular course of action.

ANDREW CLARE
CHRIS WAGSTAFF

Introduction

Imagine being given the responsibility of managing a multi-million pound portfolio of financial instruments, ranging from equities to government bonds, corporate bonds, real estate, hedge funds, private equity and derivatives. Now imagine that the success or failure of your investment strategy will determine whether hundreds, possibly thousands, of your work colleagues and others enjoy a happy retirement or not. Finally imagine that you have no formal training in economics, investment or finance. Welcome to the world of a pension fund trustee!

Trusteeship will never be easy. The 120,000 or so largely unsung heroes who are responsible for managing far in excess of £1 trillion (£1,000 billion) of assets and liabilities that reside within over 66,000 occupational pension schemes, have the ultimate objective of paying the pensions of nearly 20 million scheme members. Quite a task, and one that requires considerable confidence and competence on the part of trustees of both private and funded public sector schemes. This is especially true against the backdrop of rapidly deteriorating funding positions, not to mention the reluctance and, in many cases, the inability of a considerable number of private sector scheme sponsors to find the necessary cash in the short term to return these schemes to rude health.

When we began discussing writing this book in June 2009, we firmly believed then, and still do, that June 2009 would be remembered by many pensions professionals as the point at which the future viability of the defined benefit (DB) pension scheme was in real doubt. It was in this month that blue chips BP and Barclays made sweeping changes to their own DB schemes. The £11bn BP scheme announced its intention to join the 16,000 other UK DB schemes that had closed to *new* members since 2000, while the £13.5bn Barclays DB scheme, which was already closed to new members but with 18,000 *existing* scheme members, announced a more radical plan to close its scheme to future benefit accruals. This coincided with other chilling news. Almost one-third of the 117 DB scheme trustees surveyed in the annual Aon Consulting survey that year believed that their DB scheme would be wound up within the next ten years, while over one-third of the respondents believed that their scheme sponsor would close their scheme to future accruals. It was reported at the same time that the aggregate deficit of the then 7,800 DB schemes insured under the Pension Protection Fund's industry financed safety net, stood at over £179bn at the end of May 2009.

What had become abundantly clear by June 2009 was that those trustees, whose only answer to the rapidly widening DB scheme deficits was to go cap in hand to their scheme sponsor, could expect the same response that Oliver Twist received when he returned his empty bowl to Mr. Bumble and asked for more. What we knew then is what we know now: trustees have no option but to improve the management of both the asset and liability side of their scheme's balance sheet.

However, in our day-to-day roles as investment educators and industry commentators and, probably most importantly, in our capacities as trustees and investment committee members of the GEC (1972) Pension Scheme and Aviva Staff Pension Scheme respectively, we know full well that gaining the requisite confidence and competence to manage a pension scheme successfully is no easy task. In discharging their fiduciary duties, trustees are expected to acquire, hone and continually develop a whole host of skills – actuarial, legal and accounting are but a few that come to mind – but getting to grips with investment, with its often mystifying jargon and terminology, is by far the most challenging and arguably the most important, particularly in the light of continued high-profile scheme closures and sponsor under-funding. We also know from the many trustees with whom we regularly come into contact, that trustees do recognize that they need to continually improve their investment knowledge and organizational effectiveness if they are to manage the funds in their schemes more effectively.

This book therefore provides an objective and practical guide to the ever expanding range of markets, investments, tools and techniques to which trustees are increasingly exposed and regularly bombarded by their fund managers and advisers. To make the subject matter more accessible and more enjoyable, we have provided a number of 'break out' boxes within the book, to expand upon those areas that we think will be of particular interest. These principally draw on the regular articles that we write for the pensions and investment press.

We begin the book by looking at the occupational pensions' landscape and the challenges faced by trustees of both DB and defined contribution (DC) schemes. In so doing, we introduce our representative TGtI DB scheme. We then move on to discuss why it is important that trustees continually improve their investment knowledge and investment governance, before considering the roles of the main participants with whom trustees deal on funding and investment issues – the sponsor, the fund managers, the investment consultants and the investment bankers to name but a few.

Macroeconomics – how the economy works and its link to investment is then addressed before our focus turns to the four main traditional asset classes that form the mainstay of most occupational pension scheme portfolios – cash, bonds, equities and real estate. We examine their key characteristics, their historic risks and returns and how to establish whether each of the latter three asset classes at any point in time represents good, fair or poor value. The multi-headed beast that is risk is the next topic for consideration, along with how it can be measured, managed and sometimes mitigated: a theme we return to and expand upon throughout the book. As we will demonstrate, risk is one word but not one number and not always easily manageable.

We then consider what is undoubtedly the most important strategic investment decision of them all and therefore, the one to which trustees should devote a considerable proportion of their governance budget: the asset allocation decision. That is, whether and to what extent, based on their prospective risks and returns and suitability given the scheme's benchmark and other objectives, each asset class warrants inclusion in the asset mix.

No investment book would be complete without a detailed examination of derivatives. In many people's eyes, derivatives are synonymous with casino capitalism. However, when used responsibly, derivatives can solve a considerable number of pension scheme-specific problems. In particular, they can help to manage potentially 'unrewarded' interest rate, inflation and longevity risks that reside within pension scheme liabilities. This we consider within the next chapter dedicated to the world's most widely traded derivative instruments – swaps.

Our focus then turns to those non-traditional, or alternative, assets – hedge funds, private equity, commodities and actively managed currency – that are increasingly employed within the asset mix of most occupational pension schemes: both DB and within DC default funds. We then examine the methodology, tools and techniques that are used to assess the performance of fund managers, before moving on to focus on first active and then passive investment management techniques.

That then brings us neatly on to a widely misunderstood topic: Liability Driven Investment (LDI). Here we look at what LDI is, what it seeks to achieve, why and how and illustrate this through our TGtI DB scheme.

Then for something a little different. There is a groundswell of opinion that trustees, in acting in the best financial interests of their scheme membership should be more proactive in their investment decision making and subsequent monitoring of scheme investments, by placing more emphasis on environmental, social and corporate governance (ESG) matters. Therefore, we consider why ESG should be integral to the investment process.

In drawing on the insights provided by behavioural finance, the penultimate chapter focuses on how investors, and fund managers in particular, really approach investment decision making and highlights the pitfalls to which many regularly succumb. With this in mind, we finish by addressing the importance of fund manager selection, highlighting some of the issues that need to be borne in mind when selecting a manager.

In writing this book, our intention has always been to try to demystify the many aspects of investment, but also to present the subject in a lively, informative, accessible and relevant manner. We hope we have achieved this. In addition, and just as importantly however, we hope for many, if not all, of our readers, that this book will help to foster a lifelong interest in this most fascinating of subjects. If it does, then we will have achieved at least one of our aims.

December 2011   ANDREW CLARE

                                                              CHRIS WAGSTAFF

Chapter 1

The Pension Promise: How Do Pension Liabilities Arise?

Learning outcomes

- Understand how benefits accrue under a defined benefit pension scheme.
- Appreciate why most defined benefit schemes are closed to new members and increasingly to existing members and why benefits for those that remain open are being increasingly diluted.
- Understand how benefits accrue under a defined contribution pension scheme.
- Appreciate the risks faced by members of defined contribution schemes.
- Appreciate the size and composition of the UK's occupational pensions market.

Who believes in the pension fairy?

Most small children believe in the tooth fairy. For each little milk tooth that they put under their pillow at night, a kind-hearted fairy comes along, takes the tooth and replaces it with a £1 coin. It's a good deal for the kids – pull out a worthless and now useless tooth and get hard cash in exchange. But economically speaking, for any cash-strapped parent it is a bad deal – the money has to come from somewhere, and the tooth is worthless (well ok, it might have a sentimental value!).

One of the biggest problems facing developed economies today is that too many of its grown-ups believe in the pension fairy – a magical creature that will provide them with a pension for life, a pension that will allow them to maintain their pre-retirement lifestyle, no matter how long they live.

Hopefully this news will not come as too much of a blow to any of you, but there is no such thing as the pension fairy. Sorry. The funds needed to provide us with a pension in our old age will come from a combination of three sources, none of them magical:

- you;
- your employer; and/or
- current and future generations of taxpayers.

In this chapter we will explore how those pension entitlements for which trustees are generally responsible arise and accrue in the first place. We will also consider where the funds come from to make good this *'pension promise'*.

Pension scheme trustees are generally responsible for two types of pension provision: defined benefit (DB) and defined contribution (DC). First we consider typical DB arrangements, before moving on to a complementary analysis of DC arrangements.

Defined benefit pension arrangements

DB schemes are set up on behalf of their employees by a company, or a public sector organisation which, in pension speak, is referred to as the scheme sponsor. Some of these DB schemes are 'funded' while others are 'unfunded'. All private sector and some public sector DB schemes, such as the Local Government Pension Scheme (LGPS) for local government workers and the University Superannuation Scheme (USS) for university lecturers, are funded.[1] By 'funded' we mean that there is a pot of money that has been built up over time to fund scheme members' pensions upon and into retirement. However, public sector schemes, such as those provided for the Civil Service, the NHS, teachers and the uniformed services, are unfunded, in that the pensions paid from these schemes are principally met out of current taxes and current member contributions rather than from a fund that has accumulated in value over time. They are effectively pay-as-you-go-schemes.

Up until a decade or so ago, anyone starting a new job with an employer with a DB pension scheme would normally have been entitled to join the scheme. Employers (scheme sponsors) generally promoted the provision of the scheme as one of the benefits of working for the organisation, and presumably employees

---

[1] The University Superannuation Scheme (USS) is the second largest DB scheme in the UK.

saw it the same way (but probably didn't appreciate the value of a DB pension scheme as much as they do today – more on that later).

The clue to the nature of the pension entitlements that accrue within a DB scheme is in the name. The pension benefit is a pre-defined amount. It is generally based upon:

- the number of years that someone has been a member of the scheme;
- the value of the member's 'final pensionable salary' just before they retire; and
- a pre-specified accrual rate.

The member's 'pensionable salary' might exclude wage elements like overtime, bonuses and allowances, so that the pension itself is based upon the employee's basic salary. However, the definition of 'pensionable salary' can vary considerably from scheme to scheme. Some schemes, for instance, have imposed caps on the extent to which a pay rise is pensionable. Until recently the definition of 'final pensionable salary' was usually an average of the pensionable salary of the last three years served in the scheme. But again this can vary from scheme to scheme. Recently a number of DB schemes have moved from a 'final salary' basis to a 'career average revalued earnings' (CARE) basis.[2]

Finally, for a 'final salary' DB scheme, the accrual rate determines how much pension is accrued for each full year in the scheme. Other things equal, the higher the accrual rate the less time it takes to accrue a given amount of pension.

So how is the 'defined' pension of a DB scheme member, well, defined?

The basic principle is very simple. Suppose an employee who is about to retire, has been a member of their employer's DB pension scheme for 20 years. Suppose also that their average pensionable salary over the last three years of their time in the scheme was £30,000. And finally, suppose that the accrual rate is 1/80th ('one eightieth'). Their annual pension on retirement would be calculated as follows:

$$\text{Annual pension} = \frac{\text{number of years in scheme}}{80} \times \text{final pensionable salary}$$

$$\text{Annual pension} = \frac{20}{80} \times £30,000 = £7,50$$

---

[2] CARE works by accruing pension benefits based on a proportion of pay annually and then revaluing this accrual annually either by the average earnings index or an inflation index such as the Retail Prices Index (RPI) or Consumer Prices Index (CPI).

In addition to their annual pension entitlement, which is paid monthly (and which is potentially taxable, depending on the pensioner's other income), scheme members are also usually entitled to a tax-free lump sum on retirement. This can be calculated in a number of ways. Scheme members can usually forgo this lump sum entitlement in return for a larger final pension. However, for our example, suppose that in addition to the pensionable salary entitlement, scheme members earn 3/80th of their final salary for every full year that they are members of the scheme which they can take as a tax-free lump sum payment on retirement. The lump sum for our example scheme member on retirement would therefore be:

$$\text{Tax free lump sum} = \frac{3}{80} \times 20 \times \pounds30,000 = \pounds22,500$$

So on retirement our example scheme member would receive an annual pension of £7,500 in the first year of their retirement and a tax-free lump sum of £22,500, which they could choose to spend however they wished: maybe on a Harley Davidson, a world cruise or perhaps on a time share apartment in the Algarve?

This pension is paid until the member dies. This is very good news for the pensioner, of course, but what about inflation which will eat into the value of the pension over time? Because of this, the pension may be inflation-proofed either completely or up to a pre-defined limit. The degree of inflation protection varies from scheme to scheme. Some schemes have promised that they will raise their members' pensions in line with the Retail Prices Index (RPI) every year – though for some this has been replaced by the Consumer Prices Index (CPI) – regardless of the level of inflation. However, typically pensions are now uplifted by a maximum of 5 per cent per annum. This means that if inflation over a year is, say, 10 per cent, the annual pension will only rise by 5 per cent.

The really good news is, however, that nearly all pension entitlements have a zero inflation floor. In other words a pension would not be cut if inflation were negative. So the nominal, or absolute, value of the pension cannot fall.

Many DB pension schemes provide additional benefits to scheme members on top of an annual pension and tax-free lump sum on retirement. These usually include:

- widow/widower's benefit;
- dependents benefits;
- disability assurance, and
- life assurance.

So who pays for all of these benefits? Well it's not the pension fairy. Instead it is usually a combination of the scheme member (the employee) and the scheme sponsor (the employer). Members will make regular contributions, usually expressed as a proportion of their salary into an investment fund. For example, a member might be required to make a monthly contribution of 6 per cent of their monthly salary to the fund. Some schemes require a higher proportionate contribution from the member, while some require a lot less. There are also a dwindling few that do not require the member to contribute anything at all. These schemes are known as non-contributory schemes[3] (although, arrangements of this kind are usually reserved for top executives). The scheme sponsor will also make contributions to this investment fund, and these contributions can often be very high indeed. According to the Office for National Statistics (ONS),[4] the average contribution made by employers for their DB members was 16.6 per cent of salary at the end of 2008. It is therefore not uncommon for some scheme sponsors to contribute over 20 per cent of a member's annual salary bill to their DB pension fund. Some pay considerably more.

The trustees of the pension scheme are the guardians of these funds. They invest these funds in a range of asset classes. It is this pot of assets that is used to honour the financial commitments of the scheme – the pension, the tax-free lump sum, widow/widower's benefits and so forth. It is, therefore, vital that this investment fund is large enough to support all the pension promises. And remember a pension promise is a promise to the scheme member of an income for life. Which is quite a promise![5]

It is the objective of this book to explain all of the investment issues involved in making sure that this investment fund meets all the pension promises.

But what if the assets held within this fund are deemed to be insufficient to meet all of the promised benefits?[6] Effectively the responsibility for making up any perceived shortfall is the scheme sponsor's. This means that the burden of risk for a DB pension plan rests squarely with the scheme sponsor. We will return to this point soon below.

Deferred members

Of course, people often change jobs. When they do, they also cease to be active members of the DB pension scheme. Active members are those that are working for the scheme sponsor and are still accruing benefits within the scheme.

---

[3] The Marks & Spencer and John Lewis DB pension schemes are both non-contributory, though the former is now closed to new members.
[4] Pension Trends 2009, ONS.
[5] Since June 2003 the pension promise has been a legal guarantee by a solvent sponsor. That is, a solvent sponsor cannot wind up a less than fully funded DB scheme unless they secure a buyout of the scheme's assets and liabilities with an insurance company.
[6] In Chapter 3 we will introduce some of the investment professionals that determine whether the investment fund is sufficiently well funded to meet all of the promised benefits.

When a member leaves a company, but does not retire and draw a pension, they become a deferred member. Their pension entitlement remains with the scheme. However, the trustees of the scheme, as its guardians, have the same duty of care to deferred members as to active and retired members.

Even though deferred members make no more contributions to the investment fund, the scheme sponsor may still find itself making contributions to the fund to support the promise made to each deferred member while they were in the scheme – even though they may now be working for a competitor firm!

The deferred member's pension entitlement, based on the scheme's definition of the member's final salary, is not frozen. Indeed, this final salary amount will typically be uplifted annually by the CPI measure of inflation until the deferred member comes to draw their pension.[7] For example, suppose that after 15 years in the '1/80' scheme described above, that a member leaves the scheme for employment elsewhere. Also suppose that their final pensionable salary in the scheme was £25,000 and that they eventually retire 20 years later and draw their pension from the fund. This 'final' salary will have increased in line with inflation over these 20 years. If CPI inflation is 2 per cent per year over this 20 year period then the final salary will increase by approximately 50 per cent.[8] So the pension that the deferred member would be entitled to would be calculated approximately as:

$$\text{Annual pension} = \frac{\text{number of years in scheme}}{80}$$
$$\times (\text{final pensionable salary} \times \text{inflation uplift})$$

$$\text{Annual pension} = \frac{15}{80} \times (£25,000 \times 1.5) = £7,031.25$$

In practice, for most schemes the pension promises – or liabilities – of the pension scheme will be a mixture of past pension promises that have been made to:

- current pensioners, who are drawing their pensions;
- active members of the scheme, who are not drawing their pension, but who are (usually) making regular contributions to the investment fund and accruing benefits, and

---

[7] Although the statutory revaluation of deferred benefits requires the CPI measure of inflation to be applied, much depends on the pension scheme's rules. If the rules provide for revaluation specifically linked to the RPI, then the RPI takes precedence over the CPI. However if the rules provide for revaluation in line with the increase in the 'cost of living' and there isn't any reference to a specific inflation index, then the trustees will need to decide how to apply this going forward. Of course, the sponsor can, if they wish, apply more than the CPI statutory uplift to deferred benefits though, perhaps unsurprisingly, this is rare.

[8] For the mathematically minded, $£100 \times (1 + 0.02)^{20} \approx £150$.

- deferred members, who used to contribute to the scheme, but who have now left the employer, leaving behind a pension entitlement that has accumulated during their time in the scheme, and which will continue to grow with inflation.

So the total liabilities of the scheme will be a complex mix of these pension promises. However, in addition, many schemes have changed their benefit promises over time, though it is important to remember that such changes are not applied retrospectively. Any improvement in the pension promise, for example, changing it from a fixed nominal pension to one that is indexed to inflation, will only be applicable for newly acquired pension benefits, known as future accruals. Equally any diminution in the quality of the pension promise, for example changing the accrual rate from 1/80th to 1/100th, can only be applied prospectively and not retrospectively, so that all benefits accrued at the old 1/80th rate remain, although all future pensionable benefits will only accrue at the lower rate of 1/100th.

A further complication is related to the estimate of when each member of the scheme will draw their pension, what their final salary will be when they do, and for how long they will draw their pension. In other words, estimates of when scheme members will retire and how long they will draw a pension have to be made. The question about how long they will draw their pension for is particularly difficult. According to the ONS, in 2009 the average 65 year old male in the UK was expected to live for 17.8 years and female 20.4 years. However, regional differences can be marked. For instance, the difference between the life expectancy of a 65 year old male living in Kensington and Chelsea compared to a 65 year male living in Glasgow is 9.8 years.[9] Furthermore, in January 2010, the Department of Work and Pensions (DWP) suggested that the number of people in the UK aged 100 or over was set to double by 2020 to 22,000 and then grow more than 12-fold to 280,000 by 2050. One year on in January 2011, the DWP revealed that it expected nearly 11 million people to be alive at the time, around 17 per cent of the population, would live to 100. Of these, about 2.2 million were then aged 50 or over, of which 875,000 were aged 65 and above. This means that by 2066 the UK might be home to half a million centenarians. We consider the particular problem of longevity in Chapter 15.

Taken together, this all makes the calculation of the total liability of the scheme a very complex mathematical problem indeed. Luckily this is what the scheme actuary does. We will learn a little more about their role in Chapter 3, but basically the scheme actuary is very, very good at maths. They were the sort of kid at school that you copied your maths homework from, before chucking their school satchel on top of the bike shed.

---

[9] See http://www.statistics.gov.uk/STATBASE/Product.asp?vlnk=8841.

In the end then the total liabilities of the pension scheme are a complex mixture of past promised benefits, based on estimates of longevity and salary inflation over time, where some benefits may be linked to inflation, some not; some accrued at one rate, others at other rates; some to retired members, some to current members, and some to members that may now be working for rival companies. There are other complexities, relating to aspects of the pension promise, but the basic point is that this is a very complex problem best left to the scheme actuary.

In Exhibit 1.1 we present a snapshot of the liabilities of our representative 'TGtI' DB scheme – using the sort of picture that might be presented to trustees once the scheme actuary has crunched all the numbers. Panel A of Exhibit 1.1 shows the total liabilities (future cash payments) that have been promised up to that point in time. They have a discounted value of £100m and, as you can see from the chart, stretch out for many years. This is because anyone joining the scheme today, say at the age of 20, will not draw their pension until at least 40, probably 45, years time, from which point they may then live and therefore draw that pension for another 20, possibly even 30 or more years. This is why liabilities stretch out so far. They basically stretch out into the future until the last member of the scheme is expected to draw their final breath.

Panel A breaks down the liabilities into member type. As you can see, for the TGtI scheme it is estimated that most of the current pensioners have pretty much all shuffled off their mortal coils after 40 years. Actives and deferreds, being younger on average by definition, represent a liability for the scheme much further into the future. Deferred members can often make up a huge proportion of the total liability. For them to comprise over 60 per cent of the total liability would not be unusual. Active members by contrast often comprise only a small proportion of the total liability. This is particularly true for schemes where the employer has

Exhibit 1.1   The liabilities of the TGtI DB scheme

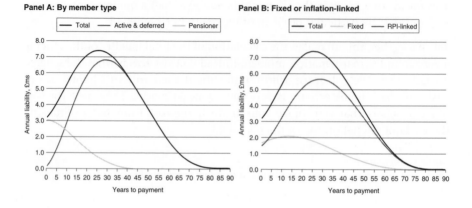

Panel A: By member type   Panel B: Fixed or inflation-linked

changed dramatically over the years, as in the case of nationalised corporations that were subsequently privatised.[10] In Exhibit 1.1 the TGtI DB scheme's pensioners make up 34 per cent of the total liability (£34m) with the rest (£66m) being due to a combination of active and deferred members.

Panel B shows the breakdown of liabilities according to whether they are indexed to inflation or not. As you can see, the non-indexed, or fixed liabilities for this particular scheme end sooner. This is because typically schemes made non-indexed pension promises in the early years of its life. This means that the pension payments made to current pensioners are predominantly fixed too. However, many schemes have made predominantly inflation-linked promises in recent years, which means that those retiring in the future are more likely to receive a pension that will rise with subsequent inflation. We should also note that in order to construct this liability picture we have to assume a value for annual inflation. In this case we have assumed that inflation will average 2.5 per cent every year for the life of the scheme (we will return to this issue in Chapter 15).

Throughout this book we explore the risks that these pension promises pose and how they relate to the investment fund that accumulates to meet them. But before we move on to discuss DC pension provision, we should just reemphasize that with a DB scheme the risk lies firmly with the sponsor. If there is deemed not to be enough money to meet all the pension promises, then the employer is required to make up the difference, as these benefits are effectively underwritten by the sponsor. However, in the event of the sponsor becoming insolvent, the scheme is admitted to the Pension Protection Fund (PPF). We consider both of these points in more detail in Chapter 3.

In recent years the burden of this risk, for reasons that we have already covered and will cover throughout the book, has proved too much for many plan sponsors, in that many have had to make huge contributions to their schemes, often greater than the dividend payments they make to their shareholders. Indeed, a number of sponsors have DB pension scheme liabilities that exceed their stock market value. Consequently, 79 per cent of sponsors now do not allow new employees to join their DB scheme, often cutting the generosity to the remaining members at the same time, though prospectively.[11] These schemes are said to be closed to new entrants. In addition, 17 per cent of DB schemes have gone a step further. They are not only closed to new members, but are also

---

[10] According to the Mercer Asset Allocation Survey and Market Profiles – European institutional market place overview, April 2010, in the UK the value of liabilities between actives, deferreds and pensioners is split 31 per cent, 34 per cent and 35 per cent, respectively.

[11] These benefit dilution measures, some of which we have already mentioned, comprise the implementation of career average revalued earnings (CARE), changing accrual rates, increasing the scheme's normal pension age (NPA), raising member contributions, capping pensionable salary rises and imposing a longevity adjustment factor to future accruals.

closed to 'future accrual'. This means that even active members cannot earn any further pension benefits under a DB formula.[12]

Increasingly then, new employees are not permitted to enter existing DB plans. Instead they are offered an alternative DC arrangement. For those schemes that have closed to future accrual, their existing members retain their pension benefits accrued in the past under the DB arrangements but their future pension accrual is offered on a DC basis. The eventual pensions of these members will therefore comprise a mixture of DB and DC pension rights.

Lord Hutton's public sector pension scheme reforms

In 2010, Chancellor George Osborne appointed, former Labour cabinet minister, Lord John Hutton, to investigate how public pension provision, both funded and unfunded, could be put on a more sustainable financial footing.

In his report on the future of public pensions, Lord Hutton made 27 recommendations to be implemented by 2015. His key proposals, all of which were agreed to by the Chancellor, were to:

- retain DB pensions but to move away from final salary to career average revalued earnings (CARE), revaluing this accrual annually by the average earnings index, while preserving benefits already accrued;
- raise the Normal Pension Age (NPA) from 60 to 65 for all but the uniformed services, for which the NPA should be raised to 60, increasing this in line with changes in the State Pension Age (SPA), and
- place a cap on the cost of public sector pension provision by employing a mechanism that would automatically increase pension contributions or reduce the benefits accrued in a particular year if the cap was breached.

In modelling the financial effect of moving from final salary to CARE, the Pensions Policy Institute found that the replacement ratio (pension income as a percentage of final salary), which currently stands at 64 per cent, would fall to 55 per cent.

Defined benefit summary

Regrettably, it would seem that the end of the DB pension scheme is probably in sight. It certainly seems likely that DB schemes will continue to close both to new entrants and to future accrual, as more and more employers seek to rid themselves of this 'burden'. However, this does not mean that we can forget

---

[12] Source of statistics: National Association of Pension Funds (NAPF), March 2011.

about them. As DB liabilities stretch out for decades before us, there will still be people drawing DB pension benefits long after most of you reading this book are pushing up the daisies – to quote from Monty Python.

Defined contribution pension arrangements

By comparison to DB, DC pension arrangements are relatively simple. However, as we will see there is no equivalent 'promise' when it comes to DC pension provision.

DC pension scheme arrangements can take several forms. An employer-sponsored DC scheme, also known as a Money Purchase scheme, can either be trust-based – that is run by trustees – or be administered by an insurance company via a Group Personal Pension Plan (GPPP), in which case it is referred to as being contract-based. Aside from these two arrangements, individuals can also manage their own personal pension via a Personal Pension Plan (PPP), some of which are known as stakeholder plans if their charges fall below an annual ceiling of 1 per cent, or a Self Invested Personal Pension Plan (SIPP), which allows the individual to invest across a wide range of different investments.

For both trust-based and contract-based employer-sponsored DC schemes, both the scheme sponsor and the scheme member make regular contributions to a member-specific investment fund. That is, although the contributions are normally pooled and managed together, each member builds up a pension pot based upon their own and the sponsor's contributions. These contributions are invested, usually in one or a number of investment funds in the expectation that each member's fund will grow over time. For trust-based schemes, these funds are selected by the trustees in conjunction with their advisers. For contract-based schemes, the sponsor selects these funds. At retirement, the member typically uses their fund to buy an annuity in the open market (this is known as an open market option) and usually takes some portion of the fund as a tax-free lump sum.[13] The size of their eventual pension will therefore be largely determined by three factors:

- the value of the DC pension pot at retirement;
- the amount of the cash withdrawn as a tax-free lump sum; and
- the current annuity rate.

---

[13] Following a change in legislation in 2011, individuals who can prove that they will be in receipt of a guaranteed minimum level of income in retirement – a Minimum Income Requirement (MIR) – of £20,000 per annum, are not required to purchase an annuity with their pension pots. Prior to this, an annuity had to be purchased by all individuals with DC pensions arrangements by age 75. Instead, those with the requisite MIR can withdraw unlimited amounts from their pension pots via 'flexible drawdown' arrangements, offered by insurance companies, from age 55.

Annuities

An annuity is a financial product offered mainly by insurance companies. In return for the pension pot that has accumulated, the insurance company will pay a regular amount to the individual, known as an annuitant, for the rest of their life. These annuities are available:

- as level payments;
- as payments linked to inflation (that is, they are 'index-linked');
- with in-built provisos that ensure that in the event of the annuitant's death some portion of the annuity payment (usually 50 per cent) continues to be paid to the annuitant's widow/widower; and
- with minimum period guarantees. That is, a guarantee that the full pension will be paid for a minimum period (usually five or ten years) even if the annuitant dies before this minimum period expires.

Exhibit 1.2 shows the average annuity payment that could be bought with £10,000 at the end of April 2011.[14] The horizontal scale shows the age of retirement for a male annuitant. The first set of bars presents the annual pension income that £10,000 could buy payable up until the death of the annuitant, with no guarantee and no index-linking. The second set of bars show the annual pension that £10,000 could buy, where the pension is payable for a minimum of five years or when the annuitant dies, and where the annuity payment rises over time with RPI inflation. This second set of annuity payments are lower initially, but with positive inflation will rise. So eventually, depending upon the rate of inflation and how long the annuitant lives, the annual payment from this annuity could end up being higher than the annuity derived from the non-indexed annual payment. The final set of bars give the non-indexed annual pension payment that £10,000 can buy, where the payment is guaranteed for a minimum of five years, and where in the event of the male annuitant's death, the annuitant's wife, assumed to be the same age as their husband, receives an annual payment of 50 per cent of the annuity.

Exhibit 1.2 demonstrates a number of important points. First, the younger the annuitant, the lower the annuity payment. This is because the insurance company will potentially have to pay the pension annuity for longer. Second, the initial payment from an index-linked annuity will be lower than for an equivalent non-indexed annuity. This is because the insurance company will

---

[14] Each payment is an average of the five best insurance company annuity offerings available at this date.

Exhibit 1.2   Annual annuity payments, per £10,000 worth of DC pension pot

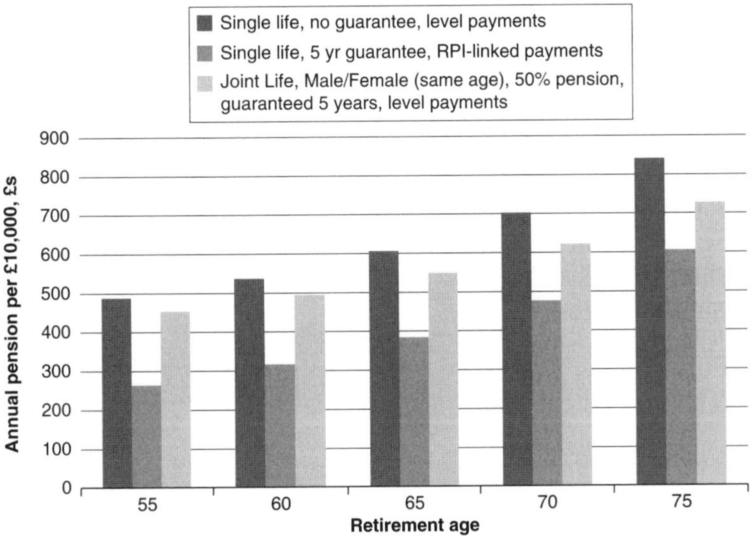

Sources: Centre for Asset Management Research, Cass Business School; and *this is money*.

have to pay higher and higher payments over time with positive inflation. The final point worth mentioning is that the more bells and whistles – guarantees, inflation-linking, widow/widower provisions etc. – attached, the lower will be the annuity. This is because each extra element becomes potentially more expensive for the insurer to provide.

So at retirement, the DC scheme member uses the pot of money that they have accumulated during their time in the scheme to purchase an annuity from an insurance company. Of course, the smaller the pension pot, the smaller the eventual annuity, but also, the lower the annuity rate the lower the eventual pension too.

Exhibit 1.3 shows the level payment and RPI-linked, single life annuity rates over time for a 65-year-old male, with no guarantee. What we can clearly see is how much these annuity rates on offer from insurance firms have declined over time. In fact, level annuity rates have halved over this 21-year period, as a result of the dramatic decline in bond yields – bonds (which we consider in Chapter 6) are used by insurance companies to back these annuities – and the equally dramatic increase in the longevity of the UK population. This means that to generate the same size annuity payment today, the annuitant's invest-ment pot needs to be around twice as big to generate the same annuity available

Exhibit 1.3   Annuity rates over time

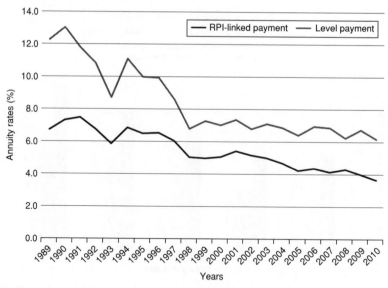

Source: Centre for Asset Management Research, Cass Business School.

in 1989.[15] This decline in annuity rates is as relevant for members of DC pension schemes as it is for sponsors of DB pension schemes.

What happens if the pension pot of a DC scheme member is not large enough to buy the pension that they expect or need at retirement? Is the employer honour bound to make up the difference? The answer is that the scheme sponsor is not honour bound to make up any perceived difference. So unlike with the DB scheme, with a DC scheme the risk of any shortfall lies firmly with the scheme member. This explains why many employers are closing down their DB schemes and are offering a DC pension scheme instead. Moreover, while the average sponsor contribution to a DB scheme is equivalent to 16.6 per cent of each member's annual salary, the equivalent figure for the average employer contribution for DC members is only 6.1 per cent.[16] Quite a difference.

---

[15] Annuity rates may be driven down by other factors in the future. One such factor is the forthcoming Solvency II Directive, which will require insurance companies probably in 2014 to back their annuities with UK government bonds (gilts) rather than higher yielding corporate bonds. Another is the decision by the European Court of Justice that the same annuity rates should be paid to men and women despite the evidence that firmly supports the latter, on average, outliving the former. A unisex market in annuities is to be created by 21 December 2012. This will mean that female annuity rates will rise but male annuity rates will fall.

[16] Pension Trends 2009, ONS.

Defined contribution default funds and lifestyling

There are two other important issues with regard to DC pension provision that we need to mention, both of which distinguish DC further from DB pension arrangements: member fund selection and lifestyling.

First, member fund selection. Throughout this book we will illustrate how DB pension scheme trustees, with the help of their advisers, allocate a DB scheme's funds between different asset classes – bonds, equities, real estate and so on. They make these choices on behalf of all their DB scheme members. However, as mentioned earlier, for their DC members, again with the help of their advisers, trustees of trust-based DC schemes instead provide a range of investment funds each with a different asset mix, from which each DC member must choose to invest their own and the sponsor's contributions. Making the 'right' decision is crucial, as, unlike DB, it is the DC member, rather than the scheme sponsor, that bears the risk of their pension pot underperforming. In practice however, because of a combination of inertia, bewilderment at the sheer choice of funds typically made available (less is definitely more when it comes to providing DC scheme members with a selection of investment funds) and the fact that most DC members are ill-prepared to make an informed decision about which fund(s) to select, most occupational DC schemes offer a default fund. The default fund, which can take a number of forms, is typically one that:

- is diversified across a range of asset classes;
- is actively managed; and
- has a clear investment objective: usually to outperform RPI inflation by five per cent per annum.

Given that the default fund should address member inertia and inexperience in actively selecting funds and cope with a wide range of investor circumstances, typically around 90 per cent of DC scheme members choose to invest in the default fund option, usually by default! Consequently, a DC scheme's default investment option is the most important decision for DC scheme trustees of trustee-based schemes and sponsors of contract-based schemes, to get right. It not only affects the greatest number of members – it is also the investment option for which trustees bear the greatest fiduciary responsibility. The challenges a default fund faces are complex. It must invest over many years in multiple asset classes and manage risks in relation to a long-dated and uncertain liability.

In selecting the default option, the DC member is usually also offered a progressively less risky asset allocation as they approach their chosen retirement age. This is known as a 'lifestyling option'. If chosen, this lifestyling option automatically moves the DC member out of the default fund and into less risky asset classes, like government bonds, usually over a five to ten year period. To see why this is done, imagine that with a few days to retirement a DC member has all of their pension pot invested in a default fund that invests heavily in equities (as many do). Now imagine the impact on the investment fund, and therefore also on the value of the annuity, if equities fell by, say, 30 per cent just before the DC member was due to buy their annuity. Such an eventuality would be disastrous for the DC member. By gradually de-risking the pension pot of the DC member over the five to ten years leading up to their retirement, it is hoped that nasty shocks on retirement can be avoided. Moreover, given that bond yields and annuity rates tend to move together, the DC member can reduce some of the risk of annuity rates moving against them as they approach retirement by investing in a bond fund.

However, because the DC member is free to choose their own asset allocation, they can opt out of the lifestyling option should they wish to do so. As such, they can de-risk their investment pot at a faster or slower pace than would happen under the lifestyling option. Moreover, as an aide to lifestyling, some DC schemes use a series of 'target retirement date' default investment funds, each of which is timed to meet a member's designated retirement age. So a 2020 target retirement date fund, for instance, would invest and de-risk as appropriate for someone seeking to retire in 2020. By contrast, a 2030 target retirement date fund would invest and de-risk in an optimal manner for someone retiring in 2030. If the member changes their target retirement date, they simply move into the appropriate target retirement date fund.

Exhibit 1.4 shows the historic performance of lifestyling for the average DC member, who has earned an average salary over the past few years. For each year when lifestyling begins (shown on the horizontal axis) our representative average salaried worker:

- is aged 55 and has ten years to retirement;
- has a pension pot equivalent to twice their annual salary;
- makes an annual contribution equivalent to 6 per cent of their annual salary to the DC default fund;
- has an employer that contributes the equivalent of 6 per cent of the member's annual salary to the DC default fund; and
- has a starting investment portfolio comprising 60 per cent equities and 40 per cent UK government bonds but by the time they retire their investment pot comprises 100 per cent UK government bonds. This is achieved over the ten years by selling 6.67 per cent of their equity holding at the end of every year, using the proceeds to increase their holdings of UK government bonds.

Exhibit 1.4   Historic performance of lifestyling

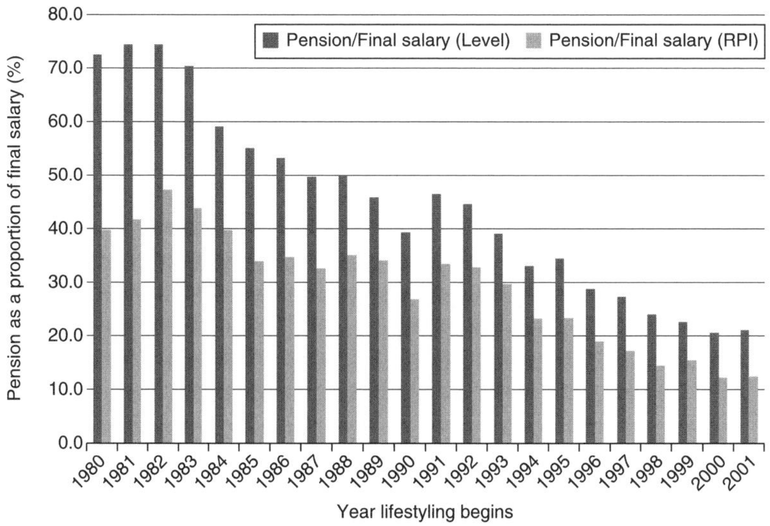

Source: Centre for Asset Management Research, Cass Business School.

The bars in Exhibit 1.4 show the size of the annuity per annum that can be bought with the pension pot at retirement as a proportion of the DC member's final year salary. This is known as the replacement ratio. To calculate this we estimate the performance of the government bond and equity markets for each ten year period, and then use the relevant annuity rates that prevailed at the time the DC member retired.

The results are quite scary, but are in line with the comment we made earlier, relating to the halving of annuity rates since 1989. Indeed, had a DC member begun their lifestyling in 1989 (acknowledging that very few DC schemes were around in 1989 – a point we come back to shortly), and assuming that they did not take any tax-free lump sum from their fund, they would have been able to purchase a level payment annuity equivalent to 46 per cent of their final salary, or an RPI-linked annuity equivalent to 33 per cent of their final salary. Contrast this with the fortunes of the equivalent individual beginning their lifestyling journey in 2001. This poor soul can only afford a level payment annuity equivalent to 22 per cent of their final salary, or a RPI-linked payment equivalent to a measly 13 per cent of their final salary. This would presumably rule out the Harley Davidson, world cruise or time share apartment in the Algarve, though not necessarily the occasional weekend on a New Forest caravan site.

The DC default fund: Improving the outcome for the DC member

The risk that a pension will not provide an acceptable standard of living is, by some distance, the biggest risk faced by DC scheme members: no one wants to live in poverty after retirement. Yet the DC default option only grapples with this towards the end of its life. Indeed, by bringing lifestyling into the equation, apart from reducing investment risk as retirement approaches, lifestyled default funds tend not to address the complexities of managing the many risks in relation to a long-dated and uncertain liability throughout the term of the individual's membership of the DC scheme. In fact, it is only by choosing opportune moments to annuitize portions of the money built up through the life of a DC scheme that the optimum result can be achieved.

The investment 'technology' needed to address some of this complexity already exists and has been tried and tested in DB schemes. Indeed, in adopting a liability-matching approach for the DC default fund, the aim is to manage risk and return throughout the investment period by investing in a well-diversified investment mix with moderate volatility, using dynamic interest rate and inflation hedges to deliver better median (average) and worse-case scenarios. These hedges we consider in Chapters 12 and 15.

The ratio of an investor's annual pension to their salary at retirement – the replacement ratio – is the key metric to consider. The key to liability-matching for DC investors is to maximize median replacement ratios, while ensuring the worst-case replacement ratio remains acceptable. Here is how it works.

The principal determinant of the replacement ratio is the amount of risk an investor takes. Modelling of different levels of risk shows that an optimal level of volatility for default funds' growth assets should be relatively moderate at around 6 per cent to 10 per cent per annum.[17] We consider volatility in Chapter 9. More risk-averse investors would adopt 6 per cent volatility to improve their worst-case outcome even though this would not maximize their median outcome. Less risk-averse investors would target 10 per cent volatility to maximize their median outcome, while accepting the risk of a worse replacement ratio.

The other two key determinants of the investment outcome are interest rates and inflation. Dynamic hedging of interest rates and inflation throughout

---

[17] 'Smarter techniques needed to ease risk of DC schemes'. Chris Wagstaff. *Financial News*, 25 April 2011.

the investment period can significantly improve median and worst-case scenarios for replacement ratios. Annuity rates tend to move in line with gilt yields and the spread on corporate bonds. When these are both high, the annuity rate – and therefore the pension received – tends to be high. So the risk of reduced income at retirement can be lessened by locking in any higher levels whenever they are available over the life of the investment: for example through interest rate swaps. The results can be startling. The optimization of replacement ratios can improve the median outcomes of lifestyle approaches by 15 per cent, reducing the worst case scenarios dramatically too.

In summary, unless DC default funds target a moderate level of volatility and use dynamic hedging throughout the investment period, then the investor's capital is at risk, sometimes substantially so.

Defined contribution starting to dominate the pensions landscape

According to Towers Watson's 2011 global pensions asset study,[18] DC schemes now account for 44 per cent of the US$26.5 trillion (£16.1tn) invested in pension schemes globally, up from 35 per cent in 2000, as the seemingly inexorable move from DB to DC continues unabated. Indeed, global DC scheme assets have grown at an annual rate of 7.5 per cent since 2000, while DB scheme assets over the same period have experienced more pedestrian annual growth of 2.9 per cent.[19] The markets with the largest proportion of DC assets are Australia, where DC scheme assets represent 81 per cent of all domestic pension assets, followed by Switzerland at 60 per cent and the US at 57 per cent.

The UK, with 40 per cent of its pension assets in DC schemes (excluding personal and stakeholder pensions), has experienced the most dramatic rate of change of any major pensions market with only 3 per cent of pension assets having been invested in DC schemes in 2000. DC schemes are then a relatively new phenomenon in the UK, certainly when compared to the more developed DC markets in the Asia Pacific region, notably Australia. Whereas 43 per cent of DC plans in Asia Pacific have been running for more than ten years, in the UK only 34 per cent have more than a ten year track record.[20]

---

[18] Towers Watson Global Pension Asset Study 2011.
[19] Compound annual growth rates: 2000 to 2010.
[20] Mercer Asset Allocation Survey and Market Profiles – European institutional market place overview, April, p.27 (2010).

As we have seen, with DB pension provision the burden of risk rests firmly with the scheme sponsor. However, with DC arrangements the risk burden lies with the scheme members. This difference is one of the main reasons why most DB schemes have closed to new entrants, while 17 per cent are estimated to have closed to future accrual too. Whether we like it or not, DC is the future and DB is the past. So much so that the UK government is launching a super DC fund – the National Employment Savings Trust (NEST),[21] loosely based on Australia's £790bn super-DC system, launched in 1992.

From October 2012, as part of a wider shake up of pension provision in the UK, UK employers will be required to enrol employees automatically into a 'qualifying workplace pension scheme'. This auto-enrolment could be to an existing company pension scheme if it meets certain criteria. If it does not or there is no company pension scheme, then employers will be required to enrol their employees into NEST, which has been designed to be a simple, low-cost pension scheme. Between October 2012 and 2017, depending on the size of the company, all UK employers will be required to contribute a minimum of 3 per cent of each employee's eligible earnings into a pension, assuming the employee does not 'opt out' of the scheme. By contrast, the Australian system is compulsory and does not allow opt outs. In addition, employees will need to pay a personal contribution of 4 per cent, with a further 1 per cent tax relief being added, taking the minimum contribution to 8 per cent of gross annual salary. By way of comparison, these contribution rates don't look that different from the 6.1 per cent and 3 per cent contributions respectively which, according to the ONS,[22] are currently paid into occupational DC schemes.

The Government estimate that about seven million, mainly lower paid, people are currently not saving enough for their retirement, and could all potentially become NEST members. More specifically, employees that will be eligible for automatic enrolment will be those who:

- are not already active members of a qualifying pension scheme;
- are aged between 22 years and the State Pension Age; and
- earn over £7,475 gross a year.

After just a few years then NEST will be the largest DC pension plan in the land – with an expected two million members by the end of 2016. It will have all the basic features and also some less common features of a typical DC scheme, including:

- a series of 'target retirement date' default investment funds – each of which is timed to meet a member's designated retirement age;

---

[21] Presumably as in 'nest egg'. Let's just hope that the egg doesn't turn out to be rotten!
[22] Pension Trends 2009, ONS.

- optional additional funds, including an ethical and a Sharia compliant fund; and
- lifestyling elements.

The shape and size of the pension industry

As the world's third largest pensions market by assets – accounting for 8.6 per cent of global pension assets (only the US and Japan are bigger, accounting for 57.8 per cent and 13.1 per cent of global pension assets respectively[23]) the UK occupational pension industry is huge. Indeed, total UK pension assets (excluding those in personal and stakeholder pensions) are estimated to be US$2,279bn (£1,381bn), equivalent to 101 per cent of UK GDP, or national output. According to the ONS, at the end of 2008 nine million people were active members of either an occupational DB or DC scheme, comprising 3.6m in the private sector and 5.4m in the public sector.[24] Furthermore, the ONS estimate that 8.8m people in the UK were in receipt of a DB and/or DC occupational pension.

Exhibit 1.5 shows how the UK's DB and DC pension schemes fit in with the wider pension landscape (excluding state pension provision). All occupational salary related schemes are DB, while all occupational money purchase schemes

Exhibit 1.5   Types of pension provision

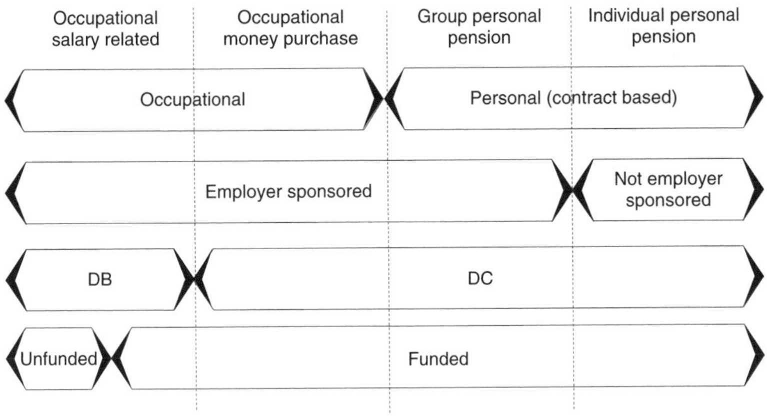

Source: Pensions Commission 2005.

---

[23] Towers Watson Global Pension Asset Study 2011.
[24] Remember that many public sector pension plans are run in the same way as private sector DB plans.

are DC. Some DB schemes – generally public sector schemes – are unfunded, while private sector DB schemes and all DC schemes are funded which means that a pot of money is set aside over time to provide the pension. All DB and DC schemes plus all group personal pension plans are sponsored by an employer. Finally individual personal pensions, while not employer sponsored (though an employer may contribute to them), are funded and are all of the DC type.

The membership split between DB and DC plans is difficult to estimate. Indeed as we explained earlier, many employees may be members of both a DB and a DC scheme. However, in a more recent report by the Pensions Regulator,[25] it was estimated that:

- 2.3 million people currently contribute to a private sector DB pension scheme (compared to 5.5m in the early 1980s);
- 1 million active members currently contribute to DC schemes;
- 2.5 million people in total have savings in DC schemes;
- annual contributions to schemes with 12 or more members amount to approximately £2.2bn, or £4,200 per active member, where 75 per cent of these contributions come from the employer; and
- around half of all DC membership is concentrated in 130 large schemes, while most DC schemes (around 44,000) are very small, with less than 12 members, accounting for just 5 per cent of total DC membership.

Key points

- Defined benefit (DB) pension schemes provide pre-defined benefits usually based on a member's 'final salary', the scheme's accrual rate and the number of years that the employee has been a member of the scheme, though a career average revalued earnings (CARE) benefits basis is becoming more common-place. These benefits are effectively guaranteed by the scheme sponsor.
- Most DB schemes are closed to new members and are increasingly being closed to existing members. Where schemes do remain open, benefits are increasingly being diluted.
- For employer-sponsored defined contribution (DC) pension schemes, which can be either trust-based or contract-based, both the scheme sponsor and the scheme member make regular contributions to a member-specific investment fund. For around 90 per cent of DC scheme members, this fund is the default fund. Most default funds employ lifestyling, while some also use target retirement date funds.

---

[25] The Pensions Regulator, DC Trust 2010.

- Because employer-sponsored DC schemes are not underwritten by the sponsor, the DC scheme member is wholly reliant on the value of the DC pension pot and prevailing annuity rates at retirement.
- The UK has the world's third largest pensions market by assets. With 60 per cent of its pension assets in DB schemes and 40 per cent in DC schemes (excluding personal and stakeholder pensions), the UK has experienced the most dramatic rate of change in the accumulation of DC scheme assets of any major pensions market.

Chapter 2

Trustee Knowledge and Understanding, and Investment Governance: What Do Trustees Need to Know?

Learning outcomes

- Appreciate the importance of trustee knowledge and understanding.
- Appreciate the need to continually improve upon your education and development and the means available to achieve this.
- Appreciate what investment governance is and the need and means by which to continually improve it.

Trustee knowledge and understanding

There's no doubt there has to be better [trustee] knowledge and understanding and it is an area of concern. We're not asking [trustees] to become financial experts but trustees need the proper depth of understanding – enough to challenge the experts who are giving them advice. I think the death of the amateur trustee has been much exaggerated – there are tens of thousands of trustees out there and they are generally prepared and willing to up their game. (Tony Hobman, Former Chief Executive, the Pensions Regulator, September 2006)

Today trustees face a multitude of challenges and increasingly complex solutions. For these reasons, Tony Blair's mantra of 'education, education, education' should resonate with trustees. Indeed, the priority given to trustee education, for those 120,000 or so unsung heroes who are ultimately responsible for well over £1 trillion of assets and liabilities[1] on behalf of nearly 20 million members[2] within over 66,000 schemes,[3] by the Pensions Regulator (tPR), ever since its inception in 2006,[4] remains as valid today as it did then. Arguably more so.

Although they may not appreciate it, the Pensions Act 2004 has made trustees one of the most powerful groups in the business world and with greater power comes greater responsibility. Nowhere is this more apparent than when powerful CEOs come knocking on a sponsoring company's door with open chequebooks, seeking a merger with or an acquisition of that company. Just ask the trustees of the Corus, Alliance Boots and Sainsbury's defined benefit (DB) scheme trustee boards, when their sponsors faced takeover bids from Tata in 2006, KKR in 2007 and Delta Two in 2007, respectively. These trustee boards, in preserving or enhancing the security of their respective pension schemes, were in a sufficiently powerful position to dictate whether the takeover was successful or not, and, if so, the terms on which the takeover would proceed.

This greater power also derives from trustees being empowered to obtain joint clearance with their sponsor from tPR when the sponsoring company proposes a 'corporate action' that could potentially deflect cash away from funding the pension scheme, or which could materially weaken the company's financial position or covenant. These corporate actions include the sponsor diverting cash away from its balance sheet or issuing debt to raise cash to pay an enhanced cash dividend to shareholders or to fund a shareholder share buyback or to finance a merger or takeover. Only if clearance is obtained before these corporate actions are implemented can these transactions proceed without any later comeback from tPR.

Trustee education

In April 2006, tPR introduced the Trustee Knowledge and Understanding (TKU) Code of Practice. Revised in 2009, this forms the basis of what trustees need to know in discharging their fiduciary duties. Based on s.247–249 of the

---

[1] Private sector trust-based occupational pension scheme assets only. Source: UBS Global Asset Management estimates to end-2009 based on data from the Office for National Statistics (ONS), ABI and HMRC.
[2] ONS OPSS Annual Report – Revised Edition 2010.
[3] NAPF, August 2008.
[4] tPR replaced its predecessor, the Occupational Pensions Regulatory Authority (OPRA), on 6 April 2006.

Pensions Act 2004,[5] its provisions are very broad,[6] though its application is self-explanatory:[7]

> *from [6] April 2006 trustees of occupational schemes will be required to be conversant with their own scheme documents, and to have knowledge and understanding (appropriate to their role as trustee) of trusts and pensions law and the principles of funding and investment . . . These requirements will apply to all trustees. However newly appointed trustees (other than corporate, professional or expert trustees) will be given six months from their date of appointment to meet the requirements.*

Although trustees are not expected to be experts in all or any one area, expertise should reside in the trustee board as a whole. A good first step in becoming TKU compliant is to complete tPR's free-to-access online Trustee Toolkit at www. trusteetoolkit.com. However, TKU cannot possibly cover everything trustees need to know. Indeed, trustees' knowledge and understanding requirements go far beyond TKU if they are to be in the best possible position to question and constructively challenge their fund managers and advisers. After all, arguably trustee rule number one should be: *never invest in anything that you do not understand*. The imperative is to gain the requisite confidence and competence to be able to ask the right questions and seek the appropriate explanations. However, if at the end of that process you still don't understand, you simply don't invest.

Trustee education beyond TKU

Without effective trustees there cannot be an effective occupational pensions system in the UK. Nowhere is this truer than in the area of investment. So how exactly do trustees raise their game to achieve the requisite confidence and competence that not only scheme members demand of them but which they demand of themselves if they are to discharge their duties in as knowledgeable and responsible manner possible?

Well, in the first instance, trustees need to establish what they need to know by benchmarking their knowledge against not only the TKU requirements but also industry press releases, such as the bi-weekly *NAPF PolicyWatch*, topical articles that appear in trustee-focused publications, such as *Engaged Investor* and *Pensions Insight*, and trustee-centric websites, like *FT SchemeXpert*, and the more popular

---

[5] The origins of the TKU Code of Practice ultimately derive from Paul Myners' review of institutional investment in November 2001. Being a Code of Practice means that while it doesn't have the force of law, it has legal effect in as far as its provisions can be applied in a tribunal or court in deciding whether a particular requirement has been met. For further information, see http://www.thepensionsregulator.gov.uk/doc-library/codes.aspx.
[6] See http://www.thepensionsregulator.gov.uk/docs/tku-indicative-syllabus-2009.pdf.
[7] The application of the TKU Code of Practice is covered more comprehensively at http://www.thepensionsregulator.gov.uk/codes/code-trustee-knowledge.aspx.

discussions on trustee community websites, such as *mallowstreet.com*. The next stage should be to conduct a Training Needs Analysis (TNA) to record what you don't know or understand and then when and how you intend to address these gaps in your knowledge by constructing a Training and Development Plan and maintaining a Learning and Development log.

As to the key sources of learning and development, especially that relating to investment, trustees are somewhat spoilt for choice in that they have access to a wide range of free-to-access educational resources. For instance, most asset managers, industry bodies and some investment consultants provide free face-to-face trustee investment training programmes, seminars and conferences and a number additionally provide dedicated investment training to individual trustee boards free of charge. The latter makes considerable sense as learning as a board can be extremely beneficial. Moreover, very little can beat the interactivity associated with face-to-face education, especially when the subject matter is complex. However, this approach doesn't appeal to everyone, not least because of the increasing demands on trustees' time and the need to travel to a central location on a specific date and at a pre-determined time. Consequently, this approach can only ever serve a small proportion of the more than one hundred thousand trustees.

To make trustee investment education much more accessible most of the same asset managers and consultants have embraced technological advances by developing a suite of online investment educational material, much of it interactive. Online investment training videos and interactive investment web seminars are also now more commonplace. This approach enables trustees to learn at their own pace, in bite sized chunks, when and at a location that is convenient for them. The proliferation of trustee community and networking websites, with their topical forums and blogs which harness 'the wisdom of the crowd' – the 'crowd' comprising trustees, pension scheme managers, asset managers, investment consultants, lawyers and academics – are also good sources of contemporary investment information.

Ideally all forms of trustee investment education should be wholly generic and free from provider product bias and should implicitly or explicitly cite its relevance to TKU and/or other trustee knowledge requirements.

However, these educational sources cannot cover everything. For example, they cannot teach trustees how to negotiate scheme funding issues with the scheme sponsor. Like any soft skill, successful negotiation requires more than just an understanding of facts and figures. On the one hand it requires firm diplomacy to avoid creating friction with the sponsor, which could otherwise damage the sponsor's willingness to support the scheme. On the other, trustees need to be sufficiently confident to lock horns with the sponsor's senior management, to whom they may well report in their day jobs.

Investment governance

Let's move away from trustee education and on to investment governance, while acknowledging that the two are intrinsically linked. Good investment governance is only possible if trustees continually improve upon their skills, expertise and organizational effectiveness as they develop a scheme's investment strategy.

However, to take a step back, scheme governance in basic terms simply means *doing things right* to ensure that the scheme is well run. At one level this is about the trustee board:

- having the right mix of skills;
- being sufficiently diverse in its composition;
- having the appropriate controls;
- making the appropriate disclosures on conflicts of interest;[8]
- being accountable;
- adopting a risk register to consider the impact on the scheme of all types of risk – financial and non-financial;
- keeping up to date with changes in legislation and regulation; and
- regularly reviewing the scheme's advisers and consultants.

That sort of thing. At another level, it is about the trustees discharging their fiduciary duties in accordance with the scheme trust deed, other scheme documents,[9] scheme rules, trust law, case law, pensions legislation, tPR regulations and Codes of Practice and abiding by 'comply or explain' best practice codes, such as the Myners principles.[10] This requires trustees to exercise their fiduciary powers carefully, fairly and impartially in the best interests of present and future scheme beneficiaries so as to ensure that the benefits accrued within the scheme can be paid.

Investment governance 1.0

Relating all of this to investment governance, again at a basic level, trustees, in having sole control over scheme investment matters, acknowledging that the

---

[8] Despite protestations to the contrary, almost all trustee boards have conflicts of interest which they need to manage. Arguably, every trustee board should have an independent trustee to help manage these conflicts, bring some independence to the board's decision making and, indeed, help the decision making process and the implementation of these decisions along.

[9] These documents include the Statement of Investment Principles (SIP) and the Statement of Funding Principles (SFP).

[10] Updated in 2008, the Myners principles are six high level principles voluntarily applied as a code of best practice. They comprise effective decision making, clear objectives, risk and liabilities, performance assessment, responsible ownership and transparency and reporting.

sponsor must be consulted on changes to investment strategy, must exercise their investment powers prudently as per the scheme trust deed, Statement of Investment Principles (SIP)[11] and the Pensions Acts. In so doing, trustees must consider the suitability of investments given the structure of the scheme's liabilities and the strength of the employer covenant, balance risk and return in the best interests of the scheme membership, give detailed consideration to the risks involved, ensuring that these risks are adequately managed and diversified, and set and monitor performance against appropriate benchmarks. Perhaps most importantly, trustees must seek appropriate professional advice in making investment decisions and not fall into the trap of believing that they themselves should act as fund managers and make decisions about individual investments.[12]

Investment governance 2.0

However, as already noted, with ever greater complexity surrounding investment solutions and investment decision making, it makes sense for trustees to move their investment governance to a more advanced level, not least because it has been suggested that it can add in excess of 1 per cent per annum to long-run risk-adjusted investment returns.[13] However, this potential for improved risk-adjusted investment performance through improved investment governance is not only contingent on *doing things right* but also on *doing the right things*.[14] After all, an advanced level of investment governance is essentially the mechanism by which trustees turn risk into reward.

Necessarily, the level of investment governance employed by a trustee board must be commensurate with its collective capabilities. Crucially, however, a more advanced level of investment governance demands a high level of organizational effectiveness if investment decisions and their implementation are to

---

[11] The SIP, which is set by the trustees, details the scheme's investment strategy and objectives, investment criteria and restrictions, strategic benchmark, asset allocation strategy and parameters, risk management policy, policy on environmental, social and corporate governance (ESG) issues and the exercise of voting rights and fund manager mandates. These outline each manager's performance objectives and risk parameters and the obligation to monitor these.

[12] In making investment decisions today, trustees should also consider the impact of those decisions on the scheme in years to come. This is particularly important for schemes as they become mature and/or close given the need to generate cash increasingly from investment income and the realisation of assets to pay members' pensions.

[13] See: Keith Ambachtsheer, 'How much is good governance worth?', *The Ambachtsheer Letter* 245, June (2006); Gordon L. Clark, and Roger Urwin, 'Best-Practice Investment Management: Lessons for Asset Owners', from the Oxford-Watson Wyatt Project on Governance, October (2007).

[14] For a more detailed consideration of what is required, see Roger Irwin, 'Best Practice in Investment Governance for Pension Funds', *QFinance*, October (2008).

be made in a more timely fashion. After all, in many aspects of investment, market timing is everything.[15]

Statement of investment beliefs

At the very least, if not already done, this requires the trustee board to delegate investment powers within defined parameters to an investment sub-committee.[16] However, if this committee is to be effective and achieve its long-term goals, it should compile a statement of its investment beliefs with the scheme's investment consultant, as an adjunct to the scheme's SIP. This statement, in articulating the committee's explicit views on a range of investment phenomena, will then provide the strategic framework for identifying those investment opportunities that best fit with these beliefs.

To fulfil this function, the statement should articulate, for example, the committee's views about how financial markets function – whether markets are efficiently priced[17] or not for instance – and should then consider the implications of these beliefs for the management of the scheme. For example, this would have a bearing on whether the scheme wishes to employ active fund managers or not. The statement should also address questions such as the committee's belief in:

- the equity risk premium – the expected long-term outperformance of equities over bonds;
- what constitutes an overvalued and undervalued asset class;
- when and how the scheme should de-risk; and
- the scheme's attitude to diversification.[18]

Given that a substantial investment in risk management[19] is an integral component of advancing the level of investment governance, the committee

---

[15] So as to assess the effectiveness of their governance and make good any shortcomings, a number of schemes have started to make use of the specialist governance appraisal services offered by most consultants. These governance consultants ensure that the trustee board and any sub-committees are getting the most of out their meetings by scrutinising the dynamics of the board, principally the way in which decisions are made and how they are implemented. We return to the dynamics of trustee decision making in Chapter 17.

[16] The size, composition and the decision-making processes of a trustee board and investment sub-committee are considered in more detail in Chapter 17.

[17] That is, whether market prices always fully reflect all that's known about the market. See Chapters 14 and 17 for a fuller explanation of market efficiency.

[18] For a detailed exposition of what a list of investment beliefs should comprise and the benefits of compiling such a list, see: Kees Koedijk and Alfred Slager, '*Investment Beliefs: A positive approach to institutional investing*', Basingstoke, Palgrave Macmillan (2010).

[19] See Chapter 9 for an explanation of the risks trustees face and how these should be managed.

also needs to ensure it has a defined risk budget[20] again clearly outlined in its investment beliefs statement. The dynamism that characterizes financial markets, investment strategies and risk management demands that the statement is regularly revisited and amended as appropriate. For example, many such statements might have needed revision after the events of 2008.

Implementing these beliefs

With its beliefs and risk budget clearly articulated, the committee can then consider whether it has the capability, expertise and appetite to look beyond simple traditional investment strategies to those that could potentially raise the scheme's expected risk-adjusted returns. If so, then it may be ideally placed to exploit a wider 'opportunity set' by investing in a wide and diverse range of asset classes and employing a whole host of investment techniques and strategies, subject to the parameters of its risk budget and, of course, its investment beliefs. Indeed, as stated earlier, the investment beliefs statement should help in identifying the investment risks taken by the scheme and in exploiting the opportunities that best meet with these beliefs.

However, in so doing, the committee may well feel the need to create one or a number of small working groups, again with well-defined delegated powers, so as to operate in a more 'fleet-of-foot' fashion or to be a 'first mover' in a particular investment market or in applying a particular strategy. Indeed, small working groups can prove especially useful when implementing a liability driven investment programme or when complex assets or investment strategies are under consideration.

Other schemes wishing to embrace a more advanced level of governance, but recognizing the limitations of time and/or expertise residing within their ranks, can appoint a dedicated Chief Investment Officer (CIO) or delegate their investment decision-making powers to a fiduciary manager.[21] After all, no one ever said trusteeship was easy.

Investment governance for defined contribution schemes

Just as there are investment governance challenges for the trustees of DB schemes, so there are those for trustees of defined contribution (DC) schemes.

---

[20] Risk budgeting is the process of setting a limit on the total amount of investment risk assumed by the scheme by setting limits on each source of investment risk that contributes to this total. This investment risk is assumed in the expectation that it will generate a return.
[21] Also known as implemented consulting, fiduciary management, which originated in Holland, is offered by a significant number of investment consultants and dedicated fiduciary managers.

As we saw in Chapter 1, a key challenge faced by the trustees of DC schemes is minimizing the risk to those DC members ill-equipped to assume the investment and annuity risks that the seemingly inexorable move from DB to DC presents. As we suggested, a DC scheme's default investment option is the most important decision for DC trustees to get right as it not only affects the greatest number of members but it is also the investment option for which DC scheme trustees bear the greatest fiduciary responsibility. Indeed, default funds should be regularly reviewed by trustees for their appropriateness, given the age profile of the scheme membership, contribution and salary levels, while regular investment performance reviews should be conducted and clear communications be sent to members.

However, DC scheme trustees also need to educate and communicate with their members better (especially those within generations X and Y[22]) about: the nuances of investing; how to make appropriate fund choices; and how best to approach the annuitization, or de-accumulation, stage of the retirement process. It is only in this way that member expectations will be both realistically anchored from the outset and ultimately met. Fortunately, technology is a great enabler of member engagement as it facilitates the employment of user-friendly online interactive financial education and financial planning tools.

The principles of good investment governance for defined contribution schemes

In March 2008 the Treasury asked the National Association of Pension Funds (NAPF) to carry out a review of the Myners principles and establish whether they were having a positive affect on scheme investment governance.

The result of the NAPF review was that the Myners principles were consolidated into six high level principles, to be voluntarily applied by schemes as before as a code of best practice, and a new industry-led Investment Governance Group (IGG) was established. The IGG, comprising pensions industry professionals, was charged with looking at ways in which engagement with and standards of investment governance could be improved across all scheme types, without any requirement for regulation. However, as the review highlighted the need for improvements in investment governance

---

[22] In contrast to the baby-boom generation (those born between 1946 and 1965), generation X (those born between 1966 and 1981) and generation Y (those born between 1982 and 1995) have, on the whole, displayed a tendency to borrow and spend their way to immediate gratification, without thinking too much about their financial future – such is the intangibility of being poor in retirement.

within DC schemes, a DC sub-group of the IGG was set up to establish a set of principles for use in both trust-based and contract-based DC.

Six principles were published in November 2010, following a formal public consultation and comprise the following:

1. *Clear roles and responsibilities*: all parties involved in running the scheme should agree what their role in the scheme's investment governance is, with the allocation of responsibilities being fully documented and made transparent to members.
2. *Effective decision making*: the critical aspects to effective decision making, such as knowledge, resources, available time and planning, should be harnessed.
3. *Appropriate investment options*: the investment options offered by the scheme should accommodate members' risk profiles and other needs without overburdening members.
4. *Appropriate default strategy*: recognized as the most important of the six principles, given that most members do not want to make asset allocation decisions, there must be sound governance of the scheme's default fund.
5. *Effective performance assessment*: the performance of the scheme's investment options should be regularly reviewed and addressed if below expectations.
6. *Clear and relevant communication to members*: principle six provides a checklist to ensure that member communications are of sufficient content, quality and frequency.

Summary

An advanced level of investment governance is essentially the mechanism by which trustees turn risk into reward. However, the level of investment governance employed by a trustee board is, by definition, commensurate with its collective capabilities and how it organizes itself. Given the intrinsic link between investment governance and education, training and development, unless sufficient time and effort is applied to the latter, a more advanced level of investment governance will never be achieved. Nor will it be if insufficient attention is paid to risk management and to the clear articulation of the scheme's investment beliefs.

Key points

- The Pension Regulator's TKU Code of Practice is a good first step in improving trustee education but does not cover everything trustees need to know.

- Trustees have access to a multitude of free-to-access educational resources.
- Governance simply means *doing things right* to ensure that the scheme is well run.
- There is a positive relationship between the level of investment governance and investment performance, which is not only contingent on *doing things right* but also on *doing the right things*.
- A statement of investment beliefs should help identify the investment risks taken by the scheme and in exploiting the opportunities that best meet with these beliefs.

Chapter 3

The Main Parties Trustees Deal with on Funding and Investment Issues: Who are the Main Pension Players?

Learning outcomes

- Know the main parties trustees have contact with on funding and investment issues and their respective roles.

Introduction

Trustees come into regular contact with a myriad of organizations and pensions professionals as they address the various funding and investment issues connected with their scheme. This chapter identifies these parties and the crucial role they play in the context of managing the investment aspects of a defined benefit (DB) scheme, though many aspects of this chapter equally apply to the running of a defined contribution (DC) scheme. Principal among those with whom trustees have direct contact, are the Pensions Regulator, the scheme sponsor, the pensions manager, the scheme secretary, scheme actuary, investment consultant, fund managers, scheme lawyer and, increasingly, an independent trustee (see Exhibit 3.1). We will now examine the role of each of these parties and a number of others.

Exhibit 3.1   The main parties trustees deal with on funding and investment issues

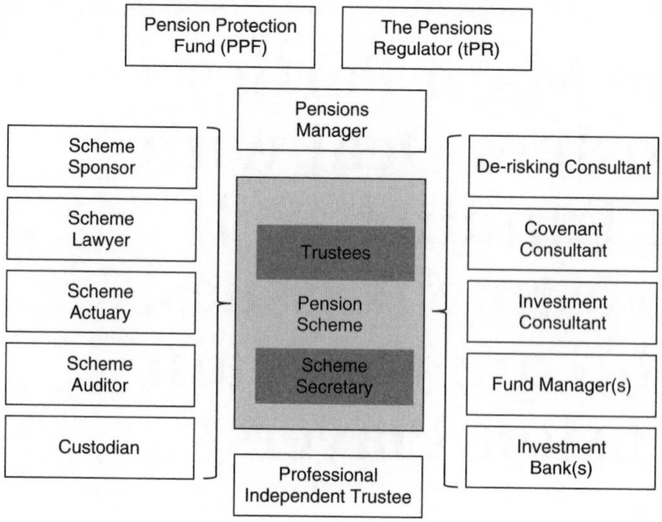

The Pensions Regulator (tPR)

A good place to start is with the Pensions Regulator (tPR). tPR is empowered by the UK government to regulate UK work-based pensions and replaced the Occupational Pensions Regulatory Authority (OPRA) in April 2006, with much wider and more flexible powers. For instance, tPR has anti-avoidance powers that enable it to force firms to make contributions to schemes of which they are the sponsor if it is believed that they have deliberately avoided their obligations.

tPR's main objectives, as set out in the Pensions Act 2004, are to:

- protect the benefits of members of work-based pension schemes;
- promote good administration and improve understanding of work-based pension schemes;
- reduce the risk of situations arising which may lead to DB schemes being admitted to the Pension Protection Fund (PPF); and
- maximize employer compliance with employer duties, such as the requirement from 2012 to automatically enrol eligible employees into a qualifying pension provision with a minimum contribution.

These objectives seek to ensure that those responsible for providing access to and managing work-based pensions fulfil their obligations. tPR works with trustees, employers, pension specialists and business advisers providing guidance and education to make clear what is expected of them and enabling them to achieve high standards.

In particular, tPR has established a number of Codes of Practice. These are standards of conduct and best practice expected of trustees in a number of areas of trusteeship. For example, the tPR Trustee Knowledge and Understanding (TKU) requirements are embodied in the TKU Code of Practice we briefly considered in Chapter 2. While not statements of law, Codes of Practice do have legal effect in that they can be used in a tribunal or in court to decide if a particular requirement has been met.

The sponsor

The sponsoring employer is central to the operation of an occupational DB pension scheme. It is the sponsor who establishes and ultimately funds the scheme. Indeed, since June 2003, the promise made to provide a pension on retirement is a legal and contractual obligation on a solvent sponsor. That is, a solvent sponsor cannot wind up a less than fully funded scheme unless they secure a buyout of the scheme's assets and liabilities with an insurance company.

While the sponsor, in assuming the investment and annuity risk for the scheme membership, underwrites the scheme, it is the trustees who determine the scheme's investment policy, though, as we noted in Chapter 2, the sponsor must be consulted on this and any proposed changes in the scheme's investment strategy. However, in practice, the sponsor can hold considerable sway over how the trustees manage the scheme's investment policy given that the sponsor's regular financial contribution to the scheme is the most important asset of most schemes. Indeed, without the financial support of the scheme sponsor – most sponsors pay significant regular monthly or annual contributions and the occasional ad hoc lump sum into their occupational DB schemes – most schemes would have to cut the promised benefits to members drastically. Therefore, the trustees' and sponsor's interests and wishes need to be aligned wherever possible. In particular, it is essential that the sponsor's appetite for investment risk is taken into account by the trustees when setting the investment strategy.

Another salient point is that the cash that sponsors contribute to the scheme cannot be withdrawn by the company at a later date. Once in, it belongs to the scheme. Given this, some sponsors wishing to support their schemes but not wishing to contribute large amounts of cash that cannot then be subsequently withdrawn if not needed, have resorted to pledging increasingly complex (and often very novel) contingent assets to their schemes. That is, assets that can be drawn on by the scheme if the need arises in the future. However, if the scheme does not need to draw on these assets, then the legal ownership of the assets remains with the scheme sponsor. So you can think of these contingent assets as being like an insurance policy. The value and risks of these assets, however, must be assessed very carefully by the scheme lawyer, scheme actuary, scheme investment consultant and the covenant consultant.

Some examples of companies pledging contingent assets to their scheme include:

- Diageo plc, which pledged 2.5 million barrels of whisky(!);
- Whitbread plc, which pledged its Premier Inn hotel chain property portfolio and the rights to a proportion of the income generated by the chain into a Special Purpose Vehicle (SPV);
- Marks Spencer and Sainsbury who made similar property pledges to their schemes;
- ITV who set up a SPV to share ownership of a subsidiary company with its scheme; and
- the most novel of them all, Uniq, the former Unigate business and now M&S's biggest sandwich supplier, which handed over 90 per cent of its share capital to the pension scheme in return for the scheme relinquishing its claim on the company.

The covenant consultant

Given the pivotal role of the sponsor in continuing to meet its financial and legal obligations to the scheme and its members in securing the scheme's ultimate viability, it is perhaps surprising how little time and effort used to be devoted to monitoring the financial strength of the sponsor and the strength of the sponsor covenant. Even more so, considering that the Pensions Act 2004 requires trustees to understand the willingness and ability of the scheme's sponsor to provide the funds needed to pay member benefits.

Arguably, it was not until the height of the financial crisis of 2008 following the failure of the investment bank Lehman Brothers, a bank considered by most as 'too big to fail', that the strength of the sponsor covenant was brought into sharp focus.[1] Following this dramatic period, the strength of the scheme covenant was duly thrust to the top of many trustee board agendas. Indeed,

---

[1] As indeed was counterparty risk. For instance, many schemes conduct over the counter derivative transactions with investment banks. From the scheme's point of view, the viability of such transactions, which variously include interest rate, inflation and credit default swaps, are wholly dependent upon the creditworthiness of the bank, the counterparty, with whom they are transacting.

what had become blatantly clear was that there was no such thing as a perfectly safe sponsoring employer. As such, the monitoring of the sponsor covenant should no longer be relegated towards the bottom of the trustee agenda and typically comprise a cursory glance at the sponsor's credit rating, share price – if it is a publicly listed company – and the most recent public statements on its trading record and prospects.

In fact, as we outline in Chapter 9, today the strength of the sponsor covenant, especially for a DB pension scheme in deficit, must arguably be the number one priority for trustees with its active monitoring ideally being undertaken by a covenant consultant who can really delve into the detail and seek the views of industry analysts. Although dedicated covenant consultants have existed for some time, their rise to prominence is a very recent phenomenon, coinciding with the heightened awareness of covenant risk. This ongoing covenant review should consider the strength and sustainability of the sponsor's credit rating(s), credit default swap spreads,[2] cash flow and profitability, all of which are greatly dependent on the viability and sustainability of the sponsor's strategy and business model and the extent to which it is able to maintain a competitive position in its chosen marketplace(s).

Another major consideration is whether the pension scheme is backed by that part of the sponsoring organization that holds the assets against which the pension scheme has recourse. This is particularly important where a UK sponsor is part of a larger overseas entity, as the UK sponsor may simply be a holding company without any assets of its own and may not have recourse to the assets of the overseas parent company. Somewhat surprisingly, many pension schemes are unwittingly backed by that part of the sponsoring organization over which the pension scheme does not have a legal claim on the sponsor's assets. This is especially true of those sponsoring organizations that operate in the service sector.

All of these things require detailed consideration, so much so that tPR has issued regulatory guidance on what is expected of trustees in assessing, monitoring and taking action on the employer covenant.[3] The guidance covers issues such as the importance of measuring the covenant; understanding a group's legal structure and an employer's legal obligations; what to consider when assessing the employer's financial position; alternative forms of scheme security; when to appoint external covenant assessors; and the importance of regular monitoring of the covenant.

---

[2] Credit default swap spreads represent the price of insuring an issuer's bonds against default.
[3] The guidance can be accessed on tPR's website: http://www.thepensionsregulator.gov. uk/guidance/monitoring-employer-support.aspx.

The Pension Protection Fund (PPF)

With the best will in the world, some companies will fail. When they do, what becomes of their DB plan?

In the event of a DB scheme sponsor becoming insolvent, the assets of the scheme and the responsibility for meeting the scheme's liabilities fall to the Pension Protection Fund (PPF). At this point, the role of the trustees ends and that of the PPF begins. However, the PPF, which became operational on 6 April 2005, is financed by a levy which is imposed on all UK DB schemes. It is in this context that most DB schemes interact with the PPF.

The formula for this levy is currently based on an assessment of the scheme sponsor's short-term risk of insolvency and the size of the scheme's liabilities. This is set in advance of each financial year and is then divided up between all insured schemes. For 2011–12 it is £600m. However, as from 2012–13 the PPF will instead set a levy for each scheme based on the risks posed by that particular scheme by applying a new formula that will focus on three key principles: stability, simplicity and smoothing. Stability, or predictability as to the size of the levy, is provided by locking-in the levy structure for three years at a time; simplicity by reducing the number of bands within which a sponsor's risk profile can fit from 100 to ten; and smoothing by using average measures for both sponsor insolvency risk and under-funding, the latter by making calculations of scheme assets and liabilities over five-year periods. This means that any temporary changes in an employer's insolvency risk score or scheme funding position would not have such a significant effect on a pension scheme's PPF levy, thereby avoiding large swings in the levy charged.

In addition, the levy will be linked to the riskiness of a scheme's investment strategy. If a scheme chooses not to invest in assets that mirror its liabilities then it will be required to recognize the risk it poses to the PPF by paying a higher levy. The PPF will therefore stress test scheme assets and liabilities to establish the investment risk potentially posed to the fund, though will require schemes with section 179 liabilities of at least £1.5bn to conduct their own bespoke analysis.[4] Also, by placing a greater emphasis on scheme funding rather than covenant strength, those sponsors with stronger covenants that choose not to fund the scheme will be penalized accordingly. The PPF will not be setting a target levy and then dividing this up between all insured schemes. Rather, it will set a levy for each scheme based on the risks posed to the PPF by that particular scheme.

---

[4] Section 179 liabilities are calculated on the basis of the premium an insurance company would charge to assume payment of PPF levels of compensation. This may be less than the full promised benefits of the scheme.

The pensions manager

If there is one individual who is invaluable to the operation of the scheme, then it is the pensions manager. Historically, the pensions manager has been an employee of the sponsor and has performed two roles – to act on behalf of the sponsor as its in-house expert and source of advice on all pension matters and also to act as secretary to the trustees.

Increasingly, it is recognized that there are inherent conflicts of interests in one person, often with a team supporting them, performing these functions for two potentially opposing parties – the sponsor and the trustees. Therefore, there is a growing consensus that these roles should be divided between two individuals or organizations. This is especially true when schemes are closed to new entrants and/ or future accrual. This is because, in all likelihood, the sponsor may not have or be prepared to secure, the necessary internal resource to fill these two roles. In which case, one or both of the functions can be, and increasingly are, outsourced.

The scheme secretary

The scheme secretary is often the trustees' first port of call whenever an investment or funding issue needs resolving. The scheme secretary works closely with the chairman of the trustees, as well as the rest of the trustees and any sub-committee chairmen, acting as the main point of contact for all parties that deal with the scheme. Many trustee chairmen will tell you that having an efficient and experienced scheme secretary is vital to the smooth running of the scheme and the trustee board.

The scheme secretary role is comparable to that of a company secretary. The scheme secretary is responsible for organizing trustee, committee and investment working group meetings, compiling agendas and papers, writing up meeting minutes and following up action points. However, the role of the scheme secretary is not restricted to these areas because they will be expected to use their broad knowledge of pensions to assist the trustees in the governance of the scheme including the preparation of risk registers, business plans, the sourcing of professional advice, liaison with regulatory bodies, including tPR, arranging TKU-complaint trustee training, preparing member communications and preparing the trustees' budget.

The scheme actuary

The scheme actuary, whose appointment is required under the Pensions Act 1995, is the named individual within an actuarial consulting firm who, among other things, regularly reports the scheme's funding level to the trustees and advises on whether there are sufficient scheme assets to meet the scheme's liabilities as they fall due.

A formal valuation of the scheme's assets and liabilities is conducted by the scheme actuary every three years in drawing up the scheme's triennial actuarial valuation. Since the assets of most pensions schemes are traded in public markets, their valuation is relatively straightforward. However, the scheme's liabilities require far more complex analysis. Some schemes have thousands of current and past members, all of whom will have a claim on the scheme that is specific to them. The actuary must not only assess the claim of each of these members, but must also make an estimate of when and for how long each member is likely to draw their pension. To estimate the likely longevity of each scheme member, the scheme actuary will make use of historic longevity trends. This complex data-intensive and numerical task is the most important that the scheme actuary performs for any scheme. So it is a good job that most actuaries love maths and number crunching – though be warned, they often seem fixated on the probability of death![5]

Once completed, and assuming there is a deficit to plug, the scheme actuary, working with the scheme's investment consultant, lawyer and pensions manager, then assists the trustees in negotiating a recovery plan and investment strategy with the scheme sponsor. The recovery plan negotiations principally focus on agreeing an appropriate contribution rate with the sponsor with the aim of plugging the deficit on a valuation basis agreeable to both the trustees and sponsor over the shortest possible recovery period without adversely affecting the sponsor's business. After all, without a viable sponsor, there won't be a viable pension scheme.[6]

Notwithstanding the viability of the sponsor's business, which is obviously a big constraining factor, the sponsor's contribution rate will also be determined by the scheme's funding ratio, the scheme's asset allocation, the extent to which the scheme has mitigated its interest rate, inflation and longevity risks, the acceptability of any contingent assets offered by the sponsor, the valuation basis adopted for the liabilities and the recovery period, which should ideally not exceed tPR's guideline of ten years. The valuation basis will largely be guided by the scheme's investment policy. As we will see in Chapter 6, other things equal, the more cautious the investment policy, the lower the discount rate and the higher the present value of the liabilities.

---

[5] Which is of course 100 per cent!
[6] The situation is not dissimilar to Colbert's dictum on levying taxes: 'The art is to pluck the maximum number of feathers, with the minimum amount of hissing from the goose.'

Once agreement has been reached between the trustees and sponsor, the scheme actuary will then work with the trustees in agreeing the recovery plan with tPR. The recovery plan must be submitted to tPR within 15 months of the triennial valuation. In agreeing the recovery plan, tPR will look for prudent assumptions, especially as regards the recovery period, investment returns, the discount rate applied to the liabilities, inflation expectations and member longevity. The trustees will then be provided with regular scheme valuations and funding updates up until the next triennial valuation to ensure that the scheme is on track to be fully funded by the end of the recovery period.

In addition, the scheme actuary calculates the scheme's PPF levy and advises on the financial implications of transactions such as buy-ins and buyouts and scheme mergers.[7]

The investment consultant

The investment consultant, like the scheme actuary, has a multi-faceted role, in that they advise the trustees on:

- the scheme's investment policy;
- the formulation of a risk budget, within which the scheme's investment policy should operate;
- identifying, measuring, managing and monitoring the various financial risks that reside within the scheme's assets and liabilities, including which to assume and which to mitigate;[8]
- the construction of a strategic benchmark, against which the scheme's asset performance is regularly assessed; and
- the appointment of new fund managers, along with the regular monitoring of existing fund managers.

The scheme's investment policy principally comprises its tactical and strategic asset allocation policy, its approach to active and passive fund management and its views on manager investment style.[9] While the scheme's investment policy and strategic benchmark continually evolve with the strength of the

---

[7] A buyout refers to the situation when part or all of a scheme's assets and liabilities are transferred to an insurance company which then underwrites the benefits. Buy-ins involve the trustees insuring part or all of its deferred and/or pensioner liabilities via an insurance company. The insurance policy for a buy-in is written in the name of the trustees and remains as part of the assets of the scheme.

[8] Risk management and risk budgets are expanded upon in Chapter 9.

[9] Asset allocation and the construction of a strategic benchmark is covered in Chapter 10, active and passive fund management is covered in Chapter 14 and investment style in Chapters 7 and 18.

sponsor covenant, the structure of the scheme's liabilities, the funding position, risk budget and risk appetite of the trustees and sponsor, it should ultimately be driven by the trustees' investment beliefs. As noted in Chapter 2, these should be documented in a statement of investment beliefs, which the investment consultant should formulate with the trustees. In so doing, the investment consultant works with the trustees in compiling, reviewing and revising the scheme's Statement of Investment Principles (SIP).

The investment consultant role should also actively monitor the quantitative and qualitative aspects of the scheme's fund manager mandates and provide the trustees with regular updates of performance and risk attribution, while assessing potential fund managers for new or existing mandates.[10]

All of the big actuarial consulting firms have an investment consulting arm, though increasingly, independent investment consultancies are emerging with many advising some of the UK's largest DB schemes. However, given the increasingly demanding investment governance requirements of running a DB scheme, as outlined in Chapter 2, the trustees of a significant minority of larger schemes have either delegated the scheme's investment policy and risk management to a fiduciary manager or appointed a dedicated Chief Investment Officer (CIO) to the scheme.

The fund managers

In 1996, the UK's top four institutional fund managers were balanced managers.[11] Balanced managers, who have reinvented themselves now as 'multi-asset managers', were entrusted to manage a scheme's entire asset portfolio, hence their dominance of the UK fund management industry in the mid-1990s. Today, however, trustees are more discerning in their asset allocation and manager selection decisions, based on the view that no one single fund manager is likely to have the necessary skills to successfully manage all asset classes across all strategies, not least because the asset universe has become so wide and disparate, extending to a whole host of 'alternative' assets. Schemes, therefore, tend to diversify across a number of fund managers when investing in a range of asset classes and/or strategies. Indeed, in 2009, only 14 per cent of UK pension scheme assets were managed by a balanced manager.[12]

---

[10] Manager monitoring and selection is comprehensively covered in Chapters 14 and 18.
[11] Based on UK pooled and segregated pension fund assets under management. Sources: FTfm 8 June 2009. Hymans Robertson Market Briefing Survey 2007.
[12] Source: Hymans Robertson Market Briefing Survey 2010.

Each fund manager will run either a pooled or segregated fund management mandate for the scheme on either an active or passive basis. Pooled mandates are managed on behalf of a number of the fund manager's clients who own shares or units in the fund. Segregated mandates, however, are run for one client only. Details of the mandate are set out in an Investment Management Agreement (IMA) which will specify the out-performance target which for an active fund management mandate is typically expressed as a financial index, such as the FTSE All Share index, plus x per cent per annum and is conventionally expressed gross of (i.e., excluding) the manager's fees. The IMA will also spell out the relevant risk parameters and fee structure.

The de-risking consultant

As intimated above, a key focus of the investment consultant is advising the trustees on identifying, measuring, managing and monitoring the many and various financial risks that reside within the scheme's assets and liabilities. Investment consultants should also help trustees to decide which risks to assume and which to mitigate. However, some larger schemes now employ specialist de-risking consultants when seeking to manage the 'unrewarded' interest rate, inflation and longevity risks within the scheme liabilities, usually via derivatives termed swap contracts. A good de-risking consultant should have the requisite investment banking and asset management contacts, negotiating skills and expertise in the swaps market to ensure that these risks are managed in the most efficient and cost effective way for the scheme. We examine swap contracts in Chapter 12 and the management and mitigation of these risks and the role of the de-risking consultant in Chapter 15.

The scheme lawyer

The scheme lawyer advises the trustees on the parameters within which they should operate, drafts and checks the scheme's documentation and flags changes in legislation and regulation, advising on the likely implications for the trustees and the scheme. From an investment perspective, the scheme lawyer's input is invaluable. The scheme lawyer will advise on the wording and parameters of the SIP (which, for most schemes, can become quite an unwieldy document), and fund manager IMAs (similarly so). They also play a crucial role in negotiating and agreeing the detailed legal documentation that is required between the scheme and investment banks when the trustees undertake a de-risking exercise involving swap contracts.

From a funding perspective, the scheme lawyer is also pivotal in working with the trustees and scheme actuary when negotiating the recovery plan with the sponsor, following the compilation of the triennial actuarial valuation. Legal input is particularly valuable in assessing the security offered by any contingent assets offered by the sponsor as a temporary funding stop gap.

The custodian

The custodian, which is typically a division of an investment bank or asset manager, arranges for the safekeeping of the scheme assets and documents of title. The vast majority of these assets will be managed by fund managers via either pooled or segregated mandates, though the scheme may invest in some assets directly.[13] The custodian deals with corporate actions, such as capital raising, and processes dividends and other income for those directly held scheme assets.

In addition, the custodian, who works closely with the investment consultant and pensions manager, provides the trustees with quarterly asset, cash flow and corporate actions reports and undertakes all appropriate scheme asset administration.

The investment banks

The investment banks, having always attracted the best and brightest people both from within the financial community and academia, are renowned for their innovative solutions to scheme funding and risk management, albeit for not inconsiderable fees. That said, many investment consultants (some of whom have an investment banking background) have become more creative in the provision of cutting edge solutions in recent years.

While some investment banks approach schemes directly with their latest ideas, most tend to do so via the scheme's investment consultant.

The scheme auditor

The scheme auditor, in auditing the scheme's annual financial statements, verifies the assets held within the scheme and the valuation accorded to them. This is particularly valuable when non-conventional assets, for which there is not a ready market, and over the counter derivatives, that is, those not traded or cleared on an exchange (more on that in Chapter 11), form part of the asset pool.

---

[13] Those assets in which a scheme may invest directly, i.e., without the intermediation of a fund manager, may include private equity, social housing and infrastructure debt, fine wines and other 'chattels' and some contingent agents, such real estate leases, pledged by the sponsor.

The scheme auditor also examines the robustness of the scheme's risk controls and identifies where there are unnecessary concentrations of risk. For instance, it may well be that the scheme has not adequately diversified its counterparty risk across a sufficient number of investment banks when mitigating scheme risks through swap contract transactions.

The professional independent trustee

Finally, we should consider a relatively new category of trustee, the professional independent trustee. As can clearly be seen from this and Chapter 2, the complexity of the trustee role and the number of advisory and other relationships has grown inexorably in recent years and will doubtless continue to do so. Coupled with the fact that as scheme deficits have grown, relationships with the sponsor have, in many cases, become more adversarial, this has pointed to the need for many trustee boards to appoint an independent trustee.

An independent trustee is likely to have a strong background in pensions and/or investment, be well informed on all contemporary pension and investment issues, bring the benefit of their experience as a trustee of other schemes to the table and most importantly, have no other connection with the sponsor, given that they will not be employees or pensioners of the scheme. Without any inherent conflicts of interest, the independent trustee should be able to advise and guide the other trustees and is in the best possible position to ask the right (and more politically difficult) questions of the scheme's advisers and sponsor.

Although there is as yet no mandatory requirement for trustee boards to have an independent trustee, the advice and guidance from tPR makes it clear that scheme governance is greatly improved by appointing one.

Key points

- Trustees come into regular contact with a myriad of parties when addressing the many and various funding and investment issues connected with their scheme. Principal among those with whom the trustees have direct contact are the Pensions Regulator, the scheme sponsor, the pensions manager, the scheme secretary, scheme actuary, investment consultant, fund managers, scheme lawyer and, increasingly, an independent trustee.
- The scheme actuary advises the trustees on the scheme's funding level and whether there are likely to be sufficient scheme assets to meet the scheme liabilities as they fall due.

- The investment consultant advises the trustees on the scheme's investment policy – principally its asset allocation – fund manager selection, risk management and risk budgeting.
- The scheme's fund managers will each run either a pooled or segregated mandate on an active or passive basis for the scheme and specify the performance target, risk parameters and fee structure of their mandate in an Investment Management Agreement (IMA).
- The scheme lawyer advises on the wording and parameters of the Statement of Investment Principles (SIP), fund manager IMAs, the detailed legal documentation around swap contracts and in assessing the security offered by contingent assets.
- The independent trustee, given a typically strong background in pensions and/or investment and an absence of any inherent conflicts of interest, is in the best possible position to ask the right (and more politically difficult) questions of the scheme's advisers and sponsor.

Chapter 4

The Macroeconomic Background to Pensions: Why Economics Matters

Learning outcomes

- An understanding of the drivers of economic growth.
- An understanding of the nature of inflation and its costs.
- An understanding of modern macroeconomic and monetary policy.
- An understanding of how economic trends and policy can influence financial markets.

What is economics?

Economics can be grandly defined as 'the study of the allocation of scarce resources among many competing ends'. In other words, the resources available to governments, corporations and consumers are generally in limited supply and somehow decisions have to be made as to how these limited resources should be allocated between those who wish to make use of them. Economics concerns itself with the processes employed by societies to allocate these resources and with the ways in which resource demand is met by resource supply. In this regard, one of the most important economic concepts is that of *opportunity cost*. For every economic decision that we make, the true cost is the other economic transactions that, as a result of this decision, are foregone. At an economy-wide level, society may wish to devote more of its resources to improving the infrastructure of its economy (for example, its transport infrastructure) than to producing consumer goods. At an individual consumer level the opportunity cost of any purchase that we make is the other goods that we could have bought with the money.

51

Economists specialize in various branches of economics. For example, 'labour economists' concentrate on the supply and demand for labour and the way in which wages and salaries are set, while industrial economists focus on the competitive structure of individual industries, and financial economists study the behaviour of the market for financial assets, like bonds and equities. However, there are two broad types of economics: *microeconomics* and *macroeconomics*.

Microeconomics is concerned with individual economic decision making. Microeconomists study the choices made by individual consumers and producers and the economic conditions that exist in individual markets. Macroeconomics is concerned with the aggregate outcome of all the individual economic decisions that take place in an economy. We can illustrate this distinction easily. The economic conditions faced by an individual company in its own market may lead that firm to hire more people. A microeconomist will look at the factors that led to this decision. If many companies come to the same decision then levels of employment will rise in the economy and unemployment may fall. A macroeconomist will look at this broader economic picture that will be the consequence of these hundreds and thousands of individual economic decisions. They will, therefore, monitor broad economic trends relating to phenomena like economic growth, unemployment, inflation and interest rates. Moreover, many macroeconomists will focus on the economic policies pursued by governments and central banks. The policy choices made can have a significant impact upon the broader economic environment and, of more interest to trustees, can have a significant impact upon the evolution and behaviour of financial markets.

It is impossible to do justice to the topic of economics in one chapter so here we will concentrate on arguably the three most important aspects of the economic environment from the perspective of a trustee: growth, inflation and macroeconomic policy.[1]

Growth

Once you start thinking about it, it is hard to think about anything else. (Robert Lucas, 1988)

By 'it' the Nobel Prize winning economist, Robert Lucas, was referring to 'economic growth'. Really what economists want to monitor are the changes in our economic well-being, or welfare over time. Can we say that our welfare has

---

[1] For a more thorough introduction to the subject the interested reader should refer to R. Lipsey and A. Chrystal, *Economics*, Oxford University Press (2003).

improved, or deteriorated from one year to the next? There are many metrics that we could use to determine the answer to this question. We could use:

- measures of educational attainment,
- levels of pollution and congestion,
- estimates of the numbers of people living below the 'poverty line',
- estimates of life expectancy, and/or
- infant mortality rates.

The United Nations Development Programme (UNDP) produces the Human Development Index (HDI).[2] The UNDP produce this index annually for over 200 countries. It combines three broad definitions of well-being related to: the length and health of the lives of a country's citizens, their educational attainment and finally, their income levels. In the last published survey Norway had the highest HDI score. The UK was ranked as the nation with the 26th highest HDI value. Of more interest is how the index has changed over longer periods of time. In 1980 Norway scored 0.90 on the index; in 2010 Norway's score had risen to 0.94. Over the same period the UK's score went from 0.74 to 0.85. So in HDI terms the welfare of UK citizens had grown by 15 per cent in nearly three decades. But compare this with China's progress. In 1980 China's HDI score was 0.39; in the most recent survey it had risen to 0.65 – representing an improvement in their HDI-measured welfare of 67 per cent.

The conventional measure of growth

Despite a potentially large list of measures of our well-being and therefore its evolution, most economists focus on a monetary measure of our perceived well-being known as Gross Domestic Product (GDP). GDP measures the amount of income generated, the total spending or the value of goods and services that an economy produces over a given period of time, usually over a calendar quarter. Before we look at how it is calculated, it is probably worth considering whether a monetary measure is a useful proxy for measuring our well-being. After all, economists are often accused of being cynics, that is, knowing the cost of everything and the value of nothing. Exhibit 4.1 shows that there may be a relationship between well-being and GDP. The horizontal axis represents annual GDP per capita, or per head of the population, while the vertical axis measures life expectancy. Each diamond on the chart represents a country. The line that we have imposed on the chart shows the broad relationship between income (as measured by GDP per capita) and life expectancy. As average annual income rises, average life expectancy rises too. It rises particularly rapidly as average income increases from lower starting levels.

---

[2] See: http://hdr.undp.org/en/.

Exhibit 4.1   Wealth and health

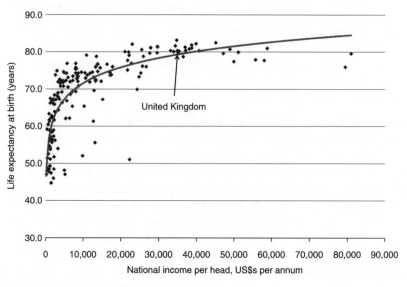

Source: *UN Human Development Report* (2010).

For example, life expectancy is around 40 to 50 years when average income is close to US$0, but rises to just under 70 years by the time average income reaches US$10,000.

This chart goes some way towards explaining Professor Lucas's comment about the importance of growth, and why less developed nations are determined to achieve high levels of GDP growth. But growth itself, measured in these terms, is actually a very modern phenomenon as Exhibit 4.2 shows. Between 0 AD and 1000 AD average growth, as measured by GDP per capita, was virtually zero across the world. By 1700, incomes in Western Europe were only twice their level in 1 AD. However, between 1700 and 1998, average incomes in Western Europe had increased by over 1,600 per cent, while in the US they had increased by over 5,000 per cent over the same period! So what happened?

Exhibit 4.2   GDP per capita, US$s, (1990 prices)

	1	1000	1500	1600	1700	1820	1870	1913	1950	1973	1998
'UK'			714	974	1250	1707	3191	4921	6907	12022	18714
'W. Europe'	450	400	774	894	1024	1232	1974	3473	4594	11534	17921
'USA'			400	400	527	1257	2445	5301	9561	16689	27331
'Japan'	400	425	500	520	570	669	737	1387	1926	11439	20413
'China'	450	450	600	600	600	600	530	552	439	839	3117

Source: Extracted from Table B-21, *The World Economy*, Maddison, OECD, 2006.

Exhibit 4.3   Relative size of world GDP (in US$) by country at the end of 2010

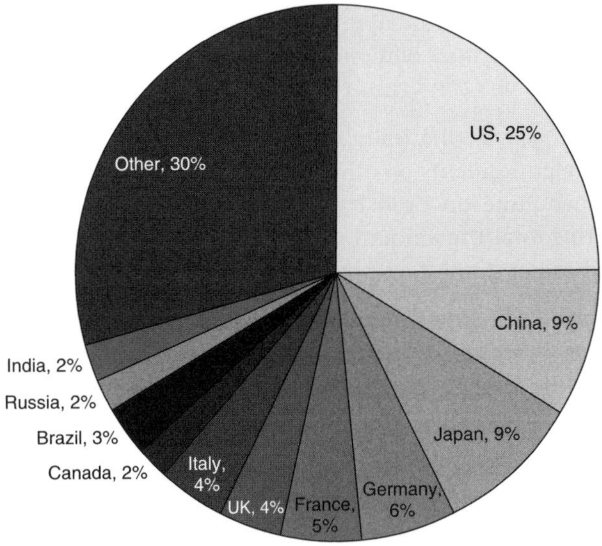

Source: Thomson Financial.

The answer is the industrial revolution. For centuries prior to this revolution, the farmer produced the same quantity of grain, year after year, the miller produced the same quantity of flour, the baker produced the same number of loaves. Then along came steam power and subsequently continuous improvements to both farming and manufacturing processes. As these processes improved so too did output and incomes, year after year. Economic growth then is inextricably linked to productivity growth. That is, the ongoing process of increasing output by combining capital (for example, machinery) and labour more and more efficiently over time.

When we think about growth in these terms it is very evident that China is currently going through its own industrial revolution today. As Exhibit 4.2 shows, between 1 AD and 1913 output and incomes were virtually unchanged in China. However, after 1973 output in China really began to take off. Today the Chinese economy is the world's second largest economy as shown in Exhibit 4.3. However, despite the rapid industrialization of the Chinese economy since the 1970s by the end 2010, GDP per head was only US$5,220 in China compared to US$48,770 in the US (Source: OECD).

Measuring GDP

Corporations are always looking for ways of producing more goods and services in a more efficient manner every year. As they do so, over long periods of time an economy's output (GDP) per capita, grows. Since GDP is a measure of the value of all these goods and services produced within an economy over a specific period of time, usually a calendar quarter, it is therefore a 'flow concept' rather than being a measure of the stock of monetary wealth in an economy. Statisticians use three ways to measure GDP – the expenditure, income and output approaches.

The *expenditure approach* basically involves adding up all of the expenditure of UK and foreign residents on all goods and services produced domestically, including expenditure on capital goods like machinery, factories and roads. Then, from this total the amount of money spent by UK residents on goods and services produced in other economies is subtracted.

The *income approach* requires that the national accounts statisticians add up all of the incomes derived from productive activity in an economy by all 'factors of production'. In practice, this means adding up all of the wages and salaries, rental income and company profits and so on, generated within the economy.

Finally, the *output approach* to the calculation of GDP involves adding up the gross value added of each sector of the economy: agriculture, manufacturing, utilities, construction and services.

In theory the three measures should produce the same answer since someone's expenditure, on someone else's output will ultimately become someone else's income. In practice, however, the complexity of collating accurate information for every single aspect of economic activity is such that differences can often exist between the three measures which can in turn lead to sizeable revisions in the measures over time, as more accurate information is collated. The most notable discrepancy is often between the expenditure and income approaches to the measurement of GDP. The measurement of income requires that all agents in an economy declare their earnings honestly to the tax authorities, while expenditure is registered whether the income has been declared or not. This discrepancy tends to be larger in less developed economies than in developed ones, where tax evasion is often seen as a birth right rather than as a criminal offence!

To illustrate the process of measuring changes in our welfare we can focus on the expenditure measure of GDP (E), as illustrated in Exhibit 4.4. Although statistical practices vary from country to country the basic process involves the calculation of the following expenditure components:

First, add up the expenditure of all households (consumers) in an economy (C). In a mature economy like the UK's, expenditure by consumers can make up almost two-thirds of total expenditure. In China this figure is estimated to be around 35 per cent. To household expenditure we then add the total expenditure of corporations and firms, referred to as investment (I). In the UK – much to

Exhibit 4.4 The expenditure components of GDP

Component	Description
C	Final consumption expenditure by households
+I	Gross fixed capital formation (investment in plant and machinery)
+G	Final consumption expenditure by the government
+X	Expenditure by foreign residents on home goods and services
−M	Expenditure by home residents on foreign goods and services
= E	Gross Domestic Product – expenditure basis

the annoyance of successive Chancellors – this figure is fairly low, around 15 per cent. In China it is estimated to be over 50 per cent (though accurate figures are elusive). To consumption and investment expenditure we then add expenditure by the government (G), which in the UK is around 40 per cent of total expenditure. We then add the expenditure of foreign residents on an economy's goods and services, known as exports (X), and subtract from that the expenditure of the economy's residents on foreign goods and services, known as imports (M).

To determine the likely path of future growth, economists will therefore take views on and monitor all of these components, using a vast array of indicators. Governments will wish to understand these trends so that they can plan their taxation and expenditure programmes. Corporations will want to understand these trends to determine their own business strategies and to inform their investment decisions.

But why should trustees be interested in growth trends?

They should be interested because economic growth can be a powerful determinant of asset prices. To put it simplistically, when economic growth is strong, or is expected to be strong, equity prices can be driven to high levels, since strong economic growth is usually (though not always) associated with strong profits growth too. Similarly, commercial real estate prices are highly geared to economic growth because a vibrant economy tends to result in greater demand for offices and industrial premises, not to mention retail outlets for consumers to spend the increased income and wealth that flows from economic growth.

Unfortunately GDP data is published with a considerable lag because it takes some time to collect. This means that it only measures how fast things have grown over a three-month period that ended anything up to three months ago. So analysts pay particular attention to more frequent data and to surveys of economic activity. For example, to arrive at a better picture of consumption trends in the UK, analysts will dissect the monthly report on retail sales and the vast array of surveys of consumer activity, that help them establish how fast consumption is currently growing and is likely to grow in the near term.

Trend growth: Growth potential

One of the most important issues in relation to economic growth is what economists refer to as *trend growth*. Politicians often refer to this as *sustainable growth*. In some respects we can think of an economy as being analogous to a marathon runner. If the runner begins the London marathon at too fast a pace then at some stage they are likely to overheat and break down. On the other hand, if they begin too slowly they are unlikely to be able to finish the race in the best time possible. A good marathon runner paces themselves for the long run, so that they neither overheat nor simply jog around the course below their full potential. Most economists agree that when an economy grows *too rapidly* it can overheat leading to inflation (more on this below), while if it grows *too slowly* some of its resources will lie unnecessarily idle, in particular there will tend to be a large pool of unemployed people. The problem lies in trying to define 'too rapidly' and 'too slowly', or in other words, trying to define the optimal, sustainable, or trend rate of growth. Since the dawn of time every Chancellor of the Exchequer in the UK has tried to increase trend growth.

So what factors determine this trend rate of GDP growth?

It will be determined by the quantities of capital (machinery, factories etc.) and labour available in an economy and perhaps more importantly, on how efficiently these are used and combined. Economists sometimes refer to this combination and the resulting synergy as *total factor productivity*.

The total output of an economy can be thought of as simply the average output of each worker multiplied by the number of workers. So economic growth can come from two sources, from:

1. an improvement in the productivity of workers. In other words, by continually finding ways to increase the output of individual workers; or
2. a continual increase in the size of the workforce. That is, by migration or by drawing members of the population, that traditionally did not form part of the workforce, into employment.

Between 1997 and 2007, often referred to as the NICE decade,[3] UK economic growth was relatively high and stable. However, much of this growth came from an expansion of the labour force. At the end of 1996 there were 10.9m

---

[3] The NICE decade was a term coined by the Bank of England Governor, Mervyn King. NICE is an acronym for Non-Inflationary Consistent Expansion.

female participants in the UK labour market, by the end of 2007 that number had risen to 12.4m (Source: Office for National Statistics). Similarly, between 2004 and 2007 significant numbers of workers migrated to the UK so boosting the labour force. Much of the growth in the UK economy during this ten-year period was due to an increase in the size of the available labour force and to its willingness, on average, to work longer hours. By contrast, growth in economies like Germany, which did not experience such significant changes in their labour market, was predominantly due to improvements in productivity.

Trend growth can be defined as the growth rate that is neither associated with an overheating economy – often characterized by high inflation – nor one that is not making full use of its potential – often characterized by high unemployment. But of course, even if the authorities – governments and central banks – were very skilful at managing their economies, growth would tend to cycle around its long-run trend rate as shown in Exhibit 4.5.

The trend GDP line in this exhibit represents the long-run sustainable growth in GDP. The actual GDP line represents the stylized growth path of GDP. There are times when the economy will be growing above trend, and times when it will be growing below trend. When it is growing above trend, economists say that there is a positive output gap. That is, the economy is producing more goods and services than is sustainable in the long run, while the converse of this is a negative output gap. Governments and central banks spend a great deal of their time considering the likely level of trend growth so that they can then work out whether there is a positive or negative output gap. If the gap is positive then further growth could be inflationary. Alternatively, if it is negative then the economy may have capacity for strong growth without inflationary consequences. Such considerations will also be of relevance to pension scheme

Exhibit 4.5 Stylized representation of the output gap

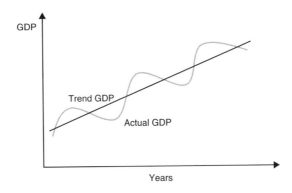

trustees and other investors since inflation will affect the returns available to investors and, with regard to pensions, will also affect the level of pension payments.

Growth summary

Positive, high and sustained economic growth – as measured by GDP – is the goal of most governments. It does not come without its costs of course, notably the depletion of the earth's natural resources, and higher levels of pollution and congestion, but nonetheless it remains the goal. However, we have also hinted that in practice it can be unstable. In other words economic good and bad times, booms and busts are phenomena to which we have become all too accustomed. Exhibit 4.6 presents year-on-year UK GDP growth since 1956. Over this period the average annual growth rate has been just under 2.4 per cent. However, there have been regular booms, particularly in the 1960s, and regular busts too. The most notable bust, or recession, over this period was the one that followed the collapse of the investment bank Lehman Brothers in September 2008. In the year that followed, UK output fell by a staggering 6 per cent.

The holy grail of growth is that it should sustain high levels of employment – it should not collapse as it did in 1979, 1991 or 2008 – and it should be non-inflationary. It is to the phenomenon of inflation that we now turn, and eventually to its relationship with economic policy and stable growth.

Exhibit 4.6   UK GDP growth since 1956

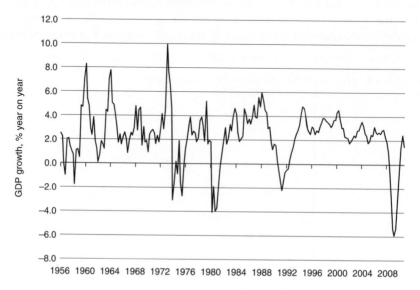

Inflation

Inflation is always and everywhere a monetary phenomenon. (Milton Friedman, 1968[4])

We began our discussion about growth with a quote from a Nobel winning economist, Robert Lucas, so it is appropriate to begin a discussion about inflation with the wise words of another Nobel laureate, the late Professor Milton Friedman. However, before we can address this comment we will need to begin to define inflation and then go on to examine its causes.

So what is inflation? It is usually measured as the percentage change over a month or a year of a price index – though it could be equally measured as the percentage change in the price of any single good or service. There are many different price indices and therefore many different measures of inflation. In practice when journalists and analysts talk about '*the*' rate of inflation they generally mean the percentage change in an index of the prices of goods and services typically purchased by consumers, or more specifically by the average household. In the UK the most important consumer price indices are the Retail Price Index (RPI) and the Consumer Prices Index (CPI). These two indices differ in two ways. First, they are based upon slightly different baskets of goods and services and second they are based upon different calculation methodologies.

Panel A in Exhibit 4.7 shows the level of a broad index of UK prices going back to 1750. Between 1750 and 1799 prices roughly doubled, but a century later they were basically unchanged. Between 1921 and 1936, they either fell every year or rose by less than 1 per cent. Between 1973 and 1981 prices tripled. We can see the history of inflation with more clarity when we look at Panel B. This shows that there have been some very significant periods of inflation around conflicts. Prices rose by 50 per cent over the first ten years of the Napoleonic wars, and doubled during World War I.

Perhaps the most interesting feature to draw from the figure is that persistent and positive inflation has been a very modern phenomenon. Until the recent credit crunch, when a short period of negative inflation was experienced, as measured by the RPI, since the 1960s the average price level has risen year after year. This phenomenon has been experienced in most other developed economies over this period too, with the exception of Japan. Before the post-World War II period, a rapid increase in prices was generally followed by a period of

---

[4] Milton Friedman. *Dollars and Deficits: Living With America's Economic Problems*, Prentice-Hall (1968).

Exhibit 4.7   Consumer prices in the UK since 1750

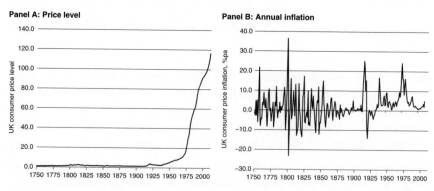

Sources: ONS, Bank of England.

rapidly falling prices. Our modern mindset finds it difficult to imagine how average prices could fall by 20 per cent or 30 per cent as they have done in the past. This is because we have lived the past 50 years or so in a period of (almost) continually rising average prices.

Before we go on to examine the ways in which governments and central banks have tried to control inflation, we should first establish why inflation matters.

Why does inflation matter?

Significant efforts have been put into controlling inflation since the major economies experienced such high levels of inflation in the 1970s. In August 1975 the UK's annual inflation rate peaked at 27 per cent. From the early 1970s then, inflation has been seen as a 'bad thing' by politicians, businessmen and consumers alike. But why? What are the costs of inflation?

At a micro level, high levels of inflation would mean businesses constantly having to change the advertised prices of their goods and services. These are known as 'menu costs'. There are also what economists refer to as 'shoe leather costs' of inflation too. In times of high inflation people would naturally tend to hold less cash, and would, therefore, wear out their shoe leather (or today more likely the engines of their 4×4s) in making frequent trips to the bank to withdraw cash. But these are relatively old arguments, used to demonstrate that inflation is bad. In a modern economy, with the Internet and with transactions becoming increasingly cashless, these costs will be lower today than they may have been in the past.

To demonstrate the possible adverse effects of inflation, imagine a world for a moment where inflation is high but where all prices in an economy are perfectly indexed to inflation, and that technology has eliminated the issues surrounding the menu and shoe leather costs of inflation. In such an economy would people care about inflation? Probably not. If average prices of goods and services rose by 10 per cent, salaries (and all other prices) would rise by the same amount, which would, therefore, make people indifferent to the price rise. In practice however, not all prices, wages, salaries, rents and so forth, are indexed, in which case people would certainly start to worry about inflation again.

What if inflation, in this world where prices are no longer perfectly indexed, is high but perfectly predictable? In this alternative, imaginary world we would have to think about inflation, but not too hard as long as we were capable of calculating the impact of the known inflation rate on all future prices. So if everyone knew that inflation would be 10 per cent over the next year, then everyone could bargain for a 10 per cent increase in their salaries to accommodate this, and firms would plan to put up the prices of their goods and services by 10 per cent. Actually, in this world an expectation of 10 per cent inflation would become a self-fulfilling prophecy.

However, in all likelihood we would worry about inflation in a world where all prices were not indexed and crucially, where inflation was high and unpredictable.[5] Arguably it is the unexpected component of inflation that is most costly. Inflation that is anticipated can be factored into wage negotiations and priced into business and financial contracts. But, when inflation turns out to be higher than is anticipated then borrowers benefit at the expense of lenders, since the real value of their borrowing declines. Conversely when inflation is lower than is anticipated, lenders benefit at the expense of borrowers, since the real value of their debt repayments rises.

If inflation is very uncertain, or very volatile, then lenders will ask for a premium to compensate them for this uncertainty and, therefore, the costs of borrowing will be higher than they would otherwise have been. Higher borrowing costs could in turn reduce economic activity as a result, for example, of associated lower levels of investment.

Most economists agree then that it is unexpected inflation, or uncertainty about the future rate of inflation, that creates most of the costs associated with the phenomenon of inflation.

It is possible that uncertainty about inflation can exacerbate the cycle of boom and bust too. Take for example, the case of an imaginary washing machine factory owner. Suppose one day the factory owner looks out at the market for washing machines and sees that the market price of washing machines has risen by

---

[5] In fact this is a crude description of the UK's inflationary backdrop in the 1970s and 1980s.

10 per cent. Faced with this information, the factory owner assumes that there has been an increase in demand for washing machines or maybe a reduction in supply. So to take advantage of the new, higher prices, they increase the capacity of the factory, employ more workers and begin to produce more washing machines. Once they have increased their productive capacity, they attempt to sell the extra machines that the factory has produced. But to their horror they find that there is no extra demand for their washing machines. Instead they realize that the 10 per cent rise in washing machine prices was caused by a general increase in all consumer prices across the economy. Now the washing machine manufacturer realizes that they have surplus stock, excess factory capacity and too many workers. So they cut back on production, lay off some of the workforce and realize that they won't need to invest in new plant or machinery for a long time. If we scale this example up, it should not be difficult to imagine how unanticipated increases, or decreases, in the general price level could exacerbate and, in some extreme cases, cause economic booms and busts.

Over the past two to three decades the consensus among economists has been that unanticipated and high levels of inflation can have an impact on real things like employment, investment and profits, and, therefore, that controlling inflation should be one of the main goals of macroeconomic policy. Before we turn to the issue of macroeconomic policy and the desire to control inflation we should first think about the causes of inflation.

The causes of inflation

We began this section with a quote from Milton Friedman. We can now return to it.

Money is just a medium of exchange[6] which makes multiple and complex transactions very simple. To explain, imagine a world without money, a world where barter is the medium of exchange. Suppose too that the price of one cow is four goats. How could inflation have an impact upon this price? The answer is that it could not. The price of the cow could rise to five goats, if cows suddenly become in short supply or if people suddenly believed that eating beef was good for them. However, this is not inflation; this is just a change in the relative price of one good with respect to another.

Now let's introduce pieces of paper into this economy that we will call money and which can be used as a medium of exchange. For the sake of argument

---

[6] Money is also a unit of account and a store of value. To perform these functions, money should be recognizable as such, durable, portable and divisible. For more detail on money and its role in the economy see R. Lipsey and A. Chrystal, *Economics*, Oxford University Press (2003).

let's call this paper 'pounds'. Suppose that the price of a goat in this economy is £25 and that the price of a cow is £100, so the cow to goat exchange rate is 1:4, as in the previous example. Now let's double the amount of money in circulation. For every piece of paper representing a pound held, everyone is now given an extra pound. Nothing in the real economy has changed; it's just that people have twice the amount of paper in their pockets than they had before. The most likely impact then is that in money terms the prices of all goods and services will also double, so that the price of a cow would rise to £200 and the price of a goat to £50. The prices of both have risen and the economy has experienced a rate of inflation of 100 per cent. However, the cow to goat exchange rate is still 1:4.

This example demonstrates that inflation is only possible where an economy uses money as a medium of exchange which is not fixed to another asset or good that is in fixed supply. It demonstrates that *'money is always and everywhere a monetary phenomenon'*. Without money, there cannot be inflation.

Too much money chasing too few goods

The barter economy example gives us a clue as to one possible cause of inflation – money. Put crudely inflation can be the result of *'too much money chasing too few goods'*, or too many pieces of paper chasing too few goods. The Quantity Theory of Money is the more sophisticated expression of this idea, upon which Friedman built his proposition.

To be honest, as theories go this is not up there with $E=MC^2$. In mathematical terms the quantity theory of money is an identity. Or in layman's terms – it is little more than the statement of the *'bleeding obvious'* (to quote Basil Fawlty[7]).

The mathematical representation of the theory looks like this:

$$M \times V = P \times T$$

The 'M' stands for the quantity of money in an economy; the 'V' stands for the number of times over a given period that a unit of the currency changes hands; the 'P' represents the average price level; and the 'T' represents the total number of transactions that take place in the economy. Effectively what this expression is telling us is that the amount of money spent over a given period is equal to the value of all the goods and services that the money is used to buy. In essence it is rather like saying '$2 \times 2 = 1 \times 4$'. It is a banal accounting

[7] For anyone fortunate enough to be under the age of 30, Basil Fawlty was the central character in the 1970s BBC comedy series *Fawlty Towers*.

identity really. And yet in the hands of highly paid economists it can become so much more!

According to some economists, if the monetary authorities – the central bank, or the central bank under the direction of the government – allow the money supply, M, to expand too rapidly then it is probable that the price level, P, will rise since the number of transactions – the number of people wishing to buy cows and goats – will be unchanged by this action. Hence they argue that inflation is a direct function of the rate of growth of the money supply and can, therefore, also be controlled by the authorities who are in charge of the supply of money – simple.

Well not quite that simple.

Although flooding an economy with additional cash could certainly lead to higher inflation, the relationship between money and prices is not that straightforward. First, an increase in the money supply could cause greater economic activity in the short term – recall the example of the washing machine manufacturer – and so a rise in M could cause T to rise too. But more importantly for this theory to 'work', the velocity of circulation of money, V, has to remain fairly constant too. If the money supply, M, increases rapidly but people simply hoard this extra cash so that the average number of times that each unit of currency changes hands falls, then the net impact on the price level, and upon the number of transactions, could be negligible.

To see how likely this is, we only need to consider the case of Japan. Beginning in 2001, the Japanese monetary authorities deliberately expanded the money supply to kick start their economy, but rather than stimulating economic activity the additional cash was simply hoarded by Japanese banks so that the additional Yen did not result in a higher number of transactions. Effectively as the 'M' in the quantity theory of money identity rose in Japan, 'V' was falling to such an extent that the increase in the money supply had only a limited impact on 'P' and 'T'. Despite the expansion of their money supply, the Japanese economy has remained mired in deflation.

There is also another more significant problem for those economists that believe that inflation is driven very mechanically by the money supply – and that is the idea that causation runs from money (M) to economic activity ($P \times T$). There is plenty of evidence to suggest that causation runs in the opposite direction, that is, from economic activity to money supply. In other words, increases (decreases) in economic activity lead to a rise (fall) in the supply of money. In fact some economists argue that saying that causation runs from money to activity is a bit like observing that there had been an increase in the sale of wedding rings and from that inferring that the subsequent increase in marriages was *caused* by the sale of these wedding rings! The cause of the weddings was, of course, love!

So the relationship between money and inflation is complex. Though most economists acknowledge that there is a relationship, there remains debate about the strength of this relationship, and the degree to which inflation can really be suppressed by controlling the rate of growth of the money supply.

Demand pull inflation

Money probably does play an important role in determining the rate of inflation, particularly in the long term, but prices might also rise as a consequence of an increase in demand. Economists refer to inflation that emanates from, for example, a sharp increase in consumer demand as 'demand pull inflation'. Whereas the monetary explanation for inflation could be characterized as: '*too much money chasing too few goods*', the demand pull explanation of inflation could be characterized as: '*too much demand chasing too few goods*'.

We have already hinted at this phenomenon when discussing the output gap, as depicted in Exhibit 4.5. When economic growth drives the economy to the point where its output is not sufficient to meet the demand of all of its citizens, a positive output gap develops and the ever increasing demand for the limited output forces the prices of these goods up and also wages and salaries, as producers compete to attract workers to satisfy the demand, as well as rents, house prices and so on.

The UK economy went through a cycle of this kind in the late-1980s. Back then, the Chancellor, Nigel Lawson, claimed that he had banished the boom and bust years of the past and that he had also managed to raise the economy's trend growth. Sound familiar? And because he believed this, he also believed that the economy could grow at the sort of fast pace that would have simply led to inflation in the past. This rapid growth can be seen in Exhibit 4.6 between 1985 and 1988. Eventually the strong demand caused the prices of goods and services, wages and salaries and house prices all to rise, and the output gap to become increasingly positive. In the end it resulted in tears with the sharp recession of the early 1990s (also evident in Exhibit 4.6) until the output gap shrank back again and the inflationary pressures gave way to a negative output gap and recession – which could be characterized as '*too little demand for too many goods*'.[8]

As inflation can be generated by increases in demand beyond the economy's capacity, and low levels of inflation can be generated when demand is too

---

[8] Lawson blamed the boom and subsequent bust on poor economic data.

weak, the macroeconomists working in government and central banks spend a great deal of time, either formally or informally, estimating the current value of the output gap.

Cost push inflation

Finally there is 'cost push inflation'. For most people this is more obvious as an explanation for why prices rise. Cost push inflation occurs when the price of an important good, service or commodity rises, causing other prices to rise too. The classic example of this type of inflation relates to the oil price shocks of the 1970s.

In 1973 OPEC restricted oil production causing the price of a barrel of oil to rise from around US$3 to US$9 literally overnight. This brought great wealth to oil producing nations – which was OPEC's aim – but increased costs for households and businesses in most other nations, both directly through an increase in energy prices and indirectly since oil and oil-based products were such an important input in other industries. The UK's annual inflation rate of 27 per cent in August 1975 was a direct result of the cost push inflation generated by OPEC's action two years earlier. A similar OPEC-related oil shock in 1979 caused UK inflation to rise rapidly again. On that occasion the oil price eventually peaked in 1981 at US$35 per barrel.

Cost push inflation might also be the result of aggressive wage bargaining. The high level of inflation that we experienced in the UK, which began with OPEC's action, was exacerbated by the trades unions who understandably wanted to increase the wages of their workers by winning 'inflation busting' pay claims. Though well intentioned at the micro level, the net effect at the macro level was the kind of inflationary self-fulfilling prophecy we mentioned earlier. Unions sought to make pay claims to compensate their members for the high inflation that they had experienced since their last pay claim, and also sought to claim enough to compensate them for the high inflation that they expected in the future too. Such behaviour virtually guaranteed that the high future inflation that they expected and for which they had bargained, would eventually appear.

Inflation summary

> *Inflation is as violent as a mugger, as frightening as an armed robber and as deadly as a hit-man.* (Ronald Reagan)

The sort of economic chaos that high and volatile inflation caused in the UK and in other developed economies in the 1970s goes some way to explain why many economic policymakers concluded that the taming of inflation should be the number one goal of macroeconomic policy. Mrs. Thatcher certainly thought so (as did her opposite number, Ronald Reagan, in the US). However, as we have discussed, there is no one, single cause of inflation. Does this matter? The answer to this question is definitely yes. In the next section of this chapter we will discuss the ways in which policymakers have sought to influence both the level of inflation and indirectly, the level of growth too, and why for this policy to be successful it is necessary for the monetary authorities to identify the source of inflation.

Macroeconomic policy

Battered and bruised by the high and volatile levels of inflation in the 1970s, governments and central banks in many developed economies, including those in the UK and the US, decided that inflation was public enemy number one. In this section we will focus on the UK authorities' attempts to get inflation under control because, in many respects, the UK's experience reads like a manual that might have been entitled: 'How *not* to control inflation'.

In the post-war years, the main weapon used to fight inflation was interest rates. When inflation started to rise (fall), interest rates were increased (decreased) causing the cost of credit to rise (fall) for companies and for householders, which eventually led to a fall (rise) in inflation. However, once OPEC had unleashed a spiral of cost push inflation, interest rate adjustments were not enough. In fact raising interest rates when inflation was rising because of an OPEC-induced increase in energy prices represented a double whammy for UK businesses and householders. Not only was the price of oil and energy rising, but the cost of credit was rising too.

In desperation UK politicians relied increasingly on cruder methods to control inflation that were ultimately doomed. These were incomes polices. An incomes policy would begin with a government announcement that, for example, no workers were allowed to receive a pay increase of greater than *x* per cent over a pre-specified period in the future. By announcing such a policy it was hoped that the vicious wage-price inflation spiral would be broken. Fine in the world of theory, but nobody lives in that world!

In the real world the result tended to be industrial strife as workers sought to derail the policy and/or seek a series of 'catch up' wage claims once the policy was lifted, so that even if the policy was successful in bringing down inflation in the short run, eventually the inflation genie would escape from the bottle once again. The last incomes policy of the Labour government of the 1970s ended with the 1978 'Winter of Discontent' – widespread strikes, fuel undelivered, bins uncollected, power cuts and the general impression that the UK was ungovernable.

If the costs of inflation were high, it seemed back then that the costs of trying to defeat it were higher still.

Mrs. Thatcher came to power in 1979 as a direct result of the collapse of the Labour government's flagship incomes policy and the 'Winter of Discontent'. Whatever her motives might have been, the number one economic policy objective of Mrs. Thatcher's administration was the defeat of inflation. Under her first two Chancellors, Geoffrey Howe and then Nigel Lawson, Mrs. Thatcher's government began what became known as the 'British Experiment'.[9] The basic idea was that inflation could be tamed by controlling the rate of growth of the money supply, and that by announcing in advance the rate of money growth that the government would target, this in turn would help to create an expectation of future money growth and inflation, and ultimately become a self-fulfilling goal.

Although the intellectual framework around this policy had the blessing of Professor Friedman and his monetarist acolytes, rooted as it was in the quantity theory of money, in order to restrict the growth of money the government had to increase the price of holding it – that is, they had to increase interest rates. As such, interest rates in the UK went up sharply, eventually peaking at 17 per cent. The net effect of this was a decline in inflation, but also a savage decline in economic activity. Unemployment rose from just over 3.5 per cent in 1979 to just over 10 per cent by 1984. Critics of this monetary experiment argued that its 'success' in bringing inflation down from around 10 per cent in 1979 to around 5 per cent by 1984, was more to do with the collapse in aggregate demand than to the successful control of the money supply. Indeed, the UK government soon became aware that controlling the rate of growth of the money supply was more difficult than it sounded. The difficulties arose because of the ingenuity of the financial sector, which essentially managed to create new forms of money to thwart the government's efforts to control its supply and growth. Eventually the Conservative government abandoned its attempts to set monetary supply growth targets and its associated attempt to control its growth in 1985.

Exchange rate targeting

With money supply targeting largely discredited, the UK government turned to another popular means of controlling inflation – exchange rate targeting. When a high inflation economy has a floating exchange rate, its currency will tend to depreciate over time against an economy with a low inflation rate. This perpetual depreciation of the currency keeps domestic exports competitive,

---

[9] See the Fifth Mais Lecture: *The British Experiment*, given by The Rt. Hon. Nigel Lawson MP, Chancellor of the Exchequer, delivered at the City University Business School (renamed in 2003 as the Cass Business School), 18 June (1984).

but perpetuates the high inflation environment. By fixing its currency to an economy where the monetary authorities enjoy a reputation for controlling inflation – many countries fix their exchange rate to the US dollar – the high inflation economy seeks to 'import' some of this credibility for itself. Once fixed, the only way that the high inflation economy can remain internationally competitive is to improve its productivity, rather than by charging lower and lower foreign currency denominated prices for its goods and services. The currency fix is usually maintained by the monetary authority by buying and selling its own currency in the open market. If the currency is depreciating then the authority must step in and buy it by selling some of its foreign currency reserves. It could also put up domestic interest rates to make its currency more attractive too. In this way it encourages others to buy the currency, thus supporting its value.

In 1990, sterling joined the fixed exchange rate regime known as the European Exchange Rate Mechanism (ERM). This meant that sterling was effectively fixed against the strongest currency in the ERM, the Deutschemark (DM). By doing so, the UK government hoped that they would effectively import the economic success and low inflation of the German economy to the inflation prone UK economy.

Since sterling was fixed at a high rate of just over DM3 to £1 and domestic demand in the UK was very strong, this meant that import growth was strong but export growth was weak. Had the pound been freely floating it would have most likely fallen in value, increasing the price of imports to UK residents and reducing the price of UK exports to overseas buyers, thus helping to restore the balance. But in a fixed exchange rate regime this is not possible. To maintain the fix, the UK government had to sell increasing amounts of its foreign currency reserves to help support sterling, and increasingly raise interest rates to make sterling more attractive to foreign investors. Eventually UK interest rates reached levels that began to choke the domestic economy. International speculators, such as George Soros, knew that such high rates of interest could not be maintained indefinitely. They began to sell the pound aggressively, making it even harder to maintain the fixed rate, until eventually the UK government had to abandon the fixed rate to allow sterling to float freely once again.

So what next? In an effort to control inflation the UK government had tried:

i.   prices and incomes policies;
ii. targeting the rate of growth of the money supply; and
iii. tying the pound to the currency of a strong, low inflation economy.

In September 1992, having crashed ignominiously out of the ERM, the UK began to target inflation directly. In May 1997, this was formalized by giving the Bank of England operational control of interest rates – that is, without the political interference of the Chancellor – and a mandate to keep inflation within well defined parameters.

The 'state of the art': Inflation targeting

Inflation targeting was first considered at the end of the 1980s and the beginning of the 1990s. The basic idea of this approach to economic policy is that a whole range of indicators (not just money growth, or the exchange rate) are monitored to assess the inflationary pressures within an economy, so that interest rates are set accordingly to achieve a published target for inflation. However, in order to strengthen the credibility of this framework, it was recognized that the responsibility for controlling interest rates and for achieving the inflation target should lie in the hands of central bankers rather than those of politicians. This is because it was felt that central bankers had more credibility than politicians when it came to controlling inflation. For example, a heavily indebted government might be tempted to 'inflate away' its debts, at the expense of debt holders. The more credible a monetary policy authority the more likely it is that it can succeed in influencing inflation expectations, such that their inflation target becomes a self-fulfilling prophecy. Exhibit 4.8 shows how inflation targeting spread in popularity as an approach to macroeconomic policy.

Exhibit 4.8   The spread of inflation targeting

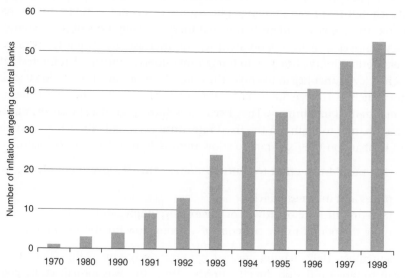

Source: G. Stern and L. Mahadeva, *Monetary Policy Frameworks in a Global Context*, London, Routledge (2000).

Exhibit 4.9 A selection of inflation targets

Country/region	Inflation target
Australia	Australian Federal Reserve's target is: inflation between 2.0% and 3.0%
Canada	Bank of Canada's target is: CPI inflation within 1.0% and 3.0%
Eurozone	ECB's target is: CPI inflation below a ceiling of 2.0%
South Korea	Bank of Korea's target for 2010–2012 is: CPI inflation within ±one percentage point of 3.0%
New Zealand	Reserve Bank of New Zealand's target is: inflation between 1.0% and 3.0%
Sweden	Riksbank's target is: CPI inflation within ±one percentage point of 2.0%
UK	Bank of England's target is: CPI inflation within ±one percentage point of 2.0%

Source: Central bank websites, available at: http://www.bis.org/cbanks.htm.

Exhibit 4.10 Inflation for a selection of mature economies

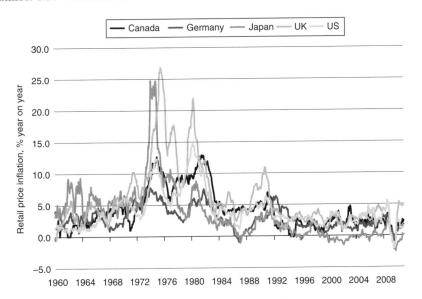

Source: Thomson Financial.

In Exhibit 4.9 we have presented a selection of inflation targets for a range of central banks. Most central banks target a broad measure of consumer price inflation, aiming to keep it at around 2 per cent over the medium term, though permit a fairly narrow range around this target. As noted above, the Bank of England was given operational responsibility for interest rates in May 1997 and, much like other independent inflation targeting central banks, aimed to be as transparent as possible with its decision making. As such, it publishes regular analysis – the *Inflation Report*[10] – where the Bank's views about growth and inflation are laid out in tortuous detail.

So how successful has inflation targeting been? Exhibit 4.10 shows the inflation experience of a number of mature economies. The inflation horrors of the 1970s are very clear from this. But since the mid-1990s the inflation experience of a range of economies has been very similar. In fact, their inflation experiences have been very closely related to their inflation targets. That is, inflation expectations have become 'well anchored'.

Arguably then, inflation targeting has been a success. The narrow-minded focus on inflation, and indeed, the focus of the narrow-minded monetary authorities – the central banks – finally seems to have seen off endemic inflation which was the scourge of policymakers, households and corporations in the 1970s and 1980s. Or have they?

The price of inflation targeting

While inflation targeting seems to have been very successful in its relatively narrow goal, some have argued that the rather simple-minded objective of containing the rate at which consumer prices rise has been at the expense of instability elsewhere. Throughout the world, while independent central bankers were watching the consumer price inflation gauge, they paid less attention to other prices. In particular to asset prices and also to the build-up of credit in the global financial system. We now know that the sharp reversal of this credit build up – that is, the credit crunch – that began to bite in the late summer of 2007, was the catalyst for the worst global recession for more than 70 years. Indeed, between 2008 and 2010 many central banks have been fighting not the spectre of inflation, but that of deflation – a persistent decline in average prices.

For the moment, not wanting to throw the baby out with the bath water, many policymakers around the world, remain wedded to the idea of inflation targeting. It is likely that its implementation will have to change in the future to take account of the remarkable post-Lehman Brothers events. Indeed, Exhibit 4.11 illustrates the extent of the impact that a financial crisis can have on the real economy and upon the performance of equity markets. The data in the exhibit are based upon the performance of the US economy following 14 severe crises between 1929 and 2001. On average, house and equity prices have fallen dramatically, GDP per head has fallen on average by 9.3 percentage points and perhaps most astonishingly, the average real cumulative increase in US government debt is 86 percentage points three years following a financial crisis.

---

[10] See: http://www.bankofengland.co.uk/publications/inflationreport/.

Exhibit 4.11   Peak-to-trough changes in the aftermath of severe financial crises

	Cumulative change (%)	Duration (years)
House prices	–36.0	5.0
Equity prices	–56.0	3.4
GDP per head	–9.3	1.9
Real government debt	–86.0	3.0

Source: C. Reinhart and K. Rogoff, *The Aftermath of Financial Crises*, Cambridge, MA, National Bureau of Economic Research (2009).

Fiscal policy

We have spent a great deal of time in this chapter discussing the issue and threat of inflation. Inflation can destroy the real value of fixed income investments and very volatile inflation can create havoc in an economy, causing employment and profits to fall. But because inflation is *'always and everywhere a monetary phenomenon'*, it has generally been felt that monetary policy is best suited to deal with inflation via the manipulation of interest rates. Until the recent financial crisis it was widely believed that fiscal policy – which refers to the government's decisions about taxation and spending – was best used to redistribute wealth throughout the economy and to provide the right incentives for individuals to work, for entrepreneurs to innovate and for existing companies to invest. Until recently then fiscal policy had taken a back seat to monetary policy. However, given the size of the public sector in most developed economies, relative to that of the economy as a whole, the fiscal framework can still have a big impact on employment, growth and profits.

Governments are both big spenders and big borrowers. There is no point therefore having a conservative monetary policy that seeks to keep inflation under control on the one hand, if the government is going to tax, borrow and spend its way into oblivion on the other. Under these circumstances monetary and fiscal policy could end up in conflict. It was for this reason that Gordon Brown, in his capacity as Chancellor, introduced his 'golden rule' after the May 1997 general election which broadly stated that over the economic cycle, as defined by the Chancellor, the government would borrow only to invest and not to fund current spending. By doing so it would also aim to keep outstanding UK government debt below 40 per cent of GDP. With this 'fiscally prudent' rule, Mr. Brown was trying to reassure the world that fiscal policy would provide a stable and supportive background for the economy and for monetary policy in its single-minded fight against the perils of inflation.

The financial crisis struck a mortal blow to this prudent fiscal framework. The depth of the crisis was so great that it caused the UK government's fiscal position to deteriorate rapidly. At the end of 2010 the fiscal deficit ballooned from around 3 per cent of GDP to 10 per cent, that is, for every £10 the government spent, £9 was raised from taxes and £1 was raised from borrowing. The increased borrowing caused the total amount of UK government debt to rise too. It is expected to peak at around 80 per cent of GDP in 2014, leaving Mr. Brown's 40 per cent threshold well behind.

Although much of the focus over the past ten years has been on monetary policy, it seems that the focus over the next ten years will be almost certainly be on the fiscal positions of developed economy governments, including that of the UK, the US, Japan and several Euro zone governments,[11] as they all attempt to pay down their enormous debts shown in Exhibit 4.12. This can only be done via a combination of tax hikes and public expenditure cuts. This fiscal austerity may well foster a much weaker growth environment over the next ten years than was experienced over the ten years leading up to the crisis. The weaker growth environment will affect the pricing and performance of UK and other developed economy financial assets, particularly cash deposit rates and government bond prices. Trustees will need to bear this in mind when looking at financial assets issued from the now highly indebted developed economies of the world.

Exhibit 4.12   Central government debt to GDP, end-2009

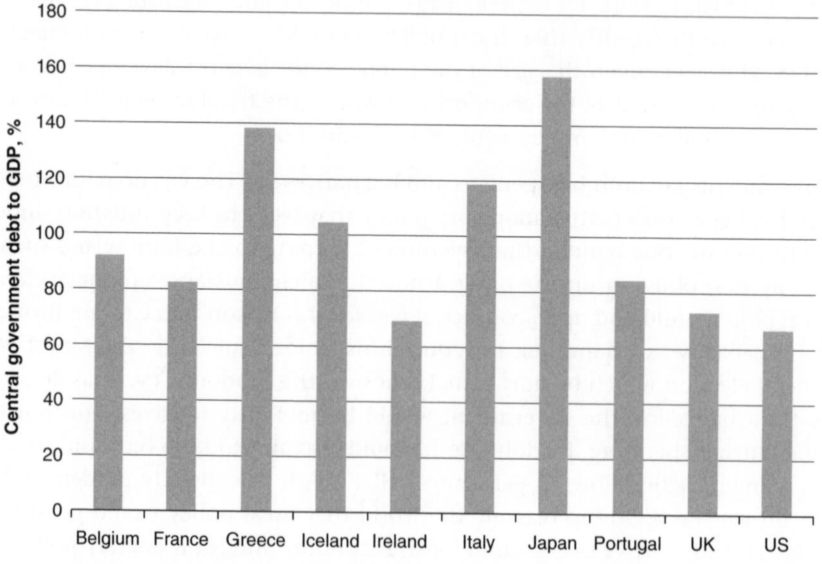

Source: World Bank (NB: Figures for Japan are for end-2008)

---

[11] Italy, Spain, Belgium, Portugal, Ireland and Greece in particular.

Summary

Sustainable and stable economic growth remains the goal of most governments, since its attainment is thought to have positive consequences for profits, employment and prosperity. But keeping inflation at bay has been the pre-eminent goal for many years because, if left to run riot, inflation can have damaging consequences for the real economy.

Though inflation targeting currently remains the policy of choice for many governments and nations, it is by no means the only overarching policy option available. Many economies prefer to operate an exchange rate targeting regime. Indeed there are a large number of currencies pegged to the US dollar including: the Hong Kong Dollar, the Chinese Renminbi, and a range of currencies issued by South American, Middle Eastern and Gulf states. Prices and incomes policies are also still used on occasions.

Economists and policymakers believed that if they could control inflation then sustainable, stable growth would almost always be the natural consequence. Monetary authorities have taken the lead in trying to control the general direction of their economies by using interest rates. While monetary policy has taken all of the limelight in macroeconomic management, fiscal policy has been used to create incentives for households and corporations to pursue certain economically desirable courses of action and to redistribute income, rather than to chart the direction of the economy. However, now that the fiscal position of many governments, including the UK's, has deteriorated so sharply, fiscal policy is likely to assume crucial importance in the years to come.

But why is any of this relevant for investors?

The answer is that all financial instruments are ultimately a claim on an underlying economy. As such, growth and inflation trends, along with the economic policy chosen by individual governments and monetary authorities will determine the return that investors will demand from holding any financial instrument over time. We will expand on this relationship in Chapter 10 where we will introduce the idea of asset allocation.

Key points

- Economics is the study of the allocation of scarce resources among many competing ends.
- Microeconomics is concerned with the choices made by individual consumers and producers and the economic conditions that exist in individual markets, whereas macroeconomics focuses on the aggregate outcome of all the individual economic decisions that take place in an economy.

- The macroeconomic goals of most governments are to generate high and sustained economic growth and employment and low inflation. The principal focus of macroeconomic policy for most governments since the 1970s has been on controlling inflation through a combination of prices and income polices, targeting the rate of growth of the money supply, exchange rate targeting and formal inflation targeting.
- Fiscal policy refers to the government's decisions about taxation and spending and has typically been used to create incentives for households and corporations to pursue certain economically desirable courses of action and to redistribute income, rather than to chart the direction of the economy.
- Financial crises can have a devastating effect on asset prices, economic growth and unemployment and typically result in a sharp deterioration of a nation's fiscal position.

Chapter 5

Cash: The Most Liquid of All the Asset Classes

Learning outcomes

- Appreciate that cash is an asset class in its own right.
- Appreciate that the active management of cash is an integral element of a scheme's overall investment strategy.
- Know the main characteristics of cash deposits and money market instruments.
- Know what constitutes a secure and stable money market fund.

Introducing traditional asset classes

In this and the next three chapters we look at four asset classes that have, to a greater or lesser extent over time, traditionally comprised a typical defined benefit (DB) scheme's asset portfolio. A few years ago we would not have needed the 'traditional' adjective at all as up until fairly recently the four asset classes that we cover were largely all that was available to pension schemes and other institutional investors as an investment medium. However, over the past decade or so the range of asset classes and related investment strategies has increased enormously. We cover the main alternative asset classes – hedge funds,[1] commodities, private equity and foreign currency – in Chapter 13. In this and the next three chapters we devote our attention in turn to cash, bonds, equities and real estate.

---

[1] Although frequently referred to as an asset class, hedge funds are not really an asset class. We explain why in Chapter 13.

Although cash is not generally held with the expectation of generating significant returns over time, it is a vital component of any scheme's asset portfolio, not least because it is the means by which regular pension payments are made to the scheme's pensioners. Pensioners prefer to be paid in cash! Whereas pension schemes traditionally allocated a portion of their funds to government bonds to generate the cash flow necessary to meet current and expected pension payments, following the collapse of the equity markets in the early-noughties, and the development of the sterling and euro corporate bond markets over the last 15 years, bonds have gradually become part of a more strategic approach to return generation and, as we explain more fully in Chapter 15, a way of managing balance sheet risks. Equities have been, and still remain for many schemes, the asset class that most trustees look to, to produce the long-term returns necessary to fund their schemes. However, in more recent times the traditional scheme reliance on equities has been called into question. The disillusionment with equities has been one of the main catalysts for the interest in alternative asset classes. Finally, the inclusion of real estate in this list of traditional asset classes may seem odd to some. There are certainly those institutional and retail investors that view real estate as an alternative asset class. But for many others, the stable cash flows generated by this asset class have long been seen as an essential part of their asset portfolio. In the end, 'traditional' and 'alternative' are in the eye of the investor beholder.

Introducing cash

All pension schemes will have an allocation to cash, even if it is simply to ensure that a suitable cash buffer is held to meet all pension payments over say a six-month period. Having such a buffer avoids the need to liquidate other, more risky and less liquid asset classes to meet pension payments, which would be less than ideal in the event of a decline in the prices of these asset classes. Pension schemes typically hold their cash in two forms: cash deposits and money market funds. Both forms allow the scheme to manage its short-term liquidity needs. That is, they enable a scheme to meet its payments to pensioners, its day-to-day operational expenses and to support the strategic and tactical buying and selling of the scheme's other assets. In addition to this ease of accessibility, cash investments should also offer capital security and a temporary safe haven for funds, especially in times of market turbulence. As such, cash investments are an asset class in their own right, while the active management of cash is an integral element of a scheme's overall investment strategy.

However, despite their flexibility and other attractions, cash investments are not normally held over the long term in the hope of generating high returns; historically cash investments have underperformed most other asset classes over the medium to long term and their long-term, real (or inflation-adjusted) return has just about been positive. According to the Credit Suisse Global Investment Returns Sourcebook 2011, between 1900 and 2010, UK cash instruments outperformed inflation on average by 1 per cent per year, but underperformed UK equities and UK government bonds by 4.3 per cent and 0.4 per cent per annum respectively.[2]

Cash deposits

Let's start by looking at cash deposits. Up until very recently, short-term bank deposit accounts were traditionally the principal means by which pension schemes held their cash. The main characteristics of these accounts are that the:

- return comprises interest income with no potential for capital growth, and
- amount invested is repaid in full at the end of the term.

In effect these accounts are no different from the current or deposit accounts that individuals can open with any high street bank.

Most pension schemes deposit their cash with a UK domiciled British bank. However, some deposits may be held with those banks that are located, but not domiciled, in the UK. Whether investing via British banks or via banks that are only located but not domiciled in the UK, trustees and their investment consultants should scrutinize the creditworthiness of the chosen deposit taking institution. Trustees should also look closely at the likely willingness of the monetary authorities or government of the country in which the bank is domiciled to step into the breach should the bank fail. The failure in 2008 of those Icelandic banks operating in the UK and the unwillingness of the Icelandic government at that time to compensate those UK pension schemes that had deposited tens of millions of pounds with these financial institutions, should serve as a salutary warning to all bank depositors.

If venturing overseas or offshore, then in addition to assessing the creditworthiness of the country's banking system, trustees should also establish:

- the costs of currency conversion and hedging the exchange rate risk;
- whether the deposit will be subject to any exchange controls that may restrict access to the money, and
- the tax treatment of interest applied to the deposit.

---

[2] Copyright © 2011 Elroy Dimson, Paul Marsh and Mike Staunton, *Triumph of the Optimists: 101 Years of Global Investment Returns*, Princeton University Press (2002).

The money markets

Increasingly, however pension schemes are turning to the money markets for the management of their cash balances. The money markets are the wholesale (as opposed to retail) markets for cash and are populated by the banks and institutional investors. The money markets enable wholesale customers to both deposit money and to borrow money over very short time horizons. The markets are characterized by the issuance, trading and redemption of short-dated negotiable, or tradable, securities[3] usually with a maturity of up to one year, with most having maturities ranging from overnight to three months.

To facilitate trading in money market instruments, most are issued in bearer form, that is, without registered title. Most are issued at a discount to their face value and are redeemed by the bearer (who may or may not be the original purchaser) at face value on maturity. The difference between the issue price and the redemption payment constitutes the return, analogous to an interest payment.

The main money market instruments are:

- Treasury Bills (T-Bills). These are arguably the most important of all money market instruments and are issued to facilitate a government's short-term financing needs. UK T-Bills are the UK government's short-term instrument for liquidity management and are issued on behalf of the UK government by its agent, the Debt Management Office (DMO). UK T-Bills are usually issued at a discount with a term of one, three or six months and redeemed at face value at maturity. They are usually highly liquid and act as the benchmark risk-free interest rate when assessing the returns potentially available on other asset types.
- The annual yield on a 91-day Treasury Bill is calculated by the following formula:

$$\left[\frac{\text{par value} - \text{issue price}}{\text{issue price}} \right] \times \frac{365}{91} \times 100$$

- So, a 91 day Treasury Bill issued at £99.75 will have an annualized yield of:

$$\left[\frac{100}{£99.75} \right] \times \frac{365}{91} \times 100 = 1.00\%$$

Although the yield on each money market instrument is calculated in a slightly different way, the calculation above is a good representation of the way in which money market instruments work.

---

[3] We use the terms 'securities' and 'instruments' interchangeably.

- *Certificates of Deposit (CDs).* A CD is a negotiable, bearer security issued by a commercial bank in exchange for cash from an investor, with a fixed term and a fixed rate of interest, set at approximately the same level as an equivalent term deposit. The investor can either retain the CD until maturity or sell the security in the money market whenever access to the money is required. However, being a fixed interest security, the sale price achieved will fluctuate depending upon (i) the perceived credit quality of the issuer of the CD and the corresponding credit spread, (ii) prevailing market yields at the time of sale, and (iii) general market liquidity for the security in question. The issuer of a CD is able to keep the cash received from the sale of the CD until the CD matures. CDs can be issued with terms of up to five years and are quoted by yield.
- *Commercial Paper.* This is the corporate equivalent of a T-Bill and is the term used to describe the unsecured, negotiable, bearer securities, or short-term promissory notes, issued by companies. They are issued at a discount to par with a maturity usually between a few days and a year and are redeemed at face value at maturity. They are quoted in the market by a discount yield.
- *Interbank market deposits.* Fixed term deposits can be made in the interbank market. The interbank market originally served the short-term deposit and borrowing needs of the commercial banks but has since been tapped into by institutional investors and large corporates with short-term cash surpluses or borrowing requirements. The term of deposits made in the interbank market can range from overnight to several years. Up until 2008 deposit yields were typically commoditized and investors were paid at LIBID – the London Interbank Bid Rate – while short-term borrowers were charged at LIBOR – the London Interbank Offered Rate. The mean of these rates is referred to as LIMEAN, the London Interbank Mean Rate. Since 2008 markets have moved away from standard LIBID/LIBOR rates and have factored in credit spreads. The credit spread tiers rates offered to investors depend upon the perceived credit quality of the deposit taker and the general supply and demand of cash at the time of the deposit.
- *Overnight repurchase agreements (repos).* These are essentially overnight secured loan agreements. Under a repo agreement the party wishing to borrow money typically sells a government bond for cash to another party but with an agreement to buy the bond back after a certain period, which can range from overnight to a few months. The difference between the lower sale price and the higher repurchase price is effectively the rate of interest charged by the lender to the borrower of cash. The advantage of lending money via a repo agreement is that if the borrower defaults the lender gets to keep the government bond. For the cash borrower the advantage is a cheaper borrowing cost, since the lender is lending money secured on the government bond. The repo is a very important source of liquidity for all financial market

institutions. The Bank of England uses the repo market in its monetary policy operations.

Schemes can use all of these instruments to earn interest on their cash balances. However, an alternative are money market funds.

Money market funds

Money market funds (MMFs) originated in the US around 40 years ago. The vast majority of funds, by value, are rated AAA/Aaa (long term)[4] and aim to provide investors with a credible alternative to a short-term fixed deposit. Quite simply, they are daily priced collective investment funds that diversify investments across a range of high credit quality, short-term money market instruments (Treasury bills, commercial paper, certificates of deposit etc.) with the principal aims of preserving investors' capital, providing liquidity and generating competitive returns, in that order. So as to meet these objectives MMFs usually have strict guidelines on:

- credit quality – MMFs typically invest in high quality money market instruments with a short term rating of at least A1/P1 (or equivalent) being the norm;
- weighted average maturity (WAM) – to limit the fund's sensitivity to interest rate changes and ensure liquidity is available for investors wishing to withdraw their investments at short notice; and
- diversification across geography, industry, issuers and instrument type to limit counterparty risk.

Indeed, by adhering to these guidelines, MMFs are able to meet their capital preservation objective by maintaining a constant net asset value (CNAV) of typically £1, €1 or US$1 per unit or share, depending on the currency in which the fund is denominated. Accounting rules allow a fund's short-term holdings below 60 days to be valued at amortized cost, rather than market value[5]. However, strict tolerances have to be complied with to ensure that a regular mark-to-market valuation remains within close proximity to the £1 amortized cost share price. Should a fund's mark-to-market price stray beyond the tolerance it may be forced to 'break the buck', that is, investors would incur capital losses. This type of event is highly unusual – normally investors get back their initial capital investment (their 'buck') plus interest – but it is happened in the past.

---

[4] We expand upon ratings shortly.
[5] There are, however, those MMFs that adopt a variable NAV by taking account of the daily market movements of the instruments in which they invest.

Towards the end of the noughties, some MMFs were unable to maintain mark-to-market prices within the allowable tolerance for a CNAV fund due to the enormous and unprecedented strains faced by markets. Some funds were forced to 'break the buck' and close to investor redemptions while a number of fund sponsors supported funds in an attempt to calm investors and markets.

Selecting a money market fund

Like most other investment funds, MMFs are formally rated and have benchmarks, against which their performance is assessed.

Ratings agencies, such as Moody's, Standard and Poor's (S&P) and Fitch, provide specific ratings to MMF funds, which are based on a variation of their standard ratings designations. So for Moody's the top rating given is designated by Aaa/MR1, while for S&P it's AAAm and Fitch, AAA/V1+. These ratings are based on criteria such as the credit quality of the fund, the experience of the manager, and the quality and robustness of the risk management process applied in running the fund.

Money market fund managers generally aim to outperform standard money market interest rates over time. This benchmark interest rate will vary depending upon the fund's currency denomination. Sterling money market fund managers typically benchmark their performance to LIBOR, or to the Sterling Overnight Interbank Average (SONIA). The benchmark for euro and dollar money market funds will typically be the Euro Overnight Interbank Average (EONIA), and the Federal Reserve Funds Rate (FFR) respectively.

Key points

- Cash investments facilitate short term liquidity management, offer capital security and a temporary safe haven for funds but from a long-term performance perspective may be unsuitable.
- Short-term bank deposits pay interest income with no potential for capital growth and repay the amount invested in full at the end of the term.
- Money market instruments are negotiable, typically have a term of less than a year to maturity and most are issued in bearer form.
- Money market funds (MMFs) diversify investments across a range of high credit quality, short-term money market instruments and aim to preserve capital, provide liquidity and generate competitive returns.
- MMFs are formally rated and have benchmarks against which their performance is assessed.

Chapter 6

Bonds: The Asset Class Trustees Fear the Most

Learning outcomes

- Understand the characteristics of a bond.
- Know who issues bonds and the types of bonds issued.
- Understand the key aspects of bond risk.
- Understand the yield curve and the influences on its shape and level.
- Understand why the analysis of bonds, bond markets and the yield curve are fundamental to the management of a pension scheme.

Introduction

Until the late-1990s bonds were seen by many pension fund trustees as relatively uninteresting, a place where funds were parked safely in order to generate the cash flows necessary to meet pensions in payment. Today things have changed. An understanding of bonds and bond markets is crucial for a proper understanding of the defined benefit (DB) pension problem. First, the allocation that schemes typically make to bonds is now very significant. In 1993, bonds made up only 10 per cent of a typical DB pension scheme's assets.[1] By the end of 2010 that figure had risen to 41 per cent.[2] Moreover, on current trends, bonds will soon make up more than 50 per cent of pension portfolios on average, a figure typical of allocations last seen in the 1960s. Indeed, a number of schemes have already allocated more than 50 per cent of their assets to bonds.

---

[1] Source: UBS Global Asset Management, Pension Fund Indicators June, p. 75 (2010).
[2] Source: Mercer Asset Allocation Study April, p. 9 (2010).

This move into bonds, largely at the expense of scheme allocations to equities, has principally been driven by two factors. First, schemes are maturing rapidly, that is, the average age of scheme members is rising. Second, pension scheme liabilities are now valued with direct reference to the valuation of bond markets.

In addition, for any scheme seeking to hedge either the interest rate risk or inflation risk inherent in their liabilities,[3] an understanding of bond analytics is crucial, as an investment in bonds can help to reduce these risks. Indeed, this is exactly what the Boots plc pension scheme famously did in 2000 when it allocated all of its assets to bonds and bond-type assets.

In other words, the world of bonds can no longer be ignored by trustees. The seemingly impenetrable language of the bond fund manager must be deciphered. This chapter will hopefully demystify the topic of bonds and who knows, after reading it you might even learn to love bonds . . . a little!

Bond characteristics

Bonds are essentially IOUs, or an acknowledgement of a debt, issued by a wide range of borrowers to raise long-term capital for a variety of reasons. Governments, both national and local, issue bonds, as do companies and supra-national agencies.[4]

Bonds are known as *fixed income securities*. This is because the amount and timing of the associated cash payments from a bond are usually fixed and known in advance. Although there are many types of bond available to investors, they share some general characteristics.

- They are typically issued at a par value – this par value is also referred to as the principal, face or nominal value of the bond.
- They usually pay a fixed interest payment to investors, known as a coupon, at regular intervals – usually either annually or semi-annually. This coupon is expressed as a percentage of the bond's par value and, unlike dividends payable to a company's ordinary shareholders,[5] must be paid without exception. So, a bond with a par value of £100 and an annual coupon of 6 per cent will pay a fixed interest payment of £6.00 every year.
- They are usually issued with a finite, fixed life and generally repay the principal loan amount when the bond is redeemed at maturity, typically at the par value. So most bonds also mature – unlike some people(!)

---

[3] We consider hedging interest rate, inflation (and longevity) risk in Chapters 12 and 15.
[4] Such as the European Bank for Reconstruction and Development (EBRD).
[5] We cover the dividends payable to the ordinary shareholders of a company in Chapter 7.

Bonds that conform to these general characteristics are sometimes referred to as *plain vanilla bonds*, because of their relatively simple structure. Furthermore, even though there are many bond types that do not conform to the plain vanilla structure, bonds are nearly always defined in terms of the style of their coupon payment. For example, bonds that pay a coupon that varies according to prevailing interest rates are known as floating rate notes (FRNs), or sometimes as variable rate bonds. We'll come back to bond types shortly.

The cash flow from plain vanilla bonds

Let's consider the cash flow generated by a plain vanilla bond. In Exhibit 6.1 we have presented the payments that an investor could expect from holding a bond with a redemption value of £100, and an *annual* coupon of £6.00, with five full years to maturity.

As we can see from the chart, the vast majority of the payment from this bond is received when it matures. This is when the principal of £100 (the par value – the original amount borrowed per bond from all investors) is paid back. For the first four years the investor would receive just the coupon payment of £6.00 (representing a coupon rate of 6 per cent on the par value of £100). On the maturity date in five years time, an investor holding a bond with a face value of £100 would receive £100 from the entity that issued the bond, plus the final coupon payment of £6.00.

Exhibit 6.1   Cash flow of plain vanilla five year bond with 6% coupon

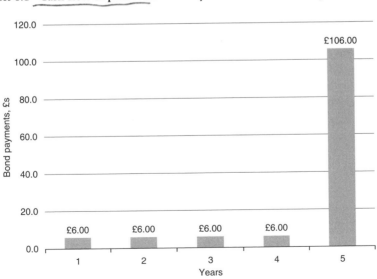

The global bond market

At the end of 2010, the global bond market stood at around US$44tn, a figure equivalent to about 70 per cent of world GDP. Exhibit 6.2 shows the growth of the global bond market over the 13 years to end-2010. Let's now take a look at the main issuers of bonds, starting with governments and government bonds.

Government bonds

Governments have used the bond markets to raise capital for many years. Indeed, until the 1970s most government bond issues, also known as sovereign debt, were related in some way to the financing of wars. The first ever government bond was issued by the British government in 1693 to fund the war against France. Today government bonds are issued by developed and emerging economy governments, to plug the gap between public spending and taxation, as the former usually exceeds the latter. You'll note from Exhibit 6.2 that the government bond market now accounts for about 70 per cent of the global bond market and has grown three-fold over this period, despite a move to more prudent fiscal policies by the developed G7 economy governments[6] in

Exhibit 6.2 Growth in the global bond market (US$bn)

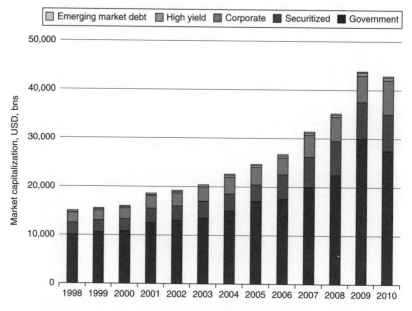

Source: UBS Global Asset Management, *Pension Fund Indicators 2011*.

---

[6] The G7 comprises the US, UK, France, Germany, Japan, Italy and Canada.

the 1990s, with the notable exception of Japan. However, a return during the noughties to fiscal profligacy and increased indebtedness by the G7 and others, exacerbated by sovereign bail outs of the banks in 2008, has accelerated the growth of the developed economy government bond market. These bailouts and the deep recession that followed will mean that the government debt of many developed economies, notably those of the US, UK and in many of the economies within and on the periphery of the Euro zone, will grow even more rapidly over the next few years.

Largely as a consequence of its size, the market for G7 government bonds is by far the most liquid of all the bond markets. Most bonds issued by G7 governments are of the plain vanilla kind (although there exist some minor differences between the bonds issued by one government and another). Gilts are the bonds issued by the UK government (having originally been issued as certificates with a gilt edge) and are generally of the plain vanilla type. Government bonds in the US, Germany and Japan are also typically plain vanilla bonds and are known respectively as Treasuries, Bunds and JGBs. Given their size and liquidity, the government bond markets of the world, and, in particular, the market for US Treasuries, act as a benchmark for all other bond markets.

In Exhibit 6.3 we present a breakdown of the global government bond market. Perhaps unsurprisingly, the three largest bond issuers – the US, Japan and the 17 Euro zone governments – are also three of the world's four largest economies. In other words, big economies have big debts! Moreover, over 80 per cent of government bond issuance is denominated in US dollars, the euro and the yen.

Exhibit 6.3 The composition of the global government bond market

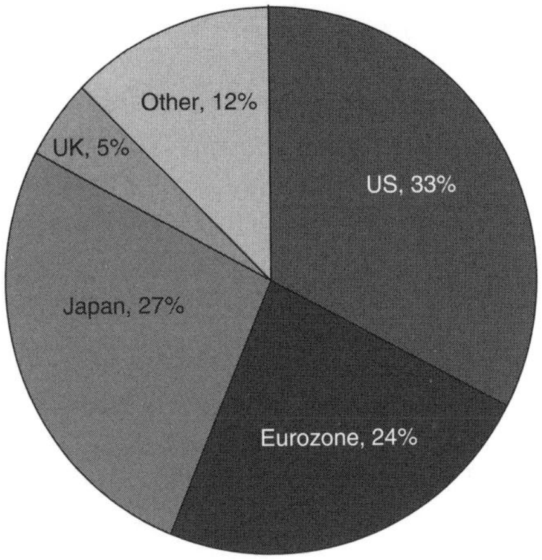

Source: UBS Global Asset Management, *Pension Fund Indicators 2011*.

The UK gilt market is also a relatively important market. By the end of 2010 the market value of outstanding gilts was, according to the Debt Management Office, £913.5bn.

In addition to developed economy government bond issuance, the governments of around 50 emerging economies also issue bonds. While the emerging government bond market is relatively embryonic, having only been in existence for a little over 20 years, it is already capitalized at around US$2.8tn, having had a market value of about US$1.1tn at the end of 2009. While most issues were originally denominated in US dollars, today most emerging economies having implemented responsible macroeconomic policies, notably fiscal policies, issue bonds in their own currencies. Indeed, the local currency bond market is the fastest growing part of the emerging debt universe and is now larger than the market denominated in US dollars. Moreover, such has been the transformation of many of these economies that over 50 per cent of emerging market government debt is now classified as 'investment grade' by the major rating agencies, although the creditworthiness of this disparate universe of countries remains more widely dispersed than that of developed economies.

Non-government issuers

Non-government issuers of bonds account for about 30 per cent of the value of the global bond market. As we can see from Exhibit 6.4 this issuance is overwhelmingly dominated by issuance by US entities, followed by those

Exhibit 6.4   The composition of the non-government bond issuers

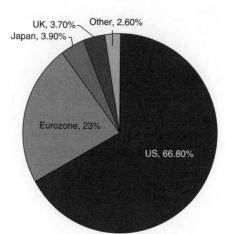

Source: UBS Global Asset Management, *Pension Fund Indicators 2011*.

issuers that are domiciled in the Euro zone, Japan and the UK. These issuers comprise:

- Supranational agencies, such as the European Investment Bank (EIB), European Bank for Reconstruction and Development (EBRD) and the International Finance Corporation (IFC) of the World Bank, who raise development capital on commercial terms for the world's poorest regions.
- Domestic and international companies, who issue bonds in both the domestic and the international Eurobond market, to finance future growth, whether organically or by acquisition and/or to restructure their finances. Corporate issuance also includes securitized, or asset backed, issues. Used mainly by banks and credit card companies, but more recently by property companies and telecoms companies, these issues package up cash flows to be contractually received in the future – such as royalties, credit card payments, mortgage repayments, rents and telephone bills – and sell this income stream as a bond. This means that rather than having to wait to receive a stream of credit card payments or mortgage repayments over time, a bank can package up these 'future receivables' into a bond and receive a capital sum today. Over the past few decades securitization has become incredibly widespread. In fact, in 1997, the rock star David Bowie, packaged up the estimated value of future royalties to be received on his 'back catalogue' for the next 10 years and sold this to a large insurance company for US$55m!
- Government agencies, such as Municipals and Local Authorities, who issue bonds mainly to finance capital expenditure, against future expected revenue receipts.
- Private Finance Initiatives (PFIs) such as public/private infrastructure companies, health authorities and so forth, who issue bonds to finance capital intensive projects.

Bond types

There are a number of different bond types. Their 'type' usually relates to the way in which they differ from a *plain vanilla* bond. Bonds can vary in many different respects – particularly with regard to the nature of the coupon payment – as a result bond issuers outline all of the specific details of their particular bond issue in a legal document that specifies the rights and obligations of both the issuer and of the bond investors. This document is known as the *bond indenture* and it will outline:

i. when coupon and redemption payments are due from the issuer in return for buying the bond;

ii. details about what constitutes a default and the procedures to be applied in the event of a default;
iii. information about any constraints upon the issuer with respect, for example, to the issuance of future debt; and
iv. the conditions under which the bond can be redeemed early, or converted into equity, etc.

These and many other details that are relevant to the issue will all be spelled out in the bond indenture.

Zero coupon bonds

Bonds that do not pay a coupon, but instead only make a single payment to investors when the bond matures are known as *zero coupon bonds*. So what is the point of buying a zero coupon bond? For an investor to realize a return from holding a zero coupon bond with say a face value of £100, which is payable at some time in the future, the bond must be issued at a 'deep discount' to its face value. In other words, at a price that is significantly less than the face value of £100. The investor realizes a return from investing in this bond through the difference between this deeply discounted price and the eventual redemption value of £100. Zero coupon bonds are typically issued by corporations that do not have the cash flow to meet regular coupon payments, and can be thought of as very long-term money market instruments since, like a money market instrument, investors are not entitled to a regular interest payment and they are issued at a discount to their face value.

Structured bonds

Some bonds that pay a fixed coupon, might also repay part of their principal throughout the life of the bond. That is, the principal is 'amortized'. These bonds are often referred to as structured bonds, since the cash flow is structured in a specific way, rather than just consisting of a regular coupon and ending with the repayment of principal when the bond matures. As such, when the bond finally matures there may be no remaining repayment of principal to be made. These bonds are often issued by Private Finance Initiatives (PFIs). The scheduled principal payments throughout the life of the bond are normally known when the bond is issued and are detailed in the bond's indenture. The structure of the payments from such bonds is often designed to complement the cash flow of the underlying project to which the capital is applied. Compared with a plain vanilla bond then, investors that hold structured bonds do not have to wait for the bond to mature before the majority of the bond's cash flow is received.

Floating Rate Notes (FRNs)

Some bonds are issued with variable rather than fixed coupon payments, where the coupon payment typically varies with some pre-specified interest rate, usually

LIBOR. These are known as *Floating Rate Notes* (FRNs), or sometimes as variable rate bonds. With these bonds if interest rates rise then the coupon payments of the bond will rise too. However, falling interest rates will lead to lower future coupon payments though the redemption value of a FRN is unaffected by the level of interest rates. The market is split between conventional, typically bank-backed, and asset-backed issuance. Asset-backed issuances can be backed by a wide variety of assets, although the majority is backed by residential mortgages.

Index-linked bonds

A bond where both the coupon and principal payment vary with a price index, usually a consumer price index, is known as an *index-linked bond*. As such, the payments from these bonds, unlike most other bonds are, to all intents and purposes, inflation-proofed since the coupon and principal payment both rise with the price index. Although some corporations with index-linked revenues, such as utilities and infrastructure companies, issue these bonds, the main issuers are developed economy governments. The UK government was the first major government to issue index-linked bonds back in 1981. These bonds are known as *index-linked gilts*, or more affectionately as *linkers*. Index-linked bonds are also issued by the governments of emerging economies, mainly Latin American governments, primarily Brazil, though governments in Eastern Europe, Africa and Asia now also issue linkers. The inflation proofing element of index-linked bonds, principally those issued by developed economy governments, utilities and infrastructure companies, has made them very popular with institutions that have to fund inflation-related liabilities, in particular pension funds and life assurance companies.

Bonds with embedded options

Some bonds confer upon either the issuer or the bondholder the right to exercise an embedded option should they wish to do so.

Those bonds that extend a right to their holders to convert their bonds into the underlying equity of the issuer, under certain pre-defined conditions, are known as *convertible* bonds. Therefore, if the company issuing a convertible bond performs well, the holder may wish to exercise their right to convert the bonds into the company's ordinary shares, thereby giving them a claim on the future profits of the firm, rather than on future coupon payments. Due to this desirable, additional feature, convertible bonds are typically issued at a lower yield than equivalent non-convertible bonds.

The other main types of bond that contain embedded options are *puttable* and *callable* bonds.

A puttable bond gives the investor the right to sell the bond back to the issuer before its maturity date: that is, the bond can be 'put back' at a pre-specified price to the issuer. An investor may put back a bond if the credit standing of the issuer has fallen since they purchased the bond, enabling them to use the cash generated from putting the bond back to buy a bond issued from a corporation with a higher credit standing. Also, the investor may put the bond back if interest rates have risen substantially in the underlying economy. By selling the bond back to the issuer they can reinvest the cash that this realizes to buy more recently issued bonds with higher coupon rates. The price at which the bond can be put back will be outlined in the bond indenture and will normally be less than the face value of the bond. The difference between the face value of the bond and its put price, known as the put penalty, can deter the investor from exercising the right to sell back the bond.

Conversely, a callable bond gives the issuer the right to buy the bond back (redeem it) early: that is, the bond can be 'called back'. An issuer may exercise its option to buy a bond back if its credit standing has improved since issuing the bond. By buying the bond back it might then be able to issue another bond with a lower coupon and hence reduce its debt burden. For similar reasons, the issuer may also call the bond back if interest rates in the relevant economy have fallen since the bond was originally issued. The price at which the bond can be called back will be outlined in the bond indenture and will normally be greater than the face value of the bond. The difference between the face value of the bond and its call price, known as the call premium, might deter the issuer from exercising the right to buy the bond back.

Eurobonds

Although in the past, investors have been able to purchase domestic corporate bonds – for example, a sterling-denominated bond issued by a UK company in the UK known as a *debenture* – these domestic corporate bond markets are now far smaller and less popular than the market for international bonds, known as the *Eurobond* market.

A *Eurobond* is a bond that is issued by a corporation in a number of markets simultaneously, and not necessarily in the home currency of the issuing entity. Governments and supranational organizations can also issue them. For example, a bond issued by a US corporation simultaneously in a number of financial centres in either yen or sterling would be referred to as a Eurobond – despite the fact that it is not being issued in euros! Eurobonds can be of any type – callable, puttable, convertible, etc. – and indeed the Eurobond market has been responsible for pioneering many new bond structures in order to meet the demands of both the issuers and the end investors. They usually pay coupons (unless they are zero coupon bonds of course) once a year, gross of any tax.

Corporate bonds and credit risk

To issue a corporate bond a company would normally need to obtain a rating of its creditworthiness (as, indeed, governments, supranational agencies, local authorities and others do when issuing bonds). *Credit ratings* can be obtained from a number of independent credit ratings agencies. While the largest and most well known of these are Moody's and Standard & Poor's (S&P), there are others such as Fitch, Dominion and AM Best.

Credit ratings are medium term forecasts of a company's future creditworthiness. That is, its ability to pay interest on ('to service') its bonds, or a particular bond issue, on the due dates and repay the principal at redemption. As such, credit ratings are based on such things as:

- how supportive the economic environment is likely to be for the company;
- the strength of its business model – which is a function of its product mix and the markets in which it operates;
- its management quality and strategy; and
- the strength of the company's finances.

To assess the strength of a company's finances requires the credit rating agencies to conduct an analysis of the company's financial statements – a process known as financial ratio analysis. This establishes the extent to which the interest payments on the company's bonds will be 'covered' by its profits and cash flow after all prior claims on its income have been met and the degree to which the company is financially geared. Financial gearing measures the ratio of the amount of bond, or debt finance employed by the company compared to the amount of its equity finance as a percentage of the total amount of capital (bond and equity finance) it employs. This matters because, as mentioned earlier, interest payments on debt must be paid regardless of the issuer's financial situation, unlike dividends payable to equity shareholders, which can be cut or simply not paid.

While a company that is highly geared financially, that is, that employs a high proportion of fixed rate debt finance, may do exceptionally well in the good times, it may well struggle in the bad times with a high interest bill to pay. Moreover, if the company is also highly operationally geared, that is, most of its costs are fixed regardless of its level of activity, then its fortunes on both the upside and downside will be magnified.

In Exhibit 6.5 we have presented S&P's and Moody's credit ratings along with a brief description of the 'meaning' of each rating. If an issuer is deemed to be of excellent credit quality it will be given a high credit rating, for example a AAA/Aaa, or 'triple-A', rating. The bonds of most developed country governments – Gilts,

Exhibit 6.5   Ratings and their definitions

S&P	Moody's	
Investment grade debt		
AAA	Aaa	Extremely strong capacity to pay
AA	Aa	High quality debt – only slightly diminished capacity to pay the principal and interest relative to previous rating
A	A	Strong capacity to pay the principal and interest, but more susceptible to adverse effects of changing economic conditions
BBB	Baa	Adequate capacity to pay the principal and interest
High yield debt		
BB, B	Ba, B	Predominantly speculative with respect to the issuer's capacity to pay the interest and principal in accordance with terms and obligations
CCC, CC	Caa, Ca	The same as above
C	C	Income bonds on which no interest is being paid
D	D	Bonds in default

Source: Moody's Investor Services.

Bunds, etc., – carry this high rating since technically governments cannot become bankrupt, as they can always print money to meet their bond obligations. There are exceptions to this rule however. Given the scale of their debts, Japanese, Greek, Spanish, Italian, Irish, Portuguese and even American government bonds are all currently rated below triple-A by the main ratings agencies. In addition, because they are part of the Euro zone, Greece, Spain, Italy, Ireland and Portugal cannot simply print their own money.

Similar to school homework grades, S&P ratings have a plus or minus suffix, while Moody's ratings have a 1, 2 or 3 suffix. So within the AA/Aa category, for example, S&P can award an organization AA+, AA or AA–, while Moody's can apply a Aa1, Aa2 or Aa3 rating. Bonds issued with a rating of BBB – by S&P and Baa3 by Moody's, or better, are referred to as 'investment grade' bonds. Those given ratings below these levels embody a significant prospect of default risk and are referred to as *high yield, speculative, non-investment grade* or *sub-investment grade* bonds. This is because investors require a higher yield on the bonds given the higher risk of default. They are also often less generously referred to as *junk bonds*!

That brings us on to our next point. Once a rating has been awarded, it is not necessarily set in stone. Indeed, the credit rating agencies employ two types of 'rating actions'.

The first are *ratings outlooks*. These are regularly updated for most investment grade bonds (government bonds and others included) and state the rating agencies' opinion on the likely direction of any ratings change over the next 18 months. Three categories are applied: positive, stable and negative. However, just as a positive ratings outlook does not guarantee a ratings upgrade, a negative ratings outlook does not always result in a ratings downgrade – they are simply opinions expressed by the credit ratings agencies at a point in time. However, they send out a clear message to the issuer concerned, especially if a negative ratings outlook is applied.

In addition, whenever the economic conditions or the business model that supported the issuer's original credit rating, fundamentally change, then the ratings agencies may conduct a formal review of the issuer's credit rating. Moody's will put the issuer on their 'Watchlist', whereas S&P will put them on 'Credit Watch'.

Financial ratio analysis

Although there is no fixed formula by which credit ratings are calculated, there is a strong relationship between credit ratings and some of the financial ratios we discussed above. A stylized example is shown in Exhibit 6.6.

From our stylized example, you can see that those companies awarded a triple-A rating (the few that still exist) have, on average:

- profits that cover their bond interest payments over 17-times;
- cash flow, after all prior claims on the company's income have been met, that exceeds the amount of debt in issue by a multiple of over 42; and
- have ultra low financial gearing, at slightly over 20 per cent.

Contrast these metrics with bonds rated triple-C, where, on average, the issuer's profits and cash flow do not cover their interest payments and future redemption payments respectively – given ratios in both cases of less than one – a situation not helped by their 70-plus per cent financial gearing!

Default rates

As you would expect, there is also a strong relationship between credit ratings and the probability of subsequent default. For instance, historically less than one in a thousand triple-A rated bonds default within ten years of being issued, whereas about 80 per cent of triple-C bonds default within the first ten years.

Exhibit 6.6   Key financial ratios by credit rating

	AAA	AA	A	BBB	BB	B	CCC
Pre-tax interest coverage, times	17.6	7.6	4.1	2.5	1.5	0.9	0.7
Free operating cash flow/Total debt, %	42.3	28	13.6	6.1	3.2	1.6	0.8
Total debt/Total capital, %	21.9	32.7	40.3	48.8	66.2	71.5	71.2

However, a default is not always as bad as it sounds. Although a default usually occurs when an issuer fails to meet their contractual interest and/or redemption payment obligations, it can also be triggered if the issuer breaches one of a number of financial ratios set out in the bond indenture. Neither should a default always result in the investor losing all of their money. Indeed, on many occasions, the default is often remedied by the issuer shortly after it occurs and even when it is not, the 'recovery rate' on most defaults average about 40 per cent of what's owed. The reason for this is that bond holders usually rank above most of the company's other stakeholders, including the company's DB pension scheme as an unsecured creditor.

Credit spreads (?)

Although credit ratings act as a guide to the likelihood of default, one criticism of credit ratings is that they are backward looking and are not adjusted in real time. By contrast, *credit spreads* are forward looking and reflect investors' assessment of creditworthiness in real time. The credit spread is the additional yield on a corporate bond, or corporate bond index, over and above the yield on an equivalent maturity government bond. While the credit spread also embodies compensation for liquidity risk and risk associated with the price volatility of the bond, it is, in the main, a reflection of the amount of credit risk inherent in the bond, which is set by the interaction of buyers and sellers in the bond market.

Exhibit 6.7   Credit spreads and default rates

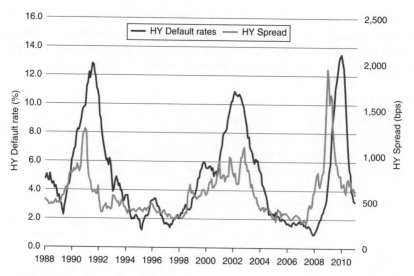

Sources: Moody's Investor Service, Merrill Lynch.

Exhibit 6.7 shows the average credit spread for US high yield bonds over US Treasuries between September 1986 and January 2010, and also the default rates in the US high yield bond market. You'll notice that the credit spread changes over time, often dramatically: in the early 1990s, early noughties and most recently over the recent credit crunch. These were all periods marked by recession, it is clear from the chart then that the spread is heavily influenced by the strength of the underlying economy: when it is weak spreads rise, when it is strong spreads fall. The chart also shows how default rates tend to rise a little after spreads rise. This is because bond market participants demand a higher premium on debt, particularly low quality debt, as the economy weakens in anticipation of future defaults.

The price of a bond

In Exhibit 6.1 we presented the cash flow that an investor could expect to receive from holding a bond with a redemption value of £100, with an annual coupon of 6 per cent and five full years to maturity. In total, the investor could expect to receive cash payments summing to £130, comprising five coupon payments of £6 and the redemption value of £100 when the bond matures. But what price would an investor be willing to pay *today* to receive those future payments? The answer to this question resides in the concept of *discounting*. Before we look at the way in which a plain vanilla a bond is priced, we will begin with an overview of discounting. Actually, discounting is not just relevant to valuing bonds, it is the fundamental process used to value *all* financial instruments.

Discounting

Most people would agree that if they were owed, say, £100, then they would rather be repaid this money today than in one year's time. This is because if they were repaid today they could deposit that money into a bank account and earn interest on that money at a rate of interest, 5 per cent for example, over the course of the next year. After a year, at a rate of interest of 5 per cent, the £100 would be worth £105 (ignoring taxes, etc.).

In this case, the future value (FV) of £100 today is £105, which can be calculated easily as follows:

$$FV = £100 \times (1 + 0.05) = £105$$

Now suppose that the same investor buys an asset today that promises to pay them £105 in one year's time. If the interest rate is unchanged then we already know that the value today of that £105 payment in one year's time is £100.

In other words, the present value (PV) of £105 in one year's time is £100. If we know the future value of the payment and the related interest rate we can calculate its present value as follows:

$$PV = \frac{£105}{(1 + 0.05)} = £100$$

To calculate the present value of this future payment, we simply divide this future value by one plus the interest rate – alternatively known as the discount rate. So, in this case, the price that this investor would pay today in return for a payment of £105 in one year's time, given a discount rate of 5 per cent, is £100.

This concept can be easily extended to take account of payments that occur at any point in the future. Suppose that the discount rate is still 5 per cent but that the payment now occurs in two rather than in one year's time. An investor is therefore now giving up receiving the cash for two years – missing out on two years' worth of interest. The future value of £100 today can be calculated as follows:

$$FV = £100 \times (1 + 0.05) \times (1 + 0.05) = £110.25$$

or

$$FV = £100 \times (1 + 0.05)^2 = £110.25$$

Alternatively, suppose an investor buys a financial instrument that promises to pay them £110.25 in two years time. If the discount rate is 5 per cent, then the present value of this payment can be calculated as follows:

$$PV = \frac{£110.25}{(1 + 0.05) \times (1 + 0.05)} = £100$$

or

$$PV = \frac{£110.25}{(1 + 0.05)^2} = £100$$

Applying the principle of discounting to price a plain vanilla bond

Consider the bond illustrated in Exhibit 6.1 again. That is, a bond with a redemption value of £100, with an annual coupon of 6 per cent and five full years to maturity. In Exhibit 6.8 we present the future values of this bond's payments again, but also show their present values.

By discounting each of these future payments at a discount rate of 6 per cent, appropriately adjusted for the time that will elapse before the payment is made, and then adding up each of these payments, we arrive at the present value of the bond. As we would expect, the present values of each cash flow are smaller than their associated future values.

Exhibit 6.8 The present and future values of a bond's payments

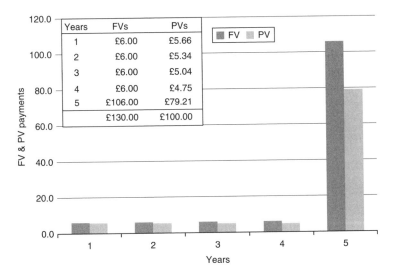

Years	FVs	PVs
1	£6.00	£5.66
2	£6.00	£5.34
3	£6.00	£5.04
4	£6.00	£4.75
5	£106.00	£79.21
	£130.00	£100.00

Notice also that the sum of the present values of all the payments from this bond, which has a face value of £100 and that pays an annual coupon of £6.00, is equal to £100 when the discount rate is 6 per cent. This is an important result: when the discount rate is equal to the coupon rate, a plain vanilla bond will have a price, or present value, equal to its par value.

Bond prices and returns

The discount rate we used to discount each of these payments is commonly referred to as the *gross redemption yield* (GRY). It is a 'gross' yield because it incorporates both the bond's coupon and its redemption, or par, value without the deduction of tax. It represents one measure of the *expected return* from the bond. It can also be thought of as the bond's *required return*, as it is set by the bond market. That is, by the interaction of buyers and sellers in the bond market. To be more specific, when an investor buys a bond, the GRY represents the annualized return on the bond that they could expect to earn if it is held until maturity:

- on the assumption that the bond issuer does not default; and
- on the assumption that the intermediate coupon payments can be reinvested at the same GRY.

The risk that these intermediate payments cannot be reinvested at the same yield is known as *reinvestment rate risk*. If future coupons can be reinvested at rates of interest that are higher than the bond's GRY when it is purchased, then the actual return that the investor will achieve will be higher than this GRY. The opposite is true if future coupons can only be reinvested at lower rates of interest.

The relationship between the bond's price and its GRY is very important. As the GRY rises, the rate at which the market discounts all future payments from the bond rises too, and so the present values of the bond's payments fall, along with the overall price of the bond. This is because the 'opportunity cost' of receiving these payments in the future, that is, the interest we forgo on these payments by being unable to invest them all today, has risen. The opposite is true when the GRY falls.

So, to summarize, there is an inverse relationship between a bond's GRY and its price. This is an important concept to grasp, and stems directly from the process of discounting.

Exhibit 6.9 shows the inverse relationship between the price of a plain vanilla bond (the vertical axis) and its GRY (the horizontal axis). As the required yield (the GRY) rises, the bond's price falls. As the required yield falls, the bond's price rises.

There are two things to observe. First, a bond with a par value of £100 and a coupon of £6.00 or 6 per cent, has a market value of £100 when the GRY, or required yield, is also 6 per cent. Second, you'll also notice that the price/yield

Exhibit 6.9   The relationship between a bond's price and the gross redemption yield

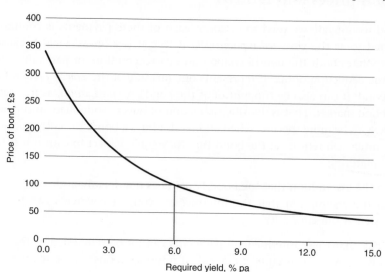

relationship is non-linear, or curvy. This curvature, or convexity, is the source of a key parameter of bond analysis known as *duration*.

Duration – the key bond risk parameter

We now know that when the discount rate on a set of future payments rises, their value to us today – their present value – falls. The discount rate that we use for calculating the present value of the payments from a bond is the GRY. This is the market-derived yield 'required' by investors. When the GRY rises, the bond price falls. When the GRY falls, the bond price rises.

Bond price volatility

For an investor, pension scheme trustee or a bond fund manager, knowing how sensitive a bond's price is if the required yield changes is very useful information. This information is embodied in a measure of bond risk known as modified duration, which is expressed as a percentage. The higher this number, the greater the sensitivity of the bond's price to a change in yield. Although duration can also be expressed in years, it is best to quote it in percentages terms.[7]

For example, if a bond has modified duration of 10 per cent, it means that for every increase in the required yield of 0.01 per cent (one basis point), the bond's price will fall by (approximately) 0.10 per cent (ten basis points). And for every decrease in the required yield of 0.01 per cent, the bond's price will rise by (approximately) 0.10 per cent. So a bond with a modified duration of 5 per cent will be less sensitive to changes in its required yield than a bond which otherwise has the same risk characteristics, but has modified duration of 10 per cent.

The best way to illustrate this is with the help of an example. Exhibit 6.10 shows the present values of the payments of two bonds. Both bonds have face values of £100, have annual coupons of £6 per annum, that is, 6 per cent, and currently have GRYs of 6 per cent. Therefore, both bonds have a current market price of £100 and only differ in terms of their maturity. One is a 10-year bond the other is a 40-year bond.

---

[7] Duration expressed in years, rather than as a percentage, is known as Macaulay duration. A bond with a Macaulay duration of, say, eight years is one where the present value of the average payment from the bond, or half of the bond cash flows, will be received in eight years time. Macaulay duration is related to modified duration for a bond that pays an annual coupon by the following equation: Macaulay duration/[1 + (GRY)], where GRY represents the gross redemption yield of the bond. Broadly speaking, the equation tells us that the Macaulay duration expressed in years will be slightly greater than the modified duration expressed in percentage terms.

Exhibit 6.10   Present value payments of 10 and 40 year maturity bonds

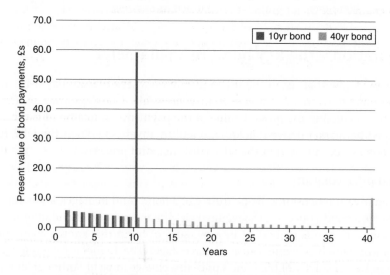

Exhibit 6.11   Interest rate risk and duration

	Required yield = 6.01%		Required yield = 5.99%	
	10-year bond	40-year bond	10-year bond	40-year bond
Price before yield change	100.00	100.00	100.00	100.00
Price after yield change	99.93	99.85	100.07	100.15
% change in price	–0.0736	–0.1503	0.0736	0.1507

The modified duration of the 10-year bond is approximately 7.36 per cent, whereas the modified duration of the 40-year bond is approximately 15.05 per cent. The two tables in Exhibit 6.11 show the new prices of the bonds if the required yield rises for both bonds by 0.01 per cent (one basis point) and when it falls for both bonds by the same amount.

As Exhibit 6.11 shows, when the required yield increases by 0.01 per cent, the 10-year bond falls by just over 0.07 percent, while the 40-year bond declines by just over 0.15 per cent; and when the required yield falls by 0.01 per cent, the 10-year bond rises by just over 0.07 per cent, while the 40-year bond increases by just over 0.15 per cent. So the bond with the higher duration – the 40-year bond – is more price sensitive to changes in the required yield than the one with the lower duration – the 10-year bond.

What influences duration?

We saw above that the longer-dated bond had the highest modified duration. There is a mathematical explanation for this, but an intuitive explanation will hopefully suffice. When the required yield on a bond changes, the impact of this change will be far greater the further away the payments are from today. This is because the change gets compounded over and over again until the size of the discount rate applied to payments that are far away becomes very large indeed.

We can see this in Exhibit 6.11. The £106 paid on the maturity of the 10-year bond has a present value of £59.25 – representing a cash discount of £46.75. However, the £106 paid by the 40-year bond at maturity has the much smaller present value of £10.34, representing a cash discount of £95.66. The much lower price is due to the fact that the same discount rate has been compounded over 40 years, rather than just ten. Therefore any change in this discount rate has a much greater impact on the longer-dated bond compared with the shorter-dated bond.

A bond's maturity is the major factor determining the modified duration of a bond (although the coupon size and the general level of interest rates in the economy will also play a part). In Exhibit 6.12 we have presented the modified duration of bonds with identical characteristics, but with a range of different maturities. As we can see, the modified duration of the bond rises with maturity. A 10-year bond has modified duration of around 7.5 per cent; a 20-year bond has modified duration of around 12.5 per cent; while a 30-year bond has duration of around 15.5 per cent. However, as the chart also shows, as the maturity of the bonds continues to increase, other things being equal, the rate at which the modified duration increases, declines. There is mathematical

Exhibit 6.12   Duration and maturity

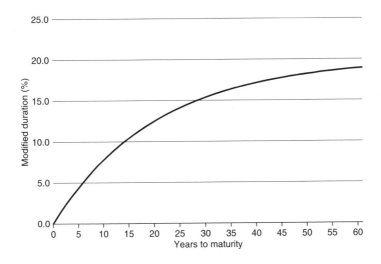

explanation for this, but again hopefully an intuitive explanation will suffice. The greater the maturity of the bond, the smaller the present value of the final payment from that bond. Whereas for a shorter-dated bond, its redemption payment has a big impact upon the bond's modified duration, for a very long-dated bond the present value of its redemption payment is already so small that even a big change in the required yield has little impact on the overall price of the bond, since the final payment already makes up such a small component of the bond's price.

The net result of this is that for plain vanilla bonds that pay only a regular coupon and the redemption value of the bond at maturity, its modified duration will be capped at around 20 per cent. This 'fact' of bond mathematics has relevance for the desire of many DB pension schemes to match the modified duration of their assets to that of their liabilities. The problem is that many schemes have liabilities that extend beyond a duration of 20 years, equivalent to a modified duration of a little under 20 per cent. We cover this point and possible solutions in Chapter 15.

Duration and bond portfolio management

Duration is a summary measure of a bond's sensitivity to yield changes. By knowing a bond's modified duration an investor can assess the amount of 'interest rate' risk that they are taking by investing in the bond. One very useful property of modified duration is that it can be used to describe the interest rate risks embodied in a portfolio of bonds too. For example, suppose that a bond fund manager holds two bonds. The first bond has a modified duration of 10 per cent, the second has a modified duration of 5 per cent. If the portfolio consists of 50 per cent of both bonds, then the modified duration of the portfolio is 7.5 per cent. In other words, it is a simple weighted average of the duration of both bonds:

$$(50\% \times 10\%) + (50\% \times 5\%) = 7.5\%$$

All bond fund managers will know the modified duration of their own portfolios. In addition, they will also know the duration of their bond benchmarks. By knowing these two metrics they can position their portfolios, so that they hopefully benefit from a changing required yield environment. For example, a government bond fund manager has a benchmark with a modified duration of 8 per cent. Suppose now that the manager believes that yields will decline in their market generally. This means that bond prices will generally rise, but it also means that the prices of longer-dated bonds with higher modified duration will tend to rise the most. To position the fund to take advantage of this move in yields, the manager could buy more long-dated bonds and sell shorter-dated bonds. This would have the effect of increasing the modified duration of the portfolio. Suppose the fund manager adds long-dated bonds to the portfolio until the modified duration of the portfolio rises to 10 per cent. If yields in the market fell by 0.01 per cent, the benchmark would typically rise by 0.08 per cent, but the portfolio would rise by 0.10 per cent. Therefore, the fund manager would outperform the benchmark by 0.02 per cent for every 0.01 per cent fall in yields. Conversely if yields were to rise instead of fall, the fund manager would underperform the benchmark. If yields rose by 0.01 per cent, the benchmark would typically fall by 0.08 per cent, and the portfolio would fall by 0.10 per cent. Therefore, the fund manager would underperform the benchmark by 0.02 per cent for every 0.01 per cent rise in yields.

This duration positioning is behind many bond fund managers' comments. When a bond fund manager says that they are 'long duration' it means that their portfolio has higher modified duration than their benchmark, because they believe that yields are more likely to fall than to rise. Conversely, when a bond fund manager says that they are 'short duration' it means that their portfolio has lower modified duration than their benchmark, because they believe that yields are more likely to rise than to fall.

> ### Duration and the valuation of pension scheme liabilities
>
> All pension schemes are committed to making a stream of future payments to their scheme members. The calculation of a scheme's liabilities to its members is extremely complex; it requires a whole host of assumptions about the future. Considerations such as:
>
> - how long each scheme member will remain within the scheme;
> - what their expected final salary or career average earnings will be;
> - how wage and price inflation will pan out; and perhaps most importantly of all
> - what is the likely post-retirement life expectancy of the scheme membership;
>
> all need to be forecasted decades into the future.
>
> Exhibit 6.13 shows a typical set of payments that a scheme might face, where each bar represents the total estimated amount of cash that the scheme will have to pay to its members in five-year periods, or 'buckets'. Each of these future payments can be discounted. It is the sum of these discounted liabilities that represents the present value of the scheme's liabilities. This gives us an idea of the value of the liabilities in today's money.
>
> The total liabilities represented in Exhibit 6.13 and faced by the scheme – the sum of all those bars – is a whopping £332,376,010. Suppose we were to use a single discount rate of 5 per cent to arrive at the present value of the liabilities

Exhibit 6.13   Typical set of pension scheme liabilities

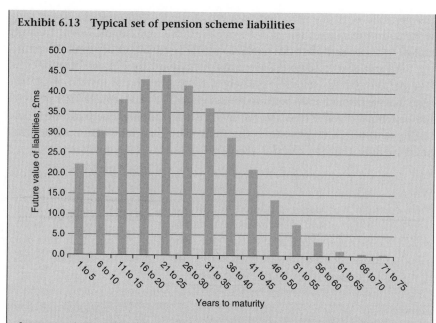

shown in the exhibit. If we were to use this discount rate the present value of these liabilities would be £107,029,378. So if the scheme can generate a 5 per cent return on its assets over this period then it will need to invest £107,029,378 today to meet the future payments.

Suppose that we used a discount rate of 4 per cent instead of 5 per cent. In this case the present value of the liabilities shown in the exhibit would rise to £128,440,461. You should note that the present value of the liabilities rises even though their future values are unchanged. So the present value of the scheme's liabilities will be sensitive to changes in the discount rate applied to them, just as the price of a bond will be sensitive to a change in the required yield on that bond. This sensitivity will be determined by the duration of the liabilities, just as the sensitivity of a bond to changes in the discount rate will be determined by its duration.

It is very easy to calculate the duration of any set of liabilities. This duration number is just a summary of the interest rate sensitivity of all of the scheme's liabilities. In this case the modified duration of the liabilities is just over 16 per cent. However, the duration of a typical scheme's liabilities is often much higher than this, often well over 20 per cent. This is because the payments promised are generally promised for a very long time indeed.

Pension fund liabilities are analogous to the payment stream generated by a very long-dated structured bond. It is because of this similarity that today scheme liabilities are treated by the FRS 17 and IAS 19 accounting standards as being bond-like. The discount rate applied is that of a high quality corporate bond yield. In the case of FRS 17 this is specified as the 15-year AA-rated corporate bond yield, although IAS 19 is not so prescriptive.

The appropriate discount rate for valuing liabilities is a highly contentious issue. As this example illustrates, small differences in the applied discount rate can dramatically alter the liability present value. Reported FRS 17/IAS 19 liability numbers are dwarfed by the much larger liability number calculated on the buyout basis, which is disclosed to the scheme membership in the mandatory summary funding statement. The buyout value of a scheme's liabilities represents the price that a third party insurer would charge for assuming all the risks of the scheme. The buyout value is higher because the discount rate used is based upon gilt yields, rather than on AA corporate bond yields. The difference between these two yields is usually around 1.5 per cent.

Yield curves and the yield curve family

The relationship between the yields on a set of bonds issued by the same issuer, or with the same risk characteristics, such as the same credit rating, but with different maturities is known as the *yield curve*. The yield curve is therefore a snapshot in time of the yields available to investors depending upon their maturity preferences. An example of a yield curve is shown in Exhibit 6.14. Each observation on the

Exhibit 6.14 **The gross redemption yields on gilts by maturity**

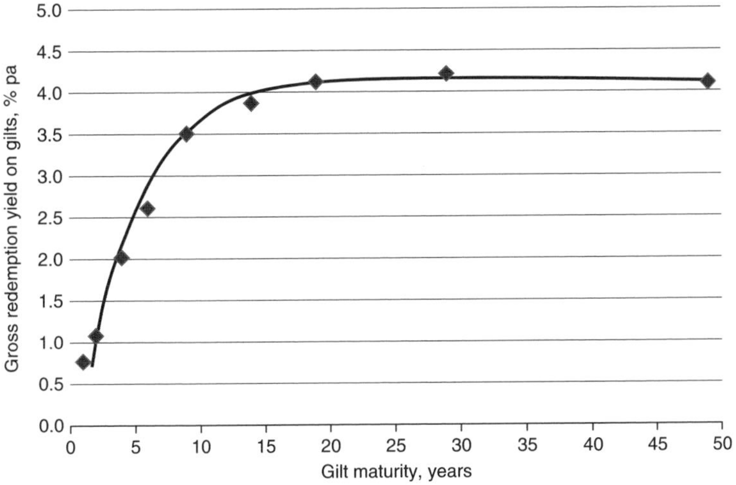

Source: Thomson Financial (31 December 2010).

chart represents the GRY of a gilt issued by the UK government. The line that joins up the dots represents the yield curve – in this case a gross redemption yield curve. A gross redemption yield curve is what most people (at least in the bond world) refer to generically as 'the yield curve'. On the day that the yields on these bonds were recorded, the yield curve was generally upward sloping. In other words, investors were willing to receive a lower yield from lending to the UK government for say ten years than from lending to it for 50 years.

A similar curve could have been drawn for US Treasuries or for Bunds. The yield curve can also be drawn for companies, as we suggested earlier, with the same credit ratings and issuing bonds in the same currency. For example, we could draw the yield curve for BBB-rated sterling bond issues and many others. So the yield curve shown here is one of many that exist at any point in time.

Perhaps the most important yield curves are those that can be derived from the government bond markets, as these set the benchmark for other bond markets. For instance, from these curves we can derive zero coupon and forward yield curves. An understanding of zero coupon and forward yield curves is central to understanding the pricing of derivative instruments such as swaps, which are increasingly being used by DB pension schemes as an alternative means to bonds by which to protect the scheme against interest rate and inflation (and longevity) risk.

The next section of this chapter is dedicated to explaining zero coupon and forward yield curves and the relationships that exist between them. While important, this section is optional reading for those of you who wish to delve into bond yields and pricing a little deeper. For those of you that do not like maths, look away now!

Zero coupon, spot or cash rates

The yields shown in Exhibit 6.15 represent the returns required by investors for holding one of five UK government bonds until maturity, where each of those bonds pay a regular coupon. However, from these coupon paying bonds we can derive the yields that would be required on a bond that does not pay coupons – that is, a zero coupon bond. The yields on zero coupon bonds are known as zero coupon rates, spot rates or sometimes cash rates.

Calculating the two-year zero coupon rate

Suppose that we know the set of GRYs on the five gilts shown in Exhibit 6.15. Furthermore, suppose that each bond is trading at its par price of £100 and that the bonds pay an annual coupon (these two assumptions just make the maths a little easier).

Exhibit 6.15   Calculating zero coupon rates

Year	Bond price	Coupon	GRY %	Zeros % (int rule)
1	100	5.00	5.00	5.00
2	100	5.25	5.25	5.26
3	100	5.50	5.50	5.52
4	100	5.75	5.75	5.79
5	100	6.00	6.00	6.06

Now suppose that an investor wants to buy the two-year coupon paying bond. We know that this bond will pay, on every £100 invested, a coupon of £5.25 after one year, and then £105.25 in the final year (comprising a coupon and principal payment). We also know that to receive these payments we have to pay a price today of £100.

By thinking about these two payments separately we can derive the implied zero coupon rates. In other words, the £100 we pay today for this bond can be represented as follows:

$$£100 = \frac{£5.25}{(1+Z1)^1} + \frac{£105.25}{(1+Z2)^2} \qquad (6.1)$$

If we thought of this two-year annual coupon paying bond as comprising two separate future payments, these payments would both have a value to an investor today – the present value. However, the present value of these two payments will depend upon the discount rate, denoted Z1, that we apply to the first payment and the discount rate, denoted Z2 that we apply to the second payment. The sum of these two present values must be equal to £100, since that is the price that the market is willing to pay for the bond that produces the combination of these two payments.

From Exhibit 6.15 we know that the discount rate that the market is currently applying to a payment from an annual coupon paying bond in one year's time is 5 per cent. This is the one-year zero coupon rate since the coupon paying bond pays no intermediate coupon. So the appropriate rate to discount the first payment made by the two-year bond is 5 per cent. Because we know this, we can now calculate the correct rate to discount the payment of £105.25 made in two years' time:

$$£100 = \frac{£5.25}{(1+0.05)^1} + \frac{£105.25}{(1+Z2)^2} \qquad (6.2)$$

The algebra necessary to reveal the value of Z2 from expression (6.2) is messy, so we will not run through it here. But for those of you that remember your algebra classes at school, expression (6.2) is just 'one equation with one unknown' – we hope the memory of that phrase is not too horrifying!

Once we have used our secondary school algebra to solve for Z2 we find out that its value turns out to be (approximately) 5.26 per cent. *Try entering this number into the formula and calculating the present values of the two payments shown in expression (6.2). They should total £100.*

Calculating the three-year zero coupon rate

We can use a similar process to calculate the three-year zero coupon rate. We know that the three-year bond will make three payments and that the sum of the present values of these payments is £100. If we think of these payments as being three separate payments, each with their own discount rate, then we can write down the following expression:

$$£100 = \frac{£5.50}{(1 + Z1)^1} + \frac{£5.50}{(1 + Z2)^2} + \frac{£105.50}{(1 + Z2)^3} \tag{6.3}$$

The bond pays an annual coupon of £5.50 at the end of three years, plus the principal value of the bond of £100 when it matures. (why zero coupon)

We already know that the appropriate discount rate for a payment in one year's time is 5 per cent. We also know that the appropriate discount rate for a payment in two years time is 5.26 per cent. Now that we know all of this we can write out the following expression which, if one is algebraically minded, should reveal the three-year zero coupon rate, Z3:

$$£100 = \frac{£5.50}{(1 + 0.05)^1} + \frac{£5.50}{(1 + 0.0526)^2} + \frac{£105.50}{(1 + Z3)^3} \tag{6.4}$$

Z3 turns out to be 5.52 per cent. We can carry on this process, which is known as bootstrapping, to reveal the four and five year zero coupon rates as follows:

$$£100 = \frac{£5.75}{(1 + 0.05)^1} + \frac{£5.75}{(1 + 0.0526)^2} + \frac{£5.75}{(1 + 0.0552)^3} + \frac{£105.75}{(1 + Z4)^4} \tag{6.5}$$

where Z4 turns out to be 5.79 per cent, so that Z5 can be revealed from the following expression:

$$£100 = \frac{£6.00}{(1 + 0.05)^1} + \frac{£6.00}{(1 + 0.0526)^2} + \frac{£6.00}{(1 + 0.0552)^3}$$
$$+ \frac{£6.00}{(1 + 0.0579)^4} + \frac{£106.00}{(1 + Z5)^5} \tag{6.6}$$

where Z5 turns out to be 6.06 per cent.

We can see from the calculations that are summarized in the last column of Exhibit 6.15 that the zero coupon, or spot, rates are higher than the GRYs on the bonds with the same maturity. In fact, when the yield curve is upwards sloping the zero coupon curve (made up of zero coupon rates) always sits above the GRY curve representing yields on coupon paying bonds. Exhibit 6.16 shows this.

The usefulness of zero coupon rates

The explanation as to why the zero coupon curve plots above the GRY, or coupon paying, curve when it is upward sloping and below when the coupon paying curve is downward sloping will become clear when we examine forward rates. But before we launch into that explanation it is worth considering why zero coupon or cash rates are so useful.

Zero coupon rates, derived by decomposing the coupon paying yield curve, represent the precise rate that we need to use to discount any payment in the future. This may be a payment in ten years' time, or in five years' time, or in 31 years' time. For example, suppose that an investor expects to receive a payment of £100m in 23 years' time. Using the 'bootstrapping' approach to construct the zero coupon curve, as we have done here, it is possible to identify the appropriate rate at which to discount this payment, so long as there are coupon paying bonds with maturities of at least 23 years. This is because the limit of the zero coupon curve is restricted to the limit of the coupon paying curve.

Exhibit 6.16   The zero coupon curve

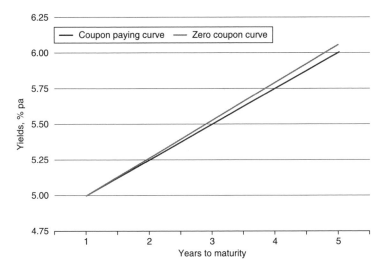

Zero coupon rates and pension fund liabilities

Zero coupon rates can be used to value the complicated liability profiles of pension schemes. So, for example, if a pension scheme knows that it must make a payment to its scheme members of £10m in ten years' time, by knowing the appropriate ten-year discount rate the present value of this liability can easily be calculated.

Forward interest rates and the forward yield curve

Zero coupon rates are also important because they allow us to uncover market interest rate expectations. We can do this by using the zero coupon rates to construct forward interest rates and forward yield curves. So what is a forward rate of interest? A forward interest rate is one that would be applied to borrowing or lending not today, but at some pre-specified time in the future for a pre-specified period. For example, a borrower may wish to borrow £100m in one year's time for a year, as opposed to wanting to borrow £100m today for a year.

How is it possible for financial markets to quote a rate of interest that will apply in the future? The answer to this question can be found in the concept of hedging and through the use of zero coupon rates. Suppose that an investor wishes to borrow £100m for one year in one year's time. The bank providing this service could agree to provide this cash for the investor by simply guessing the level of one year interest rates in one year's time. But this would be very risky. If they quote a rate of 5 per cent and one year rates turn out to be 6 per cent in one year's time, the bank will have to borrow £100m at a rate of interest of 6 per cent and then lend it out for a year at 5 per cent, incurring a loss over the year of 1 per cent × £100m = £1m.

A better way to deal with the request would instead be to borrow the £100m now in the open market for two years. This way the bank knows that it will have the funds in one year's time when the client needs them, and will be able to pay back its own borrowing in two years' time when the client pays them back. By borrowing the money in this way the bank can hedge its exposure to interest rates.

So what rate should they quote the client? This will depend upon the cost of the hedge, which, in turn, will depend upon the prevailing cost of borrowing money for two years. In other words, the two-year zero coupon, or cash rate. But it will also depend upon:

i. the interest that the bank will earn from depositing the money in a cash account for one year (since the client will not need the money in this year); and
ii. the interest that the bank can earn from the client in the second year of the arrangement.

Exhibit 6.17 Calculating forward rates

Year	Bond price	Coupon	GRY (%)	Zeros (%)	Forwards (%)
1	100	5.00	5.00	5.00	5.00
2	100	5.25	5.25	5.26	5.51
3	100	5.50	5.50	5.52	6.04
4	100	5.75	5.75	5.79	6.60
5	100	6.00	6.00	6.06	7.18

We can express this issue as follows:

Bank pays	Bank receives
£100m $\times$ $(1 + Z2)^2$ =	£100m $\times$ $(1 + Z1)^1 \times (1 + {}_1F_2)$

where ${}_1F_2$ refers to a forward rate that will last for one year and begins in one year's time. So the bank will pay Z2 for the borrowing and will receive Z1 in the first year from the market and then the rate of interest ${}_1F_2$ from the client. This means that there is a rate for forward lending that the bank can fix now, since it knows the borrowing rate for two-year money (Z2) and the lending rate for one-year money (Z1) today.

If the one-year and two-year zero coupon borrowing rates are as given in Exhibit 6.17, then we can calculate the one-year rate in one year's time (as long as we are not afraid of a little algebra). To calculate a one-year rate, one year forward we need to find a value for ${}_1F_2$ such that the bank's total payments equal its total receipts:

Bank pays	Bank receives
$(1 + 5.26\%)^2$ =	$(1 + 5.00\%) \times (1 + {}_1F_2)$
${}_1F_2$ =	5.51%

The answer to this bit of algebra is (approximately) 5.51 per cent. *Try plugging this value into the formula to verify this.*

So if the Bank quotes the client a borrowing rate of 5.51 per cent, it will neither profit nor gain. So in order to make a profit the bank will quote the client a rate of just over 5.51 per cent for this service. We can use the same logic to calculate:

- a one-year rate in two years' time:

Bank pays	Bank receives
$(1 + 5.52\%)^3$ =	$(1 + 5.26\%)^2 \times (1 + {}_2F_3)$
${}_2F_3$ =	6.04%

- a one-year rate in three years' time:

Bank pays		Bank receives
$(1 + 5.79\%)^4$	$=$	$(1 + 5.52\%)^3 \times (1 +_3F_4)$
$_3F_4$	$=$	6.60%

- a one-year rate in four years' time:

Bank pays		Bank receives
$(1 + 6.06\%)^5$	$=$	$(1 + 5.79\%)^4 \times (1 +_4F_5)$
$_4F_5$	$=$	7.18%

Exhibit 6.17 summarizes how we have been able to start with the yields and prices of coupon paying bonds, and derived zero coupon rates and then forward rates. Exhibit 6.18 shows the three yield curves, that all represent the yield or interest rate on a different type of fixed income payment. Exhibit 6.18 also shows how the forward rates sit above the zero coupon rates, and how the zero coupon rates sit above the coupon paying rates, or GRYs.

Exhibit 6.18   Coupon, zero and forward yield curves

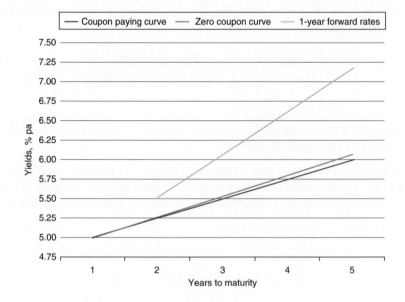

The relationship between forward and zero coupon curves

The forgoing calculations reveal an important feature about yield curves. When the coupon paying yield curve – the GRY curve – is upward sloping, interest rates and yields are generally expected to be higher in the future. The intuition for this is simple. For an investor to choose to buy a one-year zero coupon bond yielding, for example, 5 per cent, compared with a two-year zero coupon bond yielding, for example, 6 per cent, there must be some expectation that the rate of return available from another one-year bond in one year's time will be high enough to compensate them for the lower interest that they earn in the first year (5 per cent) compared with what they earn in the first year on the two-year zero coupon bond (6 per cent).

Exhibit 6.19 shows that in this case the compensation has to be around 7 per cent. In other words, one-year rates are expected to rise from 5 per cent today to 7 per cent in one year's time. Note that when the yield curve is upward sloping it generally means that there is an expectation that future rates will be higher. The converse is true if the yield curve is downward sloping. That is, there will be a general expectation that future rates will be lower.

Now that we know this, we can explain why the zero coupon curve sits above the coupon paying, or GRY curve when the latter is upward sloping and vice-versa.

Exhibit 6.19   Zero coupon and forward rates

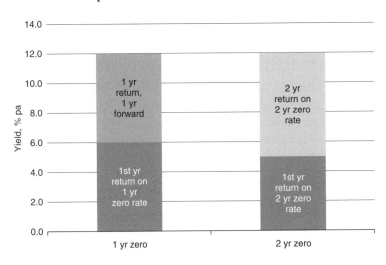

Upward sloping

When the yield curve is upward sloping imagine that an investor is faced with two choices:

- a two-year coupon paying bond, or
- a two-year zero coupon paying bond.

The upward sloping curve implies that future interest rates will be higher. Therefore, if the two bonds were offering the same yield, an investor would plump for the coupon paying bond, because the intermediate coupon(s) could be reinvested at higher rates in the future. In practice then, the two-year zero (by definition) does not pay this intermediate coupon and, therefore, investors will demand a higher yield from this bond compared with the coupon paying equivalent in order to compensate them for not being able to benefit from higher future interest rates.

Downward sloping

When the yield curve is downward sloping imagine that an investor is faced with the same two choices:

- a two-year coupon paying bond, or
- a two-year zero coupon paying bond.

This means that interest rates are expected to be lower in the future, which, in turn, means that the coupons of any coupon paying bond will be reinvested in the future at lower interest rates. To compensate investors for this the coupon paying bond has to offer a higher yield today, and, therefore, in a downward sloping yield curve environment the zero coupon curve will sit below the coupon paying curve.

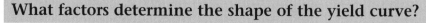

What factors determine the shape of the yield curve?

In Exhibit 6.14 we presented the GRYs on a range of UK government bonds. The chart showed that at that time the yield required on a long-dated UK government bond was higher than that required on a short-dated bond, the UK government yield curve was generally *upward sloping* at this particular time.

In Exhibit 6.20 we present the yield curves from three government bond markets, as they were on 31 December 2010. Each curve had a distinctive shape. The Japanese curve was smooth and upward sloping. The UK government curve was upward sloping until about 20 years and then began to slope downwards, while the US curve was upward sloping over the whole maturity range.

Exhibit 6.20 Yield curves for US, UK and Japanese government bond markets

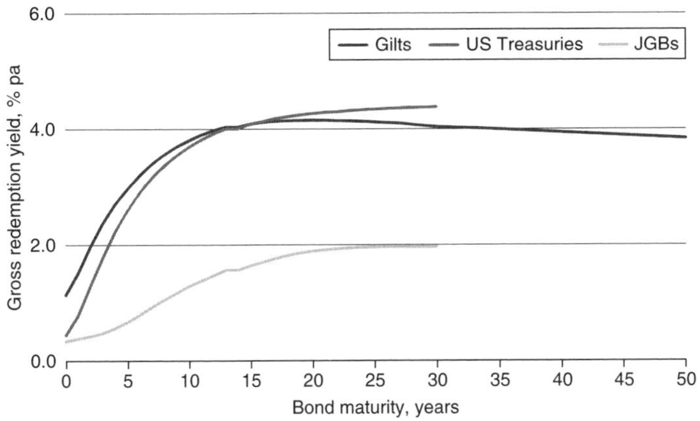

Source: Thomson Financial (31 December 2010).

What factors can explain the basic shapes of these curves? Although many issues may affect the shape of a yield curve, there are three 'theories' relating to the yield curve that economists believe explain the majority of their shape.

The liquidity preference theory

The liquidity preference theory of the yield curve relies upon borrower and lender preferences to explain the 'term structure of interest rates', or the shape of the yield curve. This theory says that to give them certainty, borrowers generally prefer to borrow over a longer time period and are, therefore, willing to pay a little more for the associated certainty relating to future borrowing costs. Conversely, because shorter term borrowing creates more uncertainty about the future cost of financing, borrowers will be inclined to pay less for these funds. For example, people that prefer to pay a higher mortgage interest rate for a fixed rate mortgage over a period of, say, five years, rather than pay the lower variable rate that might be available at the same time, are effectively paying a premium for fixing their mortgage payments with certainty over the five-year period.

The theory also considers the preferences of lenders. Lenders would prefer not to tie up their money for too long just in case a better investment opportunity arises in the future. Therefore, they will be willing to accept a lower rate of interest for short-term lending because they retain the flexibility to redeploy their resources if the opportunity arises. To encourage lenders to lend for longer periods of time and, therefore, to tie up their capital for longer, they will need to be compensated for the associated loss of liquidity.

It is for this reason that time deposits and other similar bank accounts that require us to invest our money for a pre-specified period of time generally pay higher rates of interest than current accounts. In the case of the former we lose some liquidity and require a higher rate of interest in return, while in the case of the latter our funds remain very liquid and we accept a lower rate of interest because of this.

Overall then, if borrowers prefer to borrow long and lenders prefer to lend short, then we can expect the yield curve to be upward sloping – long-term borrowing rates should be higher than short-term borrowing rates. This would appear to be a good explanation of the US and Japanese yield curves in Exhibit 6.20. However, if you look closely at the figure you will see that UK yield curve on this date starts to slope down from around the 20-year maturity point. Indeed in the past the gilt curve has often had a significant downward slope, or inversion, from this maturity point onwards, even when the curve slopes upwards over the zero to 20-year maturity range.

Another theory can help to explain why the yield curve is sometimes downward sloping.

The expectations theory of the yield curve

We have already looked at forward rates in this chapter and shown how they can be derived from underlying bond prices and yields. We also showed that when the coupon paying curve is upward sloping, forward rates are higher than the yields on both coupon paying and zero coupon bonds. Conversely, when the coupon paying curve is downward sloping, embedded in this structure are forward rates that are lower than both the yields on coupon and on zero-coupon bonds. Finally, when the yield curve environment is flat, this implies that market participants expect rates to neither rise nor fall in the future.

Another way of putting this is that:

i.   in an upward sloping yield curve environment future interest rates are expected to rise;
ii. in a downward sloping yield curve environment future interest rates are expected to fall; while
iii. in a flat yield curve environment interest rates are not expected to rise or to fall.

The expectations theory of the yield curve holds that it is the market's expectations about future short-term interest rates that dictates the shape of the yield curve.

The shape of their zero coupon government bond curves in Japan and the US, shown in Exhibit 6.20, suggest that interest rates were expected to rise in the market, since the yield curve was generally upward sloping. Given that the official 'policy rate' in Japan and the US was so low (at virtually 0 per cent in both cases) at the time, it would be consistent with the view that future Japanese and US interest rates were expected to be higher in the future.

Can the expectations theory explain the shape of the UK government yield curve, which is often very inverted, or downward sloping after the 20-year maturity point? According to the expectations theory of the yield curve, the UK curve shown in Exhibit 6.20 appears to imply that there was an expectation that interest rates would rise in the short to medium term, but begin to fall in the long term. This seems a little implausible as an explanation. While market participants will be able to form views about how a central bank will adjust interest rates in the short-term, can they really form expectations about what the short-term policy rate will be in 20 or 30 years' time?

Can liquidity preference theory explain why the long end of the UK government yield curve is often inverted? Liquidity preference theory asserts that the yield curve should be upward sloping, it cannot explain why lenders are willing to lend money to the UK government for say 50 years and earn a lower return than can be achieved by lending the money for say 20 years.

Other factors must often have a significant impact upon UK government borrowing rates since neither the liquidity preference theory, nor the expectations theory of the yield curve can provide an adequate explanation for a curve that slopes up at first and then starts to slope down again.

The market segmentation theory of the yield curve

The market segmentation theory of the yield curve effectively asserts that it is inappropriate to link the different yields in a bond market to create a single curve, because this implies that ultimately there is a relationship between, say, the yield on a one-year bond and the yield on a 30-year bond. According to this view of the yield curve, this is an inappropriate assumption to make because different market participants prefer to buy certain types of bonds. For example, general insurance companies might prefer to hold shorter-dated UK government bonds, since their liabilities (car insurance, home contents insurance, etc.) are short-term in nature. At the other end of the spectrum, pension funds have very long-dated liabilities and, therefore, are likely to prefer long-dated government bonds.

With this theory of the yield curve, supply and demand in different segments (maturities) of the market play a crucial role in determining bond prices and yields in these different segments, which can take place in isolation from one another. Therefore, one explanation of why the UK government curve often slopes up in the short to medium-term maturity spectrum and down thereafter is that there is often 'excess demand' for longer-dated UK government bonds from a group of investors that prefer long-dated bond maturities to shorter-dated ones. Many believe that this excess demand emanates from the UK's DB pension schemes that are seeking to buy these long-dated government bonds to back their long-dated liabilities.

A 'unified' theory of the yield curve

In practice, liquidity preference, interest rate expectations and supply and demand imbalances in certain parts of the yield curve will all play a part in determining the shape of the yield curve at times. When forming views about likely changes to the shape of the yield curve, bond fund managers have to use their judgement in an effort to try and predict which of these factors will be dominant over their particular investment horizon.

Summary

In this chapter we have introduced you to the 'wonderful world' of bonds. Many trustees are put off by the technical jargon that often gets thrown around by bond fund managers and by consultants with regard to these instruments. However, this asset class cannot be ignored by trustees. It is becoming a larger and larger part of most pension portfolios, and as we will see in Chapter 15, understanding the way bonds work is crucial for an understanding of Liability Driven Investment (LDI). We will also use much of the analysis we have introduced in this chapter in further chapters.

Hopefully we have demonstrated that a bond is fundamentally quite a simple financial instrument and nothing to be scared of . . . though some bond fund managers may be scary!

Key points

- There are many types of bond but generally it is the nature of the coupon payment that distinguishes one type from another.
- When bond yields go up, bond prices go down and vice versa. A bond's potential sensitivity to a change in yield is measured by its duration.
- The liabilities of a typical DB pension scheme can be thought of as being analogous to those payments due from a very long-dated, structured bond.
- We can extract zero coupon and forward yields from the prices of coupon paying bonds.
- The shape of the yield curve will be determined by borrower and lender preferences, by expectations about future interest rates, and by demand and supply conditions in different maturity segments of the market.

Chapter 7

Equities: The Traditional 'Growth' Asset Class

Learning outcomes

- Understand the key features of equities.
- Understand how equities are valued.
- Understand the concept of the equity risk premium.
- Appreciate the concept of equity investment style.
- Appreciate the importance of reinvested dividend income as a source of return.

Introduction

In the previous chapter we examined bonds as an asset class. To many, the analysis of bonds appears to be very technical, full of unfamiliar concepts like duration, spot and forward rates. Investors often feel more comfortable thinking about equities as an asset class and, indeed, consider equities to be simpler instruments. They also often consider equities to be entirely separate and distinct from bonds. In other words: bonds live in one world, equities in another and never the twain shall meet. The bad news is that equities are every bit as complex as bonds, in that a very similar analysis is equally applicable to equities as it is to bonds. Indeed, equity and bond prices share common components that make them inextricably linked. The good news is that we will begin at the beginning and then will show how thinking about equities using the same framework as used for bonds actually makes perfect sense.

What are equities?

A company's share capital can be divided into two broad categories: ordinary shares and preference shares. The former are commonly referred to as equities, stocks, or the equity share capital of the company. Shareholders' rights relating to both ordinary and preference shares are specified in a legal document known as the *Articles of Association*. This document governs the internal constitution of the company. However, given that a company is a separate legal entity, distinct from that of its shareholders, the types of business a company is permitted to conduct are specified in another document – the *Memorandum of Association*.

Both ordinary and preference shares can be issued by both public limited companies (plcs) and private limited companies (Ltd.). A plc is permitted to issue shares directly to the public and institutions, such as pension funds, and to have their shares traded on an officially recognized exchange – the *London Stock Exchange* (LSE), for example. It is these publicly listed securities issued by plcs that form the bulk of the equity holdings of UK pension schemes. By contrast, shares issued by private limited companies are typically tightly held by the company's founders, often families, though many private companies are now owned by private equity firms, often as a result of 'taking a public company private'.

Ordinary shares

> *October: This is one of the peculiarly dangerous months to [buy] stocks. The others are July, January, September, April, November, May, March, June, December, August, and February.* (Mark Twain, Pudd'nhead Wilson, 1894)

Ordinary shares are the most common type of share capital. Ordinary shares confer ownership of the company to the ordinary shareholders, who, not only participate in the company's profits and losses but, in addition, typically have voting rights that they can exercise to determine corporate policy, the desirability or otherwise of a takeover bid from another company, or to appoint new directors and so forth.[1] However, the returns attributable to the ordinary shareholders are subordinated to those of all of the company's other investors and stakeholders. These include the banks, the company's bondholders, the taxman and other 'secured creditors', not forgetting 'unsecured creditors' such as the company's DB pension scheme. This means that the returns from ordinary shares are not fixed and will depend upon the profitability of the company. In other words, the ordinary shares are the main risk capital of the company.

Companies distribute profits via dividend payments, which are usually paid twice yearly in the UK, in the form of an interim and final dividend. When an

---

[1] We consider the importance of corporate governance in Chapter 16.

investor buys ordinary shares, they are effectively buying a right to a portion of this dividend stream into the future. However, a company is not obliged to make dividend payments and many do not. Moreover, in the event of the company failing, the ordinary shareholders are similarly the last in line to be compensated. As a result of the uncertainty of the dividend stream and the possibility that the firm might fail, ordinary shareholders demand a higher *prospective* return from their holdings than bondholders do from theirs. This additional return is known as the *equity risk premium* (ERP). We return to the ERP later in the chapter. On the upside, in the event that a firm does fail, the owners of fully paid up ordinary shares are not liable for any of the company's remaining debts, as their liability is limited to the paid up value of the shares they own.[2]

Other ordinary share types

While conventional ordinary shares conform to the characteristics outlined above, there are some variations on this general structure. *Non-voting ordinary shares* are identical in most respects to conventional ordinary shares, but because they do not carry voting rights, they trade at a discount, that is, at a lower price, to their voting share equivalents.[3] Unlike most bonds, ordinary shares are not normally issued with a redemption date. Those that are, are known as *redeemable ordinary shares*. Finally, *deferred shares* usually carry additional voting rights and are often held by the original, private owners of the company so that they can retain a certain degree of control over the business. However, in return for these more powerful shares, a dividend payment can only be paid to them once a dividend payment has been made to the other ordinary shareholders.

Preference shares

Shares issued by a company with the promise of a fixed dividend payment are known as *preference shares*. The preference share dividend can be deferred, but, unlike ordinary shareholders, the preference shareholders are usually entitled to any dividend arrears. In this case the preference shares are *cumulative*. Usually these cumulative dividend arrears can only be paid once all obligations to bondholders have been met. In the event of a firm's failure, preference shareholders have a superior claim on the firm's remaining assets over ordinary shareholders, but an inferior claim to bondholders. In general then, preference shares are seen as being less risky than ordinary shares but more risky than the company's bonds, so the return required from them by investors is normally

---

[2] Some ordinary shares are initially issued in partly paid form, requiring the investor to purchase the shares in instalments according to a pre-determined timetable. Once the shares are 'fully paid up', the ordinary shareholders do not have any liability for the company's debts. Until then their liability extends to the unpaid portion of the shares.
[3] Non-voting shares are a rarity nowadays and can no longer be issued by UK companies.

lower than that required on equivalent ordinary shares, but higher than that required on the company's bonds.

There are a number of different preference share structures. *Participating preference shares* are entitled to the fixed dividend, but also a portion of the profits of the firm normally when the dividends paid on the ordinary shares have reached a certain threshold. *Redeemable preference shares* have the bond-like characteristic of being redeemable at a pre-determined point in the future. Finally, *convertible preference* shares can, under certain pre-determined conditions, be converted into the ordinary shares of the company.

The structure and size of the world's equity markets

As mentioned earlier, when we speak about 'equities' or 'stocks' we generally mean 'ordinary shares'. Also, as intimated earlier, ordinary shares are by far the largest type of equity issued by firms, and, indeed, traded in global financial markets. Exhibit 7.1 presents a list of the world's largest companies by the market value of their ordinary shares as at the end of February 2011. You will recognize most of the names in the list. In terms of 'country', US companies currently dominate the list, though two Chinese firms now rank in the top 20. In the future we will undoubtedly see more Chinese companies making it on to this

Exhibit 7.1   The world's largest companies by equity market capitalization

Company	Country of incorporation	Market Cap (£bn)
1. Exxon Mobil	US	261.8
2. Apple	US	200.0
3. Royal Dutch Shell	UK	138.1
4. Microsoft	US	137.3
5. General Electric	US	137.0
6. Berkshire Hathaway	US	132.6
7. China Construction Bank	China	129.2
8. Chevron	US	128.4
9. IBM	US	122.4
10. Google	US	121.2
11. Nestle	Switzerland	120.6
12. HSBC Holdings	UK	119.4
13. China Mobile	China	115.7
14. Walmart Stores	US	114.5
15. JP Morgan Chase	US	112.2
16. Procter & Gamble	US	108.6
17. Gazprom	Russia	106.3
18. Wells Fargo	US	104.4
19. Johnson & Johnson	US	103.8
20. AT&T	US	103.1

Source: Factset, as at 28 February 2011: MSCI All Country World Index.

list. However, the country in which a company is incorporated, or domiciled, can often be a bit misleading. For example, BP, although widely recognized as being a British company (especially when held responsible for an environmental disaster!), derives only around 10 per cent of its annual revenue from the UK. Today, it is really only a British company in the sense that its shares are listed on the LSE and it remains headquartered in London. In reality it is a global company.

In terms of the sectoral composition of the list, oil and technology companies currently dominate, while there are fewer banks in the list than there were before the recent credit crunch took a big bite out of the banking sector!

Exhibit 7.2 presents the names of the ten largest companies listed on the LSE. Mining and oil stocks dominate this list. Along with financial stocks, they also dominate the UK equity market.[4] The last column in the table gives the weight of each of these stocks within the UK equity market. This we proxy by using the FTSE All Share Index, which in comprising the top 600 or so companies listed on the LSE, is one of the broadest UK equity market benchmarks.[5] We cover equity indices in more detail in Chapter 14. HSBC Holdings, the world's second largest bank (see Exhibit 7.1), comprised 6.5 per cent of the FTSE All Share Index at the end of February 2011 while, taken together, the ten largest companies made up

Exhibit 7.2 The largest LSE listed companies by equity market capitalization

Rank	Constituent name	Sector	Market Cap (£bn)	FTSE All Share Index weight (%)
1	Royal Dutch Shell (A&B)	Oil & Gas producers	138.1	7.53
2	HSBC	Banking	119.4	6.51
3	BP	Oil & Gas producers	93.2	5.08
4	Vodafone Group	Mobile Telecommunications	90.5	4.93
5	Rio Tinto	Mining	65.8	3.59
6	GlaxoSmithkline	Pharmaceuticals & Biotechnology	61.9	3.37
7	BHP Billiton	Mining	53.7	2.93
8	BG Group	Oil & Gas producers	50.4	2.75
9	BAT	Tobacco	49.2	2.68
10	Anglo American	Mining	44.2	2.41
Total			766.4	41.80

Source: Factset, as at 28 February 2011.

[4] As at end-February 2011, these three sectors accounted for 54 per cent of the value of the FTSE All Share Index.
[5] The reason for appearing to be vague about the number of companies that comprise the FTSE All Share Index is that the criteria for companies' inclusion in the index changes periodically.

42 per cent of the entire index. This last point is worth dwelling upon, not only from a UK equity market perspective but also from a global one. There are literally thousands of companies that have publicly traded ordinary shares around the world but a disproportionate amount of the total value of global equity markets is made up of a relatively small number of large, global companies.

In Exhibit 7.3, the pie chart in Panel A shows the proportions of the world's equity markets by country of listing. At the end of 2010, 33 per cent of the world's equity markets by value, or market capitalization, comprised the ordinary shares of those companies listed in the US, while Japan at 9 per cent assumed the number two spot. In 1990, Japan accounted for 40 per cent of world stock market capitalization, while the US assumed the number two spot at 32 per cent. The UK had the third largest equity market in 2010, accounting for 7 per cent of world stock market capitalization.

However, when comparing the pie chart in Panel A with that in Panel B, which shows the world broken down by GDP (see Chapter 4), we can see that a country's equity market capitalization bears little resemblance to the relative size of its economic output, as measured by GDP. For instance, as the world's largest economy, the US accounted for 25 per cent of annual global output at the end of 2010. However, this is far less than the relative size of the US in global stock market terms. Similarly, the UK has the world's third largest stock market but only the sixth largest economy. This apparent disparity

Exhibit 7.3   Relative sizes

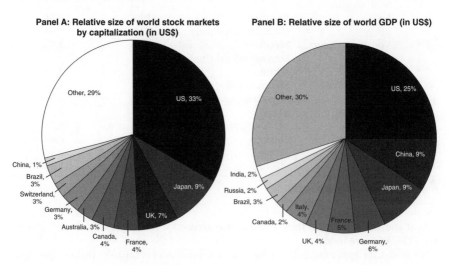

Panel A: Relative size of world stock markets by capitalization (in US$)

Panel B: Relative size of world GDP (in US$)

Source: Thomson Financial as at 31 December 2010

between stock market value and the size of an economy can be explained by three factors. First, as already mentioned above, some companies listed in the UK are truly global companies, like BP, while many others, like the Russian energy giant Rosneft, simply list on the London market to access international capital. In fact, more overseas domiciled companies have a listing on the LSE than in any other equity market.

Second, companies issue publicly traded equity to raise money to fund their businesses. However, there are other ways of raising money too, including bank and bond finance. So if the corporate culture favours alternative sources of finance, as in France and Germany, then a country's stock market will not necessarily reflect the size of the economy in which this market is situated. Third, not all corporate profits captured within the GDP data are captured by the stock market as many companies are privately held or state owned rather than publicly listed.

Before we move on to look at ways of analyzing equities, we should pause to consider the role equities play in pension portfolios. Panel A of Exhibit 7.4 shows the asset allocation breakdown of typical pension portfolios across Europe. Compared with the rest of Europe, UK pension portfolios have a high weighting towards both domestic and overseas equities and a relatively low weighting towards government bonds. However, as Panel B shows, UK pension fund equity weightings have declined over the past few years, while the weighting towards bonds has increased. Although bonds are gradually becoming the dominant asset class in pension funds (which is bad news for those of you who do not like all that technical bond talk), equities still play a vital role in both providing the potential returns needed to close the funding gap and in generating the dividend flows necessary to meet pension payments. Indeed, in 2010 dividends paid by companies listed on the LSE amounted to £56.5bn, of which 60 per cent was paid by just 15 companies.

Interestingly, while most schemes have been reducing their UK equity holdings over recent years, many have been simultaneously increasing their weighting towards overseas equities. The reason for this is three-fold. First, in contrast to many other markets, the UK equity market is very concentrated. This is evident from Exhibit 7.2, where the top ten companies in the FTSE All Share Index at end-February 2011 accounted for nearly 42 per cent of the index's value. Not only that, the top four sectors – financials, oil and gas, basic materials and consumer goods – collectively represented 65 per cent of the index. Second, this sector concentration means that many sectors are underrepresented in the UK equity market. Third, investing overseas helps diversify away these concentration risks given that most overseas equity markets do not move in perfect lockstep with the UK market.

Exhibit 7.4   Equities in pension portfolios

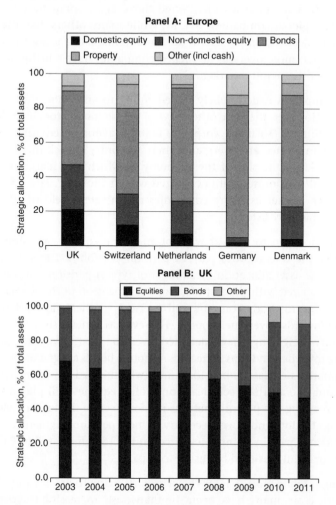

Source: Mercer European Asset Allocation Survey, May 2011.

Analyzing ordinary shares

So how do investors choose between the shares of one company and another? Or at least how do we compare them? One of the most basic ways used to compare the ordinary shares of one company with another is to compare simple financial ratios. You may recall that we showed how financial ratios can be used as a means of assessing a bond issuer's ability to service the bond(s) that it has issued – that is, pay interest as it falls due – and ultimately repay the bond(s) at redemption. Indeed, the ratings agencies use financial ratios to assist them in rating a bond issue. By contrast, financial ratios are applied to equities in an effort to compare the growth prospects of a market, sector or stock relative to another or against its own history. Although there are many metrics that can be applied to equities, the three most common are: the *dividend yield* (DY), the *price to earnings* (PE) ratio, and *price to book* (PB) ratio. Let's look at each of these in turn.

Dividend yield

As we will see later in the chapter, dividends are extremely important. Indeed, company dividend announcements are keenly anticipated by shareholders and potential investors alike, as they send out an important signal to the market about the confidence placed by the company's directors in the company's prospects. A dividend cut invariably results in the company's shares falling sharply as investors' expectations are dashed.

The *dividend yield* is the ratio of the dividend per share (DPS) paid to shareholders[6] over the previous 12 months, that is, the total of the last interim and final dividend paid, to the current share price (P):

$$\text{Dividend yield} = \frac{DPS}{P} = \frac{£0.05}{£1.00} = 5\%$$

This ratio is useful for gauging the price of the income stream from equities. For example, if the current share price is £1.00, and the last interim and final dividend totalled £0.05, then the company's dividend yield will be 5 per cent. So, for every £1 paid for an ordinary share, it might be expected to yield an annual income of £0.05. As such, an investor might prefer it to a stock with a dividend yield of 4 per cent. Although dividend yields differ considerably between markets and sectors, and can and do change over time, in the UK a dividend yield greater than 4 per cent is generally considered high – 5 per cent certainly is. Something less than about 2 per cent would be deemed low. However, there is no guarantee that a share with a high dividend yield will continue to pay the relatively high dividend payments. Indeed, a high dividend yield could reflect the fact that investors are anticipating a cut in dividend payments. This is because the share price may have fallen ahead of the anticipated cut in dividends, thereby causing the dividend yield to rise.

---

[6] Since 1997, dividends have been paid to shareholders net of tax. The tax paid can no longer be reclaimed by pension funds.

Investors that are attracted to high dividend yield paying stocks, perhaps because they wish to construct a portfolio with a high income yield (e.g., to pay pensions), but who are concerned that the high dividend yield on a company's shares may not persist, will also consider the *dividend cover ratio*. This is calculated by dividing the earnings, or profits, of the company attributed to each share, known as the earnings per share (EPS), by the dividend per share (DPS):

$$\text{Dividend cover} = \frac{\text{EPS}}{\text{DPS}} = \frac{£0.10}{£0.05} = 2$$

This ratio helps investors gauge whether the company can maintain its dividends, or even potentially increase them. For example, suppose that a company's dividend per share is again £0.05, but that the company's EPS was £0.10. This would give a dividend cover ratio of two. This means that for every £1 the company paid out in dividends last year, it earned £2. In which case, the dividend payout was twice covered by earnings.

If the earnings per share are high relative to the dividend per share – that is, the dividend cover ratio is well above one – it means that the firm is not paying out all of its earnings in the form of dividends. In such a case, other things being equal, the company will be more likely to maintain the relatively high dividend payments. Conversely, if a company's dividend cover is close to one, it means that it is paying out most of its profits in the form of dividends and also that a relatively small decline in future earnings might lead to a cut in dividends and a subsequent fall in the dividend yield. Dividend cover of less than one means that the company may have to dip into profits earned and retained in previous years in order to maintain the dividend – not normally a good sign.

Price to earnings ratio

Another very common metric for comparing equities is the price to earnings (PE) ratio. This is the ratio of the current share price to the current earnings per share (EPS) generated by the company. It is expressed as follows:

$$\text{Price to earnings ratio} = \frac{\text{P}}{\text{EPS}} = \frac{£1.00}{£0.10} = 10$$

This ratio tells investors the price they are paying for the shares as a multiple of the company's earnings. For example, if the company's share price (P) is £1.00 and its EPS is £0.10, then its PE ratio is ten. That is, investors have to pay £10 for every pound of earnings.

Investors use this ratio to compare the valuations attributed to individual equities, sectors and markets, how they compare to recent history, and as a means by which to gauge the market's expectations surrounding the company's, sector's or market's growth prospects. For instance, if a stock is trading with a low PE relative to the rest of the market, it implies that investors are not willing to pay a high price for a pound's worth of last year's earnings. This may be because the market believes that the prospect of strong earnings growth in the future is low. Alternatively, a share trading with a very high PE relative to the rest of the market indicates that investors are willing to pay a higher price for each pound's worth of last year's earnings. They may be willing to do this because they expect earnings to grow rapidly in the future.

Typically, the EPS element of the ratio refers to last year's earnings – this is known as the *historic*, or *trailing, PE ratio*. However, when the EPS is based upon an estimate of future earnings, it is referred to as the *forward, or prospective, PE ratio*. If a company's EPS is expected to grow, then its historic PE ratio will be greater than its forward PE ratio.

As with the dividend yield, what constitutes a high or low PE ratio very much depends on the market, sector or company in question and, to a large degree, the economic backdrop. However, in the UK, a company with a historic PE ratio in the high teens or above would certainly be considered expensive whereas one with a PE ratio in single figures would be deemed cheap.

Price to book ratio

The price to book (PB) ratio measures the ratio of the company's share price to its net asset value (NAV), or its assets minus its liabilities, attributed to each share. The PB ratio is expressed as follows:

$$\text{Price to book ratio} = \frac{P}{\text{NAV per share}} = \frac{£1.00}{£0.50} = 2$$

The PB ratio tells investors the extent to which the value of their shares is 'covered' by the company's net assets. Some of these assets, like office buildings, are tangible whereas others such as patents and copyrights are intangible. It also indicates the strength of investors' expectations about the company's ability to generate a high return, or not, on its net assets. The higher the ratio, the greater the expectations for growth but the lower the safety margin if things don't turn out as expected. In our example, the company's share price is £1 and the NAV per share is £0.50, so the PB ratio is two.

What constitutes a high or low PB ratio comes down to the market, sector and stock in question but a ratio of over two is typically interpreted as meaning that the company's shares are expensive, while a ratio of less than one would typically categorize the shares as being cheap.

Growth versus value

Equity markets often categorize shares as being either *growth* or *value* stocks. Growth stocks tend to trade with a high PE and PB ratio and low dividend yield relative to the rest of the market, because investors believe that the earnings of the company will grow rapidly in the future. Companies that operate in new markets with scope for expansion, for example companies in the IT sector, are often categorized as growth stocks. Conversely stocks with a low PE and PB ratio and a high current dividend yield are often categorized as value stocks – stocks where future earnings growth is expected to be relatively low. Companies that operate in mature markets with little prospect of substantial market expansion, but which still produce a stable earnings stream, utility companies for instance, might be described as value stocks. The common interpretation of these ratios is summarized in Exhibit 7.5.

It is also possible to characterize equity markets as being either value or growth too by looking at the dividend yields, PB and PE ratios on these markets as a whole. In Exhibit 7.6 we have presented the dividend yields and aggregate dividend cover on the Thomson Financial total market equity indices as they stood at the end of 2010. At just under 4 per cent, the Australian equity market has the highest dividend yield, but the lowest dividend cover with earnings of just 1.5 times dividends. By contrast the UK equity market had a relatively high dividend yield at nearly 3 per cent, plus relatively high dividend cover of just over 2.3. However, note the dividend yield in the Indian equity market which was very low at just under 1 per cent. For these markets it had the highest dividend cover, but mainly because the market was not paying a very high dividend. Why are investors willing to accept such a low dividend yield from investing in Indian equities? The answer probably lies in their view of the prospects for future Indian equity earnings.

In Exhibit 7.7 we have presented the trailing PE ratio on each of the markets shown in Exhibit 7.6, again as they stood at the end of 2010. The chart clearly shows that there is a wide range of PE ratios across these markets. For the

Exhibit 7.5   Growth versus value stocks

Ratio/yield	Value, relative to market/sector	Growth, relative to market/sector
Price to earnings ratio (PE)	Low	High
Price to book ratio (PB)	Low	High
Dividend yield	High	Low

Exhibit 7.6 Dividend yields and dividend cover for a selection of world equity markets, as at the end of 2010

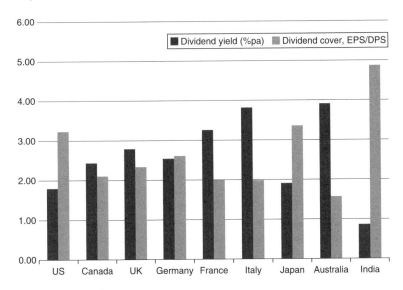

Source: Thomson Financial.

Exhibit 7.7 Trailing PE ratios for a selection of world equity markets, as at the end of 2010

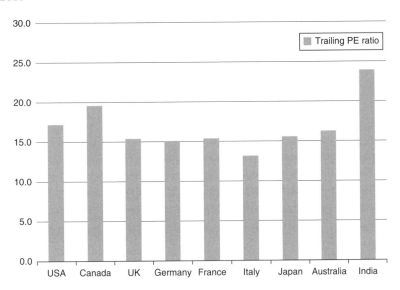

Source: Thomson Financial.

Indian market the PE ratio is 23.9. This implies that investors are willing to pay 23.9 Indian rupees for every one rupee of last year's Indian equity market earnings. Other things equal, this is a high price compared, for example, with the €13.2 that Italian equity investors are willing to pay for every €1 earned from the Italian equity market over the previous year. Investors may be willing to pay a relatively high price for Indian equity earnings if they believe that future earnings growth will be high relative to their expectations for, say, Italian earnings growth.

Some investors prefer to buy *value* stocks, while others prefer to invest in *growth* stocks. Since 1998 the total return achieved on value stocks represented by the FTSE 350 value index has been far greater than that which might have been achieved by investing in growth stocks, as represented by the FTSE 350 growth index. These total returns indices are shown in Exhibit 7.8. In January 1994, £100 invested in the FTSE 350 value index would have been worth £324 at the end of 2010, compared with just over £265 had it been invested in the FTSE 350 growth index instead. However, this does not mean that value investing always produces superior returns than growth investing, or that it will in the future. Choosing one style of investing, however, can clearly affect investment performance.

Exhibit 7.8   Value of £100 invested in January 1994 in the FTSE value and growth indices[1]

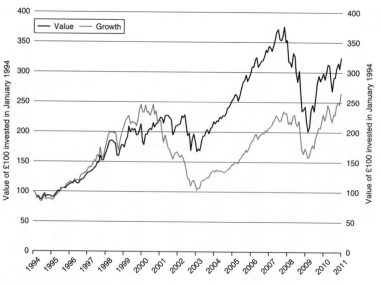

Source: Thomson Financial.

Note: [1] These indices are calculated by the FTSE organization. For information on how they categorize and then choose the value and growth stocks for the indices go to: http://www.ftse.com/Indices/Custom_Value_Partners/index.jsp.

Equity investment styles

Various equity investment styles have emerged over the years as a result of the belief that particular groups of stocks sharing one of a number of common characteristics, or *style factors*, exhibit a meaningful tendency to move together and experience long periods of out- and underperformance of the broader market. Although we return to investment style in Chapter 18, we will now briefly describe some of these equity investment styles here, and will begin with the age old debate with respect to growth versus value investing.

Growth versus value investing

Growth investing originated from the work of US Fund Manager T. Rowe Price in the 1960s, emerging as a distinctive investment style during the US *Nifty Fifty* craze of the early 1970s. Growth investing is a relatively aggressive investment style. Often growth investors and fund managers argue that what they do is to buy Growth At a Reasonable Price (GARP).[7] GARP investing centres on those companies that are perceived to offer above average earnings growth potential that has yet to be fully factored into the company's share price. One of a number of tools used by GARP managers is the PEG, or price-to-earnings-growth, ratio. This compares the GARP manager's forecasted earnings growth for the company to the company's price to earnings ratio. If the former is greater than the latter then a PEG ratio of greater than one indicates that the stock is worthy of consideration. GARP investing is also about avoiding those companies most susceptible to issuing profits warnings, as any stock trading on a high valuation that fails to meet consensus earnings expectations can be marked down savagely by the market.

Genuine GARP stocks are those companies that are able to differentiate their product or service in some way from their industry peers allowing them to command a competitive advantage and pricing power and, therefore, an ability to generate high quality earnings and above average earnings growth. This higher earnings growth, that should eventually turn into higher dividend growth, is what GARP investors are looking to benefit from. GARP investing is particularly popular with emerging market equity managers, given that within emerging markets consistently strong, high quality earnings growth purchased at the right price has historically correlated well with subsequent share price performance. In fact, over the past decade or so, GARP within emerging markets has outperformed all other investment styles.

Value investing, meanwhile, which originated from the pioneering work of Benjamin Graham and David Dodds in the 1930s[8], seeks to identify those

---

[7] Though they would say this wouldn't they?
[8] Benjamin Graham and David Dodds, *Security Analysis*, McGraw-Hill (1934).

companies that typically operate in mature markets with little prospect of substantial market expansion or rapid future growth in earnings, but which still produce a stable and relatively high dividend stream – utility stocks for example. These value stocks typically trade with a low PE and PB ratio and a high dividend yield relative to the rest of the market. Fund managers that specialize in investing in value stocks do so because they believe that in the long run these stocks will outperform other stocks, particularly growth stocks.

So which of the two styles has been the most successful over the years? It is well documented that within developed markets value outperforms growth over the very long term, though this period typically extends far beyond the investment horizon of most pension funds, let alone individual investors. According to the Credit Suisse Global Investment Returns Sourcebook 2011,[9] drawing on the top 100 companies in the UK, this outperformance has amounted to 2.9 per cent per annum over the period 1900 to 2010 and 1.7 per cent per annum between 1975 and 2010. However, this is not just a UK phenomenon. In fact, between 1975 and end-2010, using the MSCI Barra Value and Growth indices, value outperformed growth in 13 of 19 developed equity markets by an average of 2.5 per cent per annum. Between 2000 and end-2010, this outperformance among 16 of these markets rose to 3.9 per cent per annum. Over shorter horizons however, the evidence suggests that each style periodically outperforms and underperforms the other and the market.

Valuation spreads

Research, drawing on data between 1952 and 2009, suggests that '*valuation spread*s' can explain the short term out- and underperformance of active fund managers of value and growth strategies. The 'valuation spread' is defined as the difference in the valuation of the cheapest 20 per cent of stocks in the market compared to the average valuation of stocks – valuation being defined by traditional valuation measures such as price-to-earnings and price to book ratios. Since 1987, these valuation spreads have been stable, periodically deviating from their historic average by no more than one standard deviation but quickly reverting back to historic norms. However, in 2008 at the height of the financial crisis, valuation spreads approached historic highs as certain stocks and sectors, such as the banks, were hit particularly hard.

---

[9] Copyright © 2011 Elroy Dimson, Paul Marsh and Mike Staunton, *Triumph of the Optimists: 101 Years of Global Investment Returns*, Princeton University Press (2002).

The result was a marked increase in the dispersion of active fund manager returns as investment style and stock selection took on a whole new level of importance. Indeed, this dispersion of good and bad returns meant the difference between a respectable performance and one that could tarnish or even terminate a career in fund management. Moreover, as is usually the case when valuation spreads widen, only about 30 per cent of active managers collectively outperformed general equity market indices, such as the S&P 500 (in this particular research study). By contrast, when valuation spreads narrow – that is, as the valuations of the very cheapest stocks start to return to historic norms – a little over half of active fund managers outperform.

Indeed, as these valuation spreads narrowed in 2009, so 70 per cent of active fund managers outperformed the S&P 500, gross of fees. This narrowing of valuation spreads was also accompanied with an even greater dispersion of fund manager returns, as those value stocks that had suffered the most during the period of financial stress substantially outperformed those stocks that had proved the more resilient. The result was that during the first six months of 2009 96 per cent of US large-cap value managers outperformed their value benchmark, with only 16 per cent of large-cap growth managers outperforming theirs. However, the outperformance was most marked among US small-cap value managers at around 33 per cent.

Source: Empirical Research Partners LLC. October 8, 2009.

Momentum investing

Momentum investing focuses on those stocks that have recently performed well and whose price continues to gather momentum in a self-perpetuating manner. Often momentum investing is favoured by those managers whose investment decisions are principally dictated by technical analysis, or charts of share price movements. Most fund managers adopt either fundamental analysis or technical analysis to determine whether to buy, hold or sell a company's shares. Fundamental analysis revolves around crunching the numbers contained within a company's financial statements and supplementing this with company visits and meetings with senior management to determine a company's prospects and the fair value of its shares. Technical analysis, however, focuses on identifying patterns and trends in company share price charts to establish the possible future trajectory of the company's share price.

Momentum investing appeals to investors' natural tendency to extrapolate trends. Little attention is paid to the average market valuation of shares in a momentum driven market. However, momentum can turn. Investing in last year's top performing stock does not necessarily guarantee a repeat performance the following year though short-term momentum effects often exist for periods of up to 12 months. Momentum investing is more about gauging short-term market psychology and going with the market consensus, rather than analyzing the characteristics of individual stocks.

Thematic investing

Thematic investing involves identifying an economic or socio-economic trend that will eventually have an impact upon the valuations of underlying securities. For example, if a fund manager believed that advances in technology would mean that people would have increasing amounts of leisure time available in the future, then the manager might build a portfolio consisting of firms with exposure to the leisure industry, comprising travel companies and companies with an interest in casinos or leisure parks for example. This portfolio might be constructed on a global basis, that is, made up of companies from many different regions of the world, rather than comprising stocks from one particular country.

In practice, many active fund managers adopt investment themes, favouring particular industries and reflect this in their portfolios. However, these themes will change over time as financial markets evolve. By contrast, thematic investing tends to involve sticking with one or a number of particular themes.

Contrarian investing

Some fund managers will deliberately position their portfolio so that it is at odds with the consensus view. All active managers buy or overweight stocks relative to their benchmark that they expect to rise in price (we consider benchmarks in Chapter 14). However, these investments are still usually made with reference to a benchmark. By contrast, a contrarian investment manager will seek out stocks that have fallen in value significantly and hold these stocks regardless of the sector in which they trade and without reference to a benchmark index. Some people tend to associate contrarian investing with value investing but contrarian investors can also be growth investors. For instance, a growth investor may also sell a stock after a strong run in performance in the belief that the consensus view has driven the stock's price beyond its 'fair value'. Indeed, just as markets undershoot by overreacting to bad news, to the benefit of value-oriented contrarian investors who position themselves against the market consensus, they also overshoot their intrinsic value to the benefit of momentum investors.

Stock picking

Arguably the oldest style of all is that of the pure stock picker. Stock pickers are generally not concerned with larger themes or styles. They simply pick the stocks that they believe will perform well over time. They could choose stocks that they believe will benefit from a particular macroeconomic background, or those that they believe have a good business model, or those that are run by managers and entrepreneurs that they trust and believe in. This bottom-up style of investing is still quite common among traditional brokerage firms. Their portfolios often contain far fewer stocks than most equity fund managers would be comfortable holding and therefore often contain a significant amount of stock specific risk too.

The Dividend Discount Model (DDM)

Using estimates of the dividend yield and the price to earnings ratio along with other accounting-based metrics like dividend cover and the price to book ratio, is one way of analyzing equity markets. To some extent the choice between investing in equities with a high PE ratio rather than those with lower PE ratios, and perhaps high dividend yields, for example, really boils down to one's expectations about future earnings growth – regardless of the investment style of the investor.

There is one model of equity valuation that reveals the importance of dividend growth very clearly. This is the dividend discount model (DDM). This model can help investors form views about the long-term prospects of an individual equity, or equity market. The starting point for this model is the simple assertion that when we buy ordinary shares we are buying a stream of future dividends. The value of an ordinary share is then just the discounted present value of all the dividends to which the shares 'entitle' the investor. Simple!

Today's equity price (P_0) can be written like this:

$$P_0 = \frac{D_1}{(1+r)^1} + \frac{D_2}{(1+r)^2} + \frac{D_3}{(1+r)^3} + \dots + \frac{D_n}{(1+r)^n} \qquad (7.1)$$

where D_1 is the dividend to be paid in one year's time, and D_2 is the dividend to be paid in two years' time etc. These unknown future dividends all have a present value to the investor today, which can be calculated using the 'appropriate' discount rate, r. In this case, r is the return that investors require to compensate them for the risk involved in buying a portion of this dividend stream; it can be thought of as the expected return on this equity or equity market.

The problem that one encounters when trying to apply this model is that it requires us to calculate the present value of every unknown, future dividend payment where these dividend payments are made forever – since ordinary shares do not have a maturity, or redemption, date. This is a great deal of adding up to do! Luckily if we make one simplifying assumption, maths can come to our rescue. If we assume that dividends will grow at a constant rate in the future – which is not too unrealistic an assumption for a broad equity index with many stocks and sectors etc. – then the infinite sum simplifies to the following:

$$P_0 = \frac{D_1}{(r - g)} \tag{7.2}$$

where g represents the constant, real growth rate in dividends. This is a much simpler calculation to undertake. We can add some additional elements to it by considering what *r* comprises. *r* represents investors' expected, or required, return on equities. In real, or inflation adjusted, terms, what should this expected return comprise? As we know, ordinary shares are the main risk capital of the company. Therefore, investors could expect to earn more than could be achieved without risk, for example by investing in an index-linked government bond, since this type of bond does not embody either credit risk (because technically a government cannot become bankrupt[10]) or inflation risk (since the payments are inflation-protected via their link to a consumer price index, such as the Retail Prices Index).

The minimum that an investor would *expect* to receive then would be the real yield represented by a long-dated index-linked bond (*rl*), plus another element for equity risk – this is the equity risk premium (*ERP*). The equity risk premium is defined as the additional return required by equity investors over and above the real, riskless return to compensate them for equity risk. When we substitute (*rl* + *ERP*) for *r* in expression (7.2) we obtain the following:

$$P_0 = \frac{D_1}{(rl + ERP - g)} \tag{7.3}$$

Using some simple maths we can rearrange expression (7.3) to magically reveal the make-up of the mysterious equity risk premium:

$$ERP = \frac{D_1}{P_0} + g - rl \tag{7.4}$$

Expression 7.4 indicates that the equity risk premium is made up of a measure of the dividend yield, plus real dividend growth, minus the real risk-free rate of interest. At any point in time we can observe the dividend yield and the real

---

[10] This proposition has been severely tested in recent years notably by those nations that comprise the periphery of the Euro zone.

yield on a long-dated government bond (at least in the UK and in other developed markets). Therefore, the only additional information that we need to 'reveal' the equity risk premium is an estimate of future real dividend growth.

For example, on 31 December 2010 the FTSE 100 Index (the top 100 companies listed on the LSE) finished the day at 5,900, with a dividend yield of 3.0 per cent, while the real yield on a long-dated index-linked gilt was around 0.7 per cent. If we assume that the dividends paid by companies in the FTSE 100 grow in line with the trend rate of growth of the UK economy, say by 2.25 per cent, then the equity risk premium implied in the market on this date (given our assumptions) can be calculated approximately as:

$$\mathrm{ERP_{FTSE100}} = 3.0\% + 2.25\% - 0.70\% = 4.55\%$$

According to the model, the equity risk premium implied by these market values is 4.55 per cent. But, if an investor believed that the stocks represented by the FTSE 100 will produce greater earnings growth, their estimate of the premium would be higher. Also if they believed that the 0.70 per cent yield on the long-dated index-linked gilt was not representative of the real return required on these bonds, due to distortions in the market at present, and instead believed that this value should over the long term approximate the trend rate of growth of the economy too, then they may use a higher value for this figure, say 2.25 per cent, which would cause the estimated equity risk premium to decline.

We can show how the equity risk premium, dividend growth and risk-free rate assumptions interact by using a DDM matrix, which we have presented in Exhibits 7.9 and 7.10.

Each cell in Exhibit 7.9 represents a level of the FTSE 100 index that would be consistent with a real yield of 0.70 per cent, with the equity risk premium in the first row and the real dividend growth shown in column one. We have

Exhibit 7.9 A DDM matrix (based on real risk-free rate of 0.70%)

		Risk Premium					
	Long term	3.0%	3.5%	4.00%	4.55%	5.0%	5.5%
	1.50%	8045	6556	5531	4720	4214	3766
	1.75%	9077	7224	6000	5057	4481	3978
Real Growth	2.00%	10412	8045	6556	5446	4784	4214
	2.25%	–	9077	7224	5900	5130	4481
	2.50%	–	–	8045	6436	5531	4784
	2.75%	–	–	–	7080	6000	5130
	3.00%	–	–	–	–	6556	5531

Exhibit 7.10   A DDM matrix (based on real risk free rate of 2.25%)

		Risk Premium					
	Long term	2.0%	2.5%	3.00%	3.50%	4.0%	4.5%
	1.50%	6436	5446	4720	4165	3726	3371
	1.75%	7080	5900	5057	4425	3933	3540
Real Growth	2.00%	7867	6436	5446	4720	4165	3726
	2.25%	–	7080	5900	5057	4425	3933
	2.50%	–	–	6436	5446	4720	4165
	2.75%	–	–	–	5900	5057	4425
	3.00%	–	–	–	–	5446	4720

highlighted the value at the end of 2010 of the FTSE 100 that was consistent with a risk premium of 4.55 per cent and real dividend growth of 2.25 per cent. However, if an investor were to take the view that real dividend growth would be 2.5 per cent in the future then, on an unchanged risk premium, the implied fair value of the market would be 6,436, and therefore might represent a buying opportunity for the investor. Conversely, if the investor felt that the FTSE 100's real dividend growth would be 2.25 per cent over the long term, but also that they wanted 5.5 per cent per annum compensation for the risk embodied in equity markets, only if the market were to fall to 4,481, would the investor find the market attractive. And hence this investor may view the market as being overpriced, that is, offering insufficient reward.

In Exhibit 7.10 we have produced the same table, but where the real risk-free rate is assumed to be 2.25 per cent, instead of 0.70 per cent. When compared with Exhibit 7.9 for every given amount of real dividend growth, the implied equity risk premium is lower. In Exhibit 7.10 a risk premium of 3 per cent would have been consistent with the FTSE's index value of 5,900 at the end of 2010, assuming that real dividend growth would be of 2.25 per cent per annum.

The DDM is a useful tool for analyzing equity markets, although it is by no means a universally accepted tool of analysis. Its strength is its simplicity and the fact that it focuses attention very clearly on dividend growth, something that all equity investors wish to access. However, as far as critics are concerned, its weakness is also this simplicity and in particular the assumption that dividends will grow at a constant rate in the future, not least in line with the trend rate of economic growth.

Necessary adjustments to the DDM model

What if firms increase dividends temporarily? If firms increase dividends in response to a temporary increase in profitability, then the dividend yield will also rise temporarily giving the impression that the available risk premium is larger than it really is. To overcome this, users of the model try to take account of the fluctuations in the equity market dividend yield.

What if firms don't pay dividends? The UK equity market is fairly unique. UK equity investors expect firms to pay dividends. In other equity markets many firms pay little or no dividend. This means the dividend yield will be low, and that investors will need to sell shares to create a regular cash flow for themselves (if it is a regular cash flow that they need). This problem can be overcome by adjusting the model to focus on earnings (profitability) rather than on dividends.

What about share buy-backs? In some equity markets, for example the US market, firms may prefer to return cash to investors by buying back shares rather than by paying a dividend. This has the effect of giving the impression that the cash flow from the company to shareholders is low if only the dividend yield is considered. To overcome this problem, the DDM can be adjusted to take account of not only the dividend income that is paid to investors but also the cash returned under share buy-back schemes.

The professional user of the DDM will make various adjustments to the model to deal with issues like these, but the basic principle remains: the value of an equity, or an equity market, is simply the sum of the present value of all the income that that company or market will generate into perpetuity.

The equity risk premium

The DDM provides us with the additional return required by equity investors over and above the real, riskless return to compensate them for assuming equity risk, rather than the additional return that will actually be achieved. The *expected* additional return, derived by the DDM, is an *ex ante* measure of the ERP. The *actual* ERP achieved is an *ex post* ERP. And of course what you expect is not necessarily what you will get!

Equity risk has been well rewarded in the long run. According to contemporary sources,[11] the *ex post* ERP generated by the UK stock market between 1900 and 2010 has averaged just under 4 per cent per annum. However, these figures disguise the fact that the *ex post* ERP can fluctuate

---

[11] See the *Credit Suisse Global Investment Returns Sourcebook 2011* p.160 Copyright © 2011; Elroy Dimson, Paul Marsh and Mike Staunton, *Triumph of the Optimists: 101 Years of Global Investment Returns*, Princeton University Press (2002); and *Barclays Capital Equity Gilt Study 2011*, p. 92.

dramatically from year to year. For instance, in 2008 UK equities under-performed UK government bonds by 38.4 per cent. In 1975 they outper-formed by a massive 80.8 per cent![12] Moreover, the equity market can experience both long upturns, or bull markets, and long downturns, or bear markets.

By way of example, Exhibit 7.11 sets out the duration and magnitude of ten bear markets experienced by the US equity market over the last 100 years. This exhibit makes it abundantly clear that the ex-ante and ex-post equity risk premium are often very different.

Exhibit 7.11   Ten US equity bear markets over the last 100 years

Start	End	Months	S&P 500 % change
Nov 1919	Aug 1921	22	−46.6
Sep 1929	Jul 1932	34	−89.0
Mar 1937	Apr 1942	62	−60.0
May 1946	Jun 1949	37	−29.6
Aug 1956	Oct 1957	15	−21.5
Nov 1968	May 1970	18	−36.1
Jan 1973	Oct 1974	21	−48.2
Nov 1980	Aug 1982	20	−27.1
Mar 2000	Oct 2002	31	−49.1
Oct 2007	Mar 2009	17	−56.8
Average		27.7	−46.4

Sources: LMCM (2009) and Russell Napier, *Anatomy of the Bear*, Petersfield, UK, Harriman House (2007). The bear markets of 1919–1921 and 1929–1932 are based on the movements of the Dow Jones Industrial Average Index.

In addition, looking even further afield, a number of prominent equity markets around the world have suffered prolonged periods of negative real equity returns – some as long as 70 years. In other words the ERP is just that – a risk premium or a *potential* reward for assuming equity risk – it is certainly not a given.

To further illustrate this point, Exhibit 7.12 brings our analysis back to the UK and shows the real returns from UK equities against bonds and cash by decade between 1900 and 2010. The two best consecutive decades were

[12] *Credit Suisse Global Investment Returns Sourcebook 2011* p. 160 Copyright © 2011; Elroy Dimson, Paul Marsh and Mike Staunton, *Triumph of the Optimists: 101 Years of Global Investment Returns*, Princeton University Press (2002).

the 1980s and 1990s. Unfortunately the asset allocation decisions of many institutional as well as retail investors were heavily influenced by this experience. Needless to say, the performance of the UK and other developed economy equity markets over the noughties was not what most equity investors either expected or wanted.

Exhibit 7.12 Annualized, total real returns from UK equities versus bonds and cash: 1900–2010

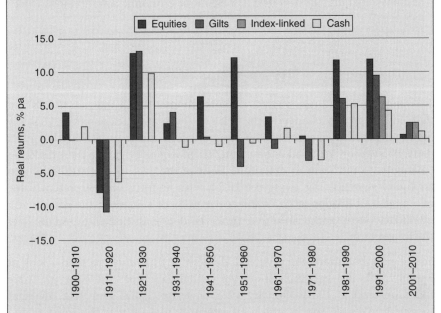

Source: Barclays Capital Equity Gilt Study 2011

The big imponderable is whether assuming equity risk will be as well rewarded in the future as it has been in the long-term past. Most commentators suspect that 3 per cent rather than 4 per cent per annum will be the long run *average ex-post* ERP.[13] However, much depends on the macroeconomic backdrop. If we are headed for a rerun of the high and volatile

---

[13] There is little hard evidence to support this view of the equity risk premium, but some evidence is presented in A. Clare, R. Priestley and S Thomas, 'Reports of β's death are premature: evidence from the UK stock market', *Journal of Banking and Finance*, Volume 22, Number 9, pp. 1207–29 (1998), which suggests that the *ex ante* risk premium on UK equities should be around 3.5 per cent per annum.

inflation of the 1970s then equity markets would probably perform poorly, even though equities represent a claim on the real economy, and thus should represent a hedge against inflation. However, as we explained in Chapter 4, as volatile inflation can damage the real economy, that is, jobs, profits and so on, equity prices may fall over such a period as the equity risk premium on equities rises. On the other hand, if we are heading for a period of Japan-style deflation and stagnation, equities will also struggle, since real profit growth will almost certainly be weak in this sort of environment. Equities generally perform best in periods of economic stability and rising prosperity.

Equity returns – the importance of dividends

The return on an ordinary share is a combination of the capital gain or loss that may arise from any change in the price of the share after purchase, plus the dividend payments received over the period in question. Given that on a daily, or even on an annual, basis, market movements, rather than dividend payments, would seem to determine most of the gain or loss attributable to an equity shareholding, using the DDM, with its focus on the present value of a stream of dividends, to establish the value of a share or the market as a whole may seem counterintuitive. However, dividends matter, especially over the longer term.

To see how important the dividend element of this return is, take a look at Exhibit 7.13. The two lines show the capital gain from the FTSE All Share Index, rebased to 100 in January 1965, and the capital gain with dividend income reinvested, that is, the total return. As the chart shows, over a long period of time this reinvested income really adds up! Indeed, £100 invested in the All Share Index with dividends reinvested until the end of 2010 would have been worth £12,000. Without the reinvested dividend the £100 would have been worth only £2,000.

Over the very long term this dividend reinvestment is even more significant. If £100 had been invested in the UK equity market during the 111 year period between 1900 and 2010, this sum, without dividends reinvested would have grown to £12,655 in nominal terms and £180 in real terms. The equivalent numbers for an investment in gilts would have been £49 and £1 – yes, £1! However, with gross dividends reinvested,[14] the respective numbers would

---

[14] Notwithstanding the fact that dividends reinvested by UK pension funds have been net, not gross, since 1997.

Exhibit 7.13   Capital gains versus total returns since January 1965

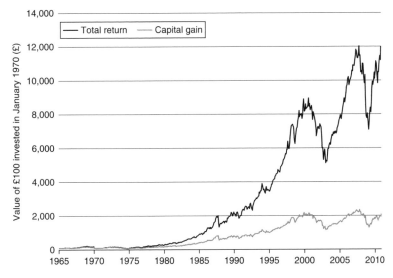

Source: Thomson Financial

have been 134 times greater at £1.7m and £24,133.[15] Although real dividend growth has, at 0.46 per cent per annum, just kept ahead of inflation, being invested in the 50 highest yielding stocks within the UK's top 100 companies between 1900 and 2010 would have delivered an annual return of 10.9 per cent against 9.5 per cent for the top 100 as a whole and 8 per cent for the 50 lowest yielding.[16]

In fact, the source of these statistics concludes that:

> *The longer the investment horizon, the more important is dividend income. For the seriously long-term investor, the value of a portfolio corresponds closely to the present value of dividends.*[17]

This explains why we use the DDM, with its focus on the present value of dividends.

---

[15] Barclays Capital Equity Gilt Study 2011 p. 95.

[16] *Credit Suisse Global Investment Returns Sourcebook 2011* p.160 Copyright © 2011; Elroy Dimson, Paul Marsh and Mike Staunton, *Triumph of the Optimists: 101 Years of Global Investment Returns*, Princeton University Press (2002).

[17] *Credit Suisse Global Investment Returns Sourcebook 2011* p.160 Copyright © 2011; Elroy Dimson, Paul Marsh and Mike Staunton, *Triumph of the Optimists: 101 Years of Global Investment Returns*, Princeton University Press (2002).

Longer term equity valuation metrics

We'll finish this chapter by looking briefly at two long-term equity valuation metrics. These are both reckoned by some investors to be good indicators of long-term equity market value. They are Tobin's Q-ratio and Shiller's real cyclically-adjusted PE ratio (CAPE). They build upon the PB and PE ratios considered earlier. Tobin's Q is similar to the PB ratio in that it measures the ratio of the value of the equity market and the net asset value (NAV) of the underlying companies that comprise the market. If the ratio is one, then the market value of the companies in aggregate equals their NAV. If more than one, then this indicates that it would be cheaper to buy the net assets of these companies rather than to buy their shares in the market. Professor Robert Shiller's CAPE which is shown in Exhibit 7.14 is derived in the same way as the PE ratio we considered earlier but where 'P' represents the *real* price of the equity market and where the 'E' is a ten-year moving average of the market's *real* earnings. Deflating the real equity price by a moving average of real earnings irons out the short-term volatility in this indicator over time.

Research has shown that the higher these ratios are, the poorer subsequent equity returns will be over the next ten years or so and vice versa. In fact,

Exhibit 7.14   Robert Shiller's cyclically adjusted PE ratio (CAPE) for the US equity market

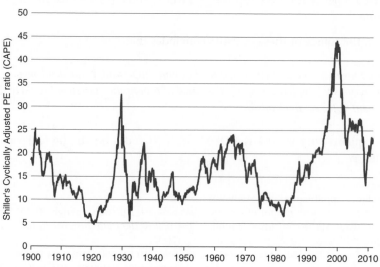

Source: http://www.econ.yale.edu/~shiller/data.htm.

drawing on US equity market data from 1900 to 2008,[18] in the case of Tobin's Q-ratio, if the equity market is trading above one or, in the case of the Shiller real cyclically-adjusted PE ratio, the equity market is trading much above its long-run average real cyclically-adjusted PE ratio, then subsequent equity returns will be poor. This is well illustrated by the fact that, as a consequence of the equity market becoming severely overvalued on both measures (and most others besides) in 1999, when the dot.com boom was in full swing, equities were the worst performing asset class in both the UK and US by some margin (with both also underperforming inflation) during the ten year period from 1999 to 2008.

Key points

- As the main risk capital of the company, the returns attributable to the ordinary shareholders are subordinated to those of all of the company's other investors and stakeholders.
- A disproportionate amount of the total value of global equity markets comprises a relatively small number of dominant sectors and large global companies.
- Financial ratios help investors compare the growth prospects of a market, sector or stock relative to another or against its own history.
- Equity markets often categorize shares as being either growth or value stocks. Growth stocks tend to trade with a high price to earnings and price to book ratio and low dividend yield relative to the rest of the market, while value stocks display the opposite characteristics.
- Reinvested dividend income is by far the most important source of return for equities in the long run. In fact, reinvested dividend income and equity market valuations tend to determine subsequent total equity market returns.

---

[18] See the Barclays Capital Equity Gilt Study 2009, pp. 5–8.

Chapter 8

Real Estate: Putting Your Faith in Bricks and Mortar

Learning outcomes

- Appreciate the distinguishing features of real estate.
- Appreciate the case for investing in real estate.
- Know the means by which to gain an exposure to real estate.
- Appreciate the diversity of the real estate market.
- Appreciate the case for globally diversifying into real estate.

Introduction

Real estate[1] matters. From an economic perspective it matters because it represents about a quarter of annual fixed investment in the UK. It also generates over 10 per cent of the UK's tax revenues. Moreover, the universe of investible commercial property in the UK is worth over £200bn, making it the fourth largest in the world after the US, Japan and Germany.[2] From a business perspective it matters too because it accounts for about 30 per cent of companies' tangible assets and is the second biggest revenue cost for firms after labour. However, most importantly for institutional investors, like pension schemes, real estate matters because it has been one of the top performing asset classes over the longer term

---

[1] We use the terms 'real estate' and 'property' interchangeably.
[2] Source: IPD Global Index 31 December 2009. The estimated value of the UK real estate market at 31 December 2009 was US$341.7bn.

and has a low correlation with the returns of most other asset classes.[3] Yet, since 1991, the average percentage of defined benefit (DB) pension scheme allocations to real estate has been in single digits, in stark contrast to its popularity in the 1970s and 1980s when it was considered to be an ideal hedge against inflation.

Distinguishing features

Real estate is unique among the more traditional, or mainstream, asset classes[4] because it has a number of key distinguishing features – some that work for it, some that work against it. These are:

- **Heterogeneity** – given that each property is unique in terms of location, structure and design, the real estate market can be segmented into an enormous number of individual markets. Because of this and the fact that there is a wide dispersion of returns not only between but also within the various real estate sectors, most of the value derived from real estate investment, around 80 per cent in fact, is attributable to selecting the 'right' building(s), rather than being in the 'right' country and/or sector. So, unlike with equity investment, for example, stock selection is usually viewed as being more important than sector allocation.
- **Illiquidity** – owing to its heterogeneity, real estate is not traded in a centralized market place or on an exchange. By contrast, most money market instruments, bonds and equities are traded 'remotely' in markets or on exchanges linked via computer feeds, rather than on a physical trading floor. As a consequence, real estate is a highly illiquid asset. This illiquidity extends to both making purchases and sales and results in annual turnover rates (annual real estate sales as a percentage of the total real estate investment market) of less than 20 per cent for direct investment in real estate in the UK. Moreover, this illiquidity is periodically exacerbated by investors either piling into the asset class at the same time, as in the mid-noughties, or simultaneously rushing for the exit as in 2007/8.
- **Valuation** – real estate's heterogeneity, illiquidity and the fact that the price at which many real estate transactions take place is not made public, means that continuous and reliable price data is unavailable, thereby making the markets' assessment of value unclear. In practice, valuations are made in

---

[3] Correlation measures the extent to which the returns of two asset classes, say equities and real estate, move together (or not). The lower this co-movement, the greater the level of diversification achieved by combining these asset classes. We cover correlation and diversification in Chapter 9.

[4] Though given its near absence in many DB pension scheme portfolios, many industry practitioners and commentators treat real estate as an alternative asset class.

relation to comparable properties, recent market transactions or, more typically, by discounting the often complex expected net cash flows attributable to a property from leasing it. While valuing a property by discounting the future net cash flows attributable to it means it is no different in principle from the methodology applied to the valuation of most other asset classes, there are many elements and uncertainties that uniquely apply to real estate cash flows. On the revenue side, there is the need to forecast vacancy rates and the risk of tenant default, which, obviously, becomes more complex when dealing with a large shopping centre with, say, 200 tenants. Then on the cost side, there are the various maintenance and operating costs and fees that need to be taken into account. Finally, there's the perennial problem, applicable to the valuation of most assets classes, of setting an appropriate discount rate to be applied to these cash flows. Real estate price indices, constructed by property index providers, such as Investment Property Databank (IPD), on a sample of regularly valued properties, exist as a guide.

- **High transactions costs** – owing to its heterogeneity, illiquidity and the way in which it is valued, real estate transactions, unlike those assets traded on an exchange, incur substantial transactions costs, such as professional fees and stamp duty land tax. In the UK, these typically amount to about 6 per cent on purchase and 1.5 per cent on sale, not to mention other costs such as property search costs. That is the time and money spent finding the right property in the right location and at the right price is a consequence of the heterogeneous nature of real estate and it not being traded in a price transparent centralized marketplace.

- **High ongoing costs** – unlike most other asset classes, an investment in real estate also has high ongoing costs, such as maintenance, management and operating costs and fees on rent reviews, valuations and lettings, etc. Having said this, in the UK, the tenant is usually responsible for repairing the building and for the majority of its running costs.

- **Indivisible** – if accessed directly, real estate can only be purchased in large discrete units. This renders diversification difficult unless a considerable investment is being made in the asset class. However, real estate can also be accessed indirectly. That is, an investment can be pooled with that of other investors – making diversification much easier.

- **Subject to deterioration and obsolescence** – buildings, more so than the land on which they are situated, can deteriorate or become obsolete. However, buildings can be improved through 'active management', whether by refurbishment, changing the building's use, extending or improving a lease or even redevelopment. This is a valuable feature of property investment, as, for example, try as hard as you like, you won't be able to improve the basic features of a gilt!

- **Land is finite** – as Mark Twain once said, 'buy land, they're not making it anymore.' Unlike most other asset classes, the supply of land is finite and its availability can be further restricted by legislation and local planning regulations. However, to counter this, brownfield sites – land mainly in the industrial heartlands that was formerly thought of as being unfit or uneconomic for redevelopment – and derelict land have steadily been developed, with urban regeneration also becoming an established theme.

Freehold and leasehold

In England and Wales, an interest in property can either take the form of a freehold or leasehold interest.

Freehold

The freeholder of a property has the right to use or dispose of the property as they wish, albeit subject to legislation, local planning laws or any covenants that specifically apply to the property.

Leasehold

The freeholder can create a lesser interest in the property known as a leasehold interest. The leaseholder, or tenant, to whom this interest is conferred, has the right to use the property for a specific period subject to the terms of the lease and the payment of rent. Unless prevented from doing so under the terms of the lease, the leaseholder can also create a sublease and act as the head lessee to a sub-tenant.

Once the lease has expired, the freeholder assumes full rights over the property.

The case for real estate

Most people tend to think of real estate as simply comprising residential housing, offices, shops and industrial buildings. Important as these sectors are, the real estate universe is incredibly diverse in its composition and global reach. Moreover, as intimated earlier, it can be accessed both directly and indirectly – in the latter case via a range of investment media.

However, before looking at the real estate universe and the various ways in which an exposure to real estate can be obtained, let's take a look at its key attractions:

- **An attractive income stream** – an investment in real estate is principally an investment in a relatively high and stable income stream, with the potential for income growth, given the standard practice, at least in the UK, for rents to be revised upwards-only with five-year reviews. Rental income yields are typically a little higher than the yields available from gilts of an equivalent term, though much depends on the expected growth in rental income and the level of real estate prices. As with equity dividend yields, the higher the expected rate of (rental) income growth and the level of (real estate) prices, the lower the initial yield. Indeed, the yield compression that accompanied peak real estate values in early-2007 saw rental yields dip below gilt yields. In the longer run, while UK commercial property yields have averaged a shade under 7 per cent per annum, rental income growth, unlike equity dividend growth, has tended to underperform inflation. For a long lease granted to a high quality tenant in an established location, this income stream looks similar to that of a long-dated index-linked bond, suitably adjusted to reflect the creditworthiness of the tenant and the illiquid nature of the investment. Equally, however, where a short lease is granted to a low quality tenant in a less well-established location, this cash flow can more closely resemble that of a stream of equity dividends.

As income typically accounts for around 75+ per cent of long-run real estate returns in the UK, the return attributable to capital growth is usually quite modest, despite capital values being positively correlated with economic growth. Crucially, the long-run total return from UK real estate has typically outperformed inflation and gilts though it has underperformed equities. That said, real estate was the top performing traditional UK asset class of the noughties.[5]

When making an investment in real estate, UK pension funds tend to focus on commercial property, rather than on residential property, because of the former's relatively secure and reliable cash flow. By contrast, the returns from residential housing are largely based around changes in capital values. This is in sharp contrast to countries such as the US, Japan, France, Germany, the Netherlands and Switzerland, where institutional investment in residential housing is popular. That said, prime residential housing in central London at one end of the spectrum and social housing at the other are two areas of the UK residential housing market in which UK DB schemes increasingly have an interest – the latter in particular, given the relatively secure inflation-linked cash flows generated by this sector of the real estate market.

- **Tangibility** – the traditional 'bricks and mortar' qualities of real estate are attractive to investors from a capital security perspective and the scope this potentially provides to enhance a property's value through active management, as outlined earlier. Moreover, if untenanted, the building can always be realized.

---

[5] IPD / Factset. Data for the period 1 January 2000 to 31 December 2010.

- **Low volatility**[6] – notwithstanding the dramatic upturn in the volatility of real estate prices in the late-noughties, real estate has historically generated less volatile returns than those of other asset classes. However, the caveat here is that, unlike those other asset classes, such as bonds and equities, most of which are traded in public markets, real estate prices are not marked-to-market on a daily basis, let alone in real time. Rather, real estate is valued periodically, usually monthly, by independent valuers who use principles laid down in the Red Book of the Royal Institution of Chartered Surveyors. This means that the variation in prices is smoothed over time. If bonds and equities were valued by taking their month-end values from one month to the next, rather than their daily closing prices, then the volatility of bond and equity prices would be significantly less than currently reported.
- **Low correlation with other asset classes** – real estate tends to perform differently from other asset types, which makes it valuable as a way of diversifying risk. This principally derives from the recurrent but irregular upswings and downswings in the property cycle, triggered by oscillations in economic growth, to which the property cycle is closely correlated, and amplified by time lags in property construction. These cycles tend to run for eight to ten years but are highly variable in length and amplitude. However, the low correlation of real estate returns with those of other asset classes are flattered to a degree because of the artificial smoothing of property prices resulting from periodic valuations.
- **Sustainability** – many aspects of the real estate market are now managed on sustainable lines, with, as we noted earlier, development increasingly taking place on brownfield sites and more sustainably sourced materials being used in the construction process allied to more environmentally-aware construction methodologies.[7]

Investing in real estate

As we noted above, the real estate universe is incredibly diverse in nature and can be accessed both directly and indirectly via a range of investment media. We'll now look at the way in which an exposure to real estate can be achieved and then each of the sectors in which pension schemes invest.

Investment vehicles

There are essentially three main ways in which pension schemes can achieve an exposure to real estate: directly, indirectly via unlisted funds and publicly-listed shares, and via derivatives.

---

[6] We cover volatility in Chapter 9.

[7] We consider the importance of adopting sustainable investment policies in Chapter 16.

- **Direct investment** – investing directly in real estate, via a segregated mandate, has many advantages: a bespoke portfolio, direct control of the assets within the portfolio and scope for active management. However, to do so in a diversified manner, so as to avoid the specific risks attached to individual properties, requires a minimum investment of around £100m (£200m if looking to invest globally). In addition, there are high management and information costs.
- **Indirect investment** – for those pension schemes (the vast majority) with substantially less than £100m to invest, gaining an exposure to real estate via indirect investment, by pooling their investment with others in a diversified property portfolio, is a more realistic proposition. It also provides the investor with much improved liquidity. However, pooled investors do not have direct control over the property portfolio in which they invest and the actions of their fellow pooled investors can sometimes negate some of these advantages. For instance, the improved liquidity associated with pooled investment is lost if a sizeable number of investors simultaneously decide to redeem their investment, as in 2007/8. We consider this within the operation of pooled funds below.

There are a number of different indirect investment options open to pension funds including: unlisted property funds, Fund-of-Funds (FoFs), multi-manager funds, publicly-traded Real Estate Investment Trusts (REITs) and REIT funds, property company shares and property investment trusts. Let's look at each of these briefly in turn.

- o *Unlisted property funds* – these pooled investment funds are typically categorized as either balanced or specialist. Balanced funds, as the name suggests, diversify across a wide range of real estate sectors and often geographically. Specialist funds, however, have a specific geographical or sector focus. Examples include a focus on shopping centres, healthcare, student accommodation, retail warehouse parks, prime residential property, urban regeneration and sustainable development.

Unlisted property funds are unitized, or divided into shares or units, with each share or unit conferring an equally proportional share of the fund's net asset value (NAV). These shares/units are usually priced daily, based on the most recent valuation of the properties held in the portfolio.

Balanced funds typically adopt an 'open-ended' structure. That is, they normally permit daily entry to and exit from the fund, subject to the balance between investors moving into and those moving out of the fund. Given the illiquid nature of the fund's underlying assets, exiting the fund may, on occasion, be subject to restrictions, as was the case with many funds during the very difficult markets in 2007/8. In fact, many investors had to wait for up to six months to redeem their investment.

Although each unit/share will reflect the net asset value (NAV) per unit/share of the fund, the fund will typically be dual priced – that is, with different prices for entry and exit. The difference in these prices is termed a bid/offer spread. This reflects the transactions costs incurred by the fund in buying and selling the underlying assets and to manage the fund's cash flow as investors move into and out of the fund. Alternatively, entry to and exit from the fund may be based on a single price, albeit with an implicit bid/offer spread built into the 'single price', effectively making it dual priced! Given that this bid/offer spread can be in the order of 6 per cent, further serves to highlight the long-term nature of an investment in property.

The offer price is the price at which investors buy the shares/units and the bid price is that at which they sell. Depending upon the balance between those seeking to buy and those seeking to sell, these funds often attempt to redress the balance by periodically adapting their pricing basis. That is, they tend to adopt an offer pricing basis if there are more buyers than sellers and a bid basis if there are more sellers than buyers.

A fund will usually price on an offer basis when cash flows are positive. Pricing a fund on an offer basis means that buyers pay the maximum permissible price to access the fund, while those redeeming their shares/units receive a more generous price than the minimum possible bid price. A bid basis, however, which seeks to stem a tide of redemptions from the fund, gives sellers the minimum permissible price, while a more generous offer price seeks to entice buyers. If an investor buys into the fund while it is priced on an offer basis and sells out when priced on a bid basis they will incur the full bid/offer spread. However, if they were to buy when the fund is priced on a bid basis and sell when priced on an offer basis, then the bid/offer spread would be substantially less. In many cases the spread can be mitigated by 'matching' buyers and sellers so that the full costs of buying and selling do not have to be met. Many fund managers do this by managing a 'box' of units/shares, whereby redeemed shares/units are held by the fund manager in anticipation of potential buyers. However, in practice, this is not always possible.

Suffice to say, the whole purpose of adapting the pricing basis is to ensure that all investors are treated as fairly as possible – not least loyal long-term investors who should not be disadvantaged by letting new investors into the fund too cheaply or paying too generous a price to those redeeming their shares/units.

By contrast, specialist funds usually adopt a 'closed-ended' structure. Unlike an open-ended structure, the fund will have a defined size at inception and a finite term, usually between five and seven years. What this means in practice is that investors cannot move into and out of the fund until the fund is wound up at its expiry date, unless a seller can be matched with a buyer. However, the key benefit of this structure is that the fund manager can take a longer-term view of the market by not having to manage the balance between investors buying and those selling shares/units and the implications this would otherwise have on the fund's cash flow. Additionally, these funds can, and usually do, employ gearing, or leverage, to enhance potential returns.

o *Fund of Funds (FoFs) and multi-manager* – because there are more than 1,500 unlisted real estate funds globally and because investors appreciate that a single fund manager cannot have expertise in all sectors of the real estate market, the popularity of FoFs and multi-manager funds has grown considerably in recent years.

Both FoFs and multi-manager funds aim to sort the wheat from the chaff by actively selecting and monitoring those real estate funds, listed shares and managers that best meet their risk and return criteria. This not only requires an extensive knowledge of the real estate funds market and an in-depth appreciation of local market practices and legal structures but also the qualities that define a good fund manager.[8] For the investor, the FoFs and multi-manager approaches mean even greater diversification and professional management, albeit at the cost of an additional layer of fees for the due diligence and ongoing management of the portfolio.

FoFs differ from multi-manager funds in several respects. FoFs are particularly suitable for smaller institutional investors and adopt 'off the peg' discretionary management, whereby all investors invest in the same mix of underlying funds. By contrast, multi-manager funds usually require an investment in excess of £25m given the bespoke nature of the portfolio constructed for the investor, which will take account of the investor's specific risk/reward objective and, indeed, other criteria, such as a focus on sustainability.

o *Real Estate Investment Trusts (REITs) and REIT funds* – a REIT is a property company that manages a real estate portfolio and operates in accordance with REIT regulations. The REIT regulations are intended to ensure the company is primarily engaged in property investment, rather than in development or other non-property related activities with restrictions placed on the amount of borrowing, or gearing. Examples of property companies that have converted themselves into REITs include British Land and Land Securities.

While REITs themselves were introduced in the UK in January 2007, they are not exclusive to the UK. North America, Australia and Holland all launched REITs a long time ago, while in the past few years countries such as France, Hong Kong, Italy and Japan have launched similar vehicles.

---

[8] We consider what makes a good fund manager in some detail in Chapter 18.

REITs can be very tax efficient because the property company pays no corporation or capital gains tax on the profits made from property investment, but must pay out at least 90 per cent of its property income to shareholders. Dividends from REITs are treated as income to the investor but pension funds can register to receive gross rather than net dividends.[9]

As REITs are listed property companies that trade on a stock exchange they are subject to continual market scrutiny, making them very transparent. They are also generally very liquid though the price of this liquidity is that the share price will usually differ from the company's Net Asset Value (NAV), that is, the value attributed to the underlying properties. If there are more investors seeking to buy than those seeking to sell the shares, as in 2007 and 2010, then the shares can often trade at a premium to their NAV, if the converse is true, as it was in 2008/9, then the shares will trade at a discount to the NAV.

As a consequence of being listed, REITs are significantly more volatile than direct property investments or unlisted property funds and in the short run perform more like equities than property. However, in the long-term, their performance is more closely correlated with property than with equities. As such they can often act as a good leading indicator of the commercial bricks-and-mortar property market.

- o *Property company shares* – the shares of those listed property companies that cannot or do not choose to convert to a REIT, trade alongside REITs on a number of stock exchanges. Like REITs, property company shares tend to perform like equities in the short term but in the long run typically perform in line with the real estate market.

- o *Property investment trusts* – also known as property investment companies, property investment trusts invest in real estate directly and indirectly. They are very similar to REITs in that they are listed companies, offer daily liquidity and also trade at premiums and discounts to their NAV.

- **Derivatives** – property derivatives, which principally comprise total return swaps and forward contracts, are based on country and sector indices constructed by the IPD and other established property index providers. While it is rare for pension schemes to gain access to the real estate market via derivatives, asset allocators and property fund managers sometimes use the property derivatives markets as a means by which to gain a market exposure to real estate or hedge an underlying exposure to the asset class. Trading in property derivatives is popular in the US, Japan and Australia, while the UK dominates property derivative trading within Europe.

---

[9] This contrasts with UK equity dividends that are paid to pension funds net of tax.

The property market risk premium

In Chapter 7 we looked at how to derive the value of an equity, or indeed, the whole equity market. We argued that one or the other was simply the sum of all the discounted future dividend payments that the equity (market) could be expected to generate over time. Then by making some simplifying assumptions about dividend growth we showed that we could reveal the equity risk premium (ERP) – the prospective outperformance of equities of a risk-free asset such as government bonds – to be:

$$ERP = DY + g - rl$$

In other words the equity risk premium can be thought of as comprising three elements the current dividend yield (DY); the real, constant growth rate of future dividends (g); and the yield on a long-dated, inflation-proofed risk-free bond. For the UK this would be the yield on a long-dated index-linked gilt (rl). While we acknowledge that there are problems with this simplification of such a complex phenomenon, it serves as a good rule of thumb for equity market valuation. For example, the ERP was very low prior to the collapse of the high tech bubble, indicating that outperformance of UK equities over UK government bonds would be commensurately low, as has turned out to be the case. However, can this model be applied to the valuation of property?

The answer to this question is yes. Real estate is simply another asset that produces a cash flow; in this case rental income and not dividend income. When an investor buys commercial property or buys into a commercial property fund, then they are buying the right to a stream of future income. There are some tweaks that need to be applied to this discounted cash flow view of property valuation, but essentially the same principles hold. This also means that by using similar logic, we can define a property market risk premium (PRP) that can be applied to the analysis of the broader market:

$$PRP = RY + gr - rl$$

where RY is rental yield; and gr represents real rental growth over time. To identify the property market risk premium then, all we need to do is to estimate, or make an educated guess, at the likely growth in real rental income over time, since we already know the other two elements of the right hand side of the PRP formula. When calculating the ERP, it is normally assumed that dividend growth is closely correlated with the real growth of the underlying economy from which companies derive their earnings. However, when it comes to commercial property, many analysts assume that real rental growth will be zero (or close to it) on average over time. This does not mean that they expect rental growth to be zero, but instead that they expect it to grow in line with inflation over long periods of time. If this is true (and we make no claims here to its validity one way or another) then the PRP expression is relatively simple: for the UK commercial property market it is simply the difference between the current rental yield and the yield on a long-dated index-linked gilt, since gr is equal to zero.

In Exhibit 8.1 we present the historic value of the property risk premium for the entire UK commercial property market plus its main sub-divisions – retail, offices and industrial – going back to 1990. The chart shows that at the beginning of this period the premia on offer were very low. This period of very low premia was followed by a property market crash. The main commercial property index for the UK market fell by around 10 per cent in the early 1990s, with the offices sector falling most, by almost 15 per cent from peak to trough. The collapse in prices propelled the PRP up as capital values fell indicating that property represented much better forward-looking value by 1993/94. The UK property market risk premia remained high through most of the 1990s, but began to decline once again during the noughties and the credit bubble – a period when credit was cheap for those wishing to buy residential and commercial property. Following the collapse of Lehman

Exhibit 8.1   UK commercial property risk premia

Source: IPD.

Brothers in September 2008, property risk premia rose once again as property prices once more collapsed. So those buying commercial property in 2006/07 when the property market risk premium was low once again, experienced significant losses on their property portfolios. Despite the subsequent recovery in the market, by the end of 2010 the premium on offer still seemed to be quite attractive compared to history. However, please take note, we are not offering investment advice here, just a form of analysis that we believe is a useful metric which can help investors decide when to and when not to buy commercial property.

Investment styles

Just as an equity fund manager may employ one of a number of investment styles, such as value or growth, so too do real estate managers in managing unlisted real estate funds. These styles can broadly be divided into core, value-added and opportunistic.

A core investment style typically focuses on investing in a diversified manner in mature sectors and countries, employing little or no gearing to potentially enhance returns and deriving a high proportion of the fund's return through income. Value-added, however, takes a more holistic approach to countries and sectors; usually employs some leverage; and returns a balance of income and capital appreciation. In addition, value, unlike core, also usually has a moderate exposure to property redevelopment projects. By contrast, an opportunistic investment style adopts a highly focused approach to individual markets and sectors; usually employs considerable gearing (borrowing to invest); has a high exposure to development and active management; and, as a consequence, derives much of its return from capital appreciation.

Real estate market sectors

The UK real estate market comprises commercial property, residential property and other sectors, such as leisure complexes, agricultural property and infrastructure. We now cover each of these in turn before looking at an area of the real estate market that is increasingly being picked up on pension scheme radars – that of liability-linked income (LLI) assets.

- **Commercial property** – commercial property is the mainstay of the real estate market and comprises freehold and long leasehold interests in high street shops, supermarkets, shopping centres, retail parks, retail warehouse parks, offices, business parks and industrial storage and distribution warehouses. These are, in turn, categorized into three broad categories: retail, offices and industrial.

    o *Retail* – at over 50 per cent of the UK real estate market by value, retail real estate is the largest sector of the UK commercial property market. Retail comprises shops, shopping centres, retail parks and retail warehouse parks and in the UK is split evenly by value between these three sectors. Of course, the three big risks of investing in retail property are its dependence on consumer spending, locational risk and, of course, the constant threat posed by Internet shopping. In the latter case, if shoppers' focus is directed elsewhere, then the value of the property can decline quickly.

    o *Offices* – represent 30 per cent by value of the UK real estate market, 60 per cent of which are located in the City of London and London's West End. Given the London office market's reliance on the economically sensitive finance and business services industries, offices are the most cyclical area of the UK real estate market. Therefore, diversification is achieved by combining London offices with regional offices that are not so reliant on the UK's finance and business services sector.

    o *Industrial* – this sector of the UK commercial property market, which comprises leases on industrial parks, industrial warehouses and distribution centres, accounts for 15 per cent of the UK real estate market.

- **Residential** – as noted earlier, although UK pension funds have tended not to focus on residential housing, as evidenced by the sector accounting for less than 1 per cent of the UK real estate market, prime London residential housing and, perhaps more importantly, social housing are increasingly being targeted by pension schemes.

- **Other** – around 4 per cent of the UK real estate market comprises other sectors, such as leisure complexes, student accommodation, care homes, agricultural property, woodland and infrastructure.

- **Liability-linked income (LLI) assets** – trustees and their advisers are constantly re-evaluating how best to meet their funding objectives by generating suitably strong long-term investment returns and hedging the interest rate and inflation risks within their scheme liabilities by securing liability matching cash flows.[10] As they do so, there is increasing interest in a recently emerged subset of the real estate market. These are termed liability-linked income (LLI) assets. This real estate niche captures aspects of each of the sectors we have already considered and principally comprises long-lease real estate, ground leases, social infrastructure and social housing.

---

[10] We revisit LLI assets in Chapter 15.

The defining feature of LLI assets is that they provide predictable long-term income streams, typically in excess of 15 years but in some cases beyond 75 years. Added to the fact that these income streams are also usually inflation-linked, mainly to the Retail Prices Index (RPI), or include fixed uplifts, means that they can provide a good hedge against inflation and interest rate risks.

Moreover, these cash flows are secured against physical or operating assets (the security often being far in excess of the value of the underlying investment) or a government/quasi-government covenant. All of these features make these cash flows particularly appropriate for paying pensions far into the future. In addition, there is little, if any, reliance on the potential for capital values to increase. Indeed, unlike the return from a dated bond, the capital sum invested is typically amortized, or built, into the cash flows paid to the pension scheme over the term of the investment. This means that at the end of the investment term, the pension scheme doesn't usually receive the residual value of the underlying property.

However, as no secondary market currently exists for LLI assets, this means that pension schemes are effectively locked into the asset for the duration of the investment's term. The illiquidity of an asset which provides a secure long-term income stream may not be as much of a concern to long-term investors, compared to those with a shorter investment horizon, particularly if it accounts for a relatively small percentage of the pension scheme's assets. Nevertheless, to compensate investors for their illiquid nature, LLI assets typically offer a significant 'liquidity premium'. That is, they offer more attractive yields and potentially higher returns than are attainable from – albeit more liquid – gilts and index-linked gilts and many secured corporate bonds, of a similar risk profile, as well as some diversification benefits.

LLI assets under the microscope

We now briefly introduce the key characteristics of the different types of LLI assets.

Long-lease real estate

Long-lease real estate assets are like a typical real estate asset but differ in three respects. First, lease-lengths are at least 15 years and often 20 years plus. Second, tenants offer very strong covenants, because they are either government-backed in some way, or are offered by the strongest performing and most secure corporations. Third, leases are drafted to deliver a strong degree of certainty of income flows with rents based on the RPI or fixed uplifts rather than open market reviews. By meeting all three of these criteria, long-lease real estate can offer pension funds long-dated, index-linked cash flows to help meet their liabilities. This is their core appeal. However, while long-lease real estate is low risk relative to most other real estate assets, it is more risky than some other LLI assets. Compared to ground rents, for example, lease lengths are relatively short and the residual value of the underlying property will have a material impact on an investment decision.

The trend for banks and supermarkets to engage in sale and leaseback programmes of their property portfolios over recent years has generated more opportunities in long-lease real estate. Typically, a lease to one of the largest supermarkets in the UK would offer an initial yield slightly above that offered by gilts with RPI rental uplifts over a term of at least 25 years, providing a pension fund with a constant stream of real cash flows to match its inflation-linked liabilities.

Ground leases

A ground lease, or ground rent, is typically a very long-term (that is, 75 years or more) lease of land, often undeveloped land. The lessee constructs and/or operates office blocks, residential accommodation or shopping centres, for example, on a site and pays the lessor rent. Ground rents are usually paid annually or semi-annually and typically represent 0.1 to 0.25 per cent of the leasehold value of the property. They thereby provide a steady and highly predictable cash flow.

In the event of default, the lessor would typically terminate the lease, making it the owner of any improvements on the land, such as property developments. So the incentives for tenants to avoid default are extremely high, and, as ground rents are typically very small in absolute terms, arrears are usually extremely low. Furthermore, if default does occur, the lessor can assume they will be more than adequately compensated.

Depending on how it is written, a ground lease can expose the holder to income risks. For example, some ground rents are linked to 'rents received' or 'rents receivable' from the leases of on-site developments while others are based on open market reviews, meaning income could decline if rental values fall or vacancies increase. Furthermore, investors can focus on ground leases that offer fixed or RPI-linked uplifts. Availability of such leases is improving as developers are learning to draft ground leases to ensure that they are attractive to potential ground lease investors.

As individual ground leases are often of relatively low value, a large number of transactions have to be processed and managed in order to invest significant funds. Investment in existing ground lease portfolios, therefore, seems the most efficient means of gaining exposure to the sector as it allows large economies of scale in administration and management, risk diversification by sector, tenant and geography and the smoothing of returns.

Social infrastructure

Social infrastructure is generally defined as those monopolistic assets that provide no or limited exposure to the economic use of underlying infrastructure assets. Typically their income is dependent only on their provision, usually to the state. Social infrastructure includes schools, hospitals and other healthcare, social housing, prisons and other government buildings – such as libraries, offices and police stations. This contrasts with 'economic infrastructure', such as many road and rail assets, most electricity, gas and water utilities, ports and airports for which income flows are typically dependent on usage levels.

Although high barriers to entry and the monopolistic characteristics of economic infrastructure usually bring stability to financial performance, they do not have the security of income that social infrastructure provides. Given that the rate of default on social infrastructure assets has been historically very low and the rates of recovery high,[11] investors can have a very strong degree of confidence in future income flows.

The characteristics of social infrastructure are similar to long-lease property, but the counterparty is generally state-backed and contractual agreements are particularly long at typically over 30 years. The income streams they provide are, therefore, considered very secure, and standard practice is to link them to the RPI. It is generally accepted that higher spending on many types of infrastructure is required, but high costs and the scarcity of state funding means that pension fund capital is likely to play an increasing role.

Given its low correlation with traditional asset classes and more traditional real estate, social infrastructure can also add diversity to an investment portfolio.

---

[11] For the UK, according to Robert Bain, in an article in *Infrastructure Investor,* February 2011, of the 667 UK PFI (Private Finance Initiative) projects on the Treasury's Signed Projects List, the number of defaults has been minimal. This can be explained by the strong contractual framework and the level of due diligence and security which is included in these transactions. For a more global perspective, see: *Default and Recovery Rates for Project Finance Bank Loans, 1983–2008*, Moody's, October (2010) and *Project Finance Consortium Study: Default and Recovery Trends From 1990 Through 2009*, S&P, November (2010).

Social housing

Social housing leases are seen as a much needed solution to the housing development funding crisis in the UK and are therefore expected to be a growing source of very low risk income streams.

Investment in social housing is made via a Registered Provider (RP), a not-for-profit organization, formerly known as a Registered Social Landlord (RSL). As with long-lease property and social infrastructure, contractual agreements are particularly long term, typically over 30 years. In addition, the income streams they provide are considered very secure and benefit from RPI uplifts. Moreover, the amortizing nature of social housing leases means that the return of the pension scheme's investment capital is built into the cash flows received by the scheme over the investment term. Therefore, the residual value of the property at the end of the lease is of relatively little importance.

Due to the regulated nature of the social housing sector, in the event of an RP defaulting, the government has historically arranged for the defaulting RP to be taken over by a stronger RP. Failing that, the counterparty to the leases, usually a real estate fund manager, would manage the individual properties to ensure that the pension scheme continued to receive the contractual cash flows. Moreover, as individual properties became vacant, they could be sold in the open market at an open market value. That is, at a value significantly higher than the 'existing use' value at which they were acquired.

Investing globally in real estate

While most UK pension funds have kept their money close to home when investing in real estate, more recently there has been a move towards diversifying real estate exposure globally given a greater appreciation of the valuable diversification opportunities available. After all, the UK real estate market only accounts for around 8 per cent of the value of the global investible universe of US$4.4tn, with the Americas accounting for 40 per cent, continental Europe and the Nordics 35 per cent and Asia Pacific 17 per cent (see Panel A of Exhibit 8.2). Panel B of the same exhibit shows that the global sector split differs from the UK, with offices at 42 per cent (UK 30 per cent), retail at 26 per cent (UK 50 per cent), industrial at 12 per cent (UK 15 per cent), residential at 15 per cent (UK 1 per cent) and 'other' at 5 per cent (UK 4 per cent).

This diversification not only arises from this wider and more diverse opportunity set, but also from property cycles not being globally synchronized and the differences in the principal drivers of real estate markets between countries and regions, such as income and wealth levels, demographics and rates of

Exhibit 8.2   **The structure of the real estate market**

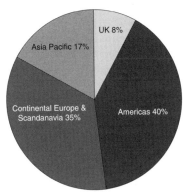

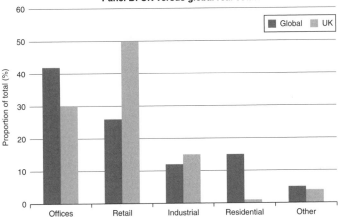

Source: IPD Global Property Index 31 December 2009.

urbanization. Indeed, the correlation between regional real estate markets can be very low, given the wide spreads between country and sector level perform- ance, unlike that between sectors in a single country. However, when investing overseas, investors need to be familiar with the many different local practices, legal structures and risks: principally currency, tax and geo-political risk.

As to returns, as is the case in the UK, most other real estate markets derive well over 75 per cent of their long-run returns from income streams, while capital appreciation similarly flows from the positive relationship between capital growth and GDP growth. Again, as in the UK, longer-run returns should be between those of equities and government bonds.

Concluding comments

As an asset class, real estate has provided positive real long-term returns allied to low volatility and a reliable income stream. An exposure to real estate can also provide diversification benefits owing to its low correlation to both traditional and alternative asset classes. However, owing to its illiquidity and high transactions costs on transfer, real estate is the archetypal long-term investment.

Key points

- Real estate has some unique distinguishing features, with heterogeneity, illiquidity and subjective valuation being key among them.
- An investment in real estate is an investment in a long-term income stream, which, in the UK, typically benefits from five year upward-only rent reviews, fixed or inflation-linked uplifts.
- There are essentially three main ways in which pension schemes can achieve an exposure to real estate: directly, indirectly via unlisted funds and publicly-listed shares and via derivatives.
- The real estate market comprises commercial property, residential property and other areas such as leisure complexes, infrastructure and woodland. Liability-linked income assets, which principally comprise long-lease real estate, ground leases, social infrastructure and social housing populate a number of these sectors.
- With the UK real estate market accounting for less than 10 per cent of the global property market, property cycles not being globally synchronized and with differences in the principal drivers of real estate markets between countries and regions, there is arguably a strong case for diversifying into overseas real estate.

Chapter 9

Risk and Risk Management: Trustees as Risk Managers

Learning outcomes

- Appreciate that risk can be measured in a number of ways.
- Know the key measures of risk-adjusted return.
- Understand how diversification works.
- Understand the meaning and shortcomings of Value at Risk.
- Understand that not all risks are quantifiable.
- Appreciate the range of soft risks trustees face.
- Appreciate that risk management is not an exact science.

Risk is one word but not one number

Risk is a difficult concept to define. Most textbooks typically define risk as the range of uncertainty surrounding an expectation about a future outcome. For example, investors may expect UK equities to return 8 per cent per annum on average over each of the next ten years, but as we know events rarely unfold as we expect; the lower the likelihood of our expectation being realized the greater the risk. An alternative way of thinking about risk is that it is the potential for suffering a loss. For example, history has shown us that investing in equities can lead to substantial losses; the greater the potential for loss, the greater the risk.

Perhaps a less conventional place to start when thinking about risk are the 'wise' words of Donald Rumsfeld:

> *There are known knowns. These are the things that we know. There are the known unknowns. That is to say, there are things that we know we don't know. But there*

are also unknown unknowns. These are the things we don't know we don't know.
(Donald Rumsfeld, Former US Secretary of Defence, 2002)

Although ridiculed at the time, Rumsfeld was simply trying to point out that while the sources of some risks – the *known unknowns* – might even be quantifiable, others – the *unknown unknowns* – the bolts from the blue, or the 'Black Swans'[1] – cannot always be anticipated, let alone quantified.[2]

Pension scheme trustees have to deal with both categories of risk, some of which were rarely considered before the financial crisis of 2008. Indeed, the financial crisis brought previously poorly considered risks such as the strength of the sponsor covenant, liquidity risk and counterparty risk, into sharp focus. It also highlighted the need for trustees to re-evaluate the risk models that had failed to capture adequately even the *known unknowns* properly. In short, the ongoing measurement, management and monitoring of risk has been firmly thrust to the top of the trustee agenda.

In this chapter we will begin by dealing with the concept of risk as it is taught in business schools today. Finance academics have spent the past 60 years trying to find ways of quantifying and measuring risk and to be honest, despite their best efforts, they have not made a huge amount of progress. However, the risk measures that have been developed are a useful guide to the known, unknowns that are inherent in asset prices – including all of those covered in Chapter 10 – and in particular, those that reside in portfolios of financial assets.

However, as indicated above, risk cannot easily be distilled into one simple number. In the second part of this chapter we will outline those risks that are more difficult to quantify.

---

[1] The term 'Black Swan' was popularized by Nassim Nicholas Taleb in his books: *Fooled by Randomness. The Hidden Role of Chance in Life and in the Markets*, Random House (2004) and *The Black Swan: The Impact of the Highly Improbable*, Penguin (2007). The term originates from the 18th century philosopher David Hume, though it is often attributed to the 19th century philosopher John Stuart Mill.

[2] In 1921, economist Frank Knight in *Risk, Uncertainty and Profit* distinguished uncertainty, an unmeasurable risk as he termed it, or an *unknown unknown* in Rumsfeld-speak, from one that is measurable – a known unknown. In fact, today an unmeasurable risk is termed *Knightian uncertainty*. John Maynard Keynes in 1937 also distinguished uncertain events (unknown unknowns) from those that are probable (known unknowns). As Keynes put it, an uncertain event is one where '*there is no scientific basis on which to form any calculable probability whatever. We simply do not know.*'

Not so 'modern portfolio theory'

Modern portfolio theory (MPT) has had an important influence on the way that the fund management industry constructs, manages and analyzes investment portfolios. MPT itself has its roots in the work of economists in the 1950s and 1960s – and in that sense it is not all that modern! In particular, the work of Professor Harry Markowitz in the 1950s has had an extraordinary influence on investment management practices today. Markowitz showed that investors could reduce the investment risks that they took by combining assets into portfolios so that the risks embodied in the portfolio were lower than the sum of the risks inherent in each individual asset. This insight relied crucially upon the *correlation* between risky assets.[3] The returns on some assets are highly correlated, which means that their returns tend to move together over time. However, when returns are less well correlated, Markowitz showed that the risk involved in holding these assets together in a portfolio is lower than the sum of individual risks of each asset in the portfolio. Today most investors, including pension funds, hold portfolios that can often consist of hundreds of individual assets.

Markowitz also explained the idea of an *efficient portfolio*: a concept used by many of the risk optimizer models employed by today's fund managers, asset allocators and investment advisers. An efficient portfolio is one that generates the highest expected return from a set of assets for a desired level of risk. Alternatively, an efficient portfolio could be described as one that embodies the lowest level of risk for any required return.

Measuring risk

The return on an individual asset is just the difference in the value of the asset at the end of the period compared with the value at the beginning of the period, plus any income earned from holding that asset, divided by the value of the asset value at the start of the period. The average of this return over time is often used as a useful summary measure of an asset's performance. The historic average return is often used as a proxy for future expected returns. Even when it is not, when investment professionals talk about expected return, they generally mean the expected average return over a particular period.

---

[3] Risk, or risky, assets are those that are not risk-free. Indeed, very few assets are. Therefore, the expected return on a risky asset should incorporate one or a number of risk premia as potential compensation for assuming these risks. For example, corporate bond investors would expect to be compensated for the possibility of the issuer defaulting on their obligations, for the relative illiquidity of the bonds and for the volatility in the price of the bonds. We consider risk premia in Chapter 10.

Exhibit 9.1   Returns from assets A and B and from a portfolio consisting of 50% in asset A and 50% in asset B

	Returns					Squared deviations					
	Year 1 (%)	Year 2 (%)	Year 3 (%)	Year 4 (%)	Average (%)	Year 1 (%)	Year 2 (%)	Year 3 (%)	Year 4 (%)	Sum (%)	Std. dev. (%)
Asset A	9.00	0.00	10.00	1.00	5.00	0.16	0.25	0.25	0.16	0.82	5.23
Asset B	0.00	10.00	0.00	8.00	4.50	0.20	0.30	0.20	0.12	0.83	5.26
Portfolio	4.50	5.00	5.00	4.50	4.75	0.001	0.001	0.001	0.001	0.003	0.29

In Exhibit 9.1 we present the returns achieved over each of four years on assets A and B, plus the return achieved on an equally weighted portfolio of assets A and B over the same four years. The average return over these four years on asset A is 5 per cent, on asset B is 4.5 per cent and on the equally weighted portfolio is 4.75 per cent, as shown in the sixth column of the table. We could use these averages as proxies for expectations of future returns if we feel the sample period is truly representative of the sort of returns these assets and this portfolio will generate in the future.

But what about expected risk?

Measuring the risk embodied in these two assets and in the portfolio is slightly more complicated. When referring to risk, or measuring it, the early proponents of modern portfolio theory argued for a measure known as *standard deviation*. This statistical calculation is used to measure how widely dispersed a set of observations is around the average result. In an investment context it measures the dispersion of the returns on an asset, or portfolio of assets, around the average return.

Standard deviation can be described crudely as: *the weighted sum of the squared deviations of each return observation from its average.*

To illustrate the calculation consider the returns from assets A and B and from the portfolio consisting of investments in assets A and B in Exhibit 9.1 again. To calculate the standard deviation of return we must first calculate the difference between the actual return achieved in each year and the average return; we then multiply this value by itself. The results of these calculations are shown in the columns headed 'squared deviations'.[4] The reason for taking the squared standard deviation for each asset's return (the difference between the actual return from each asset in each year and the average return) is to ensure that positive and negative differences are treated equally. The squared deviation is known as the

---

[4] This point is more evident from Exhibit 9.4 later in the chapter.

variance. So for example the squared deviation of the return for asset A in year 1 is calculated as:

Squared deviation for asset A in year 1 = (Year 1 return – average return)²
  = (9.00% – 5.00%)² = 0.16%

These individual squared deviations are then added up as shown in the column headed 'Sum'. This 'sum' is literally the sum of the squared return deviations from the average return. To obtain the standard deviation for each return series, the sum of squared deviations is then divided by the number of observations minus one,[5] and then the square root of this value is taken to arrive at the standard deviation. For example, the standard deviation of asset A is calculated as:

$$\text{Std. deviation of asset A} = \sqrt{\frac{\text{sum of squared deviations}}{\text{number of observations} - 1}}$$

$$\text{Std. deviation of asset A} = \sqrt{\frac{0.82\%}{4 - 1}} = 5.23\%$$

The standard deviations calculated and shown in Exhibit 9.1 demonstrate how much more volatile each individual asset is compared with an equally-weighted combination of them.

Standard deviation is often used as a proxy for the expected risk embodied in an individual asset or in a portfolio of assets. But what does it mean?

Interpreting standard deviation

As long as the returns produced by an asset or portfolio are fairly evenly distributed around their average return, that is, they are distributed in a kind of bell shape, then standard deviation has a useful and intuitive interpretation. For example, the range represented by one standard deviation either side of the average represents 67 per cent of all the observations. In other words, 67 per cent of the time the returns on that asset would be between plus and minus one standard deviation of the average return. This is perhaps best illustrated with the diagram shown in Exhibit 9.2, which shows this bell-shaped distribution of returns for an asset. This is the *normal distribution*. It is a distribution

---

[5] The reason for dividing the sum by 'minus one' is because this data represents a sample of the returns rather than every return recorded, which is known as the population. By subtracting one from the number of observations enables us to obtain a good approximation of the standard deviation of the population of returns from these two assets.

Exhibit 9.2   The classic bell-shaped normal distribution

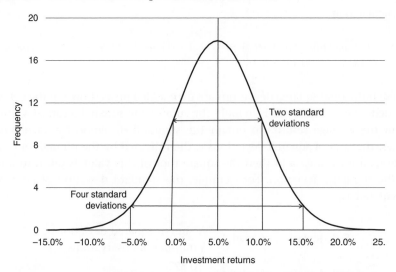

that appears frequently in nature. For example, were you to take a trip to the Antarctic to measure the heights of all the male Emperor penguins in a colony, you would almost certainly find that their heights are distributed in the bell shape similar to that in Exhibit 9.2, with penguin height on the horizontal axis and the number of penguins at this height on the vertical axis. Alternatively, rather than going to these extremes to prove this to yourself you could simply take our word for it!

The bell-shaped curve in Exhibit 9.2 represents the distribution of returns of an asset that experienced an average return of 5 per cent per annum, with a standard deviation of 5 per cent – very similar to the average return and standard deviation of asset A in Exhibit 9.1. One standard deviation either side of this average is a range of 0 to 10 per cent. As we know, with a normally distributed series, 67 per cent of the time the returns on this asset would be expected to be within this range. Two standard deviations either side of the mean represents a range of –5 per cent to 15 per cent. With a normally distributed series, 95 per cent of the time the returns on this asset would be expected to be within this range.

The larger the standard deviation, the wider the range of realized returns from an asset, an asset class, or from an investment portfolio. Conversely the lower the standard deviation, the smaller the range of realized returns. Exhibit 9.3 shows the standard deviation of several major equity markets as well as the standard deviation of a group of emerging equity markets. The data used to calculate the risk, or standard deviation, represented by these markets spanned the period January 1990 to December 2010.

Exhibit 9.3 The standard deviation on a range of equity markets, 1990–2010

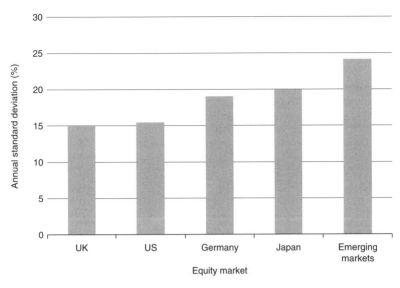

Source: Thomson Financial.

Generally speaking, assets, asset classes or investment portfolios whose returns have had, or are expected to have, a high standard deviation of returns are characterized as high risk. In Exhibit 9.3 the returns generated by emerging equity markets since 1990 have been the most volatile (risky) while those generated by the UK equity market have been the least risky over the same period.

Covariance and correlation

We have already hinted above that the way in which risky assets move together (or not) is important. In Exhibit 9.1 we can see that in years when asset A generally does well, asset B performs poorly and vice versa. When held together by an investor in equal proportions we can see that the resulting risk – standard deviation – is much lower than the risk inherent in asset A or in asset B. In this case the portfolio has benefited from the imperfect correlation between assets A and B. By imperfect, we mean that they do not produce the same return as one another year after year. In fact, the correlation between them was negative.

Covariance can be used as a measure of how risky assets, or asset classes, co-vary, or move together (or not). We can calculate a standardized measure of this covariance called the *correlation coefficient*. In Exhibit 9.4 we have laid out the steps needed to calculate the correlation of assets A and B shown in Exhibit 9.1. This is rather convoluted, so you need to pay attention, but it's not actually that complicated.

Exhibit 9.4   Calculating covariance and correlation

	Returns					Deviations			
	Year 1 (%)	Year 2 (%)	Year 3 (%)	Year 4 (%)	Ave (%)	Year 1 (%)	Year 2 (%)	Year 3 (%)	Year 4 (%)
Asset A	9	0	10	1	5.0	4.0	−5.0	5.0	−4.0
Asset B	0	10	0	8	4.5	−4.5	5.5	−4.5	3.5

	Multiplied deviations				Covar	Correl
	−0.18	−0.28	−0.23	−0.14	−0.205%	−0.75

The first few columns of Exhibit 9.4 show the annual returns for assets A and B again, along with the average return. The columns headed 'deviations', simply show for each year and for each asset the difference between the actual return and the average return of each asset. So for example, the deviation between actual and average return in year 1 for asset A is: (9% − 5%) = 4%.

The bottom row of the columns headed 'Multiple deviations' is just the return deviation for asset A in each year, multiplied by the deviation for asset B in the same year. So for example, in year 1 we have: (4.0% × −4.5%) = −0.18%. The covariance between the returns on assets A and B are then given as the average of each of these multiplications. This comes to approximately −2.05%. This is not a very intuitive value. However the minus sign in the covariance term means that on average the returns in each year tend to move in opposite directions. That is, when the return on one is positive, the return on the other tends to be negative. A more intuitive measure of this tendency for returns to move together is the correlation coefficient. The correlation coefficient is a standardized measure of covariance and it can be calculated as follows:

$$\text{correlation between assets A and B} = \frac{\text{Covariance (A,B)}}{(\text{std. dev. A} \times \text{std. dev. B})}$$

$$\text{correlation between assets A and B} = \frac{-2.05\%}{5.23\% \times 5.26\%} \approx -0.75$$

The correlation coefficient between assets A and B is therefore −0.75.

How do we interpret a correlation coefficient? The good news is that it is a standardized measure which has a maximum value of 1 and a minimum value of −1. If the correlation coefficient is equal to:

- 1.0, then the returns on the assets are perfectly correlated – they move one for one with one another over time;
- 0, then the returns are said to be completely uncorrelated. That is, their returns are unrelated to one another;

Exhibit 9.5   The correlation between the UK equity market and other major equity markets, 1990–2010

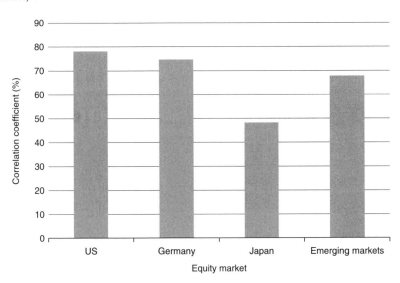

Source: Thomson Financial.

- –1.0, then the returns are said to be perfectly negatively correlated. That is, when the return on one asset is, say, –5 per cent, the return on the other will be +5 per cent.

The more positive the correlation coefficient, the more two assets, asset classes or portfolios move together. In our simple example the returns on the two assets are almost, but not quite, perfectly negatively correlated.

In Exhibit 9.5, using the same data used to generate the measures of standard deviation shown in Exhibit 9.3, we present the correlation between the returns on the UK equity market and each of the other equity markets.

The returns generated by the UK equity market are most highly correlated with (most similar to) those generated by the US equity market, while they are the least similar to those generated by the Japanese equity market over this period.

Diversification

Now that we understand how 'modern portfolio' theorists recommend measuring risk, we can move on to the important concept of diversification.

The idea of *diversification* has its roots in the old saying 'Don't put all your eggs in one basket'. The investment equivalent of this, as Harry Markowitz showed in 1952, is 'Don't invest all your wealth in one risky asset'. To illustrate the concept of diversification and the advantages that it can bring in terms of risk reduction, consider the performance of the two risky assets A and B over the four years shown in Exhibit 9.1 again. Asset A produces an average return of 5 per cent over the four years but has two bad years where it produced returns of zero and 1 per cent. Asset B also has two good years and two bad years and produces an average return of 4.5 per cent. For both assets the returns vary quite dramatically from one year to the next.

However, now consider the final row in Exhibit 9.1. This is the return produced by a portfolio that consisted of 50 per cent in asset A and 50 per cent in asset B. The portfolio produces a lower return than asset A, but a higher return than asset B. Most importantly, however, we can see that the yearly returns from the portfolio are far less volatile than those from holding either asset A or asset B in isolation. This is because when asset A had a bad year, asset B had a good year and vice versa.

In other words, the returns on the two assets were not highly correlated, so combinations of the two assets produced lower overall risk, or volatility – represented here by standard deviation – than either of the two assets held individually.

Combining assets that are not perfectly correlated (that is, they do not move together to produce the same return in all periods) can reduce the overall risk in a portfolio. By combining assets into portfolios, finance researchers have found that risk can be reduced significantly. However, they also found that there comes a point where, for example, adding further individual equities to an equity portfolio does not reduce volatility further. This point is illustrated in Exhibit 9.6.

Exhibit 9.6 shows a stylized representation of what happens to the standard deviation of a portfolio as more assets are added to it. As the exhibit indicates, the average standard deviation – or volatility – is highest for a single asset portfolio whereas the volatility of portfolios comprising progressively larger numbers of assets falls, quite sharply at first, so that the standard deviation of a 10 or 15 asset portfolio is significantly lower than that for a one asset portfolio. However, the rate at which portfolio standard deviation declines as more assets are added to the portfolio reaches a kind of floor, such that the inclusion of additional assets cannot further reduce average portfolio standard deviation by any significant degree.

The sharp decline in portfolio standard deviation comes about from imperfect correlations among the assets. The standard deviation that can be eliminated by holding a diversifiable portfolio is called, unsurprisingly, 'diversifiable risk' or 'unsystematic risk', since it can be diversified away. The portfolio volatility

Exhibit 9.6 Stylized representation of the limit to portfolio diversification

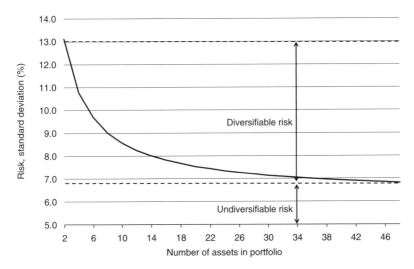

that cannot be diversified away is known as 'undiversifiable risk', or 'systematic risk'. Indeed, one of the great insights of the early portfolio theorists, like Markowitz, was that we can distinguish between the two types of risk:

- diversifiable, or unsystematic risk, and
- undiversifiable, or systematic risk,

where the former risk can be all but eliminated by holding a diversified portfolio of assets, while the latter cannot be eliminated from a portfolio of risky assets. In other words, by holding larger and larger numbers of individual equities in an equity portfolio the risk inherent in that portfolio might be expected to decline. The same holds true for holding larger and larger numbers of corporate bonds in a bond portfolio, or more and more hedge funds in a fund of hedge funds portfolio, or more and more alternative asset classes.[6] However, not all risk can be eliminated. No matter how diversified investors' portfolios were in October 1987, UK equity portfolios all fell by around 30 per cent when the market crashed. Systematic risk, also known as 'market risk', remains even in a well diversified portfolio.

Perhaps the most important message from modern portfolio theory with regard to unsystematic and systematic risk, is that over long periods of time

---

[6] 'How many alternatives should you have in your investment basket?', A. Clare and N. Motson, *CAMR*, Cass Business School, London (2009).

investors are not rewarded for bearing unsystematic risk, but can expect to be rewarded for bearing systematic risk.

Efficient portfolios

When combining assets into portfolios, Markowitz showed how unsystematic risk can gradually be diversified away by adding more and more additional assets.

Using average return and standard deviation to describe return and risk, Markowitz also showed how some portfolios were more *efficient* than others. In other words, for every level of risk there will be one combination of assets that will produce the highest return. This portfolio would be more efficient than all others. This is because we assume that investors would prefer to hold the portfolio with the highest return with a certain amount of risk, than to hold a portfolio with a lower return, but with the same amount of risk. The return on the former portfolio would be more efficient since the same return is produced but at a lower level of risk. This analysis gave rise to the concept of an *efficient frontier*. That is, by combining assets and exploiting the different risk and return characteristics of each security, one can identify a whole set of efficient portfolios.

A typical efficient frontier is shown in Exhibit 9.7. The frontier has been calculated using:

- expectations of the returns on a set of assets;
- expectations of the standard deviation of returns on each asset; and
- an assumption about the correlation between the expected returns on these assets.

Only portfolio combinations that plot on the upper portion of this frontier are efficient. For example, portfolios A and B have the same standard deviation of return. But portfolio A has an expected return of 5.5 per cent, while portfolio B has a return of 4 per cent. Clearly in this case portfolio A is more efficient than portfolio B, since the same risk is expected to produce a higher return.

Efficient frontiers can be constructed from individual assets, or by using the risk and return characteristics of broad asset categories like equities, bonds, real estate etc. *Asset allocators* make use of efficient frontier analysis when constructing *strategic benchmarks* in the *asset allocation* process. In addition, many of the risk tools used by fund managers have 'optimizer routines' that are designed to help managers choose combinations of assets that produce the highest return for a given risk tolerance.

Exhibit 9.7   An efficient frontier of risky assets

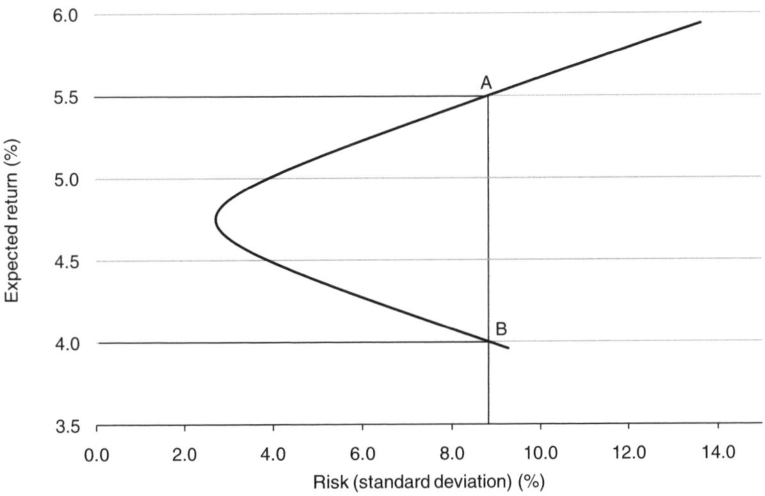

What determines the shape and position of the frontier?

Although the expected returns and standard deviations of the combined assets or asset classes under consideration are key inputs, it is the expected correlations between the returns on these assets that are the most important determinant of the efficient frontier's shape and position within a mean-variance chart. When portfolio managers and investment advisers construct efficient frontiers they typically use historic values for the standard deviations of the assets under consideration and historically determined correlations between the asset classes, as proxies for expected correlations. While they may be relatively stable in the long run, correlations between asset classes in particular, can break down very quickly in times of financial market crisis. Indeed, this is what happened during the recent liquidity and credit crisis. At such times, the prices of all risky assets tend to fall in unison, just at the time when the benefits of diversification are most needed. In fact, with the exception of bonds issued by developed economy governments and gold, all other asset classes experienced significant losses during 2008.

The position of the efficient frontier can change as we add or subtract assets to and from the investment mix. For example, if we were to add additional assets that have a low correlation with the original set of assets, then as long as their expected returns are similar to those of the assets already under consideration the efficient frontier should shift towards the northwest corner (the most desirable corner) of the mean-variance chart. The addition of such assets means that for any given level of risk, investors can achieve a higher expected return.

It is argued by many that the risk-return trade-off for pension scheme portfolios can be enhanced by adding asset classes such as commodities and hedge funds to the asset mix. We will return to such issues when we discuss asset allocation and alternative asset classes in Chapters 10 and 13 respectively.

Deriving the efficient frontier

The efficient frontier is plotted as a two-dimensional chart, with the portfolio's expected return on the vertical axis and the portfolio's expected risk, as quantified by the expected standard deviation of the portfolio's return, on the horizontal axis. This can be done by using two equations, one for the portfolio's expected return and one for the portfolio's expected risk for all of the different combinations of the assets within the portfolio. Thankfully, today we have computing power to do this for us but this wasn't always the case!

We demonstrate here how these calculations can be undertaken for a portfolio with just two risky assets. First, the easy bit. A portfolio's expected return $E(R_p)$ is given by the weighted average of the expected returns from the individual assets in the portfolio. For a portfolio containing just two assets, $w_1E(R_1)$ is the weighted return from asset 1 and $w_2E(R_2)$ is the weighted return from asset 2. w_1 and w_2 are simply the proportions of the portfolio invested in asset 1 and 2 respectively. So if the portfolio has a 50 per cent weighting towards asset 1 and a 50 per cent weighting towards asset 2, then the portfolio's expected return is simply 50 per cent of the expected return from asset 1 added to 50 per cent of the expected return from asset 2: nothing more complicated from that. The expected return on this portfolio will therefore be given by expression (9.1):

$$E(R_p) = w_1E(R_1) + w_2E(R_2) \tag{9.1}$$

Now for the slightly more challenging bit. The risk for this two asset portfolio, that is its variance, or the standard deviation squared (standard deviation is denoted by σ), can be calculated by expression (9.2):

$$\sigma_p^2 = w_1^2\sigma_1^2 + w_2^2\sigma_2^2 + 2w_1w_2\sigma_1\sigma_2\rho_{1,2} \tag{9.2}$$

where $w_1^2\sigma_1^2$ and $w_2^2\sigma_2^2$ are the weighted variances of assets 1 and 2 respectively, and $\sigma_1\sigma_2\rho_{1,2}$ is the covariance between assets 1 and 2. You'll see that the covariance contains the correlation coefficient between asset 1 and 2, denoted by $\rho_{1,2}$.

Let's bring this together in a worked example.

Asset	E(R)	Variance	Standard deviation
1	0.075	2.56%	16.0%
2	0.112	4.41%	21.0%

25% of the portfolio is invested in asset 1 and 75% is invested in asset 2. Correlation coefficient between assets 1 and 2 = 0.37

We know that the portfolio return is given by expression (9.1) so the expected return on the portfolio is:

$$E(R_p) = (0.25 \times 7.5\%) + (0.75 \times 11.2\%) = 10.28\%$$

We know that the portfolio variance is given by expression (9.2), so the portfolio variance is:

$$\sigma_p^2 = [(25\%)^2 \times (2.56\%)] + [(75\%)^2 \times (4.41\%)]$$
$$+ (2 \times 25\% \times 75\% \times 16\% \times 21\% \times 0.37) \approx 310.7\%$$

The portfolio standard deviation is $\sqrt{310.7\%} \approx 17.63\%$.

You'll note that 17.6 per cent is less than the 19.75 per cent weighted average of the standard deviations of assets 1 and 2 [(0.25 × 16) + (0.75 × 21) = 19.75%]. This is to be expected with a correlation coefficient between the two assets far below plus one.

To create the efficient frontier for assets 1 and 2, the above calculations would need to be repeated for all possible weightings of the two assets within the portfolio. To do this with many, many assets would be very difficult in the manner outlined above. However, luckily computers can manage this relatively easily.

Reward and risk

The efficient frontier links the concept of reward and risk. We assume that trustees and other investors want to be rewarded for taking risks. There are people in this world that love risk and care little for the return. You can find them at any gamblers anonymous meeting!

Modern portfolio theory has produced a number of convenient measures of risk-adjusted return that are used frequently by fund managers, investment advisers and by most investment professionals. They are all attempts at quantifying the amount of prospective reward on offer in comparison to the prospective risk that derives from an asset or portfolio of assets. They are sometimes referred to as reward-to-risk ratios.

Sharpe ratio

A key measure of risk-adjusted return that draws on the volatility of returns is the Sharpe ratio, suggested by the Nobel laureate William Sharpe. The Sharpe ratio calculates the unit of return for the portfolio or individual asset over and above that available from a risk-free asset, per unit of measured risk. The risk-free asset is normally taken to be the yield on a Treasury bill. It can be calculated in the following way:

$$\text{Sharpe ratio} = \frac{\text{asset return} - \text{risk-free rate}}{\text{standard deviation of asset return}}$$

The higher the Sharpe ratio for an asset or a portfolio, the higher the return per unit of risk. In fact, the efficient portfolio idea that we introduced earlier is directly related to the Sharpe ratio. Each efficient portfolio is the portfolio with the highest Sharpe ratio out of all available portfolios with the same risk. The Sharpe ratio is frequently reported by fund managers when they report the performance of their own funds and when investment advisers provide their regular updates on the performance of scheme managers.

The information ratio

Although the Sharpe ratio is widely reported, perhaps the measure most commonly used to quantify the reward-to-risk ratio in the investment industry today is the *information ratio*. However, when used in the context of portfolios, rather than comparing the return on the fund with the return on a risk-free asset, the comparison is between the return on the fund and the return on the fund's benchmark index. The risk parameter is different too. Rather than being the standard deviation of the fund's return, as in the case of the Sharpe ratio, it is instead the standard deviation of the difference in return between the fund and the fund's benchmark index.

The information ratio of a portfolio, IR_p, can be calculated as follows:

$$IR_P = \frac{\bar{R}_P - \bar{R}_B}{\sigma(R_{Pt} - R_{Bt})}$$

where $\bar{R}_P$ is the average return from the fund, $\bar{R}_B$ is the average return on the fund's benchmark and $\sigma(R_{Pt} - R_{Bt})$ is the standard deviation of the difference between the return on the fund and the return on the fund's benchmark. Other things equal, the larger the difference between the return on the fund and its benchmark (the numerator), and the lower the standard deviation of this difference (the denominator), the higher the information ratio. A fund manager that manages a fund with a high information ratio is therefore adding more value to the fund per unit of risk (or deviation from the benchmark) than another manager that achieves a lower information ratio.

Exhibit 9.8   Information ratios on selection of UK equity funds

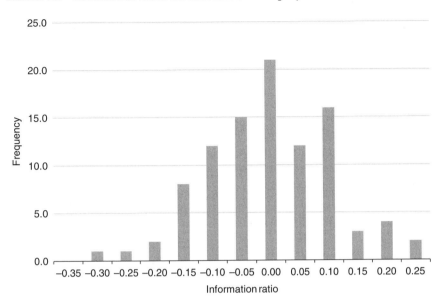

In Exhibit 9.8 we present the information ratios of a range of almost 100 UK equity funds. The ratios were calculated using returns data, gross of fees, from January 2000 to December 2010, and where the benchmark was presumed to be the FTSE All Share index. The exhibit shows that the funds with the best risk-adjusted performances achieved information ratios just above 0.2 over this period, while around 40 produced ratios that were negative, which means that the funds underperformed the All Share index over this period – they subtracted value for their investors. The average information ratio for these funds over this five-year period was just under zero.

The information ratio is a useful reward-to-risk measure. However, be warned, many UK fund managers and investment professionals refer to it as 'tracking error'. This is rather confusing because as we will see in Chapter 14, elsewhere the term tracking error is simply taken to be the difference between the average return on a portfolio and the average return on its benchmark. That is, $(\overline{R}_p - \overline{R}_B)$ – the numerator in the information ratio expression above.

The Capital Asset Pricing Model (CAPM) and risk-adjusted returns

Arguably the most famous, but also the most criticized, model in finance is the *Capital Asset Pricing Model* (CAPM). This model was developed in the 1960s and was a direct development of modern portfolio theory's mean-variance analysis.

A full derivation and description of this model is beyond the scope of this book, but we can highlight the main features of this model and show how it is used as the basis for calculating risk-adjusted returns.

The basic intuition of the CAPM is that the risk inherent in any asset or portfolio can be summarized by its relationship with 'market risk'. That is the idea of 'systematic risk' that we discussed earlier. Market risk is that element of risk that cannot be diversified away by holding a large portfolio of risky assets. Although market risk is more difficult to define than one might expect, equity practitioners generally use a broad equity index as a proxy for market risk. For UK equities, industry professionals might use the FTSE All Share index; for US equities they might use the S&P 500 Composite index.

If we can accept that these broad indices are suitable proxies for market risk, then according to the CAPM, on average, the expected return in excess of a risk free return on any risky portfolio, or asset, can be described as follows:

$$E(R_i) - R_f = \alpha_0 + \beta_i \times (E(R_m) - R_f)$$

where $E(R_i)$ is the expected return on risky asset i; R_f is the return achievable on a risk-free asset, like a government T-bill, over the same period; $E(R_m)$ is the expected return on the market; $(E(R_m) - R_f)$ is the expected return on the market over and above the risk-free rate of return, known as the *market risk premium;* and β_i is a parameter that maps the relationship between market risk and the return on the asset. This is known as the beta. α_0 in this expression – the *alpha* – should be equal to zero, but we will explain what alpha signifies once we have explored the significance of beta.

Within the CAPM the beta coefficient, which is the model's crucial parameter, comprises the following components:

$$\beta_i = \frac{Cov_{i,m}}{Var_m}$$

This looks complicated but it's simply the covariance between the expected excess return[7] on asset i and the expected excess return on the market, all divided by the variance (the standard deviation squared) of the expected excess return on the market. Since the denominator in this expression is the same for all assets, it's really the covariance of an asset's or a portfolio's return with the return on the market that determines the value of beta.

Although, technically speaking the CAPM is couched in terms of 'expectations', in practice most users of the CAPM simply calculate an asset's beta by using

---

[7] By 'excess' we mean the return in excess of the risk-free return.

historic data. That is, calculating the covariance of an asset's return with the return on the market using past data, and calculating the variance of the return on the market using data from the same sample period.

What does a 'high' or a 'low' beta signify?

According to the CAPM there is only one source of systematic risk and that is 'market risk'. But that does not mean that all assets are as risky as the market. Some will be less risky, others more so. For example, if on average, the return on a fund moves very closely with the return on the market over time then the fund's beta coefficient will be equal to one. In this sense then, an asset with a beta of one embodies the same amount of risk as the market, since their returns will tend to move together over time.

If the performance of an asset is more volatile than the return on the wider market such that, for example, when the market goes up by 1 per cent the fund goes up by 1.5 per cent and when the market goes down by 1 per cent the fund produces a return of minus 1.5 per cent then the beta coefficient will be greater than one, basically because the fund's returns are more volatile than the returns produced by the wider market. The converse is true if the returns are less volatile. That is, the fund's beta will be less than one.

According to the CAPM then, a portfolio that has a calculated beta of 1.5 embodies more risk than a portfolio that has a beta of 0.5 since, if the CAPM is broadly correct, a fall in the market of 5 per cent would be accompanied by a fall of 7.5 per cent for the former, but only a fall of 2.5 per cent in the case of the latter.[8]

In Exhibit 9.9 we present the betas produced by the same set of UK equity funds that we used to calculate information ratios in Exhibit 9.8. The betas were calculated using returns data from January 2000 to December 2010, and where the proxy for market risk was presumed to be the FTSE All Share index. The average beta for these funds was 0.98. Over this period some managers had betas as low as 0.813, while others had betas as high as 1.20.

In summary, beta is a measure of systematic risk embodied in an individual security or portfolio.

---

[8] Some have argued that stock betas are largely determined by the operational and financial gearing of the company: the higher the gearing the greater the stock's beta. Financial gearing is the amount of debt finance as a proportion of the total capital employed by the company. The greater the proportional amount of debt finance, the higher the financial gearing and the greater the company's interest payments, which must be met out of its cash flow, regardless of the company's rate of cash flow generation. Other things being equal, the greater the financial gearing, the riskier the company. Operational gearing is the rate at which profits and losses accrue as a result of the size of a company's fixed costs as a proportion of its total costs. Other things being equal, the higher the proportional amount of fixed costs, the more quickly profits and losses accrue, hence the riskier the company.

Exhibit 9.9   CAPM betas on selection of UK equity pension funds

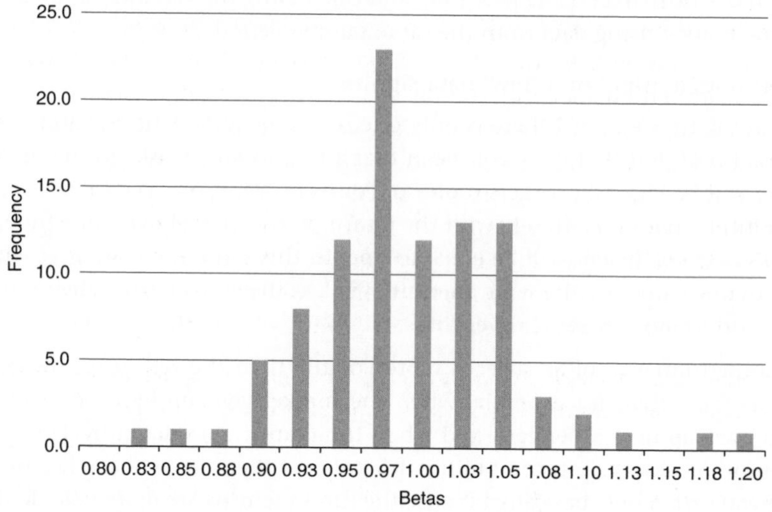

But what about alpha?

Recall the basic CAPM relationship again:

$$E(R_i) - R_f = \alpha_0 + \beta_i \times (E(R_m) - R_f)$$

According to the CAPM if one can make an educated guess about the likely return on a proxy for the market over time, then if we also know the risk-free rate of interest and the CAPM beta of the portfolio then we can work out the expected return on this portfolio. Nothing else should be required. In this case α_0 – the alpha – or risk-adjusted excess return, should equal zero. In other words, all the information needed to forecast the return on the portfolio is embodied in the CAPM's other parameters. Therefore, the expected excess return on any asset – that is, over and above the risk-free rate of return – should be equal to its beta multiplied by the expected excess return – the 'risk premium' – on the market.

Industry practitioners include the alpha coefficient in the CAPM expression when they calculate CAPM betas as a test that the basic relationship holds. Evidence that alpha is not zero can be taken as evidence that 'something else' influences returns, over and above the market return itself. Fund managers would like to convince us that positive alpha is the result of their skill as a fund manager. So often alpha is referred to as a measure of 'fund manager skill'. However, the existence of alpha may also indicate that the CAPM as a risk model is not adequate to capture all the risks taken by the fund manager.

Nonetheless, calculating alpha, and testing whether it is equal to zero or not is an important part of calculating risk-adjusted returns.

Using alpha

In the late 1960s Michael Jensen showed how the CAPM could be used to determine whether a fund manager added value to their portfolio. That is, whether a fund manager had alpha.

Suppose that we are analyzing the monthly returns produced by a fund manager over the past ten years on a portfolio of UK equities. Using this data, plus data on the return from a proxy for the market and the return achieved from a risk-free asset over this period, we can calculate the fund manager's beta coefficient. Suppose that the beta coefficient turned out to be 1.2. This means that, on average, the fund manager's portfolio was around 20 per cent more volatile than the return on the market over the same period, which in turn means that the assets held by the fund manager in the portfolio were more volatile than the market itself.

Suppose also that the excess return on the market over this same period was 10 per cent per year, while the return on the fund manager's portfolio was 12 per cent per year. We can use the basic CAPM expression to determine how well the manager performed over this period:

$$E(R_i) - R_f = \alpha_0 + \beta_i \times (E(R_m) - R_f)$$
$$12\% = 0\% + 1.2 \times (10\%)$$

The average return of 12 per cent achieved by the fund manager was the return that would be 'predicted' by the CAPM. In other words, the fund manager achieved a higher return than the return produced by the wider market, but took greater risks than were embodied in the market to achieve these returns, as evidenced by the fact that the beta on the portfolio was 1.2.

Now consider the same set of circumstances, but assume that the fund manager achieved a return of 13 per cent per year over this period instead of 12 per cent.

$$E(r_i) - R_f = \alpha_0 + \beta_i \times (E(R_m) - R_f)$$
$$13\% = 1.0\% + 1.2 \times (10\%)$$

With a beta of 1.2 the fund manager took on enough market risk to produce a return of 12 per cent, but the actual return was 13 per cent. The fund manager's alpha was therefore 1 per cent in this case. The manager added something to the portfolio that was unrelated to the risks that they took. This 1 per cent could have been the result of the fund manager's skill, because this additional 1 per cent return was added without taking on additional market risk.

When a fund manager is said to produce 'alpha' on a consistent basis, what is meant by this is that the fund manager regularly adds value to the portfolio through their innate skills as a manager, without incurring commensurately higher risks. However, when using alpha as a measure of a fund manager's risk-adjusted performance there are two issues of particular importance that must be borne in mind. First and foremost the CAPM may not be a valid model of risk. Other models of risk have been developed over the years and the use of one of these models may have produced very different results than those presented in Exhibit 9.9. Second, a fund manager may have produced a high alpha over a particular period, but the performance might have been due as much to good fortune as to good fund management. University researchers have produced many statistical models and tools in an effort to distinguish fund manager skill from luck.[9] We return to this point in Chapters 14 and 18.

Multi-factor risk models

The CAPM helps an investment analyst identify the systematic risk in a portfolio. It is often referred to as a 'single factor' model. This is because the model implies that systematic risk can be represented, or captured by a single factor – the return on the market. However, there exist other models that attempt to capture systematic risk using more than just one factor.

Effectively, these risk models decompose and quantify the extent of the risks to which the portfolio is exposed into multiple sources. Some models use a number of pre-determined risk factors, such as economic growth, the oil price, the exchange rate, while others use unspecified factors that aim to highlight risks common to a number of stocks in the portfolio but do not label them. Other multi-factor risk models drill down into the DNA of the portfolio by identifying the extent of the portfolio's investment style, for example, analyzing their exposure to small cap stocks.

Full descriptions of these more complex models are beyond the scope of this book,[10] not least because it requires considerable expertise to estimate these models and more still to interpret their results. However, they all attempt to do

---

[9] K. Cuthbertson, D. Nitzsche and N. O'Sullivan, 'Mutual Fund Performance: Skill or Luck?' *Journal of Empirical Finance* (2008). Available at: http://papers.ssrn.com/sol3/papers.cfm?abstract_id=665744.
[10] For an early example of the application of a multi-factor model for the UK equity market see 'Macroeconomic factors, the APT and the UK stock market', A. Clare and S. Thomas, *Journal of Business Finance and Accounting* (1994).

the same thing: to distinguish between systematic risk, unsystematic risk and manager skill ('alpha').

The Treynor ratio

As well as calculating a fund's alpha to determine the fund manager's skill, analysts also use another measure of risk-adjusted performance that is based upon the CAPM. This is the Treynor ratio, which is very similar in spirit to the Sharpe ratio. Rather than dividing the excess return on a fund by the standard deviation of the fund's return to calculate the Sharpe ratio, to calculate the Treynor ratio the excess return on the fund needs to be divided by its beta.

The expression for the Treynor ratio, T_P, is given as:

$$T_P = \frac{\bar{R}_P - \bar{R}_f}{\beta_P}$$

where $\bar{R}_P$ is the average return on the portfolio over a given period; $\bar{R}_f$ is the average return from a risk-free asset over the same period; and β_P is the fund's 'beta coefficient'. The average return from a risk-free asset is subtracted from the average return on the portfolio because the difference between the two represents the reward for risk taking. This means that the Treynor ratio can be negative if the return on the fund is negative, or if the average return on a risk-free asset over the period in question is higher than the average return on the portfolio over the same period. But perhaps more importantly, the higher the fund's beta, other things equal, the lower the Treynor ratio and the worse the fund manager's risk-adjusted performance.

Value at Risk (VaR)

For many years, the Sharpe ratio, Treynor ratio and measures of alpha and beta were seen as being adequate descriptions of asset and portfolio risk. However, in the late-1980s the idea of Value at Risk (VaR) was introduced. The appeal of VaR is its apparent simplicity. It provides investors with a single, easily comprehendible cash value to the question: *How much can we lose if the worst comes to the worst?*

For example, a VaR calculation may enable us to assert that: *There is no more than a 5 per cent chance that a loss greater than 8 per cent of the portfolio's current value will be incurred over the next 12 months.*

Another way of putting this is: *We are 95 per cent confident that a loss no greater than 8 per cent of the portfolio's current value will be incurred over the next 12 months.*

Arguably this is easier to grasp as a measure of risk than saying that a portfolio's expected standard deviation is 6 per cent. While few people understand the concept of standard deviation, let alone what it would mean to have portfolio standard deviation of 6 per cent versus one with 8 per cent, everyone understands what a loss is and can compare one loss with another easily enough. VaR also focuses the investor's mind on the element of uncertainty in which they are most interested – losses. We could just as easily calculate a VaR value indicating the likelihood and magnitude of a possible gain, but this is not what is typically done. Instead VaR focuses on the likelihood of a bad event occurring and also on how bad that bad outcome might be. VaR focuses on potential loss, and can be expressed as a percentage or in absolute terms. Its flexibility as a measure of risk means that it is now applied to a whole host of financial phenomena. In the pensions' world, VaR can be used to quantify the downside risk attached to a particular asset, the scheme's asset portfolio, its liabilities or its funding position.

So how do we go about calculating a VaR value? Assume for the moment that the returns on a portfolio are, or have been, normally distributed over time. VaR calculations are typically made with 95 per cent or 99 per cent confidence, referred to as VaR95 and VaR99 respectively, which in turn correspond to points on the normal distribution curve 1.96 standard deviations and 2.33 standard deviations below the mean. VaR is calculated as follows:

$$\text{VaR} = \text{confidence level in standard deviations}$$
$$\times (\text{daily standard deviation} \times \sqrt{\text{days}})$$

So, for example, if we wanted to establish the VaR99 of a £10m portfolio, which has an annual volatility of 12.18 per cent then:

$$\text{VaR99} = 2.33 \times (12.18\%) = 28.38\%$$

From this, we could make VaR-like statements, such as:

We are confident that there is only a 1 per cent chance that the portfolio will lose more than 28.38 per cent of its current value, or approximately £2.84m, over the next 12 months.

Let's try to apply VaR in practice then. On Monday, 19 October 1987 the UK equity market fell by 10.37%. Based upon daily returns data up until that date this event was a 'twelve and a half standard deviation event'. In other words, based upon the idea that daily UK equity returns were normally distributed from 1970 to October 16 1987, a fall of 10.37% in one day was twelve and a half standard deviations from the historic daily mean return. Take another look at Exhibit 9.2 to see just how far two standard deviation events are from the normal distribution's mean. Now imagine how far twelve and a half standard deviations are away from the centre of that distribution.

So using the normal distribution, what were the chances of this catastrophic event happening? Should it have been a once in a 25 year event? A once in a 50 year event? A once in 100 year event?

Astonishingly, calculating the likelihood of this event, based on this data, and on the assumption that equity returns are normally distributed, strains the limits of an Excel spreadsheet. Under these conditions the event turns out to be a once in 1.06×10^{33} year event! And no, that is not a typo. For those of you that are unfamiliar with this notation to arrive at the number long hand all you have to do is multiply 1.06 by 10, 33 times. You could say that investors were very unlucky to experience an event of such astonishing, apparent rarity. Alternatively, you could say that the assumption that financial returns are normally distributed is just plain wrong.

Indeed, the point we make here is not actually specific to VaR, it is really a point relating to the assumption that financial market returns are normally distributed over time. They are not and basing assessments of risk on this assumption can be a very dangerous game to play indeed.

Fat tails – Skewness

The fact that financial market returns are not normally distributed means that in practice we have to use more sophisticated methods to derive a VaR that won't leave us with egg all over on our investment faces. Most importantly we need to take account of something called skewness. Skewed return distributions will tend to indicate a higher probability of the sort of event that happened in October 1987. The distributions are not bell-shaped, or symmetric, but asymmetric. Exhibit 9.10 is a stylized version of a return series that is negatively skewed. That is, large negative monthly returns are more frequent and therefore more probable than implied under the (false) assumption that returns are normally distributed.

The returns from many risky assets, such as equities, are negatively skewed. Although there are plenty of return values concentrated at the higher end of the returns distribution, as you would expect, there are typically a number of extreme negative outcomes, at the lower end. You should also note that while it is quite possible for two portfolios to have the same mean and standard deviation, they may well have different skewness characteristics.[11]

---

[11] For an example of this see Gary B. Gorton and K. Geert Rouwenhorst, 'Facts and Fantasies About Commodity Futures', *Financial Analysts Journal*, Volume 62, Number 2, pp. 47–68 (2006). In this research the authors constructed an equally weighted index of monthly returns of commodity futures for the period July 1959 to December 2004. While they exhibited the same return and standard deviation as the S&P 500, the distribution of returns was positively skewed whereas that for the S&P 500 was negatively skewed.

Exhibit 9.10   Negatively skewed returns

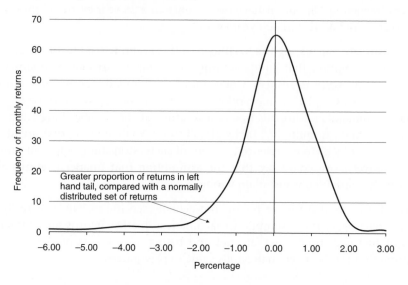

There are much more sophisticated ways of generating VaR statistics than we have used here, that do not assume that returns are normally distributed. However, no matter how sophisticated they are, these measures should still allow for the possibility that asset class returns can be very negative at times. In other words, they must allow for the large losses that have historically plagued financial markets and take full account of the *known unknowns* in asset prices.

Other complementary risk metrics

The existence of these nasty 'tail events' means that VaR, like any risk measure, should not be used in isolation. One very simplistic, but powerful way of enhancing our view of the risks inherent in investment portfolios and in a pension scheme's liabilities too is to undertake stress, or scenario, tests.

These tests are very simple to calculate. They are designed to answer questions like:

> *What would happen to the value of my asset portfolio and/or liabilities if we were to experience a re-run of the capital market events brought about by the:*

- *October 1987 stock market crash;*
- *Asian financial crisis of 1997;*
- *Russian debt crisis of 1998;*
- *collapse of the high tech bubble in the early-noughties; or the*
- *collapse of Lehman Brothers in September 2008;*

or any extreme market event that might conceivably happen again in a similar way in the future?

Calculating what would happen to your portfolio today if asset prices moved once again as they did in a past crisis period can be a very sobering exercise indeed, and we would encourage all trustees to undergo such an exercise.

Quantitative risk measures summary

There are many ways to measure risk. No single measure is perfect or even adequate. Risk might be one word but it is like a hydra – watching one head (one aspect of risk) is not sufficient – all the heads need to be watched if trustees wish to avoid being bitten. The complex nature and interaction of risks means that risk cannot be distilled into a single number. Furthermore, when modelling risk, it is important to understand the basis of the model and the assumptions made. Changing the assumptions does not necessarily affect the underlying risks but could impact how the risks are reported.

Other, less quantifiable risks

The preceding discussion concentrated on many of the measures available to quantify the *known unknowns*, for example, the uncertainty surrounding the likely returns that an investment in equities might produce. Even though we explained the issues and problems related to fat tails in asset returns in the context of VaR, it is important to understand that *all* these measures struggle with the issue of non-normality, or the fat tails that typify investment returns. While trustees need to have these risk metrics at their fingertips, they need to take a more holistic view of the risks that surround a typical scheme. That is because, arguably, there are other risks that are even harder to quantify.

There are three risks in particular that need to be monitored carefully. These relate to:

- the covenant of the scheme sponsor;
- financial market liquidity; and
- counterparty risk.

The sponsor covenant

Until defined benefit (DB) scheme deficits became widespread in the early part of this century, sponsor covenant risk appeared to be a known quantity for many trustees. Most assumed that it posed little risk to their scheme – since the scheme actuary and investment consultant told them that the scheme had sufficient assets to meet future liabilities, and in some cases that they had surplus assets – that is, too much money! Today, however, sponsor covenant risk is no longer a *known known*, rather it is very much a *known unknown*.

Indeed, as we noted in Chapter 3, the strength of the sponsor's covenant, especially for a DB pension scheme in deficit, should arguably be the number one risk to monitor. After all, as we pointed out in Chapter 1, most DB scheme sponsors contribute a significant amount of money to support their scheme every year. While individual scheme members typically contribute 6 per cent of their gross salary to the scheme, scheme sponsors can contribute in excess of 20 per cent of the total gross salary bill annually to the scheme. Moreover, a scheme's exposure to the financial health of the scheme sponsor is analogous to an investor holding an equity portfolio consisting of just one equity shareholding. Nonetheless, this is the exposure with which most schemes have to live.

The scheme sponsor is usually the most important asset that the scheme 'owns'. Without a scheme sponsor that can commit to such support, the viability of a scheme can quickly be called into question.[12] As such, trustees should keep this covenant under regular review with its active monitoring ideally being undertaken by a covenant consultant.

As noted in Chapter 3, any covenant review should consider whether the pension scheme is backed by that part of the sponsoring organization that holds the assets against which the pension scheme has recourse. Somewhat surprisingly, many pension schemes are unwittingly backed by that part of the sponsoring organization over which the pension scheme does not have any legal claim on the sponsor's assets! This is especially true of those sponsoring organizations that operate in the service sector. As well as being aware of the scheme's legal backing, the trustees and/or covenant consultant should also monitor the sponsor's credit rating(s), credit default swap spreads,[13] cash flow and profitability. Furthermore, because the sponsor's ability to support the scheme will depend on the viability and sustainability of its strategy and business model and the extent to which it is able to maintain a competitive position in its chosen marketplace(s), this should be monitored too. For example, if the sponsor embarks on an ambitious investment programme, or on a series of corporate acquisitions, if these destroy value (which they often do) then the strength of the sponsor covenant will be commensurately weaker.

---

[12] For a discussion of the issues, and for quantification of the degree to which a typical scheme is reliant on the sponsor's contribution see: A. Brigden et al., 'Coping with uncertainty and the importance of the Sponsor's covenant: The case of defined-benefit pension plans', ABI Research Paper Number 9 (2008).

[13] Credit default swap spreads are the price of insuring an issuer's bonds against default.

Moreover, following the recent economic crisis, many UK private sector DB schemes have suffered some deterioration in the quality of their sponsor covenant as the priority of many corporates has been to conserve cash on their balance sheets to fund their operations rather than the pension scheme. This has resulted in novel and increasingly complex contingent assets being pledged to schemes as a temporary stop gap in the funding of pension scheme deficits.

As we noted in Chapter 3, good examples of this trend towards the pledging of contingent assets include:

- Diageo plc which pledged 2.5 million barrels of whisky to its scheme;
- Whitbread plc which put its Premier Inn hotel chain property portfolio and the rights to a proportion of the income generated from the chain, into a Special Purpose Vehicle (SPV);
- Marks & Spencer and Sainsbury pledging part of their property portfolios to their respective schemes;
- ITV using a SPV to share ownership of a subsidiary company; and
- the most novel of them all, Uniq, the former Unigate business and now M&S's biggest sandwich supplier, handing over 90 per cent of its share capital to the pension scheme in return for the scheme relinquishing its claim on the company.

These complex, contingent assets put additional burdens on the governance budget of a trustee board. That is, they increase the amount of time that needs to be devoted to the analysis of the scheme's assets and require trustees to upgrade their knowledge and skill so that they can continue to oversee the operation of the scheme.

Liquidity risk

Liquidity risk arises when it proves difficult to realize an asset at the quoted market price because two-way trading in the asset has dried up. In instances like this there may be many sellers but few, if any, buyers. This usually leads to a sharp fall in the prices of risky assets (as in 2008) and a widening of dealing spreads. Indeed, liquidity risk had largely been forgotten by most market participants until the full force of the credit crisis was felt in late-2008 when the liquidity in most asset markets dried up completely. In other words, it was one of Rumsfeld's *unknown unknowns* for many investors in 2008.

Liquidity is a particularly important issue for pension schemes. At a minimum they must have sufficient liquid assets – the most obvious being cash – to be able to pay pension benefits in full and on time, though the liquidity needs of each scheme will vary. Schemes that are cash flow positive – that is, schemes that receive more income from members than they pay out to pensioners – may only require a relatively small liquidity buffer. However, the less cash flow positive a scheme the greater the liquidity buffer required. Cash flow negative schemes, by definition, have to pay benefits from selling regular and growing amounts of their asset bases. Having to pay benefits by selling assets that are very depressed in value – as they were in 2008 – can lead to a deadweight loss. That is an effective loss that cannot be made up by the performance of the remaining assets of the fund in the future – once sold at a loss, that is that.

So why not keep all assets in highly liquid assets such as cash and government bonds? The answer is that these assets tend to produce very low long-run real returns. Most schemes need their asset base to grow at rates substantially above that which they could expect from these assets if they are to meet their mainly inflation-linked liabilities that are subject to continually improving scheme member longevity. There is a balance to be struck then. A liquidity buffer is needed to pay benefits from month to month and to protect those benefits in times of financial market stress. However, this buffer is costly – in terms of a loss in expected return. So schemes now typically set liquidity buffers large enough to:

- meet x months of benefit payments,
- to withstand a 1 in 20 year nasty shock, or
- to withstand the impact of a re-run of 2008 and so forth.

Counterparty risk

Counterparty risk is another risk that was poorly considered before the financial crisis of 2008. For many, it was yet another *unknown unknown* in 2008. After all, what were the chances of a very large blue chip investment bank failing, what were the chances of a large retail bank being on the verge of failing and what were the chances of one of the world's largest insurers failing? Yet, Lehman Brothers failed. Lloyds-TSB, RBS and other banks around the world were only saved following government intervention. Additionally one of the world's largest insurers, AIG, went under.

Counterparty risk is related to, but is different from corporate default risk. It really refers to the plumbing of the financial system. In most transactions – particularly with regard to derivative contracts – financial institutions make connections, or act as intermediaries, between buyers and sellers. We rely on them to execute these transactions in an efficient manner. If one of them fails, literally hundreds of thousands of financial transactions can fail, leaving one side of each of many of these transactions facing losses. For example, some investors who had dealt with Lehman Brothers in September 2008 were left substantially out of pocket when the US investment bank, failed. Moreover, once the complexity of many deals was unwound, investors found that rather than, say, XYZ Bank being their counterparty to a trade, the ultimate counterparty was Lehman Brothers. In fact, a number of hedge funds found this out to their cost.

Counterparty risk can be quantified by reference to credit rating agency credit ratings, credit spreads and credit default swap spreads. Credit ratings are scaled from AAA/Aaa1 (the notation used depends on which credit rating agency has issued the credit rating) to D, with BBB-/Baa3 representing the dividing line between investment grade and sub-investment grade ratings. Credit spreads quantify the extra yield an investor can receive over and above the yield on AAA/Aaa1-rated government bonds, such as UK gilts. Credit default swap spreads are the price of insuring an issuer's bonds against default. All of this data can be provided by your investment consultant and fund manager(s). The lower the rating and the higher the spreads, the greater the perceived counterparty and/or default risk. However, be warned, none of these indicators gave any real indication that Lehman Brothers was about to fail until it was about to happen. The best way to deal with counterparty risk is probably to spread exposure to a range of counterparties rather than to rely on just one – no matter how highly rated that one might be.

Following the financial crisis of 2008, most pension schemes have reviewed their counterparty exposures and have tried to reduce any concentrations by using a wider range of counterparties and by making sure collateral arrangements are sound, and are revalued on a daily basis. Given that we are unlikely to get much warning before any future collapse of a major financial institution, it is just as well to review these arrangements on a regular basis.

Soft risks

Unfortunately there are other risks too; risks that we might term as *soft risks*. Perhaps an inappropriate term, since it makes them sound rather benign, but they are not. These soft risks are arguably even less visible than those outlined above. However, despite this they can still result in equally disastrous outcomes if not properly monitored and managed.

Agency risks

The risk that those third parties to whom trustees delegate their duties do not discharge them in a responsible manner are called agency risks. For example, in Chapter 3 we introduced the fund manager. Most pension schemes entrust their assets to these professional asset managers – for which they charge a fee of course. The scheme is therefore reliant on their professionalism and also on their ability to protect and grow the assets under their management. We will look at their proven abilities to do this in Chapters 14 and 18. However, another element of fund manager(s) risk is their susceptibility to behavioural biases, or to sub-optimal behaviour. Such biases can lead to sub-optimal portfolio construction and poor performance. Although we consider these biases in more detail in Chapter 17, they include:

- blindly extrapolating perceived trends into the future;
- only relying upon the most recently available information and that which confirms a strongly held personal view;
- displaying unwarranted overconfidence in their own investing abilities;
- selling profitable investments too soon and holding on to loss making investments too long; and
- blindly following the herd.

While some of these biases can be detected by simply examining the composition of the manager's portfolio over several months, nothing beats questioning the manager face-to-face on their investment philosophy and process.[14]

As well as meeting fund managers regularly to make sure they are doing their jobs properly, trustees should also meet with other third party service providers too, for example, their global custodian – the financial institution responsible for recording and 'storing' the scheme's assets. Meeting regularly with your scheme actuary and investment consultant goes without saying. Often it is a good idea to ask such providers to pitch for scheme business every few years, or when the trustees are unhappy with an aspect of the service provided (or not). As well as reviewing the incumbent provider, this gives trustees the opportunity to compare others with them and to learn about how practices might vary from one provider to the next. Although this can be time consuming, it is a necessary process if agency risks are to be managed effectively.

Poor decision making and focus

There are also risks surrounding the trustee decision making process. In Chapter 17, we explain how poor decision making can result from insufficient Board diversity and poor chairmanship. Getting the composition of the Board right and the method by which decisions are made spot on is absolutely essential. Spending too much time on unnecessary detail and focusing on the issues that make little, if any, impact on the bottom line at the expense of the big picture will serve members poorly. This is a particular feature of decision making by committee in many walks of life.

Governance

Good governance is a pre-requisite for any governing body. It applies equally to the boards of corporations, to government departments and to trustee boards.

---

[14] We consider fund manager philosophies and processes in Chapter 18.

It is important then that trustees make sure their governance is effective and efficient. For example, most committees meet regularly, usually quarterly, but sometimes semi-annually and increasingly monthly. As financial markets move rapidly, trustees need to be confident that the frequency of the meetings does not hamper their ability to respond accordingly. Investment advisers are frequently frustrated at the time it takes trustee boards to come to a view and make a decision. Often the delay is due to a lack of knowledge. Here is a typical problem:

- the investment adviser recommends an investment in a new asset class – let's say emerging market government debt (EMD) for the sake of argument;
- at least one board member is unfamiliar with EMD, but has read in the media that EMD is riskier than UK gilts;
- before coming to a decision, this trustee and now others on the board ask for training on this asset class;
- after much negotiation, a training day is arranged that everyone can attend; and
- finally at the next meeting – perhaps six months on – now fully trained a decision is made, but unfortunately the compelling case for investing in EMD has now gone. Other investors have entered the market and pushed the price up.

This is just one example of how not having the requisite understanding and skill set on the board can hamper decision making. This particular issue might be resolved by setting up an investment sub-committee, populated with people that are more familiar with investment markets. This inevitably means more time and effort, but the costs of poorly implemented decisions (and inertia) can be very high indeed.

A related issue is that of succession planning. As membership of trustee boards changes over time, it is important to plan for the changes. A board does not want to lose its resident expert on say swaps, or on say, Environmental, Social and Corporate Governance (ESG) issues. The requisite replacements should be lined up before changes take place, not after, and ideally these people should be fully trained *before* they join the board.

Summary: A word of warning

Let us begin by summarizing this chapter on risk with the wise, but rather discouraging words of Nobel laureate, Edmund Phelps:

> *Risk assessment and risk management models were never well founded . . . There was mystique to the idea that market participants knew the price to put on this or that risk. But it is impossible to imagine that such a complex system could be*

> *understood in such detail and with such amazing correctness . . . the requirements for information . . . have gone beyond our abilities to gather it.* (Edmund Phelps, 2009, Nobel Prize for Economics 2006)

Since the 1970s some of the best and brightest minds in finance have attempted to define and manage risk better and to avoid investment disasters through detailed risk modelling and financial engineering. However, risk management still remains far from being an exact science. In fact, arguably there has been a fundamental misunderstanding of risk. Some very clever people – who should have been clever enough to know better – have perpetuated the idea that all risk is manageable. In reality, much risk management is arguably still based on a very old framework,[15] one that requires the accurate calculation of the probability of all possible outcomes!

Pablo Triana suggests in his highly readable book, *Lecturing Birds on Flying: Can Mathematical Theories Destroy the Financial Markets?*, that the analytics within risk models did not just fail, but decisively contributed to the financial crisis of 2008 and many other crises before that. To quote him from the Financial Times:[16]

> *In fact, it is reasonable to argue that the worst market crises since 1929 were all aided, abetted and directly caused by flawed analytical concoctions.*

For trustees it is important to bear in mind that the mathematics applied in risk management by these super intelligent mathematicians can only take us so far. Ultimately, there is a big role for judgement and intuition.

However, we'd like to finish where we started – with reference to the 'wise' words of Donald Rumsfeld. Preparing oneself for the *known unknowns* is difficult but not impossible. The preparation needed, however, involves a holistic approach to risk management. More than one risk measure is needed and a single-minded reliance on quantitative risk measures is definitely a mistake.

But what about the *unknown unknowns*? How do trustees prepare for these since, by definition, they have no frame of reference? Arguably while having a robust risk management framework and experienced advisers can help, the bottom line is that it is essential to brace yourself for the unexpected. History can prove instructive, but it may not necessarily be a good guide to the future.

---

[15] For instance, the mainstay of risk management, as we know, revolves around the normal distribution, which was originally documented by a French mathematician Abraham de Moivre in 1733 in his *Doctrine of Chances*. Similarly, the basis of portfolio construction still rests on the work of Harry Markowitz in his 1952 paper entitled 'Portfolio Selection'.

[16] *Financial Times*, 29 November, p. 17 (2010).

Key points

- Risk is a difficult concept to define and cannot be distilled into one simple number. While the sources of some risks – the *known unknowns* – might even be quantifiable, others – the *unknown unknowns* – cannot be anticipated, let alone quantified.
- Standard deviation measures the dispersion of the returns on an asset, or portfolio of assets, around the average return and is based on the assumption that investment returns are normally distributed.
- In constructing an efficient frontier, although the expected returns and standard deviations of the combined assets, or asset classes, under consideration are key inputs, it is the expected correlations between the returns on these assets that are the most important determinant of the efficient frontier's shape and position within a mean-variance chart.
- Reward-to-risk ratios quantify the amount of prospective reward in comparison to the prospective risk that derives from an asset or portfolio of assets.
- Those risks that are hard to quantify but need to be monitored carefully include sponsor covenant risk, financial market liquidity and counterparty risk. In addition, there are soft risks such as agency risks and governance risks that also need to be considered.
- Risk management remains far from being an exact science in that not all risks can be identified and managed.

Chapter 10

Asset Allocation: The Big Decision

Learning outcomes

- Understand the importance of the asset allocation decision.
- Understand the building block approach to strategic asset allocation (SAA) and the challenges it presents.
- Understand how tactical asset allocation (TAA) differs from strategic asset allocation.
- Understand how tactical asset allocation could be implemented.

Introduction

Asset allocation is one of *the* really big decisions that trustees need to get right. It involves making choices between broad asset classes. Traditionally, for most institutional investors, including pension funds, the process of asset allocation principally involved choosing between equities and bonds. We looked at each of these traditional asset classes in Chapters 5 to 8. Further allocation decisions were then usually taken within these broad asset classes, for example, within the equity category a choice might be made between domestic versus overseas equities, or within the bond category, between government and corporate bonds.

However, today, as well as being able to choose between these traditional, or mainstream, asset classes, investors can now choose from a range of 'alternative' asset classes too. The term 'alternative' is really applied to all those asset classes that were not part of a typical institutional portfolio in the past. These 'alternative' asset classes might now include commodities, private equity, currency, infrastructure assets and hedge funds (although strictly speaking hedge funds are not an asset class, rather a skill set). Over the past ten years or so, the finance industry has developed investment vehicles that allow investors, both small and large, to obtain access to these alternative sources of risk and return. Whether each of these traditional and alternative asset classes should be managed on an active or passive basis is another issue,[1] but it is secondary to the core asset allocation decision.

In this chapter we will begin by concentrating on the issues that an asset allocator has to consider when coming to a judgement about the likely future returns and risks relating to these traditional asset classes, by developing a consistent, intellectual framework for this decision making process. That is, the views that they must form to inform their strategic asset allocation decisions. We will then move on to consider a more active asset allocation process – tactical asset allocation. In Chapter 13 we will show how alternative assets classes might be integrated into this same framework.

Asset allocation in practice

Asset allocation is generally practiced by investment professionals who manage portfolios that combine asset classes. Life assurance companies employ asset allocation techniques to manage their multi-asset class portfolios which they use to back their life funds and most asset management companies offer multi-asset class 'balanced funds' or 'diversified growth funds' for their institutional clients, such as pension schemes. Finally, investment consultants typically advise pension fund trustees on the appropriate mix for their pension fund assets.

But how difficult is asset allocation?

Exhibit 10.1 shows the real, or inflation-adjusted, value of £100 invested in three UK asset classes over the past 100 years or so, where the income from these assets has been reinvested over time.

According to Barclays Capital, £100 invested in the UK equity market at end-1899 with the gross dividend income reinvested over time, would have been worth £24,133 in real terms by the end of 2010. Over the same 111-year period an investment in gilts and in cash, with coupons and interest income reinvested, would only have been worth £369 and £286 respectively in real terms.[2] On the face of this evidence then, the asset allocation decision appears rather straightforward: *invest in equities and don't bother with government bonds or cash.*

---

[1] We consider the active versus passive decision in Chapter 14.
[2] *Barclays Capital Equity Gilt Study 2011*, p.95.

Exhibit 10.1   **Real accumulated total returns**

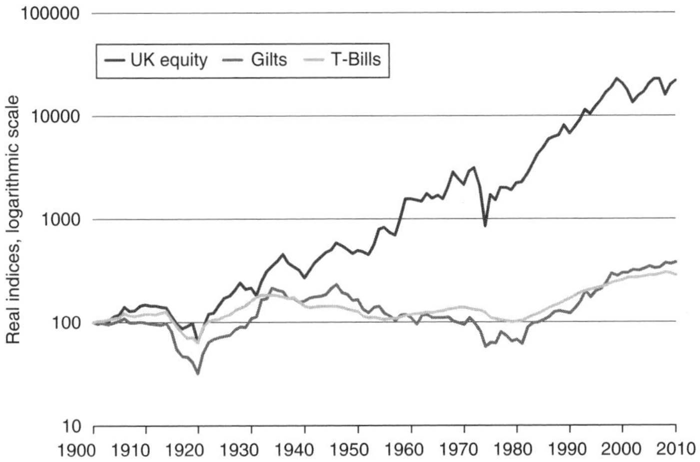

Source: Barclays Capital.

Indeed, during the 1980s and 1990s many institutional investors, including the UK pensions industry, came to the conclusion that equities were the most appropriate or desirable asset to hold.

We can see this in Exhibit 10.2, which presents the broad asset allocation break-down of the UK's defined benefit (DB) pension schemes from 2003 to 2011. In 2003 equities comprised 68 per cent of the total long-term holdings of pension funds, and although this proportion has fallen since then, they still made up 47 per cent of pension fund investments in 2011. Exhibit 10.2 also shows how the asset mix has changed over this ten-year period. Bonds now make up a greater proportion of total holdings. There are a number of reasons why the asset mix has shifted, but one factor behind the move is the belief that the very strong, real returns produced by the world's major equity markets over the past few decades, as shown for UK equities in Exhibit 10.1, are unlikely to be repeated in the future. This view has been supported by the performance of developed economy equity markets over the noughties. The FTSE 100 ended the decade down by 22 per cent. The slightly better news is that when dividends are taken into account, the FTSE 100 produced a positive return of 9 per cent over the decade – nearly 1 per cent a year – while the broader FTSE All Share Index managed 18 per cent. By contrast the MSCI Emerging Markets Index doubled over the same period – though with substantially more volatility. Given this, when looking to allocate funds between one asset class and another how does one come to a view about potential returns, particularly over the long term, which is arguably the horizon on which most institutional investors should be focussing? Furthermore, how can an investor come to a view about the likely risks associated with long-term investments?

Exhibit 10.2   Long-term asset holdings of UK DB pension schemes

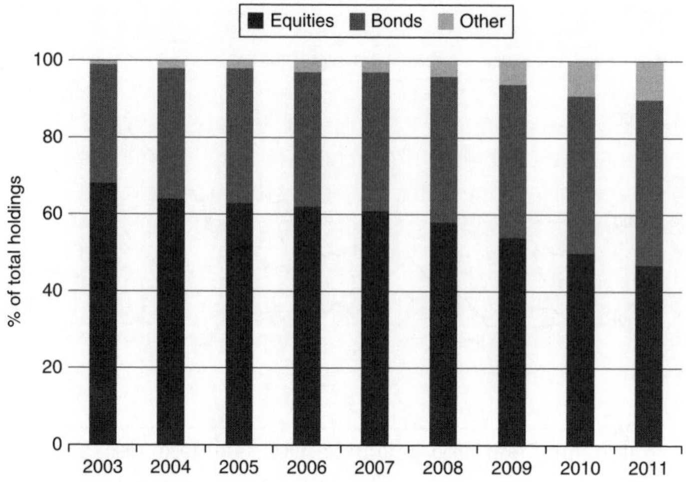

Source: Mercer European Asset Allocation Survey, May 2011.

These are questions that asset allocation professionals have to address – whether they like it or not – before coming to a view about the most appropriate asset mix, whether for a pension fund, for a Life Assurer's life fund, or indeed for any situation where the liabilities are very long term in nature.

The asset allocation process necessary to come to such views is often referred to as *strategic asset allocation.*

Strategic asset allocation

The importance of the strategic asset allocation (SAA) decision cannot be over-stated. Work on this topic in the 1980s[3] suggested that a broadly conventional SAA that employs conventional active management to manage mainstream asset classes can 'explain' over 90 per cent of a portfolio's returns over time. In addition, a later study recently concluded that around 100 per cent of pension fund returns are attributable to SAA.[4]

So SAA really is *the* big investment decision.

---

[3] Gary P. Brinson, L. Randolph Hood and Gilbert L. Beebower, 'Determinants of Portfolio Performance', *The Financial Analysts Journal*, July/August (1986).
[4] Roger G. Ibbotson and Paul D. Kaplan, 'Does Asset Allocation Policy Explain 40%, 90% or 100% of Performance?', *The Financial Analysts Journal*, January/February (2000).

However, most practitioners of strategic asset allocation do not see asset alloca-tion as a way of simply maximizing the potential return on an investment fund. A simple, return maximizing strategy, with no regard for the underlying volatility of an investment fund, might lead to an asset mix that is very heavily weighted towards equities. But, most investors, including pension fund trustees, do care about the risks taken in achieving returns because most investors are risk averse and because they have liabilities that need to be met through time. Other things equal, most investors would prefer a portfolio that produces a less volatile set of returns than one that produces higher return volatility.

Therefore, most asset allocation practitioners aim to achieve not the highest return, but instead the highest *risk-adjusted return* on the funds under manage-ment. That is, achieving the highest return for a given and acceptable level of risk. We can illustrate this objective by reintroducing the mean-variance efficient frontier that we described in Chapter 9.

We present an example of an efficient frontier in Exhibit 10.3.

Each dot in Exhibit 10.3 represents the expected return and expected standard deviation (or risk) for a particular asset class. The curved line represents the maximum expected return that can be achieved by combining these asset classes for any given level of expected standard deviation, or risk. Higher return is achievable with lower risk as long as the returns on the various asset classes used to produce the frontier are imperfectly correlated. In other words, where the returns are not expected to move up or down in perfect unison over time.

The goal of SAA is to identify the return requirements of the fund and then to combine asset classes in such a way that the expected return is produced with

Exhibit 10.3   A mean-variance efficient frontier for asset classes

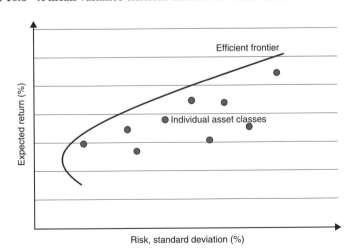

the lowest volatility. In other words, the goal is to identify the efficient frontier for any given group of asset classes. To do this, asset allocators have to come to a view about the following three factors required to build the frontier:

i.   the expected return on the asset classes under consideration;
ii. the likely volatility of these asset class returns; and
iii. the likely correlations between asset class returns.

Once the asset allocator has come to a view about these issues the frontier can be constructed and the 'optimal' client portfolio can be identified. Clearly this will be a highly subjective exercise. There is no correct way of coming to views about the future performance and associated risks of a set of asset classes. However, in this chapter we will attempt to outline the key issues on which asset allocators need to form views, before they can undertake an SAA exercise.

Long-term expected returns

For most economists the expected return on an asset class, or an individual asset, will comprise three components. Therefore to come to a view about expected long-term returns one needs to come to a view about these individual elements. These components are:

i.   the expected riskless, real return;
ii. expected inflation; and
iii. the expected risk premium.

Of course expected returns may not always equate to actual returns, but at least the framework that we will discuss here gives asset allocators a starting point and a framework for thinking about these important issues.

The expected, riskless real return

The first component of return is possibly conceptually the hardest to grasp. Imagine a world where there is no inflation, nor any investment risk. In this world investors would still require a return on their investments. Why is this? When we invest our cash today, we cannot then use it to buy goods and services. This means that there is an opportunity cost to all investing. This opportunity cost is related to the consumption that we forego by handing over our cash to another party as part of an investment. Therefore, even if there is no inflation in an economy and no risk, investors will still require a real return on this investment. We can think of this as the first component of expected return, which will be common to all investments, since all investment requires us to give up consumption today for consumption at some time in the future. So how high, or low should this expected riskless real return be?

Economists argue that this component of expected return should be closely related to the expected real, long-term growth rate of the underlying economy. In aggregate, the growth rate of the economy is the opportunity cost foregone for consuming today rather than at some stage in the future. However, if the expected riskless real return is closely related to the growth rate of the underlying economy, this just prompts another question: what is the long-term potential growth rate of an economy? As discussed in Chapter 4, trend growth is the rate at which an economy can grow without causing inflation to accelerate or alternatively unemployment to rise.

Luckily the trend rate of economic growth for most, if not all, major economies is quite stable over time. For example, the UK economy has tended to grow at an average annual real rate of around 2.25 per cent. Surprisingly enough, it seems that quite dramatic changes to an economy are required to alter this trend rate of growth even by small amounts. The advent of rail travel, the invention of the car and the telephone, the arrival of the computer and finally the Internet have all failed to make a significant difference to the underlying trend rate of growth of the UK economy. A rather sobering thought. In fact, for the UK we have to go back to the Industrial Revolution[5] to find a change that made a significant impact on UK trend growth.

So trend growth tends to be quite stable for mature economies like the UK's and even for more dynamic economies like that of the US. This does not mean that the rate of trend growth will be the same across all of these economies. Some economies will have a trend rate of growth that is more rapid than others. This, in turn, means that the expected real return in each economy should be different too. However, as Panel A in Exhibit 10.4 shows, for most developed economies, economic growth has been between 2 and 3 per cent over the past 40 years or so. US economic growth has been faster than, for example, UK economic growth over this period.

If these trends continue into the future, and remember these are well-established trends, then when we invest money, the minimum we should expect to receive would be a real return of between 2 to 3 per cent per year, depending upon the developed economy in which we undertake the investment – this is where the discretion of the asset allocator comes in. One asset allocator might believe that US trend growth is 3 per cent, another that it is 2 per cent. The point is that each asset allocator needs to come to a view about this component of expected return, and then needs to be able to justify this view to their colleagues and clients.

Some indirect confirmation of this view might be derived from the market for index-linked government bonds. These bonds are to all intents and purposes

---

[5] The Industrial Revolution of 1780 to 1840 introduced stream power and the mechanization of a whole range of previously labour intensive tasks, enhancing productivity as it progressed.

Exhibit 10.4   Real growth and real yields

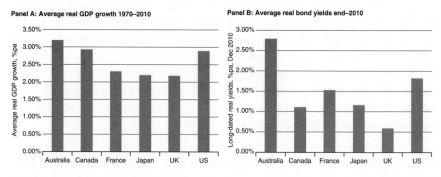

Source: Bloomberg, Thomson Financial.

inflation-proofed and technically at least, carry no default risk since governments can always print money to meet the payment commitments.[6] Investing in these bonds is like investing in a world without risk and inflation. Panel B of Exhibit 10.4 presents the average real yields on a range of long-dated index-linked government bonds at the end of 2010. The yields are not zero. Instead they range from just over 0.5 percent in the UK, to just under 3 per cent in Australia. These bonds do not present a perfect proxy for the expected real return since in many cases these bonds are rather rare and, as such, tend to trade at relatively high prices and low yields. This is the main reason why the real yield on UK government bonds is so very low. Nevertheless in the past, particularly prior to the credit crisis, the real yields on these bonds have tended to be between 1.5 and 2.5 per cent – more or less in line with historic growth trends. Of course we should not forget that the data in Panel A is backward looking, while the real yields demanded on long-dated government bonds at the end of 2010 involve a forward-looking assessment of growth. Read like this, Panel B could be taken as an indication that at the end of 2010 bond market participants were expecting lower economic growth in the future than had been experienced in the past from these developed economies. In other words, they may be viewing the collapse of the credit bubble as being a paradigm shifting event with regard to economic growth.

Expected inflation

We imagined a world without inflation and risk, and argued that even in this world that investors would expect a real return on their investments. As we

---

[6] Although this is not true of Euro zone governments, who do not control their currency, the euro.

know, inflation is a fact of life. The general price level has tended to rise over time in most economies, particularly since the oil shocks of the 1970s. This general increase in price levels erodes the purchasing power of cash over time. As a result of this, investors will require compensation for this erosion of their spending power and will price assets such that their prospective returns will compensate them for any anticipated inflation. This compensation will be required by investors for all investments where the cash flows are not inflation protected.

We saw in Chapter 4 just how volatile inflation has been over the years, but also that that volatility seems to have been lower since central banks have been given responsibility for targeting it. It remains to be seen whether inflation volatility will remain low in a post-credit crunch world, but at the time of writing, inflation expectations still appear to be in line with the inflation experience of the past ten to 15 years, rather than reflecting fears of a return to the inflation of the 1970s.

Panel A of Exhibit 10.5 shows a selection of break-even inflation rates. That is, the difference between the yield on a conventional government bond and an index-linked bond of the same maturity. Although this is not a perfect representation of the inflation expectations of financial market participants, these indicators can be taken as the market's forecast of inflation over the horizon of these bonds. Panel B shows an alternative measure of expected inflation for a selection of economies which is based upon a survey of business leaders, trade unionists and so forth.

We could either use measures such as those shown in Exhibit 10.5 (or combinations of them) as an estimate of future inflation, or alternatively, where a

Exhibit 10.5   Two measures of inflation expectations

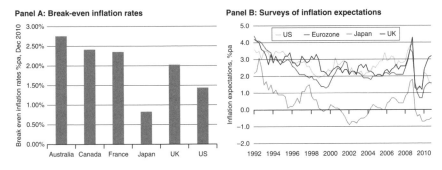

Source: Bloomberg, Thomson Financial.

central bank has an inflation target, we could use this as the proxy for expected inflation. We discussed inflation targeting in Chapter 4. The degree to which any investor would wish to rely on a central bank's inflation target as a proxy for expected inflation would depend very much on the credibility of the central bank. Where the central bank has had a long and successful track record in keeping inflation under control, an asset allocator (or any investor) might place significant weight on this target.

Alternatively, an asset allocator may not have any faith in financial market, survey-based or central bank target-based proxies of expected inflation, and will form views that are entirely independent of any of these sources. Again, the point we are trying to make here is that however one arrives at these views they must be arrived at in some way or another. Arguably coming to a view about future inflation is easier today than it was in the 1970s, but then again . . .

The expected return on cash

So far we have looked at the first two components of expected return, the:

i. expected riskless real return, and
ii. expected inflation.

When we add these two components together for an economy we arrive at a proxy for the required return on a cash deposit over time. Suppose for example, that we believe that the UK long-term, real annual economic growth rate is 2.25 per cent and that UK inflation will average 2 per cent in the long term. Given these views, the long-term return on cash continuously deposited in very short-dated deposit accounts with very secure financial institutions (assuming such entities exist now!) that would be sufficient to compensate us for real economic growth and inflation would be 4.25 per cent (2.25 per cent plus 2 per cent). Equally, suppose that we believed that real Japanese economic growth will be 1.5 per cent in the future and that inflation will average 0.5 per cent. In this case the return on similar cash deposits necessary to compensate investors would be much lower, at around 2 per cent (1.5 per cent plus 0.5 per cent). Using this simple framework, different asset allocators may arrive at very different cash return expectations depending upon their underlying assumptions.

The sum of the real return and expected inflation components of return is often referred to by economists as the 'neutral policy rate', or 'neutral rate of interest'. This is because it will tend to be the rate of interest that neither stimulates economic growth nor detracts from it. Over time interest rates will tend to cycle around this neutral rate. When the economy is weak, interest rates may fall below this neutral rate as the monetary authorities try to stimulate

Exhibit 10.6   Bank of England's policy rate

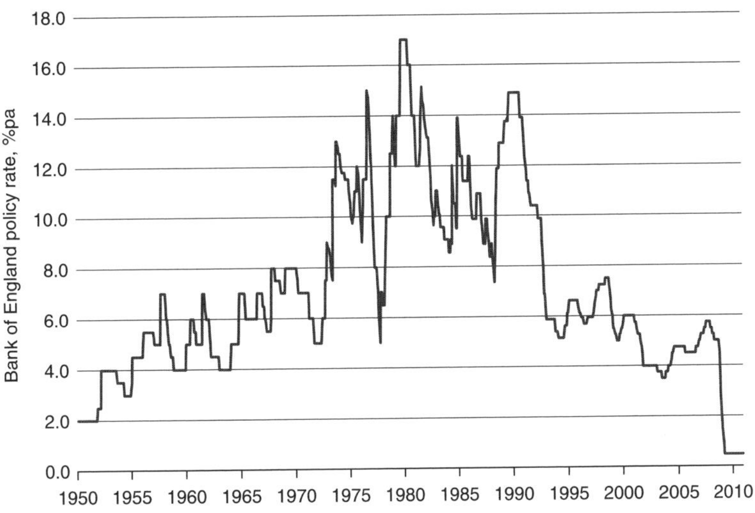

the economy. When the economy overheats, interest rates may rise above their neutral level as the monetary authorities try to reduce economic growth.

In Exhibit 10.6 we have presented the policy rate for the UK stretching back to 1951. There was a rising trend in the UK's policy rate over the 1950s and 1960s. This gradual increase in interest rates was largely due to the gradual increase in inflation over this period. Then came the 1970s and 1980s. Over these two decades, average interest rates were much higher than in the earlier post-war period. This was because inflation was not only high but so were inflation expectations. Therefore, investors and other economic agents demanded a higher nominal interest rate on cash balances in compensation for the loss in purchasing power that resulted from such high levels of inflation.

More recently, as inflation has fallen, and with the successful introduction of an inflation target – originally set at 2.5 per cent RPI(X) inflation and now 2 per cent CPI inflation – interest rates have cycled around 4.50 per cent to 4.75 per cent. Following the recent financial crisis the Bank of England's Monetary Policy Committee's (MPC) extraordinary response is evident; rates were slashed well below the neutral rate in an effort to kick start the economy.

Risk premia

The first two components of long-term expected returns make up the neutral policy rate and can be broadly thought of as the long-term return that investors and asset allocators might expect from cash deposits over time. In fact, this expected return on cash is the basis for the return expected on all risky investments. It is the minimum that we would expect from a (more or less) riskless investment. So investors will expect an additional return, over and above the neutral rate of interest, for investing in risky asset classes. This additional return is known as a *risk premium*. It is this risk premium that distinguishes the expected return on one risky asset class from another, since the risks inherent in these asset classes will differ depending upon the type of investment that they represent.

The assessment of the 'fair' risk premium on each asset class is one of the key judgements that an asset allocator has to make in coming to a view about the appropriate strategic asset allocation.

Index-linked government bonds

As we noted earlier, index-linked bonds issued by developed economy governments involve no credit risk, since 'technically' governments cannot become bankrupt, because they can always print money to pay their debts if they need to.[7] Furthermore, investors do not need to worry about future inflation since the payments from these bonds are automatically adjusted for inflation. The return required on an index-linked bond then will be very closely related to the trend rate of economic growth in the underlying economy. Given that there is (almost) no inflation risk or credit risk in these bonds, there is no need for investors to seek compensation for these risks when investing in these bonds.

However, this does not mean that the returns on these bonds will not contain a risk premium. This is because there is always the possibility that an investor may have misjudged the trend rate of growth of the economy. However, rightly or wrongly, most asset allocators assume that this premium, if it does exist, is small particularly compared with the risk premium required on conventional government bonds.

Conventional government bonds – the inflation risk premium

As explained above, theoretically there is no credit risk involved in buying most government bonds, since they can always print money to pay their

---

[7] With the exception of course of Euro zone governments, who, as we noted earlier, do not have control of their own currency, the euro.

debts should the need arise. If this is true, what are the risks involved in holding developed economy government bonds? Perhaps the main risk is that inflation will turn out to be very different from the levels initially envisaged. Consequently, the additional return required by investors for holding long-dated government bonds over and above the neutral rate of interest is often referred to as the 'inflation risk premium' – the extra return required due to the uncertainty related to future inflation. This risk premium could, of course, incorporate uncertainty about future real economic growth or, in these post-credit crunch times, uncertainty about the creditworthiness of governments! However, we will continue to refer to it as the inflation risk premium.

Unfortunately, it is impossible to say how big or small this premium really is, or should be. But we can get some idea by performing the following experiment. Suppose we can assume that the real return on an index-linked government bond is a good proxy for the market's assessment of the real, long-term growth potential of an economy. If we then subtract this yield from the yield on a conventional government bond with a similar maturity, and then subtract from this a measure of inflation expectations, perhaps derived from a survey of investor inflation expectations, what is left over is the extra return investors require for holding a conventional government bond over and above the real required return and the return in compensation for expected inflation. This calculation can be summarized as follows:

Yield on conventional government bond

minus

Yield on index-linked government bond of similar maturity

minus

Survey-based measure of inflation expectations

equals

The 'inflation risk premium'

In Exhibit 10.7 we have presented a calculation of this kind for the UK government bond market. There are a number of points worth noting with respect to this particular representation of the inflation risk premium. First, it is certainly imperfect, since it shows that the premium is negative at times. This makes little practical sense since, if accurate, it would imply that in compensation for future uncertainty about inflation (or other factors) investors are willing to receive a lower return! Second, putting aside these

Exhibit 10.7   Measure of the inflation risk premium for gilts

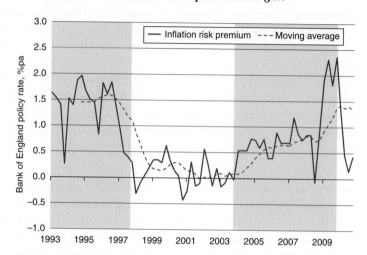

negative values for the moment, there are three distinct periods that we should consider.

i.   The period 1993 to mid-1997: the series averages just under 1.5 per cent. This is the average level of compensation that investors required over this period in compensation for risk, largely the risk associated with future inflation.

ii. Mid-1997 to 2004: the series averaged around 0.25 per cent.

iii. The period 2004 to 2009, where the premium averaged around 0.75 per cent.

What might have caused the shifts in the level of the inflation risk premium over time? One of the most important influences on the premium at any point in time will be the market's perception of the credibility of the government and of the monetary policy authority. If they can be trusted to deliver stable growth and inflation, then this suggests that the premium demanded from government debt should be lower than otherwise might be the case.

In May 1997 the MPC was given the power to set interest rates with the remit that they should target inflation. Prior to this the responsibility for setting interest rates and controlling inflation rested with the Chancellor of the Exchequer. It seems very likely that the fall in the inflation risk premium after 1997 was at least partially due to the fact that financial market participants had more faith in the central bank's willingness and ability to control inflation than they had in politicians. This might explain why the premium fell.

In the same vein, the gradual rise in the premium since 2004 could be interpreted as a sign that investors have become progressively less convinced about the ability of the Bank of England to achieve its inflation target, and/or the ability of the government to pursue policies that will ensure stable growth over time. Having recently gone through the deepest recession in 70 years, it is perhaps not surprising that this premium has risen. In fact, perhaps it is surprising that it has not risen further.

Summary so far

The sum of the expected riskless real return, inflation expectations and the inflation risk premium together comprise investors' required return on long-dated government bonds. This also means that changes in the perception of these components can change the overall return expectation. Furthermore, the values of these components will differ from one government bond market to another, since economies differ too, and, as such, they can go a long way to explaining the differences in the yields on bonds issued by different governments.

Corporate bonds – the credit risk premium

We highlighted the fact that governments that issue bonds in their own currency need never default on these debts, if they can print money to meet the payments – though this strategy would not go down well with bond holders! However, corporations issue bonds too but, unlike governments, they cannot print cash to meet their payment obligations – well, not legally anyway. There is a real risk that they may default on their obligations, that is, they might miss a coupon payment or become bankrupt. Because of this risk, investors demand a credit premium.

The credit premium is an additional return that investors demand, over and above the return that they would require from a government bond issued in the same currency and with the same maturity. This means that the total return required on a corporate bond incorporates all the components that go into making up the required return on government bonds discussed above, plus a credit premium. But how big is this credit premium?

The premium itself will vary from corporate bond issuer to issuer. We have already briefly explained the concept of credit quality and the role that ratings agencies like Moody's and Standard and Poor's play in assessing creditworthiness in Chapter 6. When determining the premium to be demanded on a particular corporate bond, credit analysts will consider much the same factors as the ratings agencies. These factors fall into three broad categories: firm specific, market specific and economic. Credit analysts will assess the following firm specific factors, using detailed balance sheet statements and profit and loss accounts:

i. liquidity,
ii. leverage, and
iii. profitability

Liquidity relates to a firm's ability to generate cash to make its regular coupon payments. To assess this, credit analysts may look at the ratio of the firm's regular cash flow to the interest payable on its debts. The higher this ratio, the more confident the credit analysts may be that a firm will be able to meet its coupon payments. Leverage refers to the total amount of debt that the firm has relative to its total capital. So for example, analysts may look at the ratio of a company's total debt to ordinary shareholder funds. The lower this value the greater would be the analyst's confidence that the firm is creditworthy. Finally, a highly profitable firm would be less likely to have to default on its debt than a firm with weak profitability. To assess profitability, analysts might look at the ratio of company profits to total sales or capital employed, the higher these ratios the more profitable the firm.

There are, of course many, many financial ratios that analysts might consider, but basically the three broad categories address one simple issue: what is the issuing firm's ability to pay?

Exhibit 10.8 shows the results of research conducted by the ratings agency Moody's, on their own ratings. Each bar shows the proportion of bonds of a particular rating that default within five, ten, 15 and 20 years respectively after first receiving that rating. For example, no bond that has been rated Aaa by Moody's between 1970 and 2001 has defaulted in the subsequent five years following the award of this Aaa rating. However, as time progresses the

Exhibit 10.8   Average cumulative issuer-weighted global default rates 1970 to 2008

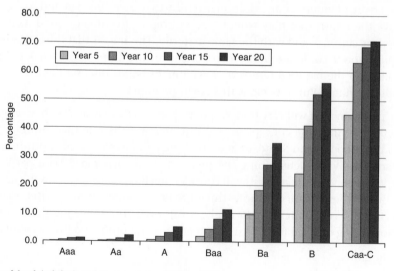

Source: Moody's default and recovery rates, 1920 to 2008.

default rate rises in all categories, and it is likely that as it does so those that were originally rated Aaa and eventually defaulted were probably progressively downgraded by the agency as they became less creditworthy.

The overwhelming message from Exhibit 10.8 is that default rates rise across all horizons, as the initial rating gets lower and lower. Remember from Chapter 6 that bonds that receive a rating of Baa 3 or above on the Moody's scale are referred to as investment grade bonds. From Ba1 downwards the occurrence of subsequent default rises dramatically. This is why the bonds issued by these firms are categorized as speculative grade or high yield bonds.

Other things equal, as the ability to pay declines, the extra return – the credit risk premium – demanded by investors over the return required on a government bond with a similar maturity, will rise. Panel A of Exhibit 10.9 shows the credit premium on a range of corporate bonds by rating category and for three broad maturity categories. We can see clearly that for both one- to three-year debt, for seven- to ten-year debt and for debt that matures beyond 15 years, as the rating declines the premium rises. However, you can also see that on the day this snapshot of credit premia was taken, the credit curve was downward sloping. In other words, the credit premium on longer-dated debt with the same credit rating was lower when compared to short-dated debt. This is a fairly unusual situation since the longer the maturity of any debt, the greater the chance that the issuer will default on it.

Panel B of Exhibit 10.9 shows how the economic environment can influence the credit premium too. Corporations will tend to fail more frequently in a tough economic environment, particularly during recessions. The economic slowdown of the early-noughties caused the premium on BBB bonds to rise to around 4 per cent, well above the credit premia demanded on higher rated bonds. However,

Exhibit 10.9   Credit premia

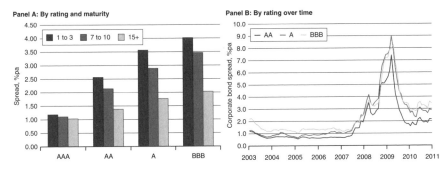

Source: Thomson Financial.

as the economy recovered and corporate profitability rose, credit premia shrank once again, until along came the global credit crunch.

The onset of the liquidity crisis caused investors to question the ability of companies (and governments) to repay their debts and they therefore demanded a much larger credit premium as Panel B shows. As the crisis reached its peak, the premium demanded on BBB-rated sterling corporate bonds over UK government bonds was 9 per cent. Just prior to the crisis the premium was around one per cent. Panel B also shows how the credit premia fell once the global financial system was stabilized and the UK economy began to recover.

Although the recent credit crisis was an extreme event, the credit risk premium does tend to ebb and flow with the economic environment, so that in bad economic times even companies with a strong 'ability to pay' will see the required premium on their corporate debt rise and conversely, companies with a poor 'ability to pay' will see the credit premium on their debt shrink in economic good times.

Equities – the equity risk premium

You may recall from Chapter 7, that the return that investors expect from their equity investments over and above the return on a long dated-government bond is referred to as the equity risk premium (ERP). Many elements influence the size of this premium at any one time. However, it is worth considering why investors need this additional return at all.

First, unlike with developed economy government bonds, there is a chance that the firm that has issued the equity might fail, in which case equity investors would normally lose all of their investment; equity being the risk capital of the company. Second, unlike the cash flows that investors receive from most government and corporate bonds, the cash flows from equities are not fixed and are far more uncertain. The dividends and share buybacks that comprise the cash flow from equities will tend to rise and fall with the profitability and cash flow of the firm, despite the company's best efforts to grow, or least maintain, its dividends over time. This profitability will be influenced by many factors over time, not least the performance of the domestic and world economy. It is for these two basic reasons that investors require an ERP.

Unfortunately there is no way of knowing for sure the value of this ERP. Many asset allocators use the Dividend Discount Model (DDM) we explored in Chapter 7 to help them assess the size of the ERP inherent in an equity market. As you may recall, the basic proposition of the model is that when one buys equities, one effectively buys the right to a stream of dividend payments into the future. The sum of the discounted, or present, value of these dividend payments should therefore be equal to the value of the equity, or equity market that produces this stream of payments.

Although we will not repeat the explanation of the model here, according to the DDM the ERP for an individual equity can be expressed as follows:

$$\text{ERP} = \text{current dividend yield} + \text{real long-term dividend growth} \\ - \text{real long-term risk-free rate}$$

If we think of an equity market as just being like one giant individual equity, which generates an earnings, or dividend, stream then we can use this model to derive the value of the ERP implied on the whole market by plugging in the appropriate numbers to the simple formula.

We know the current dividend yield on the market at any time. This is calculated and published on a daily basis. We can also observe a proxy for the real, long-term risk-free rate. This will be just the yield on a long-dated, index-linked government bond. The only truly unknown element on the right hand side of this expression is the real long-term growth rate of dividends. Any investor, or asset allocator, wishing to make use of this model would therefore have to find some way of identifying the likely value of this element of the model.

So what logic can be brought to bear on this issue?

If we assume that in the long run, dividend growth is similar to underlying economic growth, then we can approximate the growth rate in real dividends with an estimate of trend economic growth, which, as we know, tends to be quite stable over time. If the payouts to equity shareholders grew faster than the underlying economy then eventually profits would account for the entire income of the economy! So while profits may grow faster than the economy at certain stages of the business cycle, over the long term many economists and asset allocators use underlying economic growth as a proxy for underlying dividend growth.

As an example, suppose that the current dividend yield on a broad developed economy equity market index is 4 per cent; that the yield on a long-dated, index-linked government bond from the same economy is 2.25 per cent; and that an asset allocator estimates that trend real economic and dividend growth will be 2.50 per cent per annum into the future. Using the DDM, the asset allocator may come to the view that the equity risk premium on offer in this market is:

$$\text{ERP} = 4.00\% + 2.50\% - 2.25\% = 4.25\%$$

If the DDM is a good model and if the asset allocator's assumptions are correct, then the implication of these calculations is that this equity market will, on average, outperform the return on long-dated index-linked government bonds issued in the same economy by 4.25 per cent per year over the long term.

By adopting this approach across a wide range of equity markets, asset allocators can identify those markets that offer the highest equity risk premium.

Issues related to the DDM

In practice applying the DDM is more complicated than the impression given here. For instance:

i.   the calculation might be affected if companies decide to increase dividends temporarily, causing the current dividend yield to rise, and making the risk premium look bigger than it really is;

ii. users of this model will also have to take into account cash that is distributed by companies in non-dividend forms, such as share buy-backs; and

iii. perhaps the most important issue: what if the profits earned by the firms are not derived from the domestic economy but from another economy that is growing much faster?

The model user has to take account of all of these and other factors to arrive at a value for the ERP for a particular equity market. But this approach at least gives a consistent framework for thinking about the likely returns from equity.

Putting it all together

Once an investor or asset allocator has come to a view about all of the components of long-run expected returns, they can then be put together to arrive at expected return estimates for a range of asset classes. We have only considered cash, developed economy government bonds, corporate bonds and equities here, but the asset allocator would apply a similar process to arrive at the expected returns on real estate, developing economy government bonds and so on.

In Exhibit 10.10 we have presented some typical return components for a developed economy for illustrative purposes. Our hypothetical asset allocator believes that:

i.   trend growth in the economy in question is 2.25 per cent;

ii. that inflation will average 2 per cent in the long run;

iii. that the inflation risk premium is 0.50 per cent; and

iv. that the equity risk premium is 3 per cent.

Putting all of these components together produces the expected long-run returns on index-linked and conventional bonds, on cash and on equities in this economy, shown on the right hand side of the exhibit.

Exhibit 10.10 Example of the 'building block approach' to forecasting long-run asset class returns

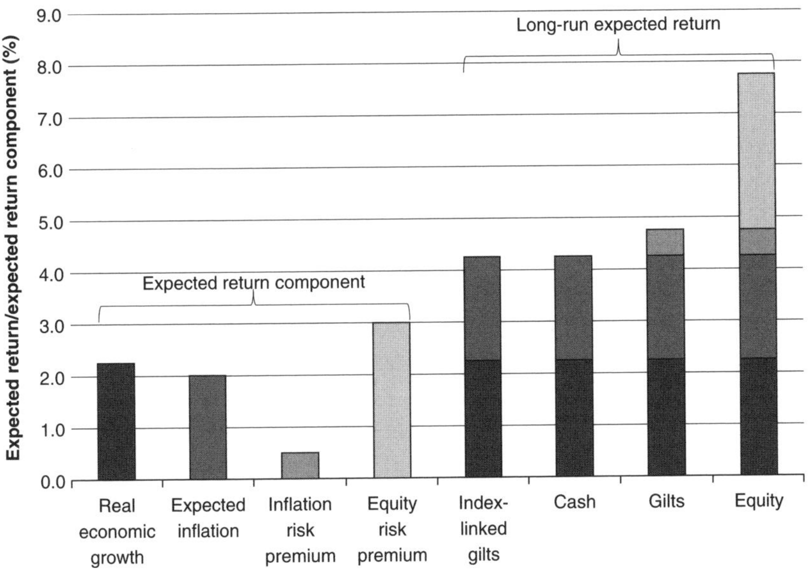

What could change an asset allocator's view of expected returns?

There are a number of factors that might cause an asset allocator to change their view on these components. Real economic growth might rise with the invention of new productivity enhancing devices or if immigration rises significantly. The converse might be true if an economy fails to innovate or adopt new technologies, or if there is significant migration from the economy. One's view of the outlook for inflation might alter with a change in the way that monetary policy is conducted. For example, a switch from targeting inflation to targeting growth, might affect one's view of the inflation outlook. Similarly, a change in the control of monetary policy from government officials to independent central bankers or vice versa, might change the way investors forecast inflation and change the levels of that forecast. In addition, a change of personnel in charge of monetary policy might also change the uncertainty about future inflation and might therefore change the level of the inflation risk premium too, as it seemed to do in the UK when the MPC was given the task of controlling UK inflation (see Exhibit 10.7).

Volatility and correlations

Having established the process for determining the expected returns on the set of asset classes under consideration, the asset allocator has effectively produced one-half of the inputs necessary to draw the mean-variance efficient frontier. Before the frontier can be drawn, investors must come to a view about the likely volatility of the returns from each asset class over time and, just as crucially, the correlation of these returns with every other asset class. The lower the correlation the greater the possibility for building portfolios which produce less volatile returns than any individual asset class for any given level of expected return.

To produce estimates of long-term expected returns via the building block approach, asset allocators try to use forward-looking information. That is, forecasts of future economic and dividend growth, forecasts of future inflation etc. Unfortunately, when it comes to forecasting the return volatility of an asset class and the correlation of its future returns with those of all other asset classes, many asset allocators do not use forward-looking information.

In order to arrive at estimates of future volatilities and correlations many asset allocators use history as a guide. In other words, asset allocators often use the historic return volatility, over a pre-determined period, as a proxy for future volatility. The same approach can also be used to arrive at estimates of future return correlations, simply by calculating the actual correlations over the same pre-specified period. This is by far the simplest method for obtaining the 'risk' inputs to construct a mean-variance efficient frontier. However, this method is not without its problems. Most notably with respect to asset class volatility and correlations, history can at times be a very bad guide to the future.

In Panel A of Exhibit 10.11 we have presented the monthly volatility (standard deviation) of the return on both the UK and the US stock markets since 1970. Each point on the line represents the standard deviation of these returns calculated over the previous five years.[8] US stock market volatility has been relatively stable over this period, ranging between 3 to 6 per cent for most of this period. The increase in volatility following the collapse of the dot.com bubble in the early part of this millennium is clearly evident, as is the collapse of Lehman Brothers in September 2008 and the advent of the credit crisis at the end of this sample period.

By contrast, using the same calculation methodology, the volatility of the UK equity market over the same period has ranged between around 3 per cent and nearly 11 per cent. However, since the early 1980s UK equity market volatility has been very similar to that in the US, but clearly the time period that is chosen to estimate the volatility can have a big influence on one's conclusions.

The same is true for the estimation of correlations too. In Panel B of Exhibit 10.11 we present an estimate of the changing correlation between UK and US

---

[8] We use five years here for illustration purposes, but could easily have chosen another sample period, say ten years, to make the same point.

Exhibit 10.11 Volatility and correlations over time

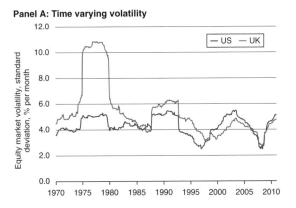

Panel A: Time varying volatility

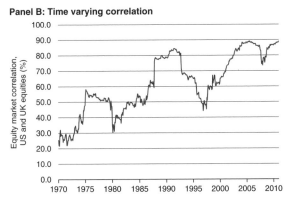

Panel B: Time varying correlation

Source: Thomson Financial.

equity returns since 1970. Each point on the line represents an estimate of the return correlation between these two asset classes, calculated using data for the preceding five years. Over time the correlation appears to have risen, although there have been two periods when the correlation between these two major equity markets fell substantially. In the early 1980s, the correlation was only around 0.4 (40 per cent). The correlation fell quite sharply in the mid-1990s to just below 0.5, before rising to just under 0.9 more recently.

If we accept this methodology as a way of proxying for expected future correlation, the final point in Panel B – 0.90 – implies that the return on UK and US equities will move almost together in the future. Given the globalization of equity markets over the past 30 years, with many UK and US companies deriving their earnings from outside of their domestic markets, perhaps this is a reasonable assumption to make? But if this is the asset allocator's view, then they may also come to the view that there is little point in diversifying out of UK equities and into US equities. Instead they might seek out other equity markets, or indeed other asset classes, that have had a lower historic correlation with UK equities, in the hope that this correlation will remain low in the future. These are the kinds of issues that an asset allocator has to resolve, before finally producing the mean-variance frontier that will enable them to construct a strategic investment portfolio.[9]

Putting it all together to produce a strategic investment portfolio

Having come to a view about expected returns, volatilities and correlations of the asset classes of interest, it is then a relatively straightforward task to build and then to present a mean-variance efficient frontier based upon this information. We constructed an efficient frontier in Chapter 9. However, even when the frontier has been constructed, the strategic asset allocation exercise is still incomplete. The asset allocator needs to establish the level of return that their client requires, or the level of risk that the investor is willing to accept from the portfolio.

In Exhibit 10.12 we have highlighted two points, A and B, on a hypothetical efficient frontier. Suppose that the asset allocator's client wishes to achieve a return represented by point E in the exhibit that can be produced by portfolio A. Using this model the asset allocator can construct a portfolio to achieve this goal, given the assumptions that they have made in constructing the frontier. This portfolio would be expected to experience the level of volatility given at point C in the exhibit. Now suppose that the client wishes the asset allocator to construct a portfolio with an expected return equal to point F, but with a portfolio volatility equal to C. Given the asset allocator's assumptions, this is not possible. But using this model the asset allocator can demonstrate to the client the amount of risk that they would have to accept in order to achieve the return given at point F, represented by point D in the exhibit. In this case some compromise might need to be made.

However, once the client has agreed the level of risk for a given level of expected return, the asset allocator can construct the associated portfolio. The asset class weights in this portfolio can be seen as the 'strategic' weights for the client portfolio. In other words, they represent the basic shape of the portfolio for the longer term and it is hoped that the portfolio will produce the long-term returns expected of it, and with the expected level of risk. This does not mean

---

[9] There are more sophisticated, scenario-based ways of generating asset class volatilities and correlations, but a description of these techniques is beyond the scope of this book.

Exhibit 10.12 Choosing a position on the efficient frontier

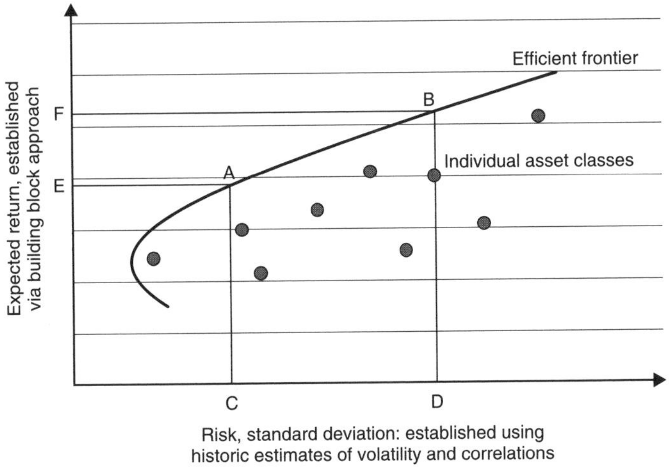

that these weights should be fixed for all time, but rather that any change in these weights would tend to be evolutionary, rather than revolutionary.

Strategic versus tactical asset allocation

This strategic portfolio can be seen as the benchmark portfolio for tactical asset allocation (TAA) decisions. For the sake of example, suppose that the most appropriate strategic portfolio for a client turns out to be one which has a weight of 80 per cent in UK equities and 20 per cent in gilts. Suppose also that the asset allocator believes that gilts are currently 'overvalued' and that UK equities are currently 'undervalued'. Given this view, a TAA decision may be taken to invest say 5 per cent less in gilts and 5 per cent extra in UK equities.

The asset allocator may be correct in their view, in which case if UK equities rise in value and gilts subsequently fall in value a subsequent decision might be taken to sell the additional UK equities and to buy back the gilts that were sold with the proceeds from the equity sale. This would bring the portfolio back to its strategic benchmark weights of 80/20 UK equities and gilts respectively, but would have added value to the portfolio by:

i. having additional exposure to UK equities that rose in value, and
ii. lower exposure to UK gilts that fell in value.

Of course, the decision might not have paid off, and the success of such TAA decisions will depend upon the asset allocator's skill in identifying over and underpriced asset markets and in timing market movements. The process that each practitioner of TAA will use will vary a great deal depending upon the experience and skill set of the investment professional involved. Regardless of the process used, the basic objective of TAA is to add value to a fund over and above the return expected from the strategic asset class positions that were determined by the SAA process.

The importance of strategic versus tactical asset allocation

Tactical asset allocation, if applied successfully, is one way of adding value over the longer term to a multi-asset class portfolio that has been designed along strategic lines to achieve a certain level of return for a given level of risk. For most institutional investors the more important decision is the strategic one. We can demonstrate this with a simple example.

Suppose that two investors choose to invest their funds in the different strategic proportions shown in Panel A of Exhibit 10.13. However, at the start of the year, investor A decides to increase the weighting in equities to 81 per cent and to reduce the weighting in bonds to 19 per cent. Investor B makes a tactical asset allocation decision to increase their weighting in bonds to 51 per cent and to reduce the weighting in equities to 49 per cent. They both hold these two tactical positions over the course of the following year.

Over this year now suppose that equities fall by 30 per cent and bonds rise in value by 10 per cent, as shown in the final column of Panel A. In Panel B of Exhibit 10.13 we calculate the return on the portfolio (i) had the TAA decisions not been made (i.e., SAA only), and (ii) with the TAA decision having been made (i.e., SAA and TAA). Without the TAA decision, Investor A would have experienced a loss of 22 per cent over the year, and Investor B a loss of 10 per cent. By getting the TAA decision correct, Investor B reduces their overall loss by

Exhibit 10.13   The importance of strategic asset allocation

	Strategic benchmarks		TAA over/under weights		Asset class
	Investor A (%)	Investor B (%)	Investor A (%)	Investor B (%)	Performance (%)
Panel A					
Equities	80	50	1	−1	−30
Bonds	20	50	−1	1	10

	Investor A (%)	Investor B (%)
Panel B		
Performance – SAA only	−22.00	−10.0
Performance – SAA and TAA	−22.4	−9.6
Difference	−0.40	0.40

0.4 per cent, while investor A, who makes an equal but opposite TAA decision, loses an additional 0.4 per cent over the year.

The purpose of this simple example is to demonstrate that the vast majority of the performance for both investors came from the SAA decision. If an asset allocator gets their assessment of the market and timing correct, they normally only add a small amount to the overall portfolio performance. Most of the total performance comes from the strategic positioning. This does not mean that the additional performance that might be gained through TAA decisions is not worth having. On the contrary, an additional 0.5 per cent to 1 per cent per year added to the performance of a fund compounds over the long term can make a big difference to the absolute value of that fund. But it does mean that it is worth trying to get the SAA correct first, before trying to add value via TAA decisions.

Strategic asset allocation summary

Hopefully so far this chapter has managed to convince you that it is possible to develop an approach to SAA that is internally consistent, and also that the SAA decision, on the whole, is a very important decision to get right. However, even if TAA decisions can only add a small amount of value over the years – a little can add up to a lot with the power of compounding. So it is worth exploring the methods and techniques used by TAA professionals.

Even if you believe that TAA professionals cannot add value consistently over time, those practicing SAA will still have to consider their tactics too. For example, suppose after a strategic review of an investor's needs it is decided that their portfolio should change from an 80/20 equity/bond split to a 50/50 split. In other words, that equities should be sold in favour of bonds. In the world of investment, timing is everything; there will be a right and a wrong time to make such a switch and the tools of the TAA can help inform this decision.

In the next section of this chapter we will outline a typical TAA process, to illustrate the kinds of issues that TAA professionals consider and the kind of framework that they might use. In practice, there will be as many TAA processes as there are TAA professionals, but hopefully the following will help to illustrate some of the key features of a TAA process.

A tactical asset allocation process

TAA seeks to identify an asset class that is likely to outperform another asset class, usually over a short timeframe relative to strategic asset class weights. Once this opportunity is identified the investor will make the over/underweight

238 The Trustee Guide to Investment

decision with regard to these two asset classes (see Exhibit 10.13). However, identifying these opportunities, implementing the appropriate strategy and getting this decision right is easier said than done. So what factors might a TAA professional consider before making such decisions?

Broadly speaking they will form their view and implement it, based on one or all of the following sets of considerations:

- the economic cycle;
- valuations;
- market sentiment; and
- technical factors.

In each case the TAA professional may consider many different indicators of these four broad areas, bringing them all together to form one coherent view. Before we explore a way of establishing a possible process for combining all of these indicators, let's begin by exploring the set of four broad influences on asset prices.

The economic cycle

As we discussed in Chapter 4, economic growth tends to cycle around a positive trend rate of growth over time. As the economy evolves in this manner so do the cash flows from some asset classes and the level of risk aversion among investors. For example, when the economy is expanding rapidly, company profits tend to rise which, in turn, means that the dividends paid by companies increase. It also means that corporations are less likely to default on their loan or corporate bond obligations. When an economy is expanding rapidly, when corporate profits are rising and perhaps when unemployment is falling too, consumers and investors tend to feel more confident about the world and they are, therefore, often willing to accept greater risks. So, higher risk asset classes like equity and lower grade corporate debt tend to rise in value and outperform lower risk asset classes like government bonds. The converse is true when the economy is slowing down or is in recession.

Although this is clearly an oversimplification of the complex relationship between the economy and asset prices, there is a relationship. Because of this, asset allocators will spend a great deal of time trying to ascertain the economy's position in the economic cycle. To do this, they will monitor a whole range of economic statistics relating to growth, unemployment and inflation. The main problem with these data is that they are only available with a lag – given the time it takes to collate them. So asset allocators will also monitor forward-looking indicators of economic activity such as surveys of consumer and business confidence.

Valuations

The issue of asset class 'value' is a difficult one. You often hear market commentators state that a market is over or undervalued. But what does this mean? It probably means different things to different people, but one interpretation of the remark is that an overvalued asset class is either too highly priced given the income stream that it has generated in the past and is expected to generate in the future, and that the price of an undervalued asset class is too low given the cash flow that it has generated in the past and likely to generate in the future.

If the asset allocator's assessment is correct, then allocating funds to undervalued asset classes and reducing exposure to overvalued asset classes will tend to add value for their clients over time. Since value is a relative concept, the sorts of indicators that are used to establish the value in an asset class tend to compare the price of that asset class relative to its cash flow. For example, the dividend yield on a broad equity market index is usually expressed as the dividend income paid out by the index's constituents over the previous 12 months divided by the market value of the index. So when this dividend yield is high relative to history, it suggests that buying this stream of dividends is cheap, relative to the price for this income stream in the past.

Asset allocators might also compare the income yield on one market relative to another. So, for example, when the equity dividend yield is low relative to the yield on government bonds compared with their respective historic levels, this might be taken to indicate that equities are 'expensive' relative to government bonds, a view that would have obvious implications for asset allocation.

The problem with using these yields and relative yields is that to establish whether they are too high or too low, they need to be compared with their historic levels. However, some would argue that history is a poor guide to the future, whereas others, who tend to put a great deal of faith in these indicators of value, argue that the historic levels of these indicators are ignored at investors' peril.

To illustrate this difficulty, recall the dot.com bubble of the late-1990s. At the time, the Price to Earnings (PE) ratio of many equity markets was very, very high relative to history. As we mentioned in Chapter 7, the PE ratio for an equity market can be interpreted as the price investors are willing to pay for each unit of earnings that the market has recently generated. As Exhibit 10.14 shows, the PE on the S&P 500 rose to just over 30 just before the bubble burst, well above its average level up until the inflation of this bubble. Those investors that trusted the valuation metric argued that the market was overvalued.

However, there were those – particularly the market strategists within investment banks – who argued that things were different this time around and that

Exhibit 10.14   The PE ratio on the US stock market

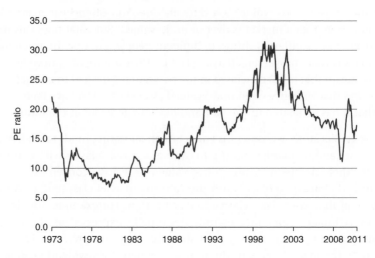

Source: Thomson Financial.

because of this the PE ratio could be sustainably higher than it had been in the past.[10] They argued that recessions had been consigned to the history books by the adoption of sensible macroeconomic policies; that inflation had finally been tamed (remember this was the late-1990s) and that the Internet had raised the productivity of the US economy to such an extent that corporate profits would grow much more rapidly in the future. So US equities were not expensive after all. Oh, and by the way, it was the investment banks that relied on equity sales for their own profitability. The moral of the story is: beware of investment bankers talking their own book!

In the end, all investors realized that the investment bankers' stories were just that, or worse still, that they were malicious lies – we'll let you decide which – but in the end the US equity market fell sharply, as did the US equity market PE ratio.

Coming to a view about the appropriate valuation of any financial market is very difficult and it's not just equity markets that pose a problem in this regard. Recall the building block approach to arriving at the appropriate yield on a government bond that we discussed earlier in this chapter. All other things equal, if one asset allocator believes that US trend economic growth is 3 per cent and another 2 per cent, they will often come to different views about whether the US government bond market is over or undervalued, and will

---

[10] In fact, this is exactly what Yale professor, Irving Fisher, argued on the eve of the Great Crash of October 1929.

make different asset allocation decisions with regard to this asset class. It is also often difficult to understand the 'value' in a market because of market sentiment which can sometimes be overly optimistic, while at other times it can be overly pessimistic.

Sentiment

The difficult job of untangling valuation from sentiment can be best illustrated with reference to, former US Federal Reserve Committee Chairman, Alan Greenspan's now famous comment about 'irrational exuberance'. Mr. Greenspan suggested in December 1996 that US equity market investors were displaying signs of irrational exuberance – a typical Delphic Greenspan phrase that meant that he felt that the market was overvalued. Any investor that listened to Mr. Greenspan then would have been very disappointed to see the market rise another 105 per cent[11] over the next three-and-a-half years. In the end it seems that Mr. Greenspan was right, but strong sentiment, or irrational exuberance, continued to propel the market onward and upward.

The lesson is clear: being 'right' about the market's value while ignoring market sentiment can be very costly in investment terms, at least in the short run. 'Overvalued' markets can continue to rise in value, while 'undervalued' markets can fall further. John Maynard Keynes, the British economist, also a very successful investor, has been credited with two important insights into the discipline of investing:

- *Market irrationality and you*: Keynes pointed out that the markets can remain irrational for longer than you can remain solvent.
- *The beauty contest analogy*: Keynes likened investing to being a judge in a beauty contest, but where the task of the judge was not to identify the contestant that they believed to be the most beautiful, but where instead the task was to pick the contestant that they believed the *other* judges would deem to be the most beautiful.

Both of these insights are worth bearing in mind, and both refer to the importance of market sentiment.[12] So how does one read market sentiment accurately?

To read market sentiment, TAA professionals monitor a whole range of different indicators. Two such indicators are shown in Exhibit 10.15. In Panel A we have presented a representation of earnings momentum. When the momentum in corporate earnings is positive – that is, when corporate earnings are growing – investor sentiment tends to be positive. The opposite is true when

---

[11] That is, 105 per cent, just in case you thought that was a misprint. When it came to investing, Mr Greenspan was an excellent central banker!

[12] We cover the fascinating topic of behavioural finance in more detail in Chapter 17.

Exhibit 10.15   Indicators of market sentiment

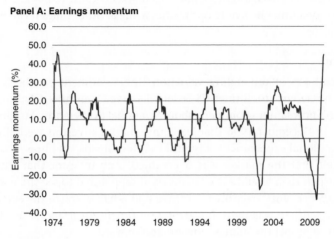

Panel A: Earnings momentum

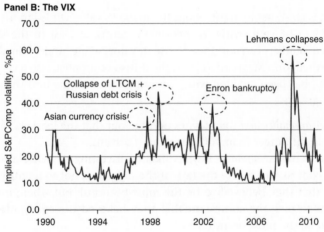

Panel B: The VIX

earnings are shrinking. Panel B of Exhibit 10.15 shows a bellwether measure of sentiment – the VIX. At any point in time, the VIX is a measure of the market's assessment of how volatile investors expect the S&P 500 will be over the following 12 months. The VIX is known as '*the fear gauge*' – given that volatility is a measure of uncertainty – and is derived from the pricing of S&P 500 index options. We can see clearly from Panel B that the value of this series tends to be very high during times of financial market distress. We have circled a few such points on the chart. At these peaks, investment sentiment is usually very weak and the prices of high risk asset classes fall at such times. Buying high risk asset classes, such as equities, as the VIX peaks has paid off handsomely in the past – but that is easier said than done. Identifying the peak is the trick. That is, identifying when market sentiment will turn.

Technical indicators

So judgments about the economic cycle, valuations and sentiment will all play a part in TAA decisions. To these considerations we can add a final set which relate to 'technical' aspects of the markets.

Sometimes these can relate to short-term buying or selling pressures, perhaps created by regulatory decisions. By anticipating in advance when certain groups of investors might be forced to buy or sell assets, the tactical asset allocator can position their investments to benefit from the move. Ultimately this forced buying or selling will end and the relevant asset price will return to some 'fair value', but before then its price might rise or fall dramatically well above or below this fair value.

But as well as judging these buying and selling pressures, there are many investors who believe that asset prices follow patterns that can be identified. As such, asset allocators may develop measures that seek to exploit these patterns. One of the most common techniques is to calculate 'moving averages' of asset prices and to set buy and sell thresholds around these averages. The line labelled '30 day moving average' in panel A of Exhibit 10.16 represents the 30 day moving average of the FTSE 100 index. The line labelled 'FTSE 100' represents the index itself. The rule that the asset allocator might use could be:

> *underweight UK stocks when it is x per cent above its x month moving average, and buy stocks when it is y per cent below its x month moving average*

or some rule of this kind. These rules can be easily calculated for most asset classes and individual assets.[13]

Each bar in Panel B of Exhibit 10.16 represents the average return for a month, or group of months, on the UK stock market from 1963 to 2009. It shows that the best months to be invested in UK equities are April followed by January. But in fact it also shows how poor returns are between May and October. Hence the old stock market expression: *sell in May and go away*. A successful equity investment strategy might have simply involved overweighting equities at the end of October and underweighting them at the end of April.

---

[13] For recent evidence on these rules see Owain ap Gwilym, Andrew Clare, James Seaton and Stephen Thomas, 'Price and Momentum as Robust Tactical Approaches to Global Equity Investing', *Journal of Investing,* Fall (2010); and Owain ap Gwilym, Andrew Clare, James Seaton and Stephen Thomas, 'Tactical 'Equity Investing Across Bull and Bear Markets', *Journal of Investing* (2011).

Exhibit 10.16   Technical indicators

Panel A: Moving average indicator

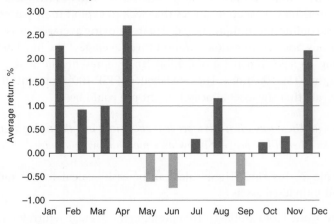

Panel B: Seasonality

The point to bear in mind with regard to such indicators is that there is little underlying economic or investment logic to them. However, there may be some behavioural explanations as to why they might work, that is, their success may have something to do with investor psychology. We will explore investor psychology, also often referred to as behavioural finance, in more detail in Chapter 17. These rules might also be self-fulfilling prophecies to some extent; if enough investors believe that they work, investment decisions based upon these beliefs might ensure that they do.

However, for the purposes of this discussion it is sufficient to note that these technical indicators will, to a greater or lesser extent, form part of the information set that asset allocators will use to make their TAA decisions.

Putting it all together: The scorecard approach

Each asset allocator will use their own range of indicators to identify tactical investment opportunities. Some will use literally hundreds of these indicators. All of this information could be very confusing unless a coherent process for putting it all together in a manageable way can be identified.

Just as every asset allocator will use a set of indicators unique to them and their process, each of them will have a unique way of combining all of this diverse and sometimes contradictory information. We will now describe one possible way of doing this. It is not *the* correct way of approaching this problem, because there is no correct way, nor is it the only way, because there is an infinite number of ways that could be used, but it is not untypical of the approaches used, and we will refer to it as the *Scorecard Approach*.

The idea of the scorecard approach is to standardize the myriad of diverse indicators so that they can be analyzed on a comparable basis. After this standardization, the relationship between the indicators and the markets of interest can be established. Let's begin with the standardization.

Step 1

Each indicator will have a different average value, and will experience different volatility over time. This makes it difficult to compare even a percentage change in one indicator with regard to another. To make them comparable, each indicator can be transformed as follows:

$$Z = \frac{X_i - \bar{X}}{\sigma_X}$$

where X_i represents the current value of an indicator, $\bar{X}$ represents the average value of the indicator and σ_X represents the standard deviation of the indicator. This transformation produces a value Z which measures the difference between the indicator's value at any point in time relative to its average, compared with its volatility. A value for Z of, say, two, might mean that the current indicator is more than two standard deviations away from its average value. If the variable is distributed normally, this will happen only 5 per cent of the time (see Chapter 9), suggesting that the indicator is at an unusually high level.

Exhibit 10.17 shows an indicator that we have transformed using this method. In this case it is the headline measure derived from the survey of US business confidence conducted by the Purchasing Managers Index (PMI). As you can see the transformed measure is centred around zero and has peaks that are bounded (more or less) by two. So if an indicator has a Z score of two, or minus two we know that its value relative to its past value is extreme.

Exhibit 10.17   Transforming the US PMI survey into a TAA indicator

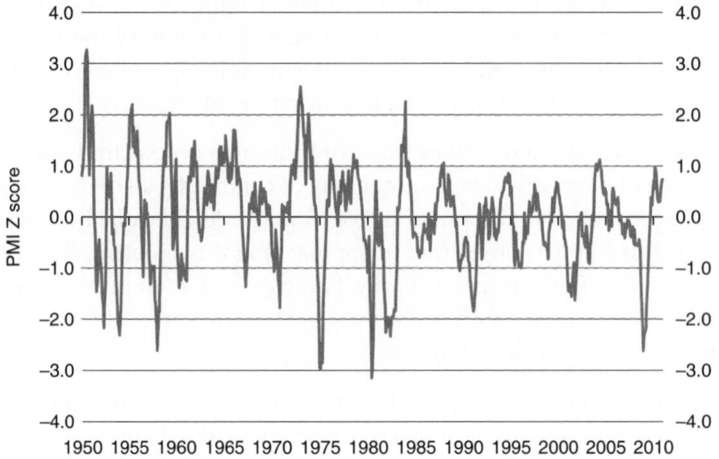

Step 2

After transforming all of the indicators into 'Z scores' the next step is to establish the relationship between the indicators and the markets, or asset classes of interest. These relationships can be identified using statistical analysis that we will not describe here, but for the purposes of illustration let's assume that the transformed version of the US PMI survey shown in Exhibit 10.17 is a good indicator of the relative performance of US equities and US Treasuries, such that when the indicator is two or more, US equities always outperform US Treasuries, and that the converse is true when the indicator is minus two or below. If we are satisfied that this relationship is stable and reliable then we can establish a 'score' for this 'bet'. For example see Exhibit 10.18.

This process needs to be repeated for all of the indicators that the asset allocator believes can help identify the relative value of US equities versus US Treasuries. However, the 'scores' of each of these indicators will almost certainly be different. To overcome this difficulty, the asset allocator can take a simple average of each of these scores – perhaps by category – or a weighted average of the indicators, where more weight is given to more reliable indicators of this TAA bet. The end result of this might be a 'scorecard' for the US equity/Treasury TAA as in Exhibit 10.19.

The scorecard in Exhibit 10.19 shows that the set of economic indicators used for this investment decision favour an investment in US equities, since the average Z score of the indicators is two. It shows that the valuation indicators have a lower average – suggesting perhaps that US equity prices are already high, or that Treasury prices are already quite low. However, the strongest equity 'buy

Exhibit 10.18 TAA action

Indicator score	TAA Action
2 (or above)	Overweight US equities, underweight US Treasuries
Between 1 & 2	Maintain any overweight in US equities
0	No over, or underweight positions
Between –1 & –2	Maintain any overweight in US Treasuries
–2 (or below)	Overweight US Treasuries, underweight US equities

Exhibit 10.19 Scorecard for US equities vs. Treasuries TAA bet

Indicator	Score
Economic cycle	2
Valuation	1
Sentiment	3
'Technicals'	2
Average	2
Recommendation	Buy US equities, sell Treasuries

signal' is coming from the sentiment indicators which have an average Z score of three – which is very high. The average of the technical indicators also favours US equities. Overall, the average score of these individual averages is two, so in this case, if the investor had any faith in their own process they would take an overweight position in US equities and an underweight one in Treasuries.

Step 3

Steps 1 and 2 need to be repeated for all asset class bets that the TAA professional wishes to consider. The end result will be a series of tactical bets based upon the sets of average Z scores that have been back-tested appropriately for their reliability.

Asset allocation summary

In this chapter we have tried to outline a framework for both strategic and tactical asset allocation. We have presented it in as methodical and logical a way as we can, but in the end we must remember that both strategic and tactical asset allocation as disciplines are more art than science. If there were a simple formula for getting it right – and we knew that formula – we wouldn't be writing this book! What we have presented instead is a way of thinking about both SAA and TAA, a way of monitoring decisions, and therefore a way of monitoring the success or otherwise of those decisions.

To put it another way, implementing a successful strategic and tactical asset allocation strategy is a bit like setting out on a voyage of discovery, with an imperfect map that can be refined and improved once the journey begins. Christopher Columbus started with an imperfect map of the world, but still managed to discover the riches of the American continent . . . even though he was looking for another route to the riches of the East Indies!

Key points

- Asset allocation involves making choices between both traditional and alternative asset classes and is one of *the* really big decisions that trustees need to get right. The strategic asset allocation (SAA) decision is more important than the tactical asset allocation (TAA) decision.
- SAA seeks to achieve the highest return for a given and acceptable level of risk. Expected long-term returns are derived via a forward-looking building block approach that takes a view about the expected riskless real return, expected inflation and the expected risk premium. By contrast, estimates of future volatilities and correlations typically use history as a guide.
- TAA seeks to add value to a fund, over and above the return expected from the strategic asset class positions that were determined by the SAA process, by identifying an asset class that is likely to outperform another asset class, usually over a short timeframe relative to the strategic asset class weights.
- TAA can be implemented using a scorecard approach based on consideration of the economic cycle, valuations, market sentiment and technical factors.
- SAA and TAA as disciplines are more art than science.

Chapter 11

Derivatives: Instruments of Mass Destruction?

Learning outcomes

- Appreciate the misconceptions that surround derivatives.
- Appreciate the difference between an over the counter and an exchange traded derivatives contract.
- Understand how forward and futures contracts, options and credit derivatives work and how they can be used by pension schemes.

Introduction

Let's start with a particularly big number: US$651 trillion. That figure is over ten times greater than the annual output of the global economy and around 20 times the size of the global equity market and the global bond market. That figure was the notional value of outstanding derivatives contracts globally at 30 June 2010.[1] This notional value is the exposure a derivative gives the investor to an underlying asset or market.

Many investors associate derivatives with casino capitalism and tabloid front page headlines, such as 'Nick Leeson – the man that broke Barings Bank'. They also associate them with the excesses of the investment banking community and now with the credit crunch, intrinsically linked as it was with *credit derivatives*. Investors, therefore, understand that derivatives have both the capability to create large losses very rapidly and the potential to destabilize the global

---

[1] BIS semi-annual derivatives statistics, 30 June 2010.

financial system itself. Indeed, derivatives' tarnished image wasn't helped by Warren Buffett, the world's third richest man, labelling derivatives in 2002 as 'financial weapons of mass destruction'[2]. Moreover, the sheer amount of jargon that is synonymous with derivatives simply exacerbates the aura of mystique that surrounds these financial instruments.

It is certainly true that derivatives can be used to increase exposures to market risk very rapidly and cheaply, thus simultaneously magnifying gains and losses accordingly. However, just as a car is a useful means of getting from A to B in the hands of sensible driver, it can be a lethal weapon in the hands of an irresponsible joy rider. When used properly, derivatives can facilitate a move from one investment exposure to another more safely and more efficiently than by using 'cash' securities, such as bonds and equities. Indeed, from a pension fund perspective, derivatives should be viewed as risk management tools.

Where pension mandates allow, fund managers can use derivatives in a number of ways. For example, to:

- hedge, or insure, against market exposures to various asset classes moving against the scheme;
- hedge against the interest rate, inflation and longevity risks within the scheme liabilities moving against the scheme;
- adjust market exposures cheaply and efficiently according to their active views;
- maintain required market exposures during fund transfers and transitions; and
- take advantage of any perceived mispricing between a derivative and the market for the underlying asset.

Due to this, pension funds have been making greater use of derivatives over the past few years, both indirectly by allowing their fund managers to use them to enhance or to risk manage performance, but also increasingly for more direct risk management purposes, as they seek to achieve a better match between their assets and liabilities.[3]

In this chapter we will explore three types of derivative instrument – *forwards*, *futures* and *options* – focusing mainly on the latter two, and we will conclude with Credit Default Swaps (CDSs), as these are the building block of many credit derivative instruments. In Chapter 12 we will explore another type of derivative: swaps.

Forwards and futures

Forward contracts pre-date futures contracts. Whereas forwards can be traced back to the Ancients, futures were established in 1848 on what is the world's

---

[2] Berkshire Hathaway letter to shareholders 2002, p. 15.
[3] We cover this in Chapter 15.

oldest and what was the world's largest derivatives exchange, the Chicago Board of Trade (CBoT).

Forwards and futures contracts are analytically very similar but differ mainly in the way in which they are traded.

A *forward contract* obliges the holder of the contract to buy an asset or commodity at a pre-specified time and price in the future from the seller of the forward contract. It is an obligation, or a legally binding agreement, between two parties and is traded *over the counter* (OTC), or *off exchange*; typically being intermediated by an investment bank. The counterparty to a forward contract is usually another investor. OTC contracts account for 90 per cent of the outstanding notional value of the derivatives market[4] and are attractive to investors, like pension schemes, owing to their bespoke nature. That is, they can be built around the unique requirements of the investor.

A *futures contract* has the same basic features as a forward contract, but is a standardized form of forward contract that is traded on a recognized derivatives exchange, such as London's NYSE Euronext exchange.[5] As such, it is known as an exchange traded derivative. Exchange traded derivatives account for 10 per cent of the outstanding notional value of the derivatives market[6] and are typically traded via remote electronic trading systems that feed into an exchange, rather than being traded on a physical exchange floor by traders donning brightly coloured jackets. The introduction of electronic trading platforms replaced open outcry trading around the turn of the noughties. Regardless of whether an investor is buying or selling a futures contract, the counterparty to the trade is the exchange itself, or rather the *clearing house* attached to the exchange. Indeed, the clearing house, in acting as the *central counterparty* to the exchange, underwrites, or guarantees, every trade executed on the exchange. With OTC contracts, like forwards, the counterparty is another investor which means that the counterparty risk[7] is usually higher with a forward contract compared with a futures contract with otherwise similar characteristics.[8]

When an investor agrees to buy an asset in the future at an agreed price today, the investor is said to be taking a 'long' position in the forward or futures

---

[4] BIS semi-annual derivatives statistics, 30 June 2010.
[5] This exchange was formerly known as the London International Financial Futures Exchange (LIFFE).
[6] BIS semi-annual derivatives statistics, 30 June 2010.
[7] We cover counterparty risk in Chapter 9.
[8] Clearing houses are well capitalized and have insurance policies upon which to draw if they are unable to meet their liabilities. Although OTC contracts are usually collateralized daily, with cash or G4-nation sovereign bonds (the G4-nations comprise the UK, US, France and Germany) typically passing between the counterparties to make good daily gains and losses, they are subject to intra-day counterparty risk.

contract. In this way the investor can gain exposure to the underlying asset without making a 'cash purchase'. That is, without buying the underlying asset[9] at the 'spot price' prevailing in the market in which the underlying asset trades. Equally, by taking a 'short' position in the contract, where the investor agrees to sell an asset in the future at an agreed price today, one can obtain a 'negative' exposure to the underlying asset without having to sell it. In this way an investor taking a short position via a forward or futures contract can benefit from a fall in the price of the underlying asset; something that cannot be achieved by simply buying the underlying asset. We should point out at this stage, perhaps counter-intuitively, that most financial futures markets don't provide a view of future cash market values. They are simply a different means of gaining an exposure to the cash market or to hedge a cash market exposure. This will become clearer when we look at how the price of a futures contract is derived.

For example, suppose that an investor enters into a long forward contract agreeing to pay £50 for an asset in six months time. If in six months time the underlying asset is trading at a price of £60, the holder of the long forward contract buys the asset from the seller of the forward contract at a price of £50 and can then sell it in the open market for £60 for an immediate gain of £10. The seller of the forward contract would lose an equal amount. However, had the asset fallen in price over this period the holder of the contract would have made a loss, while the seller would have made a gain of the same magnitude. This simple example illustrates how forwards and futures markets are a 'zero sum game'. That is, for every gain for one investor, there is an equal and opposite loss for another.

So by buying the forward contract, or by being 'long in the forward contract', the investor benefits when the underlying asset price rises, in much the same way as they would benefit from buying the asset directly instead of taking a long position in the forward contract. Almost exactly, but not quite the same for the following reason. To buy the asset, one usually has to pay the full value of that asset today. But when taking a long forward position, or buying a futures contract, to all intents and purposes the money that would have been used to buy the asset in the cash market can remain in the investor's bank account earning them interest.

Thus forwards and futures contracts, and, in fact, most derivatives contracts, give investors leveraged, or geared, access to an underlying economic exposure. Leveraged, because they do not have to commit the funds to the purchase at the outset of the contract. It is as if they are 'buying' the asset or exposure with borrowed money. Leverage is a very, very important aspect of derivatives positions.

---

[9] Throughout the chapter we use the terms underlying asset, cash market and cash purchase interchangeably.

Exhibit 11.1   The profit/loss from forward/futures positions

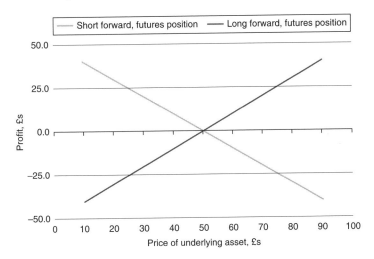

Although there are some minor differences involved in undertaking the same trade in a futures market, the general economic exposures are identical. The payoffs from long and short forward and futures positions are shown in Exhibit 11.1.

Exhibit 11.1 shows that long positions in the forward or futures contract gain when the underlying asset rises in value. Conversely short positions in futures/forward contracts profit as the underlying asset price falls. This is an important feature of these contracts. As noted earlier, they allow investors to benefit from price falls, a benefit that cannot be achieved by simply buying the underlying asset. The ability to create 'short' positions is a very important feature of derivatives. Creating a short position, that will produce a profit for an investor if the price of the underlying asset falls, is usually very expensive in the underlying market.

You will also notice that the profit/loss, or payoff profiles for the long and the short positions, (each being drawn at 45 degrees to the horizontal breakeven line) are diametrically opposed. This illustrates the 'zero sum game' between gains and losses we mentioned earlier.

We will now focus more specifically on futures contracts.

Hedging with futures

The principal use of futures is to hedge an existing market exposure. That is, they can act as a form of insurance against the price of an asset falling.

Exhibit 11.2   Hedging a cash position with a futures contract

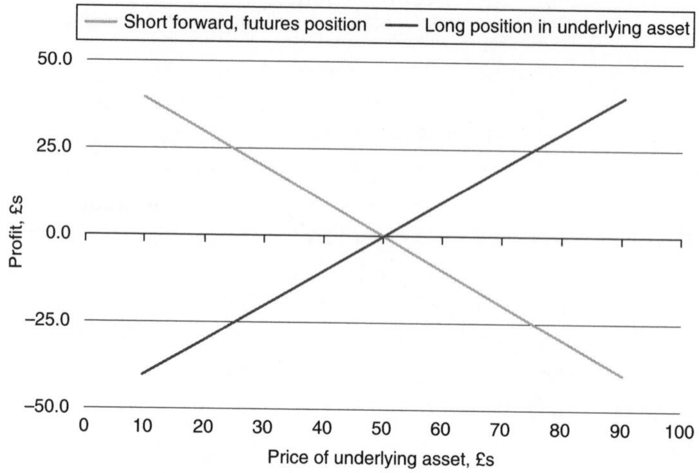

In Exhibit 11.2 the line labelled 'long position in underlying asset' represents the gain or loss on a cash investment in a particular asset. If we buy the asset for a price of £50 and it rises in value to a price of £60, we can sell it in the open market at £60 and make a £10 gain. However, if the price of the asset falls to £40 and the investor is forced to sell it at this point then they will realize a loss of £10.

Now suppose that the asset is held by the investor at a price of £50. To protect the value of the asset the investor could sell a futures contract on the asset at a price of £50. The payoff from this short futures position is given by the line labelled 'short futures position' in Exhibit 11.2. Now if the price of the underlying asset falls to £40, the £10 loss on the cash position is offset by the £10 gain from the futures contract. This gain comes about because the investor effectively sells the asset via the futures contract at a price of £50 and can buy the asset back, if they choose to, at a price of £40.

Closing out

Despite being a legally binding obligation, futures can be 'closed out' before expiry if the market exposure they provide the investor is no longer appropriate. Indeed, most are. For instance, if an investor with a long position in the underlying asset and a short futures position in place to hedge this exposure, wishes to close out this futures position because the losses incurred on this position are negating a subsequent rise in the underlying asset price, they can do so by *buying* a future on the same underlying asset with the same expiry date.

Futures positions are closed out with the clearing house that underwrites each contract and which acts as the central counterparty, or opposite side, to each contract. The futures position can typically be closed out by *either* side very quickly and at the price prevailing at the time on the derivatives exchange.[10]

Futures margins

When a futures position is taken out, both parties to the trade must deposit an amount of money with the clearing house, to protect the clearing house against one or other of the parties defaulting on the day in which the futures contracts are executed. This is known as the *initial margin*. Initial margin usually comprises cash or other non-cash collateral acceptable to the clearing house, such as G4-nation sovereign bonds.[11] Although the initial margin is periodically set by the derivatives exchange, it typically represents only a small percentage of the notional value of the futures contract. This notional value is essentially the exposure each party has to the underlying asset. By only posting a small deposit rather than committing 100 per cent of one's cash to obtain a market exposure means that futures positions are leveraged.

In addition, margin payments are made between the parties at the beginning of each trading day to settle profits and losses that arose from movements in the futures price at the close of the previous trading day. This is called a *variation margin*. The variation margin is paid in cash. If the long position has gained at the expense of the short position, as a result of the futures price rising, variation margin passes from the investor holding the short position to the investor holding the long position and vice versa via margin accounts. By settling profits and losses in this way, the clearing house is further protected in the event of one or both parties defaulting. The initial and variation margin processes are standardized by the derivatives exchanges on which the futures contract is traded. Once the contract expires or is closed out and all variation margin payments have been settled between the parties, the initial margin is returned, often with interest.[12]

---

[10] By contrast, forward contracts are closed out with the investment bank that typically acts as the intermediary in the transaction. The speed and price at which the forward contract can be closed out is dependent upon the stance taken by the investment bank and the liquidity of the market in which it operates.

[11] The G4 nations comprise the UK, US, France and Germany.

[12] With forward contracts, while there is no standardized margining process, an independent custodian is typically used by the parties to the contract for posting collateral. This process will be documented in the ISDA (International Swaps and Derivatives Association) agreement that is agreed between the parties. All OTC derivatives are governed by ISDA agreements. These are standardized documents which define the relationship and the specific terms of the agreement between the pension scheme and the investment bank. We cover ISDA agreements in Chapter 15.

We will now move on to consider two very important futures contracts to illustrate how futures work. The first is the equity index futures contract, and the second is the long bond futures contract.

Equity index futures contracts

Equity index futures contracts enable investors to take leveraged views on the likely direction of a whole range of equity indices. For example, FTSE 100 index futures contracts are traded on the NYSE Euronext derivatives exchange and allow investors to either profit from the movement in the index, or hedge their exposure to changes in the UK equity market. In this section we will concentrate upon the mechanics of this contract and highlight how the gains and losses can occur.

Exhibit 11.3 shows the contract specifications of two popular equity index futures contracts. When an investor buys a FTSE 100 index futures contract for delivery at some time in the future, the investor does not receive an equity portfolio when the contract matures. Instead the investor receives compensation in the form of cash variation margin from the seller of the contract if the contract has increased in price over the holding period, or alternatively makes a compensating payment of cash to the seller if it has fallen in price. The compensation, set by the exchange, is based upon FTSE 100 index points. For a FTSE 100 index future, the standardized minimum price movement, known as the tick, is 0.5 of an index point, which has a value of £5 – that is, a full index point has a value of £10. To see how pricing the index points in this way facilitates trading we will go through a simple example.

Suppose that the June 2012 FTSE 100 index futures contract is trading at a price of 6,300. Each index point is worth £10. So by purchasing one FTSE 100 contract, an investor is in effect, buying the right to buy £63,000 (6,300 × £10) worth of FTSE 100 equities in June 2012.

Now suppose that an investor purchases 100 June 2012 FTSE 100 index futures contracts at the price of 6,300, effectively buying the right to buy £6,300,000 worth of FTSE 100 equities.

Exhibit 11.3   **Typical equity futures contract specifications**

	FTSE 100 Index futures	CAC 40 Index futures
Quotation	Index points	Index points
Index point	£10	€10
Min tick value	£5	€5
Deliverable months	Mar, Jun, Sep & Dec	All months

For this transaction, the investor would need to pay the initial margin to the clearing house to cover the possible price movements that could occur on the day in which the trade is executed.

But the investor does not need to wait until June to realize any profit (or loss).

Suppose that only hours after the investor bought the 100 contracts at the price of 6,300, some good news about the future profitability of UK plc is released and the price of FTSE 100 index futures rises to 6,400.

To realize their profit, the investor would then close out their position by *selling* 100 June 2012 futures contracts at the higher price of 6,400, and the following amount would be added to their margin account:

No. of contracts × (contract selling price – contract purchase price)
× price per index point

$$100 \times (6,400 - 6,300) \times £10 = £100,000$$

The investor could then withdraw their initial margin from their account, plus the £100,000 profit on the trade.

In this example the investor benefits from a rise in the UK equity market without having to buy UK equities directly. But of course, if the equity market and the futures contracts price had fallen the investor might have had to close out their position at a loss.

Futures pricing

To price a futures contract, four numbers are required:

- the price of the underlying asset that trades in the cash market;
- the income yield of the underlying asset;
- money market interest rates; and
- the term of the futures contact.

Once these are known, the calculation is relatively straightforward. Suppose that an investor wishes to sell a FTSE 100 index futures contract with a three-month term. Suppose also that we know that the FTSE 100 index is currently trading at, say, 6,300, that the dividend yield is 3.5 per cent per annum and the three-month money market rate is 0.5 per cent per annum.

Now suppose that an investor wishes to sell one contract when the FTSE 100 is at 6,200. Thus the investor would effectively be committed to selling a portfolio of equities priced today at £62,000 (remember that each index point costs £10). What price should they ask for this portfolio in three months' time? Well, in three months' time the investor has to deliver cash equivalent to the value of the FTSE 100 in three months' time. The best way for the investor to hedge this exposure would be to buy a portfolio of FTSE 100 equities today. In this way if the price rises between now and three months' time they will not have to pay more for the equities. So the price the investor will charge for the equities will be equal to today's price for this basket of equities, plus the interest rate cost of buying and holding these equities for three months. The futures seller will benefit from dividends paid over this period, so this benefit will need to be subtracted from the futures price. The futures price (F) will be given approximately as:

$$F = S + (S \times r \times t) - (S \times dy \times t)$$

where S is the price paid for the portfolio at the start of the three months; r is the annual rate of interest; t is the time to maturity of the futures contract, expressed as a percentage of one year; and dy is the dividend yield on the index. If we plug the numbers in we get:

$$F = £62,000 + (£62,000 \times 0.5\% \times 0.25) - (£62,000 \times 3.5\% \times 0.25)$$
$$= £61,535$$

Since each index point equals £10, the futures seller is selling the index at a level of 6,153.5. This is said to be the *fair value* of the index in three months' time. You will note that it is trading at a discount to the value of the index today. This is because the interest cost is much lower than the benefit derived from the dividend income. If the interest rate had been higher than the dividend yield then the futures contract would be trading at a premium to the current, spot price of the FTSE. And of course if they are equal then the futures price will be equal to the current spot price of the index.

In practice however, the futures price will deviate from the 'fair' price calculated using the expression above. There are a number of reasons for this. First and foremost, it is not costless to hedge the futures position by buying the 100 shares in the equity market. So the actual futures price and 'fair' futures price can drift apart until that point at which arbitragers (those that seek to exploit perceived risk-free pricing anomalies) can use the cash market to make a profit from the divergence, that is, the difference gets so big that profits can still be made despite the associated transactions costs. Second, dividends are not known with certainty, so the seller of the futures contract will have to guess at the likely dividend that would be received. Conversely, equity index futures buyers have to guess at the amount of dividend they would not receive by buying the futures contract as opposed to buying the actual shares.

The propensity for a difference between the fair, 'arbitrage free' futures price and the actual futures price is known as *basis risk*. Basis risk exists in all futures contracts. Normally it is relatively small, but in times of financial distress, that is, when it might be very costly to fund a futures position, or impossible to hedge it, the basis risk can be very large indeed.

Another thing to bear in mind is that when the future's term expires – three months in our example – the futures price will converge to that of the FTSE 100 index. That is, whatever the value of the FTSE 100 index three months hence. You'll see from our equation that because the futures contract has a term of three months, the annual income differential is multiplied by 0.25: representing one-quarter of a year. However, as the term of the futures contract approaches expiry, so this 0.25 becomes an increasingly smaller number until it becomes zero at expiry. Multiply anything by zero and you end up with zero. So, if the FTSE 100 index three months hence is, say, 6,400, then this will be the value of the futures contract. Therefore, the buyer of the futures contract, having bought at 6,153.5 when the cash market was 6,200, would have made a profit, paid via daily variation margin by the seller of the contract, of 246.5 index points (6,400 – 6,153.5) at £10 per point, that is, £2,465.

However, the most important thing to note from this example is that a futures price is NOT a prediction of the future. Instead the futures price simply reflects the relative costs of hedging the futures position over its life. This is true of most financial futures, including the long bond futures contracts that we consider next.

Long bond futures contracts

Equity index futures are an example of a cash settled futures contract. That is, investors gain or lose some cash amount that is based upon the value of the underlying asset. Most financial futures are cash settled in this way – it makes life simple. However, some financial futures contracts and most commodities futures contracts are physically settled. This means that at the end of the life of the contract the buyer of the contract is committed to paying the seller of the contract the agreed cash amount and in return the futures seller is committed to delivering the asset to the futures buyer. The most important financial futures contract that involves physical delivery, rather than cash settlement, is the long bond futures contract.

A bond futures contract commits the buyer of the futures to the future purchase of a notional long-dated government bond. If an investor has bought a long bond futures contract and holds it until its maturity date (though most are closed out before expiry), then they will have to pay over the requisite cash amount and accept delivery of the contracted amount of the underlying government bond.

Exhibit 11.4 shows the details of two popular bond futures contracts. Let's consider the long gilt futures contract. Buying a long gilt futures contract commits the buyer to purchase £100,000 worth of a notional 6 per cent

Exhibit 11.4   Long bond futures contract specifications

	CBOT 30-year T-bond	NYSE Euronext long gilt
Notional	6% coupon notional Treasury	6% coupon notional gilt
Contract size	$100,000	£100,000
Contract price	$1,000	£100
Min tick value	1/32 of $1,000 = $31.625	0.01% of contract = £10
Deliverable	Between 15 and 25 years	8 years and 9 months to 13 years

coupon gilt. The minimum price movement of the contract is 0.01 per cent (or one basis point), giving a minimum tick value of £10. The contract is written on a notional bond, but since the contract is for physical settlement of actual bonds, these bonds need to be available to deliver to settle the contract. For the long gilt futures contract the seller can choose to deliver 'eligible' gilts with a maturity between eight years and nine months and 13 years. The exchange publishes a list of these eligible bonds.

The fact that the seller of a long bond futures contract can choose to deliver from a range of bonds has some very important consequences for the pricing of bond futures contracts. The seller of the bond futures contract would always choose to deliver the cheapest of the eligible bonds. The consequences of this 'cheapest to deliver' phenomenon are quite complex so we will not go into them here. But this is an important issue to be aware of.

Trading gilt futures contracts

The process for calculating gains and losses on gilt futures trades is fairly straightforward.

- Suppose that in June 2012 an investor believes that a forthcoming announcement is going to show that UK inflation has been higher than the market expects.
- In anticipation of this the investor sells 100 NYSE Euronext December 2012 long gilt futures contracts at a price of 105.50. This commits the investor to delivering a portfolio of £10,000,000 worth of notional 6 per cent gilts in December 2012.
- The RPI report comes out the next day and does show that inflationary pressures are stronger than the market had believed. Bond prices fall, and the long gilt futures contract falls too, to 105.10.
- The investor immediately closes their position by buying back the 100 December 2012 contracts. This leads to the following trading profit:

Profit on futures = (ticks gained/lost) × tick value × number of contracts
Profit on futures = ((105.50 − 105.10) × 100) × £10.00 × 100 = £40,000

Of course, once again, had the price moved in the opposite direction the investor might have had to close the position at a loss. But this example shows how, by selling bond futures contracts, the investor managed to gain from a fall in the market price of gilts. In other words, the investor profited from shorting the market.

We have now seen how two important futures contracts work, one that is cash settled – the FTSE 100 index futures contract – and one which is physically settled, the long gilt futures contract.

Hedging using equity index futures

NYSE Euronext FTSE 100 futures contracts can be used to hedge a portfolio of UK equities against movements in the underlying equity market. The 'quality' and effectiveness of the hedge will depend mainly upon how closely related the equity portfolio to be hedged is with the equities represented by the FTSE 100 equity index. We know that when the price of the equity futures contract falls, those investors who have sold these futures contracts will gain. Therefore in order to limit the impact of a generalized fall in the equity market on an equity portfolio, an equity fund manager could 'protect' their position by selling equity index futures contracts. In this way, a fall in the general equity market will create a loss in the equity portfolio, but a profit on the short futures positions. The question then is: how many equity futures contracts does the fund manager need to sell to protect the whole value of the portfolio? The answer to this depends upon the size of the equity portfolio to be hedged. The number of contracts needed (N) can be calculated easily as follows:

$$N = \frac{\text{Face value of equity exposure}}{\text{Face value of futures contracts}}$$

Let's illustrate the use of this hedging formula with an example. Suppose that a fund manager manages a portfolio of UK equities with a market value of £50m. In March 2012 the manager wishes to hedge the portfolio until June 2012. The FTSE 100 has just closed at an index value of 6,100. To hedge the portfolio the manager knows that they need to sell June 2012 FTSE 100 futures contracts. These are currently trading at a price of 6,120 index points. Since every index point is valued at £10, selling one futures contract is like selling a portfolio of UK equities worth:

$$£61,200 = £10 \times 6,120$$

Therefore to create an equal and opposite position in futures, given that the equity portfolio is valued at £50m, the fund manager has to sell the following whole number of futures contracts:

$$N = \frac{£50,000,000}{£61,200} = 817$$

So the fund manager needs to sell 817 futures contracts, since 817 of these contracts at a price of £61,200 creates a gross position of £50m.

The market falls to 5,500

But the proof of the pudding, as they say, is in the eating. At the expiry of the June futures contract, the FTSE 100 futures contract and the FTSE 100 index will have the same value. Suppose then that at this expiry date the futures contract and index both equal 5,500. In this case the equity market has fallen by nearly 10 per cent. Assuming that the fund manager's portfolio has suffered the same fall as the FTSE 100 index, then the value of the fund manager's portfolio will be:

$$£45,081,967 = £50,000,000 \times (5,500/6,100)$$

representing a loss of:

$$£4,918,033 = £50,000,000 - £45,081,967$$

But the futures contracts could be closed out at a profit, since the fund manager took a short position in the contracts and the market has fallen. The profit on the futures position is given by:

$$\text{Profit} = \text{No. of contracts} \times (\text{No. of index points gained}) \\ \times \text{value of an index point} \\ £5,065,400 = 817 \times (6120 - 5500) \times £10$$

When we take into account the change in the value of the portfolio and the gain/loss on the futures, the net position is a small gain of:

$$£147,367 = £5,065,400 - £4,918,033$$

The futures contracts have therefore protected the fund manager's portfolio from a fall in the equity market of nearly 10 per cent. But what if the market had risen over that period?

The market rises to 6,500

Let's assume now that at expiry the June futures contract and the FTSE 100 both equal 6,500. In this case the equity market has risen by over 6.5 per cent. Assuming that the fund manager's portfolio has benefited from the same rise as the FTSE 100 index, then the value of the fund manager's portfolio will be:

$$£53,278,689 = £50,000,000 \times (6,500/6,100)$$

representing a gain of:

$$£3,278,689 = £53,278,689 - £50,000,000$$

But the futures contracts would now have to be closed out at a loss, since the fund manager took a short position in the contracts and the market has risen. The loss on the futures position is given by:

$$\text{Loss} = \text{No. of contracts} \times (\text{No. of index points lost})$$
$$\times \text{value of an index point}$$
$$£3,104,600 = 817 \times (6,120 - 6,500) \times £10$$

When we take into account the change in the value of the portfolio and the gain/loss on the futures position, the net position is a small gain of:

$$£174,089 = £3,278,689 - £3,104,600$$

In this case the futures have prevented the fund manager from benefiting from a 6.5 per cent rise in the underlying equity market. This represents one of the main drawbacks of hedging with futures contracts. Although these derivatives can protect investors from downside risk, at the same time they do not allow investors to benefit from positive movements in the underlying markets.

Options

Options can be either OTC or exchange traded derivatives. As OTC instruments, options can be traced back to the Ancients. However, as exchange traded instruments, they are a relatively recent phenomenon, having originated on the Chicago Board Options Exchange (CBOE) in 1973. An option contract gives the buyer, or holder, of the contract either the right to buy or to sell an asset at or before a pre-specified date in the future at a pre-specified price, known as the strike or exercise price. An option that conveys the right to buy is known as a *call option*, while an option that conveys the right to sell is known as a *put option*.

This sounds very similar to the rights granted to investors under forwards and futures contracts. However, forwards and futures contracts represent obligations (unless the contracts are closed out before maturity). With option contracts the holder has the right, not the obligation, to exercise the option. Hence, option holders will only exercise their options if it is profitable to do so. If not, they will let their options expire worthless.

Although the option holder is not obliged to exercise the option, the writer, or seller, of the option – the market participant that grants the option to the holder – is obliged to buy or sell the underlying asset should the option holder wish to exercise their option. For this service the option writer charges a fee, known as an *option premium.* This is not a deposit, but a non-returnable payment exchanged for the right to exercise a future transaction.

How do call options work?

Suppose that an investor buys a call option on the ordinary shares of ABC plc, which gives them the right to buy the stock for £50 in 3 months time. The option writer charges an option premium of £5 in return for selling the call option. This optional purchase price of £50 is the exercise or strike price.

The line labelled 'long call' in Exhibit 11.5 shows the payoff profile for the holder, or buyer of this call option. If at the expiry date of the option the price of the stock is lower than the strike price of £50 then the option holder will not exercise their option, since it would be cheaper to buy the stock in the open market. In this instance the option will expire *out-of-the-money* and the investor will not recover the £5 premium paid.

However, if the stock price at the option's expiry date is £55, then the investor will exercise the *in-the-money* option by buying the stock from the option writer at the exercise price of £50 and will then make a £5 profit by selling the stock on the open market for £55. However, since the investor paid £5 for the option initially, this means that they break even. If the stock ends the period above £55 the investor makes a cash profit. Finally, if the stock was priced at £50, then the option would be *at-the-money*, as notwithstanding the £5 option

Exhibit 11.5 The profit/loss at expiry for a call option on the ordinary shares of ABC plc

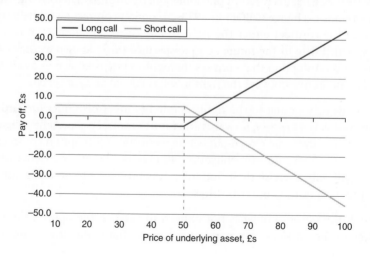

premium paid, the call option holder should be indifferent between buying the stock in the cash market or via the option. You should note that when designating an option, in-, out- or at-the-money, the option premium is not taken into account. Rather the designation derives from the difference, if any, between the price of the underlying asset and the exercise price.

There are two points in particular worth noting about the payoff profile for a call option. First, the investor has limited downside (the option premium paid) and virtually unlimited upside potential, since the value of the ordinary shares could theoretically rise without limit over the term of the option.

Second, the payoff profile for the option writer shown by the line labelled 'short call' in Exhibit 11.5 is the mirror image of that for the option holder. That is, limited upside (the option premium received) and almost unlimited downside. If the option is not exercised the option writer gets to keep the premium. If the stock price rises to £55 at the time of expiry, the option writer would have to buy the asset in the open market for £55 and sell it to the option holder for £50, thereby incurring a £5 capital loss that is offset by the £5 premium.

How do put options work?

Suppose that an investor buys a put option on the ordinary shares of XYZ plc, which gives them the right to sell the stock for £50 in three months time. The option writer charges a premium of £5 in return for selling this put option.

The line labelled 'long put' in Exhibit 11.6 shows the payoff profile for the holder, or buyer, of this put option. If at the expiry date of the option the price

Exhibit 11.6 The profit/loss at expiry for a put option on the ordinary shares of XYZ plc

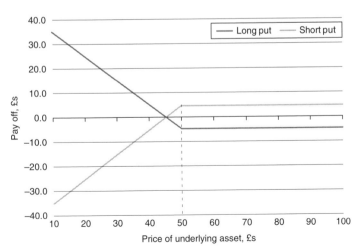

of the stock is higher than the strike price of £50 then the option holder will not exercise their option, since they would have to buy the stock at, say, £55 in the open market (or already be holding the stock worth £55) and then sell it to the option writer for £50. In this instance the option will expire *out-of-the-money* and the investor will not recover the £5 premium paid.

If the stock price at the expiry date of the option is £45, then the holder will exercise the *in-the-money* option, buying the stock in the open market for £45 (or already be holding the stock worth £45) and then selling it to the option writer at a price of £50 making a £5 profit in the process. However, since the holder paid £5 for the option initially, this means that they break even. If the stock ends the period below £45 the holder makes a profit.

Once again there are two points in particular worth noting about the payoff profile for a put option. First, the put holder has limited downside (the option premium paid) and almost unlimited upside potential. Second, the payoff profile for the option writer, shown by the line labelled 'short put' in Exhibit 11.6, is the mirror image of that for the option buyer. If the option is not exercised, the option writer gets to keep the premium. If the stock price falls to £45 at the time of expiry, the option writer would have to buy the asset from the put holder for £50 and sell it in the open market for £45, thereby incurring a £5 capital loss, offset by the £5 premium received.

Market exposure

The difference between the two positions – the long call and the long put positions – is that the holder of a call will benefit if the asset price rises above the strike or exercise price, whereas the put holder will benefit if the stock falls below the strike or exercise price. Investors who believe an asset or market will tend to rise over time will be more inclined to buy call options, whereas an investor expecting a fall in asset values might be tempted to buy put options. Put options are typically used to hedge individual assets or portfolios of assets against market movements (as an alternative to taking a short futures/forward position).

An example: Options on FTSE 100 index futures contracts

Options on FTSE 100 index futures contracts are traded on the NYSE Euronext derivatives exchange. They enable investors to buy or sell, put and call options on the UK equity market. The fact that one can trade options on futures contracts sounds complicated, but given that the relationship between equity futures and the equity index itself is, as we saw earlier, usually very close indeed, this is analogous to trading options on the underlying equity market. Buying and selling the options on futures contracts means that the transactions can be settled in cash rather than through the exchange of actual shares, which makes the process simpler, less costly and more liquid.

At any point in time there is a whole range of put and call options on the FTSE 100 index available for trading. There are up to eight maturities trading at any one time, with approximately three months between each maturity date. As well as a range of maturity dates there are also a range of exercise prices too, usually every 50 index points.

So for example, an investor could buy a July 2012 call option on the FTSE 100 futures contract with a ~~strike price of 7,000~~. Or they might be able to buy a December 2012 put option on the FTSE 100 futures contract with a strike price of 6,000.

Exhibit 11.7 shows the range of options available on the July 2011 FTSE 100 index futures contract in June 2011, which at the time had only 21 days until expiry. The premiums on these options contracts are quoted in index points.

Exhibit 11.7 shows the call premiums for all of the options with this expiry date. The exhibit clearly shows that the call option with the highest premium has a strike price of 5,600. Purchasing this call option gives the investor the right to buy July 2011 FTSE 100 index futures contracts at a price of 5,600 index points. The premium on this contract is high because on this particular day this futures contract was trading well above this strike level, at a price of 5,766. Therefore, investors would be willing to pay a high price for this option because there would be a strong possibility that it would be exercisable at a

Exhibit 11.7   Option premium on July 2011 FTSE 100 index futures

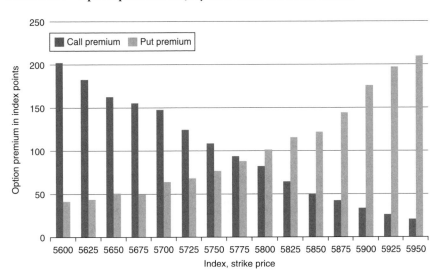

Source: NYSE Euronext (June 2011).

profit. This call option is 'in-the-money' because the price of the underlying asset is higher than the exercise price. But the exhibit also shows that as the exercise price rises, the value of the call option falls, since there is an increasingly greater prospect that it will not be exercisable at a profit.

The converse is true for the put options on the same futures contract. These are also shown in Exhibit 11.7. With 21 days to go to the option's expiry, the holder of a put option on this contract with a strike price of 5,950, and the futures price on this day at 5,766, would have had the greatest prospect of being able to exercise the option at a profit. The holder would have been able to sell the futures contact to the writer of the put option for a price of 5,950 and then close out the position by buying it back in the open market at a lower price. But as the strike price falls, the value of the option falls too since the greater the prospect that the option will expire out-of-the-money.

Payoff profile for options on FTSE 100 index futures contracts

Trading FTSE 100 index options contracts is similar in principle to trading the underlying futures contract. The premiums on these options are priced in index points and each index point is valued at £10. So if an investor wished to buy a July 2011 call with a strike price of 5,850, the quoted price of 50 index points means that each option would have a premium of £500. Each option would confer the right to buy one FTSE 100 index futures contract at a price of 5,850. In effect, this gives the holder the right to buy a portfolio of UK equities at a price of £58,500.

The payoff diagram for this particular option is shown in Exhibit 11.8. The premium is 50 index points and the exercise price is 5,850 index points. The option will only be exercised if the futures contract price is above 5,850 when the contract expires. If the index is lower than this at expiry the option will expire worthless and the investor that paid 50 index points for the option would lose this premium. If the index expires above this level, however, the option can be exercised at a profit.

If the option expires when the futures index price is 5,900, the investor will break even. For every option purchased the investor will be able to buy the futures contract at a price of 5,850 and sell it in the open market at a price of 5,900, making a 50 index point profit on each contract. However, the option premium, which is non-refundable, cost 50 index points. Therefore, the net profit would be zero. For expiry values above 5,900, however, the call option holder makes a profit.

In essence then, these options have payoff profiles that are identical to those explained in Exhibits 11.5 and 11.6 earlier. It's just that the payoff profile here is depicted in equity index points.

Exhibit 11.8 Option payoff diagram

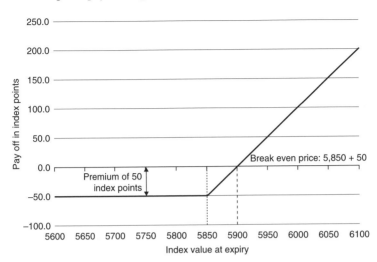

Trading options on FTSE 100 index futures contracts (?)

If an investor does not wish to wait until the option expires to capitalise on any gains (or take any losses), how are these options contracts traded?

- Suppose an investor buys 100 call options with an expiry of July 2011, with a strike price of 5,850 and for a premium of 50 index points today.
- Now suppose that the following day some good news hits the UK equity market and that the FTSE 100 index futures price rises. Because of this there is now a greater prospect that the option will be exercised at a profit, which in turn causes the option premium to rise to 55 index points.
- The option holder could realize a profit by closing out their position by selling 100 call options with an expiry of July 2011, with a strike price of 5,850 at the new price of 55 index points.   you sell yor opder right
- The profit to the investor would be calculated as follows:

No. of contracts × (option selling price − option purchase price)
× price per index point

$$100 \times (55 - 50) \times £10 = £5,000$$

- The investor could realize this £5,000 profit without having to wait for the contract to expire.

Options can be used to hedge financial market risk. We will now explain how they do this by using derivatives on the FTSE 100 equity index to illustrate the key points once again.

Hedging with FTSE 100 options contracts (|,)

NYSE Euronext options on FTSE 100 futures contracts can be also used to hedge the risks associated with a UK equity portfolio. But as with the FTSE 100 futures contracts the quality and effectiveness of the hedge will depend upon how closely related the underlying UK equity portfolio is to the FTSE 100 index.

We saw earlier how futures contracts can be used to eliminate much of the downside risk associated with an investment portfolio, as long as the investor sells the appropriate number of contracts. However, we also saw how a hedge implemented using futures eliminates upside potential too. It is for this reason that investors may wish to use options rather than futures contracts to hedge portfolio risk, since such a hedge can be implemented leaving the potential for gains if the underlying market or asset rises in value. However, as with anything in life, something worth having comes at a price. But before we explain this 'price', we should first consider the type of option strategy required to limit downside risk.

We know that when a market or asset falls in value, the holder of a put option profits from this decline. Therefore to hedge a portfolio of UK equities an investor can buy NYSE Euronext FTSE 100 put option contracts. But the question once again is how many of these contracts need to be purchased. The answer to this depends upon the size of the equity portfolio to be hedged. The number of contracts needed (N) can be calculated easily as follows:

$$N = \frac{\text{Face value of equity exposure}}{\text{Face value of index option}}$$

Once again the idea is that the investor *buys* enough contracts such that an exposure equal and opposite to the exposure represented by holding the equity portfolio can be created. Using this hedging formula can be best illustrated with an example.

Suppose that a fund manager manages a portfolio of UK equities with a market value of £50m. In June 2011 the manager wishes to hedge the portfolio, that is, protect it from a fall in the equity market, until July 2011. The FTSE 100 has just closed at an index value of 5,900. To hedge the portfolio the manager knows that they need to buy July 2011 FTSE 100 put option contracts. The manager chooses to buy these put options with a strike price of 5,675. These are currently trading at a price of 50 index points. This means that the manager will find it worthwhile to exercise the options if the FTSE 100 index falls below 5,675. The price of each put is £500, since an index point is worth £10 and the puts are priced at 50 index points.

The manager needs to purchase the following whole number of put contracts:

$$N = \frac{£50,000,000}{5900 \times £10} = 847$$

Notice that we have used the FTSE index level of 5,900 rather than the FTSE 100 put option strike price of 5,675 as the denominator in this calculation. Also, unlike implementing a futures hedge, there is an upfront, non-returnable cost to effecting the hedge. This is the difference between hedging with futures and hedging with options. Given that the manager needs to buy 847 puts, the total, up-front cost of putting on the hedge is:

$$£423,500 = 847 \times £500$$

But there is a benefit to this cost as Exhibit 11.9 demonstrates.

However, before we explain this benefit, first consider the line labelled 'P/L on portfolio'. This line represents the profit or loss on the underlying equity portfolio, assuming that it moves one for one with the FTSE 100 index. If at the expiry of the put options the FTSE 100 index has not moved and remains at 5,900, the gain on the equity portfolio will be zero, and so the line crosses the horizontal axis at 5,900.

The line labelled 'options' represents the pay-off from the option position. If the option expires with the FTSE 100 above the strike price of 5,675, the options expire worthless and the manager's net position on the options is a

Exhibit 11.9 Individual and combined pay-off profiles

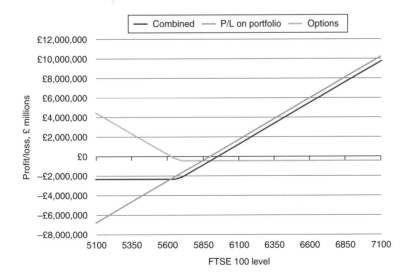

loss of £423,500 – the cost of the hedge. However, as the index drops below the option exercise price, it becomes worthwhile for the manager to exercise them. Since the manager pays 50 index points for the options the manager breaks even if the index has fallen to a value of 5,625 (5,675 – 50) at the options' expiry. The profit on the options position is calculated as follows:

$$\text{Profit} = \text{Number of contracts} \times \text{index points gained} \times \text{price of index point}$$
$$£423,500 = 847 \times 50 \times 10$$

which equals the initial cost of the options. However, if the index is below this level at the time that the options expire, the fund manager's option position produces a net profit.

But it is not the individual positions that are relevant, rather it is the combined options and equity portfolio position that matters. This combined position is shown by the line labelled 'combined'. The combination of the put options and the portfolio creates a floor at the exercise price of the put option. Basically as the index falls past this point, every £1 that the equity portfolio falls is compensated for by a £1 gain on the option position. However, unlike the futures hedge, the portfolio can benefit from a generalized rise in the equity market. In fact, if the market has risen by 50 index points to 5,950 at the time that the option expires, the fund manager has broken even. This is because the gain on the equity portfolio (which rises by approximately 0.85%) is equal to the cost of the hedge at this time. In other words:

$$\text{Portfolio gain} = \text{Initial value of portfolio} \times \text{\% change in market}$$
$$£423,500 = £50,000,000 \times (0.85\%)$$

However, if the index rises above this level the fund manager begins to make a profit on the portfolio.

The benefit then of hedging with put options is that the strategy does not cap the upside potential, but does protect much of the downside risk (depending upon the option cost and the strike price). This is the benefit that investors are sometimes willing to pay for, where that cost is the total upfront option premium.

Credit default swaps

Derivatives are very special financial contracts. They can facilitate access to the underlying asset, or cash market, without the requirement for a cash investment. In other words, investors can get leveraged access to the underlying asset classes.

They also allow investors to take short positions that are often more difficult to achieve in the cash market. For example, by selling a futures contract, or by buying a put option on an asset, an investor can benefit if the market price of that asset falls.

Credit default swaps (CDSs) can also facilitate access to an underlying cash market, without the need for a significant cash investment. In addition, as with other derivatives, investors can easily create short positions too. But the real attraction of CDSs is that they facilitate the trading of credit risk. A CDS can separate the credit risk inherent in a corporate bond from the general interest rate risk that is embodied in all fixed income securities.

CDSs as insurance

Before we explain the mechanics of a CDS we can consider the way in which insurance contracts work. For example, in return for insuring one's car, an insurance company will require us to pay them a regular premium. This premium will usually be a fraction of the value of the car. If the car is involved in an accident and is written off, then the insurance company will usually pay us a cash sum equal to the insured value of the car. At this point, the car, or what is left of it, belongs to the insurance company who will try to salvage some value from the wreckage by selling what remains to a scrap dealer.

In many respects CDSs work along the same lines. An investor can buy a CDS from another investor, where the 'insured event' is the default on a bond issued by a particular entity: typically a company or a government. In return for this 'insurance', the seller of the CDS will require that the buyer pays a regular premium. This arrangement is shown in Exhibit 11.10.

Exhibit 11.10 A typical CDS structure

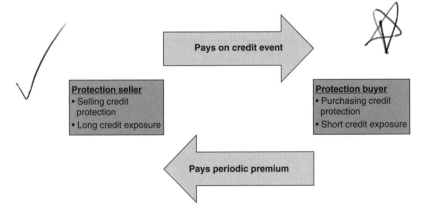

The protection buyer makes a periodic payment (usually quarterly) to the protection seller. In the event that there is a default on the bond referenced in the CDS agreement, the periodic payments cease, the protection buyer delivers the defaulted bond to the protection seller, and the protection seller makes a one-off payment for the notional amount of the bond insured. The protection seller then becomes the owner of the bond and has a legal claim on the remaining assets of the entity – let's assume a corporation – issuing the bond. If this corporation has marketable assets, then the recovery value may be high and the protection seller may be able to earn back much of the cash that it had to pay to the CDS buyer.

So, in the same way that we can buy insurance to eliminate most of the financial consequences of our house burning down, or against crashing our car etc., CDSs allow institutions like banks to insure loans that they have made to other entities, and can allow investors, like pension schemes, to buy protection against the default on a bond, or portfolio of bonds, they may hold.

What's special about CDS 'insurance'?

However, there are some subtle differences between general insurance contracts and CDS contracts. First, an individual can insure their own home or car, but it is illegal for them to insure someone else's home or car. To do this, the individual must have an insurable interest. Second, an individual can insure their car once with one insurance company, but it is illegal for them to insure the car again with a second or third insurer and then to make multiple claims in the event of a car accident.

With a CDS an investor can buy insurance relating to the default of a particular bond or loan, even if they do not own the bond or if they have not made the loan. That is, they can make a 'naked' transaction in a CDS despite not having an insurable interest.[13] Furthermore, they can continue to buy insurance from as many CDS sellers as they like, effectively buying multiple insurance contracts that insure them against, indeed, profit from, the issuing entity defaulting.

If we could add up the sum assured of every car in the UK, it should come to no more than the total market value of insured cars. However, it is very possible that the total amount of insurance bought and sold on the debt of any particular company via CDS contracts could exceed the market value of that debt. Thus CDSs (along with other credit derivatives) can greatly exacerbate the amount of total investor exposure to credit risk. These contracts, therefore, played a part in the inflation of the credit bubble that eventually burst in 2008, giving

---

[13] At the time of writing, the EU's Economic and Monetary Affairs Committee had just voted on a ban on 'naked' sovereign bond CDS transactions.

way to the credit crisis. However, as we pointed out at the start of this chapter, derivatives are only dangerous in the wrong hands. Used properly, CDSs are an important risk management tool.

CDS payments

Suppose that France Telecom has issued a ten-year bond. A CDS contract could be struck such that an investor 'insures' themselves against a France Telecom default. Let's suppose that an investor wishes to insure themselves to a notional value of €10m of this ten-year bond for the next ten years. The premium would be quoted in basis points (bp) – a basis point is $1/100^{th}$ of 1 per cent – per annum and would be payable on a quarterly basis based upon the €10m notional sum insured for ten years. If the premium is quoted as 50bp per annum, the quarterly payment to insure this notional amount of France Telecom bonds would, therefore, be:

$$50bp/4 \times €10m = €12,500$$

This premium would be payable on a quarterly basis for the next ten years until the ten years had elapsed, or until France Telecom defaulted. In the event of the default, the CDS buyer would deliver the France Telecom bond with a notional value of €10m, and would, in turn, receive a cash payment of €10m from the protection seller. At this point the CDS premiums would cease.

CDS maturities

Even though the CDS in the example above is written with reference to a ten year France Telecom bond, CDSs are typically traded with five different maturity terms (though this has increased to ten for some credits recently). In the same way that we may purchase insurance for our car for a period of one year even though the car may well have an economic life exceeding one year, the CDS maturity terms can vary according to the period over which the CDS buyer wishes to have the 'insurance'. Once that period has elapsed the contract expires, in the same way that our car insurance usually expires after 12 months.

The market for CDSs is so large and liquid now that on many corporate names there is a full range of CDS terms available and quoted at all times. In Exhibit 11.11 we present the CDS spreads that prevailed on Royal Bank of Scotland debt before the credit crunch and in October 2008 at the height of the credit crunch. In July 2007, the cost of taking out insurance against the Royal Bank of Scotland default-ing over the subsequent ten years was just under 40 basis points per annum. But by October 2008 the cost had risen to just over 250 basis points per annum.

Exhibit 11.11   Royal Bank of Scotland plc CDS spreads

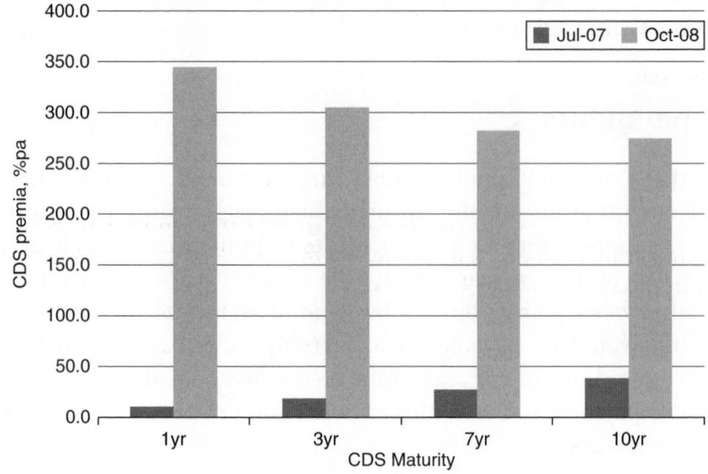

Exhibit 11.11 also demonstrates one of the key advantages of CDSs over investing in corporate bonds directly. An investor may wish to gain access to the credit risk embodied in an entity over three years. However, a three year bond may not be in existence, but by selling the three year CDS on the corporation they can access this credit exposure over the desired period, and earn a reward in the form of the premium for doing so.

Trading CDSs

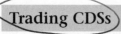

We can revisit the France Telecom example above to show how investors can gain or lose from trading CDSs.

- Suppose that an investor sells a ten year CDS contract on France Telecom. In return they will receive 50bp per annum on the notional amount that they sell.
- Now suppose that a few days later France Telecom's credit quality improves. This means that the premium charged for insuring France Telecom debt should fall, since the likelihood of a default will be lower, by definition.
- Suppose then that the CDS premium on the same France Telecom bond for a period of ten years falls from 50bp to 40bp.
- The seller of the CDS at 50bp can now lock in a profit by buying another CDS with identical terms from another investor at a premium of 40bp. In this way the investor effectively locks in a profit of 10bp per annum for ten years on the notional CDS contract amount. The investor has, therefore, benefited

bond ↓ ↑ karim ali'ni?

from an improvement in France Telecom's credit quality in the same way that the holder of the bond would have benefited. *Hence, sellers of CDSs are said to be long credit exposure, since they benefit when credit quality improves.*

However, had France Telecom's credit quality deteriorated instead then the investor looking to close their position would have to do so at a loss.

- Now consider the position of the buyer of protection, that is the investor paying 50bp to protect against a France Telecom default.
- If France Telecom's credit deteriorates, so that the ten-year France Telecom CDS spread increases to, say, 60bp, the investor can lock in a profit, by selling a ten-year CDS with identical terms on France Telecom at 60bp.
- In this case the investor benefits from a deterioration in credit quality in a similar way that an investor that is short the France Telecom bond might also do.

Using CDSs, investors can benefit from both a narrowing in credit spreads, by selling the CDS, and from a widening in the spread, by buying the CDS. This risk can be accessed without the need to buy a corporate bond in the cash market, thus giving investors leveraged access to credit risk.

Issues with respect to CDSs

CDSs can give investors access to the majority of the credit premium without having to invest in corporate bonds directly. This means that a pension fund holding a portfolio of gilts but wishing to hold a portfolio of corporate bonds instead can now effect this transformation using CDSs. So rather than incurring the significant transactions costs involved in selling the gilts and then purchasing the corporate bonds, they can simply sell CDSs on the corporate names upon which they wish to have exposure. In return they will receive the premiums on all those names from CDS buyers.

There are some issues worth noting with respect to using CDSs though. We can touch on some of them briefly:

- The vast majority of CDSs that are available are denominated in either US dollars or in euros. Therefore, a pension fund wishing to build up exposure to sterling corporate bonds by selling CDSs will, in effect, contract to receive premiums in euros, which means that the foreign exchange risk involved may need to be hedged.
- CDSs are currently OTC instruments. This means that investors need to consider carefully the counterparty risk involved.
- CDSs are currently physically settled. This means that in the event of any default, the CDS buyer has to deliver the specified bond of the referenced

corporate entity. However, given that there is technically no limit to the number of CDS contracts that can be written there may not be enough bonds to go around.

- CDSs may be written on a bond that the corporate entity decides to buy back. In this case there may remain CDS contracts written on a bond that no longer exists.

Summary

In this chapter we began by looking at futures and options contracts. Using the FTSE 100 index derivatives contracts we showed how these contracts can be used to hedge underlying financial market risk. They can of course be used to enhance this risk recklessly too, but it is to be hoped that trustees do not have this goal in mind! We also considered credit default swaps. These are the building blocks of many credit derivative instruments, and again can be used for risk management purposes, though again in the wrong hands could become the catalyst of economic disaster.

Key points

- For many uninformed commentators, derivatives represent the worst excesses of 'casino capitalism'. However, when used properly, derivatives can aid risk management.
- Derivatives can be used to increase exposures to market risk very rapidly and cheaply, facilitate a move from one investment exposure to another more safely and more efficiently than by using the 'cash' market and as a means by which to hedge cash market exposures.
- Embedded in a derivative contract is normally a 'zero sum game', that is, for every gain for one investor, there is an equal and opposite loss for another.
- Forwards and futures are obligations and are analytically very similar except that forwards are bespoke, over the counter (OTC) contracts and futures are standardized and exchange traded. By contrast, for the buyer of an option, options represent a right not an obligation. For the seller, however, they represent an obligation. Options can be traded OTC or on an exchange.
- Credit default swaps can facilitate access to an underlying credit market, without the need for a significant cash investment and provide protection against a bond, or portfolio of bonds, defaulting.

Chapter 12

Interest Rate and Inflation Swaps: Swapping Payments You Don't Want for Those That You Do

Learning outcomes

- An understanding of the basic mechanics of interest rate and inflation swaps.
- An understanding of how these swaps can be used for risk management purposes.
- An understanding of the economic exposure and key risks with respect to these instruments.
- An understanding of the investment context of using swaps.

Introduction

Many years ago, the BBC launched a Saturday morning children's show call *Multi-coloured Swap Shop*. It was presented by the then Radio 1 DJ Noel Edmonds, and quickly became a favourite with children up and down the country. Children would ring through to the show in the hope of swapping a toy or game that they no longer wanted (or one that belonged to a sibling!) for one that they did – hence the name of the show. A very simple concept – one that proved to be very popular with children growing up in the 1970s.

Believe it or not, interest rate swap contracts are a very simple concept too. In essence one can enter a swap contract by contacting an investment bank (acting in the role of Noel Edmonds) and offering to part with one stream of future payments for another. Simple. You give away a payment stream you do not want for one that you do want. For example, a UK pension fund might be receiving coupon income from a euro-denominated corporate bond portfolio. But with sterling-based liabilities it might wish to swap this stream of euro income for one denominated in sterling. This can be arranged very easily via an investment bank acting as the swap counterparty. This is known as a foreign currency swap. Of course, for the swap to work it requires another entity that is willing to receive payments in euros in return for making payments in sterling.

Swaps are really this simple. The complicated bit comes from determining the basis for the swap. In our example this means determining what sterling cash flow is equivalent to a euro cash flow. Complications also arise in valuing the two parts of the swap over time. But the principle remains: pay away the cash flow that you do not want, in exchange for one that you do want.

In this chapter we will focus on two types of swap that are now used quite extensively for risk management purposes, and which have both become synonymous with de-risking and Liability Driven Investment (LDI), which we discuss in Chapter 15:

i. fixed for floating interest rate swaps, and
ii. inflation swaps.

Swap contracts have become an important feature in the defined benefit (DB) pensions landscape over the past few years. This is because they can be used to help manage some of the risks that a DB pension fund faces. There are two risks in particular. The first is interest rate risk. When interest rates fall the present value of a scheme's liabilities usually rise by more than the value of its assets. This is because the duration of a typical pension scheme's liabilities is usually much longer than the duration of any bond assets that it might hold. An interest rate swap can help to create a situation whereby the net position of a pension fund's assets and liabilities are largely unaffected by the fall or rise of interest rates in the wider economy.

The second risk relates to inflation. A significant proportion of the DB pensions payable in the future are inflation protected, or index-linked, to some degree. This means that the pension in payment will tend to rise with future inflation. Higher future inflation will, therefore, increase the cash payments that the pension fund's assets will have to generate. An inflation swap can reduce or even eliminate the vast majority of the inflation risk to which a scheme may be exposed.

As we explain in Chapter 15, both interest rate and inflation risk are seen as being long-term 'unrewarded risks'. This is why trustee advisers have encouraged their clients to use swaps to remove or at least reduce these exposures.

Swap basics

One of the most important features of a swap contract is that usually at the outset of the contract no monies are exchanged. This is because the two payment streams are priced in such a way that they are equal at the outset of the contract.[1] Hence, an investor can swap a fixed payment stream today, priced at say £1bn, for a stream of floating interest payments also priced today at £1bn. All advisory fees and swap transaction costs, except swap spreads, are excluded from the calculation.

The mechanics of a swap can be daunting, as can the terminology, so we will begin by running through the key points.

An investor, such as a DB pension scheme, may enter into a 'fixed for floating' swap. This means that one of the swap counterparties agrees to make a set of fixed interest payments to another, and in return receives a set of payments based upon a floating rate of interest. We normally define each of the swap counterparties with reference to the fixed interest payment. In other words, when a counterparty to a swap is referred to as the 'fixed receiver' it means that they receive a fixed rate of interest and pay a floating rating of interest; while the other is referred to as the 'fixed payer'. A DB pension scheme seeking to immunize itself against the adverse impact of falling interest rates on the present value of its liabilities, would be a fixed receiver. Another important parameter in the swap is its 'notional' amount. Interest payments of nearly all kinds are regular payments expressed as a proportion of an original borrowed amount. Even though no borrowing or lending takes place under an interest rate swap, a notional borrowing amount must be specified, so that the regular interest payments can be calculated. These regular interest payments are usually made quarterly or semi-annually.[2] Finally, like any regular borrowing or lending we need to specify the term over which the lending or borrowing will take place. So, just as with a bond, a swap will have a maturity, a period over which the interest payments must be made and, once reached, the point at which they cease.

---

[1] In finance-speak, the net present value (NPV) of the two payment streams are equal to one another and therefore cancel one another out.

[2] Sterling interest rate swaps are normally based upon semi-annual payments.

Exhibit 12.1   The two legs of an interest rate swap

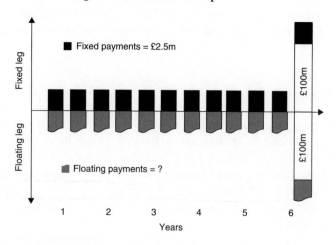

In the example in Exhibit 12.1 we have depicted the cash flows for a £100m, six-year fixed for floating swap. One counterparty is the fixed receiver and agrees to receive a set of fixed cash flows at a rate of 5 per cent semi-annually for the next six years. This means that they can expect to receive a regular annual payment of £2.5m every half year from the fixed payer. They are also due the £100m at the end of the life of the swap. So they are 'buying' this set of fixed payments. This set of payments looks just like the set of payments we encountered for a plain vanilla bond. They can be valued in just the same way, discounting each payment at the appropriate rate, summing them all together to arrive at a present value for the fixed payments.

So being a fixed receiver is analogous to buying a bond with a fixed coupon payment. However, unlike the buyer of a six-year annual coupon paying bond, the fixed receiver is required to make a set of floating interest payments to the fixed payer and then to pay that notional amount of the swap at the end of six years. Because both investors have to pay one another a notional amount of £100m at the end of the term, these two payments cancel one another out, as shown in Exhibit 12.1.   *principle ·*

Conceptually, the most complex issue with regard to this swap is the set of floating rate payments. At each pre-determined interest rate date (semi-annual in this example), the fixed interest payment is known in advance (£2.5m in this example) but the floating rate payment will be determined by the level of a reference interest rate at that time. This reference rate is usually LIBOR. If the swap payments are quarterly, then it will be three-month LIBOR, if they are semi-annual then it will be based upon six-month LIBOR.

We said earlier that at the outset of the swap, the present value of each leg is identical. It is a relatively simple matter to find the present value of a set of fixed payments. But how does one find the present value of a set of interest payments where the reference interest rate is as yet unknown? We will come to the full answer to this question below, but for now we can simply state that these floating interest rate payments are derived from the forward curve introduced in Chapter 6. Using the forward curve we can determine what the payments are expected to be, and then calculate their present value appropriately.

The important point here is not the complicated mathematics that is required to calculate the present value of the floating leg of the swap, but the economic exposure that arises from the swap. Look again at Exhibit 12.1. Forget for the moment the floating leg, the fixed receiver is in the same position as an investor that has bought a plain vanilla bond paying fixed coupons. Conversely, forget for the moment the fixed leg of the swap, the floating receiver (the fixed payer) is in the same position as an investor that has bought a floating rate note (FRN, see Chapter 6).

When interest rates rise, the present value of a fixed coupon bond falls, but because the coupons to be received on a floating rate bond will be expected to rise, its value rises relative to the value of the fixed coupon bond. The opposite effect happens when interest rates fall. Therefore, since a fixed receiver experiences a loss when interest rates rise and a gain when they fall, they effectively have a long bond exposure.

Swap collateral

At the outset of the swap, the two legs have the same present value. But as interest rates fluctuate, the value of the two legs will fluctuate too. Suppose after a swap is struck that interest rates fall. In this case the present value of the fixed leg will rise relative to the present value of the floating leg. So the present value of these fixed payments due to the fixed receiver rises, but the present value of the floating payments that the fixed receiver must make, falls. In this case a payment will be made by the fixed payer to the fixed receiver to compensate them for the fact that the leg of the swap that the fixed receiver owns is now more valuable than the leg that the fixed payer owns. If a DB pension scheme is the fixed receiver, then this payment will offset the rise in the scheme's liabilities, resulting from the fall in interest rates, against which the swap is written. This payment, known as collateral, is equal to the net change in the value of the two legs and is made into a secure collateral account.

The reason why collateral is posted between the counterparties is because swaps are over the counter (OTC) derivatives. Unlike exchange traded derivatives, OTC derivative trades are not subject to the margining rules that apply to the standardized derivatives traded on derivative exchanges and are not guaranteed by a central counterparty.[3] So, in the event that the fixed payer became insolvent the money in the collateral account would belong to the fixed receiver. The collateral flows in and out of the collateral account will be determined by the fluctuation in interest rates across the yield curve over time. When the yield curve falls, the fixed payer will pay into the account; when it rises the fixed receiver will pay into the account. These collateral flows, that depend upon the relative values of the two legs of the swap at each point in time, can be calculated and made on monthly, weekly, or on a daily basis. In practice, especially after the Lehman Brothers' bankruptcy in September 2008, collateral is usually exchanged on a daily basis. The more frequently collateral is calculated and exchanged, the lower the risk of a loss in the event that one of the swap counterparties fails. For a swap that is valued against yield curve movements, or 'marked to market', on a daily basis, any loss stemming from bankruptcy should be confined to one day's worth of yield curve movements.

The collateral flows are thus a crucial concept when it comes to swaps. After all, the notional amount of an interest rate swap is not exchanged, nor are the regular interest payments – one swap counterparty does not make a literal interest payment to the other and receive one in return. Under an interest rate swap it is only regular collateral that is exchanged, and the size of these collateral flows is determined by the movements in the relevant interest rates.

So what can be used as collateral? Given that the collateral in a collateral account is essentially meant to protect each counterparty from the credit, or default, risk of the other, it is normal to post high-quality, highly-liquid G4-nation sovereign bonds[4] or cash as collateral. Lower quality assets, for example those corporate bonds with a high degree of credit risk, may fall in value between marking the swap to market. Worse still, the bond issuers might even default themselves. If bonds other than G4 sovereigns are acceptable to the counterparties, either unilaterally or bilaterally, then the bonds are typically given a 'haircut'. That is, the bonds' market value is marked down, often quite significantly. So in market value terms, swap counterparties effectively have to post more collateral if they post lower quality bonds. What constitutes acceptable collateral and the frequency with which it should pass between the counterparties is determined by the terms agreed within the Credit Support Annex of an ISDA (International Swaps and Derivatives Association) agreement.

---

[3] However, following the Lehman Brothers' bankruptcy in September 2008, regulators have made it clear that they would like to see a number of OTC swap contacts move on to derivative exchanges. When this happens, these contracts will be subject to margining and will be guaranteed by the central counterparty to the exchange.

[4] The G4 nations comprise the UK, US, France and Germany.

All OTC derivatives are governed by ISDA agreements. These are standardized documents which define the relationship and the specific terms of the agreement between the pension scheme and the investment bank.

Interest rate swaps and bond fund management

Bond fund managers can use swaps to adjust their exposure to interest rates. For example, if the fund manager expects interest rates to fall, they may enter into a swap as the fixed receiver. If interest rates fall in line with their views, the present value of the fixed payments will rise relative to the present value of the floating rate payments. In this case, collateral will flow to the fund manager. Conversely, if the manager takes the opposite view, they may enter the swap as the fixed payer. If interest rates then rise in line with their views, the present value of the fixed payments will fall relative to the floating rate leg of the swap. And again collateral will flow to the fund manager. Where their mandates permit then, bond fund managers can, for example, adjust their exposure to interest rates by lengthening the duration of their portfolio – buying long-dated and selling shorter-dated bonds – in advance of an anticipated fall in the yield curve. However, the transactions costs involved from buying and selling bonds can be prohibitive, whereas the transactions costs for making this adjustment in the swaps market can be considerably lower.

Swap summary so far

There are a number of crucial points to remember with respect to interest rate swaps:

i.   at the outset of the swap, the two legs of the swap have the same present value;
ii. the swap counterparty is characterized according to whether they are receiving or paying the fixed component of the swap;
iii. the swap payments are based on a notional amount of borrowing that is never exchanged;
iv. the interest payments are never exchanged either. What is exchanged is the collateral. This collateral protects each swap counterparty from the credit risk of the other; and
v.   bond fund managers can use interest rate swaps to manage their exposure to interest rates, often more efficiently and cheaply than they can by trading in the underlying bond market.

So far (hopefully), so good. In the next section of this chapter we will explain where swaps rates come from. In other words how we work out the terms for swapping a set of fixed interest payments for a set of unknown floating rate interest payments.

What is *the* swap rate?

The market for swaps, which principally comprises investment banks, is now very, very large indeed and very liquid. Indeed, according to the Bank for International Settlements (BIS), the notional value of interest rate swaps outstanding as at end-December 2010 was $364.4 trillion.[5] The swaps market, the trading rules which are set by the International Swap and Derivative Association (ISDA), offers a continuous quotation for swapping fixed payments for floating payments over a range of maturities. This is reflected in Exhibit 12.2. This chart presents the five-year sterling swap rate. This is the fixed interest, sterling payment that the market is willing to make in return for semi-annual sterling payments based upon six-month LIBOR over the next five years. Conversely, it is the sterling fixed rate of interest that an investor could expect to receive in return for committing to a semi-annual sterling payment based upon six-month LIBOR over the next five years.

In late-1994, the five-year swap rate was 9 per cent. By the end of 2010 the fixed rate offered for the set of floating payments was just 2.63 per cent. The fall in swap rates over this time reflected the general fall in interest rates over this period, and then latterly the financial crisis that had forced most central banks to slash their policy rates to (near) zero, as they tried to kick start their

Exhibit 12.2   The five year sterling swap rate

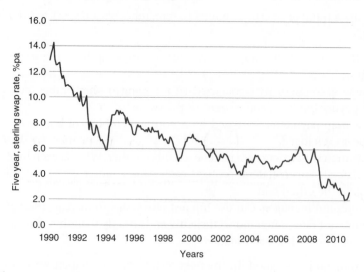

Source: Thomson Financial.

---

[5] Bank for International Settlements semi-annual derivatives statistics, 31 December 2010.

economies following the global recession that followed the Lehman Brothers collapse.

These swap rates are quoted continuously in all major currencies for a range of maturities. They are not only relevant to sophisticated financial market participants. They also have a direct impact upon the fixed interest mortgage deals offered by mortgage lenders. Using the swap market, mortgage lenders can swap the fixed mortgage interest rate payments they receive from borrowers (mortgagees) for a set of floating rate payments. In this way the money they receive rises and falls with interest rates as the interest payments they make to their depositors and other creditors also rise and fall. If they did not enter swaps of this kind, then a rise in interest rates would require them to make higher payments to their creditors, but their fixed payment receipts would not rise, leaving the mortgage lender with a funding shortfall. The five-year sterling swap rate shown in Exhibit 12.2 therefore plays a big role in the fixed mortgage deals offered to mortgagees.

The break out box entitled 'Calculating a five-year swap rate' shows the basic principle that underlies swap rates of the kind shown in Exhibit 12.2. However, if you want to avoid the maths, you should skip forward to the next section in the chapter entitled 'inflation swaps'.

Calculating a five-year swap rate

The value of a fixed for floating interest rate swap is equal to zero at the outset of the contract. This is because the present value of the fixed payments and the present value of the set of floating rate payments are set so that this is the case. But how can we determine the value of the floating rate side of the swap, since the floating rate payments in the future will depend, by definition, on the future prevailing interest rates? If interest rates are high in the future then the derived floating rate payments will be high too. Conversely if interest rates fall over the life of the swap then the floating rate payments will be commensurately lower.

The answer to the problem lies in the forward rates that we can derive from the yield curve and which were explained in Chapter 6.

Suppose that we are trying to establish the appropriate fixed rate for a five-year swap, where payments are 'exchanged' every year for five years. If we know the relevant zero coupon rates given in column (2) of Exhibit 12.3, we can calculate the one year forward rates that will determine the floating payments over the life of the swap. This is because they are the market's best guess today of one year rates in the future. These are shown in column (3) of Exhibit 12.3.

Exhibit 12.3   Pricing a five year zero swap based on £100m notional

Maturity (yrs)	(2) Zero (%)	(3) Forward (%)	(4) Floating payments (£)	(5) PV (Floating) (£)	(6) Fixed payments (£)	(7) PV (Fixed) (£)
1	4.50	4.50	4,500,000	4,306,220	6,379,772	6,105,045
2	4.75	≈5.00	5,000,598	4,557,366	6,379,772	5,786,575
3	5.00	≈5.50	5,501,791	4,752,654	6,379,772	5,432,824
4	5.25	≈6.00	6,003,577	4,892,397	6,379,772	5,052,695
5	5.50	≈6.51	106,505,952	81,491,363	106,379,772	77,622,862
				100,000,000		100,000,000
					Net	0

If the swap has a notional value of £100m and the floating rates are given by the forward rates in column (3) then the floating payments are relatively easy to calculate.

The first floating rate payment is determined by the prevailing one year rate of interest which is 4.5 per cent; which means that the payment will be:

$$£100m \times 4.5\% = £4.5m$$

The second floating payment will be determined by the one year rate in one year's time, which is (approximately) 5 per cent. Which means that year two's floating rate payment will be approximately £5m, and so on.

The final payment includes the interest payment based upon the forward rate of 6.51 per cent (approximately), plus the 'repayment' of the notional amount of £100m.

But the payments based upon these forward rates will occur in the future. To derive their value to us today we must discount them using the zero coupon rates shown in column (2). The present values of these floating payments are shown in column (5). They sum to £100m. In other words, if an investor were offered these payments today, they would be willing to pay £100m for them.

The five-year swap rate is that fixed rate of interest (or fixed coupon) which will produce the same present value for the fixed payments based upon £100m too. In this case the five-year swap rate that equates the two sets of payments is approximately 6.38 per cent[6]. These payments, plus the

---

[6] It is very easy to find this value using a computer. The alternative would be a process of trial and error, that is, substituting values for the fixed rate, and adjusting it each time until the net figure in column (7) of Exhibit 12.3 equalled zero. However, we do not recommend this unless you have a great deal of time on your hands!

'payment' of £100m at the end of the fifth year are shown in column (6). The payments that this fixed rate produces also need to be discounted by using the appropriate zero coupon rates once again. The present values of these fixed payments are shown in column (7), and they sum to £100,000,000 too (subject to rounding).

Thus, with a swap rate of 6.38 per cent, the net present value of the swap is equal to zero. At this point in time the 'fair' five-year swap rate is 6.38 per cent.

Inflation swaps

One of the most important swaps for pension funds is the inflation swap. These contracts have attracted the attention of pension fund trustees because a significant amount of the pension promises made by UK DB pension schemes are inflation-linked. That is, scheme members are entitled to a pension in retirement that will rise with inflation, while deferred members also have their pension entitlement linked to inflation, thus helping to ensure that the value of the pension is not eroded by inflation. Inflation swaps can help pension funds manage the risk associated with the inflation element of the pension promise.

These inflation-linked pension promises are often made with limits upon the amount of inflation-related uplift that the pensioner can benefit from. These are known as limited price indexation (LPI) pension promises. A common LPI pension promise might be LPI (0, 5). This means that the pension in payment can rise by as much as 5 per cent depending upon the inflation background, but cannot be uplifted by more than this in any one year. Conversely, the pension cannot be reduced if inflation becomes negative, that is, falls below zero.

As a result of these inflation-related promises many pension schemes are exposed to increases in future inflation since the pension payments they will need to make will rise with inflation. Some schemes have used inflation swaps to minimize the risk to their schemes from higher future inflation. Of course the inflation exposure would not exist if a pension scheme could get another party to commit to making the inflation-related payments for them. In effect this is what happens with an inflation swap. The swap counterparty agrees to make inflation-linked payments to the pension fund. In return, the pension fund commits to making a fixed payment to the swap counterparty. The cost to the pension fund is the fixed payment it must make for the life of the swap.

Exhibit 12.4   The two legs of an inflation swap

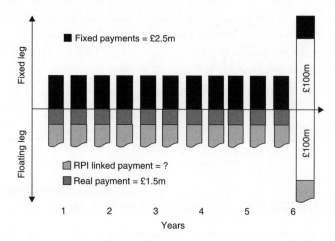

The basic principle of the inflation swap is the same as for the interest rate swap described earlier. The key difference is that the payments on the 'floating leg' of an inflation swap are determined, not by the prevailing interest rate, but instead by the level of a consumer price index, usually the Retail Price Index (RPI), though CPI-linked swaps have recently become available.

At the outset of an inflation swap no payments change hands. This is because the swap is set, or struck, so that the present value of the fixed leg of the swap is equal to the present value of the floating, or inflation, leg of the swap. Again, the swap payments are based upon a notional amount, say £100m, over a fixed period, say five years. In this case the uncertainty in the swap is not the future level of interest rates but the future level of a price index.

The fixed payer in an inflation swap might pay a fixed rate of, say, 5 per cent per annum, in return. So rather than receiving a set of payments related to future short-term interest rates, they would instead receive an inflation-proofed payment. This payment would be made up of two components: a regular payment based upon a real rate of interest, say 3 per cent, plus compensation for any inflation that might be experienced over that time. This 'compensation' comes in two forms. First, the inflation-linked coupons will rise with inflation. Second the notional amount of the swap will also rise with inflation. This is identical to the way in which an index-linked bond protects investors from inflation.

The two legs of a six year semi-annual, inflation swap are shown in Exhibit 12.4. The fixed payment is based upon an interest rate of 5 per cent; therefore semi-annual payments are approximately equal to £2.5m every half year. The real interest rate within this swap is 3 per cent. If inflation, assumed to be RPI, turns out to be zero over the six-year horizon, at every six month interval the fixed payer will only receive £1.5m. However, the higher inflation turns out to be, the larger will be the compensating RPI-linked payments. The difference between the real rate and the fixed rate of interest paid by the pension scheme is known as the *break even inflation rate*. This is a *very* important concept.

Before we explore the idea of the break even inflation rate we should consider the shape of the payment profiles shown in Exhibit 12.4. The fixed receiver is entitled to a set of payments that look just like those from a plain vanilla bond. The fixed payer is entitled to a set of payments that look like the payments from an index-linked bond.

At the outset of the swap, its net present value is zero. This is because the present value of the fixed leg of the swap is equal to the present value of the floating, or inflation, leg of the swap. Valuing the fixed leg is relatively simple. The value of the inflation leg will depend upon the assumption, or market expectation about future inflation, as measured by RPI.

Once again, as with the more straightforward interest rate swap that we explored earlier, it is not the regular interest payments that are exchanged. Instead, collateral flows between the two counterparties, as the two legs of the swap change in value; essentially as the value of index-linked bonds change relative to conventional, fixed coupon bonds. A fixed payer in an inflation swap, has essentially bought an index-linked bond and simultaneously sold a fixed coupon bond of the same maturity. Conversely, a fixed receiver has bought a fixed coupon bond and has sold an index-linked bond. The performance of the swap over time for each of the counterparties will therefore depend on the relative performance of these two bonds.

The importance of the break even inflation rate

Now let's return to the concept of the break even inflation rate. Suppose that an investor can choose between two five-year bonds both priced at £100. The first pays a fixed coupon of 5 per cent per year, that is, £5 per annum. The second is an index-linked bond that pays a real coupon of 3 per cent per annum and where all the bond's payments are indexed to a consumer price index. Let's assume this is RPI. Which bond should the investor buy? The answer to this question depends very much on the investor's expectations for inflation over the next five years. Broadly speaking, if inflation turns out to be:

i.   lower than 2 per cent per annum, the total return on the conventional, non-indexed bond will be higher over the five years, than on the index-linked bond;

ii. higher than 2 per cent per annum, the total return on the indexed bond will be higher over the five years than that on the conventional bond;

iii. equal to 2 per cent per annum over the five years then the two bonds will have returned the same, hence an inflation rate of 2 per cent over the life of the two bonds represents the rate of inflation such that the investor in the index-linked bond *breaks even* relative to the holder of the conventional bond.

In this example the two bonds can be thought of as the two legs of the five-year inflation swap shown in Exhibit 12.4. Both of these legs can be valued just as we showed in Chapter 6. In practice, collateral will flow between the two counterparties as the present values of the two legs vary over time. If inflation does turn out to be higher than the initial break even inflation rate of the swap then collateral will flow from the counterparty receiving the fixed payment to the one receiving the RPI-linked payments – the pension scheme. The converse is true if inflation turns out to be lower.

Investors wishing to protect themselves from future inflation should become *'fixed payers in an inflation swap'*, so that the collateral compensates them for inflation outcomes that are higher than the initial break even inflation rate embedded in the swap. But – and this is important – if they believe that inflation will turn out to be lower than implied in the break-even inflation rate of the swap then, as long as they turn out to be correct, they will not benefit in an investment context from becoming the fixed payer in the inflation swap.

The next section of this chapter is for those of you who wish to delve deeper into how swaps can be used by DB schemes. For those of you who would prefer not to delve any deeper, you should fast forward to the section entitled 'The investment context of interest rate and inflation swaps' (p. 301).

Using swaps to transform cash flow profiles

The interest rate and inflation swaps described above can be used to transform the cash flow profile of a typical bond portfolio, so that it more closely matches a set of pension liabilities. Pension schemes have made increasing use of swaps to:

i.   extend the duration of their portfolios;
ii. protect the real value of their assets (inflation hedging), and
iii. to ensure that the asset and liability cash profiles are more closely aligned (cash flow matching).

The next section shows how swap contracts can be used to achieve these goals.

Extending portfolio duration   (Bond Ldtr)

Interest rate swaps can be used to extend the duration of a scheme's asset portfolio. Suppose that a pension scheme holds a portfolio of investment grade corporate bonds that will generate the cash flows shown in Panel A of Exhibit 12.5. This portfolio has a current market value of £20m and modified duration of 10 per cent. However, let us suppose that the scheme wishes to extend the duration to 20 per cent. This may be because the scheme's trustees expect interest rates to fall and know that the higher the modified duration, the greater the rise in the value of the portfolio for a given fall in interest rates. They could do this by selling the portfolio and by buying a 20-year maturity zero coupon bond with the sale proceeds, since this would have duration of (virtually) 20 per cent. But let us instead assume that the scheme wishes to keep the portfolio of bonds, for reasons that will become clear by the end of this example. So instead of selling the portfolio and buying a 20-year zero coupon bond, they enter into *two* swap transactions.

Let us assume that the portfolio of bonds produces a regular fixed annual payment of 5 per cent, and also that the 20-year interest rate swap rate is 5 per cent (this just keeps the arithmetic simple). The two swaps that they enter are:

i. to become the 'fixed payer' − at a rate of 5 per cent per annum − and the floating rate receiver, where they receive LIBOR, on the notional value of this swap which is £20m.

Exhibit 12.5   Extending duration using swaps

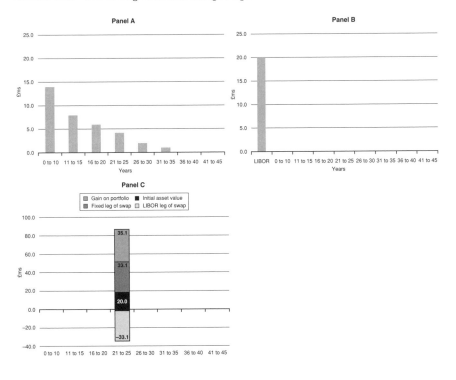

ii. then to become the 'fixed rate receiver' – paying LIBOR – to receive one single fixed payment of £20m in 20 years' time.

Panel B of Exhibit 12.5 shows the effective average maturity of the scheme's assets after the first swap. The investor effectively now owns a pool of cash that will earn them LIBOR over the next 20 years. Panel C shows the position after the second swap after 20 years. The investor has paid away the floating rate of interest received from the first swap for 20 years, but has received a fixed rate of interest of 5 per cent. The bar in Panel C represents the rolled up value of these positions in 20 years time. In other words, the net position that will determine whether the scheme gets to keep any collateral that has accumulated over that time or has to pay the accumulated collateral to the swap counterparties.

To make the maths easy, if we assume that LIBOR averaged 5 per cent over the 20-year period, then the money owed on the floating leg of the swap after 20 years would be just over £33m, but the money earned over the same period on the fixed leg of the swap would also be about £33m.[7] This is what Panel C shows.

The floating rate payments have been perfectly offset by the fixed payment receipts. But the underlying corporate bond assets, which are still owned by the investor, should have grown too. If we assume that they have been managed by a fund manager that has managed to outperform LIBOR (5 per cent) by 0.2 per cent after fees over the 20 years, then the portfolio of corporate bonds will be worth just over £55m in 20 years' time.[8] Since, in our example, the two sets of swap payments have cancelled one another out over this time, the scheme is left with a cash amount of just over £55m in 20 years' time. By keeping the corporate bond portfolio rather than selling the bonds, the scheme has managed to benefit from the excess return of the bond portfolio compared to the return on cash over time. This would be the main reason to keep hold of the portfolio of corporate bonds and not to sell them for one 20-year zero coupon bond. The scheme has also extended the duration of its original pool of corporate bond assets to 20 years.

Looking at the swap in this way makes it clear that the return on the underlying pool of assets must at least match LIBOR over this period, otherwise the scheme will experience a net loss on the swap.

---

[7] The actual figure would be £33,065,954, which is calculated as follows: [(£20m $\times$ $(1+0.05)^{20}$) – £20m] = £33,065,954.

[8] The actual figure is £55,124,516, which is calculated as follows: [(£20m $\times$ $(1+0.052)^{20}$] = £55,124,516.

Collateral flows   ~~Bond~~ \

Panel C of Exhibit 12.5 shows the final position of the two sets of cash flows and the asset value in 20 years' time. However, over the intervening 20-year period there would have been collateral flows associated with the two swaps:

- Swap 1: Scheme pays annual fixed payments and receives annual LIBOR payments.
- Swap 2: Scheme pays annual LIBOR payments and receives one fixed payment.

The two sets of LIBOR payments clearly net out to zero. But collateral will flow between the scheme and the counterparty as the yield curve moves up and down.[9]

- *Yield curve shifts down*: Suppose that there is a parallel shift down in the yield curve of 1 per cent. There will also be a 10 per cent increase in the value of the bond portfolio, given a modified duration of 10 per cent. However, the scheme will also benefit from a collateral inflow since the present value of the 20-year fixed payment also rises. The swap therefore magnifies the effect of the interest rate decline on the scheme's assets. But of course this 'gain' on the swap portfolio needs to be set against the rise in the present value of the liabilities that the decline in interest rates would bring about.
- *Yield curve shifts up*: Suppose that there is a parallel shift up in the yield curve of 1 per cent. There will also be a 10 per cent decrease in the value of the bond portfolio. However, the scheme will also have to pay money into their collateral account because the present value of the 20-year fixed payment would also fall. The swap therefore magnifies the effect of the interest rate increase on the scheme's assets. But of course this 'loss' on the swap portfolio needs to be set against the fall in the present value of the liabilities, that the rise in interest rates would bring about.

By entering into a swap arrangement of this kind the scheme has effectively 'bought' some protection against falling interest rates. Recall that a fall in the yield curve of 1 per cent would increase the present value of a typical scheme's liabilities by around 20 per cent since the modified duration of a typical pension scheme's liabilities is around 20 per cent. But really what it has done is align the risks in its asset portfolio more closely with those inherent in its liabilities.

What are the pros and cons of this approach?

First, the pros.

- The investor can effectively lock into a fixed return over the horizon of the swap.

---

[9] Twists in the yield curve will also cause collateral to flow from one party to the other.

- The duration of a corporate bond portfolio is extended. Effectively the scheme is swapping an asset with a cash flow profile shown in Panel A of Exhibit 12.5 with one that has the profile of Panel C, so that the duration of the assets has been extended, and without incurring the expense of selling all the bonds to buy a single, 20-year maturity zero coupon bond.
- The investor retains the flexibility of ownership of the underlying bond portfolio, so that an active manager can manage this portfolio. The better the bond fund manager's performance in excess of LIBOR (after fees) the higher will be the eventual funds available in 20 years time.
- The whole process can be repeated to produce zero coupon payments at other maturities as required, so that the investor's assets can be 'shaped' to meet specific future liabilities. In the case of a pension scheme, the specific pension liabilities.

Next, the cons.

- We have assumed that the fund manager outperforms LIBOR by 0.2 per cent per year. What if the manager underperforms LIBOR, perhaps because of widespread corporate bond defaults? In this case, some of the bond assets will have to be sold to meet the shortfall.
- Although the regular exchange of collateral helps to reduce swap counterparty risk, the more frequent the better. The real cost associated with the failure of one of the swap counterparties would be the cost of re-establishing the swap with another counterparty at rates that might be highly disadvantageous, as was the case for some investors when Lehman Brothers crashed in September 2008.
- Although the swap is effectively based upon a pool of investment-grade corporate bonds, swap counterparties would usually prefer to receive government bonds as collateral. Therefore, if these bonds, even with a 'haircut' applied to their market value, are considered unacceptable as collateral, a portfolio of government bonds would have to be held that would be sufficient to meet expected collateral calls. The more government bonds that need to be held to meet collateral payments the lower will be the expected return on the scheme's total asset portfolio.

Swaps are a very flexible way of managing risks and, as our example demonstrated, can be 'overlaid' on existing assets and need not disturb the day-to-day management of other asset classes. The example also assumes that there is a corporate bond pool that fully backs the swap position. That is, the value of the investment-grade corporate bond portfolio and the notional value of the swap was £20m in each case. But this is not strictly necessary.

The approach could vary in two key ways:

i. the investment-grade corporate bond portfolio used to 'fund' the swaps could have been smaller, as long as there are sufficient funds to generate the fixed cash flows. Any eligible assets could form the basis for the swap, though only high-quality assets can be used as collateral. In this case the investor would have a leveraged exposure. That is, nominal exposure to the swap market of £20m funded by, for example, a bond portfolio of say £10m.

ii. the pool of assets could have been a portfolio of commercial property, high yield bonds or even equity. Once again, as long as these assets can generate sufficient funds to meet the regular fixed cash flows, any assets could form the basis for the swap, though we re-emphasize that only high-quality assets can be used as collateral.——

Bonds!.

The advantage of a leveraged position is that investors can get more 'bang for their buck'. For example, using its £20m of corporate bond assets, the investor could have entered into nominal swaps worth £40m rather than £20m, effectively creating a much larger 'bullet' payment in 20 years time, doubling the duration exposure. The risk is greater because the collateral flows of a £40m notional swap would be twice those of a £20m swap, so that in extreme circumstances the pool of assets set aside for the purposes of meeting collateral calls could become exhausted.

The advantage of funding the swap with, for example, high yield bonds is that one would expect the underlying portfolio of assets to grow at a faster rate over time than a portfolio of investment-grade corporate bonds. The drawback would be the possibility of higher default rates.

In summary, this example has explained how a long-dated, fixed interest payment can be created by using fairly straightforward swaps. But what if an investor wished to create a long-dated payment that was inflation-proofed too? The worked example that follows shows how this is a relatively simple step.

Gaining inflation exposure

We have now explained how interest rate swaps can be used to extend the duration of an underlying bond portfolio. These swaps can therefore help to protect schemes against interest rate volatility, by bringing the duration of the assets more closely in line with the duration of the liabilities. However, as we saw in Chapter 1, a very significant proportion of a typical pension fund's liabilities are linked to the RPI. This means that their exposure to inflation is very significant. Because of this, pension schemes seek to invest in real assets where they can. That is, assets whose values should rise at least in line with inflation over time. However, these assets rarely offer a perfect match. Inflation swaps on the other hand can help to match this exposure very closely indeed. In the worked example set out below we will show how any investor can create a long-dated inflation-proofed, zero coupon payment analogous to the zero coupon fixed payment shown in Panel C of Exhibit 12.5.

You will recall that Panels A to C in Exhibit 12.5 showed how a long-dated, fixed interest payment can be created. But with the addition of one further swap we can turn this single fixed payment shown in Panel C of Exhibit 12.5 to a single, inflation-proofed payment. If we assume that the floating and fixed leg of the swap in Exhibit 12.5 Panel C cancel one another out and that we expect our manager to outperform LIBOR by 0.2 per cent over time, then the net effect is that a pool of assets worth just over £55m in 20 years would be available to the scheme − as shown in Panel A of Exhibit 12.6.

Let us now suppose that the investor adds another swap where they become the fixed rate payer and RPI receiver for the next 20 years. The 20-year fixed swap rate is 5 per cent, which means that the investor commits to paying 5 per cent on £20m annually for the next 20 years. Let us now suppose that the real 20 year swap rate is 2.5 per cent. This means that the investor will receive a real return of 2.5 per cent for the next 20 years and, crucially, that the break even inflation rate is 2.5 per cent. This in turn means that the scheme will be protected against inflation outturns that are greater than 2.5 per cent.

Now let's suppose further that the inflation rate does average 2.5 per cent over the 20-year period of the swap. Thus the investor pays 5 per cent fixed and receives 5 per cent (2.5 per cent real plus 2.5 per cent inflation) so the two legs of the swap 'cancel' one another out over the 20 years. Panel A of Exhibit 12.6 shows the starting position, before the swap is put on; a position that is equivalent to the scheme's position in Panel C of Exhibit 12.5. The end position in Panel B of Exhibit 12.6 shows that the receipts from the inflation leg of the swap have been perfectly offset by the fixed interest payments. Leaving the scheme with a fund worth just over £55m. So not very exciting really. But this demonstrates that this third swap effectively ensures that the scheme will have a payment of circa £55m in 20 years' time if inflation averages 2.5 per cent. But the benefit of the inflation swap to the pension scheme is shown in Panel C of Exhibit 12.6.

Suppose that instead of averaging 2.5 per cent over the 20 years, inflation averages 3.5 per cent instead. Panel C shows the net effect for the scheme. The receipts on the swap accumulate to approximately £44.1m over the 20 years while the cumulated payments remain fixed at £33.1m. So by the end of 20 years there would be an additional £11m in the collateral pool for the investor. This is enough to compensate them for the extra 1 per cent inflation, over and above the break-even inflation rate of 2.5 per cent, experienced over the 20 years. This 'profit' on the swap position however, would be offset by higher liability payments on the other. The swap has therefore helped to bring the assets of the scheme further into line with its inflation-linked liabilities, in this case, those inflation-linked liabilities that are due to be paid in 20 years' time.

Exhibit 12.6   Using inflation swaps

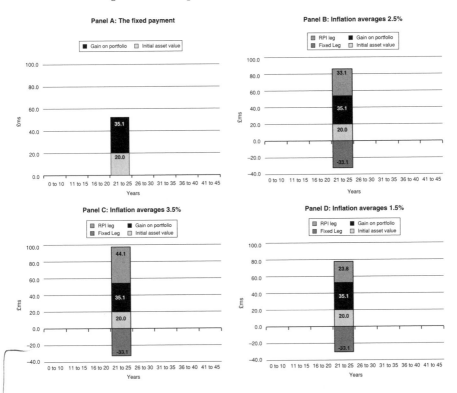

Now let us assume that inflation averaged 1.5 per cent over the 20 year period, instead of 2.5 per cent. Panel D shows the net effect for the investor after 20 years. Now the accumulated inflation leg of the swap comes to approximately £23.8m, compared with the accumulated payment on the fixed leg of £33.1m. This means that the accumulated collateral pool would be worth £9.3m in favour of the swap counterparty, that is, the scheme would end up owing £9.3m to their swap counterparty. This 'loss' on the swap position however, would be offset to some extent by lower liability payments on the other. This demonstrates again how the swap has helped to bring the assets of the scheme further into line with its 20-year, inflation-linked liabilities.

Hopefully this worked example has demonstrated a number of issues:

i.   entering into an inflation swap offers the investor protection against inflation being higher than the break even inflation rate, in this case 2.5 per cent, over the swap horizon;

ii. the swap effectively 'guarantees' a real return, in this case 2.5 per cent, over the horizon of the swap; and

iii. if an investor believes that inflation will be lower than implied by the break even inflation rate over the swap horizon, they would be better off in return terms from not entering into the swap.

Collateral flows

Again the charts in Exhibit 12.6 represent the cumulated net effect of the growth in the assets and the cash flows from the swaps after 20 years, based on assumptions about all the key rates of return. In the intervening period, collateral will flow between the scheme and the various swap counterparties. The collateral flows will derive from the following swap positions:

- Swap 1: Scheme pays annual fixed payments and receives annual LIBOR payments
- Swap 2: Scheme pays annual LIBOR payments and receives fixed payments
- Swap 3: Scheme pays annual fixed payments and receives annual inflation swap rate

where the inflation swap rate comprises a real rate plus (RPI) inflation.

The scheme will still pay, or receive collateral as the yield curve shifts up and down (or twists) because of swaps 1 and 2. However, there is an additional element to the collateral flow now that relates to the break even inflation rate:

- *Break even inflation rate rises:* Suppose that the break even inflation rate rises. In this case the scheme will receive collateral since it effectively 'owns' a zero coupon, inflation-proofed bond. Its value, relative to that of a non-indexed zero coupon bond of the same maturity, will have risen.
- *Break even inflation rate falls:* Suppose that the break even inflation rate falls. In this case the scheme will pay collateral since it effectively 'owns' a zero coupon, inflation-proofed bond. Its value, relative to that of a non-indexed zero coupon bond of the same maturity will have fallen.

This example shows that to the extent that break even inflation rates reflect actual inflation, pension schemes can protect themselves against rising inflation by entering into a swap of this nature. As inflation rises, so will the present value of the scheme's inflation-linked liabilities. However a rise in the collateral that results from a simultaneous rise in break even inflation rates would increase the value of the scheme's assets, at least partially offsetting the increase in the value of the liabilities.

What are the pros and cons of this approach?

First, the pros.

- It allows the scheme to lock into a real rate of return which offers inflation protection against inflation outturns above the break even inflation rate;
- It offers a relatively simple way of managing inflation exposure.

Next, the cons.

- Again, the approach shares the cons of the duration-lengthening swap relating to counterparty risk, collateral calls, and the performance of the underlying assets.

The investment context of interest rate and inflation swaps (?)

The examples above showed how it is possible to use interest rate swaps to hedge against interest rate risk, and how to use inflation swaps to hedge against inflation risk. It is important to remember however, that there is an investment context to such hedging activities. One set of investment considerations relate to 'timing', while another relates to the 'price' of the hedging. The two are related.

It's in the timing .

Suppose that a scheme hedges its interest rate risk by using interest rate swaps. That is, movements in the yield curve have a neutral impact on the funding position of the scheme. Now suppose that there is a large upward shift in the yield curve. Since the scheme has hedged its interest rate exposure, this has no effect on the scheme's funding position. However, had the scheme not hedged its interest rate exposure – that is, increased the duration of its assets so that they matched the duration of its liabilities – the value of its liabilities would have fallen by more than the value of its assets and its funding position would have improved accordingly. As with most aspects of investment – timing is everything.

. . . and in the price

Suppose, that a scheme enters into a duration extending interest rate swap, where it locks into a fixed rate of interest of 3 per cent. However, because the yield curve is downward sloping at the long end, the yield on shorter maturity swaps (and bonds) is much higher. By entering into a duration-lengthening swap the scheme would be paying a relatively high price for a long-dated payment, relative to the price of shorter-dated payments.

Similarly, now suppose that a scheme hedges its inflation exposure with an inflation swap, when the implied real rate is 1 per cent and the break even inflation rate is 4 per cent. This means that the scheme will protect itself from inflation outturns above 4 per cent. But it also means that it will be locking in a real return of 1 per cent. If the scheme can earn a real return greater than this from other investments, then the inflation protection is bought at a high price.

In both cases, the price for hedging either interest rate risk in the first case and inflation risk in the second can fluctuate just like the price of all investments. Since the price might fall in the future, it might then be a question of timing, but if not then schemes may need to make hard decisions about the price they are willing to pay to eliminate or just reduce such long-term 'unrewarded risks'.

Summary

Although they may seem quite complex to the uninitiated, the essence of both interest rate and inflation swaps is simple: interest payments determined on one basis are swapped for those determined on a different basis. The difficulty comes in understanding that the notional value and even the interest payments are not actually swapped. Instead, under the terms of the swap, it is collateral that passes between the two swap counterparties, where this collateral is determined by the relative values of each leg of the swap. This collateral provides protection against adverse moves in interest or inflation rates, but also helps to protect each counterparty from default risk.

Key points

- The principle behind swap contracts is very simple: you exchange one stream of future payments you do not want for another that you do.
- Swap contracts are used by defined benefit (DB) pension schemes to manage the long-term unrewarded interest rate and inflation risks they face.
- Swap contracts have a number of important features: no monies are exchanged at the outset of the contract because the two payment streams are priced in such a way that they are equal at the outset of the contract; the swap counterparties are defined by whether they are a fixed payer or fixed receiver and the swap payments are based upon a notional amount that is never exchanged. What is exchanged is the collateral based upon the daily price movement of the swap contract. This collateral protects each swap counterparty from the risk of the other defaulting.
- An interest rate, or fixed for floating swap commits the fixed payer to a series of fixed interest payments and the fixed receiver to a series of payments based upon LIBOR over the term of the contract. The fixed receiver could be a DB scheme seeking protection against falling interest rates.

- An inflation swap commits the fixed payer to making a series of fixed payments, in return for a set of payments comprising a real interest rate and the actual inflation rate, while the fixed receiver receives fixed payments over the term of the contract, and commits to making payments made up of a real rate of interest and inflation over time. The fixed payer could be a DB scheme seeking protection against rising inflation.

Chapter 13

Alternative Asset Classes: An Alternative to What?

Learning outcomes

- Appreciate what constitutes an alternative asset class and the wide and disparate nature of the alternatives universe.
- Understand the key characteristics and nuances of hedge funds, private equity, commodities and foreign exchange and their potential risks, returns and diversification benefits.
- Appreciate the additional governance burden that the necessary due diligence and monitoring of alternative asset classes entails and the short-comings in the available data.

Why invest in alternative asset classes?

During the late-1990s many of the UK's defined benefit (DB) pension schemes had a surplus of assets over liabilities. Many scheme sponsors felt so confident about the financial positions of their schemes that they took frequent contribution holidays. The main source of these surpluses was the double-digit performances of global equity markets during the 1980s and 1990s. Equities had performed so well up until that point that it seemed that this asset class – along with a relatively low weighting in government bonds to cover existing pension payments – could be relied upon to produce virtually all of the cash flows needed to meet pension promises. Back then, no alternative to equities was available, but then again, no alternative seemed necessary.

Exhibit 13.1   The UK stock market since 1900

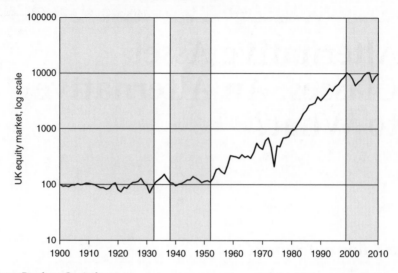

Source: Barclays Capital.

However, with the collapse of global equity markets between 2000 and early 2003 and with the associated rise in bond prices, not to mention the introduction of mark-to-market accounting,[1] widespread DB deficits emerged. Today equities no longer appear to be the answer to every DB trustee's prayers. The DB pensions industry, along with many other investors, were so dazzled by the performance of equities over the 1980s and 1990s that they didn't consider the prospect of equities failing to deliver, not just for one year, but over many.

Exhibit 13.1 shows the level of a UK equities index going back to 1900. Looking back on this long history of UK equity investing we can see that there have been extended periods when the market (and others) made no progress whatsoever. This includes the period that began in late-1999, when most developed

---

[1] The introduction of mark-to-market accounting standard FRS 17, in November 2000, represented a marked departure from the SSAP 24 accounting methodology that preceded it. Under SSAP 24, asset values were calculated triennially by employing an actuarially-smoothed valuation process to eliminate the effect of short-term market volatility on asset values, while liabilities were discounted by the historic return from equities. When, under FRS 17, assets were calculated annually at their market values (thereby capturing short-term market volatility) and liabilities were discounted by the AA bond yield (rather than the higher historic return from equities), that's when the double whammy of dramatic falls in global equity markets and declining bond yields gave rise to gaping DB scheme deficits.

economy equity markets reached their highest points. For example, the FTSE 100 reached its highest point – 6,999.99 – at the market close on 31 December 1999. Since then the index has traded well below this level. The Japanese equity market index, the Nikkei, reached its peak of 38,915.87 in December 1989 and has traded well below that level for the last 20 or so years.

Today there is a wide range of 'alternative' asset classes available to both institutional and retail investors. The adjective 'alternative' was originally used to differentiate certain investments from the traditional asset classes of government bonds and developed economy equities. However, there is no official, agreed definition of what constitutes an alternative asset class. For some institutional investors, real estate is an alternative investment class, but for those that have invested in real estate for many years, it is a traditional asset class. In other words, alternative asset classes are very much in the eye of the investment beholder. Having said this, most institutional investors would still consider:

- hedge funds,
- private equity,
- commodities,
- foreign exchange,
- global tactical asset allocation (GTAA),
- high yield bonds,
- infrastructure, and
- emerging market debt.

as typical examples of 'alternative' asset classes, or in the case of hedge funds and GTAA, alternative, or non-traditional ways of generating returns.

Most alternative asset classes are simply alternative investment claims on the underlying real economy. The real economy is that part of the economy which relates to the production and sale of actual goods and services. When an investor has a claim on the real economy it means that they own some part of the means of producing goods and services, or alternatively, that they have at least part ownership of physical assets. For example, the ownership of publicly traded equities gives the owner a claim on some portion of the assets of that firm and therefore a claim on the profitability that those assets can generate over time. So ownership of equities represents ownership of underlying, real assets. But the ownership of a portion of a Scandinavian forest also represents ownership of a real, or physical asset. From an investor's perspective, real assets only really differ in the type of cash flow that they are expected to generate. In the case of equity ownership, the cash flow comes in the form of a dividend; in the case of a tract of timberland, it comes from the sale of timber over time as the forest is harvested.

The Yale Endowment Fund

Over the past few years, the UK DB industry has been gradually diversifying its claims on the real economy, away from the real claim represented by publicly traded equities towards these alternative claims. As they have gradually adopted the idea of diversification into these alternative asset classes,[2] one investment fund has been frequently held up by advisers as a shining example of the potential benefits of diversifying investment portfolios away from traditional asset classes: the Yale University Endowment Fund. Over the ten years to June 2009 the Yale fund had produced an annual net return of 11.8 per cent, while over the 20 years to June 2009 it had generated a net return of 13.4 per cent per annum. To put this into perspective, a passive investment in a 'traditional' sterling-denominated equity/bond portfolio would have produced a gross annual return of 1.6 per cent and 6.7 per cent over the ten and 20 years to June 2009.

So how did the Yale fund achieve this impressive performance?

The Yale Endowment Fund was an early adopter in the alternatives 'space', having implemented a highly diversified approach to investing over 20 years ago. Exhibit 13.2 shows the fund's broad asset allocation as at June 2009. Its stated aim in holding this mix of assets is to achieve 'the highest expected return for a given level of risk'. As we can see, it looks very different from a typical DB portfolio. Only 7.5 per cent is allocated to domestic (US) equities, and of the 9.8 per cent allocated to foreign equity, a significant proportion of this is dedicated to emerging equity markets. The endowment's allocation to fixed income at 4 per cent is also very different from the allocations of other institutional investors, even those of other university endowment funds, where the average fixed income holding is just over 21 per cent. In total then, asset classes that together often comprise close to 100 per cent of traditional institutional allocations comprise at most 21 per cent of Yale's allocation.

As you can see, rather than relying on traditional asset classes, the Yale fund has significant allocations to alternative asset classes. Nearly one-quarter of Yale's portfolio is allocated to absolute return strategies. These strategies, which principally comprise an allocation to hedge funds, seek to provide positive returns in all market conditions. The fund first made a significant allocation to this strategy in 1990 and remains attracted to it because 'absolute return investments have historically provided returns largely independent of overall market moves'. Along with its commitment and belief in hedge funds, the Yale endowment also has

---

[2] For evidence of diversification benefits in the context of alternative asset classes see A. Clare and N. Motson, 'How Many Alternative Eggs Should You Put in Your Investment Basket?', CAMR Working Paper, Cass Business School, London (2009).

Exhibit 13.2   The Yale Endowment Fund's current asset allocation

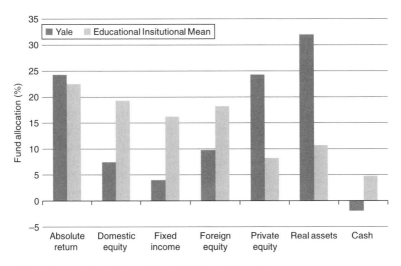

Source: Yale Endowment Fund Annual Report, 2009 available online.

almost 25 per cent of its assets invested in both venture capital and leveraged private equity buyout vehicles (which, along with hedge funds, we consider later in this chapter). Its investment in private equity, therefore, dwarfs its investment in publicly traded equity and is testament to the Yale investment committee's belief that private equity fund managers can 'exploit market inefficiencies'. Finally, the fund has 32 per cent of its assets dedicated to real assets. This portion of the fund comprises a variety of investments, including real estate, oil and gas, and timberland. The main attraction of these investments for the Yale fund is their 'inflation hedging properties'. However, they also argue that the illiquid nature of these investments means that they can potentially earn an additional return – an illiquidity premium – from them.

Arguably over 80 per cent of the Yale endowment portfolio is invested in illiquid assets – real assets, absolute return strategies and private equity. By making investments that are seemingly too complex for other investors to analyze or where most investors are put off by the illiquid nature of the investment, the Yale fund hopes to earn this illiquidity premium. As indicated above, their largely illiquid assets have earned far more for them over 20 years than the ex-post risk premium earned from liquid assets, like publicly traded equity. For example, since inception their private equity investments have generated an annual return of 30.4 per cent. Yale's view is effectively that they are long-term investors who can afford a certain amount of illiquidity in their fund, which enables them to add value by earning an illiquidity premium where it arises.

Is the Yale approach suitable for the UK DB industry?

There is no doubt that the illiquid nature of much of the Yale portfolio would not be suitable for some mature UK pension schemes that may be cash flow negative. In other words, pension schemes that have been closed to new entrants and/or future accruals for some time. This is perhaps why even those pension schemes that have embraced the idea of a diversified investment strategy across alternative asset classes have not replicated the Yale asset allocation. However, this does not mean that small, mature schemes cannot benefit from a more diversified approach to investing. It's just that the challenges to achieving the benefits may greater, but no less worthwhile once achieved.

So what is it that we need from these alternative asset classes and can they help solve the deficit crisis facing today's DB industry?

Risk and return

Arguably most investors are looking for two things by diversifying out of traditional asset classes like bonds and equities. The first is higher return. There has been much talk in the investment industry over the past few years about how equity returns in the future will be lower than they have been in the past. The second thing that investors are looking for is lower correlations between the asset classes they hold in their investment portfolios, so that investment returns are potentially less volatile than would be the case if relying on just one asset class.

In effect, investors hope that by diversifying into alternative asset classes they will be pushing out the mean-variance efficient frontier on their portfolios, as shown in Exhibit 13.3. That is, allowing them to achieve a greater return without an increase in portfolio volatility, or conversely allowing them to reduce the volatility of their portfolios without reducing the associated expected return. The stylized shift up in the mean-variance frontier implied in Exhibit 13.3 could stem from two possible sources: either from the fact that expected returns from alternative asset classes are greater than for equities and bonds, or because it is expected that the returns on alternative asset classes will be weakly correlated with the returns on traditional asset classes. However, it could be a combination of these two sources.

In this chapter we focus on four of the most popular alternative asset classes: hedge funds, commodities, private equity and foreign exchange. As outlined earlier, there are others, such as GTAA, infrastructure, emerging market debt

Exhibit 13.3   Alternatives and the mean-variance efficient frontier – a stylized example

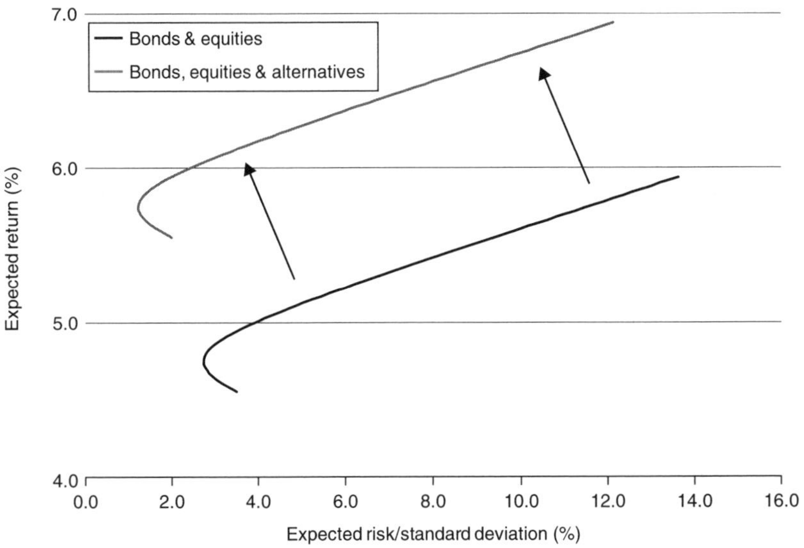

and high yield corporate bonds,[3] but the four that we cover here are sufficient to illustrate the issues that arise when non-traditional asset classes are added to a conventional portfolio of assets.[4]

Hedge funds

How it all started

The hedge fund story started in 1949 when a sociologist and financial journalist, Dr. Alfred Winslow Jones, in researching an article for *Fortune* magazine, recognized the difficulty of correctly calling the direction of the equity market at any point in time. So he adopted an investment strategy which, by taking a long position in those stocks he considered undervalued and poised to outperform and a short position in those he believed were overvalued and set to underperform, relied entirely on stock selection for its investment returns. That is, market risk was taken out of the equation, or hedged – hence the term 'hedge fund'.

---

[3] See the Mercer asset allocation survey, May 2011 for the types and percentage allocations UK DB schemes make to alternative asset classes.

[4] For evidence of the potential benefits of a diversified approach to investing for pension funds see Brigden, Clare and Dhar, 'By How Much can a Diversified Approach to Investing Improve the Prospects of Reducing a defined-benefit Pension Deficit?', *Pensions*, pp. 136–50 (2008).

(However, for some unknown reason the final 'd' in 'hedged' was dropped). Jones started his *long/short* fund, the fortunes of which were largely derived independently of the direction the market took, with four co-investors and initial capital of US$100,000. Such was Jones' belief in his strategy, that he leveraged his fund, with borrowed money, to magnify the fund's potential returns and introduced a performance fee of 20 per cent, levied on all gains. To facilitate this structure, thereby sidestepping the reporting and other regulatory requirements of the US Securities and Exchange Commission (SEC), Jones structured his fund as a limited partnership, which meant limiting the fund to 99 limited partners, or investors. Such was Jones' inventiveness that limited partnerships, leverage and performance fees still characterize the hedge fund industry today.

Little was known about Jones' hedge fund until, an article was published in *Fortune* magazine detailing Jones' accomplishments.[5] Having delivered a total return of 670 per cent over the previous ten years, the fund had performed extraordinarily well and was some way ahead of the best performing mutual fund. This marked the dawn of the hedge fund industry. By 1968, around 140 hedge funds had been established but many were wiped out by the deep and protracted equity bear market of 1969/70. Jones himself did not escape this episode unscathed but his fund emerged from the bear market mostly intact.

By the 1980s, the growth in derivative use provided the catalyst for a renewed expansion of the hedge fund industry though the really explosive growth phase came in the noughties, as investors sought solace from the equity bear market of 2000 to early-2003. Driven on by investor demand, the growth of the hedge fund industry flourished on the back of cheap credit and a deeper derivatives market, which both facilitated the use of leverage and the ability to devise more innovative strategies to exploit market anomalies. However, it was the extent to which this leverage was relied upon to generate potentially supersized returns and the illiquid nature of the investment strategies employed in the run up to the credit crisis that led to the industry's annus horriblis in 2008, which we discuss later in the chapter.

According to Hedge Fund Research (HFR), one of a number of independent bodies that collate information about hedge funds, by the end of 2010 there were over 7,000 known hedge funds globally. As Exhibit 13.4 shows, the growth in hedge fund numbers had been exponential up until 2007. While the onset of the financial crisis curtailed this growth in numbers dramatically, despite this HFR estimate that the hedge fund industry manages funds totalling around US$2 trillion.

---

[5] Carol J. Loomis, 'The Jones Nobody Keeps Up With', *Fortune Magazine*, April (1966).

Exhibit 13.4   Global hedge fund numbers

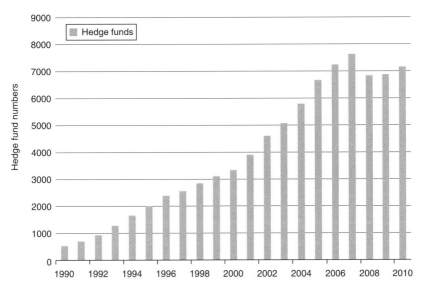

Source: Hedge Fund Research.

But what is a hedge fund? Unfortunately there is no generally agreed definition of what constitutes a *hedge fund*, although some have tried.

> *Hedge funds may be defined as unregulated pools of capital, generally with fewer than 100 investors that invest in any asset class as well as derivative securities and use long and short positions, as well as leverage.* (Morgan Stanley Dean Witter, 'Why hedge funds make sense', Witter Research, January 2001)

In fact the term 'hedge fund' is used to describe an incredibly wide range of investment strategies, quite often strategies that do not involve hedging at all! Some hedge funds specialize in trading 'distressed securities', others in emerging market securities, or in particular aspects of the fixed income or equity markets. Others define themselves according to the strategies that they employ, for example *market neutral*, *arbitrage* and *event driven* (to name but a few). Today there are hedge funds operating in all corners of the world's capital markets, though many of these funds are run out of Greenwich (US) and Mayfair (UK). Exhibit 13.5 shows how the composition of the hedge fund market, broken down by one of a number of possible categorizations, has changed since 1990.

The sheer number and variety of hedge fund strategies means that categorizing hedge funds is not easy. Moreover, this challenge is compounded by the fact

Exhibit 13.5   Hedge fund strategies

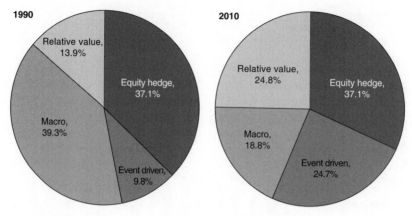

Source: Hedge Fund Research.

that each manager runs their hedge fund in their own unique way (or at least claim to) often in a manner that sometimes does not entirely correspond to its categorization.

Although hedge funds can be sliced and diced in numerous ways, and while not definitive, we will stick with the HFR categorization as depicted in Exhibit 13.5, to briefly explain the investment objectives of the main hedge fund strategies.

Equity hedge

This was A.W. Jones' original hedge fund strategy. Also known as long/short equity, an equity hedge strategy takes long positions in those stocks that are favoured and short positions in those that are not. Given the different skill and mind sets, not to mention risk management framework, that shorting demands,[6] compared to 'going long a stock', most equity hedge managers inevitably have a long bias to their portfolios. This means that most tend to assume a substantial element of market risk, or beta, in their portfolios. In other words, their portfolios are rarely hedged to any great degree against the direction of the equity market. Those that are broadly hedged against general market movements, however, are referred to as *market neutral funds*.

---

[6] In contrast to taking a long position in a stock, where the worse-case scenario is losing the price paid for the stock, short selling, if not properly risk managed, can result in potentially unlimited losses because technically there is no upper limit to the price.

Event driven

Event driven strategies focus on making money from various aspects of corporate activity, such as mergers and acquisitions and corporate restructuring. For instance, if the hedge fund manager believes that a takeover bid for a company will be successful, they will take a long position in the target company and a short position in the bidder, given that bidders invariably overpay for acquisitions. A corporate restructuring fund might focus on buying securities in those companies that have filed for Chapter 11 bankruptcy in the US where, in the eyes of the fund manager, the pessimism surrounding the prospects of these companies has been overdone.

Macro

Macro funds, also known as directional strategy funds, take large leveraged positions, typically using derivatives, to back the manager's views on perceived macroeconomic shifts and trends, such as the likely direction of interest rates or the likely movement of one currency against another. Indeed, sterling's ignominious exit from the European Exchange Rate Mechanism (ERM) in September 1992 introduced the world to the macro hedge fund. George Soros' macro fund – the Quantum Fund – netted a cool £1bn when it sold sterling in great quantities in September 1992, a feat that also earned Mr. Soros the title of 'the man who broke the Bank of England'.

Relative value

Relative value funds are based on the notion of arbitrage, also known as the law of one price. An arbitrage opportunity arises when two securities that provide the same economic exposure have different prices. In these circumstances it is possible to make a risk-free profit by simultaneously selling the overpriced asset and buying the underpriced one. In practice, this strategy, which principally comprises *fixed income arbitrage* and *convertible arbitrage*, exploits the price differences between two securities, usually within credit and sovereign fixed income markets that provide a similar, but not the same, economic exposure to a particular asset.

Hedge funds versus traditional investment funds

Perhaps the best way to describe hedge funds is to compare and contrast them with traditional investment funds.

- *Management style*: Hedge funds are actively managed investment funds with flexible investment policies that seek to achieve positive returns in all market conditions. The benchmark, or 'hurdle rate', for these absolute returns is often defined in terms of the prevailing cash rate, represented by LIBOR. So a hedge fund might target an annual return of 'LIBOR + 10 per cent'. That is, a return of 10 per cent over and above what cash would have earned for an investor, though some (remarkably) only target LIBOR itself.

- A small number of hedge funds are run as cloned funds, or *alternative beta funds*. These funds attempt to emulate the performance of top performing hedge fund strategies by using a combination of derivatives and money market instruments to replicate the 'return sources' and 'risk exposures' assumed by the latter. The result is a lower cost and more liquid structure than the fund(s) replicated, though given that these replication strategies involve much experimentation to determine the optimum model inputs, performance of cloned funds has, perhaps inevitably, lagged that of the wider industry since their inception in 2004.
- By comparison, traditional investment funds, managed for institutional clients, such as pension funds, on either a pooled or segregated basis, usually have a very restrictive investment policy, typically with a return target expressed relative to a broad financial market index, like the FTSE All Share index, with tightly defined risk parameters, such as tracking error limits. Moreover, as we outline in Chapter 14, these funds are increasingly passively managed.
- *Fees*: Hedge funds typically levy both an annual management charge (AMC) and a performance-related fee, though cloned funds usually only charge an AMC. This performance related fee usually applies to returns achieved above a certain pre-specified, absolute level. '2 and 20' is still a common hedge fund fee structure, though is less prevalent than it was pre-credit crisis. This means that the hedge fund will charge an annual fee of 2 per cent of the funds under management, plus 20 per cent of the return achieved above the fund's benchmark over the year.[7]

Exhibit 13.6 shows how performance fees are calculated. The wavy line is meant to represent the value of a fund which rises and falls over time. At the end of year one, the fund's first high water mark is established. Assuming this is above the fund's benchmark, the 20 per cent performance fee is calculated on the difference between the benchmark and the high water mark and is then paid out to the manager at the end of the year. Over the second year, fees continue to accrue but ultimately the fund's performance falls back by the end of the year, causing it to end the year below the high water mark set at the end of year one. This means that no performance fee is payable at the end of year two. Performance fees only begin to accrue in the third year once the fund's performance has breached the high water mark set at the end of year one. At the end of year three, performance fees are paid out on that element of the fund's performance above its year one high water

---

[7] For a discussion about the nature and impact of hedge fund performance fees see: C. Brooks, A. Clare and N. Motson, 'The Gross Truth About Hedge Fund Performance and Risk: The Impact of Incentive Fees', *The Journal of Alternative Investments* (2008).

Exhibit 13.6   The interaction between the hedge fund performance fee and high water marks

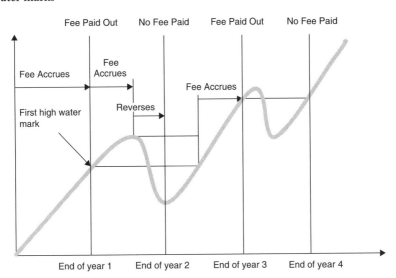

Source: C. Brooks, A. Clare and N. Motson, 'The Gross Truth About Hedge Fund Performance and Risk: The Impact of Incentive Fees', *Journal of Alternative Investments* (2008).

mark. At the end of year three a new high water mark is established. The relationship between the high water mark and performance fee is designed to ensure that investors only pay once for the same performance.

By contrast, the fees that traditional fund managers charge are typically related to the size of funds under management – the larger the pool of funds under management, the larger the fee income. While performance fees are sometimes applied these are usually restricted to specialist mandates. However, for a hedge fund, often operating in a market niche with a correspondingly niche strategy, a large fund-size may hinder the manager's ability to execute the trades that they wish to undertake. Indeed, the world's largest hedge funds are a mere fraction of the size of the world's largest asset managers and traditional investment funds. At end-June 2010, the world's largest hedge fund manager was JP Morgan with assets under management (AuM) of US$53.5bn, followed by Bridgewater Associates at US$43.6bn and Paulson & Co at US$32bn; by contrast, the three largest asset managers at end-2009 were BlackRock with AuM of US$3.35tn, State Street Global at US$1.91tn and Allianz Group at US$1.86tn.[8] Most will have an optimum

---

[8] *Financial Times*, 12 August, p. 17 (2010); The P&I/Towers Watson 'The World's 500 Largest Asset Managers' Year-End 2009.

fund size in mind, 'hard closing' the fund to new investment when this optimum size is reached.

- *Typical investors*: The investor base for traditional investment funds encompasses all investors, large and small. By contrast, hedge funds have traditionally targeted high net worth individuals (HNWI) and family offices, and have, since the beginning of the noughties, increasingly marketed their funds to institutional investors, such as pension schemes, endowments and foundations. While the minimum investment subscription to invest directly in hedge funds is still too high for most retail investors and smaller pension funds, access to 'Newcits' funds, that employ some key hedge fund techniques with commensurately lower fees, has been provided in recent years by both traditional fund managers and hedge fund managers alike.[9]
- *Liquidity*: Just as accessing a hedge fund can be difficult, so can exiting. Hedge funds typically lock-in investor funds for an initial, pre-specified period and also require that investors give notice before funds can be withdrawn after this period. This is a direct consequence of the illiquid financial markets and instruments in which they principally invest. By contrast, traditional investment funds are far more liquid, given the greater liquidity of the assets in which they typically invest.
- *Transparency*: The legal structures of hedge funds are designed to reduce the extent of regulatory scrutiny and associated reporting, whereas the financial market regulations that traditional investment funds are subject to make them very transparent by comparison.

The difference between hedge funds and traditional investment funds are summarized in Exhibit 13.7.

The structure of the hedge fund industry

As Exhibit 13.4 showed, hedge fund numbers have expanded rapidly, along with the amount of money the industry manages. Moreover, the structure of the industry has certainly changed since the early 1990s, with strategies such as macro giving way to event driven and relative value. Of the thousands of hedge funds that exist today, many are relatively small. We can see the breakdown of the size structure of the hedge fund industry in Exhibit 13.8.

According to HFR nearly 80 per cent of all funds at the end of 2010 had less than US$100m under management whereas just over 8 per cent of funds had in excess of US$500m under management.

---

[9] Newcits, which are colloquially referred to as 'hedge fund-lite', are authorized by the Financial Services Authority and must meet with the stringent investment strategy and disclosure requirements of the UCITS III Directive, which applies to all funds marketed to the general public in the European Economic Area. Newcits are so-called because of their UCITS status.

Exhibit 13.7   Hedge funds versus traditional investment funds

	Traditional investment funds	Hedge funds
Management style	Active/pseudo active/passive	Active/cloned
Investment policy	Heavily restricted by mandate and regulations	Very flexible/typically leveraged
Return targets	Normally small annual percentage above benchmark (active), or identical to benchmark (index)	Target is absolute percentage return with aim of achieving this, regardless of market conditions
Fees	Based on funds under management (and occasionally a performance-related component)	Based on funds under management and performance-related component
Economies of scale	The bigger the funds, the larger the fees	Nature of activity means often an optimum fund size
Investor base	All	HNWI, family offices and institutional investors
Liquidity	Normally investors can enter/leave funds at any time	Highly restricted, enabling funds to invest in highly illiquid markets and instruments
Legal structure	Usually subject to raft of financial market regulations. High degree of transparency	Organized to reduce regulatory obligations. Poor degree of transparency

Exhibit 13.8   Estimated proportion of funds by asset size, 2010

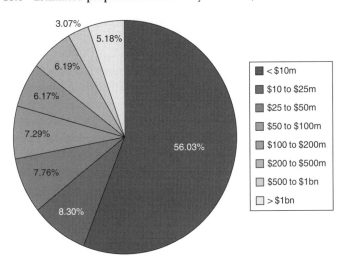

Pie chart values:
- 56.03% — < $10m
- 8.30% — $10 to $25m
- 7.76% — $25 to $50m
- 7.29% — $50 to $100m
- 6.17% — $100 to $200m
- 6.19% — $200 to $500m
- 3.07% — $500 to $1bn
- 5.18% — > $1bn

Source: Hedge Fund Research.

Fund of funds

There is a dazzling array of hedge funds available to institutional investors today, many using fairly sophisticated investment strategies. For an institutional investor, attempting to choose between them can seem a daunting task, though a number of hedge fund consultants exist to assist with manager search and selection and the associated due diligence (for a not inconsiderable fee). Furthermore, many institutional investors are unwilling to put all their eggs into one hedge fund basket as that would mean possibly relying on the trading skills of one or two individuals. As a result of this, many institutional investors have chosen to invest in hedge funds via the 'fund of funds' route.

The fund manager of a fund of funds will invest the funds entrusted to them into a wide range of individual hedge funds with divergent strategies, though the returns, and associated risks to the investor will therefore be dependent upon the quality of the hedge funds chosen by the fund of funds manager. The advantage for the investor is that their money will be spread across a number of hedge fund managers, where each one may be employing different strategies and operating in very different areas of the capital markets. Another advantage of this approach is that by pooling assets in this way, the minimum investment amount for investors may be considerably lower than that for any individual hedge fund.

For this service the investor pays a fee to the manager of the fund of funds. This manager will in turn be charged a fee by the hedge funds in which they invest on behalf of their clients. The disadvantage of accessing hedge fund returns in this manner then, is that the investor pays two sets of fees. That is, an AMC and a performance fee, typically on a '1 and 10' basis, on top of the '2 and 20' paid to the underlying hedge fund managers. However, despite this, Exhibit 13.9 shows how popular hedge funds of funds have become over the past few years. By the end of 2010 this hedge fund investment avenue comprised over 2,000 funds.

Hedge funds and the credit crunch

Exhibit 13.10 shows the number of new hedge fund launches along with the number of hedge fund closures (liquidations) since 1996. New hedge fund launches peaked in 2005 at over 2,000. However, hedge fund liquidations peaked in 2008 at just under 1,500, as the credit crunch took hold. Just over a further 1,000 disappeared in 2009. The increase in net hedge fund numbers between 2001 and 2007 was partly driven by investor demand. At the beginning of the noughties investors were disappointed with the performance of equity markets and were looking for an alternative source of return uncorrelated with equity markets. The hedge fund 'promise' of an absolute return regardless of market conditions seemed attractive. Another source of this growth was the ease with which hedge funds could borrow money to invest – via a range of strategies. The 2008/09 liquidity crisis led to widespread losses across the industry, not just

Exhibit 13.9   Global hedge fund of funds numbers

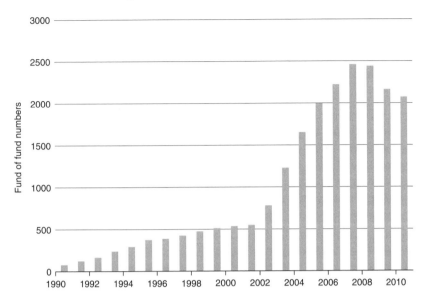

Source: Hedge Fund Research.

Exhibit 13.10   Global hedge fund launches and closures, to 2010

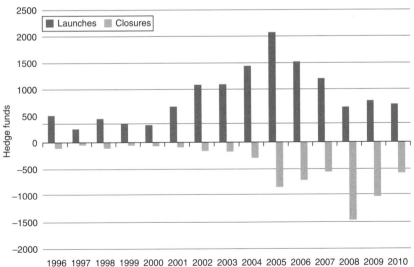

Source: Hedge Fund Research.

because the assets that they held fell in value, but also because many of their strategies required markets to remain very liquid and, more crucially, required cheap leverage. A series of temporary short-selling bans imposed by the regulators of most of the world's stock exchanges on particular cohorts of stocks, largely financials, between late-2008 and early/mid-2009, also compromised many hedge fund strategies.

The losses in the industry over this period caused many investors, despite the many and various attempts by hedge fund managers to stem the tide of redemptions, to withdraw their money from hedge funds, leading to the widespread closures shown in Exhibit 13.10. However, despite the industry as a whole suffering a weighted average loss of 19.1 per cent in 2008 – its first annual loss, or 'drawdown', since 1998 – the industry swiftly recovered in 2009, posting an average performance of 18.6 per cent, followed by another double-digit gain of 11 per cent in 2010.[10]

Picking up nickels in front of a steam roller

Prior to the credit crunch, relative value managers were accused of 'picking up nickels in front of a steam roller'. In other words, their trades regularly added small amounts to performance, though these increments became smaller and smaller over time as competition in the relative value 'space' increased. To enhance their returns, relative value funds began employing considerable amounts of leverage to magnify potential gains from arbitrage opportunities in credit and sovereign fixed income markets. However, crucially they had ignored the potential consequences of market liquidity drying up – the steam roller. The steam roller eventually caught up with many of these managers: market liquidity dried up and credit was almost impossible to come by. This meant that market positions had to be closed out at disadvantageous prices. Fixed income arbitrage funds posted an average loss of 28.8 per cent in 2008. However, those funds that survived this period managed to claw these losses back. Fixed income arbitrage funds recorded average performances of 27.4 per cent and 12.5 per cent in 2009 and 2010, respectively.[11] Other funds however were left flattened on the tarmac.

Performance data biases

Although we consider the analysis of performance data in more detail in Chapter 14, the analysis of hedge fund performance data has particular

---

[10] Dow Jones Credit Suisse Hedge Fund Index.
[11] Dow Jones Credit Suisse Hedge Fund Index.

challenges. There exist a number of well documented biases in the reported data. These are as follows:

- *Index coverage*: There are a number of hedge fund performance databases, none of which provides performance data that is representative of the entire industry. Moreover, some of this data, the historic data in particular, has not been audited or independently verified.
- *Non-representative data*: Most hedge fund performance data has a relatively short history.
- *Survivorship bias*: Survivorship bias exists within any performance data series and results from the data only capturing the performance of those 'winners' that have remained in business throughout the period of analysis, ignoring that of those that have fallen by the wayside. As a consequence, performance is flattered. For hedge funds, this bias can be quite pronounced given the number of funds that go into liquidation, as illustrated in Exhibit 13.10.
- *Self-selection bias*: As the reporting of performance to hedge fund databases is entirely voluntary, many new funds and some top-performing hedge funds closed to new business do not report their performances, or have not done so in the past.
- *Backfill bias*: Once new funds have established a good track record they then begin reporting their performances to the index compilers. The performance databases backdate previously unreported performance into the data which, by definition, tends to be good. Unsurprisingly, funds with a poor record do not report their performance. This backfill bias causes the returns on the compiled indices to be upwardly biased since they exclude funds that have performed poorly in the past.

Private equity

Private equity is another alternative investment class that has attracted a good deal of institutional investor interest. Private equity funds exist to provide private (rather than public) equity capital for companies requiring finance. As Exhibit 13.11 shows, this capital is provided by a wide range of investor types, including pension funds.

When private equity is sought by a start-up, or by companies in the early stages of development, it is known as venture capital. These firms may turn to venture capitalists for financing when they themselves are unable to raise equity via a public listing, issue debt, or take out bank loans if their nascent cash flows will not support leverage. In return for providing appropriate capital for the business, the venture capitalist will own a proportion of the company's equity and therefore have a claim on a proportion of the firm's profits.

Exhibit 13.11   Sources of private equity funds

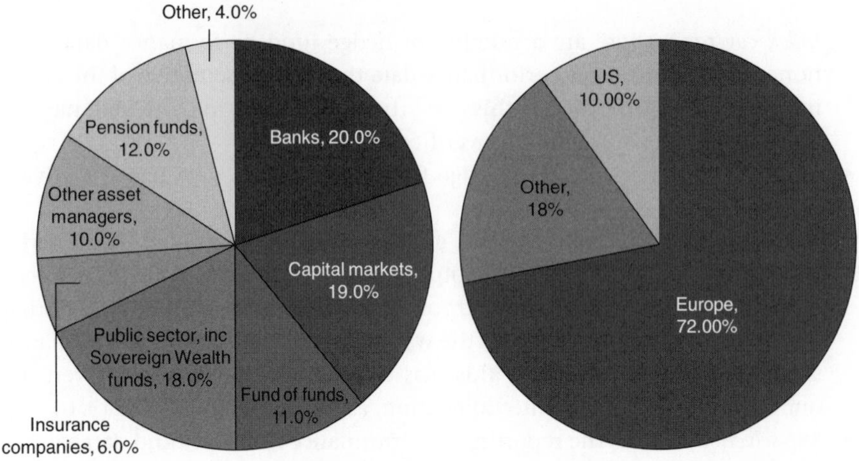

Other, 4.0%

Pension funds, 12.0%

Other asset managers, 10.0%

Banks, 20.0%

Capital markets, 19.0%

Public sector, inc Sovereign Wealth funds, 18.0%

Fund of funds, 11.0%

Insurance companies, 6.0%

US, 10.00%

Other, 18%

Europe, 72.00%

Source: European Venture Capital Association, 2010.

But private equity companies also buy existing, well-established firms too, sometimes in collaboration with the existing management of the company and also in collaboration with other private equity funds. These private equity firms are known as buyout funds, since they literally buyout the existing owners in whole or part – either the equity shareholders of the publicly traded shares if it is a publicly quoted company, or the owners of the privately held shares if the firm is unquoted.

As the targets are very different, the average size of a private equity buyout deal will be much larger than the average deals undertaken by venture capital funds. Indeed, immediately prior to the credit crunch, private equity buyout funds made the headlines as they bid for bigger and bigger household names at increasingly eye-watering prices.

Typical private equity structure

The majority of the capital, or 'war chest', that comprises the funds available for the private equity fund will be provided by banks, long-term investors such as life assurance companies, pension funds and endowments and also wealthy individuals. The private equity fund managers will typically provide a small proportion of the capital too.

Exhibit 13.12 shows the structure of a typical fund. The fund itself is registered as a limited partnership where the partners are the suppliers of capital. The private equity manager is the general partner and the investors, limited partners. From

Exhibit 13.12   Simplified private equity fund structure

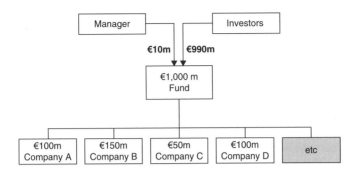

the date of the fund's inception, the private equity fund manager will usually levy an annual management charge (AMC) of between 1.5 per cent and 2.5 per cent of the fund's value for managing the fund, and will typically also be entitled to a 20 per cent share of the total profit made by the fund's investments. However, usually this profit share, or 'carried interest', is only payable when the fund achieves a certain minimum return, known as the 'hurdle rate', which can be anywhere between about 6 to 8 per cent, and is only payable once the original capital and the realized profits have been returned to the limited partners.

Once the funds have been raised, the private equity fund managers will look for suitable investments. Identifying suitable targets may take some time, which means that three to five years may elapse before all the capital raised has been 'drawn down' or 'put into the ground'. If the companies that the private equity fund manager buy can be sold at a later date, whether by a stock exchange floatation, or a secondary buyout to another private equity group, at a profit, then the private equity fund's investors should profit too. Of course, if the investments do not turn out to be profitable then the returns to investors will suffer commensurately. Usually the fund will have a target lifespan where the aim is to return all monies to investors after a certain period, seven to 12 years being common.

How do private equity firms generate returns for investors?

There are a number of ways in which private equity firms generate returns for themselves as managers and for their investors. The first source of profit is, of course, the difference between what they pay for a firm, or for a stake in a firm, and what they sell it for subsequently. But private equity managers would argue that they do more than just 'buy well'. So what else do they do?

In the case of venture capital, the private equity firm can bring a whole range of management expertise ranging from finance to marketing that might otherwise be missing in a company with a small number of employees. The existing employees may be expert in some newly developing scientific technology but not necessarily in business management. By bringing this expertise to start-up companies the private equity firm can help expand the business and make it more profitable.

How is it possible to buy a publicly traded company that is analyzed by thousands of analysts, fund managers and investors and then to sell it back to that same publicly traded equity market at some time in the future and make a profit? Private equity managers argue that they bring more expertise to the running of that business than the incumbent management. They would also argue that they have a longer time horizon in mind than managers of publicly traded companies who are often under pressure from equity market participants to increase profitability quickly. Out of the glare and alleged short-termist scrutiny of the public equity markets, private equity managers argue that they have more time and scope to improve the longer-term value of the firm by, for example, focusing on the firm's core business by selling unprofitable aspects of the business or perhaps by bringing stricter cost controls to bear. Changes like these are all designed to increase the firm's long-run profitability.

It is also argued (by the private equity industry) that the private equity ownership model – with its simplified ownership structure and active, engaged investors with their long-term strategic focus – better aligns the interests of owners, managers and employees and largely eliminates the agency problem that exists between the directors and shareholders of publicly traded companies. Moreover, with strong corporate governance and without the need to enter into lengthy consultations with the disparate shareholder base that characterizes many public companies when seeking to embark on corporate actions such as mergers, acquisitions and spin-offs, private equity managers claim to be able to operate in a more fleet-of-foot and empowered fashion than their quoted company counterparts. Given this and because of the attractive remuneration packages private equity firms offer, these funds are in a good position to attract and retain talented managers.

Private buyout firms and leverage

Perhaps one of the most important tools used by private equity buyout funds is leverage. So how does this leverage work? A simplified example can illustrate the way in which leverage can enhance a firm's profitability. Suppose that there exists a firm with a current market value of £100m, which is all equity financed and that generates net profits of £10m per year. If a private equity firm were to buy this company for £100m with cash then it would yield a net return of 10 per cent on this investment in the first year. However, if instead of buying the company in an all-cash deal, the private equity firm puts up £50m in cash and borrows the remaining £50m at a rate of interest of say, 6 per cent, then the return on this investment increases dramatically. Rather than earning £10m in

Exhibit 13.13 Leverage and firm profitability

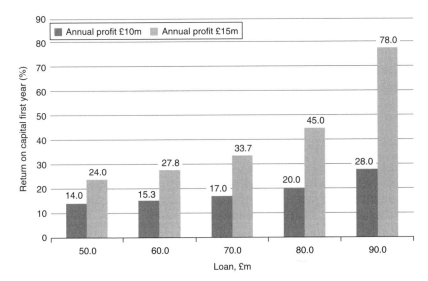

the first year on an investment of £100m, the private equity firm would instead be earning £10m on an investment of £50m. However, interest payments will now need to be paid on the loan. When this is taken into account, the return on capital invested in the first year turns out to be 14 per cent (Note: the calculations assume no repayment of loan principal in the first year).

In Exhibit 13.13 the first bar in the chart represents the return on capital, from buying this company with a £50m loan charged at 6 per cent. Successive bars, labelled 'Annual profit £10m' show the same rate of return calculation but with progressively higher borrowing. In the calculations used to produce the chart we also assume that the loan rate increases by 0.5 per cent for every extra £10m borrowed, so that the loan rate for the £90m loan is 8 per cent. The bars show how the returns from this company can be enhanced via leverage. So, if the loan is £90m and the rate of interest is 8 per cent, then an interest charge of £7.2m must be deducted from the £10m profit generated by the company. The residual £2.8m expressed as a percentage of the £10m of equity capital invested is 28 per cent. The bars labelled 'annual profit £15m' represent the same basic calculations but here we assume that via changes to the firm's structure, the firm instead produces a profit of £15m in the first year. The increase in profitability enhances the leveraged returns yet further.

The risk involved in using debt in this way is that if the firm's profitability falls, it may not have the funds available to meet the interest payments and repayment of the loan principal. In this case the firm's creditors (its bondholders, the banks, the pension scheme, etc.) may force the firm into liquidation, in which case the equity owners would usually lose all of their invested capital.

Leverage is therefore a double-edged sword; a sword that the buyout industry wields in the hope that it can help to enhance returns on their investments. It has been shown that the performance of good buyout funds does not hinge exclusively on cheap and plentiful leverage.[12] However, it seems very likely that some of the worst performing buyout funds rely almost exclusively on this as a means of generating returns.

Private equity and the performance J-curve

One important feature of private equity investment is its tendency to produce low or negative cash flows for investors during the early years of the investment, followed by a period of positive cash flow and returns. Typically private equity firms will raise money from interested investors, even though this money is generally not needed immediately. It is only drawn down by the private equity fund as investible opportunities arise. Moreover, this capital commitment usually comprises a series of annual commitments rather than just a single commitment at the fund's launch. In the early years of the fund, negative returns can be a function of management fees which, at between 1.5 and 2.5 per cent, are similar to those typically charged by a hedge fund, and because the investments that the fund makes may take some time to produce positive cash flow as the businesses are restructured. If the private equity manager has invested shrewdly then the fund's investments will then begin to show unrealized gains, as the value of the purchased firms rise, until finally this value is realized, for example, via an initial public offering, trade sale or as a secondary buyout by another private equity firm.

Exhibit 13.14 shows a stylized version of the returns achieved from investing in a private equity fund. In the early years the fund draws down the committed capital from investors to acquire and restructure firms, while generating only limited amounts of cash flow and/or profit. Eventually the negative cash flow is replaced with a positive one as the original capital is returned to investors with realized profits. A private equity firm will normally target a break-even point, the point at which the investment becomes self-sustaining or 'evergreen', usually between three and eight years after the initial capital raising. Clearly the faster the private equity manager can turn a negative net cash flow into a positive one the less time the investor has to wait for a return on their investment.

A key point worth noting is that while investors can directly control the amount committed to a private equity fund, they have no control over the pace

---

[12] One such study is by Viral V. Acharya and Conor Kehoe, 'Corporate Governance and Value Creation: Evidence from Private Equity' April, London Business School and CEPR (2008).

Exhibit 13.14 The private equity J-curve

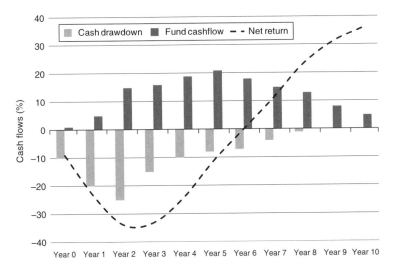

of investment because the timing of investments and realizations is entirely at the discretion of the private equity firm. Therefore, the investor's economic exposure to private equity at any time is usually not in line with their desired strategic allocation.

Private equity and the credit crunch

One of the most significant features of the credit bubble that led to the credit crunch was the amount of private equity activity that took place. The ease with which cheap credit was made available meant that leveraged deals – that is, where the buyout firm uses a significant amount of borrowed money to buy companies – were rife. Before the credit bubble burst, deals were being completed with more than 90 per cent of the purchase price being borrowed. With the onset of the credit crunch, the economics of leveraged private equity deals changed dramatically. So much so that such private equity activity ground to a halt. Furthermore, deals had been put together with the expectation that they could be refinanced at similarly cheap levels. The withdrawal of credit meant that many deals that looked profitable before the credit bubble burst, now look less so.

All this means that private equity funds launched in the good times, might struggle to produce good returns for investors, since:

- private equity managers may have overpaid for companies;
- more expensive, post-credit crunch financing might have a detrimental impact on projected cash flows; and
- committed capital may not be put to use very quickly.

Conversely, many funds launched after the worst of the crisis had passed, may have picked up companies and assets at rock bottom prices and would have been forced to finance their deals at realistic interest rates. In other words, as with all investments, timing is everything.[13]

Private equity performance

In the world of private equity, while timing matters, as evidenced by the often marked differences in performance between funds launched in different 'vintage years',[14] so does manager and strategy selection. In other words, selecting the right manager and the right fund at the right time is crucial. Historic performance data[15] suggests that:

- buyout funds outperform venture capital funds;
- large buyout funds outperform small buyout funds;
- long-standing funds outperform younger funds;
- returns are positively skewed towards top performing funds; and
- performance persistency exists at both ends of the performance spectrum. That is, good and bad performance repeat over time.

In other words, an investment in private equity is an investment in a skill set rather than an asset class, just as it is with hedge funds. Focusing on the penultimate bullet point, over the period 1980 to 2008, research found that while the median buyout manager delivered an annual return of zero, the arithmetic average annual performance of the top 25 per cent of managers was a staggering 22.7 per cent.[16] For those of you who are not familiar with the differences between an arithmetic average and a median, these figures indicate that a huge proportion of private equity managers added little or no value whatsoever, while a small proportion of good managers, added value on a massive scale.[17] The problem is that accessing these top performing managers is not always possible since, as with hedge funds, many close to new business and tend to stick with a fixed client base when starting a new fund.

[13] Kaplan, S. and A. Schoar, 'Private Equity Performance: Returns, Persistence and Capital Flows', *Journal of Finance*, August, pp. 1791–823, (2005) found that private equity funds created in boom years are more likely to perform poorly. Also see the *BVCA Private Equity and Venture Capital Performance Measurement Survey* 2009.

[14] See the *BVCA Private Equity and Venture Capital Performance Measurement Survey* 2009.

[15] EVCA/Thomson Reuters, *2008 Pan-European Private Equity Performance Benchmarks Survey* of 1,331 individual funds formed 1980–2008. S. Kaplan and A. Schoar, 'Private equity performance: Returns, Persistence and Capital Flows', *Journal of Finance*, August, pp. 1791–823, (2005). Private Equity Intelligence Limited, 2008.

[16] EVCA/Thomson Reuters '2008 Pan-European Private Equity Performance Benchmarks Survey' of 1,331 individual funds formed 1980–2008.

[17] Private Equity Intelligence Limited 2008.

Another point to bear in mind when analyzing private equity returns is the fact that they are stated in IRR (Internal Rate of Return) terms. These returns can be distorted by the size and timing of cash flows into and out of the fund and the estimated value of existing investments. This means they are not directly comparable to returns from public equity markets or funds that invest in publicly traded securities. (We look at performance measurement in Chapter 14.)

Finally, given the diversity and inherent illiquidity of private equity funds, it is difficult to obtain robust estimates of the volatility of private equity returns and the correlation of these returns with other asset classes. However, most studies suggest that private equity returns do provide some diversification when combined with other asset classes.

Accessing private equity

Pension schemes can access private equity, via:

- segregated accounts,
- a fund of funds approach, or
- publicly quoted investment trusts.

Most pension funds adopt the fund of funds route given the substantially lower annual capital commitment when compared to direct or segregated investment and the greater degree of diversification this medium offers to most investors. Fund of funds can also offer access to top performing funds that might otherwise not be within reach of smaller investors. Although each of the other routes have their merits, investing in private equity via a segregated mandate can involve significant management fees. Although the investment trust route offers the investor greater liquidity than becoming a limited partner of a fund, the investor is typically tied to a single provider with little control over vintage year exposure and must accept that the investment trust share price can often trade a discount to the net asset value of their investment.

Commodities

The rapid industrialization of the Chinese and Indian economies over the past few years has led to a sharp increase in the global demand for many commodities. This increase in demand for raw materials from newly developing economies coincided with a period of relatively constrained raw material supply. Taken together the increase in demand for raw materials and the weak capacity from raw material producers to satisfy this higher demand has led to a rapid increase in many commodity prices since 2003. The sharp increase in many commodity prices came at the tail end of the equity bear market of the early noughties, the latter having led many investors to the conclusion that

Exhibit 13.15   The price of tin and copper

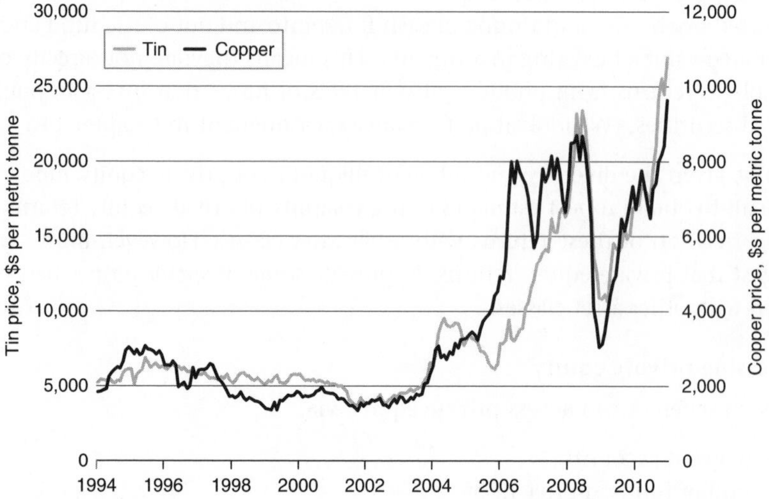

Source: Thomson Financial.

an exposure to commodities might improve the overall performance of their portfolios. In Exhibit 13.15 we present two commodities, tin and copper, the prices of which have both increased quite dramatically since 2003.

How do you invest in commodities?

Unlike financial instruments such as bonds and equities, where the ownership can be maintained in electronic formats by global custodians, investing in physical commodities poses some obvious problems. Where would the average investor store a US$50m investment in oil, or worse still, in a perishable commodity like grain? Then there's the insurance to consider.

There are two main ways in which investors can obtain exposure to commodities, without having to buy and then store and insure them. The first realistic option might be to construct a portfolio of ordinary shares where the companies comprising this portfolio are directly involved in the commodities business. For example, an investor wishing to add exposure to energy-related commodities might buy the ordinary shares of British Petroleum, British Gas, Royal Dutch Shell for example. Typically when energy prices rise, the profits of these companies rise too, and in this way the investor would benefit indirectly from the rise in energy prices.

However, sometimes due to a range of factors such as regulation, or due to certain company-specific issues, the returns on the equities of these companies can be poorly correlated with commodity prices. For example, in 2004 when the

Exhibit 13.16   Composition of two commodity indices

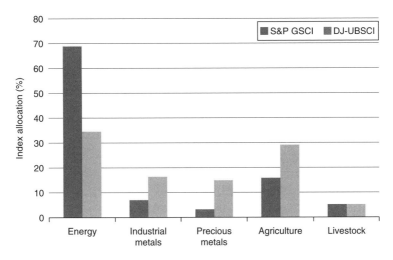

Source: S&P GSCI, DJ-UBSCI.

oil price was rising rapidly the ordinary shares of Royal Dutch Shell were falling, because the Anglo-Dutch energy company had to restate the size of its untapped oil reserves.

As a result of these issues many investors choose to gain exposure to commodities by engaging a fund manager to invest in commodity futures on their behalf. These commodity futures funds are usually constructed to track, or to benchmark themselves against, an index of commodity prices, where the index itself is also created out of commodity futures by a commodities index provider like Dow Jones-UBS or S&P-Goldman Sachs.

In Exhibit 13.16 we have presented two of the most popular commodity futures indices, the S&P GSCI and the DJ-UBSCI, the weightings of which to the various commodity types differ quite markedly. For instance, an investor choosing to mimic the DJ-UBSCI would have a far lower exposure to energy-related products than one who chose instead to replicate the returns on the S&P GSCI. The investment strategy of those investment funds that track or benchmark themselves against these indices, involves buying the appropriate number of nearest to maturity commodity futures, and then selling these contracts ('rolling them over') before they expire to purchase the next nearest to maturity contract. In this way the investor obtains exposure to commodity price changes reflected in the futures contracts without ever having to hold the commodities.

On the whole, as Exhibit 13.17 shows, the commodity indices seem to track changes in the commodity market quite well. Indeed, both indices began to rise sharply after early 2002.

Exhibit 13.17   Commodity futures index performance

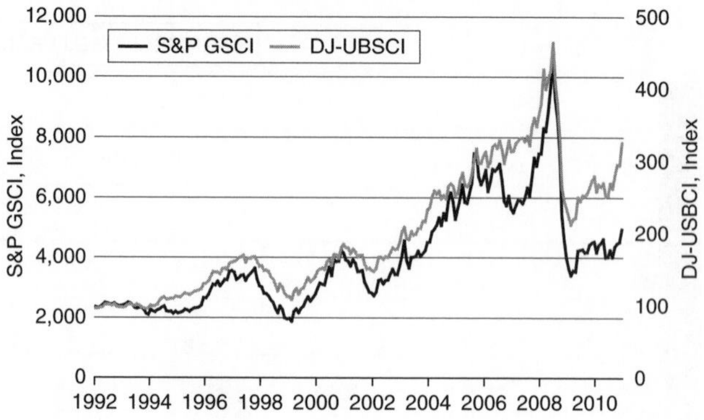

Source: Thomson Financial.

Other sources of commodity futures return

Investing in commodity futures contracts is seen by many investors as a convenient way of gaining exposure to the underlying commodities because it circumvents the storage and insurance problems associated with direct investment. It also avoids exposure to a small group of commodity-related companies whose fortunes are partly dictated by the general direction of equity markets. However, investing in commodities via commodity futures does involve some other factors and considerations that should be borne in mind.

First, when we enter into a futures contract, rather than commit capital to the total value of the commodities exposure, we only need to put up sufficient cash to meet the initial margin, which, as we saw in Chapter 11, usually accounts for a small percentage of the value of the exposure assumed. This means that the rest of the cash laid aside for the commodity investment can be placed into a money market deposit and earn interest. The total return reported on commodities indices includes the interest that can be earned from only having to put up a small portion of the cash as margin. Therefore, some of the return that an investor will earn will have nothing to do with changes in commodity prices but will instead be related to the prevailing level of interest rates.

Second, the continual rolling over of one futures contract to the next, means that the returns achieved will also be a function of the shape of the futures curve. For instance, if the futures curve is upward sloping, or 'in contango' (that is, the futures are trading at a higher price than the underlying commodities), then selling the nearest to maturity contract for the more expensive, next nearest contract, as the former approaches maturity, will create regular and predictable,

Exhibit 13.18   The price of copper and the cumulative gain from investing in copper futures

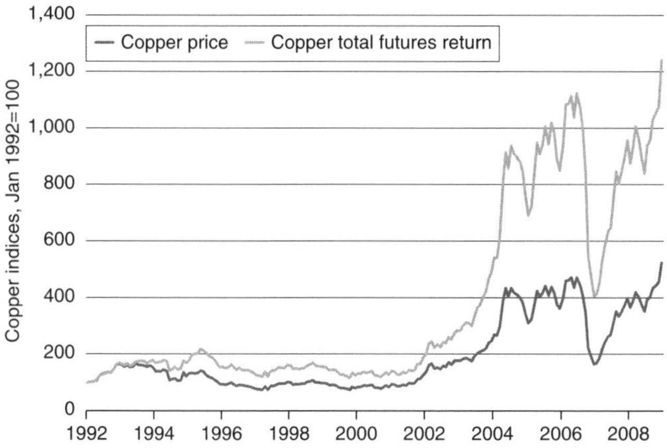

Source: Thomson Financial

capital losses for investors. This is known as 'negative roll'. So, when the futures curve is upward sloping, for the investor to break even, the commodities price would need to rise by the difference in the price of the next nearest to maturity contract and the one that is about to expire. Conversely, if the futures curve is downward sloping (the futures market is 'in backwardation'), the roll over procedure would involve selling the more expensive nearest to maturity contract for the cheaper, next nearest to maturity contract as the former approaches maturity, thus creating regular and predictable, capital gains for investors. This is known as 'positive roll'.

As inferred above, at times the shape of the futures curve can have a big influence on the returns achieved by commodities futures funds. Indeed, for much of the commodities bull market, commodity futures contracts have traded in contango as a result of the sheer weight of money being invested in commodities via the futures. In Exhibit 13.18 we demonstrate this issue. We present an index of the price of copper on the one hand and the cumulative gain from investing in copper futures over time. The two series look very different from one another. Between 1992 and 2010 the price of copper increased by a factor of five; over the same period the cumulative gain from investing in copper futures was 1,200 per cent.

Finally, it is worth noting the findings of an interesting paper that considered the risks and returns of commodity futures, analyzed over the period July 1959 to December 2004, during which the futures markets largely traded in backwardation.[18] The study, which measured the monthly returns from an equally weighted index of commodity futures, found that while they exhibited the same annual return and standard deviation as the S&P 500 index, the distribution of returns was positively skewed whereas that for the S&P 500 was negatively skewed. In addition, commodity futures were also found to be positively correlated with both expected and unexpected inflation.

These results may not necessarily hold in the future. The period 1959 to 2004 is a period where commodities were not seen as an investible asset class by most investors. However, since 2004 more and more investors have added commodities investments to their portfolios. There is now clear evidence to suggest that the correlations between commodities and traditional risky asset classes such as equities have risen. Take the period following the collapse of the investment bank, Lehman Brothers. Investors the world over tried to reduce their exposure to all risky asset classes, including commodities. Thus, commodity prices fell sharply along with other risky asset classes. In other words, as investors see commodities increasingly as an asset class, rather than as a consumption good, the higher will be the correlation between commodities and other asset classes.

Foreign exchange

Every three years, the Bank for International Settlements (BIS) conducts a global survey into the size and structure of the foreign exchange (forex) markets. In its most recent survey, released in December 2010,[19] BIS revealed that the global *daily* turnover in forex and related derivative instruments had risen by 20 per cent from its 2007 level to US$3.98 trillion. That equates to an annual turnover of nearly US$1 quadrillion (that's one thousand trillion dollars). With a daily turnover ten times as great as that for global equities and five times that for daily global trading in US Treasuries, the forex market is by far the world's largest financial market.

Other BIS findings

The December 2010 BIS triennial review into the size and structure of the forex market found that London continued to dominate the trading of forex and related derivatives, accounting for 37 per cent of global daily turnover. At US$1,584bn, this equates to 140 times the daily volume of trading on the London Stock Exchange. New York was the next largest forex centre with

---

[18] Gary B. Gorton and K. Geert Rouwenhorst, 'Facts and Fantasies About Commodity Futures', *Financial Analysts Journal*, Volume 62, Number 2, pp. 47–68, April (2006).
[19] BIS Triennial Central Bank Survey Report on global foreign exchange market activity in 2010, December 2010.

an 18 per cent market share and then Tokyo and Singapore with market shares of 6 and 5 per cent, respectively.

The world's most actively traded currency remained the US dollar. It featured in 84.9 per cent of all currency trades, with the euro, yen and sterling featuring in 39.1 per cent, 19 per cent and 12.9 per cent of trades respectively. Of the commodity-related currencies, the Australian dollar, accounting for 7.6 per cent of trades, was the most prominent. You will note that as currencies trade in pairs, this data series adds up to 200, rather than 100, per cent. The most popular currency pairs trade remained that of the dollar/euro.

When investing overseas, as UK pension funds and other investor types increasingly do, increasing amounts of foreign currency risk are progressively introduced to the portfolio, leaving investors faced with three basic choices. These are to:

- simply accept and bear the risk associated with exchange rate movements;
- use foreign currency derivatives to hedge the foreign exchange risk; or
- see foreign exchange risk as a potential source of additional return and foreign exchange as an asset class in its own right.

Exhibit 13.19 shows the annualized standard deviation of the US, Europe (ex UK) and Japanese stock markets from January 1990 to December 2010, assuming that the currency risk has been hedged for a sterling-based investor. That is, the volatility that a sterling-based investor would have experienced by investing in these equity market indices on a currency hedged basis. The exhibit also shows the annualized standard deviation associated with these equity markets for a sterling-based investor where the exchange rate risk remains unhedged. As we can see over this period choosing to leave overseas equity investments unhedged can have an impact on the volatility of the returns.

However, risk is only one side of the coin. The question is whether this risk can be turned into return.

Active currency management

Today active currency management is seen as another potential source of return. Moreover, unlike many other alternative investments, as the world's largest financial market, the forex market offers superior transparency and liquidity.

Currency overlay

For a pension scheme with overseas assets, an active currency overlay requires the fund manager to take views about the portfolio's currency exposures. Those foreign currency exposures that the manager believes will benefit the scheme

Exhibit 13.19   Volatility of hedged and unhedged equity returns

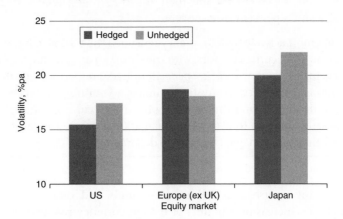

are left unhedged, while the others are hedged. On those occasions when the fund manager has no strongly held views about any currency, they might wish to 'return to benchmark' by hedging all currency exposure. In this respect then, active currency management is no different to actively managing say, a portfolio of equities. Currency 'bets' that pay off will benefit the fund, while those that do not will subtract value from it. Just like any active fund manager, the active currency overlay manager will use information from a range of sources when they take currency positions. For example, these might include views about:

- currency 'fundamentals' – a consideration of the likely impact of current and future interest rate and/or inflation differentials between economies;
- political factors that might have a bearing on a government's approach to its currency; and
- technical factors, such as the recent direction of one currency's value against another.

In fact, active currency overlay managers have an almost infinite number of indicators to choose from.

Specialist currency fund managers

Another way of adding value through currency might be to hedge the foreign currency exposure of a fund using foreign exchange derivatives, and then to appoint a specialist currency fund manager who would be tasked with adding value by managing currency independently of the scheme's other asset holdings. This approach treats foreign exchange as an asset class in its own right. That is, as an additional source of risk and return.

As currency markets are principally populated by organizations, such as central banks, importers, exporters and companies and institutions investing overseas that are simply seeking to hedge currency exposure rather than to make a profit from trading currency, (not forgetting holidaymakers who simply need spending money), active currency management aims to exploit the pricing anomalies that can sometimes arise as a consequence of this activity, and to earn the premium that these hedgers are willing to pay to eliminate forex risk from their balance sheets. Currency funds typically try to add value by employing one of three investment styles: *carry*, *momentum* and *fundamental*.

- *Carry*: a carry approach to currency management involves borrowing, or short selling, lower yielding currencies while simultaneously buying the currencies of economies with high interest rates. Because Japanese interest rates have been at, or very close to, zero in recent years, the yen has been the favourite currency to short sell for carry trade purposes, while high yielding commodity-related currencies, such as the Australian dollar, have been favoured for the long-carry position. The difference between the interest paid on the borrowed currency and that earned on the invested currency is 'the carry'.
- *Momentum*: momentum currency trades involve assessing the underlying direction of a currency in an attempt to identify how long the currency will continue to move in a particular direction against another, typically using moving average calculations.
- *Fundamental*: fundamental currency management techniques attempt to identify currencies that are over or undervalued relative to some estimated fundamental value. For example, given the size of the US current account deficit today, a value currency strategy might be to sell the US dollar against currencies that have an associated current account surplus.

Exhibit 13.20 gives one example of the kind of indicator that a manager focusing on currency fundamentals might consider. The line represents the ratio of the price of a basket of goods and services in the US to the price of a basket of goods and services in the UK, represented by the US CPI (Consumer Prices Index) and the UK RPI (Retail Prices Index), respectively. It therefore represents the price of a basket of US products relative to a basket of UK products – in other words, a rate of exchange. Because UK inflation has been higher on average than in the US over the period under consideration, the price of the UK basket has risen relative to the US basket and hence the 'rate of exchange' has fallen, by around half over that period. According to a well-known theory of exchange rates, purchasing power parity (PPP), the actual exchange rate should equate the average price of goods in one currency relative to another. In other words, the US dollar sterling exchange rate should broadly reflect the relative values of goods in the two economies, represented by the line labelled 'US CPI/UK RPI'. As we can see from the exhibit, the actual US dollar/sterling exchange rate has indeed trended down with the ratio of US consumer prices to UK prices since 1973.

Exhibit 13.20   Dollar/sterling exchange rate, and ratio of US versus UK consumer price indices

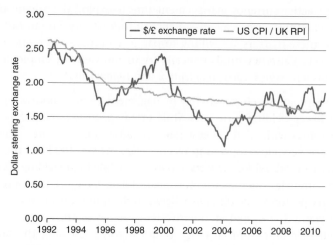

Source: Thomson Financial.

The line in Exhibit 13.20 then, can be thought of as one fundamental measure of the value of the dollar relative to the pound. We can see that although the two series trend together over the long term, there are long periods when the actual exchange rate is a very different from the one implied by the ratio of the two inflation indices. One interpretation of the relationship between these two series is that when the exchange rate is above the line derived from the price indices, the pound is overvalued relative to the dollar, but is undervalued relative to the dollar when the exchange rate is below the line derived from the price indices. A valuation-oriented fund manager may use measures like the one presented in this exhibit to try and identify over and undervalued currencies and, by doing so, seek to add value by buying undervalued currencies and selling overvalued currencies.

Currency management performance evaluation

Whether trustees prefer to use a currency overlay manager, or a specialist currency fund manager (and there is no reason why both cannot be used) the key aspect of these approaches to currency is that it is seen as an asset class in its own right, rather than as a residual equity or bond market risk. However, regardless of which approach is chosen, one issue remains – *how does one measure performance?*

With the active management of an equity portfolio, performance can be benchmarked against a relevant equity index such as the S&P 500 or the FTSE 100. Specifying a currency benchmark is much harder. If, for example, the active currency overlay manager can return to benchmark by hedging all currency exposure, the benchmark return should be a return of zero. This is why it is often suggested that a positive return on currency is 'pure alpha', implying that there was no market/systematic – or beta – risk involved in the activity. However, this is misleading. While some of a currency fund manager's positive return may be unrelated to risk, this should not be taken to mean that currency returns are achieved with no risk – just as there is no simple, objective way of separating the true alpha from any market risk. Furthermore, currency positions can be taken without the need for a capital investment, since a long position in one currency automatically implies an offsetting short position in another. Therefore any return on 'capital invested' is virtually either an infinitely positive or an infinitely negative return.

The investment community is now beginning to address ways of benchmarking currency fund management so that currency performance can be measured and return targets can be set. However, despite these knotty issues, there is still no doubt that currency should be seen as an asset class in its own right. As such, the foreign exchange market offers pension schemes another alternative and legitimate way of adding value to their portfolios if they choose to manage it actively, rather than just ignoring it, or hedging it away entirely.

Integrating alternatives with traditional asset classes

The preceding discussion highlighted some of the peculiar features of four alternative asset classes. While each has its own unique attractions, investing in alternative asset classes can also bring about a whole series of headaches for trustees, and other investors. Aspirin might be required for any one, or all of the following reasons:

- inadequate historical return data,
- opacity,
- illiquidity,
- high fees, and
- additional due diligence burden.

Return history

As we inferred when considering hedge funds, many alternative investment categories have a relatively short history or at least a short history of accurate performance data. This causes two problems. First, investors have little historic guide as to the likely return and volatility of these asset classes. Coming to a view about expected return and volatility is hard enough for asset classes for which we have decades of return data; for the hedge fund industry and for currency managers we have arguably, at best, ten to 15 years worth of reasonably reliable return data. Having such poor historic data also means that it is difficult to come to a view about the likely return correlation between alternative asset classes and traditional asset classes, not least because only a meaningful allocation to alternatives will change the characteristics of the portfolio. All of this information is vital if we are to understand the impact that adding alternative asset classes could have on the mean-variance frontier (see Exhibit 13.3).

Opacity

Although it is not always obvious to clients what an equity fund manager does all day,[20] it is not that difficult to understand the broad approach that they use to try and add value. Stocks, whose prices are normally quoted in national newspapers, are bought and sold; ones that the manager thinks will go down in price are sold, while those that the manager thinks will go up in price are bought. This is, of course, a simplification of what an equity manager does, but the performance of most equity managers can be monitored simply by observing broad equity indices. If the index has risen by 10 per cent over a period, then the manager's portfolio should have risen by a similar amount, more or less.

As hedge fund managers use a wide range of very complex instruments and strategies, it is not possible to follow their general progress in the national press. Worse still, for mere mortals, even asking a hedge fund manager for an explanation of their strategy leaves most with no better idea. Hedge funds are a very opaque investment.[21]

The performance of a private equity fund is also very difficult to judge over time. The companies that they buy are not traded on public markets. Their values over time, and therefore the value of the fund too, are estimated by accountants, but ultimately a business is only worth what someone else is willing to pay for it. It is only really at the end of the life of the fund that investors realize whether the accountant's valuation is shared by the rest of the world. Even commodity investing is not as straightforward as it might seem, even though we can easily track the price of commodities in the financial press. This is because most investors access this source of return via commodity futures funds, the returns on which often only bear a weak resemblance to the price changes in the underlying commodities.

---

[20] Why don't equity fund managers look out of the window in the morning? Because then they'd have nothing to do in the afternoon!

[21] Before the credit crisis, it was not unusual for a hedge fund manager to respond to questioning about their investment strategy with 'I do what I do'. One positive outcome of the crisis is that hedge fund managers, in seeking to attract investment from long-term institutional investors such as pension funds, have become more open about their investment processes.

Illiquidity

One of the main criticisms aimed at alternative asset classes is that they are illiquid. Hedge funds often tie in their investors for one or two years and after that period, allow only quarterly redemptions, with a calendar quarter's warning. Private equity investment is essentially locked up for the term of the fund; ten years would be typical. It is also difficult to disinvest from infrastructure projects or from property related assets.

Trustees naturally fear having their assets tied up in asset classes that cannot be converted easily into cash to pay benefits. However, there is an emerging consensus that trustees should establish an 'illiquidity budget'; that proportion of their assets that they believe they can afford to have tied up for a significant length of time. For schemes that are very cash flow negative, this proportion might be very low indeed, but for less constrained schemes, the proportion could be relatively large.

Why have an 'illiquidity budget' at all? Why bother with such illiquid assets? The reason why investors should consider illiquid assets – particularly investors with a long-investment horizon – is the prospect of earning an 'illiquidity premium'. Arguably at least some of the success of the Yale University endowment over the past two decades has been due to their willingness to invest in illiquid assets that other investors have either shunned or to which they have not been able to gain access. The weaker demand for illiquid asset classes means that they can be purchased at a lower price than otherwise would be the case, by those who can absorb the illiquidity.

As long-term investors, pension funds should not fear illiquidity, rather they should embrace it.

Fees

We have already highlighted the issue of fees with regard to both hedge funds and private equity funds. Indeed, hedge funds have been described as a *'remuneration package dressed up as an investment vehicle'*. The same accusation could be aimed at private equity funds too. In the end investors have to weigh up the likely net return from investing in alternative asset classes, consider how the returns that are expected to be generated will correlate with the other asset classes in the portfolio, and then weigh up the costs against the potential benefits. Though fees might be negotiable, the best hedge fund and private equity managers for example, are less likely to be prepared to negotiate whereas the less able, or desperate ones might!

Due diligence

The novelty and complexity of some alternative investment asset classes means that trustees and other investors new to this area often need to go through a training programme to introduce them to the characteristics of hedge funds, to the nuances of currency trading or to the economics of commodities. Indeed many investment advisory firms have had to put their own staff through such training over the past few years, given their lack of expertise in these investments too. Without a background in this area or adequate training, the due diligence and monitoring of alternative asset class investments can take up a disproportionate amount of trustee governance – disproportionate that is, because typically trustees commit only limited amounts of time to new investment opportunities initially.

Of course, the monitoring of such investments, and also the process of choosing appropriate investment vehicles and managers in the first place, can be sub-contracted to specialist firms, with appropriate input from the scheme's investment consultant. But ultimately there is no way around the impact on the governance budget. Integrating alternative asset classes will increase the time needed to monitor and oversee the investment portfolio. This has to be budgeted for in terms of both time and money.

Summary

The list of 'headaches' detailed above do not apply to all alternatives, but there is no doubt that alternatives do bring about additional problems for trustees. We have tried to summarize which alternative asset classes suffer from each issue in Exhibit 13.21. This is not meant to be the definitive word on alternative asset class characteristics, but it might be helpful as a guide.

Exhibit 13.21   Alternative investment headaches

Asset Class	Headache			
	Is historic return data limited?	Is return generation opaque?	Are the investments Illiquid?	Will the fees make your eyes water?
Hedge funds	Yes	Usually	Yes	Yes
Private equity	Yes	Yes	Yes, very	Yes
Commodity futures funds	Yes	No, but it is complex	No	No
Foreign exchange funds	Yes	The source of alpha is opaque	No	No
Infrastructure	No	No	Yes	Possibly
Emerging market debt	A little	No	No	No

Key points

- The Yale University Endowment Fund is held up as a shining example of the potential benefits of diversifying investment portfolios away from traditional asset classes and into alternative asset classes, having implemented a highly diversified approach to investing over 20 years ago.
- Hedge funds are not only difficult to define and categorize, given the wide and disparate range of strategies offered, but given the low correlation between and within the attempted categorization of strategies means that hedge funds are a skill set rather than an asset class. The analysis of hedge fund performance is complicated by the various biases within the returns data.
- Private equity principally comprises venture capital and buyout funds. While the latter typically outperform the former, the performance of buyout funds is highly dependent on the year in which the fund was launched, how long the fund has been established and its past performance, given that returns are positively skewed towards top performing funds, and performance persistency exists at both ends of the performance spectrum.
- Commodities are typically accessed by investors via commodity futures funds, in order to avoid the storage and insurance costs associated with investing in physical commodities. However, the performance of commodity futures rarely resemble the performance of the underlying commodities, upon which they are based, and are highly dependent on the shape of the futures curve.
- The foreign exchange market is the world's largest and one of the most liquid and transparent. Although as a zero sum game with no defined risk premium, active currency management should have an expected return of zero.
- A combination of inadequate historical return data, opacity and illiquidity, along with the importance of strategy and manager selection make the due diligence and monitoring requirements of investing in alternative asset classes particularly onerous. For hedge funds and private equity, the fee structure is also a major consideration.

Chapter 14

Portfolio Management: Analyzing and Generating Returns

Learning outcomes

- Understand the methodology behind and differences between money-weighted and time-weighted rates of return.
- Know the methods by which equity indices are constructed and the shortcomings of each method.
- Know the characteristics of an effective benchmark.
- Know how to decompose fund manager performance and better understand the sources of portfolio performance.
- Understand the methodologies that underpin the process of performance evaluation.
- Appreciate the advantages and limitations of both active and passive fund management.

Introduction

In Chapters 5 to 8 we looked at the risk and return characteristics of the 'traditional' asset classes that are available for investment, and in Chapter 13 we introduced and discussed the risk and return characteristics of some less traditional, or alternative, asset classes. Taken together, and often combined with some of the derivatives discussed in Chapters 11 and 12, today these asset classes comprise the vast majority of the holdings of most pension funds.

In the past, it was not uncommon for pension schemes to manage their own investment portfolios – a small number still do. However, today most pension schemes outsource the management of these assets to a specialist fund manager. Equally, as we noted in Chapter 3, in the past it was not uncommon for a single fund management company to manage all of the assets of a scheme, that is, its cash, bond and equity assets in a 'balanced fund'. However, today it is much more common to appoint specialist managers for each asset class, indeed for larger schemes it is very common to have each asset class managed by multiple managers, where each individual manager is responsible for managing a portion of a scheme's equity assets for example. Multiple managers may be appointed to spread 'manager risk'. Because most pension fund assets are now managed by third party fund managers, trustees need to be able to monitor the performance of these managers.

We will begin this chapter by introducing the topic of performance evaluation, that is, the methodology, tools and techniques that are used to assess the performance of fund managers. We will then move on to focus on active fund management, where we will examine the evidence that active fund managers can add value to investment portfolios. We will then examine passive investment management techniques, before concluding the chapter with a discussion of how active and passive fund management techniques can be combined.

Performance evaluation

Investors are naturally keen to know the performance of the funds that they have entrusted to an investment management company. However, knowing the return achieved is only part of the process of performance evaluation. Investors will also want to know how their particular fund manager has performed relative to both an independent benchmark and against their peers. They will also want to know how the fund manager achieved the performance and also what risks were taken to achieve the returns. Once the investment manager's clients have all of this information they can determine whether they wish:

- the manager to pursue a different strategy,
- to change the fund manager's performance target, or
- most importantly, whether they wish to continue with a manager.

Exhibit 14.1 is a stylized representation of the performance evaluation process, which begins with the measurement of absolute return, then the assessment of relative return, followed by an attribution of the returns achieved, and finally involves an assessment of the risks assumed in generating the returns.

Exhibit 14.1   The process of performance evaluation

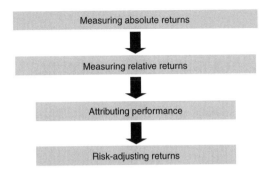

Measuring absolute returns

Calculating the return on a managed fund might seem like a simple enough task. For example, suppose that a fund manager is entrusted with the management of a portfolio of UK equities valued at £100m at the start of a year. At the end of the year the fund's value has risen to £110m. We can calculate the change in the value of this portfolio as follows:

$$R = \left(\frac{MV_1 - MV_0}{MV_0} \right) = \left(\frac{£110m - £100m}{£100m} \right) \times 100\% = 10\%$$

where MV_0 represents the initial value of the fund and MV_1 represents the end of year value of the fund. The percentage change in the value of this fund is 10 per cent. But does this really represent the return achieved by the fund manager? 10 per cent would represent the fund manager's absolute performance, as long as there were no in- or outflows of cash during the course of the year. However, fund in- and outflows are inevitable and can arise from a number of sources including:

- dividend payments,
- coupon payments,
- client withdrawals, and
- client deposits.

Let us suppose that the equity fund received an additional inflow of client money of £5m at the end of the first half of the year. This means that part of the growth in the fund over this period had nothing to do with the fund manager's abilities. It also means that we need to calculate fund returns in such a way that allows for the in- and outflows that occur over the fund's lifetime.

Two of the most common methods involve the calculation of a money-weighted rate of return (MWRR), or the calculation of a time-weighted rate of return (TWRR).

Money-weighted rate of return (MWRR)

The MWRR calculation is an *internal rate of return*. This means that all monies in the fund are assumed to have grown at the same rate, although account is taken of the size and timing of each cash flow. The formula for the MWRR is as follows:

$$MV_0(1+r) + \sum_{t=0}^{1} C_t(1+r \times t) = MV_1$$

where MV_0 and MV_1 again represent the initial and end year values of the fund respectively; C represents either a deposit or withdrawal; t represents the proportion of the time period over which C has been invested; and r is the MWRR. If we return to our simple example, if there are no fund in- or outflows, and the fund begins the year with a value of £100m and ends the year with a value of £110m then the MWRR, r, clearly equals 0.1, or 10 per cent

$$MV_0 (1 + r) = MV_1$$
$$£100m(1 + 0.1) = £110m$$

The complicated looking expression involving the cash flows, C, simply takes account of the size of the cash flow and then applies a rate of return to this cash flow, but only for the period that the cash is managed by the fund manager. So for example, if the money is received halfway through the year, 0.5 of the year remains, and the money therefore earns the return r, for half of the year only, so t = 0.5.

We can show how the formula works by revisiting the return on the same fund, but now assuming that the fund manager receives the cash inflow of £5m half way through the year. The calculation of the MWRR now looks like this:

$$MV_0 (1 + r) + C_t \times (1 + r \times t) = MV_1$$
$$£100m(1 + r) + £5m(1 + r \times 0.5) = £110m$$
$$MWRR = r = 4.88\%$$

The manager achieves a rate of return of r on £100m over the full year, but the rate of return of r on the £5m deposit for just half a year.

The first thing to notice is that the fund manager's return is significantly less than the 10 per cent that we calculated without taking into account the £5m inflow. This expression can be augmented to allow for withdrawals, that is, allowing for negative values for C, and for multiple cash in- and outflows, as long as we know when the cash flows occur, so that we know the period over which the manager managed the funds.

However, although this is a relatively simple calculation, the assumption that all monies grow at the same rate of return throughout the measurement period is unreasonable, especially as the measurement period increases. According to the MWRR calculation above, the manager achieved a return of 4.88 per cent on £100m for one year, and a return of 4.88 per cent on £5m for half a year. In reality the fund manager is very unlikely to achieve the same return throughout the entire period.

As a result of the deficiencies of the MWRR calculation, most organizations now calculate a time-weighted rate of return (TWRR).

Time-weighted rate of return (TWRR)

The TWRR calculation divides the overall measurement period, for example one year, into sub-periods, representing one month, week, or day of that year. Each sub-period is allowed to have a separate rate of return. These sub-period returns are then used to calculate the return for the whole period under consideration. The timing of each individual cash flow is identified and then associated with the sub-period in which it occurs.

The expression needed to calculate a TWRR is as follows:

$$r = \left[\frac{MV_{t1}}{MV_0} \times \frac{MV_{t2}}{MV_{t1} + C_{t1}} \times \cdots \times \frac{MV_1}{MV_{tn} + C_{tn}} \right] - 1$$

where MV_0 and MV_1 again represent the initial and end year values of the fund respectively; MV_{t1} represents the value of the fund at the end of the first sub-period, MV_{t2} represents the value of the fund at the end of sub-period two and so on; and C_{t1} represents either a deposit or withdrawal at the end of sub-period one, C_{t2} represents a fund deposit or withdrawal at the end of sub-period two and so on; n represents the number of sub-periods, 12 if monthly, 52 if weekly etc.; and r represents the TWRR on the fund.

We can use this formula to calculate the return achieved by the fund manager who receives the £5m cash inflow halfway through the year, but to do this we need another crucial piece of information: the value of the fund just before the £5m was received. Let us assume that at the end of the first half of the year, immediately before the £5m inflow, that the fund has a market value of £95m.

With this additional piece of information we can calculate the TWRR of this fund as follows:

$$r = \left[\frac{MV_{t1}}{MV_0} \times \frac{MV_1}{MV_{t2}} \right] - 1$$

$$r = \left[\frac{£95m}{£100m} \times \frac{£110m}{£100m} \right] - 1$$

$$r = 0.045 \text{ or } 4.50\%$$

In this case we have split the one year period up into two, since the £5m inflow occurs after the first six months of this period. We know that the fund had a value of £100m (MV_0) at the start; had a value of £110m (MV_1) at the end of the year; had a value of £95m (MV_{t1}) at the end of the first half of the year; and a value of £100m (MV_{t2} = £95m + £5m) at the start of the second half of the year. When we plug these values into the formula we find that the fund return was 4.50 per cent.

We can see from the TWRR formula that the return achieved over the two halves of the year was very different. The fund manager managed to turn £100m at the start of the year into £95m over the next six months, but, over the second six month period they managed to turn £100m into £110m. Taken together the performance was 4.50 per cent.

TWRR versus MWRR

In our example the TWRR was 0.38 per cent lower than the return calculated for the same fund using the MWRR technique. The problem with the MWRR technique is that it assumes that the same return was achieved on all funds under management throughout the entire period. This is very unlikely to be the case. As the timing of the cash in or outflow can influence the return, most performance measurement (though not all) uses the TWRR method of calculation.

Measuring relative returns

Once returns have been calculated, the fund's investors will wish to know how the fund manager has performed relative to a financial market benchmark, such as the FTSE 100 index. It is very common practice in all industries and, indeed, in many walks of life to benchmark performance. By using benchmarks we can assess the quality and/or quantity of a company's output by comparing this output to that of its peers and competitors. The output of the fund management industry that we wish to assess is the returns that they generate from our investments.

We will deal with the issue of active versus passive fund management shortly, but we should emphasize that passive fund managers always require a defined benchmark, while nearly all active fund managers manage their funds relative to a benchmark too.[1] Basically a passive fund manager manages their fund so that it replicates the performance of a financial market index. On the other hand an active fund manager manages their fund in order to outperform a financial market index, or some other benchmark.

To be effective a financial market benchmark should meet certain criteria, namely:

- *Investable*: the benchmark should comprise assets that can be bought and sold by the fund manager. For a passive fund manager the presence of assets that could not be bought would, of course, make the process of forming a portfolio to track the benchmark passively extremely difficult, if not impossible. For an active fund manager with a target to outperform the benchmark by a certain pre-determined amount, the inability to hold some of the benchmark's assets would make this task very difficult. As we'll see in Chapter 18, the better active managers are more 'benchmark aware' than 'benchmark constrained' in that they seek to outperform their benchmark by taking 'off-benchmark positions' in securities not represented in the benchmark. Moreover, the issue of investability is not as straightforward as it may seem. For example, not all of the shares issued by a publicly traded company are freely available for trading. As a result of this, many of the index providers now produce *free float* indices to take account of the proportion of a constituent's shares that are freely floating and which are therefore available for the manager to buy.
- *Compatibility*: a pension scheme may not wish to invest in assets that embody credit, or default, risk and may be willing to accept a relatively low return on its assets, perhaps as part of their strategy to fund the payments to current pensioners. In this case, a UK government bond benchmark might be most compatible with their preferences. A benchmark that comprised emerging market equities would not be so compatible.
- *Clarity*: the rules governing the construction of the benchmark, for example, those rules relating to the weighting of individual index constituents and the method used to calculate index returns should be clear and unambiguous.

---

[1] As we saw in Chapter 13, hedge fund managers do not manage their funds according to a financial market benchmark.

This clarity should also extend to the process used for additions to and withdrawals from the index.

- *Pre-specification*: the benchmark should be specified in advance of any mandate, so that the manager is clear about the objectives of their clients and so that they can construct the portfolio that is most appropriate for these objectives. You would be amazed at how many fund managers try to change the definition of their benchmark over time, to make their own performance relative to the benchmark look better than it really is. Perhaps you're not amazed, but either way, trustees should resist 'benchmark creep' when the fund manager tries it on.

Many organizations produce financial market indices that meet the criterion necessary to allow trustees and other investors to compare the absolute performance produced by their fund manager with that generated by the wider market. We will now review some common indices and then some of the issues relating to their construction.

Equity indices

The main UK equity indices are constructed and provided by FTSE International. The FTSE 100 comprises the 100 largest stocks quoted on the London Stock Exchange (LSE); the FTSE 250 comprises the next 250 largest LSE companies; the FTSE 350 comprises the FTSE 100 and the FTSE 250; and the FTSE-Small Cap index consists of stocks quoted on the LSE but which are not large enough to be included in the FTSE 350. Finally, the FTSE All Share index comprises the FTSE 100, FTSE 250 and the FTSE Small Cap indices and accounts for the vast majority of all stocks quoted on the LSE by market value. The composition of each FTSE index is shown in Exhibit 14.2. The FTSE 100 makes up around 80 per cent of the FTSE All Share. Those stocks that do not meet the All Share's criteria make up a further index called the FTSE Fledgling index.

In addition to being able to monitor broad equity market trends using these indices, equity indices are also available along industrial classification lines,

Exhibit 14.2 Composition of FTSE Indices

Index	Constituents	% of FTSE All Share
FTSE 100	100 largest LSE listed companies	80.0
FTSE 250	The next largest 250 LSE listed companies	15.0
FTSE 350	FTSE 100 plus FTSE 250	95.0
FTSE SmallCap	FTSE All Share minus FTSE 350	5.0
FTSE All Share	FTSE 350 plus FTSE SmallCap	100.0
FTSE Fledgling	Stocks that do not meet the size criteria for FTSE All Share	1.5

both within a particular country and globally. This makes it possible, for instance, for investors to compare the performance of global IT stocks with the performance of UK IT stocks.

Bond indices

Many leading investment banks, such as Goldman Sachs and Barclays Capital, produce bond indices for developed economy government, corporate and emerging economy bond markets. Traditionally the main index providers for the UK's bond market had been the FTSE organization. However, the increase in size and popularity over the last ten years of the Eurobond market has led to a demand for a wider range of indices for this market. A relatively new organization, IBOXX, is now the industry standard provider of Eurobond indices. In addition, IBOXX also constructs a wide range of indices on government bond markets too. Finally, as well as aggregate bond indices that are designed to cover the market as a whole, bond indices are also available according to maturity, credit rating, currency and industrial category.

Other indices

As well as producing bond and equity indices, index providers like FTSE International, Standard and Poor's (S&P), MSCI, and many others, produce indices for virtually every asset class, including cash, currencies, commercial property, hedge funds, private equity, commodities amongst others.

Peer group benchmarks

Despite the widespread availability of indices covering virtually every conceivable sector and aspect of the world's financial markets, some investors prefer to compare their fund managers not against objective benchmarks constructed by organizations like FTSE International, but instead to their fund manager's peers. That is, comparing the performance of one manager of UK equities with other managers of UK equities. Each manager is then assigned a performance ranking within their particular sector of the financial markets.

The performance of individual fund managers are collected and then ranked by independent organizations like the WM Company, who then publish these results, thus allowing investors to see the rankings of their particular fund manager, relative to other managers that they could have chosen!

Index weightings and return averaging

One of the important decisions that an index provider has to make is which weights they should apply to the individual components of the index. This is true whether they are constructing equity, bond, or commodity indices.

To illustrate the choices available and the consequences for the indices themselves, we can consider three different approaches that have been applied to some of the world's best known equity indices, namely:

- *Price weighting*: both the Dow Jones Industrial Average Index of large US equities and the Japanese Nikkei 225 weight their individual components by stock market price. This means that a stock with a price of say US$100 will have a greater influence on the index than one with a stock price of US$1, regardless of whether the latter company has a larger market capitalization, or stock market value, than the former.
- *Equal weighting*: an alternative to price-weighting an index is to apply an equal weighting to all the stocks in the index. The FT30, which used to have a very high media profile and which comprises 30 of the largest stocks listed on the London Stock Exchange, applies an equal weighting to these stocks.
- *Market capitalization weighting*: most of the capital market indices created in recent years have been weighted according to the market capitalization of the constituents. With regard to equity indices, it is the largest companies that have the greatest influence over the index. The FTSE 100 and the S&P 500 Composite index, which comprises the 500 largest stocks listed on the New York Stock Exchange (NYSE), are both market value, or market capitalization-weighted, indices. With regard to bond indices, the weights are usually determined by the size of the issued debt, so the larger the market value of a company's debt, the greater will be its weighting in the index – a point we will return to at the end of this chapter.

In addition to there being a number of ways of choosing the constituent weights, there are also two methods that can be used to average returns to calculate the changes in the index. Some indices like the FTSE 100 index use arithmetic averaging to calculate index changes, while others like the FT 30 are constructed using geometric averaging.

Suppose we have an index that comprises three stocks. An arithmetic average of the returns over that period could be calculated as follows:

$$\text{Index return} = \frac{r_1 + r_2 + r_3}{3}$$

where r_1, r_2 and r_3 are the returns on the three assets over the period in question. By dividing the sum of these returns by the number of stocks, the arithmetic average is achieved to give the index return. A geometric average return can be calculated as follows:

$$\text{Index return} = [(1 + r_1) \times (1 + r_2) \times (1 + r_3)]^{1/3} - 1$$

In this case the returns are multiplied together and then raised to the power of 'one over the number of observations' which in this case is again three. Also note that we have effectively assumed that the weights on the returns of each stock in the index are equal.

But the choice of weighting and the method used to average returns can have a big influence on the way that the index reflects the underlying performance of the constituents. We can illustrate this with a very simple example.

In Exhibit 14.3 we present the prices of three shares that make up an index. At the start of the period the price of all three stocks is 100p. However, the largest stock is stock A because it has 800 shares outstanding compared with only the 100 shares outstanding for stocks B and C. This means that in market capitalization terms, stock A makes up 80 per cent of this particular market while the other two stocks only each account for 10 per cent. However, in price weighted terms they have equal weights.

Now suppose that stock B's share price falls to zero because the company goes into liquidation, but the share price of stocks A and B are unchanged over the same period. The impact that this change has on three different indices is shown in Exhibit 14.4.

The value of an arithmetic, price weighted index would fall to 66.67 since one-third of the index had disappeared over that period. The price of an equally

Exhibit 14.3   Index construction example

	Stock		
	A	B	C
Initial price	100	100	100
Number of shares	800	100	100
Market weight	80%	10%	10%
Price weight	33%	33%	33%

Exhibit 14.4   Impact of price change on indices

Period	Stock			Index		
	A	B	C	Price Arithmetic (e.g., DJIA)	Equal Geometric (e.g., FT 30)	Market cap Arithmetic (e.g., FTSE 100)
t0	100	100	100	100	100	100
t1	100	0	100	66.67	0	90

weighted geometric index would fall to zero. This is because the returns are multiplied together using their weights, and since the weight of stock B in the index falls to zero, multiplying through this expression by zero results in a new index value of zero. However, the value of the market capitalization-weighted arithmetic return index, like the FTSE 100, falls by 10 per cent, since stock B is now worthless and it made up 10 per cent of the original index. Therefore the change in the value of the market capitalization-weighted index accurately reflects the percentage change in the market value of a portfolio consisting of 80 per cent in stock A and 10 per cent in both stocks B and C over this period. It is for this reason that many investors prefer to benchmark their own portfolios to market capitalization-weighted indices.

Performance attribution

By comparing the performance, for example, of a UK equity fund manager with the performance of an appropriate UK equity index, the fund manager's clients can gain an idea of how well the fund manager is performing relative to the market in general. So benchmarks form the basis of *performance measurement*.

Additionally benchmarks can be used to delve further into the DNA of the fund manager's performance. By using appropriate financial market indices the fund manager's performance can be decomposed to reveal where the performance did or did not come from. Depending upon the nature of the fund, the performance itself might come from asset allocation, sector selection, stock selection, or currency exposure. The performance of a bond fund might in addition be broken down into decisions regarding duration and those concerning the yield curve.

Knowing where the fund manager's performance was derived from is useful information for the clients of the fund and for the investment management company too. For example, if a fund manager is good at stock selection, but less proficient with sector selection, another fund manager may be asked to advise on the sector selection aspect of the portfolio, allowing the original fund manager to concentrate on stock selection.

Performance attribution example

To show how performance attribution works, consider a fund manager that has just won a defined benefit (DB) pension mandate to manage £100m. The mandate makes it clear to the manager that the benchmark for these funds comprises three financial market indices: the FTSE 100, the S&P 500 and the Nikkei 225 indices. The mandate also specifies that the performance of the benchmark will equal 60 per cent of the performance of the FTSE 100, 30 per cent of the S&P 500 and 10 per cent of the performance of the Nikkei 225.

$$\text{Benchmark composition} = (60\% \times \text{FTSE } 100) + (30\% \times \text{S\&P } 500)$$
$$+ (10\% \times \text{Nikkei } 225)$$

The fund manager is asked to outperform this particular benchmark by 1 per cent per annum.

Over the course of the year the three financial indices produce the returns shown in Exhibit 14.5. Over the full year the benchmark generated a return of 14 per cent, which comprised a relatively even return of 6.6 per cent in the first half of the year and 7.4 per cent in the second half. However, the components of the benchmark produced a more volatile return over these two periods, particularly the Japanese index which was up 15 per cent over the first half of the year, but down 10 per cent over the second half.

Over the full year the fund manager achieved a return of 15 per cent, meaning they satisfied the mandate since it required a performance of 'benchmark + 1%'.

Where did this performance come from? To understand this we need more information about the fund manager's decisions throughout the year. We need to know the proportions of the funds that the manager allocated to UK, US and Japanese equities over the course of the year.

In Exhibit 14.6 we have presented this fund manager's broad allocation between the three markets. In this case the fund manager held the equities in 'benchmark proportions' for the first half of the year.

Exhibit 14.5   Index and benchmark performances over year

Index	Weight (%)	Returns		
		1st 6 months (%)	2nd 6 months (%)	Full Year (%)
FTSE 100	60	6.0	10.0	16.0
S&P 500	30	5.0	8.0	13.0
Nikkei 225	10	15.0	−10.0	5.0
Benchmark	100	6.6	7.4	14.0

Exhibit 14.6   Fund manager asset allocation decision

	Fund allocations	
	1st 6 months (%)	2nd 6 months (%)
UK equities	60	50
US equities	30	20
Japanese equities	10	30
	100	100

However, at the beginning of the second-half of the year, the fund manager reduced the proportion of both UK and US equities by 10 percentage points each and increased the holding of Japanese equities by 20 percentage points.

We can calculate the return that the fund manager would have achieved by adopting these revised equity weightings, by using the returns achieved by the indices; in other words assuming that the fund manager had passive holdings in each of the equity markets. In the first half of the year the fund would have achieved the following return:

$$\text{Return in 1st 6 months} = (60\% \times \text{FTSE 100}) + (30\% \times \text{S\&P 500})$$
$$+ (10\% \times \text{Nikkei 225})$$
$$\text{Return in 1st 6 months} = (60\% \times 6\%) + (30\% \times 5\%) + (10\% \times 15\%) = 6.60\%$$

In the second half of the year the fund would have achieved the following return:

$$\text{Return in 2nd 6 months} = (50\% \times \text{FTSE 100}) + (20\% \times \text{S\&P 500})$$
$$+ (30\% \times \text{Nikkei 225})$$
$$\text{Return in 2nd 6 months} = (50\% \times 10\%) + (20\% \times 8\%)$$
$$+ (30\% \times -10\%) = 3.60\%$$

Giving a grand total of approximately 10.2 per cent for the full year.

However, the fund manager achieved a return of 15 per cent, which means that 4.8 per cent of the return came from a source that was not due to the broad asset allocation decisions that the fund manager made. In fact, had the manager held the equity funds passively, but in line with the benchmark proportions they would have achieved a return of 14 per cent over the year. This means that the fund manager's asset allocation decisions 'cost' the fund 3.8 per cent. This is easy to see from the decision to switch 10 per cent out of UK and US equities into Japanese equities, just after the Japanese market had risen by 15 per cent over the previous six months and just before it fell by 10 per cent over the following six months.

We can use the performance of the indices along with the fund manager's broad allocations and actual performance to attribute the performance of the fund manager over the two halves of the year. This attribution analysis is shown in Exhibit 14.7. In the last column of Exhibit 14.7 in Panel A, the fund manager achieved a return of 15 per cent, the benchmark produced a return of 14 per cent, but the return on the indices invested passively in accordance with the fund manager's asset allocation produced a return of only 10.2 per cent. In the final column of Panel B we can break down this performance for the year. The fund manager's asset allocation decision would have led to underperformance

Exhibit 14.7   Attribution analysis

	Returns		
	1st 6 months (%)	2nd 6 months (%)	Full Year (%)
		Panel A	
Fund return	**10.00**	**5.00**	15.00
Benchmark return	6.60	7.40	14.00
Manager allocation return	6.60	3.60	10.20
		Panel B	
Return difference			
Asset allocation	0.00	−3.80	−3.80
Stock selection	3.40	1.40	4.80
Total under/over performance	3.40	−2.40	1.00

of 3.8 per cent, but the fund manager's actual performance suggests that they added value to the fund over and above the asset allocation decision by 4.8 per cent over the year.

We can break down the performance over the two halves of the year too. The relevant figures for the first half of the year are in column one of Exhibit 14.7. The fund returned 10 per cent in the first six months of the year, compared to an increase in the benchmark of 6.6 per cent. Since the fund manager held the fund in benchmark proportions over this period, the additional return of 3.40 per cent (10% – 6.6%) probably came from sound stock selection.

Over the second half of the year the fund returned 5 per cent, while the benchmark increased by 7.40 per cent. However, funds held passively in the asset allocation proportions chosen by the manager returned just 3.60 per cent (due to the fall in the Japanese stock market). This means that the manager's asset allocation decision cost the fund 3.80 per cent in the second half of the year, but because overall the fund underperformed the benchmark by 2.40 per cent this means that the manager added 1.40 per cent to the fund, probably in the form of stock selection.

This analysis allows us to see that the fund manager's asset allocation decisions added no value to the fund in the first half of the year, and reduced the value of the fund relative to the benchmark in the second half of the year. By contrast, the manager's stock selection added value to the fund in both periods of the year, although more value was added in the first period.

Further attribution analysis

In the example above we have assumed that the return not due to the manager's asset allocation decision was instead attributable to stock selection. However, since this is a portfolio of international equities the additional return may have been due to changes in exchange rates over the period. With a more detailed attribution analysis we could, for example, have revealed how much of the performance was due to exchange rate movements, or how much of the performance on the Japanese fund was due to sector selection.

Modern performance attribution software gives fund management companies the requisite tools to examine the detail of a fund to reveal all of this performance information. In doing so, the company may conclude that a particular fund manager is very good at stock selection but very bad at sector selection. Given this information they might ask another manager with better sector selection skills to make sector related decisions, allowing the original manager to continue to pick stocks and therefore to continue to add value.

Risk-adjusting returns

Benchmarks can be used to monitor relative performance and can also be used to identify the sources of a fund manager's outperformance or underperformance. Another way of comparing the performance of fund managers and understanding the source of portfolio performance involves the risk-adjustment of returns. We discussed the following, most commonly used measures of risk-adjusted performance in Chapter 9:

- the Sharpe ratio;
- the Treynor ratio;
- the Jensen measure of performance (based upon alpha); and
- the information ratio.

Usually in analyzing the risk-adjusted performance of a fund manager, investment advisers will typically look at more than one measure. Each measure can tell us something different about the performance of the fund manager. To illustrate this point, consider the following example.

Two fund managers, let's call them Bill and Ted, each manage a portfolio of UK equities, and are both benchmarked against the FTSE All Share index. Over one year, when the risk-free rate was 4 per cent, the funds managed by Bill and Ted produce the performance statistics shown in Exhibit 14.8.

Exhibit 14.8   Bill and Ted's performance

	Bill	Ted
Performance	10%	10%
Standard deviation	8%	6%
Sharpe Ratio	0.75	1.00
Beta	1.0	1.2
Treynor ratio	0.06	0.05

Both managers produce a return of 10 per cent over the year. In this respect then their performances are identical and an investor may view them as equally skilful. However, Bill produced this performance with higher volatility (standard deviation). In which case, Bill's Sharpe ratio is lower than that of Ted's. In this regard Ted is the superior performer. However, the betas on their funds were not identical either – Bill achieved his return with a lower beta. Given this, the Treynor ratio indicates that Bill is the superior performer since he managed to produce the highest Treynor ratio.

First, what explains the difference? Bill's fund had a lower beta but a higher standard deviation. This indicates that Bill took more stock specific risk and probably more off-benchmark bets than Ted and that more of his performance came from stock picking compared with Ted's performance. Ted's fund, with the higher beta, was probably more exposed to a general rise in the market than was Bill's fund. So which one performed best? The answer is that it depends on what investors were expecting: a good stock picker (Bill) or someone that can judge the mood of the overall market better (Ted).

Performance evaluation summary

Performance evaluation is an essential part of the fund management process. We need to understand what performance the fund manager has produced and how. By having a robust evaluation process we can make sure that the fund managers are delivering on their promises. We can also use the same information to choose new fund managers too, though this will be the main topic of Chapter 18.

Active fund management

As we discuss in more detail later in the chapter and in Chapter 17, the basic premise of active fund management is that markets are not efficient. That is, securities are not correctly priced, at least not all of the time. Active managers seek to exploit these inefficiencies to outperform the market by taking 'active bets'. That is, by assuming positions in stocks that are different to their weight within an index or in those stocks not represented at all within an index. The latter, as we noted earlier, are known as off-benchmark bets. The extent to which the active manager's portfolio differs from any index to which they are benchmarked is known as the manager's *active risk*. This is typically measured, or quantified, by what fund managers refer to as 'tracking error'.[2] You may

---

[2] For a passive fund manager, tracking error is simply the difference between the return on the portfolio and the return on the tracked index.

recall from Chapter 6 that the term 'tracking error' has two meanings. For an active fund manager, tracking error can be expressed as follows:

$$\text{Active fund manager tracking error} = \sigma(R_P - R_B)$$

For the eagle-eyed among you, this definition of tracking error is the denominator (the bottom half) of the formula for the information ratio that we met in Chapter 9. It is the standard deviation (σ) of the return difference (R_P–R_B) between the manager's portfolio and their benchmark. It is usually expressed as an annual percentage. Many active fund managers will try to target this value – that is, to keep the deviation in their portfolio returns within a certain range of the return on their benchmark. The bigger the targeted value, the more allowance they have for deviating from their benchmark and the more active they are. For an investment grade corporate bond portfolio a typical targeted tracking error might be between 0.75 per cent and 1 per cent, while for equity portfolios tracking errors of 3 to 4 per cent are commonplace. However, a few 'truly active' or 'high conviction' equity fund managers target tracking errors as high as 6 to 8 per cent.

However, increasingly the fund manager's active risk is being measured by the manager's 'active share'. Active share is simply that percentage of the manager's portfolio that differs from the composition of the index that the manager seeks to outperform: 0 per cent being not at all and 100 per cent being totally different in all respects. Despite arguably being a much simpler measure of how active the manager is, few managers currently target this value though a number of investment consultants do.

To summarize, the higher the active share and the tracking error numbers, the more active the fund manager's investment style.[3]

So how do they do it?

Active managers seek to outperform the index against which their performance is assessed by constructing a portfolio that differs from the composition of their benchmark index. Active managers might adopt a process similar to the one illustrated in Exhibit 14.9.

The active investment process usually starts with the manager identifying the universe of assets that comprise the index, against which their performance is to be judged. They then proceed to choose from this universe those assets that best fit the characteristics of their preferred investment style and the requirements of their investors. They do this by screening out those assets that fail

---

[3] For more on fund manager investment styles see Chapters 7 and 18.

Exhibit 14.9 A stylized representation of a typical active management process

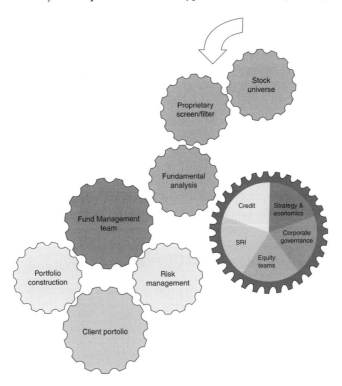

to meet a pre-defined range of criteria. Next, this narrower set of assets may then be subjected to proprietary, or in-house, qualitative or quantitative analysis in order to determine which of the securities should be included within the portfolio. This requires the manager to assess the valuation and prospects of each asset, which may involve meeting with the company's management, arranging site visits to the company's operations and crunching the numbers within the company's financial statements.

In some cases, the manager will also employ technical analysis – analyzing security price and trading volume charts – in order to get a better feel for where the security's price is heading. In larger asset manager organizations, the manager may also cross reference their investment views with those of their credit analysts (if they are constructing an equity portfolio), or their equity analysts (if they are constructing a corporate bond portfolio), corporate governance and sustainable and responsible investment teams, and with their economists and financial market strategists, who may all have assessed the company and the environment in which the company operates from a different angle. The manager will then often work with either their in-house risk management team or with risk management software in order to build a portfolio that fits with their fund's published outperformance target and other risk parameters.

It is important to note that this should be a dynamic, rather than a static process; some active fund managers turn over the composition of their portfolios by more than 100 per cent in a year. We look at the significance of portfolio turnover in Chapters 17 and 18. However, regardless of how active they are, all good active fund managers should have an investment process based upon a sound investment philosophy – encompassing some, if not all, of the elements represented in Exhibit 14.9 – that they should adhere to in their day-to-day work, and which they should be able to explain to trustee boards and other investors. We consider the importance of the manager's investment philosophy and process in Chapter 18.

Active fund manager performance

Selecting managers according to past performance figures first and brand second is widely acknowledged to be a poor way to select a manager.[4]

The key advantage of investing in actively managed portfolios is that they can be designed to meet the specific risk and return criteria, income targets and investment styles of their clients. Active fund managers should be able to profit from both prevailing and prospective market conditions and avoid the over-priced market favourites that periodically dominate the composition of many market capitalization-weighted indices (more on that later in the chapter). Moreover, they should be able to take advantage of diversification opportunities and can construct portfolios in a risk efficient manner, with the help of their in-house risk team or risk management software.

However, one of the biggest criticisms levelled at active fund managers is that many of them are just 'index huggers' – which sounds sweet enough since everyone likes a hug. However, investors should avoid index huggers if possible. Fund managers that index hug run portfolios that look very similar to the index against which their performance is judged, but charge the higher fees associated with actively managed funds.[5] By not assuming any meaningful tracking error and having a particularly low active share, they almost manage their portfolios

---

[4] P. Myners, *Report on Institutional Investments*, H.M. Treasury, London (2001).
[5] Those active fund managers that index hug seek safety in numbers just in case things go badly wrong. As John Maynard Keynes said: 'It is better to fail conventionally than to succeed unconventionally.'

on a passive basis, but charge active fees for the privilege. If ever there was a formula that was destined to underperform, this is it.

The main argument for truly active fund management then (rather than their index hugging imitators) is that active managers have the skills necessary to 'beat the market', that is, to beat relevant broad market indices and to outperform their peers. Of course there is a fundamental problem with this claim. The sum of all fund managers managing a particular asset class pretty much *is* the market, they cannot all outperform it. Similarly every fund manager cannot beat every other fund manager. On average then we might expect half of active fund managers to 'beat' the market and half to 'lose' to it. By definition half of the fund managers will beat the other half. Looked at like this then the grand active fund management game, for which many investors pay significant fees is a zero sum game . . . before fees. After fees it must, by definition, be a negative sum game for investors – though not for the fund management companies of course! This means that after fees we should expect more than half of all active fund managers to underperform the market.

If the main claim of active fund managers is that they can 'beat the market' and/or their peers, what is the evidence for this claim?

For many years now the academic literature has produced research paper after research paper dedicated to examining the performance of active fund managers, with the aim of understanding whether active fund managers have skill and whether they provide investors with value for money.[6] To illustrate the typical findings in these research papers we have constructed our own database of fund manager performance. Using the Morningstar database of fund performance we constructed a database of all those active UK managers that managed a portfolio of large-cap UK equities. To be included in the data set we required each fund to have ten full years of return data up until December 2010.[7] This gave us a sample of 97 funds in total. Exhibit 14.10 shows the proportion of funds that outperformed their benchmark over each full calendar year. As we can see, in most years far less than half of the 97 funds outperformed the FTSE All Share benchmark. The best year for this sample of managers was 2001. In total return terms, the UK equity market fell by just over 12 per cent in 2001, with 42 per cent of the fund managers in this sample performing worse than

---

[6] For a review of this vast literature see K. Cuthbertson, D. Nitzsche, and N. O'Sullivan (2008), 'UK mutual fund performance: Skill or luck?', *Journal of Empirical Finance*, 15(4), pp. 613–63. You will also see from reading this contribution that much of the research has been undertaken using data on the performance of equity funds.

[7] Our database therefore has some survivorship bias in it, that is, it will tend to include the relatively more successful funds. Less successful funds will close over time. Overall then, our performance statistics might be biased upwards.

Exhibit 14.10   Proportion of managers outperforming their benchmark each year

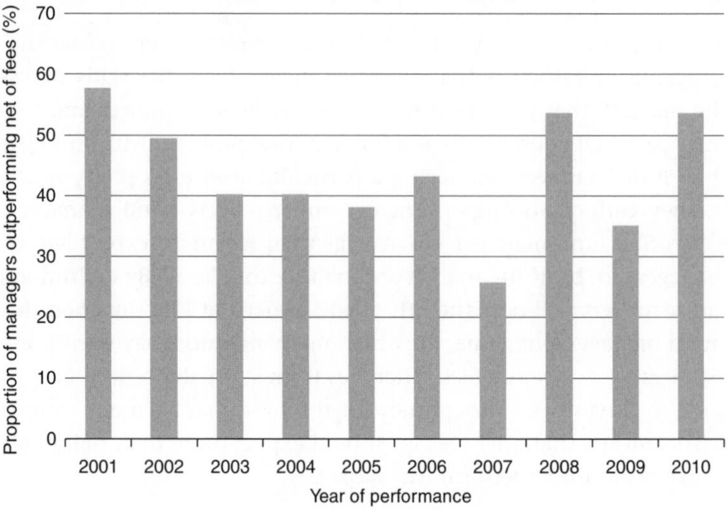

this. However, 2007 was the worst year for this sample of highly paid active managers as only 26 per cent of them outperformed the UK equity market that year.

The results presented in Exhibit 14.10 are fairly typical of the sorts of results documented in many research papers. Every year, after fees, usually less than half of fund managers outperform a relevant benchmark, which is what one would expect given that they are all playing a negative sum game. What is perhaps more surprising is that this figure can sometimes be substantially lower than 50 per cent as illustrated above by the performance of this set of funds in 2009 and in particular 2007.

Performance persistence

Of course outperforming a benchmark over a one year period is good – better than underperforming it anyway. However, we generally do not invest with fund managers for one year at a time. We generally invest with them with the view to having them manage our funds for many years. What we want then is a manager that, at a minimum, can outperform their benchmark every year. University researchers have addressed this issue too. Many papers focus on what the academic community call performance persistence, that is, the tendency for positive (or negative) performance to persist over time. The very consistent finding from this branch of the performance literature is that positive performance tends not to persist over time, but that negative performance does. In other words, choose a good fund manager with a good track record today and they may continue to outperform, at least for a short period for their investors. However, choose a fund manager with a bad performance track record and you are almost guaranteed to have invested in a fund that will continue to underperform. This puts another spin on the following phrase: 'past performance is no guarantee of future performance'.

The vast majority of academic evidence on performance persistence suggests instead that the following phrase might be more appropriate: 'past negative performance is an almost cast iron guarantee of future negative performance, while past positive performance probably won't lead to positive performance, but it might if you're lucky'.

Using the same sample of 97 funds we have tried to illustrate this issue of persistency. The results of our performance persistence experiment are shown in Exhibit 14.11. The bars in this exhibit labelled 'Outperforming next year', show the proportion of managers that outperform the market two years in a row. So the first bar shows that 40 per cent of the managers outperformed the market in 2001 and 2002 – remember from Exhibit 14.10 that 58 per cent outperformed the market in 2001. The next bar in this series shows the proportion of managers that outperformed the market in 2002 and 2003. This figure is only 23 per cent. The next set of bars, labelled 'Outperforming over three years', represents the proportion of managers that outperform the market three years

Exhibit 14.11   Performance persistence

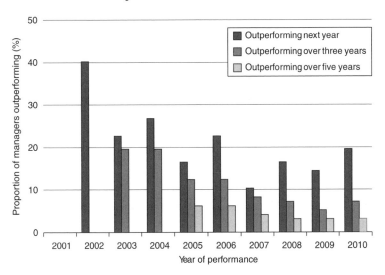

in a row. The first bar in this series shows that only 20 per cent of the managers in our sample outperformed in the years 2001, 2002 and 2003. Finally the last set of bars labelled 'Outperforming over five years' represents the performance of fund managers that outperform the market every year for five years. The first bar in this series shows that only 6 per cent of the managers in our sample outperformed in the years 2001, 2002, 2003, 2004 and 2005.

The clear message from Exhibit 14.11 is that fund managers find it very difficult to outperform the market on a consistent basis. Only a very small proportion of managers manage to outperform year after year. Again, the results shown in this exhibit are typical of others that have been found using different sample periods and performance data from different markets.

The search for alpha

Fund managers that outperform their benchmark in a year usually claim to 'have alpha' (though we have already seen above how ephemeral this outperformance can be). So, for example, of the sample of 97 funds analyzed for Exhibit 14.10 in 2010, 52 might have claimed to have 'produced alpha' for their clients. But beating the benchmark does not constitute the production of alpha.

First, alpha is the return achieved over and above the risk taken by the fund manager. A fund may well have outperformed its benchmark, but this outperformance may have been achieved by taking great risks. Alpha then, is a conditional concept. It is the excess performance conditional upon the risks taken. Recall from Chapter 9 the CAPM equation, shown below:

$$E(R_i) - R_f = \alpha_0 + \beta_i \times (E(R_m) - R_f)$$

While fund managers can outperform their benchmark by taking on more market risk, that is running a portfolio with a beta that is higher than one, within the framework of the CAPM, manager skill – alpha – is defined by the extent to which the fund manager's performance differs from the expected return which is risk-adjusted for the fund manager's beta.

To illustrate the difference between beating a benchmark, and then beating a benchmark adjusted for risk, take a look at Exhibit 14.12 where we present the distribution of monthly alphas, calculated using the formula above, using the last three years of data in our sample, that is, for years 2008, 2009 and 2010. Normally, for reasons that are too boring to go into here, we require at least three years of data to calculate alphas and betas. Over this period 45 per cent of the managers in our sample beat their benchmark – which is quite high. However, how many of them produced positive alpha? Exhibit 14.12 shows

Exhibit 14.12   Distribution of monthly alphas over 2008–2010

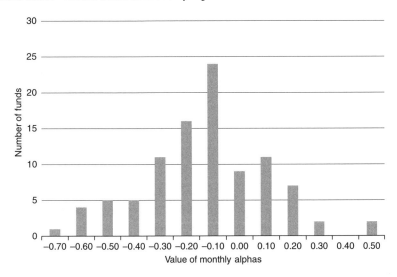

that only 22 of the 97 produced a positive alpha. In other words, after adjusting for risk most produced negative alpha, and only 22 added value to their portfolios after adjusting for the risks that they took on.

Again, the results presented in Exhibit 14.12 are typical of those that have been published in many academic papers over the years. The number of managers that produce alpha is considerably lower than the proportion that outperform a benchmark. There is another hurdle that fund managers must clear before academic researchers would be satisfied with a fund manager's claim that they had produced genuine alpha. We will return to this issue later, but it is conceivable that a manager might have produced alpha over a particular period,but maybe they had one or two months where they got lucky – biasing their returns and the measurement of their alpha upwards. Of course, it is better to have a lucky fund manager than an unlucky one, but it is surely better to have a genuinely talented one rather than a lucky one? When we apply the appropriate tests to each positive alpha produced by our sample of funds, we find that only four of the 22 had produced positive alpha on a regular, consistent enough basis over this three-year period for us to be able to declare that the alpha was produced through skill and not luck. This result should not surprise us, since Exhibit 14.11 showed us that only 7 per cent of managers beat the benchmark in 2008, 2009 and in 2010.

So from a sample of 97, over this three-year period we find that only four funds produced additional value for their investors, adjusting for the risks they took and accounting for the possible existence of luck. This is a very typical finding of academic studies of active fund manager performance.

Fund manager viewpoints

The following question was posed to Lucy Kellaway's *Financial Times* agony aunt column, which is aimed at giving much needed advice to the tortured souls of the finance industry. A particularly angst ridden fund manager asked:

> *I am a fund manager in the UK. My job is great: flexible and well paid. My problem is that I don't believe it's possible to outperform other fund managers with any consistency. I believe the industry is based on the lie that fund managers add value through skill, rather than luck – which makes it hard to keep motivated. Should I move – even though I can't think of anything else I want to do – or should I accept the idea that work is not meant to be meaningful?* (Fund manager, male, 34)

One reader replied:

> *Your question suggests you are a failure as a fund manager. As someone who has outperformed every year for 14 years, I know your statement is false. If you can't find a way of changing your investment approach . . . you should get out.* (Fund manager, male, 39)

While another offered an alternative solution:

> *I suggest you breed immediately. The increased financial pressure and the shortage of sleep will quickly assuage any regrets you have about lack of skill in your job* (Financier, male, 31)

Unfortunately we do not know whether the troubled manager took either piece of advice.

Source: The Lucy Kellaway Column, *Financial Times*, 3 April, p. 16 (2008).

Are the academic tests fair?

It is difficult to overstate how many academic papers over the past 40 years have concluded that genuine alpha is a very rare commodity indeed. In fact, what most of this impressive body of work finds is that locating managers with genuine positive alpha is hard, but identifying those with genuine negative alpha is relatively easy!

However, in defence of the active fund management industry, we believe that the results of this performance evaluation research are slightly biased towards not finding genuine, positive alpha. This is because the empirical tests are usually run using fund returns. Yet we know that fund managers move around a great deal. To see why this might affect the results of these tests, consider a fund that has been in existence for ten years. An academic researcher analyses the monthly returns produced by this fund and concludes that the alpha generated by the fund was zero. However, what the researcher does not know is that for the first five years the fund was managed by a manager that produced positive alpha of 1 per cent per year. This impressive manager then left and another manager took over. This second manager was less impressive and produced negative alpha for five years equivalent to –1 per cent per annum. The average alpha of the fund over ten years was therefore zero, but this average masks the performance of the alpha producing fund manager. The point we are trying to make is that managers may matter, and to be able to make claims – that many academics make – that the active fund management industry does not produce alpha, we need to evaluate not just the performance of funds but also the performance of fund managers too.

Some academics have begun to pay more attention to fund manager performance rather than just fund performance. This is not easy, since what is generally available is fund rather than fund manager performance data. However, Exhibit 14.13 shows that fund managers do matter; it also shows what happens when a good fund manager leaves a fund too.[8]

The data in Exhibit 14.13 is based upon the three-year performance of UK equity funds before the manager leaves and then the subsequent three-year period after the manager leaves. Panel A shows the average *cumulative* performance of the best performing 10 per cent of managers, out of a sample of nearly 250 leavers. From 36 months prior to the time when the manager leaves up until the time of the departure (t = 0), the average cumulative performance over and above the benchmark is nearly 40 per cent. These managers were (by definition) performing well before they left. However, after they leave it is a different story. The chart shows that the average cumulative abnormal performance of the subsequent three years is virtually zero, as depicted by a line with a relatively shallow slope in contrast to that before t = 0 with a steep slope. This

---

[8] This exhibit is based upon the results contained in A. Clare, S. Sapuric and N. Todorovic, *Changing Horses in Midstream: A Note on the Impact of UK Manager Changes on Fund Performance*, Centre for Asset Management Research, Cass Business School, London (2010).

Exhibit 14.13   Cumulative return in excess of benchmark

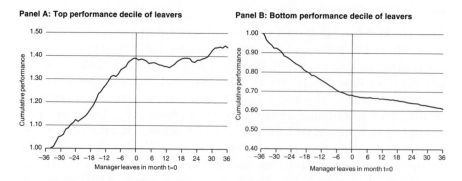

result implies that some fund managers are high performers, and that their departure can have a severe impact on the fund's performance. Panel B of the same exhibit shows a similar analysis of the 10 per cent of worst performing managers. By definition, prior to their departure these managers are subtracting value from the fund on a regular basis as they underperform their benchmark on average by almost an accumulated 35 per cent over three years. Then they leave. On average the performance of the fund continues to be poor, but the rate of value subtraction at least appears to slow down.

The analysis in Exhibit 14.13 shows that managers can make a difference. It also shows that while finding a good active manager is important, investors must also make sure they are aware of changes of fund management personnel.

The performance of pension fund managers

Much of the evidence discussed above has been derived using the returns generated by investment funds designed for retail investors. By contrast there has been relatively little research conducted using the unitized investment funds available to pension schemes. There are some notable exceptions to this rule though.

In 2004, the investment performance evaluation company, WM Performance Services conducted a study of active versus passive UK equity manager performance based on UK pension fund returns between 1994 and 2003.[9] An analysis of 818 UK equity funds was performed with a combined asset value of £140bn. These comprised 56 index funds with a total value of £28bn and 762 active funds with a total value of £112bn. What they found was that over this

---

[9] See WM Performance Services, *A Comparison of Active and Passive Management*, July (2004).

ten-year period *before fees* the median UK active manager performed broadly in line with the median passive manager, who, unsurprisingly, performed in line with the FTSE All Share Index. However, what they also found, again *before fees*, was that the top 25 per cent of active managers consistently outperformed the average passive manager year in year out, with the top 5 per cent outperforming by a considerable margin. However, in keeping with the results presented in Exhibit 14.13 above, these top performing managers changed from year to year. In fact, over the three discrete periods of 1995 – 1997, 1998 – 2000 and 2001 – 2003, only 2 per cent of UK active managers in the study managed to generate an information ratio in excess of the industry norm of 0.5.[10]

In another paper using CAPS data spanning March 1983 to December 1997, Tonks[11] examined the quarterly returns of over 2,100 UK equity segregated corporate pension funds. In contrast to some of the results mentioned above he found evidence of significant persistence in fund manager performance over a one-year horizon as well as weaker evidence of persistence over longer time periods. Excluding fund manager fees (which he assumed to average 0.4 per cent per annum) Tonks found that the top 20 per cent of pension fund managers over the previous 12 months generated 0.6 per cent outperformance over the following 12 months. A number of studies have suggested that the short-term performance persistence of outperforming managers is in part due to positive stock price momentum effects. That is, the positive effect of stocks that performed well in the past 12 months continuing to do so over the following 12 months. However, despite Tonks' findings in this study, he concluded in this and in a later 2007 study,[12] that analyzed the performance of over 9,300 US equity mutual funds between 1962 and 2004, that poor performers were still more likely to remain at the bottom of performance tables longer than top performers at the top. That is, performance persistency was more likely to be observed over the longer term among poor rather than top performers.

The gradual erosion of positive performance persistence over longer time horizons for top performers might be explained by two phenomena. First, like most performance studies, Tonks' data was based on the performance delivered by the fund management company rather than an individual manager or team of managers, who may well have moved on to another company during the period of analysis. Second, good performance often results in the manager being swamped by investors' cash. This influx of cash could conceivably force

---

[10] See Chapter 9 for a definition of the information ratio.
[11] See I. Tonks, 'Performance Persistence of Pension Fund Managers', *Journal of Business*, Volume 18, Number 6, November (2005).
[12] See J. B. Berk and I. Tonks, 'Return Persistence and Fund Flows in the Worst Performing Mutual Funds', July (2007), unpublished.

managers to depart from their previously successful strategy. Indeed, a good fund manager should know and advertise the capacity of their investment strategy and should close their fund to new investment when this capacity is reached. So, why does negative performance persist? Some have argued that the longer-term persistency of poor performance may be due to investors' unwillingness to withdraw their funds immediately in the hope that the performance will improve. To be honest this phenomena is difficult to rationalize.

Finally, a 2011 study of the performance of unitized investment vehicles available to UK pension funds,[13] again based on CAPS return data, examined the performance of over 500 equity funds, encompassing all the major categories ranging from plain vanilla UK equities, to Asia Pacific ex-Japan. Over each sample period and asset class that they examined, usually fewer than 10 per cent of managers produced a positive alpha that was not due to luck. In addition, and in keeping with the evidence discussed above, they also found little evidence of positive performance persistence. Finally the researchers performed tests of the market timing abilities of the managers of these funds. Specifically they investigated whether the managers of these funds managed to increase the beta of their fund in a market upturn, and reduce it in a market downturn. Managers often talk about 'overweighting cyclical stocks in an upturn', that is, buying stocks that benefit from strong economic growth, or conversely 'overweighting defensive stocks in a market downturn', that is, buying stocks that perform relatively well in a tough economic climate. However, they found no evidence that managers were capable of doing this. In fact quite the contrary, they found strong evidence to suggest that these managers were mistiming their exposure to the market – taking on more systematic risk in a downturn and less in an upturn.

Active fund management summary

Active fund management is a negative sum game. This means that if a trustee or other investor were to choose a manager at random, there exists a lower than 50 per cent chance that they will pick one that will outperform a relevant benchmark. The chances of choosing one at random that will outperform a benchmark year after year is substantially lower than 50 per cent as our simple experiments in this chapter showed, and as many academic researchers have also shown. So if your chances of choosing a manager that outperforms are that low, are you better off employing a chimp to run your portfolios? After

---

[13] A. Clare, K. Cuthbertson and D. Nitzsche, 'An Empirical Investigation into the Performance of UK Pension Fund Managers', *Journal of Pension Economics and Finance*, (2011), 9(4), pp. 533–47.

all, they would be considerably cheaper. The answer is almost certainly no. The main problem for active fund managers is that they are competing against a set of highly intelligent peers. They all have to run faster and faster, just to stand still.

The evidence in this chapter does indicate that despite the fierce competition among highly educated and intelligent active fund managers there are almost certainly some that stand out from the crowd, just as Lionel Messi does when he plays football at the highest level and as Usain Bolt does when he competes against the fastest runners on the planet. In Chapter 18 we will go through some of the processes needed to identify the Lionel Messi's and Usain Bolt's of the active fund management world.

However, many trustee boards and other investors prefer not to have to spend their valuable time and energy looking for genuine high octane active fund managers. For them, the research has shown them that these fund managers are hard to find and troublesome to monitor – and sometimes impossible to understand! It is for these reasons that many institutional and retail investors prefer to invest on a passive basis.

Passive fund management

Passive investing or index tracking as it is also known, generally involves constructing a portfolio of securities that tracks, or replicates, the performance of a financial market index. Why would anyone want to do this? Surely all investors want their fund manager to outperform the market? The answer is that the fundamental philosophy underlying passive investing is that financial markets are so efficient that managers cannot outperform them over long periods of time, and particularly once fund management fees have been taken into account.

This notion of efficiency is articulated by and encapsulated in the Efficient Markets Hypothesis (EMH).[14] This hypothesis states that on average, market prices reflect all available and relevant information and therefore move independently of past prices as investors react rationally and instantaneously to new market news. If correct, the EMH has obvious, damning implications for those investors and fund managers that are seeking to outperform the market. Indeed, if market prices continually reflect everything known or knowable

---

[14] The idea of price efficient markets dates back to the pioneering work of Alfred Cowes in the 1930s, Harry Roberts and Harry Markowitz in the 1950s and was then further developed through the 1960s and 1970s by Eugene Fama and others.

about the market's constituent securities, causing them to move in a random fashion, then investors cannot hope to beat the market consistently unless they are very lucky, or unless they are prepared to take higher risks.

So if market prices do evolve in this random manner, what is the point of trying to second guess the market? Indeed, under such circumstances the rational thing to do is to simply go with the flow and to hold a portfolio that simply replicates the market. Given that the aim of index tracking is to do just that, success in the world of index tracking is measured by how closely the fund manager has tracked the performance of their chosen index.

Indexing methods

Index tracker funds can adopt one of three tracking methodologies:

- *Full replication*: This involves the fund holding every security in the index in accordance with each constituent's index weighting. Only the very largest funds use this method given the cost of buying and holding every constituent in the index. By its very nature, a full-replication strategy should produce minimal tracking error, although discrepancies sometimes arise, due to management and transaction expenses. Most funds tracking major national index benchmarks that predominately contain large-cap liquid stocks, such as the FTSE 100, or a bond index consisting of government bonds, such as the IBOXX £ Gilts All Maturities index, would use full replication, subject to the size of the fund.

- *Stratified sampling*: Sometimes, however, full replication is not feasible, due to the illiquidity of the underlying securities, the sheer size of the index or country-specific tax laws for foreign holdings. In these cases a stratified sampling approach to the problem can be applied. Stratified sampling involves the application of statistical techniques to select a subset of the stocks in the index that reflect the characteristics of the index as closely as possible. Stratified funds typically overweight larger more liquid stocks and hold fewer, if any, of the smaller illiquid names in the index. In so doing, this methodology balances an acceptable level of tracking error against the lower resulting transactions costs and allows the portfolio to match the basic characteristics of the index without full replication. Stratified sampling is a popular methodology for tracking indices with a large number of constituents, such as the S&P 500, FTSE All Share and MSCI World index and those that benchmark the performance of smaller companies.

- *Synthetic indexing*: Synthetic index tracking funds usually use one of two derivative instruments to track the chosen index: either a combination of futures contracts and cash or a total return swap. Both approaches generally perform their function admirably and at a reasonably low cost. However, most passive fund managers tend not to use synthetic indexing because of certain issues that can arise in the pricing of futures, and because of the counterparty risk and the illiquidity associated with total return swaps.

What are the key advantages of index tracking funds?

Index tracking funds have a number of key advantages as a means of gaining exposure to equity markets. Arguably principal among these is that they minimize the risk of underperforming any chosen index, assuming that the fund's management costs and fees are low and the tracking methodology employed results in minimal tracking error. They therefore, provide investors with beta risk, where that beta should be equal to one. Second, transactions costs are relatively low because they normally do not need to transact as frequently as an active fund manager. They generally only need to transact when:

- the fund receives new money from investors;
- investors wish to redeem their holding;
- when dividends from the underlying constituents are reinvested; and
- the composition of the index being tracked changes, as many do quarterly.[15]

Costs are also kept low because index tracking fund managers do not need to pay implicitly for the research provided by investment banks in the form of high transactions costs. The large passive managers, in particular, can negotiate these transactions costs down with investment banks, well below the levels typically charged to active fund managers. Finally, costs are also low because they do not have to constantly search for and hire very expensive active fund managers. If you'll forgive the football analogy, index tracking fund managers can make do with Championship players, and have no need to attract, what many would perceive, their overpaid Premiership equivalents.

As the cost of doing business for passive fund managers is lower than for active fund managers, these lower costs can be passed on to passive investors in the form of lower fund management charges. To put it a little unkindly, what you get from a good passive fund manager is cheap and cheerful beta. Or as others have put it: 'you get what it says on the tin.'

What are the key disadvantages of index tracking funds?

So if you get what it says on the tin, what are the disadvantages or drawbacks of passive investing?

We discussed index construction above. Basically if a benchmark is easily replicable, fund managers can use it as a basis for passive management. However, as

---

[15] The FTSE 100 and 250 have quarterly reshuffles of their constituents. Usually only a few FTSE 100 constituents change places with those from the FTSE 250 as a result of their respective performances. In addition, if one company merges with another or is taken over then the vacancy left in the index is filled by a new constituent.

we demonstrated in Exhibit 14.4, only market capitalization-weighted indices, and not price weighted and equally weighted indices, perform like an actual investment portfolio. It is because of this realistic investment performance that fund managers generally choose to track market capitalization-weighted indices. However, tracking market capitalization-weighted indices is not without its problems. Indeed, during the heady days of the dot.com bubble in the late-1990s, a key flaw inherent within the construction of market capitalization indices became apparent. That is, market capitalization indices lead to more money being allocated to overvalued sectors and stocks and less to those likely to be undervalued with a resulting drag on performance.

For instance, let's assume that two companies – Company A and Company B – both have a fundamental value of £100m. However, if the price of A has been driven up temporarily to £120m and B down to £80m, then a market cap-weighted index allocation would create a portfolio comprising 60 per cent of A and 40 per cent of B. Therefore, 60 per cent of the portfolio would be allocated to an asset that had just risen sharply in value and which was overvalued, and only 40 per cent to an asset that had just fallen sharply in value, and which was undervalued. This does not appear on the face of it to be much of a formula for generating superior long-term returns!

Furthermore, during the dot.com era this misallocation problem was particularly acute. With so much money at the time flowing into index tracking strategies, if an index constituent did not make all of its share capital available to investors, then the stock's restricted supply against the backdrop of captive demand from index tracking funds could result in the shares becoming overvalued – sometimes severely so. This was especially true of those technology companies that, at the height of the dotcom boom, were launched on to the market to widespread public acclaim.[16] You know the companies we mean, they all had silly names like 'I've-got-a-great idea.com', not to mention incomprehensible business models.[17]

As index tracking funds clambered to weight their funds appropriately with these dot.com stocks and as other investors frantically brought into the dot.com new economic era story too, so the demand for these stocks pushed up their prices very sharply. As they did so, index tracking funds were forced to allocate yet more of their funds to these overpriced favourites, as the sheer weight of money propelled their market capitalizations to even greater heights.

---

[16] A considerable number of dotcom companies that came to market in the late-1990s were owned by large parent companies and some governments that restricted the supply of shares on the market in the hope of releasing further tranches of the shares in due course at considerably higher prices.

[17] In both respects, this era mirrored that of the South Sea bubble era of the 1720s.

Conversely they allocated less and less money to 'old economy' equities – that is, those companies that did old fashioned things like making products and employing people. These old economy stocks fell in value as passive funds (and other investors) continued to sell their shares as their index weightings declined. This, in turn, caused further index weighting declines and yet more selling!

Although the damage had been done, in an effort to address this demand-supply imbalance, the major equity index providers later introduced 'free float' indices. Free float indices dictate a pro-rata index weighting for those stocks with less than 100 per cent of their issued capital available for investment. So, within the FTSE market cap-weighted indices, for example, if a company makes between 50 and 75 per cent of its share capital available to the market and its market cap at current prices represents, say, 5 per cent of the index, then its weighting within the index is reduced to 3.75 per cent. That is, 75 per cent of 5 per cent. However, while this reduces the impact of the misallocation problem, it doesn't eliminate it completely.

Leading on from this, by choosing a market-cap-weighted index, investors often expose themselves to highly concentrated portfolios and, therefore, don't fully benefit from diversification. Indeed, as we saw in chapter 7 it's not unusual for the top ten stocks within the FTSE 100 to account for around 50 per cent of the index and the largest four sectors to capture about 60 per cent of the index's value.

Another disadvantage of passive funds is that market underperformance is almost certainly guaranteed. This is because passive fund managers still charge a fee – they are not providing a social service! If they have done their job properly then the investor will receive the benchmark return, minus any fees. In addition, whereas most indices treat dividends as having been paid when the constituent company declares the dividend – that is, when the company's stock goes 'ex-dividend' (xd) – a passive fund can't account for this dividend until the company has actually paid the dividend and the passive fund has actually received it. This tends to be around six to ten weeks after the dividend has been declared. This can cause the fund to underperform the index that it is tracking.[18]

There are also a couple of intellectual arguments that work against the principle of index tracking funds too. The first is that while the largest constituents

---

[18] However, as index tracker funds know the amount and payment date of the dividend income when the company's shares are declared ex-dividend (xd) they often buy futures contracts in the company on the 'xd day' to hedge the amount of dividend income due. The initial margin, or small cash deposit, required to be paid when purchasing futures is funded from the index fund's existing cash balances.

within an index, notably a market-cap-weighted index, often comprise those companies that are perceived to be the most successful businesses in their fields, there is no guarantee that this success will be repeated in the future. Indeed, rapid product innovation and lower barriers to entry for potential new industry entrants means that industry pre-eminence can often be a temporary phenomenon. Therefore, this year's winners may not necessarily be next year's, and yet by investing in these companies on a market capitalization-weighted basis, investors are effectively placing the biggest bets on these companies. They are buying into past winners. This inherent problem of market-cap-weighted indices can be overcome to some degree by tracking *fundamentally-weighted indices* that focus on a range of company performance metrics that change relatively slowly, such as sales, earnings, book value, cash flow, and dividends, rather than the market value of the company.

The second problem relates to the growing popularity of index funds. The greater the proportion of passive versus active management in any particular market, the greater the chance that passive managers will underperform actively managed funds. Why is this? Well, for index funds to outperform actively managed funds, the markets in which they invest need to be efficient. Ironically, this efficiency is the result of active managers researching the market in the hope of outperforming it. Essentially index funds take a 'free ride' on all of the hard work and effort of active fund managers. However, if money is allocated away from active towards passive management, a point may come when the market is not being sufficiently well researched, resulting in the market becoming inefficient and active management coming into its own again. At least that's the theory.

Fundamentally-weighted equity indices

Fundamentally-weighted equity indices originated from the ideas of Professor Robert Arnott of Research Associates in the mid-noughties.

The basic idea behind fundamentally-weighted indices is that companies should be represented in equity indices in accordance with the size of their real world attributes rather than their market capitalization as these provide a more accurate estimation of a company's fair or intrinsic value. These attributes, or fundamental factors, typically comprise a combination of a company's revenues, earnings, cash flow, net asset value, dividends and number of employees.

The result is a portfolio of stocks that can look very different from the composition of a market cap-weighted equity index, in that it overweights, or gives greater prominence to value and small-cap stocks and underweights growth and large-cap stocks relative to a market capitalization index. Perhaps unsurprisingly then, this has culminated in fundamentally-weighted indices generally outperforming their market-cap weighted counterparts, though a notable exception was in 2008 when the banks, with their strong pre-crisis fundamentals, were a big overweight.

One drawback is the additional costs associated with this form of index construction when compared to those associated with market cap-weighted indices. First, given their typically higher weighting towards smaller companies, the index is less liquid. Second, the index requires more frequent active rebalancing of its constituents, because the turnover of stocks within the index is about double that of a market cap-weighted index. However, most of this turnover tends to be in the index's larger and more liquid stocks rather than the smaller more illiquid stocks.

As a result of the additional active management involved in the construction and tracking of a fundamentally weighted index, higher transactions costs and fees are incurred. However, the proponents of fundamentally-weighted indices argue that the added performance of this approach generally offsets the extra costs involved.

The big problem with passive investing

As we've seen, there are a number of problems with passive investing, both practical and theoretical. But arguably the biggest drawback of passive investing is that as well as tracking the market up (less manager fees) – which is good – passive funds slavishly track the market down too – which is not so good. It is arguably for this reason that some investors prefer to hire an active fund manager to manage their funds.

Combining active and passive management

Although we've considered active and passive management as being distinctly different approaches to fund management, which they are, that is not to say that the techniques cannot be combined. Indeed, just as fundamental indexing extends active management into passive management, there are three other well practiced strategies that also do this:

- *Index tilting*: index tilting involves passive managers tilting, or overlaying their portfolios with small active positions, or 'bets'. So, if they are positive on stock A with a 5 per cent index weighting and less so on stock B with a 3 per cent index weighting, they may hold, say, 5.2 per cent in A and 2.8 per cent in B. Typically, index tilted portfolios will have a small outperformance, or tracking error, target: 0.1 per cent not being unusual. Arguably a portfolio adopting an index tilted approach doesn't look that much different from an actively managed portfolio where the manager index hugs – that is, takes low conviction stock positions in relation to the index. The big difference, however, is in the fees charged – the former usually charging considerably lower fees than the latter.

- *Enhanced indexation*: with enhanced indexation the manager engages in other activities to generate fee income for the fund. These can comprise writing out-of-the-money call options on selected stocks held in the portfolio, underwriting new share issues and stock lending. Given this additional activity, these portfolios usually have an outperformance target over the index of around 1 per cent.
- *Core-satellite portfolios*: as the name suggests, these portfolios are run on the basis of a core index tracker fund combined with several smaller actively managed funds, acting as the 'satellites'. With aggressive outperformance targets, these active funds are typically focused on the less efficient areas of the world's equity markets with the aim of generating performance uncorrelated with the index core or with each other.

Passive investment techniques can be applied to cash, bond, equity and even commodity investments. So are there some asset classes that lend themselves more readily to passive investment as opposed to active?

Arguably, the more efficient the market in question, the greater the scrutiny of this market, and the greater the number of scrutineers (investment analysts and fund managers), the more likely it is the market is efficient and the less likely it is that any individual manager will be able to spot a profitable investment opportunity before anyone else. This is why some investment consultants recommend that blue chip, or large-cap developed economy equity portfolios are managed on a passive basis. These passive portfolios are the archetypal index core within a core-satellite approach to portfolio construction. However, the same consultants might recommend emerging market equity portfolios to be managed on an active basis, given that many of these markets will be analyzed by fewer investors and will have idiosyncrasies that require an expert's eye, and therefore offer greater opportunity for active manager skill to shine through. In other words, they might be more inefficient. These portfolios might comprise the satellite component of a core-satellite approach to portfolio construction.

With regard to government bond portfolios, many investment consultants again recommend investing on a passive basis. This is because the opportunities to outperform for, say, a manager of a gilt portfolio is extremely limited, given the amount of scrutiny that the market is subjected to, the limited number of bonds and the fact that there is only one issuer to analyze – the UK government.

Some investment consultants would argue that corporate bond portfolios should always be managed actively. This is because individual corporate bonds are market capitalization-weighted within corporate bond indices. This tends to mean that the bonds with the biggest weights have been issued by the companies with the largest debts! So investment on a passive basis would involve investing most in the biggest debtors – not a particularly smart investment strategy.

Many trustee boards look at the active versus passive decision then on an asset class by asset class basis. They often construct asset portfolios that consist of both actively and passively managed asset classes. Although on the face of it active and passively managed funds seem to be polar opposites, when we look at a typical pension scheme asset portfolio the two approaches usually sit together on the asset side of the balance sheet. Exhibit 14.14 shows the proportion of UK DB pension fund assets that were managed passively in 2006. The data are based upon the Investment Management Association's (IMA) 2006 annual survey[19] which asked the vast majority of the UK's fund management industry to specify the type of pension fund mandates they currently manage. The survey responses accounted for £343bn of all UK pension fund assets under management. As the exhibit shows, nearly one-third of all

Exhibit 14.14   UK pension fund client mandates

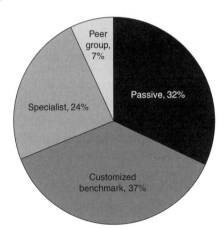

Source: Investment Management Association.

---

[19] Unfortunately we were unable to find more recent data on this split.

pension assets covered by this survey were managed passively as indexed funds in 2006, while just over one-third had customized benchmarks which could be passive, actively managed, or a mixture of both. A small percentage were managed according to peer group benchmarks, while nearly one-quarter were 'specialist mandates' which means that the funds had a specific asset class or geographic exposure.

These data seem to suggest that passive investing is likely to remain a feature of the pensions' investment landscape and for as long as it does, the active versus passive debate will rage on.

Trend following: clever passive or passive active?

Another interesting take on the passive versus active debate is an approach that has attracted considerable interest recently based upon a technique known as trend following.[20] The idea is quite simple, can be applied to any financial market index, any set of financial market indices and can be explained as follows:

- choose a financial market index, for example, the S&P 500;
- calculate the average price of the index over a pre-determined period;
- if the index price today is above this average, then invest in the market;
- however if it is below this level, disinvest and place the proceeds in cash;
- repeat this process over time.

Exhibit 14.15 shows the results of following this process using the S&P 500 as the financial market index over a very interesting period of history – 1925 to 1941. Over this period the S&P 500 produced an annual return of 5.61 per cent per annum, with annualized volatility of 26.47 per cent per annum. By contrast the trend following rule produced an annual return of 10.86 per cent with annualized volatility of 16.37 per cent. The rule works because it managed to track the market up when the market was trending up, but avoided some of the worst downturns over this period, staying in cash instead. So it combined the best aspects of passive investing and managed to avoid most of the main drawback of passive investing – that is, tracking the market down.

---

[20] See O. ap Gwilym, J. Seaton and S. Thomas, 'Price and Momentum as Robust Tactical Approaches to Global Equity Investing', *Journal of Investments, forthcoming,* 2011.

Exhibit 14.15 Trend following applied to the S&P500 (1925–1941)

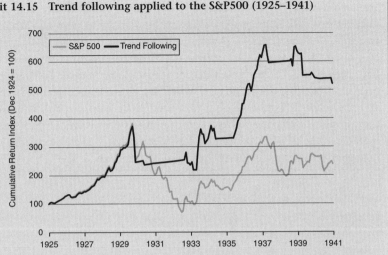

Exhibit 14.16 shows that this rule has worked in the recent past too. In this case the trend following rule has been applied to 24 equally-weighted developed economy equity markets (net of fees), and its performance is compared against the MSCI World index (gross of fees) over the period 2001 to 2010. The MSCI World index (in sterling terms) produced an annual return over this ten-year period of 1.87 per cent with annualized volatility of 16.64 per cent. By contrast the trend following rule produced an annual return of 6.60 per cent with annualized volatility of 9.59 per cent.

Exhibit 14.16 Trend following applied to 24 developed economy equity markets

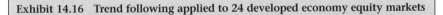

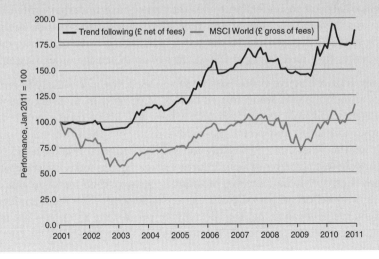

Similar findings – that is, that trend following rules applied in this way produce returns at least as good as a passive buy-and-hold strategy with around two-thirds of the volatility – have been found using a wide range of asset classes and over often very different economic environments. Of course, past performance is no guarantee of future performance. Furthermore, if everyone did this, the trends on which the rules depend would disappear, and the markets would become very inefficient, in much the same way as they would if everyone tracked equity markets passively. Nevertheless, this is an idea that is catching on. It can be viewed either as clever passive or risk managed active management – it's kind of a hybrid.

Summary

Evaluating the performance of passive funds is rather simple. Normally the passive fund's return is just compared to the return on the benchmark. This should be very close, assuming minimal tracking error, as should all the other risk measures be, such as the fund's beta and standard deviation of returns. In fact, when most of the UK's highly efficient passive fund managers come to report on the performance of their funds at trustee meetings, it is usually quite a dull meeting. The manager says something like: over the quarter the index went up by 3 per cent, and your fund went up by 2.98 per cent. Little further explanation is normally required so that the conversation usually then turns to the weather. It is very different for active managers. If they have outperformed their targets, trustees need to understand why: did they take too many risks? Trustees also need to understand why they may have underperformed their target: was their judgment poor, did they take too few risks? If their return is very close to the performance of the index benchmark, trustees need to establish whether they have engaged the services of an expensive index hugger.

With regard to the active versus passive debate itself, the jury is likely to remain out for some time yet. Some trustee boards, supported in their argument by considerable academic research, do not believe that active fund managers can add any value at all and prefer the passive route. On the other hand others fail to see the attraction of slavishly following a financial market index, and choose to invest actively. In reality most trustee boards today sit somewhere between these two extreme views. Most invest some of their assets on a passive basis and others on an active basis. Generally speaking, the more inefficient the market is believed to be, the more likely trustees are to choose an active fund manager, while the more efficient, the more likely they are to take the passive route.

Key points

- The performance evaluation process begins with the measurement of absolute return, then the assessment of relative return, followed by an attribution of the returns achieved and finally involves an assessment of the risks assumed in generating the returns.
- Not all indices are constructed in the same way and most have severe shortcomings. While market capitalization-weighted indices appear to be the most appropriate, they can lead to more money being allocated to overvalued assets and less to those likely to be undervalued and result in concentrated portfolios that do not fully benefit from diversification. Fundamentally weighted indices can overcome these problems to some extent.
- Active fund management and passive fund management are underpinned by diametrically opposing philosophies about the efficiency of markets. Passive management treats the market as being efficient and, therefore, simply tracks the performance of the market, whereas active management takes the opposite view and so attempts to outperform the market. Whereas the active versus passive debate typically revolves around the management of equity portfolios, active fund management is widely applied to the management of most other asset classes, though the use of passive management for other asset classes is less widespread.
- Index tracking funds are an inexpensive way of gaining equity market exposure. However, as a one-size-fits-all investment, passive funds cannot necessarily cater for the differing investment style, income, risk and return needs of all investors.
- Properly executed, active management should outperform passive management but is let down by index huggers, plus high transactions costs and fees that collectively render active management a negative sum game.
- Active and passive equity fund management are not mutually exclusive in that passive management can be modestly extended into active management in the creation of index tilted portfolios, enhanced indexation and core-satellite portfolios. The two approaches are combined at a higher level too: the asset portfolios of many pension schemes comprise both actively and passively managed asset classes.

Chapter 15

Liability Driven Investment (LDI): An Exercise in Risk Management

Learning outcomes

- Understand how Liability Driven Investment (LDI) seeks to reduce a scheme's potentially unrewarded risk while capturing potentially rewarded risks.
- Understand that LDI should be both a risk management and risk re-allocation exercise.
- Understand what risks are targeted and how they are mapped and measured.
- Understand how interest rate and inflation risk can be mitigated.
- Appreciate the risk posed by improving longevity and how it can be mitigated.
- Understand what is involved in implementing a successful de-risking programme.

Introduction

The principal aim of any defined benefit (DB) pension scheme should be to meet its liabilities as they fall due. However, today most schemes are less than fully funded, principally as a result of unmatched asset/liability positions. Therefore, since the outbreak of the great pension fund deficit pandemic of the early-noughties, many trustee boards have been seeking to address this mismatch as they try to prevent any further deterioration of their scheme's funding position and plug these deficits. One way of plugging the deficit would be to ask the scheme sponsor to provide the additional contributions needed. However, those pension scheme trustees whose *only* response to widening DB scheme deficits is to go begging bowl in hand, like Oliver Twist, to their sponsoring employer are likely to meet their own Mr. Bumble and receive a similar response! In our view, the *long-term* objective of any trustee board should be to reduce its reliance upon the sponsoring employer, especially where the sponsor's financial position is weak.[1]

So how can Liability Driven Investment (LDI) help trustees achieve this objective?

Liability driven investment

LDI is not a new idea, and the principle behind LDI is rather simple. Over the 1980s and 1990s, pension schemes became accustomed to benchmarking the performance of their assets against either related financial market indices or against the performance of the asset portfolios of other pension schemes. But is matching or even beating the performance of financial market indices and other pension schemes a suitable objective? These are not irrelevant benchmarks of course, but the basic principle behind LDI is that the scheme's liabilities become its benchmark. Since every scheme faces a different set of liabilities, with an LDI approach, each scheme's benchmark is different. To some extent this is how the problem was viewed and approached in the 1950s and 1960s. With the benefit of hindsight, this approach now seems blindingly obvious. The philosophy underpinning LDI can be summarized as follows:

> *the assets are there to fund future liabilities, therefore the assets should be managed so that they perform in such a way as to maximize the likelihood that the liabilities will be met.*

Designing an asset portfolio that will perform this task will require a clear understanding of the risk and return characteristics of the assets, but also the same comprehensive understanding of the characteristics of the liabilities. That is, the assets and liabilities must be viewed together and through the same lens, or lenses. Some people do not understand why, but it is quite simple: a liability can be viewed as a negative asset. A pension scheme's liability is just someone else's asset (actually the scheme members in this case). Assets and liabilities are just different sides of the same coin.

Constructing an asset portfolio without a clear understanding of the characteristics of the liabilities that they are meant to meet would be rather like a cobbler

---

[1] The strength of the sponsor covenant has a direct impact on the scheme's risk appetite and hence its desired asset allocation. We considered the sponsor covenant in Chapters 3 and 9.

designing and making a shoe for a client before they had measured their client's feet! The chances are that the shoes won't fit. Arguably the pensions industry designed asset portfolios over the 1990s that paid too little attention to the measurements of scheme liabilities. When risky asset prices fell in the early-noughties, and pension liabilities soared, it became very clear that the assets did not fit the liabilities. The consequence was the deficit pandemic.

In Chapters 5–8 and 13 we described both the traditional and non-traditional, or alternative, asset classes that comprise pension scheme portfolios. Hopefully by now you are familiar with the asset side of the pension fund balance sheet. It usually comprises a mixture of low- and high-risk, traditional and non-traditional asset classes, and increasingly derivatives. In Chapter 1 we described how pension liabilities are generated. Here we describe the sources of the key risks embedded in a typical set of DB scheme liabilities. The three most important are:

- interest rate risk;
- inflation risk; and
- longevity risk.

Interest rate risk

As we explained in Chapter 6, we can think of the projected liabilities of any pension scheme as being analogous to the projected payments of a bond. We also saw in that chapter how we can calculate the present value of a bond: all that is required is to discount each of the bond's payments and then to add up these discounted values. What discount rate should be used? It could be argued that the discount rate should be equal to the weighted average expected return on the assets held to back the liabilities. It could be a AA-rated bond. But why not the yield on a government security, like a gilt? This may seem like semantics, but it can make a big difference to the reported size of the present value of the liabilities.

Exhibit 15.1 depicts the total present value of the liabilities of our representative DB scheme, the TGtI scheme, that we first looked at in Chapter 1 (see Exhibit 1.1), discounted on three different bases. If we assume that the TGtI scheme holds 50 per cent of its assets in equities, 30 per cent in a portfolio of sterling, investment grade corporate debt, 15 per cent in a portfolio of gilts and 5 per cent in cash, then the expected return on the assets will be relatively high and therefore the discounted present value of the liabilities will be commensurately low. If the weighted average, expected return on this asset portfolio is 6.75 per cent per annum, and we use this to discount the scheme's total liabilities, then the present value of these liabilities is just over £81m. However, discounting these liabilities using the yield on an AA-rated sterling corporate bond, which we assume here for simplicity, is 5.4 per cent, then the present value of the liabilities is £100m.

Exhibit 15.1　Impact of alternative discount rates on the TGtI scheme's liabilities

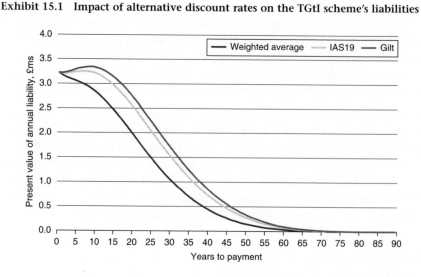

Finally, if we discount these liabilities using the yield on long-dated gilts, which we again assume for simplicity is 5 per cent, then the liabilities rise to just over £107m.[2] These simple calculations show what a dramatic impact the chosen discount rate can have on the reported value of the liabilities.

The accounting profession now recommends that a highly rated (effectively a AA-rated) sterling corporate bond yield should be used to discount scheme liabilities. The relevant accounting rules are FRS17 and IAS19; the latter having largely succeeded the former. The discount rate that is recommended for FRS 17 is equivalent to the current yield on a 15-year AA-rated sterling corporate bond, while for IAS 19 it is a 'high quality corporate bond'. When the yield, or discount rate, for a bond falls, the bond's value rises and when the discount rate rises its present value falls. Using this approach to valuation means that the scheme's liabilities will also rise and fall with the discount rate (that is, with bond yields). Viewed in this way the scheme has effectively issued a bond – a promise to pay – to its members. To the members this pension promise is an asset, to the scheme it is a liability.

So if the yields on AA-rated sterling corporate bonds fall, the accounting-based value of liabilities rises. To help reduce the impact that this would have on

---

[2] At the time of writing, gilt and sterling AA-rated corporate bond yields were much lower than this. We use the values of 5 per cent and 5.4 per cent respectively as being representative of 'steady state' values, purely for purposes of illustrating the impact that changing the basis of the discount rate can have on the present value of the liabilities.

any scheme's overall funding position (not to mention the sponsor's balance sheet), a pension fund could hold AA-rated sterling corporate bonds. In this case the rise in the value of the liabilities might be at least partially offset by the rise in the value of these bond holdings. Some schemes have sought to increase their exposure to this asset class for this very reason. Given that pension fund liabilities are *very* long-dated in nature, they have *very* high modified duration for the same reasons that a long-dated bond has high modified duration. The modified duration of the typical pension fund can be in excess of 20 per cent. Therefore 'matching' the interest rate risk would involve buying AA-rated corporate bonds with similarly *very* high modified duration. However, there are few bonds of this kind available in the market and it is for this reason that many pension schemes have sought to reduce this risk via the use of interest rate swaps, as we discussed in Chapter 12.

Inflation risk

As we discussed in Chapter 1, depending upon the scheme rules, some or all of the members' pension entitlement can be 'index-linked', or 'inflation-proofed'. This means that the value of the pension promise will rise with inflation, a feature designed to ensure that at least some portion of the pension will be protected against inflation. Exhibit 15.2 presents the impact of inflation on those of the TGtI scheme's liabilities that are linked to inflation. We first showed these in Exhibit 1.1, Panel B, when we assumed inflation to be 2.5 per cent. The lines in Exhibit 15.2 show what happens to the future values

Exhibit 15.2 The impact of inflation on the TGtI scheme's liabilities

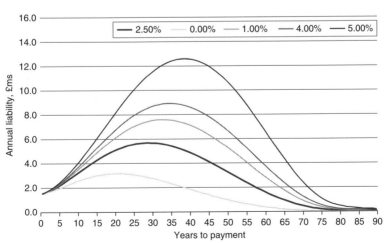

of those inflation-linked liabilities under different, average inflation outcomes over the next 80 years or so, from 0 per cent to 5 per cent. The exhibit shows just how exposed this scheme is to the ravages of even moderate inflation. To put it into perspective, with average inflation of 2.5 per cent the inflation-linked payment that the scheme would have to make in 40 years time would be £4.78m. However, with average inflation of 5 per cent per annum, the scheme would be liable for a cash payment in 40 years time of £12.53m. Quite a difference.

So the TGtI DB scheme has effectively issued an index-linked bond to its members. Again, as we discussed in Chapter 1, the inflation index most commonly used is the Retail Price Index (RPI), although recent legislation allows some schemes to apply the Consumer Price Index (CPI) to the revaluation of deferred benefits and pensions in payment instead. However, rather than rising without limit, pension payments usually embody limited price indexation (LPI), whereby pension increases are limited to 5 per cent per year. Moreover, the nominal value of the pension is also protected such that negative inflation (deflation) does not lead to a reduction in the nominal value. Pension promises of this kind are often referred to as LPI (0,5). This means that, up to a certain extent, higher inflation can increase the size of a scheme's liabilities. This will be a crucial element in the asset allocation decision process. If liabilities can potentially rise with higher inflation then holding assets whose cash flow might also rise with inflation would be one way of dealing with at least some portion of this risk.

As we intimated above, the scheme is also exposed in a deflationary environment too. Suppose that on average, consumer prices fall, so that inflation is negative. This means that the real value of any pension will rise. While this is good news for the pensioners and other members, it may be bad news for the corporate sponsor, since in a deflationary world the prices that the average company can charge for their goods and services will fall in nominal terms as will their profits. Yet the pension promise will not fall with the general price level. Furthermore, in this sort of environment, it is likely that the prices of many asset classes and the income streams that they generate will be depressed too. This 0 per cent floor to the pension promise would therefore put an increasing burden on the corporate sponsor of most schemes.

To hedge this risk, pension schemes could buy inflation-linked bonds. But these are quite rare. Of those sterling denominated index-linked bonds that have been issued, the majority are index-linked gilts and most do not have sufficiently long maturities to satisfy the matching needs of UK DB pension schemes. It is for this reason that many schemes have sought to hedge their exposure to inflation with the inflation swaps that we discussed in Chapter 12.

Longevity risk

The final key risk that is embodied in a scheme's liabilities relates to longevity. This is because the scheme is committed to making pension payments until the member dies. In addition, the scheme will usually continue to make a reduced pension payment to the scheme member's spouse until they die too. Mortality, or longevity risk then, is one of the key risks that a scheme assumes. In effect, the pension scheme has not only issued a bond to its members that exposes it to interest rate risk and usually to a considerable degree of inflation risk too, this bond also pays a coupon (a pension) with no fixed maturity date. It pays out until the member or the member's dependents die.

In a well-known paper published in *Science* magazine in 2002, Oeppen and Vaupel[3] demonstrated that life expectancy had increased by between two to two-and-a-half years per decade for the past 150 years or so in some developed economies. If successive generations continue to live longer and longer, then DB pension fund liabilities will continue to rise too. To see the impact that changing life expectancy can have on the present value of a scheme's liabilities, consider Exhibit 15.3. The total liabilities of our TGtI DB scheme are shown once again. These liabilities are based upon a standard set of assumptions about the life expectancy of the scheme's members, based upon data produced by

Exhibit 15.3 Impact of changing mortality assumptions on TGtI's liabilities

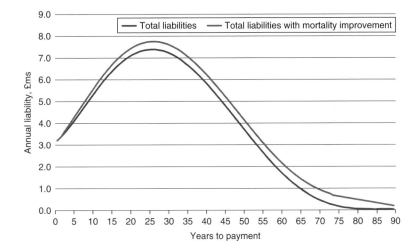

---

[3] Jim Oeppen and James W. Vaupel, 'Broken Limits to Life Expectancy', *Science*, Volume 296, Number 5570, pp. 1029–1031 (2002).

the Government's Actuarial Department (GAD). However, if we assume that each member of the scheme lives just one year longer, the liabilities increase as shown by the second line in the exhibit. In present value terms this relatively small increase in the assumption about each member's life expectancy, raises the present value of the scheme's total liabilities by around 5 per cent, from £100m to around £105m.

For the time being the real problem with this particular risk is that the financial markets do not offer standardized financial instruments to allow schemes to hedge it. Although longevity derivatives are beginning to develop along the lines required by pension funds to hedge this risk, it is really only by entering a buyout – where a third party effectively assumes ownership of the scheme's assets and takes on its liabilities – that most scheme sponsors and trustees can avoid this risk. However, buyout specialists will usually require assets equivalent to around 125–130 per cent of the present value of the IAS19-valued liabilities in return for accepting all of the risks that meeting DB liabilities entails.[4] This may sound like a lot of money, but what price would you charge for taking on the payments of a bond:

- that is exposed to interest rate risk;
- whose coupon (pension) payments rise with inflation; and
- where these coupons (pension payments) have an uncertain maturity that appears to be rising year after year?

Any takers?

We will return to hedging longevity risk later in the chapter.

What are trustees to do?

If widespread DB scheme deficits are the result of a failure of risk management, that is, a failure to match assets with liabilities, trustees must develop a better understanding of the risks that reside within both the asset and liability side of their balance sheets. Indeed, trustees need to have an understanding of the contribution that each of these risks makes to their scheme's overall risk profile. They also need to be able to test the effect of removing individual risks to ensure that any action taken does not compromise the probability of achieving the scheme's long-term funding objective. For instance, the removal of some risks – like equity risk – could also reduce future returns. This is because some risks are potentially 'rewarded'. However, the removal of other

---

[4] Scheme membership data needs to be up-to-date for the buyout provider to accurately assess the risks being assumed.

risks, such as inflation risk, may have no material impact on the scheme's future funding position. These risks are referred to as 'unrewarded' risks. The distinction between potentially rewarded and unrewarded risks is not quite as simple as this, but the basic principle holds. Once the risks are understood and calibrated, at least as far as this is possible, trustees should then develop a risk management plan. Remember the old saying: fail to plan, plan to fail!

The rest of this chapter is split into two sections. The first section we could describe as the 'science' behind LDI. The final part, however, focuses on the practical issues involved in implementing a LDI strategy, where the main aim is to de-risk a scheme's liabilities.

The science of LDI

As we noted earlier, LDI essentially involves a greater focus on the risks embodied in the scheme's liabilities, not forgetting the risks embodied in the scheme's assets and just as importantly the relationship between these risks. One of the essential elements associated with LDI is the distinction between potentially rewarded and unrewarded risks. Why are some risks assumed to be potentially rewarded while others are not?

A good example of a potentially rewarded risk is equity risk. In Chapter 7 we introduced the idea of the equity risk premium (ERP). Although it is impossible to quantify precisely, all equity investors, either explicitly or implicitly, assume that it is positive. That is, they assume that they will be rewarded over time for taking on equity risk. This reward is the extra return they expect from equities over and above what they expect on, say, government bonds. If they did not expect this positive reward over time, why would they assume equity risk? This does not mean of course that equities will definitely produce this reward year after year on a consistent basis, or even that this additional reward will be achieved at all, even over long periods of time. But by holding equities, investors expect to be rewarded accordingly.

By contrast, most advisers describe interest rate risk as being unrewarded. If we assume for the moment that a monetary authority is committed to keeping inflation under control, then both interest rates and long-term bond yields should tend to cycle around a stable level over time. So when interest rates and bond yields rise above this average, the present value of liabilities will fall, and when they fall below it, the liabilities will rise. Over time then the interest rate cycle would cause liabilities to rise and fall, but with no obvious long-term benefit to the scheme. It is argued then that since there is no reward attached to this risk it should be eliminated as far as possible.

Although definitions of LDI vary from adviser to adviser, arguably LDI focuses on two issues, in particular:

- capturing *potentially rewarded* risks that derive from: exposure to *risky* asset classes such as equities and corporate bonds; or from fund manager skill, or alpha. That is, capturing risks that should ultimately help to plug any deficit. We considered most of these risks in Chapters 5–8 and 13 when considering both traditional and alternative asset classes and alpha in Chapters 9 and 14. We return to fund manager skill in Chapter 18.
- reducing or even eliminating *unrewarded* risks, such as interest rate, inflation and longevity risk, that can cause a scheme's liabilities to rise faster than its asset base. The removal of these unrewarded risks – at an acceptable price (see Chapter 12) – should prevent any scheme deficit from widening further and, if implemented correctly, ideally should not have a material impact on the scheme's expected return or funding in the long run.

In coming to an understanding of all of the risks embodied in a scheme's assets and liabilities, including the rewarded and unrewarded ones, we need to find a way of expressing these risks. There is no perfect way of doing this – remember, risk is one word but not one number – but perhaps the most common metric used to capture the risks embodied in a scheme is Value at Risk (VaR) – the same measure that we met in Chapter 9.

Value at Risk (VaR)

To illustrate how VaR is commonly used in the pensions industry today, we will once again use our representative DB scheme, the TGtI DB scheme, first introduced in Chapter 1. Exhibit 15.4 shows the big picture position of the scheme. It has assets that have a current market value of £90m and comprise 50 per cent equities, 30 per cent in a portfolio of sterling, investment grade corporate debt, 15 per cent in a portfolio of gilts and 5 per cent in cash. Valued on an IAS19 basis, its liabilities have a present value of £100m and comprise commitments to active, deferred and pension members (see Exhibits 1.1 and 15.1). The scheme's deficit is therefore £10m. In addition, the modified duration of the scheme's gilt and corporate bond portfolio is 8 per cent, while the modified duration of its liabilities is 16.7 per cent. This is quite a mismatch, and we can illustrate the extent of it with a simple calculation. If bond yields, and therefore the discount rate applied to the scheme's liabilities, fall by 1 per cent, its liabilities will rise by approximately 16.7 per cent, causing them to increase *to* £116.7m:

$$\text{increase in liability value} = £100m \times 16.7\% = £16.7m$$

If we assume (as it is commonly assumed by consultants) that the fall in interest rates and bond yields does not affect the value of the other assets held by the scheme, then the bond portfolio will rise by 8 per cent, causing the assets to rise by:

$$\text{increase in asset value} = (\pounds 100\text{m} \times 45\%) \times 8\% = \pounds 3.6\text{m}$$

So the scheme's liabilities would be equal to £116.7m while its assets would be worth £93.6m (that is, £90m plus £3.6m). The scheme's shortfall of assets to liabilities would have risen from £10m to £23.1m, representing an increase in the deficit of over 130 per cent! Put yourselves in the shoes of the scheme sponsor and its shareholders. How would you react if someone knocked on your door to tell you that the mortgage on your home had just risen by over 130 per cent?

Of course the maths would have produced an equal and opposite result had interest rates and bond yields risen by 1 per cent (again assuming no impact on other asset classes). However, the focus here is firmly on the downside. Applying the ideas of VaR to the context of a pension scheme – with its focus on downside risk – gives some rather intuitive ways of looking at risk.

Exhibit 15.4 summarizes the extent of the mismatch between the TGtI scheme's assets and its liabilities. But we can also calculate the VaR that each asset class embodies and the VaR embodied in the liabilities too – that is, the scheme's exposure to inflation and interest rate risk – which shows more clearly the extent of the mismatch. Remember that a liability is only a negative asset. Most importantly, when tackled in this way we can calculate the overall VaR of the scheme. So while we can calculate the 95% VaR, or VaR95, for each source of

Exhibit 15.4 The TGtI scheme's unmatched asset and liability position

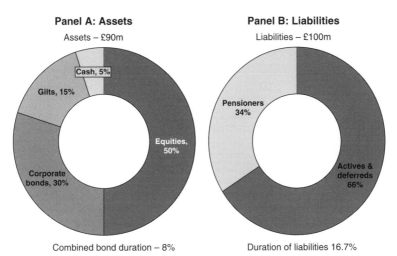

Panel A: Assets — Assets – £90m — Cash, 5%; Gilts, 15%; Corporate bonds, 30%; Equities, 50% — Combined bond duration – 8%

Panel B: Liabilities — Liabilities – £100m — Pensioners 34%; Actives & deferreds 66% — Duration of liabilities 16.7%

unrewarded and potentially rewarded risk, we can also calculate the VaR95 for the overall scheme. This is the maximum amount by which the scheme's deficit may widen as a result of its exposure to each element of risk, over the next 12 months, with a 5 per cent probability. That is, based on one or a number of adverse events that could be expected to occur on no more than 5 per cent of occasions, or no more than once in every 20 years. This is probably best explained with an example.

In Exhibit 15.5 we present each of the VaR elements for the TGtI DB scheme. The equities bar shows that there is a 5 per cent chance that a nasty equity market event could cause the scheme deficit to widen by 13 percentage points. However, the scheme's exposure to interest rates and inflation risk is larger at a combined value of 19 percentage points. Totalled, the VaR of the scheme is just over 35 per cent. But the sum is not so relevant here. These risks are not independent of one another. For example, as interest rates fall, although liability values will rise, bond prices will also rise (and so too should equity prices). The relationships that exist between all of these risks is shown by the diversification bar, which equals 13 per cent of the deficit. It represents the offsetting elements of the scheme's risks. The overall position of the scheme, taking into account the risks embodied in all of the assets and liabilities, is a VaR95 of 23 percentage points. That is: there is estimated to be a 5 per cent chance that the scheme could experience a deterioration of its funding position from 90 per cent to 67 per cent within the next year.

Exhibit 15.5   TGtI's VaR components

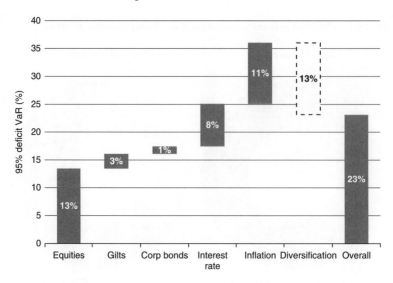

For many schemes, as for the TGtI DB scheme,[5] the VaR attributed to unrewarded risk can be very high and often higher than the VaR of the potentially rewarded risk. Just look at the contribution of interest rate and inflation risk to VaR in this typical VaR risk decomposition. If this VaR number – the *de facto* 'risk budget' – makes the trustees (and the scheme sponsor) uncomfortable, then the trustees could look to reduce the unrewarded risks. That is, risks which, if removed at an acceptable price, do not have a *material* impact upon the scheme's expected return in the *long run*. In doing this, the trustees may 'free up' some of their risk budget to accommodate exposure to more potentially rewarded risk, to improve the scheme's long-term funding position. After all, as intimated earlier, when considering potentially rewarded and unrewarded risks, LDI should be both a risk management and a risk reallocation exercise.

In Chapter 12 we showed how interest rate swaps could be used to reduce interest rate risk, and how inflation swaps could be used to reduce inflation risk. Exhibit 15.6 shows two hypothetical strategies that the trustees of the TGtI DB scheme could use to reduce the scheme's VaR, holding all else equal. The first is shown in Panel A and does not involve swaps. It simply involves selling equities and using the proceeds to increase the scheme's holdings of UK government bonds. Ultimately, if the trustees were to sell all of the scheme's equities and invest the proceeds in gilts, they could reduce the scheme's VaR95 from 23 per cent to 14.1 per cent. However, there is one obvious downside to this strategy, which is that it would reduce the expected return on the portfolio of assets. The impact on the expected return on the scheme's asset portfolio is shown in Panel B. The lower the proportion held in equities, the lower the return, and the longer it would take for the scheme to get back to a fully funded position.

Panel C in Exhibit 15.6 shows an alternative strategy. It shows the impact on the scheme's VaR that arises from hedging progressive proportions of the scheme's interest and inflation risk through swaps. By hedging all of this risk the scheme can reduce its VaR to 12 per cent. Panel D shows the impact that each hedging level has on the expected return of the portfolio. We assume that the scheme needs to hold additional gilts equivalent to 25 per cent of the notional value of the hedge as collateral. We return to this point shortly.

---

[5] To keep the analysis manageable, we have not included the VaR for the longevity risk faced by the scheme or, the interest rate and inflation basis risk. This basis risk arises as a result of most schemes valuing (discounting) their liabilities against (by) a gilt yield benchmark but using swaps to hedge the scheme's interest rate and inflation risk. As gilt yields (and the gilt yield curve) differ from and often move independently of swap rates (and the swap curve), so this basis risk arises. You might recall from Chapter 11 that basis risk arises between the pricing of the underlying asset and the derivative that is based on this underlying asset. This is a very similar phenomenon.

Exhibit 15.6   Reducing the unrewarded risk to a more palatable number

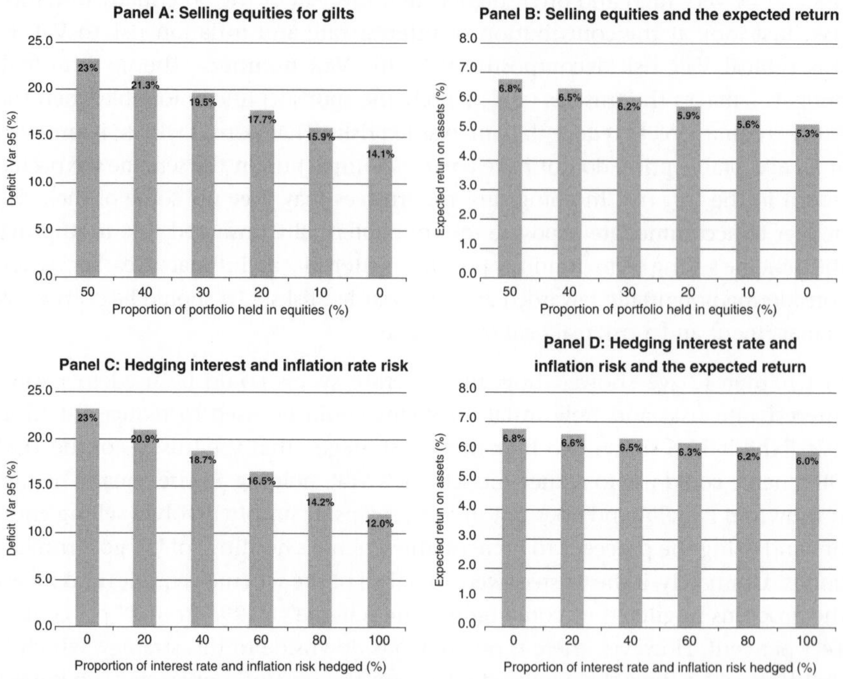

The impact on the expected return of the assets is less pronounced than that involved in selling all of the equities for gilts, this is because even with a 100 per cent interest and inflation hedge, the scheme still holds £25m of its asset portfolio in the form of equities.

This simple example illustrates one of the main attractions of swaps as a means of de-risking. While swaps do have an impact upon the expected return of the asset portfolio, it isn't quite to the same degree as selling the high expected return, high-risk asset classes to achieve similar reductions in the scheme's overall VaR.

In the end, trustees and their sponsors have to balance the desire to reduce unrewarded risk, with the need to generate enough return on their asset base to plug the scheme's deficit. There is no right answer to this dilemma. The solution will depend upon a number of factors, perhaps most importantly upon the strength of the scheme sponsor's business.

Stress/scenario testing

Another way of looking at the overall risk of a scheme involves undertaking scenario, or stress testing, exercises (we discussed these briefly in Chapter 9).

Conceptually these techniques are relatively simple. Taking the current position of the scheme as the starting point, which by definition is based upon current financial market prices, scenario testing involves looking at the likely performance of asset prices, inflation and interest rates assuming that a financial crisis occurs tomorrow. A good example might be the stock market crash of 1987, when equity prices fell by around 30 per cent over the space of three months. By imposing this fall on our scheme's current asset mix, plus all other relevant asset price movements that were associated with this event, such as any associated change in relevant bond yields, we can work out the position that the scheme would be in if the same event were to reoccur tomorrow.

Exhibit 15.7 shows the potential impact that a rerun of four separate financial market crises might have on the deficit position of the TGtI DB scheme – the great crash of October 1987, the Russian debt crisis, 9/11, and the crisis that began with the collapse of Lehmans in September 2008. In each case we have taken the relevant asset price changes that occurred during these periods of financial market distress and imposed them on both the assets and liabilities of the scheme which, as you recall has an asset portfolio worth £90m and liabilities valued on an IAS19 basis equal to £100m, and therefore is only 90 per cent funded.

The Lehmans' induced crisis has the largest impact on the funding position of the scheme, reducing funding to 71.3 per cent, while the financial market events surrounding the 9/11 tragedy reduced scheme funding the least to

Exhibit 15.7 The impact of financial market crises on TGtI's funding position

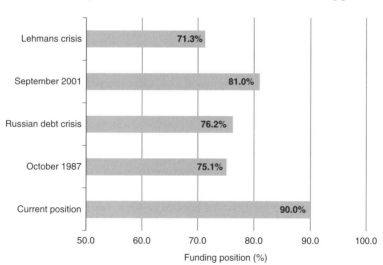

Funding position (%)

81 per cent. Analysis of this kind can give trustees a sobering view of the risks embedded in a scheme's balance sheet, and can be used to try to identify an asset portfolio and hedging strategy that can help reduce the possible impact of, for example, another Lehmans. We should also point out that these events would have had a bigger impact on average scheme funding at the time of their occurrence, since most schemes would have held more than 50 per cent of their asset portfolio in the form of equities before and up to 9/11. It is only really after this event that most schemes began to reduce their exposure to equities. Clearly the greater the proportion of a scheme's assets held in equities, the bigger the impact of such crises.

'PV01' and focusing more specifically on the risks embodied in the liabilities

Both VaR and scenario analysis are useful tools for understanding the overall risks embodied in a scheme. However, when focusing more specifically on the liabilities, analysts and investment consultants often talk about how much 'PV01' is embodied in the liabilities. (Don't worry, PV01 is not a form of bird flu, nor a social security form!) Consultants like to use confusing phrases like these to make trustees think that they are very clever, which if successful, helps to justify their hefty fees.

PV01 is simply 'the present value of one basis point', or 0.01 per cent. That is, PV01 is a measure of the impact of a one basis point, or 0.01 per cent change in interest rates or inflation on the value of the scheme's liabilities, or indeed upon the value of a scheme's bond portfolio (remember that liabilities and bonds are very similar). For a £100m liability scheme, interest rate and inflation PV01s combined of around £150k to £200k are not uncommon. For our TGtI £100m liability scheme, in the event that interest rates, or interest rate expectations, *fall* by a meagre 0.01 per cent *and* inflation, or inflation expectations, *rise* by just one basis point, then the scheme's liabilities would *rise* by about £167k. You should note that PV01 says nothing about the probability of interest rates or inflation moving by one basis point. This aspect of risk analysis relies on the scenario analysis we have just covered.

Exhibit 15.8 represents a typical PV01 chart that consultants might show trustees. They often refer to diagrams like these as PV01 (delta) ladders or PV01 risk buckets. The bar labelled 'Liabilities' in Panel A of the exhibit shows the scheme's exposure to a one basis point reduction in interest rates on the liabilities that fall due over different periods of time. For example the top bar in Panel A shows that a reduction in the discount rate of 0.01 per cent will lead to a £6,060 increase in the present value of liabilities that fall due over

Exhibit 15.8 PV01 ladders for the TGtI scheme

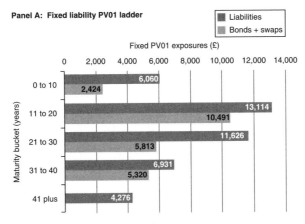

Panel A: Fixed liability PV01 ladder

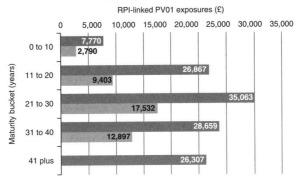

Panel B: RPI-linked liability PV01 ladder

the next ten years.[6] The bars labelled 'Liabilities' in Panel B of the exhibit show the impact of a 0.01 per cent increase in the assumed level of inflation over different liability maturity spans. So for example, the top bar shows that a one basis point increase in the assumed inflation rate on the liabilities falling due over the next ten years will be an increase in the liabilities of £7,770. The chart shows clearly where most of the risk lies in both sets of liabilities, and puts a convenient cash value on this exposure. The largest fixed liability exposure lies in the 11 to 20 year region (or maturity bucket). For the inflation-linked liabilities,

---

[6] One big shortcoming of PV01 analysis is that it does not consider the impact of changing interest rates and/or inflation on the scheme's assets other than the effect on the scheme's bond holdings. Given that many schemes still hold a considerable proportion of their assets in equities and other risky assets, arguably the consultant community should be making greater efforts to quantify the PV01 for these assets too.

the greatest PV01 risk lies in the 21 year plus region. Analysis of this kind can help trustees, with the help of their advisers, identify the correct maturity bond asset or swap needed to hedge the exposure where it is at its greatest. You will also note that the PV01 values are all much larger for the RPI-linked liabilities compared with those that are fixed.

The bars labelled 'Bonds + swaps' in Exhibit 15.8 show the impact of a one basis point decline in interest rates on the bonds and swaps held by the scheme in the case of Panel A, and the impact of a one basis point increase in inflation (or expected inflation) in the case of Panel B. For the purpose of this example we have assumed that in addition to the benefit derived from holding a bond portfolio with an average modified duration of 8 per cent, that the scheme has hedged a further 30 per cent of its combined interest rate and inflation exposure (combined PV01).

Let's now review the role that swaps can play in hedging interest rate and inflation risk for a typical scheme.

Interest rate and inflation hedging instruments

First, we should remember that interest risk can be reduced by increasing holdings of bonds, ideally, long-dated bonds, that have a modified duration (or PV01 in consultant speak) similar to that of the scheme's liabilities. Inflation-linked bonds, again with a modified duration (PV01) similar to a scheme's inflation-linked liabilities, can help to reduce inflation risk. However, swaps, unlike bonds, do not require an upfront payment to be made to effect the hedge. Instead, swaps simply derive their value, once executed, from actual or expected movements in the underlying variable – interest rates or inflation.

Unlike bonds however, they are traded as *over the counter* (OTC) instruments and, as such, are subject to counterparty risk – the risk that the other side, or 'leg' to this legally binding contract, will default. This counterparty could be one of about 15 investment banks who operate in the sterling swaps markets, none of whom has a AAA-credit rating. As a result, swaps are collateralized. That is, the daily change in the mark-to-market value of the swap is backed by the, usually daily exchange of collateral, typically cash and/or government bonds, between the swap counterparties.[7] This means that the scheme will need to maintain a sufficient amount of its assets in cash and/or government bonds to meet actual and potential collateral calls. As a rule of thumb, the scheme

---

[7] Acceptable collateral for swaps (and other most derivatives) generally comprises cash and G4-government securities. The pension scheme and investment bank are collectively known as the swap counterparties.

should hold sufficient eligible collateral for its swap positions to withstand an adverse movement in financial markets that might be experienced on 5 per cent of occasions, or once in every 20 years. However, a number of practitioners suggest maintaining eligible collateral equal to between 20 to 30 per cent of the notional value of outstanding swap positions. So if the notional value of the swaps is £100m, the scheme should hold between £20m and £30m of its assets in highly liquid, low risk, low return asset classes.

We suggested earlier that inflation and interest rate risks – which are generally viewed as unrewarded risks – could be hedged with only a limited impact on the expected return of the scheme's assets (see Exhibit 15.6). However, it is through the necessity to dedicate a proportion of the scheme assets to this collateral pool that the average return on the scheme's assets can be affected when swaps are used. Therefore, other things equal, the larger the swap-based hedge, the larger the required pool of low return, low risks assets that must be set aside as possible collateral to support the swap positions. The greater the collateral pool the higher the return on the remaining assets must be to maintain the same average expected return. In practice, this trade-off usually proves to be the key limiting factor in the amount of unrewarded risk that is hedged. It is for this reason that schemes are increasingly aligning their 'hedge ratios' – that is the percentage of the scheme's interest rate and inflation PV01 to be hedged[8] – to the scheme's funding ratio. So a funding ratio of say, 85 per cent, would result in a target hedge ratio of 85 per cent. After all, as the funding ratio improves, notwithstanding the strength of the sponsor covenant, the scheme should become progressively less reliant on the need to remain in risky assets and move into low-risk, low-return assets, such as government bonds, to both increase the hedge ratio and add to the collateral pool. In so doing, the trustees will also be locking-in the hard won gains from having invested in risky assets.

Inflation swaps

Before entering into an inflation swap, the trustees, on the advice of their investment consultant, pinpoint what proportions of which PV01 inflation buckets they wish to hedge. The scheme then enters into the required inflation swap(s) with a swap counterparty. The scheme agrees to pay a fixed rate of interest to the swap counterparty. In return, the swap counterparty agrees to pay a real rate of interest to the scheme on the same notional amount. This real rate is uplifted with inflation over time, as described in Exhibit 12.4.

---

[8] While a scheme's PV01 loosely corresponds with the scheme's VaR95, the former is a narrower measure of risk than the latter. Unlike PV01, the scheme's VaR95 extends across the scheme's liabilities and *all* of the scheme's assets, not just the scheme's bond assets.

The 15 or so investment banks[9] who operate as swap counterparties in the inflation swaps market are able to pay the inflation-linked leg of the swap because they are in a good position to source this inflation protection in the form of RPI-linked bonds, issued by organizations such as the Debt Management Office (DMO) on behalf of the UK government, utilities and infrastructure companies with RPI-linked revenues. As most of this inflation 'supply' tends to be issued with around a 30-year maturity, this is typically the most liquid area of the inflation swaps market, though the 20- and 50-year areas can also be relatively liquid at times too. The least liquid area is at the very short-dated end of market given the lack of RPI-linked issuance with sub five-year maturities. This difference in liquidity between the short and long end of the inflation swaps market is borne out in the size of the swap spreads, or the cost of transacting, in each of these areas.

Interest rate swaps

The interest rate swaps market, although much bigger and longer established than the inflation swaps market,[10] operates in much the same fashion. However, unlike the inflation swaps market, it is at its most liquid at the short-dated end of the market and least liquid at the longer-dated end, principally owing to the corresponding liquidity of the UK government bond market.

Before entering into an interest rate swap, the trustees, again on the advice of their investment consultant, identify what proportions of the PV01 interest rate buckets they wish to hedge. To hedge the interest rate exposure attached to these payments, the pension scheme pays a floating rate of interest (LIBOR) to a swap counterparty and receives a fixed payment in return. This transaction is shown in Exhibit 12.5. As explained in Chapter 12 the scheme effectively locks into a fixed rate of interest for the term of the swap.

To provide pension schemes with this fixed rate, investment banks[11] typically source fixed rate interest payments from those banks and building societies which receive fixed rate interest payments from those to whom they have granted fixed

---

[9] Despite the fragmented nature of the inflation swaps market, about 80 per cent of transactions are conducted with the top three banks.

[10] The interest rate swaps market was established in the early 1980s whereas the inflation swaps market wasn't established until 2000. With the outstanding notional value of interest rate swap contracts totalling US $364.4tn as at 31 December 2010, it is many times larger than the inflation swaps market. Source: BIS semi-annual derivatives statistics 31 December 2010.

[11] In the interest rate swaps market, the top two banks each have about a 12 per cent market share, the next ten each account for around 7 per cent of the market, leaving about 6 per cent of the market for the remaining three banks.

rate mortgages. In exchange, the investment bank pays the mortgage bank the floating rate payments received from the pension scheme. These floating rate payments can then be paid, by the mortgage bank to its depositors. Another source of fixed rate interest payments is from hedge fund managers that wish to take a directional 'bet' on interest rates over, say, the next five years. That is, the hedge fund manager pays a fixed rate and receives LIBOR in the expectation that LIBOR will, on average, exceed this fixed annual rate over the next five years.

The impact of executing interest and inflation swaps on scheme VaR

Take another look at Exhibit 15.8. The bars labelled 'Bonds and swaps' show what would happen to the combined bond assets and swap positions of the scheme as interest rates and inflation change. In this case we have assumed that the TGtI scheme has managed to hedge 30 per cent of its combined exposure to interest and inflation rates. Panel A of the exhibit shows that the scheme has hedged quite a high proportion of its fixed liabilities; that is, the two sets of bars are not so different. However, Panel B of the exhibit shows that the scheme has so far only hedged a small proportion of its inflation exposure. This is not untypical, since hedging inflation is more difficult, more costly and generally more complicated as intimated above. We can also revisit Exhibit 15.5, where we showed the VaR component parts for each major risk

Exhibit 15.9   The impact on deficit VaR of incorporating inflation and interest rate swaps

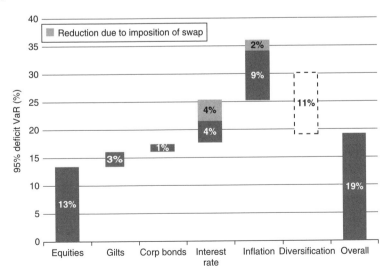

assumed by the scheme. We have now recalculated the exposures by assuming that the scheme has implemented a de-risking swap strategy that has reduced the combined interest rate and inflation exposure by 30 per cent. As Exhibit 15.9 shows, this has reduced the overall deficit VaR of the scheme deficit from 23 per cent to 19 per cent.

Aside from swaps and bonds, there are a number of other instruments that have been developed which enable a scheme to hedge inflation and interest rate risk, which we'll look at briefly towards the end of this chapter. However, there is another risk that has also been particularly unrewarding for pension schemes over the past few years and that's longevity risk. This is the risk that scheme members do not die as soon as is expected and simply draw more pension than forecast. Is it possible to hedge this risk too?

Hedging longevity risk

In January 2010 the Department of Work and Pensions (DWP) suggested that the number of people in the UK aged 100 or over was set to double by 2020 to 22,000 and then grow more than 12-fold to 280,000 by 2050. One year on, the DWP revealed that it expected nearly 11 million people alive in January 2011, around 17 per cent of the population, to live to over 100. Of these, about 2.2m were aged 50 or over, of which 875,000 were aged 65 and above. In short, this means that by 2066 the UK will have about half-a-million centenarians.[12]

With the seemingly ever increasing life expectancy trends over the past few decades there is no question in most trustees' minds that longevity risk should be hedged as long as it can be hedged without materially impacting the scheme's funding position. Many commentators suggest that underestimating the longevity of a scheme's membership by just one year adds up to 4–5 per cent to the present value of the scheme's liabilities (see Exhibit 15.3).

However, while longevity risk has long been traded in the insurance and re-insurance markets for some time, the ability to manage this risk within a pension scheme has proved to be the missing piece in the risk management jigsaw. It was either a case of insuring the pensioner liabilities – those pensions currently in payment – through a buy-in or going the whole hog with an insured buyout of

---

[12] In Chapter 1 we noted that according to the Office for National Statistics (ONS), in 2009 the average 65-year-old male in the UK was expected to live for 17.8 years and female 20.4 years. This compares with 16 years and 19.1 years respectively in 2000. However, regional differences can be marked. For instance, the difference between the life expectancy of a 65-year-old male living in Kensington and Chelsea compared to a 65-year-old male living in Glasgow in 2009 was 9.8 years. See http://www.statistics.gov.uk/STATBASE/Product.asp?vlnk=8841.

the scheme's assets and liabilities. A buy-in, or bulk-annuity contract, involves the pension scheme buying an insurance policy against the investment, interest rate, inflation and longevity risks for a particular cohort of its liabilities, typically some or all of the scheme's pensioners. This insurance policy is then held as an asset within the scheme (i.e. the trustees retain responsibility for these liabilities). A buyout involves the sponsor offloading the entire pension scheme to an insurance company. Both approaches had started to prove quite costly in 2008, notably in the wake of the bankruptcy of Lehmans and against the backdrop of a marked deterioration in scheme finances. However, things have moved forward a little recently. In 2009, Babcock International, RSA Insurance and The Royal County of Berkshire all executed longevity hedging deals, capping the longevity risk attached to the majority of their respective pensioner liabilities by using longevity swaps. These deals were then followed in early 2010 by a similar deal negotiated for the BMW (UK) pension scheme. Collectively these deals covered around £7bn of pensioner liabilities.

Longevity swaps look a lot like inflation swaps. As shown in Exhibit 15.10, they oblige a scheme to pay to an investment bank or insurance company willing to act as counterparty, a series of regular fixed payments (the 'fixed leg'), over the *expected* lifespan of the scheme's pensioners. In return the scheme receives a series of regular, variable payments (the 'floating leg') over the *actual* lifespan of the scheme members. In other words, the longer the pensioners live, the longer and the higher are the payments made to the scheme by their counterparty. Just as with an inflation swap, it is not the two sets of payments that are exchanged periodically, but instead it is the difference between the present value of each leg of the longevity swap that is exchanged between the two counterparties in the form of collateral. Ultimately if pensioner lifespans turn out to be longer than originally forecast, then the swap counterparty will end up owing money to the scheme; if they turn out to be shorter, then the scheme will end up owing money to the swap counterparty. In the former case, the scheme is compensated for the higher pension payments that it has to make; in the latter the scheme benefits from lower pension payments, but the scheme must pay the swap counterparty at least some of this benefit.

The coupons relating to the 'floating leg' of these longevity swaps can either be based upon general longevity indices, such as the JP Morgan LifeMetrics index,

Exhibit 15.10 Mechanics of a longevity swap

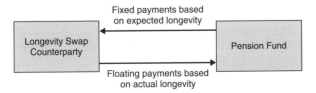

which provide protection against population-wide increases in longevity, or can be based upon estimates of the lives of a scheme's members, as was the case of the four schemes mentioned above where sufficient mortality data on the scheme membership existed. However, for many schemes, providing up-to-date membership data may prove a challenge. While the bespoke approach can provide a very close hedge for pensioner liabilities, the index approach is more suited to providing protection against active and deferred member longevity risk, where the timing and amount of pension benefits to be taken remains very unpredictable, especially if the scheme is immature. It is for this reason that this latter approach is likely to prove to be the more expensive of the two methodologies. In fact, to date, only one DB scheme – Pall (UK) – has executed an index-based swap to cover £60m of its deferred pension liabilities.

Against a backdrop of ongoing mortality improvements both the appetite for hedging longevity risk and the range of innovative solutions look set for a period of significant growth, though the market's ability to accommodate deals could very quickly hit capacity constraints. It is because of these capacity constraints that a number of pensions experts, such as David Blake of Cass Business School, have called for the UK government to issue longevity bonds linked to the future survival rate of specific cohorts of the population, for example, males aged 65 in 2010, alongside conventional and index-linked gilts. In so doing, a more liquid and transparent longevity derivatives market might develop, in the same way that the interest rate and inflation swaps markets, based principally on the conventional and index-linked gilts market, have grown exponentially in recent years. However, while a deeper, more liquid market in longevity risk might enable pension schemes to reduce this particular source of unrewarded risk, which in turn might increase the probability of meeting their liabilities, the counter argument to the UK government issuing longevity-linked bonds is strong. It would effectively mean that the taxpayer would be underwriting mortality improvements. Arguably, the state already does this via the social security and welfare system. Given this, it seems unlikely that the UK government would or should issue longevity bonds.

Arguably the crucial benefit of longevity swaps for pension schemes is that, unlike buyouts or buy-ins that can also reduce longevity risk, longevity swaps do not require the scheme to make an upfront payment to an insurance company or investment bank – allowing the scheme to retain control of its assets so that it can pursue the asset allocation strategy that best fits its recovery plan.

Given the long-term nature of the contract, when entering into a longevity swap, the necessary due diligence should be conducted around:

- the financial strength of the counterparty,
- the pricing of the deal,
- the effectiveness of the longevity hedge,

- the collateral mechanics that protect both 'legs' against counterparty risk, and
- how viable an exit strategy is, should the scheme wish to go to buyout.

Summary: the science of LDI

The science of LDI is rather complicated despite the principle behind LDI being rather simple. A scheme's assets are there to fund future liabilities, therefore the assets should be managed so that they perform in such a way as to minimize the likelihood that the liabilities will not be met.

For many, LDI is synonymous with interest rate, inflation and longevity swaps. Due to the complex nature of these contracts, most trustees require extensive training in this area though hopefully Chapter 12 has gone some way to enabling readers to develop an understanding of these contracts. However, LDI is not really only about the implementation of complicated swap contracts – though it can be. It is really about understanding the risks on both the asset and liability side of the balance sheet, plus those that reside in the quality of the scheme sponsor's covenant. Essentially it is a risk management and risk reallocation exercise. In understanding these risks, trustees and their scheme sponsors may come to the conclusion that swaps must be part of the risk managed solution, but all schemes are different and this approach may not be applicable or advisable in some cases.

There is also the issue of the price and timing of swap transactions, which we concluded with in Chapter 12, and an investment context to implementing a swap strategy that must *never* be forgotten. If you have forgotten it please go back to the last few pages of Chapter 12 again. It is very important.

Having said all this, many schemes have already begun, or intend to begin a programme of liability hedging using swaps. In other words, having looked at the risks embedded on both sides of the scheme's balance sheet, they have chosen to de-risk the scheme predominantly via the use of swaps. Given that many schemes have already come to this view, the second half of this chapter looks at some of the practical issues that are involved in this de-risking journey and the role that trustees, various third parties and practitioners play in it.

The practicalities of implementing a de-risking programme

Implementing a de-risking programme can be viewed as a dynamic seven stage process as represented in Exhibit 15.11. Although not explicitly built into Exhibit 15.11, it is absolutely essential for the trustees to gain the support of the sponsoring employer from the very start and then to work closely with

Exhibit 15.11   LDI – a seven stage process flow chart

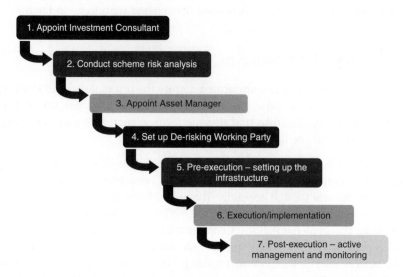

them throughout the process, keeping them fully informed of developments. We will now work through these stages in turn, starting with the appointment of the investment consultant.

The Investment Consultant

Producing the appropriate technical analysis for a de-risking programme – the VaR, the PV01s and the stress tests – all require the considerable expertise of an investment consultant with a significant understanding of swaps markets. The consultant should ideally have extensive investment banking experience and connections, since they will be responsible for sourcing the interest rate and/or inflation swaps (and/or bonds) to be executed. Your current consultant may not be up to the job, in which case a specialist de-risking or LDI investment consultant might need to be appointed. The chosen consultant will then need to work closely with the scheme actuary in gathering the scheme liability data and the scheme's custodian(s) on the asset side. Not only that, the consultant will need to be able to help the trustees measure and interpret all of the key risks and advise them on the timing and extent to which they should be reduced.[13]

---

[13] Timing is important not least because swap supply can be sporadic and the bigger the size of the swaps transaction, the greater the proportionate cost. As we mentioned earlier, the extent to which the scheme mitigates its unrewarded risk determines the amount of collateral that needs to be held as part of the scheme's assets. In extremis, this can put a constraint on the ability of the scheme to hold the risk assets it needs in order to reach full funding as per its recovery plan.

A passively implemented, or 'execute and forget', swap strategy is one that is typically executed in a liquid market via a single investment bank and once completed is left to run without any interim active management. With this type of approach the consultant helps the trustees establish 'hedging levels', or 'trigger points', for their schemes. For example, the trustees may decide to implement an inflation hedge only when the implied future inflation rates for inflation swaps are priced below their recent historic average or an interest rate swap when the fixed nominal interest rates on offer are above the recent historic average. Other schemes might base their decisions on the level of real interest rates, that take both the fixed nominal interest rate and the implied inflation rate into account, and only act when the real rate is above its recent historic average (as this implies high nominal interest rates and low implied inflation). However, when market conditions are truly inhospitable, as they were in the year following Lehman's bankruptcy in September 2008, then a more dynamic approach is needed.

A truly dynamic, or active, swap strategy is one that is implemented on an opportunistic, or tactical, basis with a number of investment banks, as and when liquidity becomes available, with the swap positions being actively managed post-execution. However, subject to the increased trustee governance requirements that this approach demands, arguably a dynamic de-risking strategy should be applied regardless of market conditions. This dynamic approach will be addressed further shortly.

Scheme risk analysis

Because we discussed the relevance of and the methodology behind producing the appropriate technical analysis for a de-risking programme – the VaR, the PV01s and the stress tests – earlier in the chapter, we won't repeat the analysis here. However, if you need a reminder of how we come to an understanding of all of the risks embodied in a scheme's assets and liabilities before moving on, please refer back to 'The science of LDI'.

The Asset Manager

The investment consultant will need to work in parallel with the appointed asset manager of the swaps portfolio. While the consultant and asset manager, collectively known as the implementation partners, often work in concert in sourcing the requisite swaps and/or bonds for the hedging, or de-risking, programme, the asset manager is solely responsible for executing the swap transactions between the pension scheme and the investment banks[14] and managing the collateral that passes between the counterparties, usually daily. The mark of a good swaps

---

[14] This is a requirement under the Pensions Act 2004.

asset manager is one who has a strong negotiating position in the swaps market, enabling them to execute the swaps at keen prices and low transactions costs with the banks, ensuring that the market is not disrupted by the execution of these swap transactions by ultimately leaving a 'silent footprint' post-execution. This only comes from experience, knowing what size of transaction to conduct at any point in time and leaving a respectable time, sometimes a week or so, between transactions.

However, the experience and skill of the implementation partners must be complemented by a sufficiently advanced level of trustee governance.

The De-risking Working Party (DWP)

Most trustee boards tend to delegate the requisite powers to work with the implementation partners in designing and implementing a de-risking programme to the investment committee. However, a dynamic de-risking strategy might require the trustees to meet and agree on the various courses of action as frequently as weekly, even daily on occasion, if the programme's implementation is to gain momentum and prove successful. In this case it might require the trustee board to form a small, dedicated de-risking working party (DWP) from the investment committee, or simply from the main board, to work with the implementation partners, with the support of the pension scheme manager and sponsor:

- in setting up the necessary infrastructure,
- on the detailed execution of the swap transactions, and
- in periodically reporting back to the investment committee, trustee board and sponsor on the reduction achieved in the scheme's interest rate and inflation exposures (PV01s), VaR95 and exposure to extreme events (stress testing).

In setting up the DWP, the trustee board or investment committee needs to take account of the skills around the table and whether the trustees selected have the time, competence and confidence to make decisions in real time. In most cases, these individuals, indeed the entire trustee board, will require extensive training from their investment consultant prior to setting up the necessary de-risking infrastructure and overseeing the execution of the swap transactions. Indeed, in some cases it may be necessary to appoint an independent trustee with the requisite experience to help out the incumbent trustees.

Pre-execution: Setting up the de-risking infrastructure

However, as intimated above, before the process of de-risking – that is, mitigating the unrewarded risks through the execution of swap contracts – can begin, the de-risking infrastructure must be set up. To do this, the DWP not only needs to work with the implementation partners and with the pension scheme manager but also with the scheme lawyers, again keeping the sponsor up-to-date with developments to carry out the following activities:

- Amend the scheme Statement of Investment Principles (SIP) to provide the authority for the scheme to execute swaps and manage the swap portfolio.
- Set up a panel of competing investment banks with whom the scheme could potentially deal. By selecting a number of counterparty banks, the scheme not only diversifies its counterparty risk but also, by keeping each of the banks on their toes, should receive priority notification of swap supply, known as swap 'axes', and achieve lower than advertised transaction costs.
- Outline the execution framework to the banks. The consultant agrees the rules of engagement and standards of behaviour with the banks and outlines the penalties of non-compliance, which ultimately means being replaced by another bank. As noted earlier, there are about 15 banks with whom the scheme can choose to deal.
- Set up the ISDA[15] counterparty documentation. As OTC instruments, swaps are governed by somewhat detailed ISDA documentation. Pension schemes are legally required to have an ISDA Master Agreement and Schedule in place before entering into any OTC derivatives contracts. These are standardized documents which define the relationship between the pension scheme and each of the investment banks with whom they potentially wish to deal and encompass the types of derivatives contracts the pension scheme will be party to. They also specify standard terms for areas including the netting of swap payments between the counterparties, the tax implications and what constitutes and what remedies a credit, or default, event on both sides. In addition, a *Credit Support Annex (CSA)* is put in place to specify the collateral requirements. However, as a negotiated document, an ISDA takes time to finalize and execute. Therefore, it makes sense to start work on the ISDA documentation as soon as the decision has been made to deal with whichever investment banks have been selected.
- Appoint a *calculation agent*. The appointment and responsibilities of the calculation agent are agreed within the ISDA documentation by the counterparties. Typically the role of the calculation agent is undertaken by the back office of an investment bank that is not acting as a swap counterparty to the pension scheme. They are charged with producing, usually daily, mark-to-market valuations for the executed swaps and calculating, typically daily, collateral requirements and the netted collateral and swap payments to be made between the counterparties.

---

[15] ISDA is the International Swaps and Derivatives Association. This is the global trade association for over the counter (OTC) derivatives and that which maintains the industry-standard ISDA documentation.

- Set up the collateral agreements. As noted earlier, collateral is generally required in the form of cash and/or government securities,[16] though there can be a unilateral or bilateral agreement between the counterparties to post and/or receive corporate bonds as collateral. Depending on the quality of the collateral, a 'haircut' may be applied to its market value to ensure that any adverse move in its price doesn't affect its ability to provide the necessary security.[17] While any collateral posted to the pension scheme is managed by the asset manager, who manages the swaps portfolio, its legal title is held by an independent third party specified in the CSA. Necessarily, any cash and/or securities held in the scheme's collateral account will earn a return, offsetting the scheme's collateral funding costs. As noted earlier, as a rule of thumb, the scheme should hold sufficient collateral within its assets to meet potential two standard deviation events – those that are expected to occur on about 5 per cent of occasions, or once in every 20 years. This equates to about 20 to 30 per cent of the notional value of the scheme's swap contracts.
- Ensure that the accounting, reporting and compliance strategies are in place. The asset manager needs to reconcile each swaps trade and periodically report the overall position to the DWP. The asset manager's compliance department oversees this and the managing of the collateral function.
- Set the de-risking timeframe. Once all of the above is in place, it is imperative that the trustee board, via the DWP, sets and sticks to a timeframe within which the scheme mitigates the agreed amount of unrewarded risk. The latter is typically expressed as both a percentage reduction in the PV01 of the scheme's inflation and interest rate risk and that of the scheme's VaR95. Trustees often set a series of de-risking targets to be met at certain stages within the defined timeframe. Other things being equal, the more advanced the trustee governance, the shorter the timeframe tends to be. As noted earlier, schemes are increasingly aligning their 'hedge ratios' – that is the percentage of the scheme's interest rate and inflation PV01 to be hedged – to the scheme's funding ratio.
- Set possible real yield trigger points. As mentioned earlier, some trustees, on the advice of their investment consultant, often set real interest rate, or real yield,[18] trigger targets, at or above which they are prepared to begin implementing their de-risking programme through the execution of swap contracts.[19] However, as

---

[16] As noted earlier, acceptable collateral for swaps (and other most derivatives) generally comprises cash and G4-nation government securities.

[17] Securities with longer dated maturities and poorer quality assets have bigger 'haircuts'.

[18] The real yield is that offered by an index-linked gilt. The terms 'real interest rate' and 'real yield' are used interchangeably.

[19] Remember, the pension scheme wishes to lock into the highest possible real interest rate as this equates to receiving the highest possible fixed interest payment from interest rate swaps and paying the lowest possible fixed payment for inflation swaps.

such targets are usually set around the long-run average for the real yield of 2.25 per cent, these can have one of two unintended consequences. The first is that a real yield of 2.25 per cent is never achieved. This has been the case in recent years for almost the entire real yield curve, thereby putting such implementation plans on hold. The second is that if, or when, a real yield of 2.25 per cent is achieved, all of a sudden a multitude of pension schemes make a beeline for the swaps market forcing real yields down again, and thus causing the hedging opportunity to disappear very quickly.

Execution and implementation

Once the de-risking infrastructure has been set up, the process of de-risking and the execution of swap contracts can begin. This aspect of the dynamic de-risking programme is illustrated in Exhibit 15.12.

However, there are a number of considerations to be made, some of which have already been noted:

- Sourcing swap supply. In an illiquid market, it is imperative to have prioritized access to swap supply. Typically, investment banks inform investment consultants and asset managers about two weeks in advance of sizeable axes coming to the market. Much comes down to selecting the 'right' banks.
- Cost. The cost of executing a swaps transaction is given by the size of the swaps contract – or the 'clip' – quoted in PV01 terms, multiplied by the swap spread expressed as an absolute number rather than in basis points. This transaction cost is factored into the present value of the swap rather than being paid by the pension scheme up front. So if a £50k PV01 inflation swap was quoted with a spread of 1.5 basis points, then the dealing cost would be £75k (£50k × 1.5). Swap spreads can vary considerably between

Exhibit 15.12   Implementing a dynamic de-risking strategy flow chart

banks, principally as a consequence of the amount of risk each is prepared to 'warehouse', or keep on its books, and the type and amount of supply they can access. However, a good asset manager should be able to negotiate down the advertised spread; and finally

- Timing is important not least because swap supply can be sporadic and the bigger the clip, the greater the spread and proportionate cost.

Once the implementation of the programme is underway, the DWP, pension scheme manager, sponsor and implementation partners should meet weekly, sometimes more frequently, if not face-to-face, then via conference call, to discuss five aspects to the de-risking programme:

- market levels, activity and trends;
- execution progress over the past week (or shorter period) and how this has impacted the scheme's risk metrics;
- de-risking opportunities arising and imminent swap supply;
- recommended swap trades to be agreed; and
- tactical refinements to the strategy.

The latter is particularly important when implementing a dynamic de-risking strategy. Tactical refinements will need to be made when the relative value of one area of the swaps curve (whether interest rates or inflation) becomes more attractive than another, subject to parameters laid down by the DWP. For example, in late-August 2008 when the interest rate swap curve was downward sloping, liquid 10–30-year interest rate swaps were priced at a discount to illiquid 50-year swaps. This meant that a pension scheme could receive a higher fixed interest rate at the 10–30-year end than at the 50-year end of the swaps curve. So for our TGtI DB scheme with PV01 buckets such as those illustrated in Exhibit 15.8, it would have made sense to have focused on 'over hedging' the ten-year end of the zero-to-ten-year interest rate PV01 bucket and the 11–30-year interest rate PV01 buckets, at the expense of 'under hedging' the 41-year plus PV01 bucket. Similarly, liquid 50-year inflation swaps were priced more cheaply than those in the more illiquid 15–30-year area, meaning that the fixed rate payable by a pension scheme at the 50-year area of the inflation swaps curve was less than that payable at the 15–30-year area. Therefore it would have made sense for our scheme to have focused on the former at the expense of the latter.

Indeed, by December 2008, as the interest rate swaps curve had steepened at the short end and had also shifted downwards, being over hedged in the 10–30-year area would have proved an extremely profitable position. In addition, a similarly sharp move by the inflation swaps curve meant that losses suffered on long-term inflation contracts would have been relatively minor compared to those on shorter-dated inflation swaps. These under- and over-hedged positions would have needed to be corrected at some stage within the desired de-risking timeframe in order to meet the scheme's risk reduction objectives but making sensible tactical relative value judgements in a risk controlled manner along the way is essential to the successful implementation of a de-risking strategy.

In addition to taking advantage of relative value opportunities across the swaps curve, a pension scheme can also benefit from tactical switches between swaps and bonds, by again employing relative value judgements. In September 2008, it had become clear that market conditions no longer favoured the use of swaps over bonds for interest rate and inflation hedging across most maturities. For instance, as shown in Exhibit 15.13, 30-year index-linked gilt yields rose above 30-year real swap rates.[20] In other words, since the break-even inflation implied by the gilt market was lower than that implied by the inflation swaps market, inflation protection could be achieved more cheaply through the index-linked gilts market than via inflation swaps. Similarly, interest rate hedging could be achieved more cost effectively by buying longer-dated gilts than by becoming a fixed receiver in a long-dated interest rate swap.

Exhibit 15.13 Responding to changes in market conditions

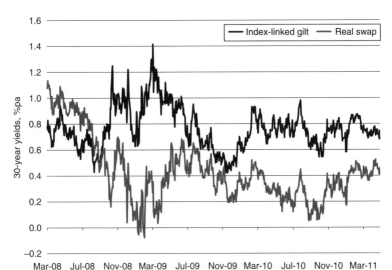

[20] The 'yield inversion' was caused by supply drying up on the swaps side and increasing on the gilts side. On the swaps side, the RPI bond issuance by utilities and infrastructure companies that underpins inflation swaps supply had begun to dry up and investment banks were not prepared to warehouse risk because their capital had been depleted by the financial crisis. In addition, Lehman's collapse on 15 September 2008 removed some investment banking capacity from the market. On the gilts side, the prospect of a dramatic upturn in new issuance to finance the government's burgeoning fiscal deficit, drove gilt prices down causing gilt yields to rise.

The key point to take away is that trustees need implementation partners who can spot relative value opportunities, and who can advise them on these opportunities. Trustees, in turn, therefore need to have the requisite skills to be able to agree to a change of tack in a timely manner. Indeed, to be successful, a truly active (dynamic), de-risking strategy is one that is highly dependent on five key factors: agility, flexibility, proximity to the market, intelligent execution and an advanced level of trustee governance; and a strong five-way partnership between the trustees, sponsor, investment consultant, asset manager and the investment banks.

New relative value opportunities

Liability-linked income (LLI) assets

Trustees and their advisers are constantly re-evaluating how best to meet their funding objectives by generating suitably strong long-term investment returns and hedging the unrewarded risks within their scheme liabilities by securing liability matching cash flows. As they do so, there is increasing interest in liability-linked income (LLI is one of the latest buzz acronyms in the pensions' world) assets, comprising:

- long-lease real estate;
- ground leases;
- social housing;
- student accommodation; and
- social infrastructure.

As we noted in Chapter 8, the defining feature of LLI assets is that they provide predictable long-term income streams, typically in excess of 15 years but in some cases they extend beyond 75 years. Added to the fact that these income streams are also usually inflation-linked, mainly to the RPI, or include fixed uplifts, means that they provide a good hedge against inflation and interest rate risks.

Moreover, these cash flows are secured against physical or operating assets (the security often being far in excess of the value of the underlying investment) or a government/quasi-government covenant. All of these features make these cash flows particularly attractive for paying pensions far into the future. In addition, there is little, if any, reliance on the potential for capital values to increase. Indeed, unlike the return from a long-dated bond, the capital sum invested is typically amortized, or built, into the cash flows paid to the pension scheme over the term of the investment. This means that at the end of the investment term, the pension scheme doesn't usually receive the residual value of the underlying property.

However, since no secondary market currently exists for LLI assets this means that pension schemes are effectively locked into the asset for the duration of the investment's term. Arguably the illiquidity of an asset, which provides a secure long-term income stream to pay pensions, should be of little concern to long-term investors, assuming that it accounts for a relatively small percentage of the pension scheme's assets. Nevertheless, to compensate investors for their illiquid nature, LLI assets typically offer a significant 'liquidity premium'. That is, they offer more attractive yields and potentially higher returns than are attainable from gilts and index-linked gilts and many secured corporate bonds, of a similar risk profile, as well as some diversification benefits. Additionally, in the case of social housing and social infrastructure, these returns are potentially enhanced yet further by virtue of the fact that, as these assets are no longer financed by governments or the banks, as they once were, new longer-term sources of finance, such as that from pension schemes, must be sought.

Gilt total return swaps

Despite a somewhat tortuous title, *gilt total return swaps* (gilt TRS) can provide pension schemes with an alternative means of reducing interest rate risk, often more cheaply than by employing bonds and swaps. The underlying mechanics are similar to an interest rate swap, in that the scheme pays a series of floating rate payments to a counterparty bank, though not in exchange for a fixed rate of interest set by the swaps market, but for the total return on a specific gilt. However, whereas for an interest rate swap the scheme makes a series of LIBOR payments to the counterparty bank, for a gilt TRS the scheme typically pays a floating rate lower than LIBOR, usually a few basis points lower, because of the way in which investment banks fund their operations. In addition, if gilts yield more than the equivalent swap, then the scheme can benefit from this yield enhancement through the gilt TRS. As TRSs are OTC derivatives, a scheme would need to use the same ISDA documentation that it uses with the same swap counterparties for its interest rate and inflation swaps.

So why don't all pension schemes use gilt TRS to mitigate their interest rate risk? Well, gilt TRS can usually only be held for up to three years, with the financing cost for pension schemes becoming increasingly less attractive the longer the term of the TRS. So if at expiry the TRS is to be 'rolled over' into a new contract, then the terms and costs will need to be renegotiated and may not be as generous as they were previously. In addition, depending on market liquidity at the time, the costs of unwinding positions before maturity can be quite significant.

Post-execution

Ultimately, the successful execution of a dynamic de-risking programme should be evidenced by the realization of the planned reduction in the scheme's interest rate and inflation PV01 sensitivity, that of its VaR95 and an improved resilience to extreme scenarios, notwithstanding any increase in general market volatility during the implementation period.[21] In addition, intelligent negotiation and execution of the swaps programme with the investment banks allied to strong trustee governance should result in substantial cost savings compared with expected transactions costs.

However, this should be seen as an ongoing process. As noted earlier, a de-risking journey should probably not be an 'execute and forget' exercise. The DWP and the implementation partners must keep everything on track by actively:

- monitoring, managing, valuing and stress testing the scheme's swaps and collateral positions;
- looking for new relative value opportunities, while remaining cognizant of the need to maintain sufficient collateral to meet potential two standard deviation events; and
- keeping in touch with, monitoring and evaluating the investment banks.

What about the growth assets?

This chapter has focused on the identification of the risks inherent in a pension scheme balance sheet and then, as a consequence of the deficit pandemic, the way in which trustees can realign the risks on both sides of the balance sheet. However, for any scheme with a deficit, simply hedging all the inflation, interest rate risk and even longevity risk will not on its own return the scheme to a fully funded position. This would be a bit like Manchester United deploying five goalkeepers and six defenders against Barcelona,[22] once they had already gone two nil down. This strategy would probably stop the situation from getting any worse (though not necessarily) but it would be unlikely to propel them to victory.

Victory for a pension scheme is the timely payment of all benefits due. Locking down all the inflation, interest rate and longevity risks, even if this were possible, would not deliver a victory on its own. The assets not dedicated to de-risking need to grow over time to plug the deficit and to achieve final victory. As we

---

[21] A general increase in market volatility will, other things being equal, result in an increase in the scheme's PV01 sensitivities, its VaR and susceptibility to extreme scenarios.
[22] This is of course against the rules of football, but possibly the only sure way of stopping Lionel Messi and his team mates.

pointed out earlier, the bigger the deficit and the smaller the proportion of remaining 'growth' assets, the harder it will be to return a scheme to a fully funded position. It is important then that trustees do not become so obsessed with the de-risking component of their investment strategy that they forget the importance of the asset allocation decisions with regard to the growth assets. Even though most schemes are well into the second half of the match and are at least one goal down, victory is still possible with sensible risk management and a judicious asset allocation strategy.

Summary

We started this chapter with an analogy drawn from Dickens' *Oliver Twist* and will finish with one. While most schemes still have a deficit to tackle and will invariably encounter some headwinds along the way, (as we know in *Oliver Twist*, Nancy was murdered, the dog was shot and Bill Sykes hung himself), schemes that engage in a LDI strategy should be considerably closer to a happier ending – as it ultimately proved for Oliver – than they would have been had they not engaged in the process. Why? Because the probability of being able to pay scheme benefits in full increases.

Key points

- The principal aim of any defined benefit (DB) pension scheme is to meet its liabilities as they fall due and to remain fully funded.
- Most DB schemes are less than fully funded, principally as a result of previously unmatched asset/liability positions.
- LDI is not a new idea, and the principle behind LDI is rather simple. A scheme's assets are there to fund future liabilities, therefore the assets should be managed so that they perform in such a way as to maximize the likelihood that the liabilities will be met.
- LDI as a risk management tool focuses on both the mitigation of unrewarded risks, comprising interest rate, inflation and longevity risk, to prevent a scheme deficit from widening and capturing a diversity of potentially rewarded risks, so as to ultimate plug the deficit.
- As there is no single approach to measuring risk, LDI views and manages these unrewarded risks through multiple risk lenses, such as Value at Risk (VaR), PV01 and scenario testing.
- Interest rate and inflation risk can be reduced by using bonds and swaps, though liability linked income assets and gilt total return swaps are increasingly being used. Each have their pros and cons and impact the scheme's asset allocation differently. Swaps can also be used to hedge longevity risk.

- The implementation of a successful de-risking programme requires:
  - o the necessary infrastructure to be set up before the programme is implemented;
  - o the trustees to form a De-risking Working Party which employs an advanced level of governance;
  - o a strong five-way partnership between the trustees, sponsor, investment consultant, asset manager and the investment banks;
  - o the timely identification and exploitation of relative value opportunities; and
  - o the ongoing monitoring and management of both sides of the pension scheme balance sheet.

Chapter 16

Integrating Environmental, Social and Corporate Governance (ESG) Factors into the Investment Decision Making Process: An Altruistic Exercise?

Learning outcomes

- Understand why and how trustees should incorporate ESG factors into their investment decisions.
- Understand what corporate governance is and why it matters.
- Appreciate the impact of good corporate governance on share price performance.
- Understand what Sustainable and Responsible Investment (SRI) is and how it differs from mainstream investing.
- Appreciate that SRI does not necessarily mean compromising on investment performance.

Introduction

The costs to pension schemes and other investors of the unsustainable risk taking, misaligned incentives, moral hazard and other issues that characterized the financial crisis of 2008 and subsequent events highlighted the importance of adopting a 'responsible' and 'activist' approach to investment. The disproportionate rise in executive remuneration, notably that of chief executives, against the backdrop of a total failure to perform, declining profits and/or a declining share price, is surely an issue that should concern all investors. Typical executive remuneration packages would make a Premiership footballer blush, especially those earned by investment bankers. *Moral hazard,* that is, reckless behaviour that is unintentionally encouraged as a consequence of a safety net, such as an insurance policy or the implicit underwriting of an activity, having been put in place, also played a big part in the crisis. For instance, immediately prior to the 2008 financial crisis, most large banks believing they were 'too big to fail' and could rely on a government bail out if things went wrong, engaged in what is best described as 'casino capitalism'. As it proved, most were bailed out, the key exceptions being Lehman Brothers and the nationalization of Northern Rock and a number of Irish and Icelandic banks. The existence of moral hazard then, should also be a key concern of investors.

The events of the crisis strongly suggest that trustees and all investors should consider Environmental, Social and Corporate Governance (ESG)[1] factors. By this, we mean ensuring that the companies in which your scheme invests adopt best practice in corporate governance and pursue sustainable and responsible business and management practices. After all, institutional investors, such as pension schemes, and the asset managers who manage their investments, have, unlike individual investors, both the financial clout and the means by which to co-ordinate their actions to promote best practice within companies. Indeed, arguably many of the issues listed above were exacerbated because the institutional investor 'landlords' were largely absent throughout the lead up to this period.[2] As such, there is now a groundswell of opinion that trustees should become more active in their approach to ESG issues when making investment decisions.

Although many investors, which may well include you, your co-trustees and many of your members, often see this as a questionable altruistic exercise, any

---

[1] ESG covers a very broad spectrum of issues, from executive remuneration, executive appointments and shareholder representation on the board, shareholder rights, corporate control and accounting practices to climate change, human rights, supply chain labour standards and business ethics.

[2] 'Absentee landlords' was a term coined by ex-City Minister Paul Myners. It was made with reference to institutional investors' lack of active engagement with the companies in which they were invested to ensure they were being run in shareholders', rather than management's, best interests and in such a way to maximize shareholder value.

scepticism should be put aside. Adopting an ESG approach to investing is all about practising good stewardship and should, when implemented correctly, lead to the generation of better quality and more sustainable long-run investment returns.

Incorporating ESG factors into investment decision making and disclosing the scheme's ESG policy

Should trustees incorporate ESG factors into their investment decision making?

Before looking at these ESG factors in more detail, the first question we need to address is whether trustees are required to bring ESG factors into their investment decision making process. As we noted in Chapter 2, while trustee investment decision-making is governed by trust law, legislation, regulation and best practice guidelines, the most common misconception that arises is that trustees' only and overriding investment objective is profit maximization. That is, to generate the best risk-adjusted investment returns possible for members to the exclusion of all other considerations.

The classic citation, wrongly used to support this position, is the case of *Cowan v Scargill (1984)*. However, given the misrepresentation of that case, in 1989 the presiding Judge took the unusual step of revisiting his judgement. Contrary to the apparent judgement he had given, the Judge confirmed, albeit in a non-binding statement, that the case did not support the thesis that profit maximization alone was consistent with the fiduciary duty of pension fund trustees and suggested that ESG factors *could* be taken into consideration by trustees. Indeed, the ruling in a subsequent case, that of *Harries v Church Commissioners (1991)*, firmly supported the Church Commissioners' explicit incorporation of ESG factors in their investment strategy and the exclusion of certain types of company from their portfolios.

However, the most effective document for promoting the integration of ESG issues into trustee investment decisions is arguably the 'Freshfields Report', published by Freshfields, the legal firm, in 2005.[3] This report was asked to consider the following question:

Is the integration of environmental, social and governance issues into investment policy (including asset allocation, portfolio construction and stock-picking or bond-picking)

---

[3] Freshfields Bruckhaus Deringer, *A Legal Framework for the Integration of Environmental, Social and Governance Issues into Institutional Investment*. UNEP Finance Initiative Asset Management Working Group, (2005).

voluntarily permitted, legally required or hampered by law and regulation; primarily as regards public and private pension funds . . .?

The Report covered nine jurisdictions – Australia, Canada, France, Germany, Italy, Japan, Spain, the UK and the US – and concluded that:

integrating ESG considerations into an investment analysis so as to more reliably predict financial performance is clearly permissible and is arguably required in all jurisdictions.

This clear conclusion has served to clarify the legality relating to pension scheme consideration of ESG issues within their investment decision making; though it should be noted that the conclusion includes an important caveat: 'so as to more reliably predict financial performance'. In other words, trustees must put financial returns to the scheme above all else, not least any ESG concerns they may have. So trustees can take account of ESG factors to: deliver improved financial returns, or where taking account of ESG factors into account produces non-financial benefits which are valued by a significant proportion of the scheme's beneficiaries, or promotes the objectives of the scheme, so long as the financial returns to all beneficiaries are not compromised.

How can trustees integrate ESG issues into their investment decision making?

So, while trustees can bring ESG considerations into their investment decision making, this of course raises the question of how trustees should go about delivering on any ESG fiduciary responsibility. After all, trustees are not routinely involved in the myriad of company meetings or those stock picking or portfolio construction decisions where ESG considerations typically arise. Issues of practicality dictate otherwise. However, the fund managers that manage pension scheme mandates are. Therefore, many pension schemes include ESG clauses within their fund manager(s) Investment Management Agreement(s) (IMAs) and require their fund manager(s) to periodically report on their ESG performance. Moreover, many fund managers are members of the United Nations Principles for Responsible Investment (UN PRI).[4] This requires that 'where consistent with fiduciary responsibilities', signatories, which can include pension schemes, should commit to integrating ESG issues into investment analysis, to being active, responsible owners by promoting good corporate practice in these areas and to reporting transparently on what actions they have taken. The UN PRI monitors delivery of its six main principles via a questionnaire. This benchmarks signatories' performance in relation to each of the PRI's principles.

---

[4] For further information on the UN PRI see http://www.unpri.org/principles.

As trustees arguably have a fiduciary duty in this area, they should require their fund managers to share the UN PRI's assessment of their performance with them at no additional cost. Indeed, this is increasingly seen as best practice.

Trustees should not assume that ESG issues are considered by all fund managers or that every manager is a signatory of the UN PRI. Ask your fund manager how they research, monitor and address ESG issues, and what the main ESG risks and opportunities are in your portfolio. In particular, be wary of fund managers who do not appear to have any interest or expertise to draw on in incorporating these issues or are unable to back up claims they make in this area.

As we mentioned above, pension schemes can become signatories to the UN PRI. The UN PRI initiative seeks to keep its membership well informed and at the forefront of the various fascinating debates on sustainable and responsible investing and on the importance of incorporating ESG factors into the investment decision making process. The UN PRI is endorsed by the National Association of Pension Funds (NAPF), which suggests that its members, in applying the UN PRI principles, could achieve improved long-term financial performance and better management of reputational risk.[5] Indeed, the UN PRI is fast becoming a de facto industry standard for responsible investment with many of the UK's largest defined benefit (DB) schemes having already signed up.

Another UN initiative is that of the United Nations Environment Programme Finance Initiative's Asset Management Working Group (UNEP FI AMWG) report which in 2009 followed up the Freshfields report.[6] Among the report's suggestions is that the fund managers and investment consultants to institutional investors, such as pension schemes, have a duty to raise ESG issues proactively within the advice that they provide and that a responsible investment option should be the default position. The report also proposes that trustees should be able to sue their investment consultants and fund managers for negligence if these issues are not properly considered, since omitting them could conceivably harm the value of long-term investment portfolios. However, there is yet to be a legal case testing the negligence risk that the report highlights.

Disclosing your pension scheme's ESG policy

Since 2005, regulations[7] have required a statement of the scheme's 'policies in relation to the extent (if at all) to which social, environmental or ethical considerations are taken into account in the selection, retention and realization of

---

[5] NAPF, Corporate Governance and Voting Policy (2007).

[6] UNEP Asset Management Working Group, 'Fiduciary Responsibility: Legal and Practical Aspects of Integrating Environmental, Social and Governance Issues into Institutional Investment', *UNEP* (2009).

[7] Section 2 of the Occupational Pension Schemes (Investment) Regulations 2005.

investments and their policy (if any) in relation to the exercise of the rights (including voting rights) attaching to the investments to be made within the scheme's Statement of Investment Principles (SIP).[8]

What ESG comprises and why it matters

Having clarified the position of whether ESG factors should be brought into the investment decision making process, let's now move on to look at exactly what these ESG factors comprise and the evidence behind whether or not their incorporation within the investment process is value adding. We'll start by taking a look at corporate governance – the G in ESG – and then move on to sustainable and responsible investing – or the environmental and social (or perhaps more correctly, sustainable) aspects of ESG – the E and the S.

Corporate governance

It matters to all of us that companies should be governed effectively. The prosperity of many of those associated with the company – whether directly as managers and employers, or indirectly as shareholders, suppliers, and customers – depends on it. (Jonathan Charkham, Member of the Cadbury Committee, *Keeping Good Company*, 1994)

Corporate governance refers to the way in which a company is governed, directed and controlled on behalf of the company's shareholders. The reason why investors need to be vigilant is because it is often all too easy for the self-interest of management to take precedence over that of the shareholders who own the company.[9] Indeed, the whole point of corporate governance is to ensure that a company's management has the right blend of skills and adopts

---

[8] These provisions are reflected in the Pension Regulator's Guidance for Trustees and the Trustee Knowledge and Understanding Code of Practice. The specific regulations that apply to the application and disclosure of a scheme adopting a corporate governance and/ or a sustainable and responsible investment policy will be discussed later in the chapter.
[9] Indeed, the father of classical economics, Adam Smith, identified this in his seminal work, *Inquiry into the Nature and Causes of the Wealth of Nations*, published in 1776. Smith argued that company directors, 'being the managers rather of other people's money than of their own, it cannot well be expected that they should watch over it with the same anxious vigilance with which the partners in a private co-partnery frequently watch over their own . . . Negligence and profusion, therefore, must always prevail, more or less in the management of the affairs of such a company' (Smith, op cit, p. 700). Essentially, a principal-agent problem arises that requires the shareholder 'principals' of a company to exercise their rights of share ownership over the company's directors – the 'agents'.

the right processes to minimize the risks that poor governance pose to maximizing long-term shareholder returns.

In the UK, corporate governance is ruled by a combination of legislation, regulation and best practice codes, though the behaviour of company boards is principally dictated by the latter. Essentially acting as two sides of one coin, these best practice codes not only provide companies with a framework within which to apply standards of best practice in relation to board composition, remuneration, accountability and shareholder relations but also encourage shareholders, such as pension schemes, to engage more actively with the companies in which they invest and exercise their voting powers responsibly so as to promote good corporate governance.

The corporate governance framework within which companies should operate

While companies and their boards are required by law to comply with the detailed provisions of legislation, such as the Companies Act 2006, rather surprisingly they are not subject to the mandatory application of codes of good practice. Companies are only obliged to explain where and why they do not follow them. This is known as the 'comply or explain' regime.

The first codification of corporate governance in the UK was provided by the Cadbury Code, which was published in 1992. This emphasized the need to ensure an appropriate balance of power between the company chairman and the chief executive and the importance of appointing independent, non-executive directors (NEDs) to the board, who could challenge company strategy and decision making processes. In 1995, the Greenbury Report followed, which dealt predominantly with the remuneration of executive directors – a topic that remains particularly thorny today. In 1998, drawing on the recommendations of previous reports on corporate governance, the Hampel Committee published the Combined Code on Corporate Governance, a code that has since been incorporated into the Financial Services Authority's (FSA) listing requirements: the FSA being the *UK Listing Authority* for companies quoted on the London Stock Exchange.[10] This included guidance on the way in which remuneration should be set, the clear definition of board roles and how shareholders should be kept fully informed of relevant company activities.

However, periodically the process and practices of corporate governance are reviewed – usually following a spate of corporate collapses and/or abuses – and so it was in 2002 when, following the calamitous events surrounding Enron,

---

[10] Listing authorities determine, apply and police the listing requirements for those companies either seeking a listing or who are already listed on the exchange of which they are the listing authority.

Worldcom and Tyco in the US, Derek Higgs was appointed to revisit corporate governance standards in the UK. Published in 2003, the Higgs Report recommended that the code of conduct established by the Hampel Committee should be further strengthened, particularly with respect to the role of NEDs. He recommended that NEDs should be truly independent, comprise half of the board, be drawn from a wider pool of talent and should act as a mechanism via which shareholders could raise concerns. Many of the recommendations of the Higgs Report have now been incorporated into the Combined Code, which, having been updated in May 2010[11] by the Financial Reporting Council (FRC) is now called the UK Corporate Governance Code.

The responsible ownership framework within which trustees should operate

> *It is not only for what we do that we are held responsible but also for what we do not do.* (Jean Bapiste Molière, 1622–1673)

As the definition of what constitutes good corporate governance has evolved, so have institutional investor attitudes, such as those of trustees, and the best practice framework within which they should operate. As noted earlier, trustees can decide the extent to which, if at all, active shareholder engagement and voting plays a role within their investment strategy. After all, the same 'comply or explain' approach that applies to companies also applies to institutional investors.

At the centre of this best practice framework is the Institutional Shareholders Committee (ISC), which comprises representatives from a number of bodies representing institutional investors, namely the Association of British Insurers (ABI), the Association of Investment Companies (IAC), the Investment Management Association (IMA) and the NAPF. The ISC is a forum which facilitates the sharing of institutional investor views and coordinates those activities that support the interests of institutional shareholders, such as pension scheme trustees.

In 1991, the ISC produced its original *The Responsibilities of Institutional Shareholders in the UK* report, in parallel with, and in anticipation of, the Cadbury Code. The report emphasized the special responsibility institutional investors had to both exercise their voting powers and ensure that its recommendations were adopted by the companies in which they invested. Through various iterations, this evolved in 2009 to become the ISC Code on

---

[11] The update included a statement of company boards' responsibilities regarding risk, a requirement for boards to increase their diversity and a recommendation that all directors of FTSE 350 companies should put themselves up for re-election every year.

The Responsibilities of Institutional Shareholders and Agents and then the *UK Stewardship Code,* issued by the FRC in July 2010.[12]

The UK Stewardship Code sets out principles and guidance for institutional investors, such as pension scheme trustees, on what constitutes good practice in engaging with the companies in which they invest. The first such investor code in the world, the UK Stewardship Code ultimately seeks to improve the quality of corporate governance and long-term returns to shareholders, such as pension schemes.

The code comprises seven principles. These are that institutional investors should:

1. publicly disclose their policy on how they will discharge their stewardship responsibilities;
2. have a robust policy on managing conflicts of interest in relation to stewardship and that this policy should be publicly disclosed;
3. monitor the companies in which they invest;
4. establish clear guidelines on when and how they will escalate their activities as a method of protecting and enhancing shareholder value;
5. be willing to act collectively with other investors where appropriate;
6. have a clear policy on voting and disclosure of voting activity; and
7. report periodically on their stewardship and voting activities.

As the above tasks are usually delegated, in the case of pension schemes, to the pension scheme's fund manager(s), the code is largely focused on UK asset managers investing on behalf of their institutional clients. However, because of the important role that pension schemes and other institutional investors can play in encouraging good stewardship, the FRC has also stated that responsibility for effective engagement does not rest with asset managers alone. Therefore, all institutional investors are encouraged to report if and how they have applied the Code, usually through delegation to their asset managers or in some cases outsourced to a corporate governance specialist[13] (with only the very largest pension funds with their own investment departments, engaging directly with companies). Therefore, all institutional investors are encouraged to report if and how they have applied the Code.

---

[12] This was in response to a recommendation by Sir David Walker, following his 2009 review of corporate governance in the financial sector. The full UK Stewardship Code is published on the FRC website at: http://www.frc.org.uk/corporate/investorgovernance.cfm.

[13] Arguably, outsourcing a scheme's corporate governance responsibilities to a corporate governance specialist, usually for a not insubstantial fee, rather than the scheme's fund manager(s), is typically at odds with what the scheme is trying to achieve, in that, unlike the scheme's fund manager(s), a corporate governance specialist will not know in which companies the fund manager(s) is/are invested.

In committing to the Code, trustees need to ensure that their fund manager(s) match up to their own corporate governance requirements as while some asset managers are already very active in stewardship and more are now planning to become so, with a considerable number having already committed to the Code,[14] trustees cannot assume this to be the case in every instance. In fact, when appointing a fund manager or a corporate governance specialist, best practice suggests that their engagement credentials and ability to add value through active shareholder engagement should be considered. Questions such as the following need to be asked:

- How does your fund manager/corporate governance specialist monitor the companies in which the scheme invests?
- Does your fund manager/corporate governance specialist:
  - o have a clear policy on voting and the disclosure of their voting policy?
  - o provide regular reports on their voting activities?
  - o have clear guidelines on when and how they escalate their engagement with the companies in which the scheme invests to protect and enhance shareholder value?

Finally, the Investment Governance Group (IGG), which maintains current best practice for trustees and is chaired by The Pensions Regulator (tPR), states that trustees of DB schemes should apply Principle 5 of the Myners Principles: Responsible Ownership[15] by adopting, or ensuring their fund managers adopt, the UK Stewardship Code (previously the ISC Code on 'The responsibilities of institutional shareholders and agents'), disclose a statement of the scheme's policy on responsible ownership within their Statement of Investment Principles (SIP) and report periodically to their scheme members on the discharging of their duties in this area.[16]

The relationship between good corporate governance and share price performance

Intuitively, better run companies, with the right blend of management and processes should produce better long-run returns. Indeed, we've hinted at this on several occasions. However, good governance in itself does not always lead to

---

[14] Since 6 December 2010, all UK authorized fund managers have been required by the FSA to produce a statement of commitment to the UK Stewardship Code or to explain why it is not appropriate to their business model.

[15] As noted in Chapter 2, the Myners Principles, which now comprise six principles, having originally comprised ten, is another voluntary code of best practice.

[16] Principle 1 of the Myners Principles requires trustees of defined contribution schemes to agree a policy on responsible ownership, to the extent it is practical given the funds offered or those under consideration, monitor its implementation and report on it to interested parties, such as members and member representatives.

good share price performance. Just as the most able, honest and well-organized management will not always succeed, the most greedy, dishonest and opportunistic managers do not always fail. However, by definition, there are less reputational and other risks involved in investing in a well-governed company in the same way that active shareholders are more likely to have greater regard for shareholder interests and maximizing long-run shareholder returns. Indeed, notwithstanding the subjectivity around what constitutes good governance and the various methodologies that can be applied in measuring it, most studies show a positive correlation between corporate governance and share price performance. That is, the quality of corporate governance has an increasingly material impact on company performance with poor corporate governance compromising the stability of this performance.[17]

The magnificent seven

Recent studies of the relationship between good corporate governance and the creation of shareholder value.

1. *Better corporate governance is reflected in significantly higher market values: Ammann, M., Oesch, D. and Schmid, November 2010:* Analyzing 64 Governance Metrics International (GMI) corporate governance attributes across over 2,300 companies between 2003 and 2008, confirmed a strong positive relationship between a company's corporate governance and the impact on its market value, given the resulting lower cost of capital that accrues to such companies.

2. *Well-governed companies deliver extra returns: Association of British Insurers (ABI), February 2008:* This study measures whether companies with investor concerns are less profitable and generate less value over time than other companies (where no concerns have been expressed). This is interesting because measurement is based not on external governance characteristics alone but also on investors' informed views at the time. The findings conclude that over a five-year period (2002–2007), shares of well-governed companies (in the view of ABI members) deliver an extra return of 0.37 per cent per month, industry-adjusted. Also, the study indicates that good governance appears to be a precursor to superior performance rather than vice versa. In addition, the study found that it takes two to three years for good or bad performance to come through.

---

[17] Hermes, the activist fund manager, maintains that in holding a stake in a company with which it engages over a three-to-five-year period, share price appreciation of between 20 and 50 per cent through improved company performance and a re-rating of the company's shares should be targeted. See FTfm, 14 February, p. 3 (2011).

3. *Identifying CEO turnover and market performance can add value:* Société Générale, March 2008: Société Générale created a basket of stocks based on the idea that companies with sound corporate governance principles that have underperformed for the last four years should see an improvement in share price performance via a change of situation or change of management. The criteria applied were (a) CEO tenure – more than three years or very recent change, (b) good governance, (c) underperformance of more than 15 per cent relative to sector for the past four years, and (d) solid financial structure. This basket of stocks outperformed its benchmark (DJStoxx50) by 11.4 per cent between April 2006 and March 2008.

4. *There is a positive equity price performance differential between the best and worst governance companies: Deutsche Bank studies 2000–2007:* Deutsche Bank's 2005 study found that the companies in the FTSE 350 index with top quintile (the top 20 per cent) governance standards outperformed the bottom quintile companies by 32 per cent over the period 2000 to 2005. The results in emerging markets can be even more dramatic. For example, above average companies in India outperformed the below average by 50.3 per cent over the three years 2004 to 2007.

5. *Governance has an effect on profitability: Governance Metrics International (GMI) 2006:* Over the one-, three- and five-year periods ending 30 June 2006, companies rated in the top 10 per cent of GMI's global database achieved a higher Return on Equity (ROE), Return on Assets (ROA) and Return on Capital (ROC) than the average for all companies rated by GMI. Furthermore, companies rated in the bottom 10 per cent achieved a lower ROE, ROA and ROC than the average for all companies rated by GMI over the same timeframe. These results suggest that there is a link between corporate governance and a company's ability to invest its capital efficiently.

6. *Companies with stronger shareholder rights earned abnormal positive returns: Harvard, Stanford and Wharton School (Gompers, P., Ishii, J. and Metrick, A.) 2003:* Gompers, Ishii and Metrick constructed a 'Governance Index' to proxy the level of shareholder rights at about 1,500 large US firms during the 1990s. An investment strategy that bought firms in the lowest decile of the index (strongest rights) and sold firms in the highest decile of the index (weakest rights) would have earned abnormal returns of 8.5 per cent per year during the sample period. Firms with stronger shareholder rights had higher valuations, profits and sales growth, lower capital expenditure and made fewer corporate acquisitions.

7. *Investors will pay a premium for well-run companies:* McKinsey 2002: This well-known McKinsey survey of institutional investors found investors would pay premiums to own well-governed companies. Premiums averaged 30 per cent in Eastern Europe and Africa and 22 per cent in Asia and Latin America.

Do institutional investors have a waning influence on corporate governance?

Despite the tightening of the codes of best practice and disclosure requirements, one cannot ignore the waning influence of UK institutional investors, such as pension funds and insurance companies, in enforcing the laudable principles of corporate governance. While in the mid-1980s around 80 per cent of the UK equity market was owned by UK institutional investors, this fell to around 40 per cent a decade ago to about 24 per cent today, split evenly between pension funds and insurance companies, as these institutions have progressively moved into overseas equities and domestic bonds.[18] With the UK equity market increasingly owned by short-term leveraged investors, such as hedge funds, though with the overwhelming majority of the market now owned by overseas investors, such as Sovereign Wealth Funds (SWFs),[19] UK pension funds no longer have the critical mass they once had in influencing the behaviour of UK companies. Moreover, while SWFs and hedge funds have a potentially greater say than UK institutions in the running of UK companies, in the main they are not inclined to engage with the companies in which they invest. Indeed, the view adopted by many hedge funds is so short term that engagement doesn't matter to them, while many SWFs, despite being long-term 'buy-and-hold' investors, consider such engagement as being tantamount to political interference. Furthermore, as noted in Chapter 14, UK pension schemes are increasingly moving away from active equity management towards index funds and some, in so doing, may not see engagement as being within their remit.

It is in all investor interests that a company is well governed by a strong board with sanctions and incentives in place for poor performance. However, as engagement can cost time and money, many institutional investors and/or their asset managers routinely overlook engagement and free-ride on the back of the engagement of others. Indeed, if every passively invested UK pension fund, short-term leveraged investor and buy-and-hold SWF adopts this hands-off approach, company management then becomes less well controlled by its shareholders than it should be. For instance, according to Pirc, the corporate governance group, all of the 2,496 directors proposed for election or re-election to FTSE 100 boards between 2006 and 2010 were appointed without opposition. In this respect, countries such as Sweden, with their shareholder-led board nomination committees, and Germany, where large shareholders are typically appointed to the company board, are ahead

---

[18] 'The Pensions Chief who says that investors are no longer a soft touch'. *Independent* online. 24 January (2011).
[19] As UK-based institutions manage around 20 per cent of the UK equity market for overseas investors, the percentages quoted for ownership of the UK equity market are not always clear cut.

of the UK. That said, the UK Corporate Governance Code recommends the annual election of FTSE 350 board directors on a 'comply or explain' basis.

According to Towers Watson, ten years ago the average investor held stocks for an average of five to eight years. Today that average has fallen to less than one year.[20] One implication of this shorter-term focus may be that companies become overly obsessed with the need to deliver short-term performance. This in turn, means that longer-run shareholder returns may suffer, as long-term planning and otherwise financially viable and value adding long-term investment projects are dispensed with. This not may not only have an adverse affect on companies at the micro level but also on the economy at a macro level.

Despite this gloomy prognosis, there is evidence that UK institutional investors remain vigilant and increasingly work in concert. Indeed, the financial crisis and the subsequent government-backed Walker review of the financial sector in 2009 seem to have moved corporate governance up the institutional agenda. For instance, during 2010 UK institutions were not slow to oppose the Prudential's proposed takeover of AIG's Asian business, seeing the deal as being substantially overpriced, while they immediately locked horns with BP's senior management over its poor risk management and health and safety record when the Deepwater Horizon disaster (2010) occurred. There was also a very public falling out between UK institutions and Vedanta, the Indian mining group, over its proposed displacement of the indigenous Orissa tribe to mine natural resources, which resulted in Vedanta adopting a more sustainable strategy and ethos.

Notwithstanding these high profile examples, engaging with company management is usually most effective when undertaken in a confidential manner and well in advance of a problem arising. After all, publicity around such discussions can be to the detriment of the desired outcomes and prevention is usually better than cure.

Sustainable and responsible investing (SRI)

An introduction

Having considered the G (corporate governance) in ESG, let's now move on to the E (the environmental) and S (the sustainable but sometimes the social) and consider the key arguments for sustainable and responsible investing (SRI). SRI strategies are increasingly being adopted by institutional investors, such as pension schemes, seeking to deliver on their ESG fiduciary responsibility and as a means by which to generate more sustainable long-run investment returns. The range of

---

[20] 'Short termism requires long-term vision', FTfm, 17 January, p. 13 (2011).

SRI products is also increasing. A few years ago primarily long-only equity funds were available. However, the range now includes balanced funds, fund of funds, absolute return and capital-protected products. SRI is also broadening its scope to include other asset classes, with a particularly notable increase in the availability of corporate bond and real estate funds. Before considering how SRI funds perform relative to 'mainstream' investment strategies and how SRI strategies are categorized, a good place to start is with the 'sustainability problem'.

The sustainability problem

In 2006, it was estimated that the world was consuming natural resources at a rate that would require 1.2 planet earths to regenerate the resources used in that year alone. If left unchecked, this consumption pattern would by 2050 require 1.8 planet earths.[21] The problem is we only have one planet earth! Voters, policy-makers and consumers increasingly recognize and express greater concern that global economic development is far from being on a sustainable footing. As such, those sustainability factors that SRI analysts and fund managers specialize in analyzing are becoming increasingly material to the valuation of investments.

Indeed, sustainable development, that which meets the needs of the present without compromising the ability of future generations to meet their own needs,[22] is a vitally important concept for long-term investors, such as pension schemes, not to mention fund managers, to grasp and incorporate within their investment decision making. After all, those companies that generate short-term financial benefits from pursuing economically unsustainable activities may well compromise the absolute value of long-term investment portfolios if they fail to make a timely transition to a more sustainable business model. However, the consideration of sustainability issues has long been criticized as being a distraction for investors seeking to achieve superior investment returns. Based on the assumption that these issues do not materially affect company valuations, this is arguably an imprudent and potential expensive position to hold. For instance, as energy costs continue to rise in a seemingly secular fashion and the response to mitigating climate change becomes increasingly global, so lower carbon producers and services will be favoured by investors.

The problem is however, that financial markets, which are key to the pursuit of sustainable development, do not yet fully encourage or reward sustainable corporate behaviour. Indeed, they continue to allocate capital to companies in a way that undermines sustainable development. There are two main related reasons for this: market inefficiency and market failure.

---

[21] WWF International Living Planet Report 2006.
[22] As defined by Brundtland, G., *Our Common Future,* World Commission on Environment and Development, p. 43 (1988).

Looking at market failure first. Markets are said to fail when the workings of the free market results in sub-optimal economic and social outcomes. That is, when market failure leads to economic resources being allocated inefficiently and/or to costs being unfairly imposed on society through the actions of others. This latter type of market failure is known as an externality and underlies this unsustainable development. An externality arises when a cost, such as pollution, rather than being assumed by those whose activities created the pollution, is instead borne by society. As unregulated free markets are the root cause of externalities, it is the responsibility of government to induce polluters and those who use resources inefficiently to take account of the effect of their activities on others, whether by limiting this activity through legislation or regulation, imposing a tax on the activity or 'internalizing' the externality. That is, creating a market for the externality and pricing it. So in the case of pollution, governments may reduce the resultant costs on society by imposing emission limits on the amount of pollution, taxing the polluters on their emissions or by 'internalizing' the externality by creating a market for pollution through initiatives such as the purchase and trading of carbon credits.

However, as a consequence of governments' failure *fully* to internalize the costs of unsustainable development, financial markets fail to price in the full economic, social and environmental costs of most corporate activity within company valuations. Moreover, these sustainable development market failures are persistent and pervasive across the global economy. For example, the valuations of oil and gas sector companies assume that their entire proven and probable reserves will be consumed/burnt without heed to the impact on global climate change. In other words, there is a market pricing inefficiency when sustainability factors are not incorporated into market prices. Indeed, just as governments' failure to fully internalize the costs of unsustainable development arguably results in the valuation of those companies that generate these externalities being overstated, so the valuation of many companies that adopt sustainable and responsible business and management policies is arguably understated.

There are three key reasons for such market inefficiency, all of which need to be addressed if market prices are to correctly differentiate sustainable businesses from the unsustainable and financial markets are to promote sustainable development. Indeed, this is exactly what financial markets should do if they are to fulfil their principal function of allocating capital efficiently between competing investment opportunities.

The first is the excessively short-term view adopted by many institutional investors, who are more concerned about the short-term costs to a company of implementing a sustainability initiative than the long-term benefits that may arise from it. This short-termism largely rests on financial markets being too near-sighted in the way they evaluate companies, evidenced by an almost obsessive focus on companies' quarterly earnings figures. This, in turn, systematically erodes incentives for companies to become sustainable businesses,[23] resulting in insufficient capital being invested to ensure their long-term health. Suffice to say that much of this short-termism emanates from pension schemes' quarterly attribution of fund manager performance.

The second key contributor to this market inefficiency (and another reason for market short-termism) is the inadequate information on which many capital allocation decisions are made by investors. Indeed, if companies do not provide an assessment of the wider sustainable development risks and opportunities associated with their activities, then how can the market assess the sustainability of that growth?

In an effort to improve disclosure, conventions like the United Nations Global Compact are now routinely taken up by leading companies around the world.[24] These companies, which *prima facie* understand that long-term shareholder value is enhanced by operating in a sustainable way and with integrity, integrate these concepts into their business policies, governance structure, strategy and incentive structures. Moreover, as the Global Compact requires a 'Communication on Progress' to be published, these companies attempts to be more sustainable (or not) can be evidenced through their disclosure to the market. However, there are major regional variations and significant differences in the quality and comparability of corporate disclosure in this area. Even for large companies where data does exist, much of the information reported is not material, not comparable and provides favourable, rather than balanced reporting. Moreover, three-to-five-year performance analysis is routinely absent.

Ultimately, however, for better market information to be made available to the financial markets and for the necessary disclosures to be made, a change to global listing rules is required. Indeed, it has been suggested that listing authorities globally need to make both corporate responsibility and strategic sustainability reporting a 'comply or explain' requirement, as well as then requiring this report or explanation to be put to the vote at the shareholders annual general meeting (AGM). While advances along these lines have been made, there is still some way to go. For instance, the UNPRI, considered earlier in the chapter, has

---

[23] According to FTfm, 7 February p. 6 (2011) 'pressure on company executives to meet short-term investor expectations has become so strong that nearly 80 per cent of chief financial officers would sacrifice future economic value to manage short-term earnings.' See John Graham, Campbell Harvey and Shivaram Rajgopal, 'Value Destruction and Financial Reporting Decisions', *Financial Analysts Journal*, Volume 62, Number 27, pp. 27–9 (2006).

[24] Underlying the UN Global Compact are ten principles that require companies to support human rights, improved labour standards, greater environmental responsibility and to work against corruption.

galvanized action by stock exchanges through its Sustainable Stock Exchanges Dialogue. Moreover, the Securities and Exchange Commission (SEC) in the US has introduced guidelines for companies to disclose their exposure to climate change, while the Johannesburg Stock Exchange became the first stock exchange to require listed companies to move towards integrated reporting.

However, simply providing this information does not guarantee that investors will be interested or ensure that they will know how to use it. This is the third key reason for the sustainability market inefficiency that arises – the lack of education among market participants on the costs and benefits of corporate sustainability. Indeed, there is greater recognition that conventional asset management analysis of companies, in addition to being too short term, is too narrow in the range of factors that are typically included in the valuation of investments. For this to change the imperative has to be to better educate market participants on the materiality of sustainability issues so that they can be factored into valuation analysis. A good place to start is with the core investment management examination syllabuses and their Continuing Professional Development (CPD) requirements.

Until the externalities arising from unsustainable activities and the three root causes of the market inefficiency around sustainability are adequately addressed, the materiality of sustainability issues will probably continue to fail to be fully factored into company valuations.

The relationship between SRI and investment performance

However, that's not to say that SRI funds are destined to underperform 'mainstream' funds. Indeed, Mercer Investment Consulting and the UNEP FI AMWG conducted a broad ranging global study of SRI academic and broker research and assessed the contribution that ESG (rather than just sustainability) factors add to investment performance.[25] The study concluded that 'the argument that integrating ESG factors into investment analysis and decision-making will only lead to underperformance simply cannot be made'. Indeed, in the foreword, the study states that:

> *Of the 16 academic studies reviewed in this report, ten showed evidence of a positive relationship between ESG factors and financial performance; two found evidence of a negative-neutral relationship; and four reported a neutral association. Pooling these results together with the 2007 report, there are 34 studies in total: 20 studies showing evidence of a neutral-positive relationship; three showing evidence*

---

[25] *Demystifying Responsible Investment Performance: A Review of Key Academic and Broker Research on ESG Factors*, Mercer Investment Consulting and the United Nations Environment Programme Finance Initiative's Asset Management Working Group (UNEP FI AMWG), p. 2 (2007, updated 2009).

of a negative-neutral relationship; eight showing evidence of a neutral relationship; and three showing evidence of a negative relationship.

However, while the jury is still out on whether there is a sufficiently marked pricing inefficiency that enables SRI funds to outperform 'conventional' funds over the long term, the belief that ESG issues are frequently material to long-term performance and rarely priced into the market continues to gather momentum. Indeed, with an increasing number of analysts seeking to exploit this inefficiency, ESG analysis will continue to grow in relevance.

Defining SRI strategies

With a number of different terms used within the SRI industry having been poorly defined and often used inconsistently, this has led to a fundamental misunderstanding of the key approaches to SRI and what each seeks to achieve. For instance, not all SRI funds have been set up with a focus on investment returns. For example, as intimated earlier, for some, the 'S' in SRI stands for Social. For others it is short for Sustainable. This is an important difference as it highlights the extent to which an investor focuses their analysis on companies contributing to and benefiting from long-term sustainable economic development, as opposed to companies undertaking socially responsible actions such as philanthropy, albeit on a voluntary basis.

Therefore, investors, such as DB pension schemes, which are primarily concerned with the financial performance of their funds, need to understand the specific investment philosophy and strategy that applies to the fund and fund manager in order to select an appropriate product and provider.

The four main SRI strategies

Some in the SRI industry can point to over ten different SRI strategies. However, they can essentially be boiled down to four: (i) avoidance, negative screening or ethical investment, (ii) positive screening, (iii) engagement, and (iv) integration.

These four main SRI strategies are summarized in Exhibit 16.1.

Combining strategies

While these four main strategies can be used independently, they can also be combined in order to develop increasingly sophisticated SRI strategies, tailored to meet individual scheme requirements. For example, for DB pension schemes, a combined approach might:

- integrate an analysis of ESG issues into the overall investment process;
- avoid some sectors on ethical grounds and/or because they are poor long-term investments and not worthy of consideration;

Exhibit 16.1 The four main SRI strategies

	Avoidance/Negative screening/Ethical investment	Positive screening	Engagement	Integration
Approach	Excluding investments that do not meet defined ethical standards.	Investing in those companies with a commitment to responsible business practices, positive products and/or services.	Engaging with companies to encourage more responsible business practices and improved ESG performance.	Capturing market inefficiencies in the valuation of sustainable and responsible businesses by integrating an analysis of how ESG issues affect corporate earnings and valuation.
Examples of this approach	Screening out exposure to tobacco, alcohol, defence and gambling.	Focusing on 'best of sector' or sustainability themed investment, e.g. environmental technology.	Direct and collaborative engagement, e.g. proxy voting at company meetings.	Examining if a company's management of climate change is priced into its shares.
Investment implications	Likely to underperform while excluded areas are performing well. The key is fund manager selection.	Can lead to a smaller company bias with volatile performance, but evidence suggests ESG thematic analysis can lead to improved performance.	Can overlay a conventional portfolio and does not necessarily impact stock selection. Dialogue on issues of concern should reduce risks and support long-term wealth creation.	If there is a sustainability market inefficiency, then integration should reduce portfolio risk and enhance returns.
Sustainability implications	Removes the potential for engagement with the companies excluded.	Can lead to companies gaining greater access to capital and cheaper financing.	Can motivate significant corporate improvement across a range of areas.	Considerable potential to promote responsible long-term business behaviour.

- positively screen a percentage of the portfolio towards companies providing sustainable goods and services on the basis that they will benefit from the long-term secular trends towards more sustainable goods and services; and
- engage with the companies that they own in order to support good ESG practices and challenge poor performance.

In addition, for defined contribution pension schemes, depending on interest, there may be scope to offer members one or a number of negatively screened ethical fund options. However, it should be noted some contradictions do emerge when combining strategies. Most obviously, screening out a company from a portfolio would mean losing the ability to engage with the company. Therefore, the key for the trustees is in understanding these implications and selecting the approach that best fits with the scheme's investment strategy.

Summary

Towards the beginning of this chapter, we mentioned that many investors, which may well include you, your co-trustees and many of your scheme members, often view the integration of ESG considerations into the investment process as a questionable, altruistic exercise. However, we hope that having read this chapter, you have now put aside any scepticism you may have had and now firmly believe that adopting an ESG approach to investing is all about practising good stewardship so as to generate better quality and more sustainable long-run investment returns.

Key points

- An investment strategy that integrates ESG factors into investment decision making is one that promotes best practice in corporate governance and sustainable and responsible business and management practices.
- Integrating ESG factors to the trustee investment decision making process is permissible and arguably required and should be disclosed within the scheme's Statement of Investment Principles.
- An ESG policy is best implemented by including an ESG clause within the fund manager(s) Investment Management Agreement(s) and requiring them to periodically report on their ESG performance.
- Corporate governance refers to the way in which a company is governed, directed and controlled on behalf of the company's shareholders. The reason why investors need to be vigilant is because it is often all too easy for the self-interest of management to take precedence over that of the shareholders who own the company.

- The ESG factors on which SRI strategies focus are becoming increasingly material to company valuations and are arguably not fully factored into market prices. This is as a consequence of the externalities arising from unsustainable activities not being fully internalized and financial markets allocating capital to companies on the basis of incomplete information.
- There are four main SRI strategies. These can be deployed independently or combined to develop increasingly sophisticated SRI strategies.

Chapter 17

Behavioural Finance: How Investors Really Make Investment Decisions

Learning outcomes

- Appreciate why the market behaves as it does and is not always price efficient.
- Understand the type of errors, or biases, that repeatedly enter into the investment decision making process, no matter how sophisticated the investor.
- Know how to interrogate your fund managers and your investment consultants in establishing how they each approach their investment decision making.

All of us think of ourselves as rational beings even in times of crisis, applying the laws of probability in a cool and calculated fashion to the choices that confront us. We like to believe we are above average in skills, intelligence, farsightedness, experience, refinement and leadership. Who admits to being an incompetent driver, a feckless debater, a stupid investor, or a person with inferior taste in clothes? . . . [but] the most important decisions we make usually occur under complex, confusing, indistinct or frightening conditions. (Peter L. Bernstein, 1998)[1]

---

[1] Peter L. Bernstein, *Against the Gods. The Remarkable Story of Risk*. New York, Wiley, p. 269 (1998).

Introduction

The fund management industry manages more than US$50 trillion of assets globally, generates more than US$160bn of revenues annually[2] and offers some of the best rewarded careers to some of the brightest and most talented individuals around. However, consistently generating outperformance of traditional benchmarks remains a challenge. Indeed, once manager fees are taken into account, active fund management industry is a 'negative sum game'. That is, there are more bad, or unskilled, managers than good, or skilled ones. As a consequence, value is detracted, rather than added by active fund management on average.

So if active fund managers cannot meet this challenge, what does this tell us about financial markets? Well, it may mean that financial markets are just too 'efficient' for most managers to be able to outperform them. However, poor performance might also be a function of human frailty, that is, behavioural biases. In this chapter we explore the behavioural biases to which all investors, including highly paid fund managers, succumb from time to time. But before we do this we begin with a review of the famous – some would say, infamous – Efficient Market Hypothesis (EMH).

The efficient market hypothesis

In an efficient financial market, security prices always fully reflect all available information. (Eugene Fama, 1970[3])

No discussion of behavioural finance could begin without consideration of the Efficient Market Hypothesis (EMH) – the backbone of finance theory since the 1960s. As we noted in Chapter 14, the idea of efficient markets dates back to the pioneering work of Alfred Cowes in the 1930s, Harry Roberts and Harry Markowitz in the 1950s and was then further developed through the 1960s and 1970s by academic luminaries such as William Sharpe and Eugene Fama. The EMH outlines three forms of efficiency – weak, semi-strong and strong. For a market to be both weak and semi-strong efficient, all past and current relevant information should be incorporated into current prices such that any new, relevant information is instantaneously factored into market prices, causing them

---

[2] Data as at 31 December 2009. Source: Boston Consulting Group, Global Asset Management 2010. The value of professionally managed assets globally at end-2009 was US$52.6tn, generating net revenues of US$164.1bn.
[3] Eugene Fama, 'Efficient Capital Markets: A Review of Theory and Empirical Work', *Journal of Finance*, Volume 25, Number 2, pp. 383–417, (1970).

to appear to move in an unpredictable fashion independently of any past price movements. If markets are both weak and semi-strong efficient then securities prices will appear to evolve in a random and unpredictable way over time. They will appear to follow a 'random walk' – a path resembling that of a drunk as they make their way home from the pub through a field on a dark night! If as well as being efficient in a weak and semi-strong form, market prices also incorporate all relevant, private information too, then the market is said to be strong form efficient. The implications of the EMH for active fund management are uncomfortable, since in such conditions managers can only beat the market consistently if they are very lucky or if they are prepared to take higher risks over time.

Embedded in the idea of a fully efficient capital market, however, are some highly questionable assumptions about how investors approach investment decision making. Investors are assumed to:

- be rational, risk averse, wealth maximizers – that is, investors only take on risk if a sufficiently acceptable investment return is in prospect;
- approach investment decision making objectively;
- have an excellent understanding of probability theory;
- be able to source, sift through and correctly interpret all relevant information to arrive at a rational view about all market prices; and
- learn from their mistakes over time so that they do not repeat them again and again.

However, all of these assumptions and the idea that we are all super-rational beings can be relatively easily dismissed by playing a couple of simple games. Let's start with the assumption that we are all rational, risk averse wealth maximizers.

What if you *conditionally* won £10,000 in pound coins – conditional in that to keep all or some of this money, you have to make a one-off non-negotiable offer to the person sitting opposite you for as much or as little of this sum as you choose. If they accept your offer, you can *both* keep the money in the proportions agreed but if they reject it, all the money passes to *us*. You are both aware of the rules of the game. If you are both rational wealth maximizers – knowing full well that we stand to gain the £10,000 if the offer is rejected – then you would, in making the offer, offer the smallest possible amount – a £1 coin – to the other person who, given the prospect of receiving something for nothing, and not assuming any risk in the process, should accept. However, when researchers conduct this experiment, this rational outcome is rarely, if ever, achieved. What tends to happen is that an offer in the region of 30 to 40 per cent of the money is made and is generally accepted. Why should that be? Well, wealth maximization in practice is a relative, not an absolute, phenomenon. While most people would be happy to receive a £1 coin for doing absolutely nothing, most would feel pretty aggrieved at seeing the person making the offer walk off with £9,999! That is, while their wealth would have increased, yours would have increased by a much greater amount. This is why, in recognizing the irrationality of the subject of the offer, the person making the offer does so by offering considerably more than £1. Indeed, this is exactly what three academics found in repeatedly playing this game with 42 economics students, who were fully aware of the notion of wealth maximization.[4]

Let's now turn to objectivity. What if you were asked to pick a whole number between zero and 100 closest to two-thirds of the average number chosen by your work colleagues? What number would you choose? For instance, if you believed the average number chosen would be 100, then you would choose 67. So what is it to be? Well, the *Financial Times* ran this 'pick a number' game among its readership[5] and had 13 as its winning entry. Was this the correct number to choose given that the game was all about second guessing what the other players are thinking? Let's think about this. If you believed the other players would on average chose 20, then you would choose 13. However, if they believed you would chose 13, they should choose two-thirds of the weighted average of all of those 20s and your 13. Ultimately, everyone should choose one but on this occasion, the (highly educated) *Financial Times* readership did not – they stopped at 13!

And finally let's test for cognizance – the ability to source, sift through and interpret information no matter what form it takes – with a couple of observation and cognitive reflection tests. Read the text below aloud to yourself:

A

BIRD

IN THE

THE BUSH

The chances are you said 'A bird in the bush', ignoring the second 'the'. Most people do.

How about counting every 'F' in the following text:

Finished files are the result of years of scientific study combined with the experience of years

---

[4] W. Guth, R. Schmittberger and B. Schwarze, *Journal of Economic Behavior and Organization*, Volume 3, Number 4, p. 367 (1982).

[5] 'Financial Planning: Win a flight to the US', *Financial Times*, 10 May (1997).

You most probably counted three. There are in fact six. Most people tend to miss the 'of's as the brain tends to process 'of' as 'ov'. In fact, identifying all six makes you a genius!

Take a guess at the ratio of the length to the width of each of the two boxes below.

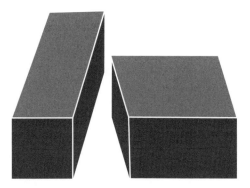

You probably guessed something around three to one for the left box and one to one for the right.

In fact, both boxes are the same. The ratio of the length to width is five to three. If you don't believe us, you should measure their dimensions. So why do they look different? Well, vertical lines look longer than horizontal lines. Also, by using three-dimensional boxes rather than just two-dimensional flat surfaces and by changing the orientation of the pictures the illusion is created that the boxes differ from one another.

And finally:

> *If a bat and ball together cost a total of £1.10 and the bat costs £1 more than the ball, how much is the ball?*

> *10p?*

> *Wrong – it's 5p, as the bat would cost £1.05. That is, £1 more.*

These last two exercises, and many others like them, test the extent to which you employ your automatic system of thought. That's the quick and easy approach to problem solving, rather than your reflective system, which is the more analytical and which uses significantly more cognitive resources. Relying too much on your automatic system of thinking often results in mistakes being made. In fact, history is littered with episodes of intelligent people who, being overly reliant on their automatic system, made some monumentally bad financial decisions. For example, Sir Isaac Newton, lost his fortune in the South Sea Bubble of 1720, commenting that 'I can calculate the motion of heavenly bodies but not the madness of men', or Professor Stephen Greenspan, who lost 30 per cent of his retirement savings in the Madoff hedge fund Ponzi scheme, having written a book entitled *Why we get duped and how to avoid it*!

Other evidence that is inconsistent with the EMH

So in the time it took you to perform the bargaining exercise, the pick a number game and the observation and cognitive reflection tests (hopefully not very long), we have now cast doubt on the three key assumptions about investor behaviour underlying the EMH. Not only that, many of the phenomena we observe in financial markets are inconsistent with the notion of the EMH. For example, there are numerous trading strategies that successfully and repeatedly exploit regularly observed pricing anomalies. One of these is the 'January effect' – that is, global equity markets tend on average to do better in January than in most other months.[6] There are also those strategies that seem to capitalize successfully upon patterns in past prices. That is, strategies that benefit from riding waves of short-term price momentum,[7] when stocks that have done well in the recent past continue to do so. There also seem to exist profitable contrarian strategies that benefit from the medium- to long-term reversal of fortunes of those top performing stocks that have got ahead of themselves and those poorly performing stocks whose prices have similarly lost touch with reality but in the opposite direction. As the economist John Kay observes: *'If you know precisely when the short term becomes the long term, this would make you very rich.'*[8]

As we noted in Chapter 7, long-run excess returns have also been observed from investing in stocks with high dividend yields rather than low yielding

---

[6] See the highly readable: Robert A. Haugen, Josef Lakonishok *The Incredible January Effect, The Stock Market's Unsolved Mystery*, Homewood IL, Dow Jones-Irwin (1988). However, in the UK, as Exhibit 10.16 shows the best month tends to be April.
[7] Financial economists Jegadeesh and Titman first identified the excess returns from price momentum in 1993. Since then, the momentum effect has been quantified globally within the Credit Suisse Global Investment Returns Sourcebook – most recently the 2011 edition pp. 49–53. See also O. ap Gwilym, A. Clare, J. Seaton and S. Thomas, 'Price and Momentum as Robust Tactical Approaches to Global Equity Investing (2009)', *Journal of Investing*, Fall (2010).
[8] John Kay, 'Markets after the age of efficiency,' *Financial Times*, 7 October, p. 17 (2009).

stocks.[9] This is also true of small capitalization stocks when compared with the long-run returns of their larger equivalents.[10] The valuation of markets at any point in time also appears to give some predictability to future returns.[11] As we also observed in Chapter 7, when market prices have risen substantially above a long-run average, their subsequent ten-year returns are typically very disappointing, but when priced below their long-run average valuation, their returns can be quite spectacular.

Markets also often exhibit excessive volatility,[12] that is, volatility well in excess of that which could be expected based upon the genuine news about the profitability of an investment over time. This excess volatility may be indicative of investor uncertainty – uncertainty as to the value of a security or the market as a whole, which culminates in investors overtrading. If markets were informationally efficient, that is, if investors correctly interpreted and instantaneously factored relevant news into security prices, then we would not observe this excessive trading between investors with different views of the same future. This observation derives from the fact that most information is rarely perfect or complete and, as identified earlier, the inability of most investors to source, sift through and correctly interpret all salient information means that arguably the consensus forecast embedded in security prices is rarely correct.

Finally, the history books are littered with frequent episodes of bubbles and subsequent crashes across a range of asset classes, from the Tulipmania of 1637 to the credit-fuelled boom and credit crunch bust of the late-noughties. These periodic episodes of 'irrational exuberance' and depressed prices, often for sustained periods, are difficult to square with the idea that capital markets are efficient.

The conclusion on market efficiency

I'd be a bum in the street with a tin cup if the markets were efficient. (Warren Buffett, 1995)[13]

---

[9] The outperformance of high yielding over low yielding stocks was identified by financial economists Fama and French in 1988. According to the Credit Suisse Global Investment Returns Sourcebook 2011 pp. 45–47, using the top 100 stocks in the UK, this amounted to 2.9 per cent per annum compound over the period 1900 to 2010 and 1.7 per cent per annum between 1975 and 2010.

[10] The 'smallcap effect' was first identified by Rolf Banz in 1981. According to the Credit Suisse Global Investment Returns Sourcebook 2011 pp. 41–45, in the UK between 1955 and end-2010, this amounted to 2.8 per cent per annum compound.

[11] See the Barclays Capital Equity Gilt Study 2009 pp. 5–9.

[12] See Robert J. Shiller, 'Do Stock Prices Move Too Much to Be Justified by Subsequent Movements in Dividends?' American *Economic Review*, Volume 71, Number 3, pp. 421–36, (1981).

[13] *Fortune*, 3 April 1995.

So perhaps markets are not so efficient, at least not *all* of the time. After all, Warren Buffett is the world's third richest man, who has amassed a US$50bn fortune through managing money over the past 50 years, to quote Mr Buffett again:

> *Observing correctly that the market was frequently efficient, [many academics and investment professionals] went on to conclude incorrectly that it was always efficient. The difference between the propositions is night and day.*[14]

Mr Buffett has made his fortune from those instances when the market has not been efficient.

Confronting the EMH school in his US bestseller of 2000, *Irrational Exuberance*, Robert Shiller, Professor of Economics at Yale, said: 'If the theory of finance is to grow in its usefulness, all economists eventually will have to grapple with the messier aspects of market reality.'[15]

What Shiller meant by this was that while it has long been known that investors do not approach investment decision making in the rational manner that the EMH suggests, for simplicity's sake it had been assumed that, on the whole, investors acted as if they did. Without a clear sense of knowing how and why investors deviated from this assumed rational behaviour, it was difficult to articulate anything rigorous or distinctive about the way in which investment decision making and markets really worked. In recent years, however, this has changed as significant advances have been made in what has become known as behavioural finance.

What is behavioural finance?

Behavioural finance is the study of human psychology in the context of investing. Some academics have tried to apply these ideas to more traditional finance models to explain observed phenomena that are inconsistent with the EMH. In contrast to the EMH, rather than making simplifying assumptions about the way that investors approach investment decision making, behavioural finance instead analyzes the way in which cognitive biases repeatedly enter investors' decision-making processes. In so doing, behavioural finance attempts to explain why security prices frequently depart from their fundamental values and why trends, patterns and simple but profitable trading strategies, that are inconsistent with the EMH, frequently arise within financial markets.

---

[14] John Kay, 'Markets after the age of efficiency', *Financial Times*, 7 October, p. 17 (2009).
[15] Robert J. Shiller, *Irrational Exuberance*. New Jersey: Princeton University Press. Preface XIX (2000).

Crucially, behavioural finance accepts that the information used by investors when making investment decisions is often incomplete and that the human mind is not a supercomputer. Moreover, a central tenet of behavioural finance is that there are very few quick learners among us.[16] When approaching invest-ment decision making we repeat mistakes with alarming regularity. According to the proponents of behavioural finance, this can often cause markets to move in predictable ways that can be profitably exploited, but it can equally cause individual security prices and markets to move in an unpredictable manner. So whereas in the EMH world, market prices are unpredictable because of investor rationality, the study of behavioural finance has taught us that our inability to learn quickly from mistakes can also result in prices becoming unpredictable. Employing the lessons learned from the study of behavioural biases within an investment decision making process then does not necessarily guarantee us a path to riches. Indeed, critics of the 'science' have argued that the main problem with the ideas that have been generated from behavioural finance is that any pattern in security prices is potentially justifiable.

The social aspect of human behaviour

Investment may be likened to those newspaper competitions in which the com-petitors have to pick out the six prettiest faces from a hundred photographs . . . not those faces which he himself finds prettiest, but those which he thinks likeliest to catch the fancy of other competitors, all of whom are looking at the problem from the same point of view . . . [they] devote [their] intelligence to anticipating what average opinion expects average opinion to be. (J. M. Keynes, 1936)[17]

Perhaps most importantly, behavioural finance, unlike the EMH, captures the social aspect of human behaviour – how we act in groups, perhaps behaviour that dates back to when we were hunter-gatherers. As John Maynard Keynes' beauty contest analogy[18] suggests, within financial markets, rather than basing our decisions on our own information and opinions, many investors tend to rely on the actions and opinions of others, particularly those who they perceive to be 'experts'. This is reinforced by the fact that there are very few independent thinkers among us. As social animals we find it difficult to stick to an opinion that differs markedly from the group and typically seek safety in numbers.

---

[16] For a variety of reasons, the composition of the market is constantly changing, as new investors enter the market and more established investors leave. This exacerbates the learning problem.
[17] J. M. Keynes, *The General Theory of Employment, Interest and Money*, London: Macmillan. p. 156 (1936).
[18] Which we first came across in Chapter 10.

Keynes had a quote for this as well: 'Worldly wisdom teaches us that it is better to fail conventionally than to succeed unconventionally'.[19]

Just look at how many sophisticated investors blindly followed others when investing in Bernie Madoff's fraudulent hedge fund operation. Then of course, there are all of those active fund managers, whose performance is judged relative to their peers and index benchmarks. So that they do not to appear out-of-line with their peer group, many follow the lead of others while a significant number position their portfolios to look not that different from the benchmarks they are seeking to outperform!

We also tend to prefer to have our actions and opinions validated by others. For instance, if you were in an unfamiliar town one evening looking for a place to eat and you saw two restaurants, one nearly full and the other empty, the chances are that you would opt for the fuller rather than the empty restaurant on the premise that if everyone else has done similarly then it must be the right decision! We will return to the social aspect of human behaviour later in the chapter when looking at the influence of others in investment decision making.

Is behavioural finance a new phenomenon?

Behavioural finance is not a new science. Academics and market practitioners have been writing about the psychology of the market for some time. In fact, one of the earliest texts on the subject dates back to 1759.[20] However, the modern day origins of behavioural finance lie in the late-1960s and 1970s when challenges to the EMH started to appear first in psychology journals and then key financial journals. When psychology professor, Daniel Kahneman, one of the founding fathers of the behavioural finance world, shared the Nobel Prize for Economics in 2002, behavioural finance was placed firmly in the limelight.

The main behavioural biases

Behavioural finance tends to segment the biases that investors succumb to into 'heuristics' and 'framing' errors, though there is a significant degree of overlap between the two and occasionally the odd contradiction. Heuristics involves applying rules of thumb, or mental short cuts, to simplify the complex reality of investment decision making. This is where the automatic system of thought,

---

[19] J. M. Keynes, *The General Theory of Employment, Interest and Money*, London: Macmillan. pp. 157–8 (1936).
[20] See Adam Smith, *The Theory of Moral Sentiments* (1759) and Charles MacKay, *Extraordinary Popular Delusions and the Madness of Crowds* (1841).

that relies on quick and easy problem solving, kicks in. Examples include basing an investment strategy on false beliefs such as 'equities *always* outperform in the long run' and that 'dips in the equity market *always* present good buying opportunities'. These statements may turn out to be true, but history tells us there are significant exceptions.[21]

Framing describes how the reference points chosen by the investor in making an investment decision, or how a problem is posed to an individual, or how they pose it to themselves, influences the decision making process itself. Take for example a pension scheme that needs to generate a 1 per cent per annum compound return over gilts for the next 20 years in order to achieve full funding. If the scheme's investment consultant articulates the decision problem in this way, the scheme's trustees might well treat the scheme's 20 year recovery plan as 20 discrete annual periods and invest in assets with low volatility in order to secure this annual 1 per cent outperformance target. If the decision problem was instead framed as needing to generate a return over gilts for the next 20 years of a little over 20 per cent, then the investment solution would probably look a lot different. In adopting a 20-year investment horizon the trustees might opt for assets that while volatile and quite illiquid in the short run would, in all likelihood, achieve the target rate of return sooner than the recovery plan required and with better inflation protection than that afforded by those assets that exhibit little short-term volatility.

Heuristics

Some of the more commonly cited heuristics, which result in sub-optimal investment decision-making, follow.

Representativeness

This is the main source of heuristic bias. Most investors, being poor at calculating and calibrating probabilities, with their limited cognitive ability, find it difficult to distinguish between random events and genuine trends and to differentiate luck from skill. Therefore, they tend to over rely on their intuition. Once again, the automatic system of thought dominates. Consequently, many investors subconsciously create and extrapolate patterns and trends from, what ultimately prove to be, a series of random events, without investigating or questioning the reasons for these supposed patterns and trends.

---

[21] For instance, the Dow Jones Industrial Average Index did not return to its 1929 high until 1954, while the equity markets of France, Germany, Japan, Spain, Italy and Belgium all experienced 50 + years periods of negative real returns during the twentieth century.

For instance, an active fund manager may have experienced a consistent run of outperformance over, say, a ten-year period. Many investors, without investigating the qualitative aspects of the manager's investment philosophy, the robustness and repeatability of their process and so on, might well attribute this outcome to skill and therefore expect this run of outperformance to continue. However, it is quite feasible that luck played a key role in this outcome and could soon run out![22] After all, if 1,000 people flip a fair coin, after ten rounds of coin flipping, there is a strong possibility that one flipper would, through pure luck, have flipped ten heads. However, had the eventual winner of this contest been identified from the outset, then in all likelihood they would have won the contest through their skilful coin flipping technique, as the odds of picking a winner from the 1,000 contestants *before* the flipping begins, are less than 0.1 per cent. Investors' inability to differentiate luck from skill is principally a consequence of confusing the minimal probability associated with naming *the* fund manager who will outperform all the others over the long term with the near certainly that one manager, as yet unknown, will outperform.

Linked to this inability to calculate probabilities correctly is a phenomenon known as *disaster myopia*. This occurs when the probability of one or a number of disastrous outcomes is severely underestimated, owing to their presumed remoteness or because they simply do not register in the popular consciousness. As such, these events are often subconsciously assigned a zero probability. For example, many of the highly leveraged financial positions taken by the banks and hedge funds in 2007 totally ignored the possibility of a 'Black Swan'[23], or an extreme event, such as the credit crisis, with a drying up of bank credit lines and market liquidity, lurking on the horizon. Indeed, this was evident from the composition of the stress test models used by the banks, many hedge funds and even the regulators on the financial positions assumed by these institutions. All had been caught with their guard down, having been seduced by the apparent secularity

---

[22] It has been suggested that 12 years of superior risk-adjusted performance is needed to prove skill with 95 per cent confidence. However, many would argue that as much as 300 months (25 years) of continuous data is needed to prove statistically the existence of skill. The problem is that only a handful of fund managers manage the same fund for anything like 12, let alone 25, years, so a detailed qualitative analysis of a manager's investment philosophy and process is absolutely essential. We examine this in more detail in Chapter 18.

[23] The term 'Black Swan' was popularized by Nassim Nicholas Taleb in his books: *Fooled by Randomness. The Hidden Role of Chance in Life and in the Markets*, Random House (2004) and *The Black Swan: The Impact of the Highly Improbable*, Penguin (2007). The term originates from the eighteenth century philosopher David Hume, though is often attributed to the nineteenth century philosopher John Stuart Mill.

of the NICE decade.[24] Once the credit crisis struck however, the probability many attributed to its reoccurrence surged to 100 per cent as the risk became salient. At this point investors had succumbed to *disaster magnification*.[25]

Representativeness also captures *confirmation bias* and the *endowment effect*, also known as *status quo bias*.[26]

Confirmation bias occurs when investors seek out evidence that confirms that they are correct in their thinking so that they ignore any evidence that suggests otherwise. The endowment effect refers to the tendency of investors to place a greater value on what they own rather than on things that they do not own. For example, many active fund managers place a greater value on and pay more attention to their overweight stock positions relative to their underweight positions and tend to know more about the former than the latter. When combined with confirmation bias, this might mean that the manager seeks out evidence that confirms that they are right to overweight stock A and underweight stock B and ignore anything that challenges this view! Good fund managers should know as much about their underweight positions as their overweight positions and should be prepared for others to challenge both.

Indeed, surrounding yourself with people with dissenting views is healthy. For this very reason, Abraham Lincoln, Barack Obama and even David Cameron all appointed a number of their eminent foes to cabinet positions. Indeed, this is probably essential if the destructive characteristics of 'groupthink' – emphasizing consensus over dissent – are to be avoided. Groupthink occurs, particularly within small groups, when decision makers are too much alike in their worldview and mindset, or when one or a number of individuals dominate the decision making process, or worse still, when some individuals decide for the group without inviting open discussion. As the philosopher Sir Karl Popper argued, in order to improve our understanding of a phenomenon, it is better to focus on falsification than verification. For instance, seeing lots of white swans does not prove that all swans are white but seeing one black swan does disprove this hypothesis. The problem is that we are not naturally inclined to falsifying information.

---

[24] The NICE (Non Inflationary Consistent Expansion) decade, which ran from 1998 to 2007, was an acronym coined by the Bank of England Governor Mervyn King. The NICE decade was characterized by economic stability and low volatility within financial markets.

[25] Just as the threat of terrorism became dramatically more salient after 9/11 and 7/7 than at any time before, it's been observed that people tend to buy flood insurance after hearing of someone affected by flooding even if they were not directly impacted by the event themselves.

[26] This has nothing to do with an ageing rock band of the same name.

Availability

Availability bias involves basing decisions solely on information that is readily available, or close at hand, without digging deeper. As such, it also overlaps with disaster myopia in that succumbing to availability bias results in placing too much or too little emphasis on the likelihood of events occurring based on recent experience or how readily they come to mind.

Affect

The affect heuristic is the probability insensitivity we experience as a result of an outcome being particularly vivid in one's mind. For instance, despite the remote prospect of your house burning down or you winning the lottery, the chances are that you have buildings and contents insurance and that you play the lottery, principally because the outcomes are vivid. That is, the unimaginable thought of your house burning down or the more pleasurable thought of you sitting on an inordinately big pile of cash and enjoying the millionaire lifestyle, means that you ignore the remote probabilities that these events will occur and rely on your emotional reaction to possible outcomes when parting with your cash. Moreover, insuring your house *and* playing the lottery goes against all of the principles of rational behaviour.

Gambler's fallacy

Gambler's fallacy involves confusing small samples of data with larger samples of the same population and is facetiously known as the 'law of small numbers'. For instance, if you flipped a fair coin 10,000 times, you would probably expect 5,000 heads and 5,000 tails to be the result. However, you would not expect the same 50/50 result to follow from ten flips of a fair coin. In the same way, just because equity markets in the long run, taking a hundred or so years of data, rise on average every two years out of three, there is no reason to believe that this is how they should behave over the next three years. Confusing the short run with the long run is exactly what happened to a number of equity strategists in 1997. At the end of 1997, after three years of double digit equity market returns, many strategists turned to the history books and incorrectly forecasted that the market would turn tail. Unfortunately for these strategists, the market continued to deliver positive returns for another two years. Similarly, at the beginning of 2002, after two years of falling markets, other strategists, on the basis of markets rising on average two years in three, forecasted positive returns for 2002 which never materialized. In short, markets don't work to timetables and are more random than most people believe.[27]

---

[27] For instance, the 508 point, or 22.6 per cent, decline in the Dow Jones Industrial Average Index on 19 October 1987 was a one in 10^{33} year event!

Anchoring

Anchoring involves placing too much emphasis on irrelevant facts and figures, simply because they conveniently fall to hand. For example, an investor may have bought a stock at 200p, which is now trading at 180p, a new low. However, it may have, in, say, the past 12 months, traded at a high of 250p. Therefore, the investor might, in considering the stock's future prospects, treat either the 200p price paid or the 250p high as price targets, despite the fact that both relate wholly to the past. Similarly, there is nothing to suggest that the stock price cannot fall below its new low of 180p. Anchoring might also explain why individual stock prices move together as much as they do, as individual stock price movements appear to be anchored to the price changes of other stocks in the same sector.[28]

Overconfidence

One of the more obvious behavioural biases relates to overconfidence. Research has shown that we tend to overestimate our knowledge, skill and ability in making investment decisions, which results in undiversified portfolios and excessive portfolio turnover to the detriment of investment returns. Overconfidence can stem from many sources. Some investors believe that success in a completely unrelated field can be extended to their investment activities. For instance, this is true of certain members of the medical profession, given their ability to heal people.

Another source of overconfidence is *hindsight bias*. Through their rose tinted spectacles, many investors convince themselves that, despite the reality, all of their investment decision making has been good. They fail to remind themselves of all the bad investment decisions they've made or else attribute these to bad luck or poor advice! There are also those who believe that they can control chance events. For instance, in attempting to throw a low number from a pair of dice, many people would throw the dice softly and vice versa for a high number. *Information overload* also tends to be a source of overconfidence. Gathering reams of information without context can lead to false empowerment and misplaced confidence and rarely improves the accuracy of decision making. In fact, it can lead to worse decisions being made. As in many aspects of life, sometimes less is more.

Adjustment conservatism

Adjustment conservatism refers to overconfidence in one's own forecasting ability. This bias is commonly found among overconfident equity analysts and fund managers who, in forecasting a company's earnings, fail to incorporate new

---

[28] See Robert J. Shiller, *Irrational Exuberance*, New Jersey: Princeton University Press, p. 138 (2000).

salient news about the company into their forecasts, despite it suggesting that something has changed. Investors might do well to heed the words of Keynes who once said: *'When somebody persuades me that I am wrong, I change my mind. What do you do?'*[29]

By becoming anchored to their forecasts and treating the news as a one-off random event, these forecasts become outdated. As a result, when the company announces its earnings, the earnings will invariably be higher or lower than many analysts or fund managers expected, often by a considerable margin. That is, there is a positive or negative 'earnings surprise'. This presents an opportunity for less overconfident investors to exploit the fact that the company's share price does not reflect everything known about the company.

However, the problem is compounded by the fact that there is a failure on the part of these overconfident investors to learn quickly from their mistakes. Indeed, there is often a succession of earnings surprises. Typically learning takes place over three consecutive quarters, though during the credit crisis in the US there were five consecutive quarters of company earnings that were posted below expectations! As suggested above, this leaves scope for those less overconfident investors to take advantage of these mistakes and make potentially considerable gains. However, these investors have to be quick because most research suggests that the majority of gains are made within three days of any earnings surprise, as investors gradually absorb the new information.

Framing

Having considered the main heuristics, let's now turn to the two main frames in the behavioural finance literature: ambiguity aversion and loss aversion.

Ambiguity aversion

In all walks of life, people much prefer to make decisions when they are in full possession of the facts and are able to quantify the risks associated with the decision. In valuing familiarity, people succumb to ambiguity aversion. In relation to investment, this typically results in portfolios adopting a 'home bias', given the familiarity of 'home' investments, causing them to overlook overseas investments and the potential benefits of international diversification. In addition, many investors invest in a company's shares purely because they use the company's product or service and therefore feel comfortable with the company. This is known as *moral anchoring* and can result in an emotional attachment to securities that should otherwise have been sold. Similarly, quality companies

---

[29] J. M. Keynes, *A Treatise on Probability*, London, Macmillan, p. 408 (1921).

are often treated as being synonymous with quality investments. That is, as with moral anchoring, sufficient consideration is not given to the, possibly inflated, valuation built into the company's share price.

Loss aversion

Loss aversion describes an asymmetric motivation to avoid losses. Traditional finance theory assumes that investors derive as much satisfaction from a 10 per cent gain as they do displeasure from a 10 per cent loss. There is now significant evidence that seems to suggest that investors derive greater displeasure from a loss than they do pleasure from an equivalent-sized gain. In other words, investors appear to be loss averse. Studies show that on average the 'pain-to-pleasure ratio' is at least two, though much depends on the size of the losses and whether the losses have been made in isolation or have been preceded by a succession of losses. This dominant motivation to avoid losses typically leads investors to sell their top-performing investments too soon and to hold on to their loss-making investments too long. Indeed, research shows that many investors sell their 'winning' stocks at twice the rate of their 'losing' stocks, thereby limiting the upside on their portfolio while potentially unrestricting the downside. This goes against the advice of the legendary fund manager Peter Lynch: *'Cut the weeds and cultivate the flowers.'*[30]

Many investors in realizing their gains too quickly as a result of 'mentally banking' their gains to avoid the regret of the gain becoming a loss, cut their flowers too soon. Moreover, by holding their loss-making investments too long in the hope that these will eventually become profitable, relying on anchors, such as the price they paid for the share or a recent high for the share price, investors end up cultivating too many weeds. Indeed, loss aversion can explain a number of spectacular debacles in recent financial history. Nick Leeson's role in bringing down Barings Bank, the two largest hedge fund losses in history – that of LTCM in 1998 and Amaranth in 2006 – and the collapse of WorldCom and Enron in 2002, can all be explained with reference to loss aversion.

Another aspect of loss aversion that results in sub-optimal investment decision making is *myopic loss aversion*: the excessive monitoring of share price movements. Given that daily securities price movements contain a lot of 'noise' rather than genuine news, this excessive monitoring can give investors an exaggerated view of the perceived riskiness, or the volatility, of an investment. This may cause many to give volatile asset classes, like equities, a wide berth and opt for other asset classes that appear to be less risky. Clearly, risk means different things to different investors. As noted earlier in this chapter, paradoxically asset classes

---

[30] *Ten Years On: Mr Bearbull.* www.investorschronicle.co.uk (accessed 23 August 2011).

such as equities that do exhibit high short-term volatility may turn out to be the least risky option for those investors with a sufficiently long time horizon. In addition, it has long been suggested that myopic loss aversion might explain why the return from equities over that from bonds – the ex post equity risk premium – tends to be considerable better over the long term than many investors initially expected.

So what can behavioural finance help explain?

In turn, these biases can individually or in combination with others help to explain why we observe:

- markets that trend for no apparent reason;
- investors being caught out by extreme adverse events;
- value stocks outperforming growth stocks in the long run;
- investors trading too often and losing out;
- abnormal returns often being made from company earnings announcements;
- investors constructing poorly diversified investment portfolios;
- investors overpaying for securities;
- investors selling their top performing securities too soon and holding their loss making securities for too long;
- equity returns often being higher than expected; and
- active fund management being a 'negative sum game'.

The latter in particular can be explained by behavioural biases, such as representativeness, overconfidence, adjustment conservatism and seeking safety in numbers that can all subtract value from investment portfolios over time.

Being influenced by others

I can calculate the motion of heavenly bodies but not the madness of crowds. (Sir Isaac Newton, 1720)

Men . . . think in herds . . . they go mad in herds, while they only recover their senses slowly, one by one. (Charles MacKay 1841)

The mass never comes up to the standard of its best member but on the contrary degrades itself to a level with the low. (Henry David Thoreau, 1849)

Anyone taken as an individual is tolerably sensible and reasonable but as a member of a crowd, he at once becomes a blockhead. (Bernard Baruch 1929)

Throughout history crowds have been viewed with suspicion. The nature of this distrust from an investment decision-making perspective is not only evident from the quotes above but also from the popularity of contrarian investment strategies that seek to do the opposite of what the crowd is doing, on the premise that the crowd in its stupidity seeks safety in numbers in adopting the consensus view. However, not everyone thinks about crowd behaviour in this way. Indeed the market consensus can at times be extremely prescient. In effect, this takes us back to the idea of efficient markets.

The wisdom of crowds

As proponents of the wisdom of crowds argue, much individual irrationality is cancelled out in the totality of the judgements made in markets. The markets may not be fully efficient but they are a form of voting mechanism that passes a constant verdict on fundamental value. We forget this at our peril. (John Plender, 2009)[31]

The overriding theme of former Morgan Stanley Chief Strategist, Barton Biggs, in his recent book, *Wealth War and Wisdom*[32] is that *'collectively the investor crowd often has superb intuition about long-term events and that those judgements should be respected and followed'*. Biggs substantiates this statement with reference to how markets anticipated events throughout World War II with amazing prescience.

Another admirer of crowds is James Surowiecki who, in his highly original and insightful book *The Wisdom of Crowds*,[33] pursues the idea that: *'Under the right circumstances, groups are remarkably intelligent, and are often smarter than the smartest people in them'*.[34] His contention is that even if most people within the group are not especially smart, well-informed or rational, the group can still reach a collectively wise decision or outcome. In fact, this collectively derived outcome should, on average, be better or more accurate than if reliance was placed on any one individual or 'expert'. This of course, goes completely against what most of us believe – that valuable knowledge is concentrated in very few hands and success is attributable to expert decision making.

[31] John Pender, 'There is still mileage in flawed market thinking', *Financial Times*, 17 June, p. 32 (2009).
[32] Barton Biggs, *Wealth, War and Wisdom*. New York, Wiley (2008).
[33] James Surowiecki, *The Wisdom of Crowds: Why the Many Are Smarter Than the Few*. London: Little, Brown. (2004).
[34] James Surowiecki, *The Wisdom of Crowds: Why the Many Are Smarter Than the Few*. London: Little, Brown. Introduction XIII (2004).

Surowiecki illustrates the wisdom of crowds with several examples and case studies but one simple example of group intelligence stands out.[35] That is the 91 per cent success rate of 'asking the audience' in the popular TV quiz show *Who Wants to be a Millionaire?*, which puts that of the 'phone a friend' expert at 65 per cent, firmly in the shade.[36] The reason why this is such a good example of group intelligence is because the outcome results from the group making a collective decision 'under the right circumstances'. That is, it captures the five conditions necessary for 'the many to be smarter than the few'. These are:

1. *Diversity*. Being different is as important as being smart because both are essential in reducing the group's collective error. Intelligence alone cannot guarantee different perspectives on a problem because smart people are too homogenous. Therefore, the group should comprise individuals who span the cultural, cognitive and socio-economic spectrums with wide and diverse social and educational backgrounds, experience, skills and expertise, not to mention race and gender. This diversity might be the source of the *Millionaire* audience, assuming that they are selected randomly.
2. *Independence*. Each individual should act independently of one other, with no one individual being decisive or dominant. Ideally, each should vote anonymously and simultaneously in using their own private information and opinions. This is exactly how the *Millionaire* voting system works.
3. *Decentralization*. There should not be any one person or central authority directing or dictating decision making. Once again, the *Millionaire* voting system works in this manner.
4. *Incentives*. Incentives help to reduce individual errors by encouraging people to participate only if they have an insight, with rewards for being right and penalties for being wrong, though these need not necessarily be financial. Arguably, the *Millionaire* audience has an incentive to keep the contestant in the hot seat so that they can continue to enjoy the show's suspense, and so that they can enjoy the contestant's winnings via osmosis.

---

[35] The classic demonstration of group intelligence arose in 1987 when Professor of Finance, Jack Treynor, ran his 'guess the number of beans in the jar' experiment with his class of 56 students. With each acting independently of the others and providing their answers simultaneously, only one of the 56 arrived at a more accurate answer than the group. With 850 beans in the jar, the group's average guess of 871 was only 2.5 per cent off the correct answer.

[36] However, it could be argued that the audience is often asked questions at an earlier stage in the game which are generally easier than those posed later in the game to the friend, when the stakes are higher.

5. *Aggregation.* There should be a mechanism by which all of this information is captured and considered, so that private judgements are turned into a collective decision. *Millionaire* uses an automated aggregation mechanism to capture the audience's voting.

Why do financial markets fail to exhibit the wisdom of the crowd?

[H]uman beings are reactive imitators . . . subject to emotional extremes of euphoria and despair [which] from time to time . . . leads to excesses and eventually to bubbles.
(Barton Biggs, 2008)[37]

In real life, however, a number of these necessary conditions can break down, resulting in the group failing to be collectively smart. This is particularly true of financial markets, despite the fact that they appear, on the face of it, to meet Surowiecki's criteria admirably. After all, financial markets comprise a large, diverse group (though maybe not as diverse as a *Millionaire* audience) of highly incentivized individuals, each apparently acting in their own self-interest, with their individual knowledge, information, opinions and views being aggregated into market prices.

The main problem is that the wisdom of the crowd is predicated on the idea that the errors that people make should be random and offsetting. That is, the errors should cancel each other out and the group should reach a wise, collective decision. However, as we suggested when considering the social aspect of human behaviour, arguably many investors, rather than act on their own private information, instead succumb to 'information cascades'. That is, they piggyback on the information, actions and opinions of others, notably those perceived to be 'experts', who may themselves have acted upon incorrect information or propagated an incorrect view. These information cascades typically perpetuate across large swathes of investors as a consequence of people being social and imitative and, as we will illustrate, decisions being made sequentially rather than simultaneously. Let's revisit a simple example we considered earlier.[38] Take a large group of people, in an unfamiliar town looking for a place to eat. They have a choice between a new Indian restaurant or a new Thai restaurant. The Indian restaurant is demonstrably better than the Thai. However, people, being social and imitative, will typically look to see what others are doing. So if the

---

[37] Barton Biggs, *Wealth, War and Wisdom*. New York, Wiley, p. 9 (2008).
[38] See Sushil Bikhchandani, David Hirshleifer, Ivo Welch, 'A Theory of Fads, Fashion, Custom and Cultural Change as Informational Cascades', *Journal of Political Economy*, Volume 100, Number 5, pp. 992–1026 (1992).

first few people are given bad information they'll go to the Thai restaurant. Even those subsequently told that the Indian restaurant is better are likely to follow the lead of the Thai diners because the Thai restaurant is crowded whereas the Indian restaurant is not. So everyone ends up making the wrong decision.

With individual errors working in the same direction, as a consequence of diversity and independence breaking down, the herding effect of information cascades culminates in collective irrationality. So it is within financial markets, especially with the explosion of financial news media sources and the markets' favourite pundits. Much of this goes back to Keynes beauty contest analogy that we considered earlier in the chapter. Anything that causes the market to lose diversity and independence *will* result in market prices losing touch with reality. As Suroweicki says: *'The best collective decisions are the product of disagreement and contest, not consensus and compromise.'*[39] Arguably, the telecoms bubble of the late-1990s was one of the most disastrous examples of a financial information cascade ever. Internet capacity was built on the assumption that Internet traffic growth would continue to grow at 1,000 per cent per annum for the foreseeable future, as it had done during 1996. However, its growth soon began to slow – dramatically. While some telecoms companies were investing on this false assumption, it seemed foolish for others not to follow – thus exacerbating the excess capacity that was created.

One result of financial markets not tapping into collective wisdom, as mentioned earlier in the chapter, are phases of excessive volatility[40] caused by uncertainty. Part of the reason for this uncertainty is the difficulty involved in guessing a company's earnings or dividends far into the future. Indeed, this is infinitely more difficult than, say, predicting the outcome of an imminent sporting event or election. (You'll recall that the value of any financial asset is the present value of the asset's expected future cash flows). Also, unlike sporting events, elections or *Millionaire*, financial markets (except for, say, imminently maturing fixed income instruments or derivatives contracts) operate in a continuum. That is, they do not work towards a known deadline. There is often no definite point in time where the correct value for the market is known for certain. This definite outcome for the other events mentioned keeps the crowd anchored to reality. Therefore, financial markets are attractive to speculators. Speculators trade securities, not because they necessarily believe the security price is wrong, they do so because they believe they can sell the security on to someone else

---

[39] James Suroweicki, *The Wisdom of Crowds: Why the Many Are Smarter Than the Few.* London: Little Brown. Introduction, XIX (2004).
[40] See Robert J. Shiller, 'Do Stock Prices Move Too Much to Be Justified by Subsequent Movements in Dividends?' The American Economic Review, Volume 71, Number 3, pp. 421–36 (1981).

for a higher price, who, in turn, believes that others will view the security more attractively than they do. This is known as the *Greater Fool Theory*, since each speculator needs a great fool to whom they can sell the security at a profit. Again Keynes' beauty contest analogy is pertinent in this regard.

Economist Colin Camerer illustrated the operation of the Greater Fool Theory by conducting an experiment where students were given the chance to trade shares in an imaginary company for 15 five minute periods.[41] Everyone was given two shares to start and money to buy more shares. Each share paid a dividend of US$0.24 at the end of each period. So if you owned the share for the entire experiment you'd receive US$3.60. Therefore, at the start of the experiment you shouldn't be prepared to pay more than US$3.60 and after period one, no more than US$3.36 etc. However, as soon as the experiment started the price of the shares jumped to US$3.50 and stayed there despite the shares' intrinsic value falling period after period. Why had the students bought at these inflated prices? One student replied: '*Sure, I knew the prices were way too high but I saw other people buying and selling at high prices. I figured I could buy, collect a dividend or two and then sell at the same price to some other idiot.*' This student, for one, was convinced that the greater fool was out there.

This experiment is interesting in that the students had all the information they needed to make the right decision and they knew when the experiment would end, yet a bubble in the shares still formed. Camerer's experiment also illustrated what we frequently observe within financial markets: that security prices can lose touch with reality for considerable periods of time when many investors believe that something will happen in the future that will justify the price paid.

This all too common situation within financial markets is not helped either by periodic bans on 'short selling', which limit investor diversity and the ability to tether financial markets to some sort of reality. That is, to drive periodic sky-rocketing markets back down to earth. After all, rising securities prices *per se* are undesirable if the market is incorrectly priced, especially if markedly so, not least because this invariably results in the inefficient allocation of investor capital. That is, too much money ends up being invested in the wrong companies and markets, inevitably with devastating consequences further down the line. You only have to look at the fallout from the dotcom bubble to see how much excess capacity resulted in the telecoms and technology industries and the sheer amount of money that was ploughed into what proved to be ventures with no real substance.

---

[41] See Colin F. Camerer, 'Taxi Drivers and Beauty Contests', *Engineering and Science*, Volume 60, Number 1 (1997).

However history tells us that being super rational in a highly irrational market, when the Greater Fool Theory can easily be applied, often comes at a high financial cost. As Keynes said, way back in 1936: *'Markets can remain irrational longer than you can remain solvent'*.

Indeed, 74 years on, the Financial Times Lex column mirrored Keynes sentiment with: *'When the herd is trampling forward . . . it is not a good idea to stand in its way.'*[42]

The expert problem

There are two classes of forecasters: Those who don't know and those who don't know they don't know. (John Kenneth Galbraith, 1993)[43]

The idea that following what the experts do and say is misguided, may seem counterintuitive. Surely relying on experts must be a good thing? Well, it would be if they were indeed experts! Philip Tetlock, a psychologist at the University of California, completed an exhaustive study of expert predictions of political and economic outcomes. In his study, Tetlock analyzed 28,000 forecasts made by 300 experts from 60 countries over 15 years. Economists were about 25 per cent of his sample.[44] He found no difference between those with a PhD and those with a first degree. Well-published professors had no advantage over journalists. Those with a big reputation produced the worst predictions. When these experts were right they attributed it to skill, depth of understanding and expertise, when they were wrong it was the situation that was to blame. Tetlock contends that experts suffer from biases, not least dismissing new information that does not fit with their beliefs. They also seem to become anchored to their pet theories and what they consider to be established chains of causation, or simple and direct relationships, between one thing and another.

Tetlock, as in an Aesop fable, divides experts into hedgehogs and foxes. The former are those operating in a very narrow field of expertise with set ideas, while the latter are those whose knowledge base is very diverse and who treat forecasting and problem solving in a flexible manner. Unsurprisingly, the latter with their cognitive diversity and open mindedness have the better record in analyzing complex problems. Those hedgehogs regarded as a real expert in their field – particularly those who are self-confident, are regularly quoted in the press, or, even worse, those who, having become accustomed to appearing on

[42] See the *Financial Times* Lex column, 14 April, p. 16 (2010).
[43] *Wall Street Journal* 22 January 1993 C1.
[44] Philip Tetlock, *Expert Political Judgement: How Good Is It? How Can We Know?*, Princeton University Press (2006).

TV, strive to be original and different by making outrageous forecasts – makes them even less reliable as forecasters. However, whether a fox or a hedgehog, rarely is a market strategist or stock market forecaster continually right for reasons we are about to consider.

The problem is that when it comes to forecasting the direction and size of market movements, there are no simple rules, only a wide range of possible outcomes with associated subjective probabilities. Indeed, most market forecasters, in succumbing to disaster myopia, fail to incorporate one key probability, the possibility of Black Swans, or extreme events, into their forecasts. There is also a tendency to over rely upon the automatic system of thought, or intuition – the quick and easy approach to problem solving. Although reliance on intuition can work well in stable environments where conditions remain largely unchanged, where cause and effect relationships are simple and straightforward, it fails, and often disastrously so, when you are dealing with a changing system in an increasingly complex world. Nowhere is this truer than when dealing with financial markets.

Financial markets are known as 'complex adaptive systems'. Usually explained within the context of how insect colonies operate,[45] complex adaptive systems have three aspects to them:

1. They comprise many heterogeneous, or diverse, agents, or individuals. For instance, bees in a hive or investors in a market.
2. These agents interact with each other, without anyone in charge. That is, they are decentralized systems in that there is no one person or central authority directing or dictating decision making.
3. The structure that emerges, the stock market for example, behaves like a higher-level system with properties and characteristics that are distinct from those of the underlying agents themselves.

In complex adaptive systems, there is no simple method for understanding the whole by studying the parts, so searching for simple agent-level causes of system-level effects is useless. Just as watching one bee or one ant will not help you understand the colony's behaviour, listening to or observing individual investors or stock market pundits will not provide a comprehensive insight into the workings of the market. In dealing with complex adaptive systems, it's the collective behaviour that matters. If you want to understand the stock market, study it at the market level since focusing on one component of a complex adaptive system without an appreciation of the system's dynamics can have

---

[45] See Peter Miller, *The Genius of Swarms*. National Geographic. July 2007, 126–147 and Thomas D. Seeley, P. Kirk Visscher and Kevin M. Passino, 'Group Decision Making in Honey Bee Swarms', *American Scientist*, Volume 94, Number 3, pp. 220–9 (2006).

unintended consequences for the whole. Take the recent bankruptcy of Lehman Brothers. The US government let Lehman's fail on 14 September 2008 since it believed that the market understood Lehman's poor financial condition and would absorb it. However, the markets recoiled at the removal of the implicit 'too big to fail' guarantee and sheer size of Lehman's losses, leading to a dramatic increase in global risk aversion. There was also a knock on effect to those areas of the market perceived to be safe. For instance, one of the oldest and largest money market funds in the US announced losses from the Lehman's debt it held, undermining confidence in the broader financial system.

In complex adaptive systems, where collective behaviour emerges from the inter-action of its constituent parts, cause and effect are proportionate most of the time. However, most complex adaptive systems are subject to abrupt, unforesee-able extreme outcomes but we fail to deal with them as we treat them as being simpler than they are.[46] Indeed, they have critical points or thresholds, called *tipping points*, where small incremental changes in the system cause it to change markedly, or disproportionately. For instance, the stock market can cope with the random removal of a few investors and the consequent loss of some diversity. However, there is a tipping point at which the loss of diversity causes a funda-mental change in the market, resulting in it failing to be collectively smart.

Using a computer simulation of 1,000 stock market investors, one academic[47] found, that as investors ride a wave of speculation and begin using similar trad-ing strategies, prices rise as a consequence of falling diversity among investors. However, as market scepticism starts to propagate and the diversity of investor views begin to proliferate, the market hits a peak and then ticks progressively lower. Once rising diversity in the market reaches a tipping point, there's a sudden strong destabilizing effect, then wham, the market takes an enormous dive. This is a fairly decent description of most market declines.

Many experts come badly undone by ignoring tipping points in their forecasts, principally as a consequence of the *problem of induction*. That is when repeated good outcomes lull us into a false sense of security and set us up for a negative surprise. For instance, if a turkey is fed for 364 days in a row, each day rein-forces the turkey's well-being until the day before Christmas or Thanksgiving when an unexpected event occurs. The same applies to the seemingly secular, stable asset correlations of the Great Moderation of 1998 to 2007 that, with few

---

[46] Complex adaptive systems, like many other phenomena in finance that are characterized by non-linear relationships, are typically treated as if they are simple and linear. After all, linear, or straight line, relationships are always easier to work with than non-linear.

[47] Blake LeBaron, 'Financial Market Efficiency in a Coevolutionary Environment' *Proceedings of the workshop on simulation of social agents: Architectures and institutions*, Argonne National Laboratories, pp. 33–51 (2000).

exceptions, rose inexorably during the financial crisis of 2007–2009. Very few experts were prepared for this. Indeed, as mentioned earlier, the philosopher Sir Karl Popper argued that to understand a phenomenon, we're better to focus on falsification than verification. For instance, eating 364 great and fulfilling meals, does not guarantee that you won't be eaten yourself on day 365!

Decision making within Trustee Boards and Investment Committees

Is there an ideal size and composition for an investment committee?

The importance attached to the size and composition of a trustee board or investment committee cannot be overstated if a pension scheme is to make the 'right' decisions to secure its long-term financial health. Indeed, despite the incentive for an investment committee to arrive at the 'right' decision, derived not only from their fiduciary duty to act in the best (financial) interests of the scheme membership, many of whom will be their work colleagues, but also from their own membership of the pension scheme, to quote a recent paper on this very subject, '*most investment committees reflect the worst of both worlds. They are large and they lack diversity*'.[48]

Interestingly, the operation of many investment committees has been likened to that of verdict-based juries – those that take a vote before any discussion and then concentrate on persuading dissenters to agree. Moreover, juries tend to be more diverse than many investment committees in their composition. Combined, these factors suggest that the current composition of many trustee boards may not be optimal.

As to committee size, given that the number of performance problems a typical investment committee encounters grow exponentially as the committee's size increases[49] and the inverse relationship between the size of the committee and each member's contribution,[50] all the evidence points to smaller committees being more effective than larger ones. Indeed, around six members is typically cited as ideal, with double figures being frowned upon. However, size is not everything. Probably of greater importance is the committee's diversity in terms of age, race, gender, socio-economic and cultural background, and education.

---

[48] See Michael J. Mauboussin, 'Investment Committees – How to Build a Team to Make Good Decisions', *LMCM*, September, p. 3 (2009).

[49] See J. Richard Hackman, *Leading Teams: Setting the Stage for Great Per*formance, Boston, MA, Harvard Business School Press, (2002).

[50] See John Payne and Arnold Wood, 'Individual Decision Making and Group Decision Processes', *The Journal of Psychology and Financial Markets*, Volume 3, Number 2, p. 94 ff. (2002).

In fact, drawing on the diverse knowledge and opinions accumulated by individuals through their varied life experiences typically outsmarts the smartest individual. Also, never underestimate the value of independent thinkers around the table. Being different is just as important as being smart.

Unfortunately, many trustee boards and investment committees, by virtue of their relatively homogenous composition and the fact that, as social animals, most of us are hardwired not to think independently means that we find it difficult to stick to a view that differs markedly from others on the committee. Consequently, many committees are destined to succumb to 'groupthink'. Groupthink, which we first considered in the context of confirmation bias earlier in the chapter, and which has been blamed for a number of catastrophic events throughout history, arises from the decision making of similar, like-minded individuals and is typically characterized by dominant personalities, closed-mindedness and pressure to adopt the group view. However, taking things to the other extreme, too much diversity can result in a board or committee experiencing problems of integration and communication, especially when dealing with complex problems where there is no simple answer. As with most things in life, it's all about finding the right balance.

How should trustee board and investment committee decisions be made?

Even after having addressed size and diversity issues, quality decision making cannot be guaranteed unless strong and unbiased leadership is demonstrated by the committee chair.

Given that democratic decisions tend to outperform dictatorial ones, the chair should encourage each individual to share their knowledge and opinions with the committee in a free and open manner. After all, it is often the information that individuals fail to share with others that holds the key to arriving at the right decision. Indeed, small groups generally have a hard time incorporating new information. Social psychologist Garold Stasser[51] ran an experiment in which a group of eight people were asked to rate the performance of 32 psychology students. Each of the eight was given two pieces of information about the students – grades and test scores – while two were given two extra

---

[51] Garold Stasser, 'The Uncertain Role of Unshared Information in Collective Choice', in Leigh L. Thompson, John M. Levine David M. Messick, eds, *Shared Cognition in Organizations. The Management of Knowledge*, Mahwah, NJ, Lawrence Erlbaum, pp. 49–69 (1999).

pieces of information and one another two. Although the group had six pieces of useful information, the ratings were based almost entirely on the two pieces of information they shared. The new information was discounted as unimportant and unreliable. The information that tends to be talked about is that which everyone already knows.

In particular, the chair should ensure that sufficient time is devoted to evaluating big picture complex problems such as those outlined above, as this is where the diversity of the committee has the potential to reach what should prove to be a more correct answer than that arrived at by any one individual. Crucially, the introverted personalities within the committee should be encouraged to contribute to the debate and given as much air time as the extroverts, with the chair ensuring that all of this information, without exception, is captured, debated, evaluated and aggregated. Dissenting views, in particular, should not be ignored in the interests of time and efficiency.

Indeed, political scientist Chandra Nemeth, in a host of studies, has shown using mock juries that the presence of a minority viewpoint, no matter whether right or wrong, makes a group's decisions more nuanced and its decision-making process more rigorous because it forces the majority to interrogate their own positions more seriously, so making the group wiser. Moreover, evidence from the study of juries suggests that where there is no minority, or a devil's advocate, view within small groups, there is a danger of group polarization. Indeed, trustees will often go along with group decisions either because they don't understand the full facts and feel foolish in asking the questions that no doubt others around the table would also like to ask, or shy away from asking these key questions because their co-trustees are big personalities or powerful executives, or both!

Interestingly, deliberation does not moderate but radicalizes people's point of view. For instance, a discussion in a group comprising risk averse people would make the group even more cautious, just as other studies show that people who had a pessimistic view of the future became even more pessimistic after deliberations. This occurs because of social comparison. That is, people constantly compare themselves to everyone else with a view to maintaining their relative position within the group. So if you start in the middle of the group and you believe the group has moved to the right, then you move to the right taking the group with you.

Even though collective decision-making can become more complicated when information is shared and evaluated, this democratic approach to group decision making has proved to be extremely valuable for the success, indeed survival, of other social animals, such as bees and ants, when deciding where to set up home for example.

The order in which people speak has a profound effect on the course of a discussion. Earlier comments tend to set the framework within which discussion occurs. As with information cascades, once the framework is in place, it is difficult for a dissenter to break it down. Quite worryingly, there is no guarantee that the most informed speaker will be most influential. Moreover, where group members know each other, deference means status usually dictates speaking patterns, despite higher status people not always knowing what they're talking about. Talkers are typically identified as being influential by default, projecting an air of confidence and expertise, despite no correlation between talkativeness and expertise!

Good decision making also incorporates 'pre-mortems' – analyzing what could go wrong once the decision is implemented – not least to minimize any subsequent decision regret.

Ultimately, the chair should refrain from swaying opinion and seek to ensure the committee reaches a decision by consensus in a decentralized fashion. Casting individual votes around the room is definitely a non-possibility. Once a decision has been made, the committee should agree on the timing of its implementation and action this accordingly. However, this is where many committees fall down badly.

Any discussion of investment committee decision-making would not be complete without looking at the contribution of experts, or advisers, to the decision making process. As we know, evidence suggests that when evaluating or forecasting complex phenomena, such as economics or financial markets, experts fare no better than informed non-experts, such as the vast majority of trustee board and investment committee members. Moreover, as intimated earlier, as social animals we tend to rely on the actions and opinions of others, especially those of perceived 'experts'. From our experience, this is especially true of trustee boards and investment committees, unless they comprise a sufficient number of independent thinkers who have the competence and competence to challenge the adviser's views.[52]

---

[52] As we noted in Chapter 2 when looking at investment governance, to assess the effectiveness of their governance and make good any shortcomings, a number of schemes have started to make use of the specialist governance appraisal services offered by most consultants. These governance consultants ensure that the trustee board and any sub-committees are getting the most of out their meetings by scrutinizing the dynamics of the board, principally the way in which decisions are made and how they are implemented.

Why hasn't behavioural finance become more mainstream?

Behavioural finance is now a popular research topic in both academic and financial institutions. Indeed, many fund managers now claim to take account of its vast and disparate array of phenomena in their investment processes – principally by recognizing and correcting their own biases and by claiming to be able to exploit those of others in the market.

However, despite the fact that behavioural finance has given us a useful perspective on financial market phenomena, there are quite a few issues that need to be borne in mind:

1. Recognizing your own biases, which means being self-critical, is never easy and often requires you to go against the consensus. As we know, as social animals it is difficult to stick to a view that is markedly different from others in the group, or market. Also, investing in accordance with Warren Buffett's mantra of: *'Be fearful when others are greedy and greedy when others are fearful'*[53] is not easy because going against the consensus never is.
2. No single bias systematically skews the market in one direction. Take overconfidence. While it may cause individuals to over-trade and to hold poorly diversified portfolios, it tells us nothing about what they're overconfident about and whether the market's going up or down. Moreover, there will invariably be offsetting trades from others overconfident about an opposing view.
3. We also still need traditional finance theory to establish the fair, or intrinsic, value of the market via concepts such as the Dividend Discount Model (DDM) and Beta, if we are to identify that prices have departed from fair value.
4. Behavioural finance, unlike many other aspects of finance, does not currently lend itself to mathematical modelling as easily as more traditional finance ideas. However, arguably this inability to translate all the understanding derived from behavioural finance into a series of equations does not necessarily detract from the valuable insights it provides. (Indeed, John Maynard Keynes rejected any sort of mathematical description of human behaviour.)
5. Perhaps more importantly, unlike the EMH, with its simple conceptual approach, no one has yet been able to consolidate what has become an extensive body of research into a simple set of unifying principles, or what academics would refer to as a falsifiable, conceptual framework.[54] There is a definite need to tie together observations of human behaviour in such a

---

[53] Berkshire Hathaway 2004 Chairman's letter.
[54] This matters to many academics who suffer from 'physics envy'. That is, they seek to apply mathematical precision or fundamental laws to phenomena which many would argue cannot be mathematically modelled unless complete rationality is assumed.

way that would facilitate the modelling of how financial market prices move in aggregate and how profitable trading opportunities can be identified and acted upon. In fact, until a more simplified conceptual approach surfaces, the EMH and behavioural finance are likely to co-exist as uncomfortable bedfellows.

What is the future for behavioural finance?

Despite its well publicized shortcomings, the behavioural finance literature continues to grow as new areas of research are explored and new methodologies are applied. Indeed, finance academics are drawing upon a range of other disciplines, as diverse as anthropology, chaos theory, the sociology of ideology and thermal dynamics, in order to improve their understanding of why and how markets evolve.

Neuroscience

One of the most exciting and truly fascinating developments in the relentless search for ways in which to understand human behaviour and beat the market, (after all, while markets may not be perfectly efficient, they are still very hard to beat) is in the area of neuroscience, where researchers have started using MRI technology to map neurological reactions to stimuli, such as making a profit or a loss. There has also been substantial testing of how chemical reactions within the brain, the release of hormones within the body and emotions determine the type and extent of financial risks people are willing to take. John Coates, a former trader and now a prominent academic, is instrumental in this area of research, which is still in its infancy.

The Adaptive Markets Hypothesis

> *It is not the strongest of the species that survives, nor the most intelligent, but the one most responsive to change.* (Charles Darwin, *On the Origin of Species*, 1859)

Another significant development is Professor Andrew Lo's *Adaptive Markets Hypothesis*. Lo argues that '*markets are neither always efficient, nor always irrational, but are adaptive.*'[55] This suggests that the EMH and behavioural finance each have merits and can co-exist on the premise that humans are neither fully rational nor psychologically unhinged and each approach captures different aspects of the same 'adaptive' system. Drawing heavily on Darwinian evolutionary biology, Lo argues that while markets can remain stable for extended

---

[55] See Andrew Lo, 'When the wisdom of crowds becomes the madness of mobs', *Financial Times*, 2 October, p. 33 (2009).

periods of time, as complex ecosystems which evolve and adapt over time, this stability can be periodically disrupted by the emergence of new financial 'species' and the extinction of others.

Just look at how conventional investment wisdom was turned on its head in the six months after the collapse of Lehman Brothers, as diversification failed, risk taking was punished and the long-run case for equities seemed to have been demolished, causing severe market dislocations, and even paralysis in some markets. Indeed, over the past few decades, investors have had to contend with and adapt to increasing complexity. For instance, by furthering the integration of financial markets, changing the way in which investors trade and facilitating the use of algorithmic trading, more sophisticated financial technologies have arguably made the formulation of market prices more complex. So investor behaviour that may seem irrational is instead behaviour that has not had time to adapt to a dynamic investment environment which produces new investment products, principles and paradigms. Against this backdrop, humans arguably work best by making guesses and by trial and error until their behaviour adapts to the new environment. If one investment strategy works then we stick with it, if not then we try another.

Will we ever get a new theory?

A theory should be as simple as possible and no simpler. (Albert Einstein, 1950)

Eugene Fama – one of the forefathers of traditional financial theory and the EMH – candidly admitted in 1998 that *'market efficiency . . . is a faulty description of price information [but] . . . market efficiency can only be replaced by a better specific model of price formation, itself potentially rejectable by empirical tests.'*[56] That is, a robust theory that explains a range of financial market facts, which in turn brings us back to the incompatibility of many behavioural finance phenomena and mathematical modelling.

This is why Paul Trickett, former Head of European Consulting at Towers Watson, believes, *'we'll get a new theory . . . but I don't think that what we see means we can throw away the existing theory'*[57] and why Tony Jackson at the Financial Times suggests: *'However broken the model, it must be maintained until an economic Newton or Einstein invents a better [one]. It could be a long*

---

[56] See Eugene Fama, 'Market Efficiency, Long-term Returns, and Behavioural Finance', *Journal of Financial Economics*, September (1998).
[57] See Paul Trickett, 'Wanted: A New Model for Markets', *Financial Times*, 22 September, p. 15 (2009).

wait.'[58] Indeed, none is likely to produce a framework that is as clean, simple and intuitive as the EMH, despite all of its shortcomings.

Key points

- The Efficient Markets Hypothesis (EMH), in assuming that investors are rational, risk averse, wealth maximizers who approach investment decision making objectively and have an excellent understanding of probability theory, asserts that everything known or knowable about a financial asset, or market, should be correctly and instantaneously factored into market prices.
- Behavioural finance is the study of human psychology in the context of investing and has become a useful way of observing *how* financial markets work in practice.
- Behavioural finance analyzes the ways in which cognitive biases, segmented into heuristics and framing errors, repeatedly enter investors' decision-making processes. It attempts to explain why asset prices frequently depart from their fundamental values and why trends, patterns and simple but profitable trading strategies, that are inconsistent with the EMH, frequently arise within financial markets.
- Crowds, under the right conditions, can be smarter than the smartest people in them, but this 'wisdom of the crowd' typically breaks down when insufficient diversity within the group results in groupthink and the herding effect of information cascades culminates in collective irrationality.
- Financial markets, as complex adaptive systems, cannot be understood by observing individual investors and are subject to abrupt, unforeseeable extreme outcomes as a result of a failure to appreciate the existence of tipping points.
- Despite its well publicized shortcomings, behavioural finance has grown as both a research topic, as new areas of research are explored and new methodologies are applied, and in its practical application within the asset management industry.

---

[58] See Tony Jackson, 'Wanted A New Model from an Economic Einstein', *Financial Times,* 29 March, p. 18 (2009).

Chapter 18

Manager Selection: How Do You Choose a Good Fund Manager?

Learning outcomes

- Understand why manager selection is important.
- Appreciate the limitations of short-term performance data as a means of assessing a manager's skill.
- Understand the difficulty of separating luck from skill and the role of mean reversion in interpreting fund performance.
- Understand the importance when evaluating a fund manager of the manager's Investment Philosophy and Process.
- Be in a better position to question your current and prospective fund managers.

Introduction

As we explained in Chapters 1 and 14, today most pension schemes delegate the responsibility for the management of their assets to professional fund managers. We also explained in Chapter 14 the basic process for evaluating their performance over time. However, this chapter focuses on the manager selection process. How do you select a fund manager(s) that will stand out from their peers, or those that will at least be a 'safe pair of hands'?

The selection process usually begins with the investment consultant scouring the fund manager universe to identify those managers that are deemed to be most capable of managing the assets in the manner required by the trustees.

In doing this they will normally ask a whole range of standard questions designed to whittle the long list down to a shorter list, not dissimilar to the sorts of questions that trustees may wish to ask and which we outline in the break out box at the end of this chapter entitled '*Assessing fund managers: The questions to ask.*' From this long list, a short-list of managers is usually identified and a beauty parade organized. Not the glamorous Eric Morley kind that are now thoroughly out of favour, but one that involves each manager on the short list making one or more presentations, where they explain why they are the best manager for the job. If you have never experienced a fund management beauty parade before be prepared for lots of sharp suits and dazzling PowerPoint wizardry.

Arguably the first decision that trustees need to make is whether they wish their funds to be managed actively or passively. If they choose the latter option then the manager selection process is relatively straightforward. We will deal with this selection issue first. Choosing an active fund manager is far more complex. We therefore devote the majority of this chapter to this more difficult task.

Selecting a passive fund manager

We explained the basic idea of passive fund management in Chapter 14. The passive manager constructs portfolios that are designed to mimic a financial market index. There are a number of techniques that can be used: full replication, that is holding all the securities in the index in their index proportions; stratified sampling, which usually involves some element of replication but also investments in representative securities that it is hoped will mimic the average movements in certain sections of the index that the manager is seeking to replicate; and replication techniques that make use of derivative instruments like futures contracts.

The passive approach is very simple in the sense that, if executed properly, it simply 'does what it says on the tin'. It is therefore a relatively simple task to evaluate the performance of the fund manager, that is, how good they have been at tracking their chosen indices. When we consider active investment below we will argue that past performance is not necessarily a good way of choosing an active fund manager. However, when evaluating competing passive fund managers, it probably is.

The largest passive fund managers in the UK are very efficient at tracking indices. The differences in the performance of the indices they track and their tracking portfolios are often only one or two basis points per year. So how do you choose between them? The answer, once you are certain that their tracking technology is sound, is fees. The passive investment product is a 'pile it high and sell it cheap' business. The economies of scale for the passive management company are virtually limitless. Passive managers therefore largely compete on fees and to a smaller degree on customer service.

Of course, you get what you pay for. As well as tracking the market up, passive managers track it down slavishly too. This is arguably why many investors prefer to have at least some of their funds managed actively.

Selecting an active fund manager

We explained in Chapter 14 that active management is almost certainly a negative sum game. That is, active managers *on average* fail to 'beat the market'. In Chapter 17 we explained how the behavioural biases displayed by most investors, including professional fund managers – since they are human too – almost certainly subtracts further value from many portfolios. So why go to all the trouble and effort of seeking out the best fund managers? The answer is that there are certainly times when having the right active fund manager can make a difference. For example, in the first six months of 2009, 70 per cent of US equity mutual funds (unit trusts) outperformed the S&P 500, with the average US fund manager focusing on US small-capitalization value stocks delivering a return of 33 per cent.[1]

By applying some intelligent due diligence, we believe that you can increase the chances of finding potentially exceptional managers who, like Warren Buffett, *more* than earn their fees over time.[2] Moreover, while this prospectively superior risk-adjusted return, or *alpha*, could be described as the icing on the cake – the strategic asset allocation decision ultimately determining the size and composition of the cake – this icing can really come into its own during periods when asset returns are modest. Furthermore, in a risk and return context, fund manager alpha is the ultimate source of uncorrelated, or diversified, return. So it is a good thing to seek out if you can.

As suggested above, when choosing a passive fund manager, past performance is likely to be quite a good guide to future performance – that is, the fund manager's 'skill' – since it is largely a mechanical process and is unlikely to diminish. However, is this true of active fund management?

---

[1] Empirical Research Partners LLC. October 8 (2009).
[2] When we say 'you', we mean with a little help from your investment consultant, delegated consultant or multi-manager.

Relying on past performance: The role of luck and skill

We have already touched on the possible existence of luck with regard to fund manager performance in Chapter 14. However, it is worth spending a little longer considering this issue. Why is past active performance not necessarily a good guide to future active performance, and therefore not necessarily a good way of choosing an active fund manager?

A simple test of whether an activity involves skill is to ask if one can lose on purpose. While you cannot purposefully lose at the casino wheel because this is a game of pure luck, you could lose on purpose at chess because this is a game of pure skill. Poker and fund management involve both skill and luck – (not that we are suggesting poker and fund management are in any way connected!) In many human endeavours, outcomes are a combination of skill and luck. However, discerning the contributions of skill and luck is not an easy task, even if analytical tools are available. In sport, for instance, even if a player's skill remains consistent, their results will be affected by changing luck. An exceptional performance is rarely repeated for any length of time as the good luck that boosted this performance will typically be absent the next time around, or certainly the time after that. Conversely, poor outcomes can reflect a lot of skill being offset by a lot of bad luck. However, over time, as luck evens out, any skill that exists will shine through. Thus luck tends to 'mean revert'. Quite simply, any activity, such as fund management, whose outcomes are determined by a combination of luck and skill, will be subject to this phenomenon. That is, an outcome that deviates from the average is typically followed by one that is closer to the average. However, to compound the problem, skill is not permanent. Indeed, it can suddenly or progressively deteriorate. In the case of athletes, skill deteriorates with age, however, in more cerebral fields, hitting a peak can take a little longer. The FIFA World Player of the Year tends to be around 26, while the average age of male sprinters winning the 100m Olympic gold is just under 24. Meanwhile psychologist Dean Simonton suggests that poets peak in their late-twenties, mathematically-minded academics at round 30 and historians in their forties.[3]

Although one would probably be right to assume that fund managers improve with age, dramatic changes in the market environment in which the manager operates might render these skills irrelevant. During both the dotcom boom of the late-1990s and the credit crisis of 2007 to 2009, a number of observers at the time questioned whether a skill set that may have helped a manager to outperform in a prior period, could be helpful during such exceptional periods. Time and

---

[3] Tim Harford, *FT Weekend magazine*, 11 September (2010).

time again, history tells us that fund managers can severely underestimate the effect of a change in the economic environment on corporate earnings and the impact this can have on individual stocks and the market as a whole.

Consider the following example, which investment manager would you rather hire: the one who recently beat the index or the one who did not? Most opt for the former. But there's no easy answer, because luck clearly plays a large but elusive role in short-term performance. However, in 2008, two US researchers in analyzing how 3,400 pension schemes, endowments and foundations hired and fired fund managers between 1994 and 2003, found a tendency to hire managers who had performed well recently and to fire managers who had recently performed badly. Somewhat disconcertingly, on average the fired manager subsequently outperformed those hired, albeit marginally, not to mention the sizeable transition costs incurred in changing managers.[4] The hired managers generated significant excess returns in the 24 months prior to their being hired, in contrast to the fired managers who had underperformed their benchmarks over the period.

The bigger the role of luck in the outcomes we observe, the larger the sample of observations one needs to distinguish skill from luck. As we noted in Chapter 17, although subject to debate, many academics would argue that around 12 years of monthly performance data for a fund manager with an information ratio of 0.5 would be needed to prove skill with 95 per cent confidence, though some would argue that about 300 months (25 years) of continuous data is needed to prove statistically the existence of skill. The problem is that very few managers have anything like a 12, let alone a 25-year track record, especially of running the same fund within the same firm. Those few that have, such as the late Nils Taube (39 years), Anthony Bolton (28 years), Bill Miller (29 years) and Neil Woodford (23 years) have proved to be among the world's most successful managers with exceptional long-run performance records, albeit punctuated with periods of short-term underperformance. Nils Taube ran his own fund from 1969 until 2006, at which point he was 78, delivering an average return of 15 per cent per annum. Anthony Bolton ran the Fidelity Special Situations Fund between 1979 and 2007, delivering an average annual return of over 19 per cent per annum. Bill Miller has run the Legg Mason Value Trust since 1982 and outperformed the S&P 500 index for 15 consecutive years between 1991 and 2005 – a feat with an ex ante one in 2.3 million probability,[5] though he subsequently underperformed between 2006 and 2008. Neil Woodford has run the Invesco Perpetual High Income Fund since 1988 and has comfortably

[4] A. Goyal and S. Wahal, 'The Selection and Termination of Investment Management Firms by Plan Sponsors', *Journal of Finance*, Volume 63, Number 4, pp. 1805–47 (2008).
[5] Source: Derek DeCloet, 'The Man Behind The Streak', *The Globe and Mail*, 21 November (2007).

outperformed the FTSE All Share index, although with periods of underperformance in 1999 and 2009.[6]

Many institutional investors (even those who should know better) have a tendency to take the line of least resistance and simply take a manager's past performance as being representative of their future performance.[7] That is, rather than examining and assessing those factors such as the manager's underlying investment philosophy and process (IP&P) in an attempt to establish the existence of skill and the repeatability of this performance, they treat good performance as sufficiently objective evidence of a good process and skill that it is likely to persist. As we already know, where the outcome of a process involves skill and luck, a good process can lead to bad outcomes and vice versa, at least for a while due to luck, which will even out over time. You should, therefore, be careful when drawing conclusions about outcomes from activities that involve luck, especially short-term results.

Investment philosophy and process (IP&P)

To reinforce our last point, investment returns have a substantial random element to them which at times will cause a poor fund manager to outperform a genuinely talented one. Because it is difficult for a prospective investor to decipher whether the alpha generated was through luck or skill, most investors simply extrapolate past performance. Arguably, true alpha generators, or skilful fund managers, should be able to differentiate themselves from, let's call them, the 'alpha pretenders' by clearly articulating their investment philosophy in a statement that captures their investment insights and value adding processes.[8]

This investment philosophy statement should comprise a set of principles that set out the manager's genuine beliefs about such things as the mechanism by which asset prices become mispriced, about the manager's capability and competitive advantage in exploiting these mispriced securities and how the manager believes alpha can be sustainably generated, ideally with examples that have borne out these beliefs in practice. These principles should, in turn, underpin the manager's investment process. A manager's investment philosophy and process (IP&P) should be distinctive, logical, consistently applied, understood, believed and adhered to across the organization. Perhaps just as

---

[6] We hasten to add that any fund managers mentioned in this chapter and any reference to their exceptional track records should not be construed as investment advice!

[7] This is known as representativeness which we discussed in Chapter 17.

[8] We outline a typical active manager's investment process in Chapter 14. For a more detailed insight into investment philosophies and processes see J. Minahan, 'The role of investment philosophy in evaluating investment managers,' *Journal of Investing*, Summer (2006).

importantly, the manager should ensure that individual and team reputations, skill sets and depth of resources fit with the IP&P as it never pays to under-deliver on something that's been promised.

Be careful, most fund managers today are skilled in the presentational art of PowerPoint. In other words, they can string together many impressive looking charts which when combined with slick presentational skills and a sharp suit can seem to represent a compelling IP&P. However, when they have left the room, following their presentation, do they just forget this presentation? It is difficult to know for sure how they put their IP&P into practice, or indeed whether the presentation is just a window dressing exercise designed to wow trustees. One way of ascertaining whether it is window dressing exercise or not is to ask for examples of how the process has worked in practice. Managers are always forthcoming with positive examples, so it is equally important to ask for examples where adhering to the philosophy did not work. Given the evidence discussed in Chapter 14, even the best fund managers get it wrong. What does the manager do under such circumstances? Do they change their philosophy, or stick to their principles? Trustees should be highly suspicious of a fund manager that claims that their process is foolproof – don't let them take you as fools.

When digging into a manager's IP&P, trustees may wish to investigate a number of issues. We will now highlight some of the most important ones.

A good investment philosophy statement . . .

- We believe that markets are inefficient as investors' behavioural biases drive prices away from their intrinsic value.
- Our philosophy is, therefore, founded on the principle that investing is the art of identifying and exploiting the difference between perception – the behaviourally driven consensus view – and reality, or intrinsic value.
- We adopt a contrarian approach to our research by identifying where intrinsic value materially deviates from consensus and, as a truly active manager, implement this view through high conviction portfolios by employing an 'investing to win' rather than an 'investing not to lose' philosophy.
- Research and portfolio construction is performed by our Team, which operates across the investment style spectrum, as a collection of small, specialist and autonomous teams, each with a genuine stakeholding in the Team's collective success.
- We believe that the combination of a contrarian approach with high conviction implementation performed by small, specialist and highly

incentivized teams is the cornerstone of sustainable outperformance and the most reliable route to delivering client expectations.

. . . and the not so good

- Our investment philosophy focuses on:
- Identifying solid investment opportunities by discovering the unexpected among the ordinary.
- Combining bottom-up research with advanced quantitative techniques.
- Taking advantage of a worldwide trading platform that enables us to use these effectively and ensure the best execution of any transaction.

Index huggers or active fund managers?

Deciding to take the active fund management route is an expensive business. It is not just the active fees, but all the time and effort that trustees must put into choosing, from among a long list, an active fund manager, and then into monitoring the chosen manager's subsequent performance. Given all the effort and cost involved, trustees need to make sure that their manager is a truly active manager and not an index hugger.

Arguably, truly active managers, unlike their index hugging counterparts, apply the three Cs to portfolio construction: contrarian, conviction and concentration. As contrarians, or independent thinkers, truly active managers continually challenge the consensus reflected in market prices. They seek to identify opportunities where their perceived fair value of a security materially differs from its market price. However, only if their analysis presents a view that is clearly differentiated from the consensus, one in which they believe with sufficiently high conviction, is this implemented into their portfolios. With high conviction comes portfolio concentration. If a high conviction idea warrants inclusion in a portfolio, then it must be implemented in a meaningful manner. Therefore, for example, most truly active equity portfolios typically contain no more than 60 or so stocks. Many contain far less. By definition, these are managers who, while aware of the benchmark against which their performance is judged, are not constrained by it. They invest to win, as evidenced by a high tracking error, rather than not to lose, as evidenced by a particularly low tracking error.

The intuitive appeal of truly active management is reinforced by hard data. Indeed, in 2009, two Yale professors developed a measure of the extent to which the composition of an active manager's portfolio differs from that of the benchmark against which they are assessed and used this to predict future performance.[9] Managers do this by widening their 'opportunity set' beyond the securities that comprise their benchmark, so long as their mandate permits this. What they found was that this 'active share' which is measured in percentage terms and scaled from 0 per cent (no different from the benchmark) to 100 per cent (completely different from the benchmark), correlated closely with fund performance and performance persistency. Indeed, drawing on the quarterly performance data of over 2,500 US equity mutual funds between 1990 and 2003, a highly concentrated, high conviction portfolio which deviated from the composition of the benchmark by over 80 per cent and had a high tracking error was typically associated with persistently strong performance in stark contrast to one with an active share below 60 per cent and a low tracking error, which infers varying degrees of index hugging.

Employing a manager with a high active share is no guarantee of future outperformance, but at least you know that you are paying active fees for an active fund manager.

Investment style

In Chapter 7 we considered the sorts of investment styles that equity investors and fund managers adopt. The style adopted by an equity fund manager will be a key component of their IP&P. While style investing can be traced back to the 1930s, having originated from the pioneering work of Benjamin Graham and David Dodds,[10] it has only really gained attention since the mid-1990s in the UK. Equity fund managers will adopt their chosen style because they believe that a particular group of stocks, sharing one of a number of common characteristics, or *style factors*, exhibit a meaningful tendency to move together and so experience periods of out and under performance of the broader market.

However, managers of other asset classes have their own styles too, though these will not necessarily have a convenient name like those associated with equity investment. For example, managers of investment grade corporate bond portfolios often do not seek to outperform their benchmarks by taking duration bets, that is, by constructing a portfolio that has a duration greater or lower than that of their benchmark. Instead they may seek to add value to their portfolio by over- or underweighting particular industries or those with particular credit ratings, while keeping the duration of their portfolio equal to that of the benchmark. Managers of commercial property portfolios might

[9] K. J. Cremers and A. Petajisto, 'How Active is Your Fund Manager? A New Measure That Predicts Performance', *Review of Financial Studies*, Volume 22, Number 9, 3329–65 (2009).
[10] Benjamin Graham and David Dodds, *Security Analysis*, New York, McGraw-Hill (1934).

also adhere to a particular style or theme too, for example, only investing in properties with particular tenant types or those that have significant development potential. We considered these in Chapter 8.

The point is that a manager's style should be clearly espoused in the IP&P. If this is how they claim to be able to add value, then trustees need to be aware of this claim and need to monitor it over time, that is, to check for what is known as *style drift*. If they are gradually changing their style over time, or indeed abandoning it completely, what does it say about their IP&P?

Style drift can be monitored by using the output from multi-factor risk models employed by most fund managers and investment consultants that scrutinize 'the DNA' of a portfolio by identifying the extent of the portfolio's investment style bias. These multi-factor risk models do this by using traditional valuation measures, such as the portfolio's average price-to-earnings ratio, price-to-book ratio, dividend yield, earnings growth prospects and the size of the stocks held, to quantify the extent to which the characteristics of the stocks held within the portfolio differ from the portfolio benchmark, so pointing to a particular investment style.

Each investment style probably demands a different mind and skill set. For example, in the same way that John Terry and Wayne Rooney could never perform at their best by swapping positions on the football pitch, most value and growth managers would find it difficult to emulate successfully their counterpart's respective defensive and attacking investment styles. Therefore, it is important to ensure that managers adhere to their chosen investment style and don't deviate from their mandate. In other words, trustees need to check that the fund management company is not playing John Terry on the left wing.

However, having said this, many fund managers argue that while each style will have a different focus, they are not always mutually exclusive. According to the legendary investor Warren Buffett, the world's third richest man, 'growth and value investing are joined at the hip'.[11] In other words, investment styles and processes may often overlap. For example, not too many value managers would ignore a stock they perceived as being cheap simply because it looked to have strong growth prospects. Equally, an investment grade corporate bond fund manager that typically seeks to keep their portfolio duration neutral may change their mind if they think that a substantial shift up or down of the yield curve is imminent. In short, no two fund managers will approach any one investment style in exactly the same manner.

---

[11] R.G. Hagstrom, *The Warren Buffet Way: Investment Strategies of the World's Greatest Investor.* John Wiley & Sons p. 95 (1995).

Another issue with regard to style is that no single style is likely to outperform over all periods. For example, equity growth investing comfortably outperformed equity value investing in the dotcom boom of the late-1990s, but subsequently underperformed once the bubble had burst. Equally, investment grade corporate bond portfolio managers that were ultra cautious in the bonds they invested in, probably outperformed more aggressive managers in 2001–2002 if they did not invest in companies like Enron, WorldCom and NTL that all defaulted over this period. Simply avoiding these blow ups would have helped performance. However, outperforming with a conservative IP&P in periods when there are no blow ups may be harder.

Rather than remaining loyal to one style then, it may pay for a fund management firm to be more pragmatic by alternating between styles, or more correctly alternating between different managers adopting different styles. This alternation is referred to as *style rotation*, and it may be a fundamental element of the IP&P. While style rotation can, at least in theory, be successfully undertaken by observing a multitude of economic and market indicators that collectively signal potential inflection points in the equity market,[12] in practice style rotation has proved to be an elusive skill.

As a result of this difficulty in identifying ex ante the style that is likely to outperform in the future, some equity fund managers adopt a *style neutral* approach to active equity fund management, such as running modular portfolios. Here, two or more sub-funds, or modules, each managed according to a distinctive investment style independently of the other companion modules, are combined to form a single fund. When well implemented, this approach, which lets growth, value and other style managers draw on their natural strengths, should offer returns that are more consistent and less volatile than the returns of the sub-funds in isolation, given the diversification of manager and investment style risk. This assumes, of course, that style drift is being closely monitored.

There's no 'I' in team

One of the first slides in a manager's beauty parade presentation is usually an impressive looking organogram that details the names, roles and background of all 'the team that would be running your portfolio, if appointed'. However, it was not always this way. In the 1990s and early to mid-noughties the asset management industry landscape was dominated by the cult of the star fund

[12] See M. Levis and N. Tessaromatic, 'Style rotation Strategies: Issues of Implementation', *Journal of Portfolio Management*, Volume 30, Number 4, pp. 160–9 (2004); A. Clare, S. Sapuric and N. Todorovic, 'Quantitative or Momentum Based Multi-Style Rotation', *Journal of Asset Management*, Volume 10, Number 6, pp. 370–81 (2010).

manager. As a marketing philosophy this seemed to make sense; in a crowded market place with little else to differentiate brands, star fund managers provided a fund management business with a competitive advantage. This point was not lost on City veteran John Duffield who, in creating asset managers Jupiter in 1985 and New Star in 2001, built much of his business proposition around the fund management superstars that he hired. You may well have seen a number of his superstars prominently profiled on billboards at railway stations during the nineties and noughties. However, as with investments generally, putting all your eggs in one superstar manager's basket, can spell disaster for the fund management firm, not to mention their investors, when the fund manager walks. Indeed, this is exactly what happened in the fund management world when star performers George Luckraft and Nigel Thomas left ABN Amro for AXA Framlington in 2002 and when Roger Guy left Gartmore in 2010. You should also revisit panel A of Exhibit 14.13 which shows what happens to the performance of a fund when a positive performer leaves.

While things can work out well for those stars who move to another fund management business, there is evidence to suggest that this is the exception rather than the rule. Indeed, many star fund managers lured from a competitor for big bucks subsequently fail to live up to the lofty expectations of their new employer. Typically when hiring the star little, if any, appreciation of the complex dynamics that made the fund manager successful in their previous organization seem to be taken into account. For example, surprisingly little, if any, consideration is given to the manager's process, the quality of the people and other resources that surrounded them and the organizational and team structures within which the manager must operate and adapt. A Harvard study of over 1,000 acclaimed equity analysts (rather than fund managers) over a decade, monitored how their performance changed once they had switched firms. The study found not only that the star's performance plunged, but also that this was accompanied with a sharp decline in the performance of the team and a fall in the asset management company's market capitalization.[13] With a string of poor performances behind them, the former star, feeling unloved, moves on, often taking the asset manager's clients with them, despite the sometimes substantial transitioning costs incurred by the client in moving money from one fund management firm to another.

This is why fund management firms now go to great lengths at beauty parades to emphasize the team aspect of their investment process. They emphasize a collegiate, or team-based, approach, where talented individuals work together

---

[13] See B. Groysberg, A. Nanda and N. Nohria, 'The Risky Business of Hiring Stars,' *Harvard Business Review*, May, pp. 92–100 (2004). Also see B. Groysberg, L. Sant and R. Abrams 'How to Minimise the Risks of Hiring Outside Stars', *Wall Street Journal*, 22 September (2008).

within small autonomous teams. In quizzing their prospective fund managers then, trustees need to understand whether and how each member of the team has a genuine stake in not only their own success but also in that of the team. Fund management companies typically do this via remuneration packages that aim to tie in the team members to the current and future success of the fund.

The idea behind this collegiate approach is clear: if one of the fund managers moves on, the team's process remains in place for the other managers to carry on from where their departed colleague left off. Just as importantly, these teams should be encouraged not to act as introspective silos but to interact with the fund management firm's other research teams so that ideas may be shared and portfolio positions challenged. Indeed, it is absolutely imperative that there exist suitable mechanisms that allow team members and other teams to challenge a manager's portfolio positions and thinking. Equally important will be the manager's willingness to listen to and act upon these challenges. For example, can the fund manager's view on a security be overridden by the sector analyst that works for them? Having an effective due diligence process can help to reduce the behavioural biases and sub-optimal decision making to which managers are all too prone (see below).

So there is no 'I' in team, and a team-based approach is what most fund managers practice. But to paraphrase Mandy Rice-Davies 'they would say that wouldn't they?'. If trustees are uncomfortable putting all their faith into the metaphorical basket of one star fund manager, and would instead prefer a fund management company with a team-based approach, they need to ask questions designed to ascertain whether it is a genuine team-based approach, or whether the whole process is highly dependent on one person, a dependency which is easy to hide within a fancy PowerPoint slide.

Behavioural biases

No examination of what makes a good fund manager would be complete without considering the extent to which a manager recognizes and corrects their own behaviour for the disparate array of behavioural biases to which investors typically succumb in a systematic fashion. Although most fund managers admit to recognizing these biases, because failing to do so would result in sub-optimal investment decision-making, only the very best actually do so in a formalized way. As we noted in Chapter 17, some of the more commonly cited biases are as follows:

- Representativeness: subconsciously creating and extrapolating patterns and trends from a series of random events, without investigating the reasons for the apparent trend.

- Availability: placing too much or too little emphasis on the likelihood of events materializing, especially the possibility of an extreme event occurring, based on how salient, or how easily visualized, the event is.
- The endowment effect: paying more attention to and knowing more about the portfolio's overweight positions than the portfolio's under-weight positions.
- Gamblers' fallacy confusing shorter-dated samples of data with longer-dated samples of the same population resulting in the formulation of incorrect notions such as markets working to timetables.
- Overconfidence: overestimating one's own investment knowledge, skill and ability, resulting in undiversified portfolios and excessive portfolio turnover to the detriment of investment returns.
- Adjustment conservatism: being overconfident in one's own forecasting ability and so failing to adjust forecasts for new salient news and being subject to a series of company earnings surprises.
- Anchoring: placing too much emphasis on irrelevant facts and figures, for example, the price paid for a stock, when considering the stock's future prospects and the price at which to sell.
- Ambiguity aversion: a preference for known, rather than unknown, risks which results in a home bias to portfolios. Ambiguity aversion can also result in moral anchoring. That is, an emotional attachment to stocks that should otherwise have been sold.
- Loss aversion: selling winning stocks too soon and holding on to losing stocks for too long.

Nothing beats questioning the manager face-to-face about their IP&P to uncover evidence of behavioural biases. Being prepared to ask questions in this area is crucial if trustees are to avoid bad fund managers.

Capacity constraints

The performance of even the best performing (quite possibly the most skilled) fund managers can be compromised by subsequent inflows of cash from investors chasing performance, because this can force the manager, overwhelmed by the sheer amount of cash, to depart from their strategy that generated the superior performance. A manager's capacity constraints – the amount of money a manager can sensibly manage – will be determined by both the characteristics of the market in which they operate and the investment style that they adopt. For instance, to operate effectively, a successful emerging markets equity or a developed markets small-cap equity fund manager may need to limit the size of assets under management to a fraction of the size of a fund managed by a large-cap developed market fund manager. This is because of the limited supply of available investments in these markets, compared to large-cap developed economy equity markets. In addition, given the relatively illiquid nature of emerging market and small-cap stocks and the much smaller free-float of such stocks (the percentage of the company's share capital made available to investors), the manager should also place a limit on the amount of each stock's free float they own. A 2 or 3 per cent limit is not unusual.

However, fund management companies generally charge a fee based on the assets under management (AuM): the larger the size of the AuM the larger the fee. Given this, fund managers find it difficult to close their fund to new business when their remuneration is so closely tied to the size of AuM and commercial pressures exist to grow these. This is particularly true of those fund managers that are the subsidiaries of large shareholder-owned organizations. Ironically, however, while in the short run growing the AuM will generate a greater level of fee income, often performance will suffer to the long-run detriment of fee income.

Good managers are those who can tell you the optimal size of their portfolio, and the level at which they intend to close their fund to new business. Once appointed, it is therefore always worth asking in subsequent meetings what new business they have attracted, from what type of client (ideally a long-term one) and ultimately about the current size of the fund versus the fund's perceived capacity. A manager that changes their story claiming that the capacity constraints previously envisaged are less onerous than previously stated should be viewed with deep suspicion.

Risk management

Risk management should be central to a manager's investment process. Good managers are those who not only manage the known and more readily quantifiable risks but also those that are not so easily forecasted and calibrated. Indeed, a good manager will constantly evaluate the macroeconomic, company specific, geopolitical, regulatory and environmental, social and corporate governance (ESG) risks to their portfolio, as well as the extent to which the portfolio is exposed to any one risk, in limiting the portfolio's downside risk.

One of the key elements of risk management is the approach taken to selling securities. We have already touched upon investor biases when it comes to selling securities that have fallen in value, that is, investors tend to hold on to these securities for too long. It is essential then that the manager has a disciplined approach to selling – this is commonly referred to as a sell discipline. It needs to be part of their overall approach to risk management.

A good sell discipline can be based upon any one or any number of the following triggers:

- a target price for the stock has been achieved;
- the stock price has fallen by a pre-determined percentage and a 'stop-loss' is triggered;
- a more compelling stock idea or theme is identified;
- the stock's fundamentals have deteriorated; or
- a previously unidentified risk becomes a concern.

Arguably fund managers spend a great deal of time monitoring the performance of their purchases, but devote far too little, if any, time to analyzing the subsequent performance of securities that they have sold. A good fund manager is not only one that buys well, but one that sells well too.

Fees

As we noted earlier, the poor performance of active fund managers will clearly not be helped by the higher transaction costs incurred in turning a portfolio over more frequently than a passively-managed portfolio and the higher management fees associated with running actively managed funds. Whereas most active managers charge a percentage annual management fee on the value of the funds under management, which reduces with the size of the funds being managed, a considerable minority also charge a not insignificant performance related fee on that element of performance that exceeds a pre-agreed hurdle rate, which in many cases is not a particularly challenging target. Unsurprisingly, the higher the fees charged, the greater the impact these fees will have on investment returns as they compound over time. To state the obvious, other things being equal, the smaller the fee, the greater the returns that accrue to you, the client.

For instance, if you had invested US$1,000 in the shares of Warren Buffett's Berkshire Hathaway fund when Mr. Buffett began running the investment company in 1965, by the end of 2009 your investment would have been worth US$4.3m. That's a compound annual return of 20.46 per cent. However, if Mr. Buffett had charged you an annual management fee of 2 per cent and a performance fee of 20 per cent on any gains, your US$4.3m would only be worth US$300,000.[14] Although this example exaggerates the point a little, in

---

[14] Terry Smith, Fundsmith, 28 September (2010).

Exhibit 18.1   Gross versus net of fee performance

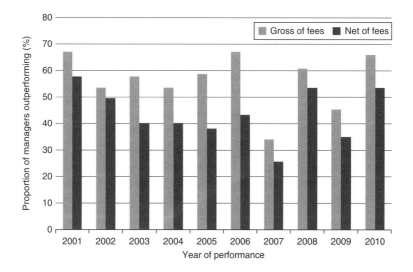

that traditional fund managers do not charge institutional clients anything like '2 and 20', it does illustrate that the level of fees you pay matters. What's more, there is no discernable relationship between the fees charged and the performance delivered, and when the manager subsequently underperforms those fees already paid are non-refundable.

Exhibit 18.1 underlines the importance of fees. Recall that in Chapter 14 (Exhibit 14.10) we looked at the number of funds out of a sample of nearly 100 UK equity large-cap managers that beat the market over each of the last ten years. The results were not very impressive in that over most calendar years most funds were beaten by the market. The results are repeated again and represented by the bars labelled 'net of fees' in the exhibit. The equivalent gross of fee performance, that is, excluding fees, is shown by the bars entitled 'gross of fees'. The performance of these managers is more impressive gross of fees of course, though the return is not adjusted for risk, but it still shows that fees make a difference. This is why it is imperative for you to negotiate fees down as far you can and structure the manager's fees so that your manager's interests are aligned with yours. For instance, if a manager is insistent on the payment of a performance fee, then one based on, say, a three-year rolling performance target with a high watermark (where a fee is only paid if the previous performance on which the fee was paid has been surpassed) rather than on annual performance without a high watermark is a good starting point.

And finally: sex

So what about sex? No thanks please, we're British. No, we mean the gender of the fund manager. Who make the best fund managers – men or women? Well, although the evidence is sketchy, according to the French investment funds association AFG, female fund managers produce more consistent and less volatile performance than their male counterparts over one, three and five years. Although according to the French research, female fund managers are rarely among the top performers, they are less likely to be among the bottom performers.[15]

The principal problem with this research, however, is the small sample size. After all, only 3 per cent of UK and 12 per cent of US fund managers are female. Despite this however, a greater percentage of female fund managers are highly rated by the fund management rating agencies – and for good reason. The behavioural finance literature confirms that women do not succumb to as many damaging behavioural biases as men. In particular, women are more analytical in their decision making. They also tend not to blindly extrapolate perceived trends that more often than not prove to be just a series of random events that look like a trend.

To shed more light on this issue, two US researchers, Barber and Odean, looked at the trading behaviour of a large number of US investors.[16] They analyzed the stocks that 66,000 retail investors bought and sold between 1991 and 1996. The average investor had a portfolio turnover of 75 per cent but the most aggressive had a turnover of 250 per cent. Between 1991 and 1996 the market returned 17.9 per cent and the average active investor 11.4 per cent. They found that the single men in their survey had the highest portfolio turnover, followed closely by married men, while both single and married women had similar low portfolio turnover statistics. Was this because single men knew the most, and were better traders? Interestingly, they found that the 20 per cent of investors that turned over their portfolios the most – largely single men – after transactions costs, earned an average return of 7 per cent over the sample period studied; while the 20 per cent of investors that turned over their portfolios the least – largely single and married women – after transactions costs, earned an average return of 18.5 per cent over the same period. We will leave the reader to draw their own conclusions from this study.

---

[15] See *FTfm*, 23 March, p. 11 (2009), and *Mail Online*, 28 March (2009).
[16] B. M. Barber and T. Odean, 'Trading Is Hazardous to Your Wealth: The Common Stock Performance of Individual Investors', *The Journal of Finance*, Volume 55, Number 2, pp. 773–806 (2000).

Assessing fund managers: the questions to ask

From our experience of working and meeting with active fund managers, we have compiled a list of the questions you should pose to identify whether a fund manager has the potential to *more than* earn their fees. These questions could form part of the beauty parade interview process, or as part of the on-going due diligence of incumbent managers. In our view, there is no substitute for seeing the whites of a fund manager's eyes in a face-to-face meeting.

1. How financially supportive is the fund manager's parent company? How much autonomy does it give to the fund manager?
2. Does the fund manager operate a star manager culture or a team-based approach? Does the culture promote genuinely creative and collaborative thinking? Does the manager have a genuine stakeholding in their own and their team's success and, if so, what form does this take?
3. Can the fund manager clearly articulate their investment philosophy and process (IP&P)?
   - What are the IP&P assumptions?
   - Has the IP&P been consistent and applied consistently over time?
   - Is the IP&P understood and adhered to throughout the organization?
   - Is there a logical, coherent rationale for why the IP&P works? Can the manager explain their performance with reference to a clearly articulated IP&P?
   - Can the manager provide examples of when the IP&P has not worked?
4. What investment style does the manager adopt and why? Does the manager adhere to this style or is there evidence of style drift? Do they style rotate?
5. How suitable is the manager's benchmark given their stated objectives and investment style?
6. What drives the manager's decision making process?
   - Which valuation metrics, e.g., dividend yield, price-to-earnings (growth) ratio, price-to-book, and valuation models, e.g., dividend discount model, do they focus on and why?
   - What quantitative and qualitative factors do they look for in a company? For example, the company has pricing power, is positioned as number one or two in the industry, generates a high free cash flow.
7. Is the manager truly active?
   - How closely does their portfolio resemble their benchmark?
     i. Are they benchmark aware but not benchmark constrained?
     ii. Do they 'invest to win rather than invest not to lose'?
     iii. Can they quantify their active share and tracking error?

- How concentrated is their portfolio? Has this concentration changed markedly over the past year and, if so, why?
- Is there evidence that only high conviction ideas are incorporated in their portfolios?

8. How does the fund manager research an idea? Are ideas generated internally to produce unique investment insights or 'bought in' from sell-side analysts? If generated internally, how is fundamental analysis and/or technical analysis employed? How often does the fund manager meet with company management?

9. Has the composition of the manager's portfolio changed over the past year? If so, how and why? What are the manager's key investment themes?

10. What is the manager's typical annual portfolio turnover? Has this increased or decreased over the year and why? If increased, is this as a consequence of client redemptions or a desire for a more concentrated portfolio or are investment themes for holding particular stocks no longer applicable?

11. Is the manager attracting new client money and are they operating at or near capacity? Does the manager know at what size of assets they should close their fund to new business? How many other clients are invested in the fund? (You shouldn't be the only one or one of only two or three clients invested in the fund).

12. What is the size, experience and stability of the team that supports the manager? Is the depth of resources adequate given the manager's investment process and the size of assets under management? What is the division between research and fund management within the team? What percentage of staff turnover has the manager experienced over the past year? What contingency and succession plans exist? Are the manager's portfolio positions effectively challenged by their peers and/or team members?

13. What behavioural biases are evident from the way the manager has managed their portfolio? For example:
   - Representativeness: are they simply trend followers?
   - Gamblers' fallacy: do they believe the market is about to change direction simply because longer-term data suggests that a correction is due?
   - The endowment effect: do they pay more attention to and know more about their overweight portfolio positions than their underweight portfolio positions?
   - Overconfidence: do they have high portfolio turnover? Do they fail to revise their forecasts when new information about a security or market comes to light?
   - Anchoring: do they use past prices as targets for their decisions to sell?
   - Ambiguity aversion: is there evidence of an emotional attachment to portfolio holdings?

- Loss aversion: do they sell their winning stocks too soon and hold on to their losing stocks for too long or add to their losing stocks to average down the price paid? Does the manager have a sell discipline? What are the triggers for this discipline?
14. What does the manager do to recognize and control their behavioural biases?
15. Does the manager have the ability to think independently and determine what's relevant? Do they have the humility to admit mistakes and rectify them?
    - Ask the manager to provide a recent example of a success story and a disaster.
    - What would the manager have done differently with hindsight?
16. What is the manager's risk management process?
17. How much time does the manager spend managing money versus that spent in client meetings?

So what makes a good fund manager?

According to award winning multi-manager John Chatfeild-Roberts,[17] there are good and bad fund managers in the same way that there are good and bad teachers. Chatfeild-Roberts' main observations are that good fund managers:

- Have the necessary skills built into them. There isn't an exam you can take to make you a good fund manager.
- Have exposure to the right skills at an early age. Examples include fund managers Mark Slater and William Littlewood, both of whom shadowed their fund manager fathers, Jim Slater and John Littlewood, before becoming fund managers themselves.
- Are inquisitive, hard working and ultra competitive.
- Have the ability to think independently and focus on what's relevant rather than become bogged down with irrelevancies.
- Have the humility to admit and rectify mistakes. After all, it can often take ruthless action to sell those severely loss making stocks that are hurting the portfolio.
- Stick to a proven IP&P even when not currently working in their favour.
- Are unconstrained in exercising their talent by being permitted to adopt high active shares and tracking errors.

---

[17] John Chatfeild-Roberts, *Fundology. The Secrets of Successful Fund Investing*, Petersfield, Harriman House (2006).

- Are sufficiently experienced, having been exposed to several market cycles.
- Are in tune with the psychology of the market.

Arguably the living embodiment of these principles is Anthony Bolton, who, as we noted earlier, in his 28 years as the manager of the Fidelity Special Situations Fund between 1979 and 2007, outperformed the FTSE All Share Index by a truly remarkable 6 per cent per annum. According to an illuminating analysis of his approach to managing his fund,[18] there is no substitute for intelligence, hard work, the ability to process a lot of information, being in tune with the psychology of the market and adopting a truly active, contrarian, low-turnover approach. Describing his process as a smorgasbord, Bolton, with the support of a loyal and experienced team, spoke with up to six company managements per day, complemented fundamental analysis with qualitative and technical analysis and took small positions in companies before taking a high conviction position.

Some final thoughts

Having considered all the issues that trustees need to bear in mind when trying to pick a good fund manager, we acknowledge that for a large number of schemes, manager search, selection and monitoring can take up a disproportionate amount of trustee investment governance for the prospective rewards. This probably explains why trustees are increasingly taking the line of least resistance and adopting passive investment strategies. However, against the backdrop of prospectively more modest real investment returns from here-on and a reluctance on the part of most corporate sponsors to plug defined benefit pension scheme deficits soon, it is perhaps more important than ever for trustees to fight for every basis point of investment return. So, if you believe that fund manager skill exists and you have the confidence to tackle the issues outlined in this chapter, then there is a good case for investing the requisite time and effort in manager selection and/or in challenging your investment consultant's manager hiring and firing decisions.

Key points

- While active fund management is a negative sum game and strategic asset allocation is the overwhelming source of long-run investment returns, selecting the right fund manager can provide a significant uncorrelated source of investment return.

---

[18] A. Bolton and J. Davis, *Investing with Anthony Bolton: The Anatomy of a Stock Market Winner*, Petersfield, Harriman House (2006).

- The duration of performance persistency among good active fund managers is greatly influenced by the extent to which investor cash inflows constrain their investment policies.
- A combination of luck, skill and investment styles determine active fund manager returns in the shorter term. However, in the longer run as luck evens out, any genuine skill will shine through. This skill can, however, take some time to prove statistically and can fluctuate and deteriorate over time.
- As the quantitative assessment of fund manager performance to determine skill is riddled with practical problems, evaluating fund managers against those key qualitative performance drivers that would appear to point to the ability to outperform over time is time well spent.
- Key issues to bear in mind are the manager's:
  o adherence to a proven investment philosophy and process;
  o stated active share and tracking error;
  o dedication to an investment style in which success has been demonstrated;
  o attitude to portfolio turnover;
  o remuneration structure and that for the fund management team, if a team-based approach is adopted or, if the management is based around a star manager, that the star is appropriately supported and shadowed; and
  o the ability to
    ▪ recognize and control their behavioural biases;
    ▪ recognize their capacity constraints;
    ▪ put risk management at the centre of all that they do; and
    ▪ charge fees that align their interests with yours.

Conclusion

In 2001, when presenting the findings of his review of institutional investment, Paul Myners quoted a prominent pensions personality who described the perception of trusteeship as being like 'community service, not dissimilar to being a scoutmaster or churchwarden'.[1] Although trusteeship may have once fitted this description, it certainly does not now. Indeed, ten years after the Myners Report trustees face a multitude of challenges and an increasingly complex set of possible solutions to these challenges.

Gone are the days when almost all defined benefit (DB) schemes used a single asset manager to run a balanced mandate for the scheme's assets against a peer-group benchmark without too much, if any, consideration being given to strategic and tactical asset allocation, let alone liability-matching, risk management and risk budgeting, the use of derivatives to mitigate risk, the merits of alternative asset classes and the active versus passive fund management decision. In addition, today's trustees must regularly moniter the sponsor covenant, evaluate counterparty and liquidity risk, scrutinize fees and transactions costs, adopt an activist investment policy towards environmental, social and corporate governance issues and take a good hard look at their investment governance. For these reasons, Tony Blair's mantra of 'education, education, education' should resonate with trustees.

There are, of course, lots of other challenges that trustees face. We suggested early on in this book that the end of active DB pension scheme provision is probably now in sight, with the burden of the DB pensions' promise proving too much for many plan sponsors. Indeed, in recent years, many corporate sponsors have had to make contributions to their DB schemes often greater than the dividend payments made to their shareholders, and a considerable number of sponsors now have DB pension scheme liabilities that far exceed their stock market value. Consequently, around 80 per cent of sponsors have closed their DB scheme to new entrants, often cutting the generosity of future scheme benefits to the remaining members at the same time. About one-fifth of DB scheme sponsors have gone one step further by closing their scheme to future accrual.

However, while this trend seems inexorable, it does not mean that we can forget about DB schemes altogether – far from it. Most DB scheme liabilities still have decades to run and DB scheme assets still account for 60 per cent of

---

[1] Brendan Maton, 'Still tirelessly calling trustees to action', *FTfm*. 8 May, p. 20 (2011).

UK pension scheme assets overall. There therefore remains a gargantuan job for trustees to perform for decades to come if the DB pension promise is to be met in full and on time.

However, defined contribution (DC) looks increasingly like the future of pension provision. DC scheme assets now account for 40 per cent of total scheme assets, having only represented a meagre 3 per cent a little over a decade ago. The DC framework presents trustees with a whole new set of opportunities and challenges to do their best by their members. Principal among these is for DC scheme trustees to get their scheme's default investment option right. After all, the default fund is not only the investment option that affects the greatest number of members, principally as a result of member inertia and financial illiteracy, but it must be capable of investing over many years in multiple asset classes, across numerous economic and investment cycles, and manage risks in relation to a long-dated and uncertain liability. While DC scheme trustees need to be in a position to provide a suitably robust default fund, indeed a suite of funds, that continually meet the needs of their scheme's ever-changing membership and their changing circumstances, they also need to tackle the root causes of this inertia and financial illiteracy, which is particularly prevalent among those members that populate generations X and Y, most of whom are ill-equipped to assume the investment and annuity risks that DC presents. The answer lies in the provision of better member education and more regular member communication, with a focus on the nuances of investing, how to make appropriate fund choices and how best to approach the annuitization, or de-accumulation, stage of the retirement process, so that member expectations are both realistically anchored from the outset and ultimately met. Fortunately, technology is a great enabler of member engagement as it facilitates the employment of user-friendly online interactive financial education and financial planning tools. DC trustees need to embrace this technology.

To do all of these things effectively – that is, to ensure that both the DB pensions promise is met and to ensure that the realistic expectations of DC members are set and met – trustees need to be sure that they are making the 'right' decisions and implementing these decisions in a timely and efficient manner. This not only means trustees continually improving their investment knowledge and their investment governance, but also knowing how to deal effectively with the many industry practitioners they come into contact with when addressing investment and funding issues and knowing how to constructively challenge the advice that they receive.

There are a number of key investment decisions that trustees need to feel comfortable making and implementing, with the appropriate advice, all of which have featured prominently in this book and all of which are essential if the end goal is to be achieved.

DB scheme trustees need to appreciate that a scheme's assets are there to fund future liabilities. Therefore the assets should be managed so that they perform in such a way as to minimize the likelihood that the liabilities will not be met. This is the philosophy behind liability driven investment (LDI) which, as a risk management and risk reallocation exercise, is all about setting a liability benchmark for the assets and understanding the risks that reside on both the asset and liability side of the balance sheet. After all, most DB schemes are less than fully funded principally as a result of historically unmatched asset and liability positions. Failing to implement a LDI philosophy can of course only have one outcome: a failure to meet the principal aim of any DB pension scheme – to meet its liabilities in full as they fall due.

In ensuring that they meet these liabilities, trustees need to pay great attention to what is undoubtedly the most important strategic investment decision of them all and therefore the one to which DB trustees should devote a considerable proportion of their governance budget: the asset allocation decision. That is, given the scheme's liability benchmark and other objectives, whether and to what extent, based upon their prospective risks, returns and suitability, each asset class warrants inclusion in the asset mix. The asset allocation decision does of course also feature prominently for DC trustees, when working with their advisers, in deciding upon and subsequently revisiting the asset mix of the scheme's default fund.

Moreover, for asset allocation decisions to be implemented efficiently, whether on a strategic or tactical basis, trustees may need to become comfortable with the integration of derivatives into their portfolios. Again, this is as true for DB trustees as it is for DC. As we know, when used responsibly, derivatives can solve a considerable number of pension scheme-specific problems usually in a more efficient and cost-effective manner than by using traditional assets.

Having made the asset allocation decision, DB trustees must then make another important choice regarding the scheme assets: whether they should be managed passively or actively or via a combination of both approaches. Once that decision has been made, the focus of attention should then turn to applying the criteria that underpins what makes a good fund manager – criteria that should guide both hiring and firing decisions. Choosing between active and passive management and the manager hiring and firing decision is the other big decision for DC trustees in providing a suite of funds, including the default fund, that meet the continually changing needs of their scheme membership.

In making these and other decisions, trustees must apply sensible risk management in a holistic manner. As we know, there is no single approach to measuring risk and risk cannot be distilled into a single number. It is a multi-headed beast. However, knowing how to measure and monitor risk in all its forms is necessary for both DB and DC trustees, as is knowing what risks to assume and which to mitigate and how.

Moreover, risk management is not just a quantitative exercise. There are numerous other risks – soft risks – that trustees need to address that are not as visible or quantifiable as those that reside on the pension scheme balance sheet but which can result in equally disastrous outcomes if not properly managed. These include poor monitoring of agency risks, poor trustee decision making resulting from insufficient board diversity, poor chairmanship and too much time being spent on unnecessary detail at the expense of the big picture. The failure to improve governance is another big risk, especially against the backdrop of more demanding asset and liability solutions and a constant flow of legislation, regulation and environmental, social and governance considerations. DB scheme trustees also need to negotiate more complex and detailed recovery plans with sponsors, that inevitably entail evaluating complex contingent assets.

With all of the above in mind, hopefully the overriding objective of this book has been met. That is, to give you, the reader, the confidence and competence to cope better with all of these and the myriad of other investment challenges presented in running a pension scheme, whether DB or DC.

However, perhaps a good point on which to finish is with two golden investment rules for any trustee. As we have already suggested, the imperative when seeking to make an investment decision is to gain the requisite confidence and competence to be able to ask the right questions and seek the appropriate explanations. However, if after extensive questioning and research, you still do not understand what is being proposed – don't invest. Golden investment rule number one is therefore: *never invest in anything you do not understand.* Golden investment rule number two is: *if it seems too good to be true, then it probably is.* Trusteeship will never be easy. However following these simple investment rules and, of course, the content of this book, will stand you in good stead to meet the increasingly complex investment challenges that trusteeship presents.

Glossary

Absolute return. An investment approach employed by fund managers that seeks to generate positive investment returns in excess of a cash or money market rate of return benchmark in all market conditions.

Accounting ratios. Ratios derived from company accounts. Accounting ratios facilitate the evaluation of a company's financial performance or financial position against that of the market, its peers or its own history, by identifying significant trends and relationships which are not immediately apparent from the financial accounts themselves.

Active management. An investment approach employed by fund managers to exploit possible market inefficiencies, with the objective of outperforming a predetermined benchmark. Contrast with passive management or index tracking.

Active members. Those members of an occupational pension scheme who are still accruing benefits in the scheme and who are usually still making regular contributions to it. Regular employer contributions to the scheme are also usually made on behalf of active members.

Active position. See: *Active risk*.

Active risk. The security holdings in an actively managed portfolio that are different from their proportions in the portfolio's benchmark and/or holdings that are not represented in the benchmark (off-benchmark positions). The greater the active risk in a portfolio the greater the chance that the portfolio will not perform like its benchmark. Also known as tracking error.

Active share. The extent to which the composition of a portfolio differs from the benchmark against which its performance is evaluated. Active share is represented as a percentage; a high percentage means a high active share.

Actuarial consultant. See: *Actuary*.

Actuary. A qualified professional who assesses the funding position of a defined benefit scheme and its ability to meet its liabilities in full as they fall due. An actuary also quantifies risk through the calculation of mathematical probabilities. See: *Scheme actuary*.

Adaptive Markets Hypothesis. A theory that suggests that investor behaviour which may seem irrational is instead behaviour that has not had time to adapt to a dynamic investment environment which frequently produces new investment products, principles and paradigms. According to the theory, in seeking to adapt successfully to the new environment, investors respond by implementing investment strategies by trial and error until their behaviour fits successfully with the new environment.

Adjustment conservatism. A behavioural bias (heuristic) relating to investors' overconfidence in their own forecasting ability which causes them to overlook new salient information.

Affect. A behavioural bias (heuristic) whereby investors experience probability insensitivity as a result of an outcome being particularly vivid in their own mind.

Aggregate demand. The total demand for goods and services within in an economy.

AGM. See: *Annual General Meeting.*

AIM. See: *Alternative Investment Market.*

Alpha. The return from a security or a portfolio in excess of a risk-adjusted benchmark return, usually derived from the Capital Asset Pricing Model.

Alternative asset classes. Those asset classes that are not considered to be traditional or mainstream. Most alternative asset classes are simply alternative investment claims on the underlying real economy.

Alternative beta funds. Funds that attempt to emulate the performance of top performing hedge fund strategies by using a combination of derivatives and money market instruments to replicate the 'return sources' and 'risk exposures' which they believe to be the source of hedge fund returns.

Alternatives. See: *Alternative asset classes.*

Alternative Investment Market (AIM). The London Stock Exchange's (LSE) market for smaller UK public limited companies. AIM has less demanding admission requirements and places less onerous continuing obligation requirements upon those companies admitted to the market than those applying for a full listing on the LSE.

Ambiguity aversion. A behavioural bias (framing error) which causes investors to have a preference for known, rather than unknown risks and to value familiarity over unfamiliarity, which can result in a 'home bias' to portfolios. Ambiguity aversion can also result in moral anchoring, that is, an emotional attachment to stocks that should otherwise have been sold.

AMC. See: *Annual management charge.*

Anchoring. A behavioural bias (heuristic) which causes investors to place too much emphasis on irrelevant facts and figures when considering the prospects for an investment, e.g. the price paid for a stock when considering the stock's future prospects and the price at which to sell, simply because they fall conveniently to hand.

Annual general meeting (AGM). The annual meeting of the directors and ordinary shareholders of a company. All companies are obliged to hold an AGM at which the shareholders receive the company's report and accounts and have the opportunity to vote on the appointment of the company's directors and auditors and the payment of a final dividend recommended by the directors.

Annual management charge (AMC). A fund management charge applied as a percentage of the value of funds under management, often pro rata on a monthly basis despite the name.

Annuity. A financial product offered mainly by insurance companies. An individual's accumulated pension pot is exchanged for an annuity which comprises a series of pre-specified regular (usually monthly) payments payable to the individual, known as an annuitant, for the rest of their life. Annuities assume a variety of forms and can be paid with term guarantees and/or index-linking.

Annuity rates. The initial annual income paid by an annuity as a proportion of the annuitant's accumulated pension pot.

Arbitrage. Deriving a risk-free profit by simultaneously buying and selling the same economic exposure to an asset in related markets where a pricing anomaly exists.

Arithmetic average. See: *Arithmetic mean.*

Arithmetic mean. What most people understand by the word 'average'. The arithmetic mean is calculated by summing a set of numbers and then by dividing this sum by the number of numbers. Unlike the median and mode, the arithmetic mean takes account of every value in the distribution and so can be distorted by extreme values. For a given set of numbers, the arithmetic mean is always higher than the geometric mean.

Articles of association. The legal document which sets out the internal constitution of a company. Included within the articles will be details of shareholder voting rights and the company's borrowing powers.

Assets. Anything owned, whether tangible or intangible, with a positive economic value from which future economic benefits are expected to flow.

Asset allocation. The distribution of a portfolio's assets across geographical regions and asset classes.

Asset backed securities (ABS). Bonds that are issued mainly by financial institutions, whose cash flows are derived from the cash flows of other assets – such as credit cards, mortgages and loans. These cash flows are said to be securitised.

Asset liability management (ALM). See: *Liability Driven Investment.*

Asset manager. Also known as an investment manager or fund manager and often just referred to as the 'manager'. An asset manager will manage either a pooled or segregated fund management mandate for a pension scheme on either an active or passive basis in accordance with the Investment Management Agreement (IMA).

At-the-money. An option whose exercise price is equal to the price of the underlying asset upon which the option is written.

AUM. Assets under management.

Authorised share capital. The maximum amount of share capital a company is entitled to issue as set out in the company's memorandum of association.

Availability. A behavioural bias (heuristic) which arises when investors base decisions on information that is readily available, or close at hand, where they place emphasis on the likelihood of events occurring depending on how salient, or how easily visualized they are.

Average holding period. See: *Portfolio turnover.*

Back office. The administrative function of a financial exchange or financial institution where securities and derivatives trades are reconciled and where transactions are processed and checked.

Backwardation. When the futures price is lower than the price of the underlying asset upon which it is based.

Balanced funds. Pooled investment funds that are diversified across traditional asset classes. Also known as managed funds.

Balance of payments. A summary of all economic transactions between one country and the rest of the world.

Balance sheet. A company's principal financial statement which shows the financial position of the company in terms of what it owns and owes.

Base currency. The currency against which the value of the another currency is quoted.

Basis. The difference between the futures price and the price of the underlying asset upon which the futures contract is based.

Basis point. A term often applied to interest rates, bond yields, spreads and fund manager fees. One basis point is 0.01%.

Basis risk. The risk that the difference between the futures price and the price of the underlying asset move independently from one another.

Bear market. A prolonged market downturn. The term is usually applied after market prices have fallen by 20% or more.

Bear spread. An option strategy that is designed to profit from a falling market. It involves simultaneously buying and selling call options on the same asset with the same expiry dates but with the purchased call option having a higher exercise price than that sold. Alternatively, by simultaneously purchasing and selling put options, again on the same asset with the same expiry dates and with the purchased put having a higher exercise price than the put option sold.

Bearer securities. Securities whose ownership is evidenced by the possession of a certificate rather than through registered title. Ownership can therefore pass from one investor to another simply with the exchange of the bearer certificate.

Beauty parade. A set of presentations made to trustees and their advisors by fund managers short listed for a fund management mandate to determine who should be awarded the mandate.

Behavioural finance. The study of human psychology in the context of investing. Behavioural finance analyses the way in which cognitive biases affect investors' decision-making processes. This discipline seeks to explain why security prices frequently depart from their fundamental values and why trends and patterns in securities prices arise that are inconsistent with the Efficient Markets Hypothesis.

Benchmark. Benchmarks comprise financial market indices, peer group benchmarks, customised benchmarks and/or the scheme's liabilities and are used to establish the risk and return parameters against which a portfolio's performance is to be assessed.

Benchmark aware. The approach taken by a truly active fund manager who is not unduly constrained in their sector and stock selection decisions by a financial market or peer group benchmark but who, nonetheless, is aware of their benchmark. Also see: *Active share*.

Benchmark creep. When a fund manager changes the definition of their benchmark over time to make their performance appear better than it really is.

Benchmarking. Using a benchmark as the basis for constructing and managing a portfolio and for subsequently assessing how well the portfolio has performed against the benchmark.

Beneficiaries. The beneficial owners of trust property, such as the members of an occupational pension scheme.

Beta. A measure of the historic or expected sensitivity of a security or portfolio to movements in 'the market'. If the security or portfolio in question has a beta of 1.5, then on average it would be expected to be 50% more volatile than the market. It can be calculated as the covariance between the excess return from a security or portfolio and the excess return on the market divided by the variance of the excess return of that market.

Bid price. The price offered by a dealer or market maker to an investor who wishes to sell a security. Also the price at which units or shares can be sold back to the manager of a collective investment scheme or mutual fund.

Bid/offer spread. The difference between the higher offer price and lower bid price of a security or investment fund. Also see: *Spread*.

Black-Scholes model. The pioneering model for option pricing developed by Fischer Black and Myron Scholes in 1973.

Black swan. In an investment context, a financial market event that occurs more frequently than might be anticipated from the assumption that financial market returns are normally distributed. Also, referred to as an extreme event, a fat tail event or as an outlier.

Blue chips. Shares of large, well known companies often with a history of steady profit and dividend growth.

Bond. A tradable interest bearing security issued by companies, governments and supranational agencies, such as the European Investment Bank (EIB), for the specific purpose of raising capital. Essentially an IOU, most bonds pay a fixed rate of interest (the coupon) until the bond is redeemed by the issuer, typically at its nominal value, on the pre-determined redemption, or maturity date.

Bond indenture. The legal document that specifies the rights and obligations of both bond issuers and investors.

Bond yield. Either the annual income return (running yield, interest yield or flat yield) or the gross redemption yield, or yield to maturity, on a bond. Bond yields move inversely to bond prices.

Bonus issue. The free issue of new ordinary shares to a company's ordinary shareholders in proportion to their existing shareholdings through the conversion, or capitalization, of the company's reserves. By proportionately reducing the market value of each existing share, a bonus issue makes the shares more marketable. Also known as a capitalization or scrip issue.

Bottom-up. Investing in individual securities based on an analysis of their specific prospects rather than by investing by drawing on a much broader macroeconomic view of the outlook for an investment. Contrast with a top-down approach to investing.

Boutiques. Small, usually owner-managed, fund management companies that typically specialise in managing money within particular markets and/or according to a particular investment style.

Break even inflation rate. The rate of inflation implied by subtracting the yield offered by an index-linked bond from the nominal yield on a conventional bond from the same issuer and with the same maturity. The break even inflation rate on government bonds is often used as a proxy for the markets' expectation of future inflation.

British Venture Capital Association (BVCA). The trade association that represents all principal sources of private and venture capital in the UK.

Bulk annuity contract. See: *Buy-in.*

Bull market. A rising market, where bad news is often disregarded.

Bull spread. An option strategy designed to profit in a bull market. This involves simultaneously buying and selling call options with the same expiry dates but with the purchased call having a lower exercise price than that sold. Alternatively, by simultaneously purchasing and selling put options, again with the same expiry dates and with the purchased put having a lower exercise price than the put sold.

Bunds. German government bonds.

Buy-in. Insuring the risks to a defined benefit scheme posed by some or all of the scheme's pensioner liabilities via an insurance company. The insurance policy for a buy-in is written in the name of the trustees and is an asset of the scheme.

Buyout. When all or part of a scheme's assets and liabilities are transferred to an insurance company which then underwrites the scheme's benefits payable to its members.

Buyout funds. Specialist private equity funds that buy out the shareholders of well established companies with a view to restructuring the firm's operations.

Buyout valuation. The valuation of a defined benefit pension scheme based on the price that an insurance company would charge for assuming all the risks of the scheme. See: *Buyout.*

Calculation agent. An investment bank that produces daily mark-to-market valuations, calculates daily collateral requirements and the netted collateral and swap payments to be made between the counterparties to a swaps contract, to which it is not itself a counterparty.

Call option. An option that confers the right of the holder to buy a specified amount of an asset at a pre-specified price on or before a pre-specified date.

Callable bonds. A term applied to those bonds that may be redeemed by the issuer prior to maturity either on a predetermined date or during a predetermined period. Usually if the bond is 'called' by the issuer, the bond holder would receive the bond's nominal value plus a additional amount known as the call premium.

Capacity constraints. The amount of money managed by a fund manager beyond which the manager believes performance may be potentially harmed. This amount will be determined by both the characteristics of the market in which the manager invests and the investment style that they adopt.

Capital asset pricing model (CAPM). An equilibrium model of asset prices that posits that the expected return on all risky assets is mainly determined by the covariance of the excess return on that asset and the excess return on the 'market'.

Capital markets. Markets in which finance is raised (the primary market) and in which related securities, for example equities and bonds, are subsequently traded (the secondary market). Today, most capital markets are not located in a centralized, physical market place. Instead they are linked by computer networks and characterized by remote electronic trading.

CAPM. See: *Capital Asset Pricing Model*.

Career Average Revalued Earnings (CARE). Where defined benefit pension scheme benefits accrue based on a proportion of annual pay, which is then revalued annually either by the average earnings index or an inflation index such as the Retail Prices Index (RPI) or Consumer Prices Index (CPI).

Carried interest. The performance fee levied by a private equity fund if the fund achieves a return in excess of the hurdle rate and if the original capital and the realised profits have been returned to the fund's investors.

Carry trade. An active approach to currency management that involves borrowing, or short selling, lower yielding currencies and buying the currencies of economies with high interest rates. The difference between the interest paid on the borrowed currency and that earned on the invested currency is 'the carry'.

Cash flow negative. Where a defined benefit pension scheme is paying out more in pensions than it is receiving from sponsor and member contributions and investment income.

Cash market. Those financial markets where securities, such as equities and bonds, are traded. Contrast with derivatives markets.

Cash securities. Financial securities such as equities and bonds that are traded on cash markets, such as stock exchanges.

CDS. See: *Credit default swap.*

Central bank. Those public institutions that operate at the heart of a nation's financial system. Central banks typically have responsibility for setting a nation's or an economic region's short-term interest rate, or policy rate, controlling the money supply, acting as the banker and lender of last resort to the banking system and managing the national debt. Many implement their policies independently of government control. The Bank of England is the UK's central bank.

Central counterparty. An institution that acts as the counterparty and guarantor to each transaction executed on the exchange to which it is affiliated. Also known as the clearing house.

Certificate of Deposit (CD). Negotiable bearer securities issued by commercial banks in exchange for fixed term deposits.

Ceteris paribus. Other things being equal. In economics, the ceteris paribus caveat is used when considering the impact of a change in one factor or variable on another variable, market or the economy as a whole, holding all other factors constant.

Cheapest to deliver. At any point in time the bond that the seller of a bond futures contract would like to deliver when the futures contract expires.

CIO. Chief Investment Officer.

City Code. The non-statutory code administered by the Panel on Takeovers and Mergers (POTAM) that applies to the overwhelming majority of UK companies involved in merger or acquisition activity. The City Code ensures that a strict timetable is adhered to and that the target company's shareholders are treated fairly and equally. Also known as the Blue Book.

Clean price. The quoted price of a bond. The clean price excludes accrued interest or interest to be deducted, as appropriate.

Clearing house. An institution that acts as the central counterparty to the exchange to which it is affiliated and facilitates the validation and settlement of transactions executed on the exchange.

Clip. The size of a swaps contract quoted in PV01 terms.

Closing out. The process of terminating an open position in a derivatives contract by entering into an equal and opposite transaction to that originally undertaken.

Collateral. Cash and acceptable non-cash assets (mainly G4 sovereign bonds) that pass between the counterparties to an over-the counter derivatives contract to cover profits and losses to date to protect each counterparty in the event of the other defaulting on their obligations.

Collective investment scheme. A diversified and professionally managed investment fund that pools the capital of a large number of investors. A unit trust or an open ended investment company (OEIC) for instance.

Combined Code. The code that seeks to promote best corporate governance practice for all public limited companies quoted on the London Stock Exchange. Also known as the Code of Best Practice. Now called the UK Corporate Governance Code.

Commercial Paper (CP). Unsecured bearer securities issued at a discount to par by public limited companies. Commercial Paper does not pay coupons, but is issued at a discount and subsequently redeemed at par.

Commission. Fee paid to an intermediary who arranges a transaction.

Commodities. Primary products or consumption assets traded on a commodities exchange. These include hard commodities such as metals and soft commodities such as grain.

Commodity futures. A futures contract based on an underlying commodity or commodity index.

Comply or explain. The regime that requires those companies which do not comply with codes of good practice (*corporate governance*) to explain to their shareholders why they do not follow them.

Compound return. Interest on interest or returns on past returns.

Concentrated portfolios. Portfolios that typically comprise considerably fewer securities than the portfolio's benchmark.

Conditional Value at Risk (cVaR). Also see: *Value at Risk.* Conditional VaR effectively considers the average loss that might occur from a set of the worst possible financial outcomes.

Consumer Price Index (CPI). A measure of the average price of goods and services consumed by UK residents. Unlike the Retail Prices Index (RPI), which is calculated as an arithmetic mean, the CPI is calculated as a geometric mean and excludes housing costs. The rate of change of the CPI is targeted by the Monetary Policy Committee.

Contango. When a futures price is higher than the price of the underlying asset upon which it is based.

Contingent asset. Assets pledged by a defined benefit scheme sponsor that can be drawn upon by the scheme under certain conditions if it experiences funding difficulties.

Contract size. The size of a transaction. Contract sizes are often standardized for derivatives.

Contract specifications. A legal document that specifies the terms of a derivatives contract. Many derivatives contracts have standard specifications.

Contrarian investing. Positioning a portfolio so that it is at odds with the market's consensus view.

Convertible arbitrage See: *Relative value.*

Convertible bonds. Bonds issued with a right to convert into either another of the issuing company's bonds or, the company's equity, both on pre-specified terms.

Convertible loan stock. Bonds issued with a right to convert into the issuing company's equity on pre-specified terms.

Convertible preference shares. Preference shares issued with a right to convert into the issuing company's equity on pre-specified terms.

Convexity. The relationship that exists between the price and required yield of a bond. The more convex the bond, the greater the price rise for a fall in its yield and the smaller the price fall for a rise in its yield. Also see: *Modified duration.*

Core-satellite An investment strategy that usually involves investing a significant proportion in a index tracker fund (the 'core') alongside a smaller proportion invested in the same asset class in an actively managed fund, or funds (the 'satellite(s)') that have aggressive outperformance targets.

Corporate bonds. Bonds issued by domestically and internationally-based (multinational) companies in both the domestic and international bond markets, to finance future growth, whether organically or by acquisition and/or to restructure their finances. Corporate issuance also includes securitized, or asset backed issues that are principally issued by banks, credit card companies, property companies and telecoms companies.

Corporate governance. The mechanism that seeks to ensure that companies are run in the best long-term interests of their shareholders. Corporate governance refers to the way in which a company is governed, directed and controlled on behalf of the company's shareholders. Also see: *Combined Code* and *UK Stewardship Code.*

Correlation. The degree of co-movement between the returns on two assets. The correlation coefficient has a value that ranges between –1 and +1. Correlation does not prove that a cause-and-effect or, indeed, a steady relationship exists between two variables as correlations can arise from pure chance. Also see: *R-squared.*

Correlation co-efficient. A metric that quantifies the degree of co-movement between the returns on two assets/asset classes/portfolios which can have a minimum value of –1 and a maximum value of +1.

Counterparty. A party to a securities transaction or derivatives contract.

Counterparty risk. The risk that the other party to a securities transaction or derivatives contract may not fulfil their obligations. Clearing houses, or central counterparties, affiliated to stock and derivative exchanges assume this counterparty risk.

Coupon. The predetermined payment from a bond usually expressed as a percentage of the bond's nominal, or par, value.

Covariance. A measure of the degree of co-movement between two securities/asset classes/portfolios. The covariance is not as intuitive as the correlation coefficient, which is bounded between –1 and +1.

Covenant. See: *Sponsor covenant.* Also a term within an agreement accompanying a bond issue placed on the issuer which if breached may require the bond to be redeemed.

Covenant consultant. A professional that monitors the ongoing strength of the sponsor covenant.

Covered calls. Where an investor writes a call option on an asset or security that they own.

CPI. See: *Consumer Price Index*.

Credit market. Predominantly the market for corporate bonds and loans.

Credit default swap (CDS). A derivative that earns the seller a regular premium for a fixed period and which provides the buyer with insurance against the default of a borrower. In the event of a default the buyer ceases to pay the CDS seller the premium, and the CDS seller pays a compensatory sum to the CDS buyer.

Credit default swap spread. The regular premium paid by a CDS buyer to the seller in return for insuring an issuer's bond against default.

Credit derivative. Derivative instruments whose pay-offs are determined by the credit worthiness of a borrower.

Credit rating. The classification by a credit rating agency of an organization's (government, supranational agency or company) ability to meet the scheduled interest payments and redemption payment for a particular bond issue made by the organization.

Credit rating agency. Those institutions, such as Standard & Poor's and Moody's, that assess the creditworthiness of an organization (government, supranational agency or corporate) and/or the ability of the organization to meet the interest payments and the redemption payment for a particular bond issue made by the organization.

Credit risk. The risk that an organisation's financial obligations will not be met in full as they fall due. Also known as default risk.

Credit premium. See: *Credit spread*.

Credit spread. The additional yield required on a corporate bond or loan over and above the yield on an equivalent maturity government bond, or that required on a government bond with less than a AAA-rating over and above the yield on an equivalent maturity AAA-rated government bond. Also known as the credit premium. Also see: *Risk premium*.

Credit Support Annex (CSA). The documentation within an ISDA agreement that specifies the collateral requirements agreed between the counterparties to an over the counter derivatives transaction.

Cumulative preference shares. Shares that usually pay a fixed rate of dividend and also confer the right to receive any dividend arrears before the ordinary shareholders become entitled to a dividend. Preference shareholders are usually entitled to the repayment of the nominal value of their shares before other shareholders in the event of the company being wound up, assuming that sufficient assets remain available for distribution.

Custodian. Typically a division of an investment bank or asset manager that arranges for the safekeeping of a pension scheme's assets and documents of title.

DCF yield. See: *Internal rate of return.*

Debenture. A corporate bond issued in the domestic bond market and secured on the issuing company's assets by way of a fixed or a floating charge.

Decile. A metric derived from a method of ranking which divides the values of the population under consideration in descending order into ten units of 10%, that is, into deciles. So, for example, the top decile of funds by performance will comprise the top 10% of performers.

Deep in-the-money. An option contract that has significant intrinsic value. That is, where the exercise price is significantly below the price of the underlying asset for a call option but significantly above the price of the underlying asset for a put option.

Deep out-of-the-money. An option contract that has no intrinsic value and whose exercise price is significantly above the price of the underlying asset for a call option or significantly below it for a put option.

Default. Default occurs when an organization fails to repay either the capital or interest or meet its specific contractual obligations on a bond or loan. The term can also be applied to the failure of a counterparty to meet their obligations under a derivatives contract.

Default risk. See: *Credit risk* and *Default.*

Default fund. The fund into which DC member contributions are invested if an active fund choice is not made by the scheme member.

Deferred members. Former active members of an occupational pension scheme, and who are not drawing a pension from the scheme.

Deficit. For example, where the present value of a defined benefit pension scheme's liabilities exceed the market value of its assets.

Defined benefit (DB) pension scheme. An occupational pension scheme that provides pre-defined benefits in retirement.

Defined contribution (DC) pension scheme. An occupational pension scheme where the benefits depend upon the amount and timing of contributions made, the performance of the fund(s) into which these contributions are invested and the prevailing annuity rate when annuitising the resulting investment fund.

De-risking consultant. Individual or firm that advises the trustees on how best to manage the 'unrewarded' interest rate, inflation and longevity risks within a scheme's liabilities in the most efficient and cost-effective way.

Derivative. An instrument whose value is based on the price of an underlying asset. Derivatives can be based on both financial and commodity assets.

Dilution levy. A potential charge that can be levied by a pooled investment fund on new investors or investors exiting the fund if the cash flows into or out of the fund are likely to be detrimental to the fund's existing investors.

Dirty price. The price of a bond that includes accrued interest.

Discount rate. The rate of interest used to establish the present value of a sum of money receivable in the future.

Diversification. The spreading of investment risk by investing across different asset classes, countries, sectors or companies. The degree of diversification is determined by the co-movement, or correlation between the assets in the portfolio.

Diversified growth funds. Pooled investment funds that are broadly diversified across both traditional and alternative asset classes and which are typically used as the default fund option within occupational defined contribution schemes. Also known as 'new balanced funds'.

Dividend. The distribution of a proportion of a company's distributable profit to its shareholders. UK listed companies usually pay dividends twice a year.

Dividend cover. A company's post-tax profits divided by the most recent dividend paid, or declared, and expressed as a multiple of the dividend.

Dividend Discount Model (DDM). An equity valuation model that values an ordinary share by considering the discounted present value of all expected future dividends.

Dividend growth rate. The rate at which a company has increased its dividend payments to its ordinary shareholders over a specified time period.

Dividend yield. The dividends paid or declared by a company over the past 12 months expressed as an annual percentage of the current share price.

Dow Jones Industrial Average (DJIA). A price weighted arithmetic index of 30 actively traded, and mainly industrial, US stocks. The oldest US equity market index of 30 leading US shares. The index is calculated by taking an unweighted average of the prices of the 30 stocks. Although unrepresentative of the composition and health of the broader US equity market owing to the way in which it is constructed and calculated, many investors treat it as the main market indicator.

Draw down. When a private equity fund invests some or all of the funds raised by drawing down from their investors' committed capital. Also referred to as 'putting the funds in the ground'.

Due diligence. Conducting a thorough investigation of the risks surrounding a potential investment or transaction and of the parties involved before investing/transacting.

Duration. A measure of the sensitivity of a bond's price to a change in yield. Referred to as Macaulay duration, when expressed in years, and modified duration, when expressed as a percentage.

Earnings. A company's post-tax profit.

Earnings per share (EPS). A company's post-tax profit divided by the number of ordinary shares it has in issue.

Earnings surprise. When a company's announced earnings exceed (positive surprise) or fail to meet (negative surprise) market forecasts of those earnings.

Economic cycle. The course an economy takes as economic growth fluctuates, or cycles over time. Also known as the business cycle.

Economic growth. The growth of GDP or GNP usually expressed in real terms over the course of a calendar quarter or year. Used as a barometer of an economy's health.

Economics. The study of the allocation of scarce resources among many competing ends and the ways in which resource demand is met by resource supply.

EONIA. See: *Euro Overnight Interbank Average.*

Efficient frontier. A convex curve plotted on a mean-variance chart representing those portfolios that offer the maximum expected return for any given level of risk (standard deviation) or the minimum level of risk (standard deviation) for any given expected return. Also known as a mean-variance efficient frontier.

Efficient Markets Hypothesis (EMH). The proposition that all relevant information about a security is incorporated correctly and instantaneously into its price. As a result of active fund managers, analysts and other investment professionals researching securities and markets, the EMH postulates that security prices move randomly and independently of past trends, in response to new relevant information.

Efficient portfolios. See: *Efficient frontier.*

EGM. See: *Extraordinary General Meeting.*

Emerging markets. The financial markets of emerging or developing economies.

Emerging market debt. The conventional and index-linked bonds issued by governments and corporates of developing economies.

Endowment. A fund, often run by a university or similar institution, comprising permanent gifts of money that are invested to further the aims of the institution.

Endowment effect. A behavioural bias (heuristic) that refers to the way in which investors pay more attention to and know more about their portfolio's overweight positions than about their portfolio's underweight positions.

Engagement. An investment approach that adopts direct and collaborative engagement with companies to encourage more responsible business practices and improved environmental, social and corporate governance performance.

Enhanced indexation. An index tracker portfolio that seeks to outperform the financial market index being tracked by the fund manager by engaging in such activities as covered call writing to generate additional fee income for the portfolio.

Environmental, social and corporate governance (ESG). Where companies adopt best practice in corporate governance and pursue sustainable and responsible business and management practices.

EPS. See: *Earnings per share.*

Euro Overnight Interbank Average (EONIA). The euro zone money markets benchmark interest rate.

Equally weighted index. Where each constituent of a portfolio or index is invested in the same proportion.

Equities. Another term for the ordinary shares of a company. See: *Equity.*

Equity. A company's ordinary share capital which confers on the holder a direct stake in the company's fortunes.

Equity derivatives. Derivatives based upon stocks and shares.

Equity risk premium (ERP). The additional return expected by investors over and above the risk-free rate for investing in equities (ex ante ERP) or the additional return actually received (ex post ERP). Also see: *Risk premium.*

ETFs. See: *Exchange Traded Funds.*

Ethical investment. An investment approach that screens out investments that do not meet predefined ethical standards.

Eurobond. International bond issues made by governments, supranational agencies and corporations, not necessarily denominated in the issuer's home currency or that of the financial centre(s) in which they are issued. Most Eurobonds are issued in bearer form through bank syndicates.

Euro zone. The economic region comprising those EU member states who have adopted the euro as their currency.

Event driven hedge funds. Hedge funds that speculate on the success of corporate mergers and takeovers, capital restructurings and turnarounds.

ex ante. Before the event.

Exchange rate. The price of one currency in terms of another.

Exchanges. Those institutions that provide a marketplace for and oversee the trading of particular securities and commodities.

Exchange traded funds (ETFs). Portfolios of shares or commodities that are traded as shares on a stock exchange.

Exchange traded derivatives. Derivatives with standardised contract specifications that are traded on a derivatives exchange.

Ex-dividend (xd). Without dividend. The period during which the purchase of shares or bonds (on which a dividend or coupon payment has been declared) does not entitle the new holder to this next dividend or interest payment.

Exercise. This happens when the holder of an option uses their right to buy (call) or sell (put) the underlying asset.

Exercise price. The price at which the right conferred by an option can be exercised by the holder against the writer. Also known as the strike price.

Expectations theory of the yield curve. The proposition that the difference between short and long-term interest rates can be explained by the course short-term interest rates are expected to take over time.

Expiry date. The last day on which a derivative can be exercised.

ex post. After the event.

Ex-rights (xr). The period during which the purchase of a company's shares does not entitle the new shareholder to participate in a rights issue announced by the issuing company. Shares are usually traded ex-rights (xr) on or within a few days of the company making the rights issue announcement.

Externality. A cost, such as pollution, being borne by society rather than being assumed by those whose activities created the pollution. See: *Market failure*.

Extraordinary General Meeting (EGM). A company meeting, other than an Annual General Meeting, at which matters that urgently require a special resolution are put to the company's shareholders.

Extreme events. See: *Black swan*.

Factors of production. The land, labour and capital employed within a particular market from which rent, wages and profits derive.

Fair value. The price at which a security is judged to be neither under nor overvalued.

Fat tails. See: *Black swan* and *Skewness*.

Federal Reserve Funds Rate (FFR). The US money markets benchmark interest rate.

FFR. See: *Federal Reserve Funds Rate*.

Financial gearing. The ratio of debt to equity employed by a company within its capital structure.

Financial future. A futures contract based on an underlying financial asset.

Financial Services Authority (FSA). The independent body that regulates the financial services industry in the UK.

Fiscal policy. The use of government spending, taxation and borrowing policies to either boost or restrain domestic demand in the economy or to promote a reallocation of resources.

Fixed income arbitrage. See: *Relative value*.

Fixed income security. See: *Bonds*.

Fixed payer. The counterparty to a swap contract who is committed to pay a series of fixed payments in exchange for receiving a series of floating, or variable, payments.

Flat rate. The annual simple rate of interest applied to a cash deposit.

Flat yield. See: *Running yield.*

Flight to quality. The movement of capital to a safe haven during periods of market turmoil to avoid capital loss.

Floating payer. The counterparty to a swap contract who is committed to pay a series of floating, or variable, payments in exchange for receiving a series of fixed payments. Also known as the fixed receiver.

Floating Rate Notes (FRNs). Debt securities issued with a variable coupon periodically referenced to a benchmark interest rate.

Foreign exchange. Collective term for foreign currency.

Forward. A derivative contract that creates a legally binding obligation between two parties for one to buy and the other to sell a pre-specified amount of an asset at a pre-specified price on a pre-specified future date. Because they are individually negotiated over-the-counter contracts, forwards are not usually traded on a derivatives exchange.

Forward exchange rate. An exchange rate set today, embodied in a forward contract, that will apply to a foreign exchange transaction at some pre-specified point in the future.

Forward price. The price set today, embodied in a forward contract, that will apply to a forward contract transaction at some pre-specified point in the future.

Forward rate. The interest rate applied to borrowing or lending at some pre-specified time in the future for a pre-specified period.

Framing errors. A subset of behavioural biases where the reference points chosen by an investor in making an investment decision, or how a problem is posed to an investor, or how they pose it to themselves, influences the decision making process itself.

Free float indices. Financial market indices that adjust a constituent's weight within an index because less than 100% of the constituent's ordinary shares are freely available for investment.

FRS 17. A financial reporting standard that requires a corporate sponsor of a defined benefit pension scheme to value the scheme's assets at their market value and its liabilities with reference to the 15 year AA-rated corporate bond yield and to disclose the resulting surplus or deficit in its company accounts.

FTSE 100. An index of the 100 largest companies by market capitalisation listed on the London Stock Exchange. Introduced with a base value of 1,000, the FTSE 100 index is calculated in real time throughout the trading day by weighting each constituent in accordance with its market capitalisation. The composition of the index is reviewed quarterly.

FTSE 250. An index of those 250 companies listed on the London Stock Exchange which, are the next largest 250 companies after the FTSE 100. The index was introduced in 1992 but now has a base date of 31/12/85 with a base value 1412.60. The FTSE 250 is calculated in the same way as the FTSE 100 and combined, the two indices form the FTSE 350.

FTSE All Share Index. An index of those companies listed on the London Stock Exchange with a market capitalization greater than that periodically determined by committee. Introduced in 1962 with a base value of 100, this index is divided into a number of key industry sectors.

Full employment level of output. See: *Potential output level*.

Full listing. Those public limited companies admitted to the London Stock Exchange's (LSE) official daily list. Companies seeking a full listing on the LSE must satisfy the UK Listing Authority's (UKLA) stringent listing requirements and continuing obligations once listed.

Full replication. An indexing method that requires an index tracker fund to hold every security in the financial market index being tracked in accordance with each constituent's index weight.

Fundamental analysis. The calculation and interpretation of yields, ratios and discounted cash flows that seek to establish the intrinsic value of a security or the 'correct' value of the broader market.

Fundamentally-weighted index. A financial market index within which the weights allocated to a company's shares is determined by factors such as the size of the company's sales revenue, cash flow and/or dividends paid.

Funded pension scheme. A defined benefit scheme for which a fund comprising contributions, assets and the investment returns deriving from those assets, has been established to meet the liabilities of the scheme.

Funding level. The market value of a defined benefit scheme's assets minus the present value of its liabilities divided by the latter.

Funding ratio. The funding level expressed as a percentage.

Fund manager. Also known as an investment manager or asset manager and often just referred to as the 'manager'. A fund manager will run either a pooled or segregated fund management mandate for a pension scheme on either an active or passive basis in accordance with the Investment Management Agreement (IMA).

Fund of funds. An investment fund that invests in a wide range of other investment funds, often with divergent strategies.

Future. A derivatives contract that creates a legally binding obligation between two parties for one to buy and the other to sell a pre-specified amount of an asset at a pre-specified price on a pre-specified future date. Futures contracts differ from forward contracts because they are standardized, exchange traded instruments.

Future value. The accumulated value of a sum of money invested today at a known rate of interest over a specific term.

G7. Seven of the world's largest industrialized nations, comprising the US, UK, France, Germany, Japan, Italy and Canada.

Gamblers fallacy. A behavioural bias (heuristic) that occurs when investors confuse small samples of data with larger samples of the same data, resulting in the formulation of incorrect notions such as the idea that markets work to timetables.

GDP. See: *Gross Domestic Product.*

Gearing. The amount of debt employed relative to equity within a company's capital structure (known as financial gearing). By increasing the amount of debt, a company can potentially enhance the return to shareholders, albeit at a higher level of risk. The term also applies: to the amount borrowed by a private equity firm relative to the purchase price of a company being bought; when investors use derivatives rather than cash securities to magnify investment returns; and to the sensitivity of an organization's profits to changes in its sales revenue given its cost structure (known as operational gearing).

General partner. The lead investor or manager of a hedge fund or private equity fund.

Geometric average. See: *Geometric mean.*

Geometric mean. A measure of central tendency established by taking the *nth* root of the product (multiplication) of *n* values. The geometric mean of a series of numbers is always less than the arithmetic mean.

Geometric progression. The product (multiplication) of *n* values.

Gilts. UK government bonds issued primarily to finance government borrowing. Also see: *Public Sector Net Cash Requirement.*

Gilt total return swaps (TRS). A short-term contract between two counterparties where one, e.g. a pension scheme, exchanges a series of floating interest rate payments (typically below LIBOR) on a notional capital sum, in return for the total return on a specific gilt from a counterparty, typically an investment bank, over a pre-specified term. As a means of reducing interest rate risk, the underlying mechanics of a gilt TRS are similar to those of an interest rate swap.

Global tactical asset allocation (GTAA). An investment approach whereby tactical investment decisions based on perceived short-term local or global opportunities are implemented via derivative instruments usually within a dedicated global tactical asset allocation fund.

GNP. See: *Gross National Product.*

Governance. The skill, expertise, organizational effectiveness and time applied by the trustees to ensure that a scheme is well run.

Government bonds. Tradable interest bearing securities primarily issued to finance the gap between a government's spending and tax receipts. Also known as sovereign bonds.

Gross Domestic Product (GDP). A measure of the level of activity within an economy. More precisely, GDP is the total amount of income generated, the total spending or the output of all final goods and services produced domestically in an economy typically during a calendar quarter or year.

Gross National Product (GNP). GDP at market prices plus net property income generated from overseas economies by UK factors of production.

Gross redemption yield (GRY). A measure of the return that could be achieved by holding a bond to maturity, given its price today, taking into account both interest payments and any capital gain or loss at maturity, assuming that the issuer does not default and the interest payments can be reinvested at the bond's GRY. Also known as the yield to maturity (YTM) or required return.

Growth stocks. Those stocks with a characteristically high price to earnings and price to book ratio and a low dividend yield relative to the rest of the market, that are perceived to offer above average earnings growth potential.

GTAA. See: *Global tactical asset allocation.*

Haircut. The reduction in the valuation applied to securities to be held as collateral. Also, the write down of the value of debt in issue as a result of a debt restructuring.

Hedge fund. An unregulated investment fund that can employ leverage and undertake investment strategies that most regulated funds cannot - short selling for instance. Given the heterogeneous nature of hedge fund strategies, hedge funds cannot be described as an asset class. Rather, they are very much a skill set given that each fund's performance is largely attributable to the hedge fund manager's skill and their management of risk.

Hedge ratio. Quantifies the extent to which a headging instrument needs to be used to eliminate a risk, such as currency, interest rate or inflation risk.

Hedging. A technique employed to reduce the impact of adverse price movements in financial assets held or in the value of liabilities to be met.

Heuristic bias. See: *Heuristics.*

Heuristics. A subset of behavioural biases that comprise those rules of thumb, or mental short cuts, that are applied by investors to simplify the complex reality of investment decision making, resulting in sub-optimal investment decision making.

High yield bonds. Tradable interest bearing securities that have a credit rating lower than BBB- (S&P)/Baa3 (Moody's) and pay higher coupons to offset the increased default risk. Often referred to as sub-investment grade, speculative, non-investment grade or less generously as 'junk bonds'.

High water mark. The investment return generated by an absolute return fund that sets the benchmark for levying any subsequent performance fees. Only if the fund's performance subsequently exceeds both the fund's hurdle rate and high water mark can performance fees be levied.

Holder. The owner of a financial security. Also the buyer of an option.

Hurdle rate. In the context of fund management, the performance benchmark adopted by those fund managers pursuing absolute return strategies. Hurdle rates are usually set with reference to a money market interest rate, such as LIBOR.

IAS19. An accounting standard that requires a corporate sponsor of a defined benefit pension scheme to value the scheme's assets at their market value and its liabilities with reference to a high quality corporate bond yield and to disclose the resulting surplus or deficit within its company accounts.

Illiquidity. See: *Liquidity.*

Illiquidity premium. The additional return expected by investors for investing in a security or an asset whose value can not easily be turned into cash.

in backwardation. See: *Backwardation.*

in contango. See: *Contango.*

Income drawdown. A financial product typically used by those individuals with larger defined contribution pensions pots who wish to draw a regular income in retirement while continuing to invest in risky assets, rather than purchase an annuity to fund their retirement income needs.

Income multiplier. The factor by which national income changes as a result of a unit change in aggregate demand.

Independent trustee. A professional trustee who advises and guides the other trustees on the pension scheme trustee board.

Index. A single number that summarizes the collective movement of certain variables, e.g. stock prices, at a point in time in relation to their average value on a base date or a single variable in relation to its base date value.

Indexation. Usually involving adjustments for the effects of inflation. Some investments benefit from explicit indexation because their returns are determined with reference to an inflation index.

Indexing. See: *Passive management.*

Index-linked bond. A bond where the interest and/or principal values are linked to an inflation index.

Index-linked gilts (ILGs). Gilts whose principal and interest payments are linked to the Retail Price Index (RPI).

Index tilting. An index tracker fund that seeks to outperform the financial market index being tracked by overlaying the portfolio with small active positions in some of the index's constituent stocks.

Index tracking. See: *Passive management.*

Index huggers. Those active fund managers who do not deviate sufficiently from their benchmark to warrant the active management fees they charge. Index huggers have low active risk and a low active share.

Inefficient market. See: *Market inefficiencies*.

Inflation. The rate of change in the general price level, reflecting the erosion in the purchasing power of money. Inflation is generally defined with reference to the annualised percentage change in a consumer price index, which comprises the prices of goods and services purchased by the average household.

Inflation risk. The risk to a defined benefit scheme of inflation being higher than expected thereby inflating the value of the scheme's liabilities. For a defined contribution scheme member, price inflation being higher than expected poses a risk for both the real value of their pension pot and the price of inflation-linked annuities.

Inflation risk premium (IRP). The additional return required by bond investors based on the volatility of inflation in the recent past. Also see: *Risk premium*.

Inflation supply. The reference made to those index-linked bonds used by investment banks to hedge their exposure to future inflation when issuing inflation swaps.

Inflation swap. A contract between two counterparties where one, e.g. a pension scheme, makes a series of fixed payments in return for a series of payments based on a real rate of interest and the actual rate of inflation from a counterparty, typically an investment bank, over a pre-specified term. An inflation swap can enable a pension scheme to lock into a real rate of interest, thereby reducing the impact on its liabilities if inflation proves to be higher than expected.

Inflation targeting. The setting of short-term interest rates by a central bank to achieve a published target for a particular measure of inflation.

Information ratio (IR). A measure of risk-adjusted return that takes the difference between the return on a portfolio and the return on the portfolio's benchmark and divides this by the standard deviation of the difference of these two sets of returns. The higher the information ratio, the higher the return per unit of risk achieved by the fund manager.

Infrastructure assets. Highly illiquid assets that comprise economic infrastructure, such as toll roads, airports and utilities and social infrastructure, such as schools and hospitals and that typically generate long-term, inflation-linked cash flows.

Initial margin. The cash or acceptable non-cash collateral deposited with the clearing house when opening certain exchange traded derivative (principally futures) positions.

Initial public offering (IPO). See: *New issue*.

Inside information. Price sensitive information about a company or security that is not yet publicly available.

Institutional Shareholders Committee (ISC). A forum that facilitates the sharing of institutional investor views and coordinates those activities that support the interests of institutional shareholders, such as pension scheme trustees.

Interbank deposits. Short-term deposits made by commercial banks, with other commercial banks.

Integration. An investment approach that captures market inefficiencies in the valuation of sustainable and responsible businesses by integrating an analysis of how environmental, social and corporate governance issues affect corporate earnings and valuation.

Interest rate parity. The mathematical relationship that exists between the spot and forward exchange rate for two currencies. This is given by the difference between their respective nominal interest rates over the term being considered.

Interest rate risk. For a DB pension scheme, the risk that falling bond yields lead to a rise in the value of its liabilities relative to its assets. For a defined contribution scheme member, it is the risk that annuity rates will fall at a greater rate than the scheme member's pension pot has risen.

Interest rate swap. A contract between two counterparties where one, e.g. a pension scheme, exchanges a series of floating interest rate payments (LIBOR) on a notional capital sum, in return for a series of fixed nominal interest payments from a counterparty, typically an investment bank, over a pre-specified term. Only the netted out interest payments, and not the capital sum, are exchanged. An interest rate swap enables a pension scheme to lock into a fixed nominal interest rate, thereby preventing a fall in nominal rates increasing the present value of its liabilities.

Internal rate of return (IRR). The discount rate that when applied to a series of cash flows produces a net present value (NPV) of zero.

International Fisher Effect. The proposition that in a world of perfect capital mobility nominal interest rates reflect expected inflation rates so that real interest rates are equal worldwide.

International Swaps and Derivatives Association (ISDA). The global trade association for over the counter derivatives.

International Swaps and Derivatives Association (ISDA) agreement. The documentation that defines the relationship, the over the counter derivatives to be used and the specific terms of the agreement between a pension scheme and an investment bank before engaging in an over the counter derivatives transaction.

Interpolation. A method by which to establish an approximate internal rate of return.

In-the-money. An option where the exercise price is below the price of the underlying asset upon which a call option is written but above the price of the underlying asset upon which a put option is written.

Investment bank. A financial institution that can provide pension schemes with risk management services and securities. They also specialise in securities market activities, underwriting new equity, corporate bond and Eurobond issues and advising on corporate mergers and acquisitions.

Investment consultant. An individual or firm that advises the trustees of a defined benefit scheme on the scheme's strategic benchmark, its investment policy, risk management and manager selection and provides risk and performance data. For a defined contribution scheme, the advice is usually restricted to manager and fund selection and the provision of risk and performance data.

Investment governance. The skill, expertise, organizational effectiveness and time applied by the trustees to maintaining and developing all aspects of a scheme's investment strategy. Also see: *Governance*.

Investment Governance Group (IGG). An NAPF-inspired committee comprising pensions industry professionals that recommends how standards of investment governance can be improved across all scheme types, without any requirement for regulation.

Investment grade. Those bonds that have a credit rating of BBB-(S&P)/Baa3 (Moody's) or better.

Investment Managers Association (IMA). The trade association for the UK institutional and retail investment funds industry.

Investment Management Agreement (IMA). An agreement that specifies the terms relating to a fund management mandate, such as the fund's objective, the performance target, the relevant risk parameters and the fee structure.

Investment philosophy. A set of principles that set out a fund manager's beliefs about how asset prices become mispriced, the manager's capability and competitive advantage in exploiting these mispriced securities and how the manager believes outperformance can be generated sustainably.

Investment process. The formalized procedures that a fund manager adheres to in their day-to-day construction and management of investment portfolios.

Investment style. Investing in those securities or physical assets that share common characteristics and a meaningful tendency for their prices to move together.

Irredeemable security. A security issued without a pre-specified redemption, or maturity date.

ISDA. See: *International Swaps and Derivatives Association*.

ISDA agreement. See: *International Swaps and Derivatives Association (ISDA) agreements*.

Issued share capital. The nominal value of a company's share capital in issue. Also known as paid up capital and called up capital.

Issuing house. An institution that facilitates the issue of securities.

January effect. The phenomenon whereby equity markets tend on average to do better in January than in most other months.

J curve. The tendency for private equity investments to produce low or negative cash flows for investors during the early years of the investment, followed by a period of positive cash flow and returns.

Jensen's alpha. See: *Alpha*.

JGBs. Japanese government bonds.

Junk bond. A bond issued by a company with poor creditworthiness and consequently a low, sub-investment grade, credit rating. Also known as a high yield bond given the size of the coupon offered as compensation for the increased risk of default.

Keynesians. Those economists who believe that markets are slow to self-correct and who often advocate the use of fiscal policy to return the economy back to a full employment level of output.

Kondratieff cycles. Long-term economic cycles of 50 years+ duration that result from innovation and investment in new technology.

Large-capitalisation stocks. The ordinary shares of those companies with large market capitalisations relative to the average capitalisation of companies within a broad equity market index.

LDI. See: *Liability Driven Investment.*

Leg. The two sides of a swap are referred to as 'legs'.

Leverage. See: *Gearing.*

Liabilities. Legally binding obligations to be met in full as they fall due. Also 'negative assets'.

Liability Driven Investment (LDI). Where a scheme's assets are managed so that they perform in such a way as to maximize the likelihood that the scheme's liabilities will be met. This requires the scheme's asset portfolio to be constructed with a clear understanding of the characteristics of the scheme's liabilities; the liabilities being the benchmark for the scheme's assets. For many, LDI is synonymous with hedging interest rate, inflation and longevity risk.

Liability linked income (LLI) assets. Those illiquid real estate and infrastructure assets that provide predictable long-term, index-linked income streams that are secured against either physical or operating assets or a government/quasi-government covenant.

LIBOR. See: *London Interbank Offered Rate.*

Lifestyling. Where defined contribution pension scheme members are automatically offered a progressively less risky asset allocation as they approach their chosen retirement age.

Limited company. A company incorporated under the Companies Acts.

Limited partners. The investors in a hedge fund or private equity fund.

Limited price indexation (LPI). When upper and lower limits are placed on the extent of inflation-linking for defined benefit scheme pensions in payment. For example, an upper limit of 5% and lower limit of 0%, that prevents the nominal value of a pension in payment being reduced if inflation falls below zero, is commonplace.

Liquid. See: *Liquidity.*

Liquidity. The ease with which a security can be converted into cash, or the ease with which a holding in an investment fund can be redeemed by an investor. Liquidity is determined by the amount of two-way trade conducted in a security; usually the more liquid a security the smaller the difference between buying and selling prices. For an investment fund, the liquidity of the underlying securities or assets held determines the ease with which investors can redeem their holdings. Liquidity also describes the amount of an investor's or a fund's financial resources held in cash.

Liquidity preference theory. The proposition that lenders have a natural preference for short-term lending causing them to demand a liquidity premium in the form of a higher return the longer the term of the lending.

Listed company. A public limited company whose shares are listed on an exchange like the London Stock Exchange's main market, or official list, and whose regulations it must comply with.

Loan stock. A corporate bond issued in the domestic bond market without any underlying collateral, or security.

London Clearing House (LCH). The institution that acts as central counterparty to all trades executed on member stock and derivative exchanges.

London Interbank Offered Rate (LIBOR). The sterling money market benchmark interest rate.

London Stock Exchange (LSE). The principal UK market for listing and trading domestic and international securities.

Long call. See: *Call option.*

Long end (of the curve). The portion of the yield curve which is typically constructed from bonds or swaps with greater than 15 years to maturity.

Longevity risk. The risk that a defined benefit scheme's members and/or their spouses will live for longer than expected so increasing the period over which pensions may have to be paid by the scheme. For a defined contribution scheme member, a general increase in expected longevity will invariably lower annuity rates.

Longevity hedge. See: *Buy-in*, *Buyout* and *Longevity swap.*

Longevity swap. A contract between a defined benefit pension scheme and an investment bank and/or an insurance company, where the pension scheme exchanges a series of regular fixed payments (the 'fixed leg') over the expected lifespan of specific cohorts of the scheme's members in return for receiving a series of regular, variable payments (the 'floating leg') linked to the actual lifespan of those same scheme members. Longevity swaps, which look a lot like inflation swaps, enable a pension scheme to lock into the prevailing level of expected scheme specific or population-wide life expectancy for particular cohorts of its scheme membership.

Long position. The position assumed in a security or derivative following its purchase. If an investor is 'long a security', they have the right to sell it. If they are long a futures contract then they have undertaken to purchase the underlying asset at a predetermined price. Long positions benefit from rising prices.

Long put. See: *Put option.*

Long/short hedge funds. A hedge fund strategy where the manager takes long positions in those securities that they consider to be undervalued and and a short positions in those they believe are overvalued. When applied in the equity market it is often called equity hedge. Also see: *Market neutral.*

Loss aversion. A behavioural bias (framing error) whereby investors have a dominant motivation to avoid losses causing them to sell their top performing investments too soon and to hold on to their loss making investments for too long.

Macaulay duration. A measure of the sensitivity of a bond's price to changes in its required yield, expressed in years.

Macro hedge funds. Hedge funds that takes positions, typically using derivatives, to back the manager's views on perceived macroeconomic shifts and trends, such as the likely direction of interest rates or the likely movement of one currency against another. Also referred to as directional strategies.

Macroeconomic policy. The use of monetary and/or fiscal policy to generate sustained economic growth, employment and low inflation.

Macroeconomics. The study of how the aggregation of decisions taken in individual markets determines phenomena such as employment and inflation. Macroeconomics is also concerned with explaining the relationship between these variables, their rates of change over time and the impact of monetary and fiscal policy on the general level of economic activity.

Mainstream asset classes. See: *Traditional asset classes.*

Manager of managers. An investment fund that invests in a wide range of other investment funds typically run by other fund managers specifically for this particular fund.

Margin. See: *Initial margin* and *variation margin.*

Marked-to-market. The process of valuing a position taken in a securities or a derivatives market by using the prevailing market price.

Marked-to-market accounting. Where defined benefit pension scheme assets are recorded annually at their market values and where liabilities are recorded by discounting them by the AA bond yield (FRS 17) or a high quality corporate bond yield (IAS 19).

Market cap. See: *Market capitalization.*

Market capitalization. The total market value of a company's shares or other securities in issue. Market capitalization is calculated by multiplying the number of shares or other securities a company has in issue by the market price of those shares or securities.

Market capitalization-weighted index. A financial market index where the index's constituents are determined by the constituents' respective market capitalizations.

Market failure. When the workings of the free market result in sub-optimal economic and social outcomes. That is, when market failure leads to economic resources being allocated inefficiently.

Market inefficiencies. When relevant information about a security is not reflected in its market price.

Market neutral hedge funds. A hedge fund strategy that takes a long position in those securities that the manager considers to be undervalued and a short position in those they believe to be overvalued, so that market risk is hedged and returns rely entirely on stock selection.

Market segmentation theory of the yield curve. The proposition that a bond market, and its related yield curve, can be divided up into distinct segments based upon term to maturity – i.e. short, medium and long term – with each segment being influenced by maturity-specific characteristics.

Market risk. That element of investment risk that cannot be diversified away. Also known as systematic risk. See: *Capital Asset Pricing Model.*

Market timing. Basing investment decisions on anticipated market movements.

Maturity. The date upon which the principal, or capital, of a security, such as a bond, becomes due for repayment.

Maximum drawdown. The size of the largest cumulative loss for an investment measured from the investment's performance peak to its low. Typically used to judge the historic risk of an investment that has an absolute return benchmark, such as a hedge fund. Also see: *Income drawdown.*

Mean. See: *Arithmetic mean* and *Geometric mean.*

Mean-variance analysis. Analyzing the expected return and standard deviation of returns for an investment. Graphically, this is usually depicted by plotting the expected return on the vertical (y) axis against the standard deviation of returns on the horizontal (x) axis. Also see: *Efficient Frontier.*

Median. A measure of central tendency established by the middle value within an ordered distribution containing an odd number of observed values or the arithmetic mean of the middle two values in an ordered distribution containing an even number of values.

Memorandum of association. The legal document that principally defines a company's powers, or objects, and its relationship with the outside world. The Memorandum also details the number and nominal value of shares the company is authorised to issue and has issued.

Microeconomics. The branch of economics that is principally concerned with the decisions made by individuals and firms in particular markets and how these interactions determine the relative prices of goods and services demanded and supplied in these markets.

Mode. A measure of central tendency established by the value or values that occur most frequently within a data distribution.

Modern Portfolio Theory (MPT). The phrase applied to the body of work that began with the pioneering work of Harry Markowitz in 1952 which seeks to understand the relationship between the expected return and risk of financial securities.

Modified duration (MD). A measure of the sensitivity of a bond's price to small changes in its yield quantified in percentage terms.

Momentum investing. Investing in those securities that have recently performed well.

Monetarists. Those economists who believe that the level of economic activity can be regulated by controlling the money supply and that fiscal policy is ineffective and possibly harmful as a macroeconomic policy tool.

Monetary policy. Principally, though not exclusively, the setting of short-term interest rates by a central bank in order to manage domestic demand and achieve price stability in the economy, via either an intermediate exchange rate or inflation target.

Monetary Policy Committee (MPC). The operationally independent body of the Bank of England established in 1997 that sets the bank's policy rate, in accordance with a medium-term target for the Consumer Price Index (CPI).

Money. Anything that is generally acceptable as a means of settling a debt. Money is typically a medium of exchange, a store of value, recognised as such, divisible, durable and portable.

Money markets. The wholesale, as opposed to retail, markets for cash that are populated by the banks and institutional investors, such as pension funds. The money markets enable wholesale customers to both deposit money and to borrow money over short time horizons. The markets are characterized by the issuance, trading and redemption of short-dated tradable securities usually with a maturity of up to one year, with most having maturities ranging from overnight to three months.

Money market instruments. Short-term securities traded in the wholesale money markets. Most are issued with maturities ranging from overnight to three months in bearer form, that is, without registered title, at a discount to their face value and are redeemed by the bearer (who may or may not be the original purchaser) at their face value on maturity. The difference between the issue price and the redemption payment constitutes the return, analogous to an interest payment made by the issuer.

Money market funds. Daily priced collective investment funds that diversify investments across a range of high credit quality, short-term money market instruments (Treasury bills, commercial paper, certificates of deposit, etc.) with the principal aim of preserving investors' capital, providing liquidity and generating competitive returns, in that order.

Money supply. The amount of money in circulation within an economy at any given time. The money supply can be defined in various ways. A narrow definition comprises the amount of notes and coins in circulation, whereas broader definitions include bank deposits. Within a developed economy with a well-established banking system, these bank deposits are lent out, with the resultant spending creating new bank deposits, which can also be lent out by the banks. This system of credit creation ultimately determines a country's money supply.

Money weighted rate of return (MWRR). The internal rate of return that equates the value of a portfolio at the start of an investment period plus the net new capital invested during the investment period with the value of the portfolio at the end of this period. The MWRR, therefore, measures the fund growth resulting from both the underlying performance of the portfolio and the size and timing of cash flows to and from the fund over this period. Contrast with the time weighted rate of return.

Moody's. A globally recognised credit rating agency.

Moody's rating. A measure of the quality and safety of a bond based on Moody's assessment of the issuer's ability to meet scheduled interest payments and the principal at redemption.

Moral hazard. The unintentional encouragement of reckless behaviour as a consequence of a safety net, such as an insurance policy or the implicit underwriting of an activity.

Multi-asset fund. See: *Diversified growth funds*.

Multi-factor risk model. Quantitative models that break down investment returns into different component parts.

Mutual fund. A pooled investment fund such as a unit trust or open ended investment company (OEIC).

Myners Report. The comprehensive report commissioned by the UK government and published in March 2001 which reviewed institutional investment in the UK. The report was formally entitled *Institutional Investment in the UK: A Review.*

Myners principles. Updated in 2008, the Myners principles comprise six high level principles that are applied voluntarily by pension schemes as a code of best practice. They relate to effective decision making, setting clear objectives, risk and liabilities, performance assessment, responsible ownership and transparency and reporting.

NAPF. See: *National Association of Pension Funds*.

NASDAQ. The second largest stock exchange in the US. NASDAQ lists certain US and international technology stocks and provides a screen based quote driven secondary market that links buyers and sellers worldwide.

National Association of Pension Funds (NAPF). The trade body that represents the interests of UK occupational pension schemes.

National debt. A government's total outstanding borrowing resulting from financing successive budget deficits, mainly through the issue of government backed securities, such as gilts and treasury bills.

National Employment Savings Trust (NEST). A simple, low(ish)-cost occupational defined contribution pension scheme into which UK employers will be required to automatically enrol those employees who are not already active members of a qualifying occupational pension scheme if they are aged between 22 years and the State Pension Age and earn over £7,475 gross a year, assuming that the existing company pension scheme does not meet certain criteria.

Negative roll. The losses that arise when investing in commodity futures as a result of the futures trading at a higher price than the underlying commodities. Therefore, selling the nearest to maturity contract for the more expensive, next nearest to maturity contract, as the former approaches maturity to maintain an exposure to the commodities market, will create regular and predictable capital losses.

Negative sum game. Where the rules of a game or investment strategy or process result in a loss for the average performer.

Negotiable security. A security whose ownership can pass freely from one party to another. Negotiable securities are, therefore, tradable.

Net asset value (NAV). The balance sheet, book value or net worth of a business. The term can also be applied to the collective market value of the underlying securities, or assets, of a collective investment fund.

Net present value (NPV). The result of subtracting the discounted, or present, value of a project's expected cash outflows from the present value of its expected cash inflows.

Neutral interest rate. The long-term return that investors might expect from cash deposits over time. This comprises the expected trend economic growth rate and the expected long-run inflation rate. Also known as the neutral policy rate.

Neutral policy rate. See: *Neutral interest rate.*

New issue. A new issue of securities, for example bonds or ordinary shares.

New paradigm. The term applied to any new economic or financial phenomena which seems to be very different from phenomena that seemed to exists in a preceding era.

New York Stock Exchange (NYSE). The world's largest market for trading equities, situated on Wall Street in New York.

Nominal interest rate. The interest rate that is observed, one that encompasses both an expected real and expected inflation component.

Nominal value. The face or par value of a security. With respect to bonds, the nominal value is the price at which a bond is issued and usually redeemed. With respect to ordinary shares it is the price below which a company's ordinary shares cannot be issued.

Non-accelerating inflation rate of unemployment (NAIRU). That level of unemployment that is consistent with a stable inflation rate.

Non-contributory pension. A pension scheme funded entirely by an employer or by the state.

Normal distribution. A distribution whose values are evenly, or symmetrically, distributed about the arithmetic mean. Depicted graphically, a normal distribution is plotted as a symmetrical, continuous, bell-shaped curve. Contrast with a skewed distribution.

Notional value. The value of the exposure to an underlying asset, interest rates or inflation provided by a derivatives contract.

Off-benchmark positions. Investing in those securities that are not represented in the portfolio's benchmark.

Offer price. The price at which a security is offered for sale by a dealer or market maker. Also the price at which investors can buy units or shares in a collective investment fund.

Open ended funds. Pooled investment funds that allow investors to enter and (usually) exit the fund freely, such as mutual funds, unit trusts and open ended investment companies.

Open ended investment company (OEIC). A diversified and professionally managed open ended collective investment fund introduced in the UK in 1997 to replace unit trusts. Unlike unit trusts, OEICs are limited companies which issue shares, rather than units, which are traded at a single price without a bid/offer spread though in practice a bid/offer spread is applied. Each share represents an equal claim on the fund's net asset value and can be purchased and redeemed at will.

Operational gearing. The sensitivity of an organization's profits to changes in its sales revenue given its cost structure.

Opportunity cost. The cost of forgoing the next best alternative course of action to that chosen. In economics, costs are defined not as financial but as opportunity costs.

Option. A derivative contract that, in exchange for the payment of a premium by one party (the holder) to another (the writer), confers the right on the holder to either buy (call option) or sell (put option) a pre-specified asset at a pre-specified price on, and sometimes before, a pre-specified future date from (call option) or to (put option) the writer.

Option combinations. A strategy requiring the simultaneous purchase or sale of both a call and a put option on the same underlying asset, sometimes with different exercise prices but always with the same expiry dates. Combinations include straddles and strangles.

Option premium. The premium paid by the holder to the writer of an option.

Option writer. The seller of an option.

Ordinary shares. See: *Equity*.

Out-of-the-money. An option where the exercise price is above the price of the underlying asset upon which a call option is written but below the price of the underlying asset upon which a put option is written.

Overconfidence. A behavioural bias (heuristic) whereby investors overestimate their own knowledge, skill and ability, resulting in poorly diversified portfolios and excessive portfolio turnover to the detriment of investment returns.

Overweight position. When an active fund manager adopts a position in a security that is larger than its weight in the benchmark.

Over the counter (OTC) derivatives. Derivatives that are not traded on a derivatives exchange.

Par value. See: *Nominal value.*

Pari passu. Of equal ranking. New ordinary shares issued under a rights issue, for instance, rank pari passu with the company's existing ordinary shares.

Passive management. An investment approach that simply tracks, or replicates, a financial market index. Also known as index tracking.

Peer group benchmark. A benchmark usually set by the median performer within a particular cohort of fund managers. Each manager within the cohort is assigned a percentile performance ranking relative to their peers for the time period under consideration.

Pensioners. Those individuals that are no longer in active employment but who are drawing a pension from either the state, a DB plan or a DC plan, or any combination of all of these.

Pension funds. The sums of money that are invested in a range of traditional and alternative asset classes for the purpose of providing their scheme members with a regular income upon reaching the scheme's normal retirement age.

Pensions manager. The individual who acts on behalf of the sponsor as its in-house expert and source of advice on all pensions matters and also acts as secretary to the trustees.

Pension promise. A legal guarantee by a solvent sponsor.

Pension Protection Fund (PPF). The statutory body that takes responsibility for meeting a defined benefit (DB) scheme's liabilities in the event of the scheme sponsor becoming insolvent. Operational since 6 April 2005, the PPF is financed by a levy which is imposed on all UK DB schemes, and by the assets of schemes whose sponsors have become insolvent.

Percentile. A method of ranking which divides the values of the population under consideration in descending order into 100 units of 1%. So the top percentile of funds by performance contains the top 1% of performers.

Performance analysis. The comparison and subsequent investigation of actual investment performance against a predetermined benchmark. Both under and outperformance should be investigated.

Performance attribution. Identifying the sources of a fund manager's performance.

Performance fee. An annual fund management fee applied as a percentage of the investment return above a predetermined hurdle rate. The fee is often only payable if the investment return has exceeded a previous high watermark.

Performance persistence. The extent to which good or bad performance repeats.

Perpetuities. An investment that provides an indefinite stream of equal pre-specified periodic payments.

Policy rate. The interest rate set by a central bank.

Pooled fund. An investment fund managed for the collective benefit of a number of pension funds.

Population. A statistical term applied to a particular group where every member or constituent of the group is included.

Portfolio Theory. See: *Modern Portfolio Theory*.

Portfolio turnover. The frequency with which securities are bought and sold within a portfolio.

Positive roll. The profits that arise when investing in commodity futures as a result of the futures trading at a lower price than the underlying commodities. Therefore, selling the nearest to maturity contract for the cheaper, next nearest to maturity contract, as the former approaches maturity so as to maintain an exposure to commodities, will create regular and predictable profits.

Positive screening. An investment approach that invests in those 'best of sector' companies with a commitment to responsible business practices, environmentally and/ or socially positive products and/or services.

Potential output level. The sustainable level of output produced by an economy when all of its resources are productively employed.

Pound cost averaging. The investing of a fixed sum of money on a regular basis which results in purchasing more of the security or investment fund when the price is low and less when the price is high.

Pre-emption rights. The rights accorded to ordinary shareholders under company law to subscribe for new ordinary shares issued by the company in which they have the share-holding, for cash before the shares are offered to outside investors.

Preference shares. Those shares issued by a company that rank ahead of ordinary shares for the payment of dividends and for capital repayment in the event of the company going into liquidation.

Premium. The amount of cash paid by the holder of an option to the writer in exchange for conferring a right. Also the difference in the spot and forward exchange rate that arises when interest rates in the base currency are higher than those in the quoted currency.

Present value. The value of a sum of money receivable in the future expressed in terms of its value today. A present value is obtained by discounting the future sum by a rate of interest known as the discount rate.

Price to book (P/B) ratio. The ratio of a company's share price to its net asset value, or its assets minus its liabilities, attributed to each share.

Price to earnings (P/E) ratio. The ratio of a company's share price to its underlying earnings per share. The P/E is used by some investors as an indication of the ability of a company to increase its earnings over time. A high P/E means the market believes the company will produce robust earnings growth. Price earnings ratios can be calculated using either the company's most recent earnings (historic or trailing P/E) or its prospective earnings (forward or prospective P/E).

Price momentum. When stocks that have performed well in the recent past continue to do so.

Price weighted index. A financial market index where the weightings allocated to each of the index's constituents are determined by the constituents' respective prices.

Prima facie. At first sight. For instance, a portfolio's past performance provides prima facie evidence of a portfolio manager's skill and investment style.

Primary market. The market for new issues or initial public offerings.

Private equity. The provision of mainly equity capital not raised on public markets to finance business start ups and companies in the early stages of development, or to buy out well-established companies with a view to restructuring the firm's operations.

Profit and loss account. A financial statement that shows how much profit a company has generated over its accounting period, what revenue was earned and what expenses were incurred and how the profit was distributed. The profit and loss account accompanies the balance sheet and cash flow statement in the company's annual report and accounts.

PSNCR. See: *Public Sector Net Cash Requirement.*

Public markets. Markets where securities can be traded by the investing public.

Public Sector Net Cash Requirement (PSNCR). The borrowing needs of the UK government, mainly met through the issue of gilts and treasury bills.

Pull to par. The natural tendency for a bond's price to approach its redemption value over time.

Purchasing power parity (PPP). The exchange rate between two countries that equates the prices of similar goods and services.

Puttable bonds. A term applied to those bonds where the holder may sell them back to the issuer prior to maturity either on a predetermined date or during a predetermined period. This right would typically be exercised by the holder following a significant rise in interest rates or if the issuer receives a credit downgrade. Usually the holder would be charged a penalty for exercising this option.

Put option. An option that confers a right on the holder to sell a specified amount of an asset at a pre-specified price on or sometimes before a pre-specified date.

PV01. The present value of one basis point. PV01 can be used to represent the sensitivity of a defined benefit scheme's liabilities to a one basis point change in interest rates across the entire yield curve. It can also measure the impact of a one basis point change in implied inflation, real yields and credit spreads on a scheme's liabilities.

PV01 (delta) ladders. See: *PV01 risk buckets.*

PV01 risk buckets. An illustration of the effect of a one basis point (0.01%) reduction in interest rates or a one basis point increase in the assumed level of inflation on a defined benefit scheme's liabilities that fall due over different periods of time (maturity buckets).

Qualitative analysis. The analysis of the quality of a company's management, its product range, intellectual property and status of labour relations in order to determine the company's future potential as an investment.

Quantitative analysis. The analysis of a company's financial statements, financial projections and valuation in order to determine the company's future potential as an investment.

Quantitative screening. A process employed by active fund managers that assists them in eliminating those securities that do not meet pre-defined criteria for investment.

Quartile. A method of ranking which divides the values of a population under consideration in descending order into four units of 25%. So the top quartile of funds by performance contains the top 25% of performers.

Quantity Theory of Money. An accounting identity that formalises the relationship between the domestic money supply and the general price level.

Quorum. The minimum number of qualifying people required to attend a meeting for any resolutions carried to be considered valid. For a shareholders general meeting this is usually two, unless the company's articles of association dictate otherwise. For a pension scheme, what constitutes a quorum is specific to the scheme.

Quoted currency. The currency whose value is expressed in terms of one unit of the base currency. The quoted currency would be currency Y for the X/Y exchange rate.

Random walk. When market prices appear to move in an unpredictable fashion independently of any past price movements. The Efficient Markets Hypothesis attributes this to markets being weak and semi-strong efficient. That is, when all past and current relevant information is assumed to be already incorporated into current prices.

Rating. See: *Credit rating.*

Ratings outlook. A rating agency's opinion on the likely direction of any ratings change for a rated organisation or its bonds in issue over the next 18 months.

Ratio analysis. The analysis of financial ratios from company accounts. Accounting ratios facilitate the evaluation of a company's financial performance or position against that of its peers, by identifying significant trends and relationships that may not be immediately apparent from the financial accounts themselves.

Real economy. That part of the economy which relates to the production and sale of goods and services.

Real estate. Residential and commercial property.

Real Estate Investment Trust (REIT). A property company that manages a real estate portfolio and operates in accordance with REIT regulations.

Real interest rate. The rate of interest adjusted for inflation.

Real return. The rate of return adjusted for inflation.

Recovery plan. For a defined benefit scheme the plan that sets out how and over what period the scheme's deficit should be eliminated.

Redeemable security. A security issued with a known maturity, or redemption, date.

Redemption. The repayment of principal to the holder of a redeemable security.

Redemption date. The date on which the issuer of a bond agrees to repay the principal to the holder. Also known as the maturity date.

Regression analysis. A statistical technique used to establish the relationship between two variables.

Reinvestment rate risk. The risk that future bond coupons will not be reinvested at the expected rate.

REIT. See: *Real Estate Investment Trust.*

Relative return. The investment performance delivered by a portfolio when compared to that of the benchmark against which the portfolio's performance is assessed.

Relative value hedge funds. Hedge funds that seek to identify risk-free profits by simultaneously buying and selling the same economic exposure to an asset in two related markets where a pricing anomaly exists.

Repo. See *Repurchase agreement.*

Representativeness. A behavioural bias (heuristic) whereby investors subconsciously create and extrapolate patterns and trends from random events, without investigating or questioning the reasons for these supposed patterns and trends. Representativeness is the main source of heuristic bias and arises as a consequence of investors being poor at calculating and calibrating probabilities, their inability to distinguish between random events and genuine trends and to differentiate luck from skill.

Repurchase agreement. The simultaneous sale and repurchase of a bond. Repurchase agreements, referred to as repos, are essentially secured loan agreements. Under a repo agreement the party wishing to borrow money typically sells a government bond for cash to another party but with an agreement to buy the bond back after a certain period, which can range from overnight to a few months. The difference between the lower sale price and the higher repurchase price is effectively the rate of interest charged by the lender to the borrower of the cash.

Reserve ratio. The proportion of deposits held by banks as reserves to meet depositor withdrawals.

Resistance level. A term used in technical analysis to describe the ceiling put on the price of a security resulting from persistent investor selling at that price level.

Retail Price Index (RPI). A measure of the cost of living, based on the cost of a representative basket of goods and services purchased by the average UK household. The RPI is calculated monthly as a headline and as an underlying rate (the latter excludes mortgage interest costs) and is published as both an index and as an annual percentage rate. Despite the introduction of the Consumer Price Index, the RPI is still the UK's most closely watched measure of inflation.

Return. The income and/or capital appreciation generated by an investment expressed as a percentage of the price paid.

Rewarded risk. The long-run return expected by investors with an exposure to risky assets, such as equities and corporate bonds.

Rights issue. The issue of new ordinary shares to a company's shareholders in proportion to each shareholder's existing shareholding, usually at a price deeply discounted to the prevailing market price. Also see: *Pre-emption rights.*

Risk. The uncertainty surrounding an expectation about a future outcome. To most investors, risk is either the possibility of making a capital loss or the opportunity cost of failing to be invested in the 'right' asset class. An element of investment risk can be reduced through diversification.

Risk appetite. The degree of uncertainty surrounding future investment returns an investor is prepared to tolerate.

Risk assets. Investments other than risk-free assets, that command a risk premium, such as equities, corporate bonds and real estate.

Risk aversion. An investor is said to be risk averse when they require higher and higher expected returns in compensation for taking on higher risk.

Risk budget. The amount of risk that a trustee board is willing to accept; often quantified by using VaR.

Risk-free assets. Assets perceived to have almost no default risk such as a AAA-rated government bond or treasury bill.

Risk-free rate. The rate of return available on a risk-free asset such as a AAA-rated government bond or treasury bill.

Risk management. Ensuring that the uncertainties surrounding future outcomes are efficiently managed within acceptable tolerances. This will entail measuring and reducing risks where appropriate.

Risk models. Models that facilitate the identification, measurement, mitigation, management and monitoring of the quantifiable risks that reside within a pension scheme's assets and liabilities.

Risk premium. The additional return expected by investors over and above the risk-free rate of return for investing in risky asset classes.

RPI. See: *Retail Price Index.*

R-squared. Derived from statistical models, and can provide a measure of the strength of the relationship between, for example, quantified by performance of a stock and that of the market in which it trades.

Running yield. The return from a bond calculated by expressing the bond's coupon as a percentage of its price. Also known as the flat yield or interest yield.

SAA. See: *Strategic asset allocation.*

Sample. A statistical term applied to a representative subset of a particular population. Samples enable inferences to be made about the population.

Scenario testing. See: *Stress testing.*

Scheme auditor. An individual or firm that verifies the value of the assets held within a pension scheme and the valuation accorded to them when auditing the scheme's annual financial statements. The scheme auditor also examines the robustness of the scheme's risk controls and identifies where there may be unnecessary concentrations of risk.

Scheme actuary. An individual or firm that advises on whether there are sufficient assets within a scheme to meet the scheme's liabilities in full as they fall due. A formal valuation of the scheme's assets and liabilities is normally conducted by the scheme actuary every three years in drawing up the scheme's triennial actuarial valuation.

Scheme lawyer. An individual or firm that advises the trustees on the parameters within which they should operate, drafts and checks the scheme's documentation and flags changes in legislation and regulation, advising on the likely implications for the trustees and the scheme.

Scheme secretary. The individual responsible for organizing trustee and committee meetings, compiling agendas and papers, writing up meeting minutes, following up action points, maintaining risk registers, preparing business plans, sourcing professional advice, liaising with regulatory bodies, including tPR, arranging TKU-complaint trustee training, preparing member communications and preparing the trustees' budget.

Screening. See: *Quantitative screening.*

Scrip dividend. Dividends paid in shares in lieu of cash.

Scrip issue. When a company offers free shares to shareholders in proportion to their existing holdings, usually by releasing retained profits or distributing the share premium reserve from its balance sheet. Although the total nominal value of shares in issue will increase, their total market value usually remains largely unchanged.

Secondary market. The market for trading securities already in issue.

Securities. See: *Security.*

Securities and Exchange Commission (SEC). A US federal agency created in 1934 to regulate all aspects of the US securities industry.

Securitisation. The packaging of rights to the future revenue stream from a collection of assets into a bond issue. See: *Asset backed securities*.

Security. A financial instrument, such as a share or a bond, issued by a company, government or other organisation that evidences a claim on or a stake in the issuer. Also, collateral taken by a lender to guarantee the repayment of a loan.

Segregated mandate. A bespoke fund management mandate run exclusively for a single pension fund.

Settlor. The creator of a trust.

Share buyback. The redemption and cancellation by a company of a proportion of its irredeemable ordinary shares subject to the permission of the High Court and agreement from HM Revenue and Customs.

Share capital. The nominal value of a company's equity or ordinary shares. A company's authorised share capital is the nominal value of equity the company may issue while issued share capital is that which the company has issued. The term share capital is often extended to include a company's preference shares.

Share split. A method by which a company can reduce the market price of its shares to make them more marketable without capitalizing its reserves. A share split simply entails the company reducing the nominal value of each of its shares in issue whilst maintaining the overall nominal value of its share capital. A share split should have the same impact on a company's share price as a bonus issue.

Sharpe ratio. A measure of risk-adjusted return that calculates the unit of return generated by a portfolio over and above that available from a risk-free asset, per unit of risk, measured by the standard deviation of return. The higher the Sharpe ratio for a portfolio, the higher the return per unit of risk and the greater the implied skill of the fund manager.

Short call. An investor is said to be 'short' a call option when they are the option writer.

Short end (of the curve). The portion of the yield curve which is typically constructed from bonds or swaps with less than 5 years to maturity.

Short position. The position assumed following the sale of a security that has been borrowed rather than owned. Short positions benefit from falling prices.

Short selling. Selling a security that has been borrowed in the expectation that it can be repurchased in the market at a lower price in the future. Also see: *Stock lending*.

Skewed distribution. See: *Skewness*.

Skewness. A distribution whose values are not evenly, or symmetrically, distributed about the arithmetic mean. Skewed distributions are often said to have 'fat tails'. Contrast with a normal distribution.

Small-capitalisation stocks. The ordinary shares of those companies with small market capitalisations relative to the average capitalisation of companies within a broad equity market index.

SONIA. See: *Sterling Overnight Interbank Average.*

Sovereign debt. Bonds issued by governments.

Sovereign Wealth Funds (SWFs). Funds that are established, owned and funded by sovereign states.

Sponsor. The organization that establishes and administers an occupational pension scheme.

Sponsor covenant. The ability of a defined benefit pension scheme sponsor to continue to meet its financial and legal obligations to the scheme and its members.

Spot exchange rate. The current exchange rate that applies to a foreign exchange transaction for immediate, or near immediate, settlement. Contrast with a forward exchange rate.

Spot market. The cash market for commodities and currencies. In contrast to futures markets, transactions in spot markets are made at prevailing market prices for immediate, or near immediate, delivery.

Spot price. The prevailing market price of a security or commodity.

Spot rate. The yield required on a zero coupon bond. Also known as a zero coupon yield. Spot rates also relate to the price of one currency in terms of another traded in the spot market.

Spread. The difference between the buying and selling price of a security or investment fund. The size of the spread provides an indication of the liquidity of the security, or investment fund. Also see: *Bid/offer spread.* A spread is also an options strategy requiring the simultaneous purchase of one or more options and the sale of another or several others on the same underlying asset with either different exercise prices and the same expiry date or the same exercise prices and different expiry dates. Spreads include bull spreads, bear spreads and butterfly spreads. Also see: *Credit spread.*

SRI. Sustainable and responsible investing.

Standard deviation. A measure of dispersion around the arithmetic mean. The square root of the variance. The volatility of an investment is usually expressed by its standard deviation of returns.

Standard & Poor's (S&P). A globally recognized credit rating agency.

Standard & Poor's 500 (S&P 500) Index. A market capitalization-weighted index that tracks the prices of 500 of the largest industrial, transport, utility and financial stocks in the US.

Star fund managers. The rock stars of the fund management world. A phenomenon of the nineties and noughties, the promotion of star fund managers was used as a key differentiator by a number of fund management houses with varying degrees of success. Contrast with a collegiate, or team-based, approach to fund management.

Statement of Funding Principles (SFP). A document that details how a defined benefit scheme intends to meet its statutory funding objective.

Statement of Investment Beliefs. An adjunct to a scheme's statement of investment principles that articulates the trustees' explicit views on a range of investment phenomena and provides the strategic framework for identifying those investment opportunities that best fit with these beliefs.

Statement of Investment Principles (SIP). A document that details a scheme's investment strategy and objectives, investment criteria and restrictions, strategic benchmark, asset allocation strategy and parameters, risk management policy, fund manager mandates and policy on environmental, social and corporate governance issues, including the exercise of voting rights.

Statutory funding objective (SFO). The requirement for a private sector defined benefit scheme to have sufficient assets to meet its liabilities in full as they fall due.

Sterling Overnight Interbank Average (SONIA). A sterling money market benchmark interest rate.

Stock. An ordinary share though the term can sometimes refer to a bond.

Stock exchange. An organized market place for issuing and trading securities.

Stock lending. Where an institutional investor, such as a pension scheme, lends securities from its portfolio against collateral to a stock borrower in return for a stock lending fee.

Stop loss. A predetermined price, typically set below the price paid for a security or its prevailing price if now higher, at which the security should be sold in the event of it falling in price.

Strategic asset allocation (SAA). The process of investing a portfolio's assets geographically and between asset classes based on the scheme's long-term views of asset class returns, volatilities and correlations. The resulting asset mix might differ from the desired strategic weights to the chosen asset classes, i.e. the strategic benchmark, owing to the implementation of tactical asset allocation decisions.

Strategic asset mix. See: *Strategic asset allocation.*

Strategic benchmark. See: *Strategic asset allocation.*

Stratified sampling. An indexing method that requires an index tracker fund to hold only a sample of those securities in the financial market index being tracked. These securities are selected using statistical techniques to ensure they reflect the characteristics of the index as closely as possible.

Stress testing. A method of testing the impact of various scenarios or events, usually extreme or 'fat tail' events such as the reoccurrence of the credit crisis, on a scheme's funding position.

Strike price. See: *Exercise price.*

STRIPS. The principal and interest payments of those designated gilts whose component parts can be traded as zero coupon bonds. STRIPS is the pneumonic for Separate Trading of Registered Interest and Principal.

Structured product. An investment product that combines an option strategy with a cash deposit. The performance of such products may be linked to an equity index with both the upside and downside potential capped, or limited.

Style drift. When an active fund manager deviates from their stated investment style.

Style factors. Those common characteristics shared by a particular group of stocks that cause the stocks to move together and so experience periods of out and underperformance of the broader market.

Style neutral. Where individual portfolios (modules), each managed by different fund managers in accordance with each manager's chosen investment style, are combined to form a single fund to provide diversification of manager and investment style risk.

Style rotation. Where a portfolio alternates between the funds of different fund managers, each of whom runs their fund in accordance with their chosen investment style. By rotating from one style to another the strategy aims to benefit from periods when one investment style outperforms others.

Sub-investment grade bonds. Bonds that have a credit rating lower than BBB- (S&P)/ Baa3 (Moody's) and pay higher coupons to offset the higher inherent default risk. Often referred to as high yield or junk bonds.

Subordinated bond. An unsecured debt instrument that in the event of the issuer defaulting will only be repaid after the claims of more senior bondholders have been met.

Subordinated loan stock. Loan stock issued by a company that ranks above its preference shares but below its unsecured creditors in the event of the company's liquidation.

Survivorship bias. The extent to which any performance data series is biased upwards because it only captures the performance of those 'winners' that have remained in business (survived) throughout the period of analysis.

Sustainable development. In an investment context, strategies that meet the needs of the present without compromising the ability of future generations to meet their own needs.

Swap. An over-the-counter derivative whereby two parties exchange a series of periodic payments based on a notional principal amount over an agreed term. Swaps can take the form of interest rate swaps, inflation swaps, longevity swaps, currency swaps, equity swaps and total return swaps.

Swap axes. Market parlance for the tranches of swaps made available by investment banks.

Swap counterparty. A party to a swap contract.

Swap rate. The fixed interest payment in a designated currency that an investor could expect to pay in return for receiving regular payments in the same currency based upon money market interest rates over a predetermined period.

Swap curve. The graphical depiction of the interest rate swap fixed leg terms or inflation swap fixed leg rates available across the entire spectrum of swap maturities.

SWFs. See: *Sovereign Wealth Funds*.

Synthetic replication. An indexing method that requires an index tracker fund to track the chosen financial market index either via a combination of cash and futures contracts, or a total return swap on the financial market index.

Systematic risk. Market risk that cannot be diversified away.

t + 3. The three day rolling settlement period over which all deals executed on the London Stock Exchange are settled.

TAA. See: *Tactical asset allocation*.

Tactical asset allocation (TAA). The process of implementing tactical investment decisions based on perceived short-term opportunities, causing the asset mix to depart from the desired strategic asset allocation, or strategic benchmark.

Tail risk. See: *Conditional Value at Risk*.

Takeover. When one company takes a controlling interest in another. Takeovers are usually contested unlike mergers.

Target date funds. A series of defined contribution funds that are each managed according to a pre-determined date upon which the investors in the fund are assumed to annuitise their pension pots.

techMARK. The London Stock Exchange market for those public limited companies committed to technological innovation that seek a full listing but do not possess a three year trading record.

Technical analysis. The analysis of charts depicting past price and trading volume movements to determine the future course of a particular market or the price of an individual security, commodity or exchange rate.

Technical provisions. The amount required to meet a defined benefit scheme's liabilities given the valuation basis applied to the liabilities agreed by the trustees.

The Pensions Regulator (tPR). The organization that regulates UK occupational pension schemes with much wider and more flexible powers than the Occupational Pensions Regulatory Authority (OPRA) that it replaced in April 2006.

Tick. The minimum price movement of a derivatives contract as specified by the derivatives exchange on which the derivative is traded.

Tick value. The monetary value of one tick.

Time value. That element of an option premium that is not intrinsic value. The term also relates to a sum of money which, by taking account of a prevailing rate of interest and the term over which the sum is to be invested or received, can be expressed as either a future value or as a present value, respectively.

Time weighted rate of return (TWRR). A measure of investment return that eliminates the distorting effect of the timing of cash flows. The TWRR is calculated by compounding the rates of return from each investment sub period, a sub period being created whenever there is a movement of capital into or out of the portfolio. Contrast with the money weighted rate of return.

TKU. See: *Trustee Knowledge and Understanding.*

Top-down. Investing on the basis of broad macroeconomic and geopolitical views. Contrast with a bottom-up approach to investing.

Total return swap (TRS). An over the counter derivative based on a notional principal amount, whereby the parties to the contract exchange a series of periodic LIBOR, or LIBOR plus, payments for a series of periodic payments representing the capital and income return of a pre-specified asset over an agreed term.

Tracker fund. A collective investment fund that seeks to replicate the performance of an equity index. Tracker funds either hold each share in the index being tracked in the same proportion as the index itself or a representative sample of shares.

Tracking error. The predetermined parameters within which the performance of an actively managed fund should typically deviate from that of the benchmark.

Traditional asset classes. Those investments that are considered to be mainstream such as cash and bonds, equities and real estate, though some bonds and real estate investments are defined as alternative assets.

Transactions costs. Those costs incurred when buying or selling securities, currencies or physical assets, such as commodities and real estate. These comprise professional fees, commissions, spreads and taxes, such as stamp duty.

Transition costs. Those costs incurred when moving a scheme's assets between different asset classes and/or fund managers. These comprise professional fees, commissions, spreads and taxes, such as stamp duty. Transitions are usually undertaken by a specialist transitions manager.

Treasuries. Bonds issued by the US Treasury on behalf of the US government.

Treasury bills. Short-term government-backed securities issued at a discount to their face value. Treasury bills do not pay coupons but are redeemed at their face value. Also see: *Money market instruments.*

Trend growth. The rate at which an economy can grow sustainably over time, that is without causing inflation to accelerate or unemployment to rise.

Treynor ratio. A measure of risk-adjusted return that calculates the unit of return generated by a portfolio over and above that available from a risk-free asset, per unit of risk, measured by the portfolio beta. The higher the Treynor ratio for a portfolio, the higher the return per unit of risk and the greater the implied skill of the fund manager.

Trigger point. Often a target interest rate or break-even inflation rate set by the trustees of a defined benefit scheme prior to executing an interest rate or inflation swap transaction.

Trustee Knowledge Understanding (TKU). In April 2006, the Pensions Regulator introduced the Trustee Knowledge and Understanding (TKU) Code of Practice based on s.247–249 of the Pensions Act 2004. Revised in 2009, this forms the basis of what trustees need to know in discharging their fiduciary duties.

Trustees. The legal owners of trust property who owe a duty of skill and care to the trust's beneficiaries.

UCITS. See: *Undertaking for Collective Investment in Transferable Securities Directive.*

UK Corporate Governance Code. See: *Combined Code.*

UK Listing Authority (UKLA). The body responsible for setting and administering the listing requirements and continuing obligations for public limited companies seeking and obtaining a full list, or quote, on the London Stock Exchange. The Financial Services Authority was appointed as the UKLA in May 2000.

UK Stewardship Code. A code of good practice issued by the FRC in July 2010 that sets out principles and guidance for institutional investors, such as pension scheme trustees, on what constitutes good practice in engaging with the companies in which they invest. The first such investor code in the world, the UK Stewardship Code ultimately seeks to improve the quality of corporate governance and long-term returns to shareholders, such as pension schemes.

Unconstrained investing. Where a fund manager has a degree of freedom in managing a portfolio whether against a relative or absolute return benchmark. Also see: *Benchmark aware.*

Underlying asset. The asset (or security) upon which a derivative is based and upon which its value is ultimately determined.

Undertaking for Collective Investment in Transferable Securities (UCITS) Directive. An EU Directive introduced in 1985 by the European parliament to enable collective investment schemes authorized in one EU member state to be freely marketed throughout the EU, subject to the marketing rules of the host state(s) and certain fund structure rules being complied with. UCITS III is the current UCITS directive.

Underweight position. When an active fund manager adopts a position in a security below its weight in the benchmark.

Unemployment. The percentage of the labour force registered as available for work but who are not working.

Unfunded pension scheme. Those public sector defined benefit pension schemes that pay members' pensions out of current tax receipts rather than from a fund comprising contributions, assets and the investment returns deriving from those assets. Also referred to as 'pay as you go' (PAYE) pensions.

UN PRI. United Nations Principles for Responsible Investment. Signatories to the UNPRI, which can include pension schemes, commit to integrating environmental, social and corporate governance issues into their investment analysis, to being active, responsible owners by promoting good corporate practice and to reporting transparently on what actions they have taken.

Unquoted company. A company not listed on a main market, such as the London Stock Exchange's main market, or official list.

Unrewarded risk. A risk that if assumed is unlikely to provide a return in the longer run. This comprises inflation risk, interest rate risk and longevity risk, which, if removed at an acceptable price, should not have a material impact upon the long-run expected return on the scheme's assets.

Unsecured bond. A debt security not secured against any of the issuer's assets. Because there is no protection for the holder in the event of the issuer defaulting, such securities carry higher coupons than equivalent secured bonds.

Unsecured debt. A loan or debt security against which the borrower, or issuer, has not pledged any security.

Unsystematic risk. The idiosyncratic risk that can be diversified away by forming portfolios.

Value at Risk (VaR). The maximum expected loss over a specified time period, typically one year, assuming a given probability. For instance, a one year VaR95 applied to a pension scheme's funding position, measures the extent to which the scheme's funding position or deficit could deteriorate over the course of the next 12 months if impacted by an event that could be expected to occur no more than once in 20 years, or on 5% of occasions. A scheme's VaR95 can be decomposed across the assets it holds and the liabilities it faces.

Value stocks. Those stocks with a characteristically low price to earnings and price to book ratio and a high dividend yield where future earnings growth is expected to be relatively low. These are typically companies that operate in mature markets with limited prospect of substantial market expansion but which still produce a stable and relatively high dividend stream.

VaR. See: *Value at Risk*.

Variance. A measure of dispersion from the mean. The standard deviation squared.

Variation margin. The cash that passes between the parties to certain open exchange traded derivative (principally futures) positions at the beginning of each trading day to settle profits and losses from the close of the previous trading day.

Venture capital. Specialist private equity capital provided to finance business start ups and companies in the early stages of development. Given the high risks involved, an equity stake and often a place on the company's Board is sought by the venture capitalist.

Vintage year. The year in which a private equity fund is launched.

VIX. A measure of the market's assessment of how volatile investors expect the S&P 500 index will be. The VIX is known as '*the fear gauge*' – given that volatility is a measure of uncertainty - and is derived from the prices of S&P 500 index options.

Volatility. A measure of the extent to which investment returns, asset prices and economic variables fluctuate. Volatility is measured by the standard deviation of these returns, prices and values.

Weighted Average Cost of Capital (WACC). The average post-tax cost of servicing a company's long-term sources of finance. The WACC acts as the discount rate for establishing the net present value of investment projects of equivalent risk to those currently undertaken by the company.

xd. See: *Ex-dividend.*

Yield. The return, though often just the income return, from an investment expressed as a percentage of its price.

Yield curve. The depiction of the relationship between the yields and the maturity of bonds either issued by the same issuer or with the same risk characteristics, such as the same credit rating.

Yield inversion. Where swaps of a particular term are more expensive than gilts, or index-linked gilts of the same maturity.

Yield to maturity (YTM). See: *Gross redemption yield.*

Zero coupon bonds (ZCBs). Bonds issued at a deep discount to their nominal value that do not pay a coupon but which are redeemed at par on a pre-specified future date.

Zero sum game. Where for every gain there is an equal and opposite loss.

z-spread. The difference in the price of swaps compared to gilts, or index-linked gilts of the same term. A positive z-spread arises if swaps are more expensive than gilts, or index-linked gilts of the same term. A negative z-spread or yield inversion arises if swaps are cheaper than gilts, or index-linked gilts of the same term.

Index

Notes: **bold** = extended discussion or term highlighted in text; B = box; e = exhibit; n = footnote.

ABN Amro   496
Abrams, R.   496n
'absentee landlords' (Myners)   430, 430n
absolute returns   308–9, 309e, **349–52**, 443
accounting   84, 111, 306n, 394, 398, 400, 405
accrual rate   3
Acharya, V.V.   328n
'active bets'   363
active fund management   348, **363–77**, 382, 389, 468, 506, 509
  capacity constraints   **498–9**
  collegiate approach   **495–7**, 504b, 507
  combined with passive management **383–6, 389**
  main advantage   367
  negative sum game   **376–7**
  outperformance of benchmark 'does not constitute 'alpha'   **370–1**, 371e
  outperformance claims: academic tests   **368–72**, 376
  outperformance claims: academic tests (fairness)   **372–4**
  performance   **366–8, 374–6**
  performance (survivorship bias)   367n
  performance persistence   **368–70**
  process   **364–6**
active fund managers   353, 377, 460, 507
  academic research   388
  appointment   **507**
  assessment (questions to ask)   **503–5b**
  attraction of new client money   504b
  cult of the star   **495–6**
  'even the best get it wrong'   491
  fees   **500–1**
  versus 'index huggers'   **492–3**
  investment to win versus investment not to lose   491b, 503b
  outperformance   493, 495, 506, 507
  requirements   **505–6**
  research methods   504b
  risk management   **499–500**

skill versus luck   462, 462n
star fund manager versus team approach   503b
stock positions (overweight versus underweight)   463
time spent in client meetings   505b
see also   equity fund managers
'active risk'   **363**, 364
'active share'   364, 493, 503b, 505, 507
adaptive markets hypothesis   **482–3**
adjustment conservatism   **465–6**, 468, **498**
affect heuristic   **464**
AFG   502
Africa   95, 440b
age   488
agency problem (publicly traded companies)   326
agency risks   **205–6**, 209
aggregate demand   70
aggregation (wisdom of crowds)   **470**
agricultural commodities   333–4e
AIG   204, 442
algebra   113–14, 117
Alliance Boots   26
Alliance Group   317
alpha (manager skill)   192, **370–2**, 400, 462, 462n, 490, 507
  genuine   372–3
  positive   376
  see also   fund manager skill
alpha coefficient (risk-adjusted excess return)   **194–6**, 197, 487
  use   **195–6**
'alpha pretenders'   490
alternative asset classes   **305–45**; 79, 156n, 185, 188, 347, 353n, 509
  data deficiencies   **341–2**
  due diligence   343–4
  fees   343
  'headaches'   344e
  illiquidity   **343**
  integration with traditional asset classes   **341–4**

alternative asset classes – *continued*
  investment advantages **305–7**
  mean-variance efficient frontier 310,
    311e
  'no official definition' 307
  opacity **342**
  risk and return **310–11**
alternative beta funds 316
altruism/philanthropy 430–1, 447, 449
AM Best (credit rating agency) 97
Amaranth (hedge fund) 467
Ambachtsheer, K. 30n
ambiguity aversion **466–7**, **498**, 504b
Ammann, M. 439b
amortization 94, 169, 172b, 424b
anchoring **465**, **498**, 504b
annual management charge (AMC) 316,
    320, 325
annuities 11, **12–14**, 17, 33
  non-indexed 12–13
  'unisex market' 14n
annuity rates 14e, 19b, 23
annuity risk 39, 510
Aon Consulting xiv
ap Gwilym, O. 243n, 386n, 456n
'April effect' (UK) 244e, 456n
arbitrage 258, **313**, 315, 322b
  fixed-income 315
Arnott, R. 382b
Articles of Association **126**
Asia 95, 440b
Asia-Pacific region 19, 172, 173e, 376
Asian crisis (1997) 200, 242e
asset allocation **211–48**; 45n, 50, 77,
    176, 188, 358, 396, 427
  expected returns (change of view) **231**
  fund manager [company] **358–61**
  practice 212–14
asset allocation decision xvi, **511**
asset allocators **186**
asset classes xvi, 5, 15–16, 46, 180–1,
    209, 389, 510
  active versus passive decision 212,
    377–8, 385–6, **386–8b**, 388, 389, 486
  correlation 156, 156n, **160**, 171b
  correlation (definition) 156n
  covariance **181–3**
  diversification 156n
  equities (traditional 'growth') **125–53**
  indices 355
  low-risk, low-return 409
  most liquid (cash) **79–85**

most-feared (bonds) **87–124**
over- versus under-valued 31
over-priced versus under-priced **235–6**,
    237–8, **239–41**, 243
real estate **155–74**
risky 336
versus 'skill set' 330, 345
volatilities and correlation **231–7**
  see also alternative asset classes
asset managers 48, 212, 317, 428, 430,
    437–8, 441
  source of private equity funds (2010)
    324e
  swaps portfolios 416e, **417–18**, 420
asset prices
  stress/scenario testing 405
assets
  fixed-income 308, 309e
  non-conventional 48
  'risk-free' 190, 192, 194, 195, 197
assets under management (AuM) 317,
    499
Association of British Insurers (ABI) 436,
    439b
at-the-money option **264–5**
Australia 19, 20, 73e, 130e, 163–4, 218,
    218–19e, 432
  dividend yield and dividend cover
    136, 137e
Australian dollar 337b, 339
availability bias **464**, **498**
average return 186, 190, 209
averaging
  arithmetic versus geometric **356–8**
Aviva Staff Pension Scheme xv
AXA Framlington 496

Babcock International 413
backfill bias (hedge funds) 323
Bain, R. 171n
'balanced funds' 212, 348, 443
balanced managers (multi-asset
    managers) 46
Bank of England 84
  control of interest rates (1997–) 71–2,
    73–4
  policy rate (1950–2010) 221e, 221
Bank of England: Monetary Policy
    Committee (MPC, 1997–) 221,
    224–5, 231
Bank for International Settlements (BIS)
    286, 410n

triennial forex survey (2010) 336, 336–7b
banking sector 129, 129e
banks 66, 82, 93, 126, 140b, 170b, 204,
 274, 327, 383b, 419
 Icelandic 81
 Irish and Icelandic 430
 source of private equity funds (2010)
 324e, 324
 sovereign bail-outs (2008) 91
 stress tests 462
Banz, R. 457n
Barber, B. M. 502
Barclays xiv
Barclays Capital 212, 355
Barclays Capital Equity Gilt Study
 (2009) 457n
 (2011) 147n, 149b, 151n, 153n, 212,
 212n, 213, 306
Barings Bank 249, 467
barriers to entry 171b, 382
barter 64, 65
Baruch, B. 468
basis risk 258–9
'Be fearful' (Buffett) 481
'beans in jar' experiment (Treynor)
 470n
bear markets 148t, 312
'beating the market' 367
beauty contest analogy (Keynes) 241,
 459, 472, 473
Beebower, G.L. 214n
behavioural biases 460–1, 487, 497–8,
 504–5b, 507
behavioural finance 451–84; 31n, 206,
 241n, 244, 363, 366, 487, 489, 491b,
 497, 502
 explanatory power 468
 mathematical modelling 'less easy' 481
 nature 458–9, 484
 'not a new science' 460
 prospects 482–3
 shortcomings 481–2
Belgium 76e
'benchmark creep' 354
benchmark index 190
'benchmark proportions' 350
benchmark return 381
benchmarks (portfolio management)
 142, 191, 352–4, 358–61, 392, 460,
 492–3, 503b, 509, 511
 active fund management 363–4
 adjusted for risk 370–1, 371e

effectiveness criteria 353–4
outperformance (active fund
 management) 367, 368e, 389
outperformance 'does not constitute
 production of alpha' 370
peer group 355
relative performance monitoring 362
sources of fund manager's
 outperformance or
 underperformance 362
benefit dilution measures 9n
Berk, J.B. 375n
Berkshire Hathaway fund 250n, 500
Bernstein, P.L. 451
best practice 29, 29n, 30n, 430, 433,
 435, 438
beta 341, 362e, 363, 370, 376, 379, 388,
 481
 'high' versus 'low' 192–4
 'higher than one' 370
beta coefficient 192–3, 195, 197
 versus corporate gearing 193n
 UK equity pension funds (2000–10)
 193, 194e
'bets' 383–4
bias 474, 481
Biggs, B. 469, 471
Bikhchandani, S. 471n
Black Swan (Taleb, 2007) 462n
black swans 176, 176n, 462, 462n, 475
BlackRock 317
Blair, A.C.L. 25, 509
Blake, D. 414
BMW (UK) pension scheme 413
board of directors
 election 441–2
 election ('comply or explain' basis) 442
board-nomination committees
 (Sweden) 441
Bolt, U. 377
Bolton, A. 489, 506
bond funds
 duration and yield curve 358
 interest rate swaps 285
bond indenture 93–4, 96, 100
bond indices 355, 356
bond mathematics 106, 108
bond portfolio management 108–11
bond prices 101–5, 122
 discounting 101–2
 discounting (application of principle to
 plain vanilla bond) 102–3

bond prices – *continued*
  and returns   **103–5**, 124
  volatility   **105–6**
bondholders   126–8, 327
bonds   **87–124**; xvi, 13, 44, 132–3, 213,
    214e, 225, 236–7, 250, 283, 287b,
    301, 310, 311e, 347, 384, 400, 406,
    407e, 411, 423, 441
  characteristics   **88–9**
  convertible   **95**, 96
  currency of denomination   112
  default rates (1970–2008)   **226–7**
  discount rate   393
  duration (key risk parameter)   **105–11**
  with embedded options   **95–6**
  'expected return' versus 'required
    return'   **103**
  global market   90–3
  high-yield   90e
  index-linked   **95**, 219, 290, 291–2, 396,
    408
  maturity   88, 89
  non-government issuers   **92–3**
  non-investment-grade bonds   **98**
  par value   88
  pension portfolios (Europe versus UK,
    2003–11)   131, 132e
  securitized   90e
  sub-investment-grade   **98**
  types   **93–6**
  variable rate   95
  see also   Bunds
boom and bust   60, 67
  adverse effects of inflation   **63–4**
Boots plc   88
bootstrapping   114, 115
borrowers
  versus lenders   63
  preferences   **121–2**, 124
Bowie, D.   93
Brazil   55e, 95, 130e
'break the buck'   84–5
break-even inflation rate   219, 219e,
    291–2, 298–9, **300**
Bridgewater Associates   317
Brigden, A.   202n, 311n
Brinson, G.P.   214n
'British Experiment' (1979–)   70, 70n
British Gas   332
British Land (REIT)   163
British Petroleum (BP)   xiv, 129, 129e,
    131, 332, 442

Brooks, C.   316–17n
Brown, G.   75–6
brownfield sites   158, 160
Brundtland, G.   443n
'buckets' (five-year periods)   109
Buffett, W.   250, **457–8**, 481, 487, 494, 500
'building block approach' (asset-class
    returns)   231e, 232, 240, 248
Bunds (German government bonds)   91,
    98, 112
  see also   corporate bonds
business cycle   229
business schools   176
buy-ins, buy-outs   45, 45n
buyout firms   **326–8**
buyout funds   324, 345
  'outperform VC funds'   330, 345
BVCA survey (2009)   330n

Cadbury Code (1992)   435, 436
Cadbury Committee (1994)   434
calculation agents   419
call options   263, **264–5**
  FTSE 100 index futures contracts
    266–8
  long call versus short call   264e, 265
  out-of-the-money   384
  payoff profile   **264–5**
call premium   96, 267e, 267–8
callable bonds   95, **96**
Camerer, C.   473
Cameron, D.   463
Canada   55e, 73e, 90e, 130e, 137e,
    218–19e, 432
capacity constraints   **498–9**, 507
Capital Asset Pricing Model (1960s–)
    191–7
  CAPM equation   370
  'single-factor model'   196
capital gains   150, 151e, 164
capital and labour   55, 58
CAPS   (Combined Actuarial Performance
    Services)   375, 376
career average related earnings (CARE)   3,
    3n, 9n, 10b, 22
'carried interest'   325
carry (investment style)   **339**
cash (chapter five)   **79–85**; 148–9b, 231e,
    347m 384, 393, 400, 401e, 408
  annualized, total real returns (UK,
    1900–2010)   149t
  expected return   **220–1**, 222

returns (UK, 1900–2010) 212, 213e
cash deposits 80, **81**
cash flow 41, 99, 99e, 147, 159, 193n, 202, 203–4, 228, 310
cash flow matching 292
cash flow profiles
 transformation using swaps **292–301**
cash flows 162, 305, 328, 329e, 329, 349–52, 424b
cash market/cash purchase 252, 252n
cash rates 112, 115
cash settled futures contract 259, 261
'casino capitalism' 430
Cass Business School (2003–) 13–14n, 17n, 70n, 185n, 308n, 373n, 414
CBOT thirty-year T-bond 260e
centenarians 7, 412
central banks 52, 59, 66, 68, 73–4, 123, 220, 231
 inflation-targeting (1970–) 72–3e
CEOs 26, 435, **440b**
Certificates of Deposit (CDs) **83**, 84
chapter 11 bankruptcy (USA) 315
Charkham, J. 434
Chatfeild-Roberts, J. 505
'cheapest to deliver' phenomenon 260
Chicago Board of Trade (CBoT) 251
Chicago Board Options Exchange (CBOE) 263
chief financial officers 445n
Chief Investment Officer (CIO) 32, 46
China 53, 54–5e, 55, 56–7, 130e, 331
 world's largest companies 128e, 128–9
Chrystal, A. 52n, 64
City University Business School 70n
Civil Service 2
Clare, A. xv, 149n, 166n, 185n, 196n, 243n, 247, 308n, 311n, 316–17n, 373n, 376n, 456n
clearing houses 251n, 255
climate change 443, 444, 448e
'clip' 421, 422
cloned hedge funds (2004–) 316, 319e
closing out **254–5**
Coates, J. 482
code of practice 27n
cognitive biases 458, 484
cognizance tests **454–6**
Colbert's dictum 44n
collateral 302, 403, 413, 416n, 419, 426
 for swaps **408–9**
collateral agreements 420, 420n

collateral flows **295**, **300–1**
Columbus, C. 248
Combined Code on Corporate Governance (Hampel Committee, 1998) 435–6
commercial paper **83**, 84
commercial property 155, 159, 165–6b, **167–8**, 174, 297, 493–4
commodities **331–6**, **345**; xvi, 79, 188, 199n, 307, 310, 342, 384
 futures contracts (physical settlement) 259
 methods of investment **332–4**
commodity futures funds 333, 345
 'headaches' 344e
commodity futures indices **333–4**
commodity futures return
 'other sources' **334–6**
communication to members
 clear and relevant **34b**
'Communication on Progress' 445
companies 131
 corporate governance framework **435–6**
 'corporations' 55–6, 56–7
 equity share capital 126
 fixed costs versus total costs 193n
 leverage and firm profitability 327e
 state-owned 131
 see also corporate governance
Companies Act (2006) 435
company secretary 43
competitive advantage 139, 496
complex adaptive systems 484
concentration (of portfolio) 504b
confidence 238, 245
confirmation bias **463**, 478
conflicts of interest 29, 29n, 43, 49, 50, 437
constant net asset value (CNAV) 84–5
Consumer Prices Index (CPI) 3n, 4, 6, 6n, **61**, 73e, 221, 290, **339–40**, 396
consumers 56, 57–8, 131
 microeconomics 52
 opportunity cost 51
consumption 216–17
contingent assets 48n, 203, 512
Continuing Professional Development (CPD) 446
contrarian investing **142**, 491–2b, 506
convertible arbitrage 315
conviction 492
copper 332e, 335e
core-satellite portfolios **384**, 389
corporate bond index 100

corporate bond portfolios   365, 385, 493–5
  tracking error (targeted)   364
corporate bonds   14n, 19b, 96, 80, 88, 90e,
    93, 111, 169, 177n, 185, 277, 284, 294,
    296–7, 400–1, 401–2e, 420, 425b, 443
  AA-rated sterling   393–5
  credit premia (by rating and
    maturity)   227e
  credit premia (by rating over time,
    2003–11)   227e
  and credit risk   **97–101**
  credit risk premium   **225–8**
  currency of denomination   280
  direct investment versus CDSs   276
  economic environment   227–8
  high-yield   307, 310–11
  impact on deficit VaR of inflation and
    interest rate swaps   411e
  see also   coupon-paying bonds
corporate default risk   204
corporate finance
  alternative sources   131
corporate governance   126, 326, 365,
    434–42, 449
  company chairman versus CEO   435
  'comply or explain' regime   435
  creation of shareholder value
    (magnificent seven)   **439–40b**
  election of directors   441–2
  framework (companies)   **435–6**
  framework (trustees)   **436–8**
  impact on share price performance
    429
  influence of institutional investors
    441–2
  nature   429
  'prevention better than cure'   442
  relationship with share price
    performance   **438–40**
  voting activity   435, 436, 437, 438
corporate governance premium   **440b**
corporate governance specialists   437–8
corporation tax   164
correlation   **160**, 171b, **177**, 184, 186,
    187, 209, 215–16, **231–7**, 310
  calculation   182e
  sophisticated techniques of
    analysis   234n
  UK equity market versus other major
    markets   183e
correlation coefficient   **181–3**, 189b
corruption   445n

Corus   26
'cost of living'   6n
counterparties   171–2b, 255, 280–2, 413,
    417, 420, 425b
  inflation swaps   289, 291
  interest rate swaps   294, 295, 296
  swap contracts   283–4, 284n, 285, 300
counterparty documentation   419
counterparty risk   40n, 49, 84, 176, **204–5**,
    209, 251, 251n, 277, 379, 408, 419, 509
coupon/s   88–9, 107, 124, 349
  definition   88
coupon-paying bonds   118, 124
  two-year   120
  see also   gilts
coupon-paying curve   115, 115e
  upward-sloping versus downward-
    sloping   122
covariance   **181–3**, 188b, 192–3
  calculation   182e
covenant consultant   38e, **40–1**, 202
Cowan v Scargill (1984)   431
Cowes, A.   377n, 452
credibility   72, 220, **224–5**
credit analysts   365
credit card companies   93
credit default swap spreads   41, 202,
    202n, 205
  definition   41n
credit default swaps (CDSs)   250, **272–8**
  counterparty risk   277
  distinguishing features   **274–5**
  foreign exchange risk   277
  as insurance   **273–5**
  issues worth noting   **277–8**
  maturities   **275–6**
  'naked' transactions   274, 274n
  OTC instruments   277
  payments   **275**
  physical settlement   277–8
  structure   273e
  trading   **276–7**
credit derivatives   **249**
credit premium   277
credit quality   **84**
credit rating agencies   85, 92, 205
credit ratings   41, 84, **85**, **97–101**, 202,
    225–6, 408, 493
  bases   **97**
  definitions   98e
  see also   ratings outlooks
credit risk   **97–101**, 273, 276, 353

credit risk premium
   corporate bonds **225–8**
credit spreads 83, **100–1**
Credit Suisse Global Investment Returns
   Sourcebook (2011) 81, 140, 147n,
   151n, 456–7n
Credit Support Annex (CSA) 419, 420
currency (actively managed) xvi
currency exposure 358
currency pairs 337b
   see also exchange rates
custodian 38e, **48**
'cut weeds, cultivate flowers' (Lynch)
   467
Cuthbertson, K. 367n, 376n
cyclically adjusted PE (CAPE) ratio 152–3

Darwin, C.R. 482
data deficiencies 156, 238, 305, 331,
   341–2, 344e, 373, 374, 385n, 414, 67n
   'inadequate information' 445, 450
   'incomplete information' 459, 484
   information 'rarely perfect' 457
   'unknown unknowns' (Rumsfeld) 176,
      208, 209
de-risking 16, 31, 280, 412, 415, **428**
de-risking consultant **47, 416**
de-risking obsession 426–7
de-risking process
   compliance 420
   setting up the infrastructure 416e,
      418–21
de-risking programmes
   changes in market conditions 423e
   dynamic strategy flow chart 421e
   execution and implementation 416e,
      421–4
   'hedging levels' or 'trigger points' 417
   new relative value opportunities **424–5b**
   'over-hedging' versus 'under-hedging'
      422–3
   post-execution 416e, **426**
   practicalities of implementation **415–27**
   relative value opportunities **422–5**, 426
   tactical refinements **422–3**
   timing 416n
   'yield inversion' 423n
de-risking timeframe **420**
De-risking Working Party (DWP) 416e,
   418, 420–2, 426, 428
deadweight loss 204
death 44, 44n

debentures **96**
debt (investment-grade) **98e**, 98
Debt Management Office (DMO) 82, 92,
   410
decentralization **470**, 475, 480b
decision-making **34b**, 484, 503b, 511
   ESG factors **431–3**
   microeconomics versus
      macroeconomics 52
   sub-optimal 497
   trustee boards and investment
      committees **477–80**
'deep discount' 94
Deepwater Horizon disaster (April 2010)
   442
default 83, 94, 98e, 157, 170–2b, 177n,
   202n, 204–5, 218, 225, 228, 255,
   274–8, 284, 296–7, 302, 495
   global rates (1970–2008) 226e, **226–7**
   recovery rate 100
default funds 22, 33, 510, 512
   see also defined contribution default
      funds
default investment option 510
default rates **99–100**
default risk 353
   'insolvency risk' 42
default strategy **34b**
deferred shares **127**
   see also equities
defined benefit (DB) schemes xiv–xvi,
   2–11, 14, 18b, 21–3, 32–3, 87, 100,
   108, 112, 124, 126, 156, 159, 280,
   358, 433, 447
   active versus passive management
      choice 512
   'additional benefits' 4
   asset allocation (2003–11) 213, 214e
   asset portfolio 79–80
   assets 19
   assets and liabilities 44, 511
   assets and liabilities (financial risk) 45
   basis 3
   benchmarks (asset-performance) 45–6
   buyout providers 398, 398n
   combined SRI strategy **447–9**
   contingent assets **39–40**
   contributions 4–5
   deferred members **5–10**
   deficits 201–2, 306, 306n, 398, 427,
      506
   deficits (and recovery plans) **44–5**

defined benefit (DB) schemes – *continued*
　definition　3
　inflation swaps　289
　interest rate and inflation swaps　281,
　　283
　investment policy　45–6
　investment strategy　39, 44
　investment strategy (riskiness)　42, 44
　'less than fully funded'　391, 427
　liabilities　7–9, 124, 510
　liabilities 'still have decades to run'
　　510
　main players　**37–50**
　pensions promise　510–11
　'principal aim'　391, 511
　private sector　203
　protection against falling interest
　　rates　302
　protection against inflation　302
　surplus of assets over liabilities　305
　swap contracts　302
　triennial actuarial valuation　**44–5**
　trusteeship　**509–13**
　see also　defined contribution schemes
defined contribution (DC) default funds
　xvi, **15–19**
　improving outcome for members
　　18–19b
　liability-matching approach　18b
defined contribution schemes　xv, 2, 10,
　11–14, 21–3, 510
　assets　19
　default investment option　33
　'domination of pensions
　　landscape'　**19–21**
　investment governance　**32–4**
　main players　37
　principles of good investment
　　governance (2010)　33–4b
　principles of good investment
　　performance　33–4b
　realistic expectations　510–11
　'trust-based' versus 'contract-based'　34b
　'trust-based' versus 'employer-sponsored'
　　11
　trusteeship　**509–13**
　see also　occupational pensions
deflation　66, 74, 150b, 396
Delta Two　26
demand　**67–8**
Department of Work and Pensions
　(DWP)　7, 412

dependents benefits　4
de-risking consultant　38, 47, 416
derivatives (chapter eleven)　**249–78**; xvi,
　47, 204, 312–13, 315–16, 334, 336,
　347, 403n, 486, 509, 511
　characterization　**272–3**
　exchange-traded　251
　'financial WMD' (Buffett)　250
　foreign currency risk　337, 338
　market size　249, 251
　over-the-counter　48
　see also　inflation swaps
derivative contracts　204
Deutsche Bank　**440b**
Deutschemark (DM)　71
Dhar, S.　311n
Diageo plc　40, 203
Dimson, E.　147n
directional strategy hedge funds　315
disaster magnification　**463**, 463n
disaster myopia　**462–3**, 464, 475
disclosure　437
discount rate　102–3, 110–11, 113–14
discounting
　bond prices　**101–3**
　plain vanilla bonds　**102–3**
'distressed securities'　313
diversification　31, 161, 168, 171b, 172–4,
　183–6, 187, 234, 308, 310, 311n, 331,
　366, 381, 389, 402e, 411e, 425b, 468,
　483
　advantages　184
　international　466
　see also　alternative asset classes
'diversified growth funds'　212
diversity (wisdom of crowds)　**470**, 472–3,
　477–8, 484, 512
dividend cover ratio　**134**
dividend discount model (DDM)　**143–6**,
　150, 151e, **228–30**, 481, 503b
　adjustments　**146–50**
　application　**230**
　matrix　145–6
dividend payments　9, **126–7**, 349, 510
　preference shares　**127–8**
dividend per share (DPS)　133, 134
dividend yield (DY)　**133–4**, 135–6, 136e,
　140, 143, 145–7, 153, 165b, 239,
　456–7, 457n, 494, 503b
　calculation　133
dividends　88, 97, 131, 213, 238, 258,
　381, 382b, 472, 473

growth 139
  importance **150–1**
  non–paying firms **147**
  paid net of tax (UK, 1997–) 133n, 150n, 164n
  re-investment **150–1**, 153
  real growth 145–6
  real long-term growth rate **229**
  REITs 164, 164n
  temporary increase **146–7**
DJStoxx50 440b
Doctrine of Chances (de Moivre, 1733) 208n
Dodds, D. 139–40, 493
Dominion (credit rating agency) 97
dotcom bubble 141–2, 153, 165b, 200, 232, 233e, 239, 380, 380n, 472–3, 488, 495
Dow Jones Industrial Average Index 148n, 356, 357e
  (1929–54) 461n
  (1987 crash) 464n
Dow Jones-UBS Commodities Index (DJ-UBSCI) 333e, 333
due diligence 163, 171n, 320, 341, **343–4**, 487, 497, 503b
  longevity swaps 414–15
Duffield, J. 496
duration
  and bond portfolio management **108–11**
  definition 108
  expression in percentages versus expression in years 105
  influences **106–8**
  key bond risk parameter **105–11**
  and maturity 107, 107e
  valuation of pension scheme liabilities **109b**
duration positioning 109

earnings momentum 241, 242e
earnings per share (EPS) **134–5**
'earnings surprise' 466
Eastern Europe 95, 440b
economic cycle 75, **238**, 247e, 248
economic growth 196, 223, 231, 376
  conventional measure **53–5**
  expected real, long-term 217
  macroeconomics **52–60**
  paradigm shifts 217, 218
  too rapid versus too slow **58**
  see also trend economic growth

economic well-being 53
economics **51–2**, 77
  definition 51
economies of scale 171b, 487
  hedge funds versus investment funds 319e
Edmonds, N. 279–80
educational attainment 53
efficient frontier **186**, 187e, 209, 215e, 215–16, 232, 234, 310, 311e
  derivation **188–9b**
  shape and position (determination) **187–8**
efficient market hypothesis (EMH) 377, **452–8**, 469, 481–4
  challenged 460
  inconsistencies with reality 458–9
  inconsistent evidence **456–7**
  'questionable assumptions' **453–6**
  'three forms of efficiency' 452
  see also market inefficiency
efficient portfolio (Markowitz) **177**, 190
Einstein, A. 483
Eleventh of September (2001) crisis 405e, 405–6, 463n
emerging market debt 90e, 307, 310
  'headaches' 344e
emerging market government debt (EMD) 207
emerging markets 139, 308, 313, 384, 440b, 498–9
  equity market (standard deviation, 1990–2010) 181e
  equity market correlation 183e
  government bonds 92
employees 4–5
  automatic enrolment (pension provision) 38
employers 2, 14, 20–3, 38
  burden of DB schemes 10–11
  see also scheme sponsors
employment 52, 60, 64
endowment effect **463**, **498**, 504b
energy 332, 333–4e, 443
Engaged Investor 27
enhanced indexation **384**, 389
Enron 242e, 435–6, 467, 495
Environmental, Social and Corporate Governance (ESG) factors **429–50**; xvi–xvii, 30n, 126, 160n, 207, 499, 509
  'broad spectrum' 430n

Environmental, Social and Corporate
  Governance (ESG) factors – *continued*
  composition and importance   **434–49**
  corporate governance   **434–42**
  incorporation into investment
    decision-making (legality)   **431–2**, 449
  incorporation into investment
    decision-making (methods)   **432–3**
  policy disclosure   **433–4**
  see also   ethical investment
equal weighting (equity indices)   **356,**
  357–8
equities (chapter seven)   **125–53**; 45n,
  88n, 228, 239, 347, 364n, 393, 456–7,
  493
  annualized, total real returns (UK,
    1900–2010)   149t
  domestic versus foreign   308, 309e
  domestic versus non-domestic   131,
    132e
  failure to deliver   306
  global (investment rules)   243–4
  impact on deficit VaR of inflation and
    interest rate swaps   411e, 412
  large-cap (UK)   367
  'negatively skewed'   199
  other references   xvi, 16–17, 81, 159,
    173, 175, 213–15, 235–7, 246, 247e,
    250, 309, 310, 311e, 384, 393, 400–6
  overseas   441
  pension portfolios (Europe versus UK,
    2003–11)   131, 132e
  returns (UK, 1900–2010)   212, 213e
  stress/scenario testing   405
  types   **126–8**
  undervalued versus overvalued   311
  see also   ordinary shares
equity analysts   365, 496
equity exposure   261, 270
equity fund managers   342, 342n
  see also   fund managers
equity funds   367n, 376
equity hedge strategy   314e, **314**
equity index futures contracts   **256–9**
  drawback   263
  hedging using   **261–3**
  pricing   **257–9**
  typical specifications   256, 256e
equity indices   **354–5**
  arithmetic versus geometric
    averaging   **356–8**
  construction   357e

equity investment styles   **139–43**
  contrarian investing   **142**
  fundamental analysis   141
  'growth' versus 'value' investing   **139–40**
  momentum investing   **141–2**
  stock picking   **142–3**
  technical analysis   141
  thematic investing   **142**
  valuation spreads   **140–1b**
equity large-cap managers   501
equity markets   80
  correlation   183e
  global (relative size, 2010)   130e
  global (structure and size)   **128–32**
  standard deviations (1990–2010)   180,
    181e
  see also   stock markets
equity mutual funds   375
equity portfolio   365
  tracking error (targeted)   364
equity prices   57, 74, 75e
  see also   share price
equity risk premium (ERP)   31, 127,
    144–6, 147–8b, 165b, **228–31**
  'potentially rewarded' risk   399
  average *ex post*   149–50b
  ex post   147–8b
equity valuation
  long-term metrics   **152–3**
ethical investment   21, 448e
  see also   sustainable and responsible
    investment
euro   337b
Euro Overnight Interbank Average
  (EONIA)   85
Eurobonds   **96**, 355
Europe   172, 173e
  equity returns: hedged and unhedged
    (volatility 1990–2010)   337, 338e
  source of private equity funds (2010)
    324e
European Bank for Reconstruction and
  Development (EBRD)   88n, 93
European Court of Justice   14n
European Economic Area   318n
European Investment Bank (EIB)   93
European Union: Economic and
  Monetary Affairs Committee   274n
Euro-zone   73e, 98, 144n
  government bonds   91, 91e
  governmental control of currency
    (lacking) 218n, 222n

non-government issuers (of bonds)
92e, 93
EVCA 330n
event-driven strategy 313, 314e, 315, 318
excess return 197
Exchange Rate Mechanism (ERM) 71, 315
exchange-rate targeting 70–2, 77, 78
exchange rates 196
  fixed versus floating 71
  portfolio management (attribution
    analysis) 361–2
  US dollar versus pound sterling 339–40
  see also foreign exchange
'execute and forget' (swap strategy) 417
'existing use' value 172b
expectations theory (of yield curve)
  122–3, 124
expected returns 186, 187e, 187, 188–9b,
  192, 209, 215e, 215–16, 230
  change of view 231
  long-term 216–25
  risk versus reward 234, 235e
  see also alpha
expected risk 178, 179, 188b
expected risk premium 248
expected risk-less real return 216–18, 225
expenditure approach (GDP measurement)
  56, 57e
'expert problem' 474–7
experts 480b
  'hedgehogs' versus 'foxes' (Tetlock)
    474–5
exports 57, 71
extending portfolio duration 292–7, 301
externalities 444, 446, 450

factors of production 56
'fail to plan, plan to fail' 399
'fair value' 142, 243, 258, 382b, 481, 492
falsification theory (Popper) 463, 477, 481
Fama, E. 377n, 452, 452n, 457n, 483
family offices 318, 319e
Fawlty Towers 65
fear gauge (VIX) 242e, 242–3
Federal Reserve Funds Rate (FFR) 85
fees 48, 157, 163, 205, 264, 281, 294,
  296, 312, 320, 328, 331, 341, 343,
  344e, 366–8, 375, 377, 379, 381,
  383b, 384, 387b, 389, 406, 437n,
  452, 487, 492–3, 499, 500–1, 503b,
  507, 509
  '2 and 20' structure 316

hedge funds versus investment
  funds 319e
  performance-related 316–17, 319e
  traditional investment funds 317
Fidelity Special Situations Fund 489, 506
fiduciary duty xv, 26–7, 29, 33, 431–3,
  442, 477
fiduciary manager 32, 46
final salary pensions 3, 6, 7, 10b, 17e, 109b
financial bubbles 471
financial crisis (1929) 208, 240n
financial crisis/credit crunch (2008–) 32,
  75–6, 78, 81, 91, 101, 129, 140b, 176,
  187, 203, 208, 218, 223, 225, 227e,
  228, 274–5, 286, 312, 324, 342n,
  383b, 429, 457, 462, 466, 488
  hedge funds 320–2
  see also Lehman Brothers
financial gearing 97, 99, 99e
financial market risk 209
  hedging 269, 270–2, 278
financial markets
  'complex adaptive systems' 475–6
  failure to exhibit 'wisdom of
    crowd' 471–4
  forecasting 475
  non-linear relationships 476n
financial ratios 97, 99, 132–3, 153, 226
Financial Reporting Council 436
Financial Services Authority (FSA) 318n,
  435, 438n
Financial Times 208, 372b, 454, 474, 483
'financial WMD' (Buffett) 250
fine wines 48n
fire 464
first movers (in investment markets) 32
fiscal deficits 423n
fiscal policy 75–6, 78
fiscal 'prudence' (Brown) 75–6
Fisher, I. 240n
Fitch 85, 97
'flexible drawdown' arrangements 11n
floating rate notes (FRNs) 89, 94–5, 283
  'asset-backed' versus 'bank-backed' 95
flood insurance 463n
'flow concept' 56
Fooled by Randomness (Taleb, 2004) 176n,
  462n
forecasters *see* 'expert problem'
forecasting 232
foreign currency reserves 71
foreign currency swap 280

foreign exchange/foreign currency   79,
    307, 310, **336–41**, **345**
  active currency management   **337**, 345
  'asset class in own right'   337, **338–40**,
    341
  currency management performance
    evaluation   **340–1**, 345
  currency overlay manager   **337–8**,
    340–1
  specialist currency fund managers
    338–40
  undervalued versus overvalued
    currencies   340
  see also   currency
foreign exchange funds
  'headaches'   344e
foreign exchange markets
  daily turnover   336
foreign exchange risk   81, 173, 277, 337
Fortune magazine   311, 312, 312n, 475n
forward contracts (derivatives)   **250–3**
  closing out   255n
  independent custodian   255n
  profit and loss   253e, 253
forward interest rates   **116–18**
  calculation   117e
  relationship with zero coupon
    curves   **119–20**
forward PE ratio   **135**
forward rates   **122–3**, 287b, 288e, 288b
forward yield curve   **116–18**, 283
forward yields   124
forwards (bespoke OTC contracts)   278
forwards and futures (derivatives)   **250–3**
forwards, futures, options   **250**
framing   **466–8**
framing errors   460, 461, 484
France   55e, 76e, 90, 90e, 130e, 131,
    137e, 159, 163, 218–19e, 251n, 432,
    461n, 502
France Telecom   **275**, 276–7
FRC [Financial Reporting Council]   **437–8**
free-riding   382, 441
'free float' indices   **353**, 381
freehold   158b, 167
French, K.   457n
Freshfields Report (2005)   **431–2**, 433
Friedman, M.   61, 64, 65, 70
FRS 17 (accounting standard)   111, 394
FT SchemeXpert   27
FT30 index   356, 357e
FTfm   439n, 445n, 502n

FTSE 100 index   145–6, 213, 352, **354**,
    356, 357e, **358–61**, 378, 381, 441
  derivatives contracts   278
  highest point (1999)   307
  moving average indicator   244e
  options contracts   **270–2**
  quarterly reshuffles   379n
  seasonality   243, 244e
FTSE 100 index futures contracts   **256–9**,
    261–3
  options   **266–8**
  options (payoff profile)   **268**, 269e
  trading options   **269**
FTSE 250 index   **354**, 379n
FTSE 350 index   436n, 440b, 442
  growth index   138, 138e
  value index   138, 138e
FTSE All-Share Index   47, 129, 129e,
    131, 150, 151e, 191–3, 213, 316, **354**,
    362e, 375, 490, 506
  benchmark   367–8
FTSE Fledgling index   354
FTSE International   354, 355
FTSE Small Cap index   **354**
full replication (indexing method)   **378**
fund management industry size   452, 452n
fund manager selection   xvii, 46n, 50,
    139, 163, 196, 205, 206, 353, 363,
    364n, 366, 377, 400, 448e, 462n,
    485–507, 512
  importance   485
  past performance as guide to future
    486, 487, **488–90**
  'fund manager skill'   **194–6**, 197, 384,
    400, 487, **488–90**, 506
  limitations of short-term data   485
  see also   alpha
fund managers   31, 37, 38e, **46–7**, 49, 141b,
    433, 437, 438, 443, 449, 451, 465–6
  'active fund-management game'   367
  active (selection)   **487**
  agency risks   **205–6**
  appointment   45
  assessment   486
  corporate (further attribution analysis)
    361–2
  corporate (performance attribution)
    358–61
  investment philosophy and
    process   485
  large-cap developed market   499
  outperformance   489

passive (selection) **486–7**
performance database (Clare and
    Wagstaff) 367, 367n, 368e
personal 375
personal (performance) **373–4**, 374e
philosophies 206, 206n
sex **502**
viewpoints **372b**
see also passive fund management
fund of funds (FoFs) 161, **163**, **320**,
    321e, 331, 443
  fees 320
  source of private equity funds
    (2010) 324e
fundamentally weighted indices **382**,
    382–3b, 389
'funded' (definition) 2
funding and investment issues
  main players **37–50**
funding stop gaps 48
'future receivables' 93
future value (FV) 101, 102, 103e, 110
futures contracts (derivatives; 1848–)
    250–3, 270, 381n, 486
  closing out **254–5**
  face value 261–2
  hedging **253–4**, 271, 272
  hedging cash position 254e
  margins **255–6**
  notional value 255
  number (N) 261–2
  'physical settlement' 259
  price (derivation) 252
  profit and loss 253e, 253
  standardized and exchange traded 278
  term 257–9
futures curve (commodities) **334–5**, 345
futures price
  'arbitrage-free' 258
  deviation from 'fair' price 258
futures pricing (F) **257–9**

G4 nations 251n, 255, 255n, 284, 408n,
    420n
G7 countries 90–1
Galbraith, J.K. 474
gamblers' fallacy **464**, **498**, 504b
Gartmore 496
gearing
  versus beta coefficient 193n
  'financial' versus 'operational' 193n
GEC (1972) Pension Scheme xv

generation baby-boom (1946–65) 33n
generation X (1966–1981) 33, 33n, 510
generation Y (1982–1995) 33, 33n, 510
geo-political risk 173
Germany 55e, 59, 90e, 91, 130e, 131,
    137e, 155, 159, 251n, 432, 441, 461n
  equity market (standard deviation,
    1990–2010) 181e
  equity market correlation 183e
  inflation (1960–2008) 73e
gilt futures contracts **259–60**, 260e
  trading **260–1**
gilt total return swaps (gilt TRS) **425b**
gilts (UK government bonds) 14n, 91–2,
    97–8, 144–5, 148b, 150, 159, 165–6b,
    169, 205, 207, 235, 277, 353, 384–5,
    393–4, 394e, 400–4, 410, 427
  annualized, total real returns
    (UK, 1900–2010) 149t
  conventional versus index-linked 414
  GRY by maturity 111e, 112
  impact on deficit VaR of inflation and
    interest rate swaps 411e
  index-linked **95**, 231e, 396, 423, 423e,
    425b
  long futures contracts **259–60**, 260e
  long-dated versus short-dated 120,
    123–4
  measure of inflation risk premium
    (1993–2009) **223–4**, 224e
  prices 113e
  returns (1900–2010) 212, 213e
  yield curve 120, 121e, 122, 123–4
  yield benchmark 403n
  yields 19b, 111
  see also government bonds
Glasgow 7, 412n
'global custodian' 206
global listing rules 445
global tactical asset allocation (GTAA)
    307, 310
globalization 233
'going long a stock' 314
gold 187
Goldman Sachs 355
good governance **206–7**
Gorton, G.B. 199n, 335–6, 336n
governance consultants 31n, 480n
Governance Index (Gompers, Ishii, and
    Metrick) 440b
Governance Metrics International (GMI)
    439b, **440b**

governance risk 209
government bonds (1693–) 16–17, 80,
    81, 83, 88, 90e, 100, 108, 112, 174,
    187, 204, 219, 251n, 259, 284, 305,
    384–5, 408–9, 420, 420n
  currency of denomination 91, 92, 96
  global market (composition, 2011) 91e
  index-linked 144–5, 217–18, 218e,
    222, 223, 229–30
  inflation-risk premium 222–5
  RPI-linked 410
  valuations 239
  yield 223
  see also bonds
Government's Actuarial Department
    (GAD) 398
governments 52, 59–60, 66, 444
  'cannot become bankrupt'
    (technically) 144, 222, 225
  fiscal policy 75–6
Graham, B. 139–40, 493
Graham, J. 445n
grain 332
Great Moderation (1998–2007) 476–7
Greater Fool Theory 473–4
Greece 76e, 98
Greenbury Report (1995) 435
Greenspan, A. 241
Greenspan, S. 456
Greenwich (USA) 313
Gross Domestic Product (GDP) 53–5
  data deficiencies 57
  expenditure components 57e
  global (relative size, 2010) 130e
  measurement 55–8
  measurement (discrepancies) 56
  measurement (methods) 56
  per capita (historical progression) 54e
  per capita (USA, 1929–2001) 74, 75e
  trend growth: growth potential 58–60
  world (relative size, 2010) 55e
gross redemption yield (GRY) 103–5,
    105n, 106e, 113e, 115, 117e, 118
  versus bond prices 104e, 104–5
  on gilts by maturity 111e, 112
gross redemption yield curve
  upward-sloping versus downward
    sloping 119–20, 121e, 122
gross redemption yield curve: determining
    factors 120–4
  expectations theory 122–3
  liquidity preference theory 121–2

market segmentation theory 123–4
'unified' theory 124
ground leases 170–1b, 174, 424b
group intelligence 470, 470n
Group Personal Pension Plan (GPPP) 11
group personal pensions 21e, 22
'groupthink' 463, 478, 484
Growth at Reasonable Price (GARP) 139
growth investing 139–40, 142
growth stocks 136–8, 153, 468
Groysberg, B. 496n
Guy, R. 496

Hackman, J.R. 477n
'haircuts' 284, 296, 420, 420n
Hampel Committee (1998) 435–6
Harries v Church Commissioners (1991)
    431
Harvard Business Review 496n
Harvard Business School 440b
Harvey, C. 445n
Haugen, R.A. 456n
hedge fund industry structure 318,
    319e
Hedge Fund Research (HFR) 312, 314n,
    314, 318, 319n
hedge funds (1949–) 311–15; xvi, 79,
    79n, 185, 188, 205, 212, 307–8, 310,
    328, 441
  asset size (2010) 318, 319e
  benchmark 316, 317e, 319e
  categorization 'not easy' 313–14
  closures 320, 321e
  and credit crunch (2008–) 320–2
  definition problems 313, 345
  fees 316, 319e, 343
  'headaches' 344e
  'high water marks' 316–17, 317e
  illiquidity 343
  industry growth (1990–2010) 312,
    313e
  versus investment funds 315–23
  investors 318, 319e
  liquidity 318, 319e
  legal structure 319e
  long and short positions 313, 314,
    314n, 315
  management style 315–16, 319e
  market-neutral 314
  minimum investment 320
  opacity 342, 342n
  performance data biases 322–3, 345

'remuneration package dressed as investment vehicle' 343
return history **341–2**
'skill set rather than asset class' 345
strategies (1990–2010) **313**, 314e
transparency issue **318**, 319e
'hedge ratios' 409, 420
hedges (interest/inflation) 18b
hedging 18–19b, 116, **253–4**, **261–3**, **270–2**
foreign currency risk 337
price **301–2**
'quality' 261
timing **301**, 302
Hermes (activist fund manager) 439n
heterogeneity (real estate) **156**, 174
heuristics 460–1, **461–6**, 484
Higgs Report (2003) 436
high net-worth individuals (HNWI) 318, 319e
high-yield bond credit spreads (USA) 100e, 101
high-yield debt **98e**, 98
high-yield default rates (USA) 100e, 101
hindsight bias **465**
Hirshleifer, D. 471n
historic PE ratio **135**
history 461, 464, 489
'not necessarily good guide to future' 208, 239, 248
Hobman, T. 25
holding companies 41
Hong Kong 163
Hong Kong dollar 77
Hood, L.R. 214n
house prices 74, 75e
Howe, G. 70
HSBC Holdings 128e, 129, 129e
human behaviour (social aspect) **459–60**
Human Development Index 53
human rights 445n
Hume, D. 176n, 462n
'hurdle rate' 315–16, 325, 500
Hutton, Lord 10b

IAS 19 (accounting standard) 111, 394, 398, 400, 405
IBOXX 355
IBOXX £ Gilts All-Maturities Index 378
Iceland 76e
'if it seems too good to be true, it probably is' **513**

illiquidity 312, 341, 344e, **343**, 378, 383b, 421, 461, 499
real estate **156**, 174
'illiquidity budget' 343
illiquidity premium 309
imitation 471–2
implementation partners (LDI) 417, 418, 421e, 422, 424
imports 57, 71
'in backwardation' (futures curve) 335–6
'in contango' (futures curve) 334
in-the-money option **264**, 265, **266**, 268
incentives (wisdom of crowds) **470**
income approach (GDP measurement) **56**
income levels 53
income stream
real estate **158–9**
income targets 366
incomes policy 69–70
independence (wisdom of crowds) **470**, 472
independent trustee 50
index coverage (hedge funds) **323**
index funds 441
index option 270
index tilting **383–4**, 389
index tracking
advantages **379**
disadvantages **379–82**
growing popularity ('problem') **382**
'lower costs' 379
methods **378–9**
misallocation problem **380–1**
same as 'passive investment' 377
index weightings and return averaging **355–8**, 389
'index-hugging' 366–7, 384, 388, 389
versus 'active fund managers' **492–3**
India 55e, 130e, 136–8, 331, 440b
induction problem **476–7**
industrial economists 52
industrial property **168**, 172, 173e
PRP (1990–2010) 166e
Industrial Revolution 55, 217
infant mortality rates 53
inflation 4, 7–9, 12–13, 18–19b, 44–5, 47, 59–60, 81, 109b, 150b, 159, 166b, 174, 204, 212, 216–21, 336, 402e
adverse effects **62–4**
definition 61
differentials (between economies) 338

inflation – *continued*
  impact on deficit VaR of inflation and
    interest rate swaps   411e
  macroeconomics   52, **61–9**
  'monetary phenomenon'   61, 65, 75
  PV01 exposure   **406–8**
  self-fulfilling prophecy   63, 68, 70
  stress/scenario testing   405
  UK versus USA   **339–40**
  unpredictability   63
inflation: causes   **64–8**
  cost-push   **68**, 69
  demand-pull   **67–8**
  'too much demand chasing too few
    goods'   **67–8**
  'too much money chasing too few
    goods'   **65–7**
inflation control: macroeconomic
    policy   **69–72**
inflation expectations/expected
    inflation   63, **218–20**, 223–5, 231,
    248, 260
  surveys   219e, 219–20
inflation hedging   156, 169, 292, **297–300**,
    309, 417, 423, 426
inflation measures   61
inflation protection   461
Inflation Report (BOE)   74
inflation risk   112, 144, 250, 280–1,
    301–2, 393, **395–6**, 398, 400, 420,
    424b, 427
  VaR   403, 403n
inflation risk premium   **222–5**, 230,
    231e
inflation swaps   280, **289–92**, 300, 396,
    403–4, 404e, 414, 420n, 421
  collateral flows   291, 292
  fixed payer versus fixed receiver   290–2,
    303
  impact on scheme VaR   **411–12**
  investment context   **301–2**
  LDI   **409–10**, 415, 427
  maturities   410
  two legs (fixed versus floating)   290e,
    290–2, 298–9, 299e
  see also   interest rate swaps
inflation swaps curve   **422**
inflation swaps market (2000–)   410n
inflation-targeting   **72–5**, 77, 78, 220
  drawbacks   **74–5**
'information cascades'   **471–2**, 480b, 484
information overload   **465**

information ratio   **190–1**, 362, 364, 375
infrastructure   51, 307, 310, 343, 344e
infrastructure companies   95, 410, 423n
infrastructure debt   48n
Infrastructure Investor   171n
'initial margin'   255, 334
initial public offering   328
'insect colony' analogy   475, 480b
institutional investors   82, 320, 323
  'comply or explain' approach   436
  influence on corporate governance
    441–2
Institutional Shareholders Committee
    (ISC)   436
instruments *see* securities
insurance   251n
  credit default swaps   **273–5**
  issuer's bonds against default   202n
insurance companies   5n, 11n, 11–13,
    39, 45n, 123, 204, 413, 414
  source of private equity funds
    (2010)   324e, 324
  'waning influence' in corporate
    governance   441
insurance costs   332, 334, 345
inter-bank market deposits   **83**
interest rate and inflation swaps   **279–303**;
    18b, 47, 88n, 250, 347, 395, 400, 403,
    415
interest rate risk   88, 106e, 108, 112, 116,
    169, 250, 280–1, 301, 302, **393–5**,
    398, 400, 420, 424b, 427, 437
  hedging   423, 426
  'unrewarded'   399
  VaR   403, 403n
interest rate swaps   19b, 301, 302, 395,
    403, 404, 414
  bond fund management   **285**
  collateral   296, 297
  extending portfolio duration   **292–7**
  'fixed for floating'   280–3, 302
  fixed payer versus fixed receiver
    293–4
  impact on scheme VaR   **411–12**
  investment context   **301–2**
  LDI   **408–9**, **410–11**, 415, 427
  market size (2010)   286
  'two legs'   282e, 283, 285, 293e
  see also   LDI
interest rate swaps curve   **422**
interest rate swaps market (1980s–)
    410n

interest rates 18–19b, 44, 52, **69**, 70–2, 77, 96, 334, 339, 402e, 417
    differentials (between economies) 338
    future 124
    impact on deficit VaR of inflation and interest rate swaps 411e
    PV01 exposure **406–8**
    stress/scenario testing 405
    'unrewarded' 47
    yields 400–1
internal rate of return (IRR) 331, **350**
International Finance Corporation (World Bank) 93
International Swaps and Derivatives Association (ISDA) 255n, 284–6, 419, 419n, 425b
    ISDA agreement: Credit Support Annex 284–5
    ISDA counterparty documentation 419
    ISDA documentation 425b
    ISDA Master Agreement and Schedule 419
internet 240, 472
intrinsic value 491b
Invesco Perpetual High Income Fund 489–90
investability issue **353**
investment 27, 64
    corporate 56–7
    price **301–2**
    timing **301**, 302
investment advisers 207
investment analysts 384
investment banks 38e, 40, 40n, 47, **48**, 49, **239–40**, 255n, 279–80, 286, 379, 413, 417, 419, 421e, 423n, 425b, 426, 428
    interest rate swaps 410–11
    swap counterparties 280, 408, 410, 410n
investment beliefs 46
    implementation **32**
    statement **31–2**
Investment Beliefs: Positive approach to institutional investment (Koedijk and Slager, 2010) 31n
investment committees
    decision-making **477–80**
    dissenting views 479b, 480b
    how decisions should be made **478–80b**
    ideal size and composition **477–8**
    leadership **478–9b**

investment consultants 37, 38e, 44, **45–6**, 48–50, 201–2, 205–6, 212, 364, 384, 409–10, 428, 433, 451, 461, 485–6, 487n, 506
    appointment 416e, **416–17**
investment decisions xvii, 30, 30n, 33, 512
    behavioural finance **451–84**
    errors or biases 451
investment education
    online material 28, 35
investment funds
    fees 317
    versus hedge funds **315–23**
    legal structure 319e
    sufficiency of funding 5
investment governance **29–34**, 35, 46, 480n, 511
    1.0 investment governance **29–30**
    2.0 investment governance **30–1**
    advanced level 29, 30, 32, 34
    appraisal services 31n
    DC schemes **32–4**
    'doing right things' **30**, 30n, 35
    'doing things right' **29**, 30, 35
    principles (DC schemes) 33–4b
    principles 2010 (DC schemes) 33–4b
Investment Governance Group (IGG) 33b, 438
    DC sub-group 34b
Investment Management Agreements (IMAs) 47, 50, 432, 449
Investment Management Association (IMA) 385, 436
investment options **34b**
investment outcome
    determinants 18–19b
investment performance
    impact of SRI 429
    relationship with SRI **446–7**
investment philosophy 365e, 366
investment philosophy and process (IP&P) **490–2**, 493–5, 498, **503b**, 505
investment philosophy statements
    good versus not-so-good **491–2b**
investment policy 39
    hedge funds versus investment funds 319e
Investment Property Databank (IPD) 157, 164, 166n
investment risk 39, 510

investment strategy   376
  contrarian   469
  false beliefs   461
investment style   **339**, 364, 364n, 366,
  389, **493–5**, 503b, 507
  real estate   **167**
investment 'technology'   18b
investment trusts   331
investment vehicles   212
  real estate   **160–4**
investor base
  hedge funds versus investment
    funds   319e
investors   xvii, 502
  biases   499
  corporate sustainability (lack of
    concern)   **446**
  hedge funds versus investment
    funds   **318**
Ireland   76e, 98
'irrational exuberance' (Greenspan,
  1996)   241, 457
Irrational Exuberance (Shiller)   458
Ishii [initials n/a]   440b
IT sector   136
Italy   55e, 76e, 90e, 98, 130e, 137e, 138,
  163, 432, 461n
ITV   40, 203

J-curve   **328–9**
Jackson, T.   483–4
'January effect'   456, 456n
Japan   21, 54–5e, 61, 66, 90e, 130, 130e,
  137e, 150b, 155, 159, 163–4, 218–19e,
  220, 339, 432, 461n
  central government debt to GDP ratio
    (2009)   76e
  credit rating   98
  equity market (standard deviation,
    1990–2010)   181e
  equity returns: hedged and unhedged
    (volatility 1990–2010)   337, 338e
  inflation (1960–2008)   73e
  non-government issuers (of bonds)
    92e, 93
Japanese Government Bonds (JGBs)   91,
  91e
  yield curve   120, 121e, 122–3
Jegadeesh, N. and Titman, S.   456n
Jensen, M.   195
Jensen measure of performance   362
Johannesburg Stock Exchange   446

John Lewis   5n
Jones, A.W.   **311–12**, 314
JP Morgan   317
JP Morgan Life-Metrics index   413–14
junk bonds   **98**
Jupiter (1985–)   496
juries   477, 479b

Kahneman, D.   460
Kaplan, S.   330n
Kay, J.   456
Kehoe, C.   328n
Kellaway, L.   372b
Kensington and Chelsea   7, 412n
Keynes, J.M.   176n, 366n, **459–60**, 466,
  472–4, 481
  'better to fail conventionally'   460
  investment insights   **241**
King, (Sir) Mervyn   58n, 463n
KKR   26
Knight, F.   176n
Knightian uncertainty   **176n**
Koedijk, K.   31n

labour   55, 58–9
labour economics   52
labour standards   445n
Lakonishok, J.   456n
land   **157–8**
Land Securities (REIT)   163
Latin America   440b
'law of one price' (arbitrage)   315
'law of small numbers' (facetious)   464
Lawson, N.   67, 70
Learning and Development log   28
'learning problem'   459, 459n
leasehold   **158b**, 167
leasing   157, **169–70b**, **170–1b**, 172b, 174
LeBaron, B.   476n
Lecturing Birds on Flying (Triana, 2009)
  208
Leeson, N.   249, 467
legal structure
  hedge funds versus investment
    funds   319e
Legg Mason Value Trust   489
Lehman Brothers   40, 60, 74, 166–7b,
  200, **204–5**, 232, 233e, 242e, 284,
  284n, 287, 296, 336, 405e, 405–6,
  413, 417, 422, 423, 430, 476, 483
  see also   financial crisis (2008–)
leisure portfolio   142

lender preferences **121–2**, 124
leverage 225, 252, 256, 312–13, 315,
  319e, 322–3, 329, 441
  definition 226
  'double-edged sword' 328
  and firm profitability **326–8**
leveraged exposure (swap markets) 297
Levis, M. 495n
Lex column (*FT*) 474
liabilities
  actives and deferreds 401e
  risks **406–8**
liability driven investment (LDI) **391–428**;
  xvi, 9, 18b, 47, 80, 88n, 108, 124,
  168n, 250n, 255n, 280–1, 511
  'capturing potentially rewarded
    risks' **400**
  de-risking 415, **428**
  eliminating unrewarded risks **400**
  focus **400**
  philosophy **392–3**, 427
  principle 415, 427
  science **399–415**
  seven-stage process flow chart 416e
  stress/scenario testing **404–6**, 416,
    417, 427
  timing 416n
  unrewarded risks 420, 427
  see also over the counter derivatives
Liability-Driven Investment Consultant
  38e, 416
liability-linked income (LLI) assets **168–9**,
  169–72b, 174, **424–5b**, 427
  characteristics **169–72b**
  liquidity premium 169
liability-matching 18b, 509
life assurance 4, 212
life expectancy 7–8, 109b, **397–8**, **412**
  versus GDP per capita **53–4**
lifestyling **15–19**, 21, 22
limited partnerships 312
limited price indexation (LPI) 289, 396
Lincoln, A. 463
linkers **95**
Lipsey, R. 52n, 64
liquidity 225–6, 255n, 337, 345
  definition 226
  hedge funds versus investment
    funds **318**, 319e
liquidity buffers 203–4
liquidity preference theory **121–2**,
  123–4

liquidity premium 169, 425b
liquidity risk 176, **203–4**, 509
listing authorities **435**
Littlewood, J. 505
livestock 333–4e
Lloyds-TSB 204
Lo, A. **482–3**
Local Government Pension Scheme
  (LGPS) 2
lock-in (investor funds) 318
London 159
  foreign exchange market 336b
  prime residential housing 168
London: City of London 168
London: Mayfair 313
London: NYSE Euronext (formerly
  LIFFE) 251
  derivatives exchange 256, 266
  futures contracts 261
  gilts 260e, 260
  options on FTSE 100 futures
    contracts 270
London: West End 168
London Interbank Bid Rate (LIBID) 83
London Interbank Mean Rate (LIMEAN)
  83
London Interbank Offered Rate (LIBOR)
  83, 85, 95, 282, 286, 293–6, 298, 300,
  302, 315–16, 410–11, 425b
London International Financial Futures
  Exchange (LIFFE) 251n
London Stock Exchange (LSE) **126**,
  129–31, 336b, 354, 356, 435
  concentration 129e, 131
  crash (October 1987) 185
  history (1900–2010) 306e, 306–7
  largest listed companies (2011)
    129–30
  volatility and correlations (1970–2010)
    232–4
long bond futures contracts **259–63**
long credit exposure **277**
'long duration' 109
'long in forward contract' 252
'long' position 251–2, 253e, 255
long position in underlying asset 254e,
  254
long-run excess returns 456
long/short fund **312**
longevity 13, 45, 47, 112, 204, 250
longevity bonds 414
longevity derivatives 398

longevity risk   393, **397–8**, 400, 403n,
     426, 427
  buy-in (bulk-annuity) contract   412–13
  insured buyout   412–13
longevity swaps
  'crucial benefit'   414
  due diligence   414–15
  'fixed leg' versus 'floating leg'   413–14,
     415
  LDI   **412–15**, 427
  mechanics   413e
longevity trends   44
loss aversion   **467–8**, **498**, 505b
losses   197–8
lottery   464
LTCM   242e, 467
Lucas, R.   52, 54
luck   196, 371, 372b, 376, 378, 453,
     461–2, 465, **488–90**, 507
Luckraft, G.   496
Lynch, P.   467

Macaulay duration   105n
MacKay, C.   460n., 468
macro strategy   314e, **315**, 318
macroeconomic policy   52, **69–72**, 240
  control of inflation   **69–72**
  exchange-rate targeting   **70–2**
  inflation-targeting   **72–5**
  inflation-targeting (drawbacks)   **74–5**
macroeconomics   **xvi**, **51–78**, 150b, 217,
     219, 238, 499
  definition   **52**
  fiscal policy   **75–6**
Madoff hedge fund   456, 460
management buy-in (MBI)   324
management style   **315–16**, 319e
'manager risk'   348
manager skill   *see*   alpha
margining rules   283–4, 284n
market anomalies   312
market capitalization   **128–31**, **356**, 357e,
     357–8, 496
market capitalization-weighted equity
     index   382–3b
  drawbacks   **380–1**
market cycles   506
market efficiency   31, 384, 388, 389
  see also   efficient market hypothesis
market exposure
  options   **266**
market failure   443, **444**

market inefficiency   443, **444–6**, 448e
  exploitation   309
market information   **445–6**
market irrationality and you
     (Keynes)   **241**, 474
market liquidity   322b
market news   377–8
market risk (beta)   185, 192, 193, 196,
     250, 311, 314, 341, **370–1**
market segmentation theory   **123–4**
market sentiment   238, **241–3**, 247e, 248
market timing   31
market-capitalization weighting   366,
     382, 385
market-neutral hedge funds   **314**
market-neutral strategy   **313**
Markowitz, H.   177, 183–6, 208n, 377n,
     452
Marks & Spencer   5n, 40, 203
mark-to-market accounting (FRS 17,
     2000–)   84–5, 160, 284, 306, 306n,
     408
Marsh, P.   147n
mathematics   7, 44, 106, 108, 112, 144,
     208
maturity   **107–8**, 111–12
maturity buckets   407e
Mauboussin, M.J.   477n
McKinsey   440b
mean-variance chart   187, 191, 209
  see also   efficient frontier
member fund selection   **15–16**
Memorandum of Association   **126**
menu costs (of inflation)   62–3
Mercer Investment Consulting   9n, 311n,
     446n
mergers and acquisitions   315
Messi, L.   377, 426n
metals (industrial)   333–4e
metals (precious)   333–4e
microeconomics   **52**, 77
migration   58, 59
Mill, J.S.   176n, 462n
Miller, B.   489
Miller, P.   475n
Minahan, J.   490n
Minimum Income Requirement (MIR)
     11n
minimum period guarantees   12, 13e
mining sector   129, 129e
modern portfolio theory (MPT)   **177**,
     185–6, 189, 191

modified duration   **105–6**, **107–8**, 395,
   400, 408
   see also   PV01
Moivre, A. de   208n
Molière, J.B.   436
momentum investing   **141–2**, **339**
monetarism   70
monetary policy   231
money   64, 64n
money market funds (MMFs)   80, **84–5**
money market instruments   xvi, 316
money market interest rates   257, 258
money markets   **82–4**
Money Purchase DC pension schemes   11
money supply   65, 66, 70, 78
money-weighted rate of return (MWRR)
   350–1, 352
monopolies   171b
Monty Python   11
Moody's   85, 97, 171n, 225
   research on their own ratings
      (1970–2008)   226e, **226–7**
Moody's Watchlist   99
moral anchoring   **466**
moral hazard   429–30
Morgan Stanley   469
   see also   MSCI
Morningstar database   367
mortgages
   fixed-interest deals   287
   interest rates   121
Motson, N.   185n, 308n, 316–17n
'moving averages' (asset prices)   243,
   244e
MRI technology   482
MSCI [Morgan Stanley Capital
   International]   355
MSCI Barra Value and Growth
   indices   140
MSCI Emerging Markets Index   213
MSCI World index   378, 387b, 387e
multi-asset managers (balanced
   managers)   46
Multi-coloured Swap Shop (BBC)   279
multi-factor risk models   **196–7**, 494
multi-manager funds   161, **163**
multiple deviations   182e, 182
Municipal and Local Authorities   93
mutual funds   312
Myners, P.   27n, 430n, 509
Myners Principles (updated 2008)   29,
   29n, 33b, 438, 438n

Myners Report (2001)   366, 509
myopic loss aversion   **467–8**

Nanda, A.   496n
National Association of Pension Funds
   (NAPF)   33b, 433, 436
   NAPF PolicyWatch   27
National Employment Savings Trust
   (NEST)   **20–1**
'negative roll' versus 'positive roll'
   (commodity futures contracts)   335
negative sum game   368, **376–7**, 389,
   452, 468
negligence   434n
negotiation skills   28
Nemeth, C.   479b
net asset value (NAV)   84n, 135, 152,
   161–2, 164, 382b
net present value (NPV)   281n, 291
Netherlands   32n, 159, 163
neuroscience   **482**
'neutral policy rate'   220–1
'neutral rate of interest'   220–1
'never invest in anything you do not
   understand'   **513**
New Star (2001–)   496
New York foreign exchange market
   336–7b
New York Stock Exchange (NYSE)   356
New Zealand   73e
'Newcits' funds   318, 318n
Newton, Sir Isaac   456, 468, 483
NHS pension scheme   2
NICE decade (1997–2007)   58–9, 463
Nifty Fifty craze (early 1970s)   **139**
Nikkei index   307, 356, **358–61**
Nitzsche, D.   367n, 376n
Nohria, N.   496n
non-executive directors (NEDs)   435–6
normal distribution   **179–80**, 198–9, 208n
   bell-shaped   180e
normal pension age (NPA)   9n, 10b
Northern Rock   430
Norway   53
noughties   101, 159, 160, 166b, 200, 213,
   251, 312, 318, 320, 331, 382b, 391,
   393, 495–6
NTL   495
'numerator' versus 'denominator'   190, 191

O'Sullivan, N.   367n
Obama, B.   463

objectivity   453, **454**, 484
Occupational Pension Schemes (Investment)
   Regulations (2005)   433, 433n
occupational pensions   xiv, xv, 21e, 21–2
   see also   pension schemes
Occupational Pensions Regulatory
   Authority (OPRA)   26n, 38
Odean, T.   502
OECD   55
Oeppen, J.   397
Oesch, D.   439b
off exchange   **251**
'off-benchmark bets'   363
'off-benchmark positions'   353
Office for National Statistics (ONS)   5, 7,
   20–1, 59, 412n
office property
   PRP (1990–2010)   166e
offices   **168**, 172, 173e
oil companies   129, 129e
oil and gas   131, 309, 444
oil price   68, 69, 196, 219, 332–3
'old economy'   381
Oliver Twist   xv, 392, 427
OPEC   68, 69
open market option   11
opinion-validation   460
opportunity cost   **51**, 104, 216–17
'opportunity set'   32, 493
'optimizer routines'   186
option premium   264–5, 269
option writer   263–4, 266
options   263–72
   exchange-traded derivatives   263
   FTSE 100 contracts (hedging)   **270–2**
   FTSE 100 index futures contracts   **266–8**
   FTSE 100 index futures contracts
      (payoff profile)   **268**, 269e
   market exposure   **266**
   OTC   263
   'a right, not an obligation'   278
   'strike' or 'exercise' price   263–4, 266–9
options contracts   278
ordinary shares   **126–7**, 128
   analysis   **132–8**
   deferred   **127**
   dividend yield   **133–4**
   'fully paid up'   127n
   growth versus value   **136–8**
   non-voting   **127**, 127n
   price-to-book ratio   **135–6**
   price-to-earnings ratio   **134–5**

redeemable   **127**
   see also   preference shares
Orissa tribe   442
Osborne, G.   10b
out of the-money expiry   **264**, 265, **266**,
   268
output approach (GDP measurement)
   56
output gap   59, 59e, 67–8
outsourcing   437, 437n
over the counter (OTC) contracts   **251**,
   251n
over the counter derivatives   48, 255n,
   285
   gilt TRSs   425b
   swaps   283–4
   see also   risk management
over the counter instruments   **408**, 419
overconfidence   **465**, 468, 481, **498**,
   504b
overheating   58, 59, 221
overnight repurchase agreements
   (repos)   **83–4**
overweighting
   cyclical stocks in upturn   376
   defensive stocks in downturn   376

Pall (UK) DB scheme   414
Passino, K.M.   475n
passive fund management   353, 509
   performance   **374–5**
   see also   pension fund managers
passive investment   360, **377–83**, **389**,
   441
   benchmark   388
   'big problem'   **383**, 386b
   'buying into past winners'   382
   combined with active
      management   **383–6**, **389**
   indexing methods   **378–9**
   market underperformance 'almost
      guaranteed'   381
   market-capitalization-weighted indexes
      (drawbacks)   **380–1**
   same as 'index tracking'   377
   techniques   348, **389**
Paulson & Co   317
pay-as-you-go schemes   2
Payne, J.   477n
payoff profile
   options on FTSE 100 index futures
      contracts   **268**, 269e

peer group benchmarks **355**, 385e, 386
peer pressure 459–60, 504b
pension fairy **1–2**
pension fund managers
  outperformance 375
  performance **374–6**
  see also private equity fund managers
pension funds 123–4
  client mandates 385e, **385–6**
  'deficit pandemic' (early–2000s) 391–2,
    393, 426
  equity-segregated (UK) 375
  extending portfolio duration **292–7**,
    301
  loss of tax relief (UK) 133n
  'should not fear illiquidity' 343
  source of private equity funds (2010)
    323, 324e, 324
  'waning influence' in corporate
    governance 441
pension industry
  funding issues **37–50**; 5n, 7, 9, 202,
    205, 348, 392n
  shape and size (UK) **21–2**, 23, 26
pension portfolios
  asset breakdown (Europe versus UK,
    2003–11) 131, 132e
  role of equities **131**, 132e
pension promise **1–23**
  cross-references 33, 202, 297, 393,
    395, 396, 485
  improvement 7
Pension Protection Fund (PPF, 2005–) xv,
  9, 38e, 38
  levies **42**, 45
  principles (stability, simplicity,
    smoothing) 42
pension scheme balance sheet
  monitoring and management 426,
    428
pension scheme liabilities **1–23**
  buyout value 111
  typical set **109–10**
  valuation **109b**
  zero coupon rates and ~ **116**
  see also scheme actuary
pension schemes 461
  assets 46
  benchmarking 392
  legal claim on sponsor's assets
    (lacking) 41, 202
  mergers 45

non-contributory 5, 5n
types 21e
work-based 38
  see also TGtI (representative DB scheme)
pensions
  employer-sponsored 21e, 22, 23
  index-linked 395
  macroeconomic background **51–78**
Pensions Acts 30
  (1995) 43
  (2004) 26–7, 38, 40, 417n
Pensions Insight 27
pensions manager 37, 38e, **43**, 44, 48,
  49, 421e, 422
Pensions Policy Institute 10b
Pensions Regulator (tPR, 2006–) 22,
  25–7, 29, 34, 37, 38e, **38–9**, 41, 43,
  49, 438
  Guidance for Trustees 434n
  guidelines 44–5
  website 41n
performance assessment **34b**
performance attribution (portfolio
  management) **358–62**
performance fees **500–1**
performance J-curve (private
  equity) **328–9**
performance measurement (portfolio
  management) **358**
performance persistence **368–70**, 376,
  375–6, 507
  outperformance 'difficult on consistent
    basis' 369e, **369–70**
Personal Pension Plan (PPP) 11
Phelps, E. 207–8
physical assets 307
'physical settlement' 259, 261, 277–8
'physics envy' 481n
'picking up nickels in front of steam
  roller' **322b**
Pirc 441
plain vanilla bonds 91, 93, 103, 108,
  282, 283, 291
  cash flow 89
  price versus GRY 104e, 104–5
plain vanilla UK equities 376
Plender, J. **469**
policy interest rates 286–7
pollution 444
pooled funds *see* unlisted property funds
pooled mandates 47, 48
Popper, Sir Karl 463, 477

'population' (of returns)   179n
portfolio composition   504b
portfolio construction
   three Cs (contrarian, conviction,
      concentration)   **492–3**
portfolio gain   272
portfolio management
   attribution analysis   361e
   benchmarks   **352–4**, 386
   clever passive versus passive
      active   **386–8**
   generating returns   **347–89**; 45–6n,
      129, 191, 196, 205, 212, 316, 331,
      441, 485–8, 490n, 491, 501
   outperformance targets   384
   performance evaluation
      (summary)   **363**
   trend following   **386–8b**
portfolio management: performance
      evaluation   **348–63, 389**
   attributing performance   349e, **358–62**,
      389
   index weightings and return
      averaging   **355–8**, 389
   measuring absolute returns   349e,
      349–52, 389
   measuring relative returns   349e,
      352–8, 389
   MWRR   **350–1**
   risk–adjusting returns   349e, **362–3**,
      389
'Portfolio Selection' (Markowitz, 1952)
      208n
portfolio turnover   366, 502, 504b, 507
portfolio volatility   310
portfolios
   efficient   **186–9**
   optimal size   **498–9**
Portugal   76e, 98
pound sterling   337b, 393–5
Povey, K.   xiii
PowerPoint   491, 497
pre-tax interest coverage   99, 99e
preference shares   126, **127–8**
   convertible   **128**
   participating   **128**
   redeemable   **128**
   see also   property company shares
Premier Inn hotel chain   40
present value (PV)   102–3, 103e, 105,
      106e, 107, 109–11, 113–14, 116, 285,
      287b, 288–9e

price efficiency   451
price level   65, 66
price momentum   456, 456n
price weighting (equity indices)   **356,**
      357
price-to-book (PB) ratio   **135–6**, 136e,
      140, 152
price-to-earnings (PE) ratio   133, **134–5**,
      136, 136e, 140, 143, 152, **239–40**,
      240e, 503b
   historic   **135**
price-to-earnings growth (PEG) ratio   139
Priestley, R.   149n
principal-agent problem   434n
private equity   xvi, 48n, 79, 307, 309e,
      310, **323–31**
   access   **331**
   and credit crunch   **329–30**
   'headaches'   344e
   illiquidity   343
   leveraged buyout vehicles   309
   manager and strategy selection   330
   performance J-curve   **328–9**
private equity firms   126, 323–4
   'break-even' point (target)   328
   'evergreen' investment point   328
   generation of returns for investors
      325–6
private equity fund managers   324
   see also   active fund managers
private equity funds
   capital 'drawn down' or 'put into
      ground'   325, 328
   fees   343
   'general partner' versus 'limited
      partners'   324–5
   opacity   342
   sources (2010)   324e
   timing   **329–30**, 330n
private equity performance   **330–1**, 345
   'average' versus 'median'   330
private equity returns
   illiquidity   331
private equity structure   **324–5**
Private Finance Initiatives (PFIs)   93, 94,
      171n
private limited companies (Ltd.)   126
private sector   21, 203
   trust-based occupational scheme
      assets   26n
probability theory   453, 461–2, 484
product innovation   382

productivity   58, 59, 71, 217n, 231, 240
professional independent trustee   37, 38e, **49**
profit-maximization   431
profitability   41, 126, 146, 147, 202, 225–6, 228, 240, 307, 326, **440b**
profits   56, 57, 64, 131, 229
  source (domestic versus foreign economy)   230
property
  diversified portfolio   161
  long-lease   171b, 172b
  terminology   155n
property companies   93
property company shares   161, **164**, 174
  see also   shares
property cycles   160, 172, 174
property derivatives   **164**
property investment companies   164
property investment trusts   161, **164**
property market crashes   166–7b
property market risk premium (PRP) **165–7b**
prospective PE ratio   **135**
protection buyer   274
Prudential   442
psychology   142, 244, 458, 459–60, 506
public limited companies (plcs)   126
public sector   21–2, 75
  pension provision   10b
  source of private equity funds (2010) 324e
public spending/government expenditure   57, 76, 90
Pudd'nhead Wilson (Twain, 1894)   126
Purchasing Managers Index (PMI)   **245–6**, 246e
purchasing power parity (PPP)   339
'pure alpha'   341
put options   **263**
  expiry   271
  FTSE 100 index futures contracts **266–8**
  'long put' versus 'short put'   **265–6**
  payoff profile   **265–6**
  pay-off profiles (individual and combined)   **271–2**
  strike price   270, 271–2
put penalty   96
puttable bonds   **95–6**
PV01 analysis   **406–8**, 409, 409n, 416–18, 420–1, 426–7

shortcoming   407n
PV01 buckets   422
PV01 interest rate buckets   410

'qualifying workplace pension scheme'   20
Quantity Theory of Money   **65–7**
  direction of causality   **66–7**
Quantum Fund   315

Rajgopal, S.   445n
'random walk'   453
'rating actions'   98
ratings outlooks   **98–9**
  see also   credit rating agencies
rationality   453–4, 459, 464, 482–3, 484
Reagan, R.   68–9
real assets   309
real economy   307
real estate   xvi, 48n, 80,**155–74**, 307, 309, 347, 393, 400, 424b, 443
  'archetypal long-term investment'   174
  attractions   **158–60**
  'attractive income stream'   **158–9**, 169, 170–2b, 174
  derivatives   **164**, 174
  deterioration   **157**
  features   **156–8**, 174
  importance   **155–6**
  long-lease   **169–70b**, 424b
  low correlation with other asset classes   **160**, 171b
  'low volatility'   **160**
  maintenance costs   **157**
  market sectors   **167–9**
  overseas   172–3, 174
  prices   57
  sustainability   **160**
  'tangibility'   **159**
  terminology   155n
  value (UK, 2009)   155n
real estate investment   **160–7**
  direct   **161**, 174
  global   **172–3**
  indirect   **161–4**, 174
  styles   **167**
Real Estate Investment Funds (REITs) 161, **163–4**
  regulations   163
  shares (discount versus premium)   164
  tax efficiency   164

real estate market
  difficult (2007–8)   156, 161
  drivers   172–3, 174
  structure (global, 2009)   173e
real yield   **420–1**
reality/real world   69, 382b, 473, 491b
recessions   240
  'too little demand for too many
    goods'   67–8
Red Book (RICS)   160
Registered Provider (RP)   172b
Registered Social Landlord (RSL)   172b
regulation factor   332–3
reinvestment rate risk   **103–4**
relative returns (portfolio
  management)   **352–8**
relative value funds
  'picking up nickels in front of steam
    roller'   **322b**
relative value opportunities   **422–5**, 426,
  428
relative value strategy   314e, **315**, 318
renminbi   77
rent   158b 159, 169–70b, 174
rental income   56, 159, 165b
rents received, rents receivable   170b
replacement ratios   17
  definition   18b
  median versus worst-case scenarios
    18–19b
  principal determinant   18b
representativeness   **461–3**, 468, 490n,
  497, 504b
reputational risk   433, 439
Research Associates   382b
residential property   159, **168**, 174
resource allocation   51, 444
*Responsibilities of Institutional Shareholders
  and Agents* (ISC, 2009)   436–7, 438
Responsibilities *of Institutional Shareholders
  in UK* (ISC, 1991)   436
responsible ownership (Myners
  Principles)   438, 438n
Retail Prices Index (RPI)   3n, 4, 6n,
  12–13, 15, 17, **61**, 144, 169, 169–72b,
  260, 290e, 290–2, 297–8, 299e, 396,
  407e, 410, 423n, 424b
  RPI (UK)   **339–40**
  RPI(X) inflation   221
retail property   **168**, 172, 173e
  PRP (1990–2010)   166e
retail sales data   57

retirement process
  annuitization (de-accumulation) stage
    33, 510
Return on Assets (ROA)   178e, 440b
  definition   177
'return to benchmark' (currency
  overlay)   338
Return on Capital (ROC)   440b
Return on Equity (ROE)   440b
'return sources'   316
return targets
  hedge funds versus investment
    funds   319e
reward-to-risk ratios   **189–91**, 209
risk   xvi, 9, 15–16, 18–19b, 29–30, 33, 35,
    38, 173, 216–18, 453, 467–8
  definition   **175–6**
  'diversifiable' versus
    'undiversifiable'   184–5, 185e
  'less quantifiable'   **201–5**
  multi-factor models   **196–7**
  potentially rewarded versus potentially
    unrewarded   **399–400**
  rewarded   398–9
  and risk management   18b, 41, 160n,
    175–209, 215, 234, 245, 251n, 362,
    364, 370, 392n, 400, 404
  'systematic' versus 'unsystematic'   184–5,
    185e, 185–6, 197
  unrewarded   281, 302, 398–9, 409,
    416n, 420, 427
risk analysis *see*   PV01
risk assessment   207
'risk budget'   45, 46, 403
risk budgeting   32, 50, 509
  definition   32n
risk burden   20
risk capital   126, 144, 153
risk controls   49
'risk exposures'   316
risk management   31–2, 34, 48, 50, 85,
    207–8, 250, 275, 314, **499–500**, 505b,
    507, 509, 511
  active fund management   365–6
  failure   398
  key element   499–500
  'outdated theory and statistics'   209
  see also   derivatives
risk measurement   176, **177–9**, 512
  quantitative   **201**
risk parameters   47
  bond duration   **105–11**

risk premia   177n, **192**, 194, **221–2**, 309, 345
risk profiles   34
risk reallocation   403, 415, 511
risk versus return/reward   188, 197, 215,
   248, 388, 389, 392, 487
   alternative asset classes   **310–11**
   criteria   366
Risk, Uncertainty and Profit (Knight,
   1921)   176n
risk 'warehousing'   422
risk-adjusted returns   **191–7**, **215**
risk-aversion   453, 476, 484, 479b
risk-less real return   248
risky asset classes   222, **400**
risky asset prices   393
risky assets   177, 177n, 181, 184, 203
Roberts, H.   377n, 452
'rolling them over'   333
Rosneft   131
Rouwenhorst, K.G.   199n, 335–6, 336n
Royal Bank of Scotland plc (RBS)   204
   CDS spreads   **275–6**
Royal County of Berkshire   413
Royal Dutch Shell   128e, 129e, 332–3
Royal Institution of Chartered Surveyors
   (RICS)   160
RSA Insurance   413
rules of game   453
Rumsfeld, D.   **175–6**, 203, 208
Russian Federation   55e 130e
Russian Federation debt crisis (1998)
   200, 242e, 405e

S&P   171n
S&P Credit Watch   99
S&P 500 index   141b, 148t, 192, 199n,
   239, 240e, 242, 244e, 336, 356, **358–61**,
   378, 386b, 387e, 487, 489
S&P Goldman Sachs Commodities Index
   (S&P GSCI)   333e, 333
safety in numbers   459–60, **468–9**
   wisdom of crowds   **469–71**
Sainsbury's   26, 40, 203
salaries   56, 63, 67
   'executive remuneration'   430
   gross bill   202
   private equity industry   326
   see also   final salary pensions
sale and leaseback programmes   170b
Sant, L.   496n
Sapuric, S.   373n
Scandinavia   172, 173e

scenario tests   200–1, **404–6**
scheme actuary   37, 38e, **43–5**, 47–9,
   201–2, 206, 416
scheme auditor   38e, **48–9**
scheme lawyer   37, 38e, 44, **47–8**, 49, 50
scheme risk analysis (LDI)   416e, **417**
scheme secretary   37, **38e**, 49, 43
scheme sponsors   2–5, 9, 15, 20, 37, 38e,
   39–40, 48, 49, 396, 398, 415, 421e,
   422, 428, 506, 512
   closure of DB schemes to new
      entrants   510
   contribution rate   44
   risk profile   42
Schmid, M.   439b
Schoar, A.   330n
Science (magazine)   397
scorecard approach   **245–7**, 248
   'bet' scores   246, 247e
   standardization of indicators ('Z' scores)
      245, 246e
   US equity v. Treasury TAA bet   246, 247e
seasonality   243, 244e
Seaton, J.   243n, 386n, 456n
secondary buyout   325, 328
sector analysts   497
sector selection   358, 362
sectors (of economy)   56
   overvalued versus undervalued   380
'secured creditors'   126
securities   82, 82n
   fixed-income   **88**
Securities and Exchange Commission
   (SEC)   312, 446
'securities' and 'instruments'   82n
Seeley, T.D.   475n
segregated accounts   331
segregated mandates   47, 48
Self-Invested Personal Pension Plan
   (SIPP)   11
self-selection bias (hedge funds)   **323**
sell discipline   **500**
service sector   41, 202
Seventh of July (2005)   463n
sex   **502**
share buy-backs   **147**, 228, 230
share price
   current (P)   133, 134, 135
   see also   equity prices
share price performance
   relationship with corporate
      governance   **438–40**

shareholder rights   440b
shareholder value   430n, 435, 437, 438
  relationship with corporate governance
    (magnificent seven)   **439–40b**
  sustainable   445
shareholders   2, 9, **126–7**, 153, 326, 441,
    445, 449
shares   353
  commodity companies   332
  ex-dividend   381, 381n
  overvalued versus undervalued   380
  see also   deferred shares
Sharia compliance   21
Sharpe, W.   452
Sharpe ratio   **190**, 197, 362, 362e, 363
Shiller, R.J.   152–3, 457n, 458, 465n, 472n
shoe leather costs (of inflation)   62–3
'short duration'   109
'short' position   252–5
short-selling   314, 314n, 322, 339
  periodic bans   473
short-termism   326, 441, 442, **444–5**, 446
'silent footprint'   418
Simonton, D.   488
Singapore   337b
'single factor' models   196
skewness   **199–200**
Slager, A.   31n
Slater, M.,   505
'small-cap' effect   457, 457n
small-cap equity   498, 499
small-capitalization value stocks   487
Smith, A.   434n, 460n
social animals   459–60, 480b, 481
social housing   48n, 168, **172b**, 174,
    424b
social infrastructure   **171b**, 172b, 174,
    424b
Société Générale   **440b**
soft risks   **205–7**, 209, 512
Solvency II Directive (forthcoming)   14n
Soros, G.   71, 315
South Korea   73e
South Sea Bubble   380n, 456
sovereign wealth funds (SWFs)   324e, 441
Spain   76n, 98, 432, 461n
Special Purpose Vehicle (SPV)   40
specialist fund management
    companies   348
specialist mandates   385e, 386
speculation/speculators   472–3, 476
speculative bonds   **98**

sponsor covenant risk   209
sponsor covenants   **40–1**, 42, 46, 176,
    201–3, 392n, 509
  regulator guidance   41, 41n
'spot price'   252
spot rates   112, 115
spouses   397
squared deviations   178e, **178–9**
SSAP 24 accounting   306n
stakeholder pensions   21
stamp duty land tax   157
standard deviation   182, 184–90, 197–8,
    199n, 209, 215, 215e, 232, 245, 336–7,
    338e, 362e, 363–4, 388, 420
  definition   **178**, 179
  equity markets   180, 181e
  interpretation   **179–81**
standard deviation squared   188b, 192
Standard and Poor's (S&P)   85, 97, 225,
    355
standardization (of TAA indicators)   **245**,
    246e
Stanford Business School   440b
Stasser, G.   **478–9b**
State Pension Age (SPA)   10b, 20
State Street Global   317
Statement of Funding Principles
    (SFP)   29n
statement of investment beliefs   35
Statement of Investment Principles
    (SIP)   29–30n, 30–1, 46–7, 50, 419,
    434, 438, 449
statistics   **178–83**, 462n, 464
status   480b
status quo bias   463
Staunton, M.   147n
Sterling Overnight Interbank Average
    (SONIA)   85
stock exchange flotation   325
stock market crashes   476
  (1987)   185, **198–9**, 200, 405, 405e
stock markets   475, 476
  see also   equity markets
stock picking   **142–3**
stock selection   358, 361e, 361–3
'stocks'   126
storage problems   332, 334, 345
strategic asset allocation (SAA)   **214–16**,
    222, **247–8**, 506, 509
  'more art than science'   247, 248
  versus TAA   **235–7**
  '*the* big decision'   **214**, 248

strategic benchmarks **186**
strategic investment portfolio **234–5**
stratified sampling (indexing method)
    378
stress tests 200–1, **404–6**
structured bonds **94**
    very long-dated 110–11, 124
student accommodation 424b
style drift **494**, 495
style factors **139**, **493–4**
style neutral approach **495**
style rotation **495**
'sum' **179**, 179n
supermarkets 170b
supra-national agencies 88
Surowiecki, J. **469–70**, 471, 472
survivorship bias **323**, 367n
sustainability 163
    real estate **160**
sustainability problem **443–6**
sustainable development (Brundtland)
    443
sustainable growth **58**, 59, 77, 78
sustainable and responsible investment
    (SRI) 429, 434, **442–9**, **450**
    combining strategies **447–449**, 450
    'comply or explain' requirement 445
    'engagement' strategy 447, 448e
    ethical investment 447, 448e, 449
    'integration' strategy 447, 448e
    positive screening 447, 448e, 449
    relationship with investment
        performance **446–7**
    'S' ('social' versus 'sustainable') 447
    strategies **447**, **448e**, 450
    strategy-definition **447**
    see also ESG factors
Sustainable Stock Exchanges
    Dialogue 446
    swap 'axes' 419, 421e
swap collateral **283–5**
swap contracts 47, 49, 50
    features **281–5**, 302
    'fixed receiver' versus 'fixed
        payer' 281–5, 302
    'notional amount' 281
swap counterparties 408n, 409
swap rates **286–9**
    calculating a five-year swap rate **287–9b**
    five-year sterling swap rate 286e
swaps (derivative instruments) xvi, 112,
    407e, 426

counterparties 302
    OTC instruments 283–4, 408, 419
    price 415
    sourcing **421**
    timing 415, 416n
    two legs 302
swaps: transformation of cash flow
    profiles **292–301**
    cash flow matching 292, **300–1**
    extending portfolio duration **292–7**
    inflation hedging 292, **297–300**
swaps portfolio
    asset manager 416e, **417–18**
Sweden 73e, 441
Switzerland 19, 130e, 159
synthetic indexing **378–9**
systematic risk **192–3**, 196

T. Rowe Price 139
tactical asset allocation (TAA) **235–7**,
    247–8, 509
    'more art than science' 247, 248
    standardization of indicators ('Z' scores)
        245, 246e
tactical asset allocation process **237–47**
    scorecard approach **245–7**
    technical indicators 238, **243–4**, 247e,
        248
takeover bids 315
'taking a public company private' 126
Taleb, N.N. 176n, 462n
tangibility
    real estate **159**
'target retirement date' (default
    investment funds) 16
target retirement date funds 22
Tata 26
Taube, N. 489
tax efficiency (REITs) 164
tax evasion 56
tax law 378
tax-free lump sum (on retirement) 4,
    11, 17
taxation 2, 4, 76, 81, 90, 96, 103, 126,
    155, 173, 444
    Colbert's dictum 44n
taxpayers 2, 414
teachers 2
teamwork 491–2b, **495–7**, 504b
technology sector 129, 129e, 380, 473
telecommunications 93, 472, 473
television 475

'term structure of interest rates'   121

Tessaromatic, N.   495n

Tetlock, P.   474

TGtI (representative DB scheme): Trustee
   Guide to Investment   xv, xvi, 422
   deficits   **400–4**
   de-risking   404
   de-risking swap strategy   412
   hedging exposure to interest and
      inflation rates   411
   liabilities (impact of alternative
      discount rates)   393, 394e
   liabilities linked to inflation   395e,
      395–6
   liabilities by member-type   8e, 8–9
   longevity risk   **397–8**
   PV01 exposure   406
   reducing unrewarded risk   403, 404e
   unmatched asset and liability
      position   401e
   unrewarded versus potentially rewarded
      risk   402–3
   VaR   **400–4**
   VaR components   402e
   weighted average expected return   393
   see also   defined benefit (DB) schemes

Thatcher, M.H.   68–9, **70**

thematic investing   **142**

Thomas, C.   xiii

Thomas, N.   496

Thomas, S.   149n, 196n, 243n, 386n,
   456n

Thomson Financial total market equity
   indices (2010)   136

Thomson Reuters   330n

Thoreau, H.D.   468

'tick' (minimum price movement)   256,
   256e
   minimum value   260e, 260

timber   307, 309

time   206, 207, 245, 326, 344, 377, 441,
   468, 507

time-weighted rate of return (TWRR)
   351–2

timing   31, **301**, 302, **329–30**, 330n, 376,
   415, 416n
   de-risking programmes   422

tin price (1994–2010)   332e

tipping points   **476**, 484

Tobin's Q-ratio   152–3

Todorovic, N.   373n

Tokyo   337b

Tonks, I.   375

'too big too fail'   40, 430, 476

total factor productivity   **58**

total return swaps   379

Towers Watson   19, 442, 483

tPR *see*   Pensions Regulator

tracking error   366, 378–9, 384, 388,
   492–3, 503b, 505, 507
   meanings   191, 363–4

tracking technology   487

trade unions   68

trailing PE ratio   **135**, 136–8

Training and Development Plan   28

Training Needs Analysis (TNA)   28

transaction costs   **157**, 162, 258, 277,
   281, 285, 378–9, 383b, 389, 418–19,
   426, 500, 502, 509
   swaps   **421–2**

transactions (total number)   65, 66

transparency   **34b**, 164, 337, 345, 414,
   432, 437
   disclosure   445
   hedge funds versus investment
      funds   318
   'opacity'   341, **342**, 344e

Treasury Bills (T-Bills, UK)   **82**, 83, 84

trend economic growth   **58–60**, 67, 145–6,
   217, 218e, 220, 222–3, 229–30, 231e,
   240–1
   definition   59
   determinants   58
   see also   economic growth

Treynor, J.   470n

Treynor ratio   **197**, 362, 362e, 363

Triana, P.   208

Trickett, P.   483

triennial actuarial valuation   48

trigger points   417, **420–1**

triple–A rating   97–8, 98e

trustee agenda   176

trustee boards   26, 27, 29, 34, 40–1, 43,
   49, 203, 377, 385, 388, 391, 418, 420
   decision-making   31n, 206, 207, **477–80**
   good governance   **206–7**
   investment sub-committees   **31–2**
   long-term objective   **392**, 427
   organizational effectiveness   30–1
   succession-planning   207
   training   207
   see also   investment committees

trustee education   25–6, **26–8**, 34
   face-to-face   28

trustee governance
link with investment governance 29
Trustee Guide to Investment
book content **xv–xvii**
book objective/purpose xv, xvii, **5**, 9,
512
'boxes' xv
trustee knowledge and understanding
(TKU) **25–8**, 43
Code of Practice **26–7**, 34, 39, 434n
and investment governance **25–35**,
46, 49, 431
Trustee Toolkit (online) 27
trustees 5, 59–60, 81, 201, 202, 403,
428
corporate governance framework **436–8**
fiduciary duties xv, 431
funding and investment issues
(main players) **37–50**
golden investment rules **512–13**
liability-driven investment **398–9**
power 26
pressure xiv
as risk managers **175–209**
'rule number one' **27**
websites 28
trusteeship **509–13**
Tulip mania (1637) 457
Twain, M. 126, 157
Tyco 436

UCITS III Directive (1985; 2002) 318n
uncertainty 121, 175, 176n, 198, 201,
223, 242, 290, 457, 472
underlying asset
income yield 257, 258
price 257
terminology 252n
see also cash market
unemployment 52, 59, 70, 217
Uniq (ex-Unigate) 40, 203
unit trusts 487
United Kingdom 53–7, 63n, 68–9, 90e,
91, 130, 130e, 133, 135, 140, 145,
147–9b, 153, 156–9, 163–4, 172b,
174–5, 219e, 228, 355, 432, 501–2
annual inflation (since 1750) 61, 62e
bond yields (average real, 2010) 218e,
218
boom and bust 67
commercial property 166b, 166e, **168**
DC schemes 19–20

dividend yield and dividend
cover 136, 137e
equity market (standard deviation,
1990–2010) 181e
fiscal deficit (2010) 76, 77
GDP growth (1956–2008) 60e
index-linked government bonds (1981–)
95
inflation (1960–2008) 73e
inflation target 73e
information ratios on equity funds
(2000–10) 191e, 191
non-government issuers (of
bonds) 92e, 93
price level (since 1750) 61, 62e
real estate market (structure,
2009) 173e
trend growth rate 217, 218e, 220
world's largest companies 128e
United Kingdom: HM Treasury 33b
United Kingdom: HM Treasury: Signed
Projects List 171n
'United Kingdom Corporate Governance
Code' (2010) 436, 442
'United Kingdom Stewardship Code'
(FRC, 2010) **437–8**, 438
United Nations
UN Development Programme
(UNDP) 53
UN Global Compact (2000) 445
UN Principles for Responsible
Investment (UNPRI) **432–3**, 445–6
UNEP Finance Initiative: Asset
Management Working Group (UNEP
FI AMWG) 433, 446, 446n
United States 21, 54–5, 55e, 69, 84,
90e, 91, 130, 130e, 137e, 141b,
147, 153, 155, 159, 164, 219e, 432,
446, 502
central government debt to GDP ratio
(2009) 76e
credit rating 98
current account deficit 339
dotcom bubble **239–40**
economic performance following crises
(1929–2001) 74, 75e
equity market (standard deviation,
1990–2010) 181e
equity market correlation 183e
equity mutual funds 375
equity returns: hedged and unhedged
(volatility 1990–2010) 337, 338e

United States – *continued*
  GDP per capita (1929–2001)   74, 75e
  government debt (1929–2001)   74, 75e
  inflation (1960–2008)   73e
  non-government issuers (of bonds)   92e
  source of private equity funds (2010)
    324e
  stock market volatility and correlations
    (1970–2010)   **232–4**
  trend growth rate   217, 218e
  US dollar   71, 337b
  US dollar (pegged currencies)   77
  US Treasuries   91, 91e, 101, 120, 121e,
    122–3, 246, 247e, 251n, 336
  US Treasuries (yield curve)   112
  world's largest companies   128, 128e
University Superannuation Scheme
  (USS)   2
unlisted property funds   **161–3**, 167
  'balanced' versus 'specialist'   161
  'box' of units/shares   162
  'close-ended' versus 'open-ended'
    structure   162–3
  dual pricing (bid/offer spread)   162
  redemption of investment   161
unlisted real estate funds   167
'unsecured creditors'   126
utility companies   95, 136, 140, 410, 423n

valuation (investment style)   **339**
valuation (real estate)   **156–7**, 174
valuation metrics   503b
valuation spreads   **140–1b**
  definition   140b
valuations   238, **239–41**, 247e, 248
value investing   **139–40**, 142
value stocks   **136–8**, 153, 468
value-added   167
value-at-risk (VaR)   **197–201**, 416, 417,
  427
  calculation   198
  fat tails – skewness   **199–200**
  complementary risk metrics   **200–1**
  LDI   **400–4**
  offsetting   402
  VaR95   **401–4**, 409n, 418, 420, 426
variance   **179**, 188–9b
'variation margin'   255
Vaupel, J.W.   397
Vedanta   442
velocity of circulation (V)   65, 66
venture capital   309, 323–6, 345

'vintage years' (private equity)   330, 331,
  345
Visscher, P.K.   475n
VIX ('fear gauge')   242e, **242–3**
volatility   **184–5**, 193, 195, 198, 213,
  215–16, 219, **231–7**, 245, 386–8b,
  426, 457, 461, 467–8, 502
  excessive   472
  history used as guide to future   **232–4**
  sophisticated techniques of
    analysis   234n
  see also   VIX

wages   56, 63, 67, 68
Wagstaff, C.   **xv**, 18n, 166n, 247
Walker, Sir David   437n
Walker review (2009)   442
Wealth of Nations (Smith, 1776)   434n
Wealth, War and Wisdom (Biggs,
  2008)   469
wealth-maximization   **453–4**, 484
weighted average maturity (WAM)   **84**
Welch, I.   471n
Wharton Business School   440b
whisky   40
Whitbread plc   40, 203
Who Wants to be a Millionaire? (television
  quiz show)   **470–1**, 474
Why we get duped and how to avoid it
  (Greenspan)   456
widow/widower   4, 12, 13
Winter of Discontent (1978–9)   69–70
wisdom of crowds   **469–71**, 482n, 484
  failure of financial markets to
    exhibit   **471–4**
  five conditions   **470–1**
Wisdom of the Crowd (Surowiecki,
  2004)   469
WM Company   355
WM Performance Services   374
women   59, **502**
Wood, A.,   477n
Woodford, N.,   489–90
working hours   59
World War II   469
WorldCom   436, 467, 495

Yale University Endowment Fund   **308–10**,
  343, 345
yen   337b, 339
yield curve   **111–12**, 124, 284, 285, 287b,
  295, 301, 494

definition 111
yield curve family **111–12**

'Z' scores 245–7
zero coupon bond **94**, 96, 119e, 119–20
zero coupon curve 115, 115e
  relationship with forward interest
    rates **119–20**

zero coupon rates **112–16**, 118
  one-year 117
  and pension fund liabilities **116**
  three-year (calculation) **114–15**
  two-year 116, 117
  two-year (calculation) **112–14**
  usefulness **115**
zero coupon yields 124